Pay Yourself First

... and give
yourself a raise,
too!
Happy Fathers Day,
1993. Eli

We thought
that you would
enjoy this book, dad.
I hope you like it.
Happy Fathers Day!
Love Julie.

Pay Yourself First

Donald Cormie
and the collapse of the
Principal Group of Companies

by
Wendy Smith

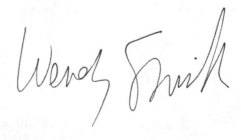

Canadian Cataloguing in Publication Data

Smith, Wendy 1952-
  Pay yourself first : Donald Cormie and the
collapse of the Principal Group of Companies
Includes bibliographical references and index.
ISBN 0-9696750-0-3

1. Cormie, Donald. 2. Principal Group Ltd.
I. Title.

HG5154.5.S58 1993   332.2'6'0971   C93-093459-8

PERMISSIONS

"Code's new conundrum" by George Koch. Copyright ©Alberta Report, 1988. Reprinted by permission of United Western Communications Ltd.
"Hi Society! Hoedown winds up day on ranch" by Maureen Hemingway. Copyright ©*The Edmonton Journal*, 1984. Reprinted by permission of *The Edmonton Journal*.
"RCMP reviews Principal complaints" by Brian Laghi and Ron Chalmers. Copyright ©*The Edmonton Journal*, 1987. Reprinted by permission of *The Edmonton Journal*.
"Subtle barriers block climb into management" by Karen Sherlock. Copyright ©*The Edmonton Journal*, 1986. Reprinted by permission of *The Edmonton Journal*.
THE MONEY RUSTLERS by Paul Grescoe and David Cruise. Copyright ©Paul Grescoe and David Cruise, 1985. Reprinted by permission of Penguin Books Canada Ltd.
"Trusts sound: Media slammed" by Peter Stockland. Copyright ©*Edmonton Sun*, 1985. Reprinted by permission of the *Edmonton Sun*.
"Western beef and mutual funds great barbeque draw" by Nicholas Lees. Copyright ©*The Edmonton Journal*, 1986. Reprinted by permission of *The Edmonton Journal*.

Published by Bruce Press
P.O. Box 493 Station P
Toronto, Ontario M5S 2T1

*I dedicate this book to the
memory of my mother
Loraine (Pachal) McIntosh (1928-1985),
with whom I learned to never trust a salesman.
And to the 67,000-plus sad but wiser Principal investors
who learned the same important lesson in 1987.
It's not enough to ask the questions,
you have to understand the answers.*

Contents

Part IV: TAKE-DOWN

Cast of Characters

THE PRINCIPAL GROUP OF COMPANIES

DONALD MERCER CORMIE, Q.C.—President and chairman of the board, Principal Group Ltd.; founding and senior partner of Cormie Kennedy, Barristers & Solicitors; director and president of Cormie Ranch Ltd./Cormie Ranch Inc., Collective Securities Ltd./Collective Securities Inc., Principal Venture Fund Ltd., Athabasca Holdings Ltd., Collective Mutual Fund Ltd.; director and chairman of Principal Savings & Trust Company Ltd.; and director of Matrix Investments Ltd., Principal Securities Management Ltd. (PSML), Allarco Energy Ltd., Principal Investors Corp. (U.S.A.) and Principal Certificate Series Inc. (U.S.A.)

JAMES MERCER (JAIMIE) CORMIE—son of Donald; vice-president (investments) and director, Principal Group Ltd.; director and president of PSML, Principal World Fund, Inc., Principal Management, Inc., Principal Cash Management Fund, Inc. and Principal Equity Fund, Inc.; director and first vice-president of Collective Securities Ltd./Collective Securities Inc; director and secretary-treasurer of Collective Mutual Fund Ltd.; and director of Cormie Ranch Ltd./Cormie Ranch Inc., Matrix Investments Ltd. and Principal Venture Fund Ltd.

JOHN MILLS CORMIE—son of Donald; vice-president (trust services), secretary-treasurer and director, Principal Group Ltd.; president of Principal Savings & Trust Company Ltd.; vice-president and director of PSML; and director of Collective Securities Ltd./Collective Securities Inc., Principal Neo-Tech Inc., Collective Mutual Fund Ltd., Principal Venture Fund Ltd. and Principal Investors Corp. (U.S.A.)

NEIL BRIAN CORMIE—son of Donald; director and president of Matrix Investments Ltd. after 1986; director and vice-president of Allarco Energy Ltd. and Cormie Ranch Ltd./Cormie Ranch Inc.; director and chairman, Drummond Brewing Company Ltd.

EIVOR CORMIE—wife of Donald; beneficial owner of Estate Loan & Finance Ltd.

KEN MARLIN—Senior vice-president (sales) and director of Principal Group Ltd.; director and president of Principal Consultants Ltd., First Investors Corporation Ltd. and Associated Investors of Canada Ltd.; director, president and chairman of Principal Neo-Tech Inc.; director and secretary-treasurer of Principal Savings & Trust Company Ltd.; and director of Principal Venture Fund Ltd., Collective Mutual Fund Ltd., Collective Securities Inc., Principal Canadian Mutual Fund Ltd. and Principal Management Ltd; director and vice-chairman of the Board of Governors of the Investment Funds Institute of Canada.

CHRISTA PETRACCA—vice-president (corporate development), Principal Group Ltd.; director of First Investors Corporation Ltd. and Associated Investors of Canada Ltd. after 1985; director and secretary-treasurer of Athabasca Holdings Ltd.; and director of Principal Savings & Trust Company Ltd., Allarco Energy Ltd. and Matrix Investments Ltd. M.B.A. University of Alberta; Chartered Accountant 1978-1992.

ROBERT PEARCE, C.A.—vice-president of Collective Securities Ltd./Collective Securities Inc.; director and secretary-treasurer of Drummond Brewing Company Ltd; director and president of Allarco Energy Ltd.; director and vice-president of PSML; and director of Principal Savings & Trust Company Ltd. and Matrix Investments Ltd.

GEORGE ABOUSSAFY—director and general manager of Principal Savings & Trust Company Ltd. 1984-1987; director of Principal Tax Services Ltd.

S. WILLIAM (BILL) JOHNSON, C.A.—vice-president (finance), Principal Group Ltd. 1984-1987.

DIANE STEFANSKI—"Department 8" bookkeeper; director, secretary and shareholder of Estate Loan & Finance Ltd.

VIRGINIA (GINNY) NICHOLSON—comptroller, Principal Group Ltd.; director and secretary-treasurer of Principal Canadian Mutual Fund Ltd. and Principal Venture Fund Ltd.; and director of Principal Neo-Tech Inc.

JUDITH (JUDE) HALVORSON—executive secretary to Donald Cormie; director, secretary and shareholder of Country Investments Ltd.; director, president and shareholder of Estate Loan & Finance Ltd.; director of Cormie Ranch Ltd./Cormie Ranch Inc.

ERIC ESPENBERG—special projects manager, Principal Group Ltd. 1985-1987; marketing and purchasing manager, Principal Group Ltd. 1977-1984; director of First Investors Corporation Ltd. and Associated Investors of Canada Ltd. 1978-1987.

BILL GREEN—mortgage broker, Alberta Mortgage Exchange Ltd. 1961-1964; mortgage portfolio manager, First Investors Corporation Ltd. 1964-1967; mortgage department manager, Principal Group Ltd. 1968-1976 and 1983-1987.

D. GRANT MITCHELL—vice-president (operations), Principal Group, until 1986; director of Principal Consultants Ltd. until 1986; director of Principal Savings & Trust Company Ltd. until 1986; elected MLA Meadowlark (Liberal) in 1986.

HUGH JAMES (JAY) MOULTON—supervisor of field services 1984-1986; vice-president of field services after 1986; director and secretary-treasurer of Principal Consultants Ltd. after 1986; director of Principal Tax Services Ltd. after 1986.

THE REGULATORS: PROVINCE OF ALBERTA

HARRY ROSE—Chairman, Alberta Securities Commission, with responsibility for regulating investment contract companies 1960s to 1973.

JOHN HART—Deputy Attorney General until the defeat of the Social Credit government in 1971; Principal Group corporate counsel during 1970s. Deceased.

JIM DARWISH, C.A.—Consumer & Corporate Affairs: auditor 1959-1965; financial analyst 1967-1972; Superintendent of Insurance and Real Estate 1972-1981 (acting deputy minister 1979); assistant deputy minister, program support 1981-1983; assistant deputy minister, program support and regional delivery 1983-1984.

JACK LYNDON—Consumer & Corporate Affairs: deputy minister 1974-1978.

BARRY MARTIN—Consumer & Corporate Affairs: deputy minister 1979-1987.

RON KAISER—Consumer & Corporate Affairs: Superintendent of Insurance 1981-1983.

TEWFIK SALEH—Consumer & Corporate Affairs: Deputy Superintendent of Insurance 1976-1981; executive director program development 1981-1983; Acting Superintendent of Insurance 1983; Superintendent of Insurance and director of financial institutions 1983-1986; Superintendent of Insurance and assistant deputy minister (financial institutions) 1986-1987.

BERNARD RODRIGUES—Consumer & Corporate Affairs: Supervisor of Investigations 1979-1982; Deputy Superintendent of Insurance 1982-1987; Superintendent of Insurance since 1987.

REG POINTE, C.A.—Consumer & Corporate Affairs: Deputy Superintendent, Insurance and Real Estate Branch 1978-1981; director of audits 1981-1983; director of trust companies 1983-1986. Treasury Department: director (now senior manager) of loan and trust companies since 1986.

GEORGE BLOCHERT, Consumer & Corporate Affairs: executive director of regional delivery 1981-1985.

AL HUTCHISON, C.A.—Consumer & Corporate Affairs: auditor 1980-1985.

BURT ELDRIDGE, C.A.—Consumer & Corporate Affairs: auditor 1976-1983; acting director of audits 1983; auditor 1983; director of audits 1984-1987; director of financial examinations since 1988.

NICK ROMALO, C.A.—Consumer & Corporate Affairs: auditor 1982-1986; Treasury Department: senior examiner, financial institutions, since 1986.

SYED ZAF BOKHARI—Consumer & Corporate Affairs: accountant 1979-1987.

ALLISTER MCPHERSON—Treasury Department: budget officer 1971-1979; Assistant Deputy Provincial Treasurer 1979-1980; Associate Deputy Provincial Treasurer (finance) 1980-1984; Deputy Provincial Treasurer (finance and revenue) since 1984, reporting first to Provincial Treasurer Lou Hyndman, and after 1986 to Provincial Treasurer Dick Johnston.

JIM DRINKWATER—Treasury Department: Assistant Deputy Treasurer (finance), reporting to Allister McPherson, until 1989.

ALFRED (Al) KALKE—Treasury Department: executive director, administration and revenue 1978-1980; Assistant Deputy Provincial Treasurer (revenue and administration) 1980-1984; Assistant Deputy Treasurer (revenue) since 1984, reporting to Allister McPherson; Acting Superintendent of Insurance 1987.

GEORGE KINSMAN—Treasury Department: director, loans and guarantees section (reporting to Jim Drinkwater) since 1981.

MARC LEMAY—Alberta Securities Commission: deputy director, filings in 1970s; director, 1982-1987; executive director of Securities Commission Board, secretariat responsible for policy development 1987-1992.

MARGUERITE CHILDS—Alberta Securities Commission: deputy director of franchises 1982-1989; senior financial policy analyst since 1989.

MARK BROWN, C.A.—Alberta Securities Commission: senior financial analyst 1983-1989; deputy director, securities analysis, 1989 to present.

THE REGULATORS: THE GOVERNMENT OF CANADA

ROBERT DE COSTER—Chairman, CDIC, 1983-1985.

CHARLES DE LERY—President, CDIC, 1984-1990.

JEAN PIERRE SABOURIN—Chief operating officer, CDIC, 1983-1986; executive vice-president and chief operating officer, CDIC, 1986-1990; president and chief executive officer, CDIC, since 1990.

ROBERT HAMMOND— Department of Insurance: Superintendent of Insurance and Pensions, 1982-1992; director, CDIC, 1982-1992.

DICK PAGE—Department of Insurance: director of the trust, loan and investment companies division, 1955-1986.

DENIS SICOTTE—Department of Insurance: senior registration and investigations officer, deposit-taking institutions sector, 1973-1992; senior compliance officer, Office of the Superintendent of Financial Institutions, since 1992.

THE REGULATORS: PROVINCE OF BRITISH COLUMBIA

ERNEST FREDERICK (BILL) SMITH, C.A.—Assistant chief accountant with the British Columbia Securities Commission during 1970s; policy analyst, Consumer and Corporate Affairs, after late 1970s; Acting Superintendent of Brokers 1986; Acting Deputy Superintendent of Brokers June-July 1986; policy analyst, Consumer and Corporate Affairs after 1986.

BILL IRWIN—Superintendent of Brokers 1962-1980.

RUPERT BULLOCK—Superintendent of Brokers 1980-1986.

EARL THOMAS JEWITT, C.A.—chief accountant, Office of the Superintendent of Brokers 1966-1979; Deputy Superintendent of Brokers 1979-1986; Acting Superintendent of Brokers January-May 1986.

DAVID EDGAR—assistant deputy minister, Consumer and Corporate Affairs; Acting Superintendent of Brokers May-June 1986.

MICHAEL ROSS, C.A.—Superintendent of Brokers July 1986 to February 1987.

DAVID SINCLAIR, C.A.—Acting Superintendent of Brokers from February 1987 to June 1, 1987.

AL DILWORTH—director of investigations and inspections, Department of Consumer and Corporate Affairs, after 1982.

THE POLITICIANS: ALBERTA

ERNEST MANNING (Social Credit)—Premier 1943-1968.

PETER LOUGHEED, Q.C. (Progressive Conservative)—Premier 1971-1985.

DON GETTY (P.C.)—Premier 1985-1992.

BOB DOWLING (P.C.)—Minister of Consumer and Corporate Affairs 1973-1975.

GRAHAM HARLE (P.C.)—Minister of Consumer and Corporate Affairs 1975-1979.

JULIAN KOZIAK, Q.C. (P.C.)—Minister of Consumer and Corporate Affairs 1979-1982; member of the first Cabinet financial institutions task force (financial institutions) 1984-1986.

CONNIE OSTERMAN (P.C.)—Minister of Consumer and Corporate Affairs 1982-1986; member of both Cabinet financial institutions task forces (financial institutions and trust companies) 1984-1986.

JAMES ALLAN (BOOMER) ADAIR (P.C.)—Minister of Consumer and Corporate Affairs February-May 1986.

ELAINE MCCOY, Q.C. (P.C.)—Minister of Consumer and Corporate Affairs 1986-1989.

MERV LEITCH, Q.C. (P.C.)— Attorney General 1971-1975; Provincial Treasurer 1975-1979; Minister of Energy and Natural Resources 1979-1983. Deceased.

LOU HYNDMAN, Q.C. (P.C.)—Treasurer 1979-1986; member of both Cabinet financial institutions task forces 1984-1986.

DICK JOHNSTON (P.C.)—Treasurer 1986-1992.

NEIL CRAWFORD, Q.C. (P.C.)—Attorney General and Government House Leader 1979-1986; member of both Cabinet financial institutions task forces 1984-1986; partner, Cormie Kennedy 1957-1968. Deceased.

THE ACCOUNTANTS

GORDON BURTON, F.C.A. (Peat Marwick Mitchell and Co.)—consultant to Alberta regulators in 1971.

DONALD MCCUTCHEN, C.A. (Deloitte Haskins & Sells)—audited Principal Group Ltd. and its subsidiaries until 1981; returned to the audit for 1984, 1985 and 1986.

DOUGLAS BRUCE PENNOCK, C.A. (Touche Ross & Co.)—auditor of Principal Group Ltd. and its subsidiaries, 1982 and 1983.

JOHN RYAN, C.A. (Coopers & Lybrand Ltd.)—consultant to Donald Cormie and the Principal Group of Companies in 1987; his firm also audited "upstairs" companies Collective Securities Ltd. and Cormie Ranch Ltd.

ANTHONIE (TONY) WOOLDRIDGE, C.A. (Price Waterhouse Ltd.)—consultant to Alberta regulators in 1987.

THE LAWYERS

JACK KENNEDY, Q.C.—founding partner and senior practising partner, Cormie Kennedy 1953-1985; agent general-Asia/Pacific for Province of Alberta in Hong Kong 1985-1991; director of Collective Mutual Fund Ltd., Principal Venture Fund Ltd. and Principal Certificate Series Inc. (U.S.A.). Deceased.

LYNN A. PATRICK—senior vice-president and general counsel, Principal Group Ltd.; director and secretary-treasurer of PSML; secretary of Matrix Investments Ltd.; and director of Principal Neo-Tech Inc., Principal Venture Fund Ltd., Principal Life Insurance Co. Travellers Acceptance Corporation, Principal Canadian Mutual Fund and Allarco Energy Ltd; partner, Cormie Kennedy 1961-1983.

WILLIAM (BILL) CONNAUTON—partner, Cormie Kennedy, until 1987; Cruickshank, Phillips, Karvellas & Connauton since 1987.

JACK N. AGRIOS, Q.C.—co-counsel, Cormie Kennedy.

GARY CAMPBELL, Q.C.—co-counsel, Cormie Kennedy. Director and secretary of County Investments Ltd. 1966-1970; director of Estate Loan and Finance and Cormie Ranch 1963-1969; president and chief executive officer of The Churchill Corporation 1981-1989; chairman of North West Trust since 1987; past-treasurer of the Progressive Conservative Association of Alberta.

SYDNEY A. BERCOV, Q.C.—Emery Jamieson, Barristers and Solicitors; consultant to Alberta regulators.

BOB DUKE—Cormie Kennedy.

C.R. HENNING—partner, Parlee, Irving, Henning, Mustard and Rodney.

KEITH FERGUSON—partner, Parlee, Irving, Henning, Mustard and Rodney, until 1987; Cruickshank, Phillips, Karvellas & Connauton since 1987.

JIM ROUT—Office of the Attorney General of Alberta.

D.W. AXLER—Office of the Attorney General of Alberta.

Introduction

I HAVE MET DONALD MERCER CORMIE only once. In 1990, during a break in one of his Edmonton court appearances, I approached him to say that I was writing a book about him, and that I hoped to interview him. Cormie told me that he knew who I was, and that I was writing a book. As far as he was concerned, "We categorize some journalists as hopeless, and you're in that category." He had no intention of speaking to me, he said; it seemed he was unhappy about certain articles I had written in 1988 about the collapse of his billion-dollar financial services empire.

I said goodbye and walked away. Then, a few seconds later, I turned to look at him. Cormie was shaking his head at his son John, seated next to him, and I could see him again mouth the word: "Hopeless."

This is, therefore, an entirely unauthorized account of the life and times of Donald Cormie.

Cormie's conglomerate, the Principal Group of Companies, collapsed during the summer of 1987. That autumn, court-appointed Inspector Bill Code began an investigation which continued for more than a year. I have relied heavily on transcripts of the 205 days of testimony, totalling 40,000 pages of evidence, heard during that inquiry. The 155 witnesses included investors, Principal salesmen, executives, accountants, business associates, provincial cabinet ministers, government officials and experts in various fields, as well as Cormie, who spent an agonizing 34 days on the witness stand.

I have also relied heavily on Code's findings. His 619-page report, a crushing condemnation of Cormie and his business practices, concluded that there was "evidence tending to show" fraud, dishonesty, oppression, unfair prejudice, unfair disregard, income tax evasion, stock market manipulation and misleading sales practices, as well as breaches of the *Investment Contracts Act* and the *Trust Companies Act*. (Code's investigation was not a judicial process and he had no power to determine criminal responsibility. Thus his mandate, as an inspector appointed under Alberta's *Business Corporations Act*, was to report to the Court of Queen's Bench of Alberta whether he had found "evidence tending to show" fraud or other reasons for the failure of Principal subsidiaries First Investors Corporation Ltd. and Associated Investors of Canada Ltd.) Code also found evidence tending to show "a grand plan" designed to cover up the severe financial problems experienced by the Principal Group companies after 1983. Both Cormie and sales chief Ken Marlin, "through their involvement in sales and marketing, perpetuated the 'disinformation' that [the group of companies] were not only healthy but facing a bright future."

Principal investment products continued to be aggressively marketed to the public for more than three years after an Alberta government auditor identified two Principal Group subsidiaries as "virtually insolvent." At the time of the collapse approximately 67,000 investors, many of them elderly or about to retire, held investment contracts worth approximately $467 million. Other investors held Principal Group promissory notes worth approximately $87 million. The investment contract holders will see approximately 85 to 90 cents on the dollar, almost half of that in the form of contributions from Alberta and other provinces; promissory noteholders expect to lose about half their investment.

Code identified an appalling regulatory failure on the part of the Alberta government, a conclusion shared in a subsequent report by the province's Ombudsman Aleck Trawick. Ombudsmen in three other provinces—British Columbia, Nova Scotia and Saskatchewan—concluded that regulatory systems failed in their jurisdictions as well. I have relied on these reports in sections of the book dealing with government involvement in the Principal Group companies over a 30-year period; particularly valuable were the reports of Trawick and B.C. Ombudsman Stephen Owen.

Sections of the book which examine accounting and auditing issues rely on the Canadian Institute of Chartered Accountants' 1988 *Report of the Commission to Study the Public's Expectations of Audits*; The Hon. Willard Estey's report into the collapse of the Northland and Canadian Commercial banks; and the report of Clarkson Gordon audit expert Richard Cormier, presented to the Code inquiry.

Sections of the book which examine stock market manipulation rely on the report of John Kolosky, former director of market operations on the Toronto Stock Exchange, who provided expert testimony at the Code inquiry.

I have incorporated several brief passages of explanation or summary from the above reports into this book without specific acknowledgement.

I have also examined many of the thousands of pages of documents submitted in evidence at the Code inquiry, and located other documents independently through searches in court houses, public archives and government offices. I have taken the liberty of correcting, without comment, the misspellings and small typographical errors which appeared in some of the documents quoted.

As well, I have interviewed dozens of people, some of whom had already testified at the inquiry, and many others who were not called to the witness stand.

Comments quoted have been taken from inquiry transcripts or other records where testimony was given under oath, unless otherwise stated. Some conversations and meetings have been reconstructed from testimony, interviews, minutes of meetings, memoranda and other records. Differing versions of events have been noted as they occur in the text.

Some of the diagrams and charts have been adapted from material included in Code's report, others from the submission of investors' special counsel Robert White to the Code inquiry.

Some of the incidents described in this book are the subject of investigation by the Royal Canadian Mounted Police. I am not in a position to express an opinion on the likely outcome of such proceedings.

Part I

Prairie Swashbuckler

1

Leap Year

February 28, 1984

JASPER AVENUE, IN EDMONTON, ALBERTA: main street in a prairie government town. Shops, cafes and office towers line the sidewalk; every few doors there's a bank, a trust company or a credit union office.

Look up, 30 storeys up. It shines like a beacon atop the money-green tower: *PRINCIPAL*, in massive gleaming letters. You can see it for miles.

This beckoning tower is Principal Plaza, corporate headquarters of the Principal Group of Companies. At street level are the offices of Principal Savings and Trust, the conglomerate's flagship company. Mounted above eye-level, a video unit endlessly loops a tape promoting Principal's investment products. To the left of a revolving door is a blue and silver sticker, emblazoned with the Canadian flag, proclaiming:

MEMBER
Canada Deposit Insurance Corporation
$60,000 maximum insurance
per person per member institution

There's a brisk flow of foot traffic into the trust company. It's RRSP season in a leap year—tomorrow is the 29th, the last day of February 1984. If you want to put money into a registered retirement savings plan for the 1983 tax year, you have to do it now.

The revolving door leads to a spacious reception area; directly ahead is the counter where trust tellers serve a snaking line of customers. When you reach the head of the line, you ask to buy an RRSP, and are pointed toward a receptionist seated at a desk at the end of the counter.

There's another queue, and you stand impatiently behind a man with a newspaper ad in his hand. It's from *The Edmonton Journal*, and it offers Principal

Trust's "no fee RRSP." The rate is 11.5% for an 18-month term. That's a great rate, a quarter per cent higher than any other institution in town. The deposit, the ad says, is CDIC-insured: guaranteed by the government of Canada.

Eventually the man reaches the desk. "If you come this way I'll introduce you to one of our investment consultants," the receptionist tells him. She leads him to the back of the room and hands him over to a good-looking, well-dressed young man seated at one of a dozen desks crowded into the space. The young man offers a firm handshake and his business card. He appears delighted at the opportunity to help a new client manage his financial affairs. "How can I help you?" he asks with a quick smile, then reaches for a company pamphlet.

"I'd like one of these," the man says, and hands over the newspaper ad. Ten minutes later he will leave the building, not with the advertised RRSP, but with a very different, extremely risky investment whose implications he won't understand for another three years.

You leave him there and exit, not by the revolving door, but through a second portal leading to the Principal Plaza foyer. The space is huge, with a mini-atrium in front of the windows. There are half a dozen elevators, and a bank of escalators to the second floor. The foyer is awash with expensive Gucci briefcases and suits.

Through the windows you see something a great deal more mundane: a bicycle messenger in a helmet and well-worn sneakers who enters the foyer and rushes for the elevators.

Slip through the doors behind him and, as the elevator climbs, take a look at the envelope in his hand. It's from someone in the provincial government, and it's addressed to the president of Principal Savings and Trust. That means the courier is going to the 29th floor.

Principal occupies the top three storeys of the office tower. The 28th floor, off-limits and top-secret, houses the corporate accounting department and a mass of computers that store account and transaction data from branch offices across the country. The computers, which fill a climate-controlled room, are protected by bullet-proof glass and a high-security system.

At the 29th floor the elevator opens into an enclosure of dark mahogany and plate glass engraved with the corporate crest. Based on the legend of St. George and the Dragon, it depicts a mounted knight with a lance skewering a clawed and fire-breathing dragon, the symbol of "fear, doubt and want." A large *P*—for Principal—is etched boldly into the knight's shield.

Two pairs of mahogany French doors lead off to left and right, but they're both locked. You have to cool your heels until an authorized employee emerges from the elevator. He approaches the doors on the left, inserts a security card, and pushes. You follow him through to an even more impressive foyer and stare, suddenly breathless, at the view before you. Principal Plaza is one of the tallest buildings in the city, and from this height commands a stunning view in all directions. At the west corner of the foyer a receptionist sits behind a half-circle desk. Over her shoulder you can see the North Saskatchewan River Valley, and beyond that the Alberta prairie.

The opulence is staggering. Across the Italian marble floor a gigantic curving staircase, carved from gleaming mahogany, sweeps grandly to the penthouse above. The two-storey foyer occupies thousands of square feet and is graced with a precious collection of Oriental artifacts, sculpture and Group of Seven and contemporary paintings.

This floor quarters several of Principal's senior executives and their support staff. The sales, mortgage and legal departments are here, as is the trust company management. It's a sprawling warren of offices, easy to get lost in if you don't know where you're going. It's almost as if it had been designed to confuse.

By the time you find your way to the trust company president's office, the courier has been and gone, and the envelope is on the president's desk. The letter, from the Alberta Director of Trust Companies, advises that federal government inspectors consider the trust company's finances to be in very bad shape, and warns that Principal Trust is in danger of losing the CDIC insurance necessary to keep its doors open.

The president can't believe it, and he sits down for a second to catch his breath. *They're always throwing their weight around, those feds,* he tells himself. They'd been closing in on Principal for some time—demanding more capital, asking questions—but this! Threatening to shut down the trust company! He picks up the phone. "This is John. Is he in? I need to see him." There's a pause. "I'll be right up."

Letter in hand, the president exits his office, then strides across the marble floor and up the stately staircase. His footsteps echo as he ascends to the penthouse, the real power centre of the Principal Group of Companies. On this floor decisions are made, money spent, careers launched and ended. The corporate president has his suite of offices here, as well as several personal support staff. The investment department is here, as is the powerful vice-president of corporate development. In the north-east corner, overlooking the urban sprawl, are an executive dining room with adjacent kitchen and an executive board room, decorated with a handsome six-panel landscape tapestry. The room is wired for action, with a video-recording system and a control panel that accesses the master computer.

The trust company president is aware of wall-mounted video cameras following his progress. As he rushes through the art-lined 30th-floor foyer he smooths his hair and straightens his tie. He nods to a secretary, then pauses at the door of the corporate president: Donald Cormie, founder and chairman of the Principal Group of Companies.

He knocks on the door, then leans inside, to see an image of himself, hand on the doorknob, flickering on a video screen. "Dad?" he says.

2

Green Plymouth

A MAN AND HIS AUTOMOBILE. At least, his girlfriend's automobile. That's the way Willard Estey remembers him. It was the end of the war, and the Harvard University campus was crowded with recently discharged soldiers, still in their threadbare uniforms and subsisting on veterans' grants and subsidized meals provided by the navy-run cafeteria.

"We walked everywhere—nobody had a car, nobody knew anybody with a car. But Don Cormie turns up with a girlfriend with a car. I figured he'd arrived in heaven. We all thought he was a millionaire." Estey chuckles as he recalls the scene: a vision of paradise to a poor Canadian air force veteran. The car was a green, four-door Plymouth with a pretty girl in the passenger seat. The girl's family, local people with a degree of pull, had managed to buy it hot off the post-war production line.

Estey entered Harvard in 1945, one semester after Donald Cormie. Both were lawyers—Estey, 25, from Saskatchewan and Cormie, 23, from Alberta—and each was at Harvard for a year to earn his Master of Laws degree. Estey remembers Cormie as "shy, quiet, but obviously smart, in the best sense of the term. He got there before I got there and left before I left. But because we were a drop of foreign oil in a big bucket of American water, we saw a fair amount of one another. And I liked him—an easy-going, interesting fellow."

To Estey, the Harvard law program was "a salt mine" that left little time for socializing. Nonetheless, Cormie managed not only to date his girlfriend and drive her Plymouth, but to marry her. The engagement, to Miss Eivor Elizabeth Ekstrom of West Somerville, Massachusetts, was announced in *The Edmonton Journal* in May 1946. The announcement detailed many of the groom's achievements and said he had been "a purser with the Canada Steamship Lines before taking post-graduate work in law at Harvard University."

The photograph accompanying this announcement created an indignant stir among some of Edmonton's young people. The photo featured Cormie, splendid in his purser's cap, looking very military. But Cormie's war-fevered peers knew that his military experience consisted of army training on the University of Alberta campus. His service as purser was actually a glamorous summer job for the seasons of 1944 and 1945. He worked on the *S.S. Noronic*, a luxury liner which cruised the Great Lakes, far from enemy gunfire. His duties included securing passengers' cash and valuables: ironic training for a man who would one day control millions of dollars of other people's money.

After graduation, Cormie packed his bride and his Harvard sheepskin into the green Plymouth and drove back home to Edmonton to practice law. Estey also headed west, to Saskatoon, where he taught at the University of Saskatchewan for a year, then went east to Bay Street in Toronto. His distinguished career culminated in an appointment to the Supreme Court of Canada, and to the chairmanship of several federal commissions of inquiry.

Estey and Cormie kept in touch through their involvement in the Canadian Bar Association. "He and I were on the same committee of the Canadian Bar one time and he looked like the old Harvard law student to me: a little more prosperous, that's all. He didn't change. He was a good-looking fellow, he dressed well and he got along well with people. Any job you gave Cormie he did it quickly and he did it well. That stood out more than anything else.

"After a while I would find that he had started a thing called First Investors. That intrigued me greatly, that one of our stray motley crowd would have such entrepreneurial instincts."

In 1987, the year before he retired from the Supreme Court, Estey was bewildered to learn that his old friend was in trouble with the Alberta government, and that his financial services empire was in ruins. Two years later Estey was in Edmonton giving a speech to the Society of Management Accountants of Canada about what happens when politicians and business leaders compromise their ethics. "They had a press conference afterward and somebody with me said: 'Do you ever look up your old friend Cormie?' And God, the press seized on that—you'd think I was associated with Al Capone. I said, 'He's a friend of mine.' I don't discontinue my friends, disconnect them, like they've been shot."

Fergus, Ontario: 1846

THE FIRST CORMIES IN CANADA, master carpenters John and Alexander, emigrated from Scotland in the 1820s. A decade later John married Ann Heggie, another Presbyterian Scot, and a decade after that the couple poured the savings of 20 years of labour—51 pounds, two shillings and six pence—into the purchase of a 100-acre farm near Fergus, Ontario, located 60 miles west of Toronto. The couple built a log house and named the property "Collessie," after the farm where Ann had been born in Scotland. Twenty-four years later, they bought a second 100-acre lot, becoming major landholders in the area.

John and Ann had three children. John Jr., the middle child, was born in 1842. At the age of 34 he married Grace Mills, 24, daughter of the town butcher, and the couple had six children.[1] The first five came spaced two years apart. Then, as Grace was turning 40, there was a surprise: an infant boy, born in 1892, named George Mills Cormie. George lived for seven years in his grandparents' log house, until his father built the gracious brick home which still stands today. (The property left Cormie hands a few decades ago. In 1983—just four years before Donald Cormie's business empire collapsed—the last Cormie in Fergus, Donald's elderly spinster cousin Anna, wrote a family history which cited a tradition of hospitality, caring and sharing. "Common traits of honesty, industry and decency have been passed down," she said.)

At the age of 20, George attended the Ontario Agricultural College in nearby Guelph. Afterward, he went to Alberta to homestead with an uncle on his mother's side, then returned to Ontario to join the provincial agricultural service. Most of his college chums had by that time enlisted, but George would later say that a broken leg had left him a little lame and ineligible for service during the first World War.[2]

In 1916, George went to work for the federal government. He moved to Edmonton as assistant to T.A. Benson, then Dominion Government poultry representative for Alberta. Two years later, when Benson was transferred to British Columbia, George was left behind in charge of the poultry division of the federal livestock branch in Alberta.

In 1918, just before his promotion, George married Mildred Bessie Mercer, the daughter of a Calgary machinist. The couple settled down in Edmonton and raised six children: three boys and three girls. The eldest, also named George, was born August 23, 1919. He was followed two years later by Gordon. The youngest son, born July 24, 1922, was christened Donald Mercer Cormie. Then came the girls: Evelyn, Allison and Helen. From the beginning, Donald was George's golden boy, a clever, highly motivated child who had plainly inherited the lion's share of his ancestors' brains and drive.

In 1925, when Donald was a toddler, George moved his family from their house in central Edmonton to a new home in the west-end sticks: to a wild and woolly place which became known as the Jasper Place Subdivision. At that time Edmonton's western city limit was marked by 149th Street. Just beyond it squatted a shantytown, occupied by a handful of families who couldn't afford, or didn't care to pay, city taxes. There were no building codes and few amenities. In those years only a couple of hundred people lived in Jasper Place. They had large gardens, plenty of animals and lots of kids.

Edmonton snobs called it Mudville, after the dirt roads that turned ʻ when it rained. When the rain stopped, a farming family hooked up a ʻ car tracks behind a team of horses, then dragged the tracks along tʻ

George bought a parcel of land on the tax-free west sidᵉ intersection of 96th Avenue, with the help of an $800 inheritaⱽ father John Jr. died earlier that year.

The Cormies' neighbours on the Edmonton side of 149th were named Young, a family that had 10 children, among them Ian, a year older than Donald. The two boys grew up together, and Ian Young remembers it as an idyllic childhood. The Cormies owned ponies named Buster and Bessie, and the Youngs had one as well. Donald and Ian roamed the countryside on horseback or bicycle, playing often in a ravine near the North Saskatchewan River delta. "We'd ride down to the river on the ponies and wear grass skirts on the weekends," Young told me. "The water weeds that grow along the river—we'd tie a bunch together and that was our grass skirts."

The Cormies, by contrast with their shantytown neighbours, were considered very well off. In 1929, as the world economy sank into depression, the federal government's Alberta-based poultry promotional program was amalgamated with the Alberta Agriculture Department. George Cormie was appointed provincial poultry inspector, and with his coveted government paycheque the family survived the early 1930s in comfort. They had a solid frame house with three or four bedrooms and a generous garden, where the children grew cabbages for money. George drove a government car. Further luxuries included a telephone, tap water pumped from a basement tank and an indoor toilet.

The Cormies owned the equivalent of a city block, about four or five acres. George built three double-decker chicken houses on 96th Avenue and raised Leghorn chickens. These are scrawny, ill-tempered little birds, tougher than shoe leather, but legendary egg-layers. George put one of his wife's brothers in charge of production, and sold (presumably self-inspected) eggs for miles around.

The Youngs and the Cormies attended the four-room Jasper Place Elementary School, a few blocks from their homes. Donald's brother Gordon was a grade ahead of him until 1931, when Donald skipped Grade 4. After that, they studied together, a year behind their brother George Jr.

Suddenly, in mid-March 1933, when Donald was ten, his mother Mildred died after a brief illness. An article in *The Edmonton Journal* described her as irreplaceable in the community. Mildred had been active in the local United Church, worked in the Jasper Place Sunday school and was treasurer of both the Royal Alexandra Hospital Aide and the Jasper Place Ladies' Aide societies. Her loss was termed "a blow felt alike in hospital circles and among her large circle of friends. She was a devoted mother, a willing worker, and, in short, a fine woman."

George was left to raise six children aged three to 14 years old, a disastrous situation for a man whose job required frequent travel. Within a year he was married again.

The bride, Emilie Schepp, was a teacher who arrived at the Jasper Place school in the autumn of 1933. She took over Donald and Gordon's sixth-grade classroom and soon became acquainted with their father. Ian Young remembers Miss Schepp as a wonderful lady and a damn good teacher and she could sing like a canary. In her ss there was no goofing around. If you did, you went up and got the yardstick ss the bum on her desk. She would pick on the biggest one, to show an example. she asked for silence that's what she wanted."

George Cormie began visiting her "and finally she started to visit him and they got married," Young said. "She continued teaching after she got married, but not for long." The new Mrs. Cormie, of German extraction, took charge of the six children with good cheer and discipline. She clearly earned a warm place in young Donald's heart, and in later years he named one of his children after her.

In November 1937, three years after his second marriage, George Cormie's government job was yanked out from under him. The Hon. D.B. Mullen, minister of agriculture in Alberta's Social Credit government, fired George without explanation and replaced him with C.W. Traves, who had been defeated the year before as a Social Credit candidate for city commissioner in Calgary.

According to a speech made by Donald Cormie in 1990,[3] George's firing was retribution for a battle waged between Social Credit Premier William Aberhart and George's uncle, managing editor of *The Edmonton Journal*. This is apparently a reference to John Mills Imrie, a Cormie relative on the Grace Mills side of the family. The *Journal* had vilified Aberhart and his Social Credit theories for years, particularly the government's "funny money" scheme. In response, Aberhart introduced *The Accurate News and Information Act*, an attempt to gag the press. Imrie rallied a hundred other papers province-wide in a massive protest against the bill. Half a year later his campaign earned the *Journal* a Pulitzer Prize for "leadership in the Defense of Freedom of the Press in Alberta," the first time the American award ever honoured a Canadian newspaper.[4] Imrie's prize-winning editorial was published October 4, 1937, a month before George Cormie was fired.

It took George only a few months to get back on his feet. He found a job for himself at the North West Mill and Feed Co. Ltd., owned by Frank McCormick of the McCormick biscuit empire, by offering to set up a new livestock feed department. The next year he was appointed plant manager, and four years later he bought the company, becoming president in 1943. George named his wife Emilie as vice-president, and Donald, a 21-year-old university student, as secretary-treasurer. The three Cormies were the company's sole directors.

It was one of many business lessons Donald Cormie learned from his father, and established a pattern that he would follow religiously for four decades: use the wife and kids on company records whenever possible; use faithful employees when necessary, but keep ultimate control close to your chest. It worked for a war-time feed mill, and it would work for a billion-dollar financial services conglomerate.

With the advent of World War II, the world market for flour began to boom, and for five years the mill operated non-stop. When the war ended and western mills were squeezed out by larger Ontario- and Quebec-based plants, George dismantled his flour-milling operation and expanded the feed mill. Much later he would tell the *Journal* that his foresight and management skills allowed him to repay his debt to the former owners five years ahead of schedule.[5] In that interview, given in 1963, George remarked that getting fired by the province at age 47 was the most wonderful thing that could have happened to him. "It enabled me to get into a profitable and happy life," he said gleefully. There is, after all, no revenge quite like success.

While George was getting established at the mill, Donald continued his studies, graduating from Victoria High School in downtown Edmonton. In 1990 Bob Purvis, the 1938-39 student union president, dug up a copy of that year's *Vic Argosy* graduation issue, and showed me a photograph of the student union. Cormie stood amid a group of school mates—most of them room representatives, like himself— instantly recognizable in the jacket, vest sweater and tie that would become his trademark. Cormie's biography read as follows:

> Sincere and cheerful, he has won many new friends at Vic. Ambition: Commercial delegate [foreign attaché]. Favourite expression: "YOU have got to prove it." Favorite occupation: singing in school.

The *Argosy*'s cover featured the motto: "Time, like an ever-rolling stream, Bears all its sons away." It was an ominous portent of the losses to come. The war had begun, and many classmates would enter into battle, never to return.

George Cormie sent his two eldest boys overseas; Donald, 17, stayed home and attended Edmonton's University of Alberta. That autumn, the campus was on a war footing. Fraternity initiations and campus club recruitment drives took a back seat to patriotic activities. Those who didn't enlist were expected to contribute as best they could. Students raised money one year for an army ambulance, the next for a mobile canteen. Compulsory army training for men was introduced in 1940, and the hockey arena was taken over as a drill hall. In 1941, women began to participate in military training, and the next year it became compulsory for them as well. On-campus air force training was added in 1942, and naval training in 1943.

Still, it was an interesting time to be on campus. With so many young men in uniform, the proportion of women to men in the classrooms had never been higher. Off-campus, the home boys were replaced by an "American invasion," as thousands of U.S. soldiers and hundreds of tons of equipment were moved into Edmonton. The city became a staging point for Alaska, and the military quickly commandeered every inch of office and storage space. The air force occupied the university student residences, pushing students out to already overcrowded boarding houses.

The situation wasn't a problem for Donald Cormie. In 1943, as crowding peaked, father George marked his purchase of the North West Mill by moving the family moved back into the city from Jasper Place. Their new house was on 90th Avenue, a few blocks from both the mill and university, so that Donald was a quick walk from his classes.

The student body was small in those years, just a couple of thousand students, and Donald Cormie became a big man on campus. He pledged the Zeta Psi fraternity, and joined a half-dozen clubs: Debating Society (secretary in 1942-43, president 1943-44); Political Science Club (executive 1942-43); the campus newspaper the *Gateway* (features editor 1943-44); Law Club (executive 1942-44); the public speaking club; the swimming club; and the outdoor club.

Cormie attended to his compulsory military training as well. In April 1941, as his 19th birthday approached, he joined the Canadian Officers Training Corps (COTC), a program which normally led to enlistment after graduation. He signed on as a lance corporal, became orderly room sergeant (responsible for administrative matters) five months later and was promoted to company sergeant major in November 1943.

In the spring of 1944, the year Cormie completed his Bachelor of Arts degree, he was prominently featured in the *Evergreen & Gold*, the university's yearbook. His graduation photo shows a distinguished-looking young man in gown and bow tie. He gazes calmly into the camera: cool, patrician, handsome. There were other photos, including a candid shot of a khaki-clad Cormie, rifle on shoulder, taken during military drill.

After graduation Cormie headed to Ontario, reporting to the *S.S. Noronic* on April 29, 1944. That autumn he returned to Edmonton to take his law degree. In November, he resigned his warrant as company sergeant major in the COTC and reverted to corporal at his own request.

That year, Cormie became editor-in-chief of the *Gateway*, and received the gold award of the students' union for outstanding executive service. He graduated second in a class of three at law school, sweeping up a basketful of honours and a scholarship that would take him to Harvard.

During the spring of 1945, as Cormie headed east—first to the *Noronic* again, then to his Harvard studies—the war ended in Europe. Japan surrendered that August, and over the next few months thousands of soldiers made the long-awaited journey home. The Loyal Edmonton Regiment, 580 men strong, arrived at the train station on October 6, 1945, to a cheering crowd of 50,000. Donald's brother Gordon was a member of the regiment, but was invalided after a shell exploded into his leg in Italy. He missed the ticker-tape parade by a month, returning home in November 1945.

The hapless red-haired George Jr., the eldest Cormie brother, never did return. He had dropped out of school after the tenth grade—doubtless a shock to his ambitious family—and hadn't seemed able to make a place for himself in the world. He drifted along: a couple of years at a school of agriculture, then a half-year at a school of engineering in Milwaukee, where he studied welding. He also spent some time on the Ontario homestead, working for his Uncle Wilbert, and is remembered in Fergus as a lively fellow, interested in good times and pretty girls.

George joined the army in November 1939, within weeks of the German invasion of Poland. The young private went through a brief electrician's course, then was shipped overseas. He landed in Scotland on the first day of 1940, and 16 months later died in a traffic accident in London.

Edmonton: 1946

EIVOR'S GREEN PLYMOUTH brought Donald Cormie and his bride across the continent to a city transformed. It was a new era of prosperity in Alberta, kindled first by the war industries, then detonated in February 1947 by Leduc Oil Well No. 1. The gusher, 13 miles southwest of Edmonton, marked the beginning of Alberta's first oil boom, whose impact was described by historian J.G. MacGregor:

In 1946, the money being invested in all phases of Alberta's development was some $122 million, of which perhaps one-fifth was going into dry holes in the futile search for oil. During the ten-year period after Leduc, the petroleum industry alone invested nearly $2.5 billion directly. On top of that, because of the rapid rise of the oil industry, other billions poured into Alberta. They were used to set up the host of new well servicing industries, the new manufacturing plants, the new homes to house the thousands who flocked in to work in the new petroleum industry, the new utilities to service these homes and the great variety of stores, institutions and government capital expenditures necessary to cope with the new era. Scores of millions rubbed off on the agricultural industry and were invested in more land and equipment. All these investments totalled some $6 billion, and all were due to the arrival of the oil age...

All this new investment swept every Albertan to a new and undreamed of standard of living. The average man, woman and child in the province in 1946 had annual income of $666; in 1956 it was $1,539. The farmer in his field, the cook in his cafe, the businessman in his board-room, and the provincial treasurer in his palace, all shared in the new prosperity.

For the first time ordinary workers had money to spare, and saving became an achievable objective in life. Donald Cormie watched the transformation with interest for a few years, then became involved in an investment certificate scheme targeted at the savings of newly prosperous citizens.

But first, Cormie articled with S. Bruce Smith, senior partner of Smith, Clement, Parlee and Whittaker. Smith, a renowned Edmonton lawyer who later became Chief Justice of Alberta, had done the legal work for George Cormie's mill company since the 1943 take-over. In October 1947, at the age of 25, Donald Cormie was admitted to the Alberta bar and joined Smith's firm, perfectly positioned to make a splash in Edmonton circles. A Harvard scholar, graduated with first-class standing and a thesis in international law, was something of a rarity. His youth was impressive too. Cormie was ahead of most of his contemporaries, now back in university scrambling to make up for the time they'd lost overseas.

Cormie hadn't gone to war, and that was a mark against him. Still, one brother had died—few knew the circumstances—and the other was wounded, so it wasn't as if the family hadn't made a contribution. (Cormie's summers on the *S.S. Noronic* would be remembered by only a few of his contemporaries. Over the years his experience would be reduced in official biographies to a vague "served in Merchant Marine 1943-44." In 1981, author Peter C. Newman would say in *The Acquisitors* that Cormie "had seen wartime service in the merchant navy," leaving readers with the impression Cormie had somehow participated in the war effort.)

Cormie's wife, however, was a definite mark in his favour. U.S. soldiers had scooped up several hundred Edmonton girls, much to the chagrin of local men. Now here was Donald Cormie bearing home an American prize—a girl with looks, charm and money. Eivor was pregnant within a couple of months of the June 1946 wedding and kept busy during the next two decades having babies. The eldest of eight children, a boy, was born May 21, 1947. His name honoured the Cormie bloodline: John Mills Cormie. Donald Robert ("Donnie") came the next year, followed in 1950 by the first girl, Allison Barbara. James Mercer ("Jaimie") was born in December 1951, followed by Neil Brian, Bruce George, Eivor Emilie ("Eivor Jr.") and, finally, Robert Ekstrom, born in 1964.

When Donald's brother Gordon returned home from the war, he went to work for his father as assistant manager in the feed mill. In 1945, while Donald was at Harvard, a company accountant had been added to the list of North West Mill directors and replaced Donald as secretary-treasurer. Two years after returning home, Gordon replaced him in turn. At war's end, father George had bought out Calgary's Anderson Grain and Feed Company, changing its name to Gold Medal Feeds Ltd. and appointing Gordon manager. In 1951, Gordon bought Gold Medal from his father and severed ties with the Edmonton mill. At this time Donald again became director and secretary of that operation and over the years would increasingly involve himself in its affairs.

Between 1949 and 1953, Donald Cormie developed his law practice and taught part-time at the University of Alberta, specializing in business law.[6] He remained with Smith's firm for seven years—among the files he handled was his father's mill company—then in 1954, struck out on his own. He took the very personable Jack Kennedy with him, and the pair founded the firm Cormie Kennedy. Kennedy, four years Cormie's junior, was a politically-connected young lawyer from a wealthy Scots family in Guelph, Ontario, a few miles from the Cormie homestead.

The partners set up their practice in the Barry Building, a two-storey office block just off Jasper Avenue. They started out doing real estate paperwork, gradually expanding into commercial and securities law. Among their first clients were Cormie's father George, his brother Gordon and their businesses; another was realtor Stan Melton, one of the Cormie boys' Jasper Place hockey chums.

3

The richest man in Babylon

HERE'S THE FABLE: On a balmy autumn evening in 1953, Donald Cormie and his friend Ralph Forster were enjoying an Edmonton Eskimos football game when the conversation turned to banking and investments. Cormie and Forster, a dignified former executive of the World Bank, discovered to their mutual delight that they both believed in saving 10% of what they earned. "We thought it might be a good idea to have a business that sold the thrift concept and so the following spring we started First Investors Corporation," Cormie told authors Paul Grescoe and David Cruise in their 1985 book *The Money Rustlers*, an admiring account of the careers of several Canadian entrepreneurs.

Cormie, Forster and some silent partners, the tale continues, tossed $10,000 each into the pot and formed First Investors, an investment certificate company. The company "grew like an eager foal." Cormie hired Saskatchewan railroader and vacuum cleaner salesman Ken Marlin and brought him to Edmonton to take over the head office. Guided by Cormie's inspired "economic cycle theory" and Marlin's genius for sales, the company became a billion-dollar financial services empire.

Not exactly true. This version, Marlin would later tell *The Edmonton Journal*, is "a bit like Soviet history, a story told by survivors." First Investors, originally named Bankers Investment Corporation Ltd., was started in February 1954 by Forster, then 56, and realtor Stan Melton, then 35. Cormie, just getting on his feet at Cormie Kennedy, got the company's legal business and became one of the partners. The idea may have originated with Forster and Cormie—both men told the football game story for many years—but it was clearly a Melton enterprise when it began.

Initially there were five major shareholders, including Melton. Forster worked for Melton as a consultant; Cormie was his lawyer; Cliff Willetts was his accountant; and Dennis Stewart worked in Melton's real estate company. The six minor shareholders were Melton real estate managers.

The company was launched with 100,000 shares, at a dollar each, and 60% were immediately allotted: Melton and Forster purchased 10,000 shares each;

Stewart had 9,998; Cormie had 9,997; Willetts had 8,000; and the other six men had 2,000 each. That gave Melton, Forster, Stewart and Cormie 15.4% each of the allotted shares; Willetts 12.3%; and the minor shareholders 3% apiece. And it generated start-up cash of $59,995. Melton became president, Cormie vice-president, and Forster was secretary.

The company, soon renamed First Investors Corporation Ltd., was designed to sell installment savings plans to people of modest means who wanted to save by putting aside a small amount each month. A typical "investment contract" or "investment certificate" would commit a person to save, say, $10 or $15 a month for five, 10 or 20 years. The money was paid to the company, which could invest the funds as it chose until the contract came due. Contract holders didn't own any part of the investments bought by the company with the contract money. The contract was simply a debt instrument, in essence an IOU, with the company owing the client a specific amount of money at maturity. The contracts paid a fixed amount of interest, close to the market rate—in those days 3% or 4%—with the provision that additional interest might be paid at the company's discretion by declaring "additional credits" when profits permitted.

At first, Forster and Stewart were the only people working full time for the company. Stewart, one of Melton's top real estate salesmen, was general manager. Forster, the group's elder statesman, was responsible for writing a procedures and policy manual which set the company's course during the early years. Without him, it is unlikely First Investors would have survived the decade.

Born in Medicine Hat, Alberta, in 1898, Forster was a world traveller and adventurer who left home in 1916 to join the army. That year, he transferred from the Canadian to the British army, serving with the Royal Tank Corps in France and Belgium until wounded and gassed in 1917. He was assigned for half a year to a war-loan propaganda and publicity unit under newspaper mogul Lord Northcliffe, the new Director of Propaganda in Enemy Lands—once called "a master of mass-suggestion"—whose corps of propaganda experts peppered Austrian and German troops with demoralizing leaflets and rumors.[1] In 1918 Forster rejoined the tank corps at the front, and that September earned the Military Cross when he led his section "with conspicuous gallantry" into battle.[2]

After the war, Forster returned home to complete his Bachelor of Arts degree at the University of Alberta. Later, he worked at the Hudson's Bay Company in Edmonton, assisting in preparations for its 250th anniversary celebration. In 1920 he returned to England, where he graduated in 1923 from the London School of Economics with a bachelor of commerce degree. Forster stayed in England for two decades, doing sales and organization work: first for an insurance company, later for a company importing and selling "electro-medical appliances"—his resume does not elaborate—then for a manufacturing firm and, finally, for a cosmetics firm.

At the outbreak of World War II, he rejoined the British army, and between 1941 and 1946 was stationed at the British Embassy in Washington, D.C., where he served as staff liaison officer between the army and the British Information Services.

Forster travelled America on speaking tours, developing connections with the film, broadcasting and publishing industries. He became a celebrated Washington host, throwing war-time receptions at the embassy attended by the Who's Who in diplomatic, political, military, business, media and entertainment circles.

After the war, Forster worked for the International Bank for Reconstruction and Development (the World Bank), created by the allied powers to rebuild the international payments system. He spent a couple of years with its public relations office (his identification card read "Media Specialist"), which was developing a speakers' bureau to send bank officials on tour. In that capacity he became acquainted with many luminaries of the international financial world, contacts that would prove invaluable in the Edmonton enterprise to come. Then in 1949, he moved to Chicago to join the British Board of Trade, where he helped promote the sale of British products in the United States.

Forster returned to Edmonton in 1953 to live with his ailing mother. Working as a consultant, he both tied Stan Melton into New York financing for his real estate company and pitched the idea of a local financial institution that would provide a pool of capital in Western Canada.

Forster was trained as an economist, but his specialty was public relations. Edmonton associates benefitted greatly from these skills, learning a great deal from him about image, publicity and self-promotion. Forster's extraordinary social and business connections—and his talent for bringing the right people together at social gatherings—also proved invaluable. Forster knew many members of the Social Credit Cabinet and during First Investors' early years he wasn't shy about calling on political friends in times of regulatory difficulty.

Forster's two-year stint with the World Bank wasn't mentioned in his *Edmonton Journal* obituary, and family members know little about that aspect of his life. But the connection was invaluable to Principal, which hyped it as a long-standing and key position. Company literature remained silent about Forster's precise duties, leaving the impression he was an executive in a formidable financial institution. In the *Principal Group Ltd. Annual Report 1971* (published in 1972) Forster's death was announced as follows:

> It is with sincere regret that Principal Group announces the passing, March 22, 1972, of Mr. Ralph P. Forster, in Edmonton. Mr. Forster became one of the founders of the Principal Group of Companies in 1954 after leaving the World Bank in the United States where he was associated for many years.

But that was many years in the future.

In 1954, Forster and Stewart set up shop in a one-room office in the Barry Building (where Donald Cormie's law office was located) and tried to sell investment certificates. It was a disaster. Despite Forster's promotional abilities and Stewart's talent as a real estate salesman, the two men were incapable of moving the product. It takes someone special to sell paper—investments are intangible, and need a special touch—and neither of them had it. Realizing they were in danger of going under, Forster wrote Ab Coyne, an old family friend in Regina, and invited him to become sales manager.

Coyne, then 42, was regional manager for Electrolux Canada Ltd. in dustbowl south Saskatchewan. During the depression he set records selling vacuum cleaners door to door in Regina; in 1936, his first year on the job, he won a gold ring—top prize at Electrolux—for his achievement.

Selling, to Coyne, was an art, a science, a thrill. "Our breed doesn't exist anymore," Coyne told me proudly in 1990. Getting a sale during the depression was like pulling teeth, "and we had training in salesmanship that you can't get today." Making it through the door was one challenge; getting a signature on the dotted line was another. Timing was everything—say just enough, but know when to stop—and there were tried-and-true tricks for every situation. "We'd meet every morning, and any salesman who made a sale had to tell about it, how he overcame the obstacles. We were taught human nature," Coyne recalled.

"For example, you've got a woman awful close to wanting it, and the husband asks, 'Do you want it, darling?' You must never let her answer, you must jump in with, 'Of course you want it.' " If one close doesn't work, "try another and another, until you break the customer down. If you don't get it, and walk out, you've lost your sale. They cool off."

When Forster contacted Coyne in 1954, he knew his friend was upset with Electrolux and might be interested in a change. Coyne had been put in charge of the south Saskatchewan territory when he returned after the war. Within a few years, he still brags, "My branch had the highest sales per salesman in any branch in the free world." Electrolux rewarded him by taking his best salesmen away and setting them up as managers inside his territory: he had been simmering ever since.

Forster brought Coyne to Edmonton and Donald Cormie made the big pitch. The potential income from the investment contract business was incredible, Cormie told him, and Coyne signed on. He stayed in Regina, opening up a First Investors office just a block from the Electrolux office. "I ran both offices at the same time. I told all my staff at both offices to keep their mouths shut, which they did." It worked until he forgot to brief a new secretary, who inadvertently told the president of Electrolux that Coyne was in his "other office." Coyne was fired by the end of the day.

Among the members of Coyne's Saskatchewan team was 32-year-old Ken Marlin, a telegrapher and train dispatcher for the Canadian Pacific Railroad who had been moonlighting as an Electrolux salesman. "Marlin had bought a floor polisher," Coyne said. "Then he had serious surgery, and he came in to say he couldn't keep up the payments. I said to him, 'Why don't you come work for me?' For three years he worked days for me and nights for the railroad." Marlin, a high-school dropout, was a hell of a salesman. He had timing, a rough charm, a sense of humour and an amiable face which gave him an aura of utter reliability.

Coyne brought Marlin and Cormie together one evening at his home. "He painted a picture that caught my imagination," Marlin said. "And when he showed me the type of certificate that they were offering the public, I recognized it as the same certificate that Western Savings & Loan, a company out of Winnipeg, had sold me 10 years earlier." Marlin had bought a $10,000 plan, to be paid over 20 years at $28 a month, and was contracted to lose a portion of his investment if he didn't continue his payments. "I remember thinking that the penalty was probably one of the most important parts of the plan because there were times in those early years when I would have probably discontinued. In talking to Don Cormie, back in '54, I said, 'Well, I think I could sell that idea because that was the smartest thing I ever did when I committed myself to pay $28 a month.' "

So Marlin added the First Investors certificates to his kit of Electrolux products and hit the pavement. That November he sold $60,000 worth of certificates and 25 vacuum cleaners. "When I added it up, I had made more money selling certificates than I had on my other two jobs." Marlin worked all night for the railroad, went home for breakfast, "then he reported to me at 8:15 a.m.," Coyne said. "He was making three times as much money working for me days as he did at nights working for the railroad. I told Ken he was going to kill himself, why didn't he quit the railroad job and start getting a decent night's sleep?

"He said to me, 'My family have always been railroaders and those who quit the railroad had financial disasters. So I'll keep that job if that's okay with you.' "

When the roof caved in at Electrolux, Coyne went to Marlin with a $1,000 cheque and an ultimatum. "I said, 'You have one minute to take that cheque, or go back to the railroad full time.' He grabbed the cheque."

Marlin went to Edmonton in January 1955 to meet the company directors. "I spent three days and came back to Regina convinced that I should leave the railroad and throw my lot with this group of young entrepreneurs," he told me. "I proceeded to hire some salesmen in Regina and by April of 1955, I had hired 15, many of them railroaders like me." In June 1955 Marlin moved to Calgary to open an office there.

After parting with Electrolux, Coyne went to Edmonton and took over the First Investors head office as general manager. Marlin was already in Calgary, and Coyne raided Electrolux of two more top salesmen. Al Wolfe, chosen by Electrolux to replace Coyne, instead took over First Investors' branch in Regina; George Fergstad, the Calgary branch manager for Electrolux, went to Red Deer for First Investors. In the fall of 1956 Marlin moved to Edmonton to become Coyne's sales manager, and they hired several other former associates, including Jim Gilhooly, who opened a branch in Moose Jaw, Saskatchewan.

Coyne and Marlin applied Electrolux sales tactics to investment certificates—door-to-door, hard-sell and emotional manipulation—and conducted accountability sessions each morning to keep sales staff on their toes. A company song included the refrain: "Savers never lose, spenders never win." The competition was incensed at their success. Insurance company salesmen, selling an insurance/savings product similar to the investment contracts, "called us a bunch of 'pots and pan men'," Coyne said. "We were taking business away from them, but we had no respect."

The key to the breakthrough was a package of five booklets with the collective title *The Babylon Course in Financial Success*. The first and most popular of the series, *The Richest Man in Babylon*, was the tale of a wealthy Babylonian named Arkad who, as a poor young scribe, persuaded the elderly money-lender Algamish to teach him the secrets of accumulating wealth. Wealth is power, Algamish lectured, and "every gold piece that you save is a slave to work for you. Every copper it earns is its child that also can earn for you. If you would become wealthy, then what you save must earn, and its children must earn, and its children's children must earn, that all may help to give to you the abundance you crave." Therefore, Algamish lectured: *A part of all you earn is yours to keep.*

It should not be less than a tenth no matter how little you earn. It can be as much more as you can afford. *Pay yourself first.* Wealth, like a tree, grows from a tiny seed. The first copper you save is the seed from which your tree of wealth shall grow, and the more faithfully you nourish and water that tree with consistent savings, the sooner may you bask in contentment beneath its shade.

Arkad learned other lessons—invest your coppers with great caution, and seek the advice of men whose daily work is handling money. If necessary, consider making provision with small payments at regular intervals. The tale was perfect, inspired, for pitching investment certificates. Packaged in simulated parchment, the booklets made simple the concepts of saving and compound interest, celebrated the work ethic and was framed in quasi-Biblical jargon that rang all the bells of First Investors' working-class prairie clientele.

For many years, Cormie claimed that it was he and Forster who brought the thrift concept to the company. Coyne says—and Marlin agrees—that is not true. "I taught them all about 10% of all you earn is yours to keep," Coyne told me. "When I was about 16, a friend of my mother's gave me a book called *The Richest Man in Babylon*. I brought that in to First Investors. I've always followed that, it always worked for me. When I was with the company, we bought more and gave them to the salesmen. People forget these things as time goes by." In 1960, First Investors acquired the booklets' Canadian copyright, then included them as an envelope stuffer with every certificate sold.

In late 1954, when Coyne was brought into the company, he was allowed to buy 5,000 shares from the First Investors treasury. Two years later, another 35,000 shares were sold among the partners, in approximately the same proportion as the initial allotment. Marlin was cut in for 3%, and Coyne held about 8%. In 1957, another 100,000 shares were sold among the partners, increasing capital to $200,000.

The next year, Stan Melton was suddenly dumped as president and director and Donald Cormie took control of the firm. More than three decades later, the details of this event are unclear. Only the major shareholders attended that fateful meeting, and only Cormie remains alive to tell his version: that the transfer of power was an amicable exchange of shares between two groups. Cormie testified that the partners, also involved in an oil and gas exploration company, decided to divide their interests. Forster, Stewart and Cormie turned over their Melton Petroleum shares in exchange for the Melton group's First Investors stock.

Minority shareholders Coyne and Marlin, however, say that according to what they were later told, the situation was a great deal more acrimonious than Cormie had indicated.

Melton, riding the post-war boom, now had 16 real estate offices in Edmonton, as well as launching Melton Petroleum. He wanted to use First Investors investment contract money to finance his development projects, but Cormie resisted. "Melton felt that First Investors existed for the benefit of the Melton group, and Don Cormie said it existed for its own purpose, not for the benefit of any other company," Marlin told me. "It became obvious the company wasn't big enough for both of them and somebody had to go."

Ab Coyne adds another twist to the story. Earlier in 1958, Coyne had left First Investors after his own unsuccessful showdown with the partners. He wanted to run the sales operation entirely without interference, and he wanted his interest in the company increased to 15%, putting him on an equal footing with the major shareholders. Frustrated in both objectives, he walked out. His revolt was sparked by the discovery that Marlin had opened several branches in southern Alberta without his knowledge, and against his wishes. For many years Coyne believed that Melton had authorized Marlin to undermine his authority, but Marlin told me that Cormie approved the plan. Ironically, because he was angry at Melton, Coyne sold his company shares to Cormie.

"After I quit, Cormie called me and asked what I'd take for my shares." Coyne accepted part payment in cash, and the rest in Melton Petroleum shares. According to Coyne, Cormie left the First Investors shares in Coyne's name in trust, so his partners wouldn't know he had control of them. With the support of Forster and Steward, Cormie controlled 45% of the shares; Coyne's 8% gave him majority control, enabling him to squeeze Melton out of the company.

At a subsequent board meeting, during a discussion of a raise for Melton, "Cormie stood up and said, 'I invoke my share rights.' Not only was there no raise for Melton, but he was fired as president," Coyne said. "This was told to me long ago by the late secretary of First Investors, Ralph Forster."

Marlin had become general manager when Coyne made his exit.[3] When it was clear there would be a fight for control, Marlin told me, both Cormie and Melton sought his support. "Melton came to me, and said he didn't know what the outcome would be: if he bought out Don Cormie, would I stay on as general manager? Half an hour later, Cormie came to my office and asked, 'Whose side are you on?' I said no one's, I was on First Investors' side."

Cormie won and Melton's name was struck as a director from First Investors' corporate records in April 1958. Cormie became president, and he, Forster and Stewart continued as company directors.[4] That month another 60,000 shares were issued (a quarter of them went to Cormie), increasing company capital to $260,000. On October 31, 1958, Cormie, Forster and Stewart signed a voting trust agreement[5] to the effect that they would vote their shares together, with the will of two prevailing over the third. By that point Melton and his colleagues had delivered their First Investors stock, and the trust agreement suggests that Cormie acquired the entire block. According to the agreement, Cormie held 162,761 shares (63%);[6] Forster had 40,000 shares (15%); and Stewart had 26,000 shares (10%). Half of the remaining 12% was held by Ken Marlin, and the other half by a couple of surviving minor partners.

By the time of Cormie's takeover, First Investors was signing up contracts at the rate of a million dollars a month, and had assets under administration totalling about $2.4 million. The operation continued to expand, and within a year the company had about 300 salesmen throughout the three western provinces. In the autumn of 1959, it moved into the United States. First Investors couldn't operate across the border, so two new companies were formed: Principal Investors Corporation, a broker-dealer, and a certificate company called Principal Certificate Series Inc. "That's where the name Principal came into it," Marlin said. "We couldn't get the name First Investors in the United States because there was already one there. An acceptable name that was registerable in all of the States turned out to be *Principal.*"

In the fall of 1959, an office was opened in Seattle, followed over the next two years by others in Oregon, Colorado and elsewhere in Washington. Expansion started in the Canadian Maritimes in the fall of 1960 with an office in Halifax, followed by St. John's, Newfoundland; Sydney, Nova Scotia; and St. John and Fredericton, New Brunswick.

In December 1959, Cormie activated a new holding company called Collective Securities Ltd. Cormie, the president, owned 64%; Forster, secretary-treasurer, held 15.5%; Stewart held 10%; Marlin held 6%; and Cormie's law partner Jack Kennedy held 4.5%.

Soon afterward, the four men sold their shares of First Investors to Collective Securities in a deal an incredulous regulator would later call a "well-watered stock transaction." (The expression refers to a carafe of wine diluted with water to make it appear to contain more than it really does.) The First Investors stock was valued at $6 a share, an astounding inflation in cost for stock in a company—never more than marginally profitable—that was worth only $1 a share a mere half-decade earlier. Of course, by recording the value of the shares at an inflated value, the book value of Collective Securities, and its credit-worthiness, were also inflated.

At the end of 1959, First Investors' capital was increased by another $246,000 with the creation of 41,000 shares acquired by Cormie's law partner Jack Kennedy. According to documents filed with the corporate registry, Kennedy paid $6 a share. In November 1960, another 17,000 shares went to Kennedy, again at $6, resulting in a total of 318,000 common shares and total share capital of $608,000.

These increases in capital were the result of regulatory pressure that began in 1958 when the Alberta Securities Commission observed that First Investors needed additional capital to meet the requirements of the *Investment Contracts Act*, enacted the year before. The Act made the commission responsible for contract companies and set out several requirements: approval of company literature by the province, the registration of salesmen, an annual audited financial statement (kept confidential by the regulators) and several financial tests, detailed in Section 8 of the Act, which became known as the "Section 8 tests." They included a minimum of $500,000 unimpaired paid-in capital; the maintenance of cash reserves for the payment of outstanding contracts; and the deposit of "qualified assets" at a bank. The wording of Section 8, discussed at greater length in Chapter 9, was ambiguous, and would lead to investors being badly misled in later years.

In September 1966, commission auditor Jim Darwish reported to his superiors that the apparent increases in First Investors' share capital since 1958 were illusory. The increases were achieved, Darwish explained, through transactions with subsidiary and parent companies, and were directly or indirectly accomplished through the use of First Investors' own funds. The 1959 increase of $246,000, for example, was manufactured by means of the following transaction: Cormie, Kennedy and Stewart sold their shares in a company called Athabasca Holdings Ltd. to their new holding company, Collective Securities, at the inflated price of $245,000; then Collective sold the Athabasca shares to First Investors for that same price. Then First Investors issued $246,000 worth of treasury shares, at $6 each, to Collective, which passed them on to Kennedy at the same price. No cash actually changed hands: it was all accomplished through an exchange of cheques and notes. (See DIAGRAM 1: *A Well-Watered Stock Transaction.*)

Darwish reported that an independent appraisal of the Athabasca shares determined their value was actually about $70,000 (Cormie, Kennedy and Stewart had earlier acquired the Athabasca shares by unloading an unprofitable real estate company into Athabasca in exchange for $240,000). The transaction effectively increased the value of the partners' investment by 3.5 times, but all was illusion. (If I buy a mongrel puppy for a dollar and sell it to you in exchange for an IOU of $1,000, and you sell the puppy to your uncle for an IOU of $1,000, and he sells the puppy back to me for an IOU of $1,000—is there $1,000 anywhere? Certainly not. There's just a mongrel puppy, a dollar bill and a lot of damp paper.) This outwardly bizarre but basically simple deal was the precursor of a string of increasingly byzantine transactions run through the Principal conglomerate in later years.[7]

By 1959, as assets under administration reached about $4 million, provincial regulators held an increasingly jaundiced view of First Investors. A memo written that year by Darwish, quoting Provincial Auditor C.K. Huckvale, said that company officers paid themselves high salaries and were withdrawing large amounts to pay off personal bank loans. A memo in 1961 complained about inflated management fees paid to companies owned or controlled by Donald Cormie. Investors knew nothing of these matters.

Cormie had little patience with regulatory interference in his money machine, and relations with government officials rapidly deteriorated. He concerned himself with the strict legality of company activities. If something was permitted under existing legislation—or, more to the point, wasn't clearly prohibited—then Cormie considered it proper to proceed. Whenever things got tight with the regulators, Cormie (and employees acting on his behalf) would reiterate his commitment to compliance with the requirements of the *Investment Contracts Act*. It was an empty pledge. The legislation, in fact, didn't require a hell of a lot and was understood, almost from the beginning, to be severely deficient. After the 1987 collapse, Alberta Ombudsman Aleck Trawick investigated the province's regulation of Cormie's companies and found:

> It is clear...that the companies very early on developed and followed a pattern of operating to the very outside limits of the legislation and of challenging the regulators on every matter raised... The companies took full advantage of the deficiencies in the [*Investment Contracts Act's*] financial requirements and the ambiguous drafting of the specific terms of the statute in order to take the opportunity to argue with the methods of calculation used by the regulators to monitor the capital, qualified assets depository and reserve requirements.

Relations with the regulators deteriorated further in 1962, when Collective Securities acquired a second investment contract company. Associated Investors of Canada Ltd., founded in 1948 in Edmonton by Harry Curlett and associates, was sold in May 1962 to Equitable Investments Corporation of Columbus, Ohio. Equitable quickly lost interest in the company and sold it to the Cormie group. At that time, Associated Investors managed assets of about $20 million, compared to First Investors' $10 million.

Unfortunately, Equitable had partly financed its purchase by having Associated Investors buy $3.6 million worth of Equitable preferred shares, almost a fifth of the company's total assets. Equitable had, in effect, taken about $3.6 million cash out of Associated Investors and replaced it with paper, using the company's own cash to take it over. (The strategy was familiar to Cormie, who had been using it himself for at least a couple of years. See below.)

Cormie, concerned that the preferred shares might not be legally qualified investments under the *Investment Contracts Act*, walked over to the Alberta Legislature and met with Premier Ernest Manning, who also held the Attorney General portfolio at that time. "When we looked at it," Cormie testified, "we were rather surprised that that would be a qualified asset even though the audit indicated that it was, except for the lack of market. So I made a point of going to—or contacting...Mr. Manning, to try and get a comfort letter that, in fact, it was a qualified asset and that if we acquired the company, we could continue to hold it and it wouldn't be against public policy for us to acquire the other company."

Manning co-operated, issuing a letter dated December 21, 1962, which advised Cormie that the Alberta Securities Commission did not question that the shares were legally qualified investments, "and has satisfied itself that they are marketable. Hence, on this score, there is no concern that these are held by Associated Investors or by First Investors, if the proposed merger is consummated."

While the Alberta government wasn't concerned, Saskatchewan's was. That province's investment contract legislation, similar to Alberta's, also laid out a number of financial tests to be applied to a company's assets. Regulators looked at the Equitable shares, decided they were not a qualified asset, and ordered that they be disposed of.

The preferred shares turned out to be almost worthless because Equitable ultimately went bankrupt, Cormie testified. As well, when he got into Associated Investors' books, he found that there were defective titles to a large number of mortgages, and interest had been accrued far past the value of several of the defaulted investments. The company took a beating totalling millions of dollars.

Cormie was furious at the loss. Rather than accept responsibility for failing to thoroughly investigate the situation prior to the acquisition, he blamed the Alberta Securities Commission (particularly auditor Darwish), who had advised Premier Manning prior to the preparation of his comfort letter.

"I am afraid that we probably had a tendency to blame the people at the commission because we felt that they owed a duty to us, as purchasing shareholders, to tell us all this, which they presumably knew or should have known," Cormie testified. "We were treating ourselves more like a certificate holder, I guess, and we thought they owed a duty to us. So we maybe started off from that point on with rather a difficult relationship in that we were critical of them and they were critical of us. I don't believe in the next 25 years that we ever got a positive report from Jim on the [contract] companies."

Prior to Cormie's acquisition, Associated Investors had always filed an annual financial statement with the corporate registry, something First Investors had never done. The last statement was filed in December 1962, as Cormie took over, and it never happened again. The contract companies had to provide audited statements to the regulators each year and did so, but they were not required to publicly disclose their financial situation. Not required: not provided.

The creation of Collective Securities in 1959 was the first step in the development of an increasingly elaborate corporate structure. Within a few years, Cormie and his associates didn't own a company or two; they owned companies which owned companies which owned companies. Some sold products or provided services to the public; a second group provided management and services to the first group. Some came to own pieces of one another, to loan one another money and to pay one another fees. Cormie's personally-owned companies were also connected to the system. Most companies further down the chain were paying fees, administration costs and dividends, and all that money was moving upwards—most of it in Cormie's direction.

Whether Cormie designed the system to be impenetrable is hard to say, but it certainly had that effect. Government officials used to speculate about what was happening behind the curtain. Some of the regulated companies had to provide information to the government, but others were completely private. In some cases it was perfectly clear what was going on. In others, officials could make an educated guess, but remained in the dark about many important matters.

In 1974 Tom Dansereau, then-Alberta's Director of Trust Companies—and responsible for the regulation of Principal's trust company, incorporated in 1965—voiced his frustration in a special report to then-Attorney General Merv Leitch which complained of Cormie's "unorthodox methods and practices of carrying on business":

> Mr. Cormie, I believe, would be most happy if he had a free hand in running his conglomerate devoid of any government legislation and its administrators. I can only assume from the information available to me, that Mr. Cormie must have spent countless hours devising ways and means to set up his empire, the Principal Group, so as to safeguard his operation from easy scrutiny and to make sure that he personally obtains by any means, the greatest return for himself.

In the early 1960s salesmen reported that customers were slipping through the net because the product range was too narrow. Accumulation plans remained popular, but many people had become interested in more sophisticated investments. Principal responded with an expanded product line, and the subsidiaries multiplied. In 1963 the first mutual fund, Collective Mutual Fund Ltd., was incorporated. That was followed in 1967 by Principal Growth Fund Ltd., and in 1969 by the Principal Venture Fund Ltd. (In the 1970s and 1980s several other mutual funds would be introduced.)

In December 1966 another layer was built into the system. Principal Group Ltd. (with Cormie as president) was inserted between Collective Securities and the subsidiaries as a holding and management company. The new company issued a million common shares, as well as 400,000 preferred shares. Many of the preferreds, which had no voting rights, were sold to the public for $25 each.[8] All but seven of the one million common shares were held by Collective Securities, with one share each held by Cormie, Stewart, Forster, Kennedy, Marlin and two men brought in from outside as executives for the contract companies.

Up the line, the shareholders of Collective Securities had remained unchanged for several years: Cormie owned 64%; Forster 15.5%; Stewart 10%; Marlin 6%; and Kennedy 4.5%. In 1967, Stewart retired and sold his shares to Cormie, increasing his ownership to 74%. (See DIAGRAM 2: *Principal Group Corporate Structure 1967.*)

The creation of Principal Group, and a new policy of providing management services to the subsidiaries on a "functional" basis, transformed the conglomerate. Over the next few years subsidiaries fired their employees or transferred them over to the parent, and all management was centralized in Principal Group. Until 1966 the two contract companies each had their own sales force and executives; after the change the companies had no direct employees. Principal Group "provided services" to the subsidiaries, then charged back the costs and salaries to each of the companies. A frustrating side-effect of this strategy, from the regulators' point of view, was that it became very difficult to determine the actual financial state of the various companies in the system.

An important component of the burgeoning system was Principal Group Ltd. subsidiary Principal Savings and Trust Company Ltd., incorporated under Alberta's *Trust Companies Act*, with Cormie as president. Principal Trust was founded with $500,000 in capital, the minimum required for registration of a trust company at that time. The company, regulated by the provincial government and insured by the federal CDIC, became the conglomerate's highly respectable flagship.

Principal Trust's original function was to act as trustee of the Hutterian Brethren Investment Trust, created to invest money on behalf of several Alberta Hutterite colonies. Hutterites, who fled Eastern Europe in the late 19th century to escape persecution for their religious and pacifist beliefs, live austere lives in communal agricultural colonies of about a hundred people. There are more than 200 colonies across the prairie provinces, many of them in southern Alberta. Members work together, build together and save together, generating huge pools of capital which are used to buy equipment and land to allow growing communities to divide.

Some Hutterite colonies had been clients of Associated Investors, and others were vigorously wooed by Ken Marlin. The colonies had originally purchased 30-year accumulation plans, but found them inflexible, and Principal proposed a new arrangement more suited to their needs. A contract between the colonies and the trust company, called a trust deed, was presented to the colonies for signature. The trust deed, approved by the colony managers who handled community business, required the investment of two-thirds of the trust funds in preferred shares of Collective Securities or any of its subsidiaries, and one third in investment certificates issued by First Investors and Associated Investors. The new trust pooled several colonies' funds and treated them somewhat like a savings account, permitting withdrawal of cash as needed. In 1966, the trust totalled $3,346,000, with $2.5 million of that held in newly created Principal Group preferred shares. By March 1967, the trust had increased by another million dollars, and it kept climbing.

The arrangement was highly advantageous to Principal, which obtained the use of cheap capital for extended periods of time. The interest paid on the funds was relatively low; on top of that Principal Trust charged the Hutterites acquisition and administration fees.

Director of Trust Companies Dansereau fought this trust arrangement for years, describing it in 1974 as "the most unconscionable agreement I have ever seen in all my years of being connected with trust companies and fiduciary matters." In 1981 he was finally successful in forcing the wind-down of the trust, and further investment by the colonies was made through Principal Group promissory notes. As a result, the opportunity was given to each colony to decide whether or not to purchase notes and to negotiate the terms of purchase, rather than allow the trustee to make arbitrary investment decisions.

By 1982, Principal Group had issued $18 million worth of notes to the colonies and began marketing them more widely to members of the public. At the Code inquiry, Marlin unabashedly admitted that the note money was often used to cover the debts and shortfalls of other parts of the conglomerate. During the inquiry, it was learned that note money was used for an even more odious purpose: to provide millions of dollars in unsecured loans to Cormie family members. (See Chapter 13.)

In 1970, the increasingly complex corporate structure was further refined. Principal's sales department was hived off to a separate company, Principal Consultants Ltd., another Principal Group subsidiary. The sales team distributed the Principal Group's entire range of financial products: the investment contracts, the trust company's term deposits and trust services, the various mutual funds and, later, Principal Group's promissory notes. In Cormie's functional system of management, Ken Marlin was both president of Principal Consultants and Principal Group vice-president of sales.

Despite the growing complexity of the structure, the operation itself remained simple. "I suppose you could say we viewed the organization as if it were one organization with many products or funds," Marlin testified. "And that, I suppose the simplistic view was, there were three departments in my mind. One was the Money-In Department, the other was a Control Department and the third was a Money-Out Department." The Money-Out Department handled investment and management of assets; the Control Department included administration, accounting, computer and legal functions; and the Money-In Department was sales. "I was responsible for the Money-In, crossing all corporate boundaries, and I simply ran it in that fashion."

Above the conglomerate—"upstairs," as it would be referred to in later years—other companies were also proliferating. In December 1955, a year and a half after the creation of First Investors, Cormie incorporated County Investments Ltd., a "tax-planning" vehicle which would become infamous during the Code inquiry as the Cormie family's "little bank."[9] In August 1956, Cormie also created Estate Loan and Finance Ltd., a family holding company.

An interesting pattern developed. The corporate registry showed Cormie as a director of each company on the day it was created —then his name was struck and he was replaced by secretaries: at Estate Loan by Bernice Metz, and at County Investments by Jean Metz, who shortly yielded the post to Bernice. The second director for each company was Cormie's accountant Ellen Howerton. In August 1960, Bernice made way for Adeline (Addy) Smith, a secretary at Cormie Kennedy. When Howerton left in 1964, she was replaced by accountant Margaret Duncan.

And so on, for 32 years: a functionary would disappear and another would arrive, thus rendering Cormie's hand invisible.

In 1956, the same month that Cormie created Estate Loan, he also entered an enterprise with Ferris George Swann, a recently graduated Edmonton engineer. Custom Camps Ltd. was created with the intention of building trailer courts and campsite facilities to house workers in the oil fields near Drayton Valley, about 50 miles from Edmonton. Immediately after Custom Camps' creation in 1956, it issued debentures (Swann loaned the company $10,000 and Cormie loaned it $5,000) and the two men elected themselves as directors. (Debentures are similar to promissory notes: basically an IOU, backed only by the credit of the issuer and unsecured by any specific asset.) The next spring Swann put in another $10,000 and Cormie put in $15,000 ($5,000 through County Investments and $10,000 through Estate Loan), making the two men equal investors. In early 1957, accountant Reginald Victor Paul, a Cormie associate, was added as a third director. A year and a half later (a few months after Melton left First Investors) Swann jumped or was pushed from the board, to be replaced by Addy Smith. Later, when Smith became director of Cormie's two other companies, she was replaced at Custom Camps by Ellen Howerton, already on the Estate Loan and County Investments rosters.

In 1962, the name of Custom Camps was changed to Cormie Ranch Ltd. The previous year Cormie had begun buying up land around Tomahawk, about 40 miles west of Edmonton, and he used the renamed company to hold and manage some of the property. After the name change, the debentures issued to Swann and Cormie were redeemed and new debentures were issued: Estate Loan immediately acquired seven of them, at a cost of $10,000 each, then acquired the remaining eight two years later.

Cormie remained director and president of Cormie Ranch throughout its existence (holding all but two of the company's common shares), but he cycled employees through the other two directorships as he had done at County Investments and Estate Loan. The same names appear on the records of all three companies. Often a person would serve simultaneously on all three boards.

During this period Cormie also created Alberta Mortgage Exchange Ltd. The company was incorporated in early 1957 with Cormie and Addy Smith as directors: Cormie held three shares and Smith held one. (Smith followed Cormie from Cormie Kennedy to First Investors, and later to Principal Group. She was dropped from the Alberta Mortgage board in 1958, and her name disappeared from the records of the last of the four upstairs companies, Estate Loan, in 1963. She later became a director of Principal Trust, and remained on its board until the 1987 collapse.)

Alberta Mortgage was in the mortgage brokerage business, and, as Cormie testified, would accept mortgage applications "then submit them to the mortgage committee of First or Associated or the trust company who would then select or accept or reject any submissions." Since the same people were running all these companies, acceptance was scarcely a challenge.

By 1965, provincial regulators were writing angry memos about Alberta Mortgage, which they felt was taking advantage of the contract companies. Alberta Mortgage was issuing discounted mortgages and selling them to First Investors after creaming much of the profit off the top. The company would issue a mortgage for, say, $10,000, but give the customer only $7,000. The interest rate was low, on the face of it, but with the discount the customer was actually paying the current rate of interest. Then Alberta Mortgage would sell the mortgage for the full $10,000 to First Investors, thus giving Alberta Mortgage an immediate profit of $3,000. First Investors ended up with a $10,000 mortgage which it would collect over the term at the low interest rate.

Marlin told me that the scheme was part of a strategy established by Cormie to avoid regulatory interference. "He had at different times stated that any surplus profits that the group made would be moved to a non-regulated area—either through dividends or management fees or discounts on mortgages—and the money left in a non-regulated company where presumably you could invest it with no restrictions and do better on it. Because if you left it in the regulated companies then the temptation of the regulators was to tell you that all the money in the company had to be invested according to the *Investment Contracts Act*. Whereas if you left the surplus money in the Principal Group then Principal Group could be creative in how it used the money."

Very creative.

From the time that First Investors was a tiny company, Cormie played these games with its funds. Over the years the games grew more complicated and the stakes grew ever larger. "The justification in my mind," he said, "was always that if First Investors or Associated Investors or the trust company needed funds to meet regulatory requirements, then the funds were injected; and that had always happened, not without some resistance and let's say pressure from the regulators, but it was a strategy to put in as little as was acceptable."

Estate Loan began collecting management fees from First Investors in December 1958, soon after Stan Melton was ousted from First Investors. First Investors' new board of directors (Cormie, Forster and Stewart) terminated a management services contract with Cormie, and replaced it with management fees of $6,410 a month to Estate Loan to manage the sales organization—despite the fact that at that time First Investors had its own office, staff and sales force.

Over the next several years the contract companies paid increasingly generous management fees and dividends, and in 1966 government regulators moved to block the activity. Jim Darwish's September 1966 report noted that Cormie, Stewart, Forster, Estate Loan and Collective Securities had taken a total of $2.8 million in "profits" out of First Investors and Associated Investors in the seven and a half years since the 1958 takeover—including $259,203 in fees and dividends from First Investors during the first half of 1966, when it had a net loss of $64,943. "In my opinion," Darwish wrote:

> for company officials to continue to make these payments with the full knowledge that profits were dependent, to a great extent, upon inter-company transactions, is a breach of their responsibility to the public.
>
> Not only were profits dependent on intercompany transactions, it was necessary for First Investors Corp. Ltd. to lend to the subsidiary company over $1,000,000, so that a dividend could be paid by the subsidiary to the parent certificate company. It appears that the public's money is being used to pay these huge dividends and management fees to the owners of the certificate company.

Darwish noted that Alberta Mortgage Exchange, which at that point owed First Investors $1,117,004, had just borrowed another $100,000 to be used as a down-payment on a downtown office building. This transaction was conducted through Alberta Mortgage because First Investors was prohibited from acquiring real estate under the *Investment Contracts Act*. This strategy—having a subsidiary or borrower do something with the contract companies' money that they were forbidden from doing themselves—was also followed in later years. Darwish further reported that First Investors had certificate liabilities of $26.9 million, while its capital, which under the *Investment Contracts Act* should have been at least $500,000, had been reduced to $3,431. He gave several reasons for this:

(1) Paying income taxes on intercompany profits, which, from the point of view of the consolidated company, have not been earned and simply constitute a writing-up of assets.
(2) Bleeding the company by its shareholders, by the payment of dividends and management fees out of paper profits.
(3) The purchase of subsidiary companies on a non-arm's length basis and placing an inflated value thereon. This transaction ostensibly created more capital, but should not be recognized as such.

That autumn the Alberta Securities Commission threatened suspension of the contract companies' licences, forcing the return of $300,000 in management fees drawn from Associated Investors during the year. According to a letter written by Darwish's boss Harry Rose to Saskatchewan regulators, Cormie promised that inter-corporate transactions would cease. They did: for about a year.

In 1968, Associated Investors borrowed money to meet maturing contracts, at the same time that it was paying significant dividends and management fees to related companies. In 1969, commission auditors complained that the financial statements of Principal Group Ltd. showed that funds borrowed from First Investors were used to reduced a debt to Principal's parent company Collective Securities. In 1970, First Investors borrowed a million dollars to pay off maturing certificates, at the same time loaning a similar amount to the parent company.

There were also deals among the private upstairs companies. (The financial records of the companies during this era are not available, and the books of Cormie Ranch and Estate Loan and Finance were never made public, so events are pieced together from corporate registry reports, scattered testimony and a few surviving memos.) In 1964, Cormie transferred his preferred shares in Collective Securities (then valued at $3.2 million) to Cormie Ranch. (The strategy is simple, and would be widely applied in coming years: if Cormie had owned the shares personally, he would have had to declare the dividends as taxable income. By having the unprofitable Cormie Ranch receive Collective dividends, he could write the income off against the ranch's operating losses.)

In 1966 Collective purchased $1 million worth of preferred shares from Cormie Ranch. The transaction, viewed by Collective shareholders as an interest-free loan to

Cormie, remained on the books until 1985, when Cormie Ranch and Collective were merged. (See Chapter 15.)

In September 1967, Ralph Forster returned from a lengthy trip and discovered that Collective Securities had made another $450,000 interest-free loan to Cormie Ranch. He wrote a protest memo to Cormie and attached a letter resigning as corporate treasurer:

> I am probably very old fashioned. I think it is the duty of a Treasurer to be vigilant in looking after the interests of all Shareholders, Majority and Minority alike. I don't think monies should be advanced without collateral and unless properly approved, authorized and minuted.
>
> In this respect as Treasurer, I have failed. The best example is that I learn from the accounts that $450,000 has been advanced to Cormie Ranch—as far as I know without consultation with Shareholders, with no meeting, approval or collateral. I don't think such casual methods are in the best interests of the Company so I attach my resignation as Treasurer, with the constructive suggestion that there are better and more efficient methods...

The next day Forster sent another memo, this time to the shareholders:

> As most of you know, for years I have been trying to arrange regular meetings of Shareholders. We all know Don is allergic to such meetings.
>
> If we are going to achieve our goals, there must be communication and we must have meetings. I suggest all Shareholders meet regularly on Fridays at 12.00 for lunch at the Glenora Club until our Agenda is cleared, and then meet monthly. I think we are at a turning point in our association and operations. I think the equities have gotten completely out of line. It is only by free and frank discussion that solutions acceptable to all Shareholders can be reached. Too much time is being wasted now thinking about these things. It should be devoted to making profits...
>
> Attached is an Agenda covering items I think should be resolved. I envisage meetings where constructive decisions are taken followed by action. Such meetings should produce a long term plan where each one of us knows where we are heading Collectively and individually.
>
> Ours has been an undertaking we should all be proud of and the parts we each have played in its creation. We have a good company. Its potential is unlimited if we all concentrate on it as we did originally. Let us all co-operate to get rid of the present unhealthy atmosphere and create one where we are again working as a team.
>
> I envy you all your youth. I still see our future as one of great opportunity.

After Forster's memos were read into evidence at the Code inquiry, Cormie testified that Forster wanted to quit—not because he was upset with the financial situation, but because he wished to travel more.

Forster's resignation wasn't accepted until a half a year later, in the spring of 1968, at which time he was also dropped as director and treasurer of both the contract companies. For several months, Forster maintained his minority interest in Collective Securities, then in August 1968 he wrote another memo. This one began by praising Cormie for "a terrific job in the last eighteen months in your drive on streamlining, reorganizing and profit making. It is a job only you could have done." Then Forster again raised the issue of interest-free loans being made to shareholders—mostly to Cormie—and complained that since "the financial demands of Cormie Ranch took precedence to the best interests of the company" the organization had declined. The $450,000 loan to the ranch "should be regularized... as I think we are all derelict of not fulfilling our duties and responsibilities as Directors." At that time, he said, the company had a total of $1,559,848 "after-tax money working, interest free, for either Cormie Ranch or a shareholder and not for the company... As I see it all shareholders pro rata are paying the costs of bank loans probably unnecessary if these sums had not been advanced."

Cormie had recently announced a new policy which required senior Principal Group officers to dispose of any investments outside the group except those requiring no management attention. The policy was targeted at Ken Marlin, who had branched out the year before with a travel agency. Forster and Marlin opposed the policy but Cormie insisted, and Marlin turned the business over to his son Rod, then 21. (Marlin Travel has since expanded into Canada's largest retail travel chain.) Around this time Marlin considered getting out, and he offered his shares to Cormie. Cormie refused the offer.

Instead, in October 1968, Marlin was allowed to buy out Jack Kennedy's interest in Collective Securities and a couple of smaller related companies. Subsequent correspondence from Marlin to Cormie indicates that Marlin paid $112,000 for the stock, and the money was loaned to him interest-free ($50,000 from Collective Securities, $32,000 from First Investors and $30,000 from Associated Investors), with the understanding that Marlin would assume a debt of $40,000 owed by Kennedy to Cormie Ranch.

In January 1969, Forster sold his common shares to Cormie, and was dropped from the Collective and Principal Group boards of directors. Cormie partly paid for the shares by transferring 500 non-voting preferred Collective shares to Forster. An entry in Forster's diary, dated June 7, 1970,[10] recorded the following:

Cormie Agreement. 9% on unpaid balance to 1976. Balance outstanding $334,000.00—Promissory Notes. Even monthly payments; Interest $2450, Principal 3151; total $5601.00. Although this is a purely personal deal realistically if anything happened to Principal Group payment would probably cease!

Two years later, in 1972, Forster died of cancer. He was memoralized with the creation of the R.P. Forster Memorial Bowl, awarded annually to the salesman with the highest total personal sales volume during the March sales campaign.

With the shares acquired from Forster and Stewart, who sold out in 1970, Cormie's ownership in Collective Securities increased to 85.5%. The balance of the shares were held by Marlin (10.5%) and accountant/corporate administrator George Berge (4%).

Three years later, Berge left the company and his shares also went to Cormie, bumping his ownership up to 89.5%. That's the way it stayed, with Marlin holding the final 10.5%, for several years, until Cormie divided 9% of his common shares between his sons John and Jaimie. When Berge left he was dropped as director and replaced by Gerard Frey, who would also be appointed a director of First Investors and president of Associated Investors. Frey and Berge were just two of many men cycled through the "downstairs" companies after the late 1960s as directors, executives and managers.

Confrontations with the regulators over the contract companies continued to escalate, and in 1971 Cormie withdrew as president and director. He hoped to stay out of sight and out of mind, but the regulators weren't fooled for very long.

Directors moved through the contract companies, and executives through Principal Group, like weekenders at a summer cottage. Most lasted less than a couple of years. Some quit, sickened at the deals they were instructed to rubber-stamp; others were fired or squeezed out. Finally, in the mid-1970s, Cormie abandoned the idea of bringing in outsiders to "manage" the contract companies. Ken Marlin was made director and president of First Investors and Associated Investors, with the assignment of smoothing over relations with regulators. In February 1978 the last of the outsiders was removed from the contract companies' boards of directors. Cormie appointed Eric Espenberg, a long-time Principal Group employee, as director and secretary-treasurer of both First Investors and Associated Investors. For several years Espenberg and Marlin served as sole directors of the two contract companies.

Espenberg, born in 1930, had been hired by Ralph Forster in 1960 to operate the office computer. He was transferred in 1966 to the office services department, becoming office manager in 1972 and purchasing manager in 1977. At the Code inquiry Cormie described him as the guy who "handled the field end, or the office supplies and things of that type." Espenberg, a high school graduate, had no business, legal or accounting background, but he was loyal, trusting and compliant.

Those qualities made Espenberg the ideal Principal company director. "I was told I was a director by John Cormie," he testified. "I was told I would be a director in name only, not in action." Did Espenberg ask what that meant? "No, I think I got the drift... Put your name on a piece of paper when it was handed to you." What were his duties as director for the two contract companies? "Just put my signature on various documents."

In short, a human pencil. Over the next nine years, Espenberg unquestioningly signed banking resolutions, cheques, contracts and authorizations of the purchase and sale of stocks, bonds and mortgages. He never attended a directors' meeting, but would receive minutes of board meetings through interoffice mail, or be summoned to the legal department for a signature. Sometimes, Espenberg testified, Cormie's secretary would appear at his desk with papers for him to sign.

The only financial information he received about the companies was at year-end, when their annual audited financial statements were presented to him and signed without discussion. Once a year there would be a meeting of the shareholders of First Investors and Associated Investors. Although Espenberg was secretary-treasurer, a member of the Principal legal staff recorded the minutes of those meetings and brought them to Espenberg for his signature. The directors' fees were discussed during the annual meeting, but Espenberg had no input into that, he said. "No, I was waiting until Mr. Cormie came up with a figure, and everybody agreed. That was it." In the final years before the collapse, the directors' fees for both contract companies totalled $4,000 per annum.

After a couple of years as director, Espenberg learned through a chance encounter with the Principal in-house lawyer that there were legal responsibilities connected to his directorships. Directors have two kinds of duties under the law: "fiduciary duties"—the obligation to act honestly and in good faith, with a view to the best interests of the company, and not for any other purpose—and duties of care, skill and diligence. It has been understood for a century that those duties cannot be shirked by leaving everything to others.

"I was shocked," Espenberg testified. "All of a sudden I found out I had quite a responsibility, I could be liable for a million dollars or more." But this didn't change the way he functioned as a director. "No, I felt that—I trusted people, I think people knew what they were doing, and I did not change."

A similar pattern held true throughout the conglomerate. As Cormie had done with his upstairs companies, he appointed Principal staff members as nominal directors of the continually-multiplying subsidiaries. By the 1980s, the employment contract of several employees included the standard phrase: "As part of the position described above, your employment will require that you act as a director or officer of one or more of the affiliated and/or subsidiary companies." The directorships paid fees ranging from a few hundred to a few thousand dollars a year: miserly compensation for the breathtaking responsibility inherent in the positions.

Control of the various subsidiaries was centralized in Principal Group, the parent company, through the "functional management" approach, and all the functional vice-presidents reported directly to Cormie. Cormie controlled the information, the pay-cheques and—through his employees—the companies.[11]

By 1971, Collective Securities' interest-free loans to Cormie Ranch had climbed to $4,030,300. That figure comes from a letter written by Marlin to Cormie in 1976, complaining of not getting a fair cut. Marlin cited the "inequitable" distribution of interest-free loans to the Collective shareholders: that is, to himself and Cormie. While Cormie had over $4 million of the company's cash, Marlin's loans totalled only $145,900, and Marlin felt the "indirect benefit" of the loans should be handed out in the same proportion as the ownership of the company: 89.5% to Cormie and 10.5% to himself.

According to Marlin's 1976 letter, Cormie Ranch had purchased $2.5 million worth of Collective Securities preferred shares in 1970 with a 10% downpayment.

> This transaction took place without my knowledge or understanding. The effect of this transaction is that I end up holding only 1% of the Collective Preferred issue while the Cormie Family end up with 94% and the full purchase price of the shares is actually being paid for by an increase in the loan to Cormie Ranch plus the dividends that have been declared and paid every year since. There are obvious inequities in this transaction that must be straightened out.

A couple of years later, Marlin was allowed to buy sufficient preferred shares to bring his share up to 10.5%.

In the early years, when sales were the primary focus of the company, Marlin and Cormie worked as a team, sometimes travelling in tandem to open new territory or to check out branch offices. During the late 1950s and early 1960s, their families sometimes spent weekends together. They seemed to be friends in those days. But as assets accumulated and companies proliferated, Cormie's attention shifted to other areas of the operation. Tax-planning and investments, both corporate and personal, became increasingly important to him. He continued to chair the sales committee, as he always had, and routinely scrutinized the sales and staff productivity reports, but he left management of the day-to-day sales activities to Marlin. The men drifted apart, and their relationship deteriorated into uneasy mutual courtesy, punctuated by occasional blowups. (The wives, Eivor Cormie and Helen Marlin, continued their friendship to the end. The two women planned to attend the Code inquiry together, until instructed by lawyers to stay apart. "I have to stop myself every day from picking up the phone and calling her," Helen Marlin told me in 1990.)

In public, Marlin liked to portray himself as Cormie's partner, but in the office there was never any doubt about who was in control. "Don's attitude was he was the major shareholder, and it operated to suit his purposes," Marlin told me. "He made no bones about that—he was the largest shareholder and he was going to arrange his affairs for the best tax benefit for himself. If we didn't like that, then that was too bad.

"In the outside world we always got along great, but in private we had some real nose-to-nose showdowns. I remember one time in the late 1950s, I was hot enough under the collar that I was following him back to his office at Cormie Kennedy, and he was trying to shake me. I was rather wound up, to the point where I said, 'For Christ's sake, Don, all I want is for you to be fair.'

"He said, 'I don't have to be fair.'

"And I said, 'Well I guess you don't.' I said, 'Is that your attitude?' and he said, 'Exactly. That's the way it's going to be. I don't have to be fair.'

"So I knew what I was dealing with. It was no mystery to me."

Despite these tensions and the furious conflicts with regulators that continued for three decades, Cormie maintained an almost unblemished public reputation. Government employees are sworn to silence, and they take that vow very seriously.

Several people, having crossed Cormie's path in a business deal, considered him a vicious cut-throat, but their views were not widely known. A couple of households wouldn't have him over the threshold, but to most Edmontonians, Cormie was an honest-to-God home-grown hero.

Marlin and Cormie sold Principal like a religion, with Cormie as the high priest of thrift. As the years passed the legend grew: Donald Cormie, a near-prescient financial wizard, "a swashbuckling Western entrepreneur"[12] with an uncanny ability to anticipate market trends. Cormie occasionally took his show on the road, and enchanted audiences paid to hear him speak about his "cyclical management strategy." Financial events, he told them, can be accurately predicted by analyzing a series of economic, social and climatic events. Everything happens in cycles of about 50 to 60 years, he explained, and if you can pinpoint where you are in the cycle you will know when to buy, when to sell and when to run: *Stick with Principal, folks, and you'll get rich—just like me.*

Over the years, Cormie's prognostications enjoyed varying success. "We had a good record at some periods and not as good at others," he admitted in testimony. "I think, you know, our record maybe doesn't look very good at this stage, but it did at one time because our mutual funds, over the last 10 years, have averaged about 20% annual compounded return. You might say anybody could do that, but if it is that easy, then everybody would be in the business."

Some of Cormie's successes were indeed dramatic. During a 1968 university lecture to sceptical business students, he predicted a tripling of commodity prices by 1975. He was off by a couple of years, but he was right, and the story got around. In 1978, at the peak of Alberta's oil boom, he predicted the collapse of oil prices and a "decline" in real estate values. He also said that the next five years would be a period of "unparalleled prosperity." He was (in order) right on the money, in the ball park and dead wrong. Unfortunately, the real estate market didn't decline in the 1980s, it crashed and burned. By 1982, the entire western economy was devastated and Cormie's companies, like everything else, were horribly scorched.

Over the years, investors poured their dollars into the Principal machine in ever multiplying numbers. Total assets under administration climbed from the original $60,000 in seed capital in 1954 to $50 million in the first decade. By 1971 assets had surpassed $100 million, and six years later had increased again to about $150 million. That was the beginning of the oil boom, and the asset values skyrocketed: $210 million in 1978; $300 million in 1979; $445 million in 1980; $505 million in 1981; $630 million in 1982. After the oil bust, there was no drop. Principal's aggressive sales force pushed assets up to $820 million in 1983; $895 million in 1984; and $950 million in 1985. Before it was all over Principal would control more than a billion dollars—most of it other people's money.

4

A suite deal for heifers

HAVE YOU EVER SEEN A BULL go peepee?" Rod Ziegler pushed his glasses back up on his nose and beamed. "It's everywhere."

Ziegler is a writer with *The Edmonton Journal*: a wide-eyed, soft-spoken guy with endless contacts in business and politics. We were talking about Donald Cormie's infamous 1983 cattle auction at the top of Principal Plaza. The memory obviously gave Ziegler lasting pleasure.

It's the audacity of the event, of course. Who but Donald Cormie would have a herd of prize Maine-Anjou heifers crammed into a highrise elevator and lifted 29 storeys up to his penthouse suite to be auctioned at the foot of a mahogany staircase? The prospect of seeing one of those precious calves pissing all over the polished marble floor was too rich to be missed.

Ziegler is now a business affairs columnist, but in 1983, when he went to watch the auction, he was the *Journal's* business editor. He wasn't on duty; a staff reporter wrote the article ("Prime cattle moo-ve up to penthouse: A suite deal for heifers") which graced the front page the next morning. Ziegler is an old family friend of the Cormies, and he just wanted to be in on the fun.

Back in the early 1960s, Ziegler told me, "My father used to go grouse-shooting, and this guy Cormie was buying up all the grouse-shooting land. So my dad called him up and asked if he could shoot there." Cormie said sure, and the Zieglers became welcome guests at the future Cormie Ranch, where Ziegler remembers hanging out as a teenager with Cormie's sons Neil and Bruce.

The 15,000-acre ranch is located in the watershed between Lake Wabamun and the North Saskatchewan River. A still sometimes-marshy spread, the land was mosquito-infested swamp when Cormie picked it up. An English colonel, a previous owner of some of the property, had hired hundreds of Chinese railway workers in the 1920s to dig a huge ditch in efforts to drain Low Water Lake, which forms the largest portion of the ranch.[1] Cormie continued to drain the land and started building his prestigious cattle breeding operation.

Cormie ran 2,000 head of imported pure-bred cattle—Maine-Anjou, Simmental, Charolais and Polled Hereford—which he bred for the bull semen. The pride of the fleet was Signal, a Swiss-born Simmental that earned the ranch $3.2 million, siring 150,000 offspring in a 13-year career. In the mid-1970s, the ranch moved into embryo transplants as well, aided by Principal Group's computers, which tracked the history, growth and value of every animal.

The staircase auction was actually the brainstorm of Bill MacLeod, the ranch's Main-Anjou herdsman, who was involved in planning a reception for delegates to the World Maine-Anjou conference in Red Deer that same week. "I was in the office one day and I thought it would be a good idea to have it there," MacLeod told me. "I talked to Neil first, and then I asked Don himself and after he thought about it for a while he thought it might be a good plan.

"So we started training the calves at the ranch—the usual halter breaking and that sort of thing, but then we had to get them used to the kind of a ride they were going to have in the elevator. So we put them in a horse trailer and took them up and down the road over a bridge that was there that had quite a jump to it. That's how they got used to the up and down motion.

"Then we just put 'em in the elevator and sent 'em up."

Cattlemen from all over North American were feted at a reception and buffet dinner. Sporting cowboy hats and business suits, more than 200 guests watched videos of ranch activities and a feature film of the cattle to be sold. Then they leaned over the mahogany railing on the Plaza's penthouse level and watched the animals parade below them. Ranch hands stood by with brooms and mops at the ready, instantly eliminating any indiscretions from the marble floor.

The auction was a very hot story. It hit the national and international television news that night, and was the talk of the cattle world for years: a wonderful boost to Cormie's already larger-than-life reputation.

In the 25 years since taking over First Investors from Stan Melton, Donald Cormie had become a wealthy and powerful man. Like his ancestors, he took comfort in land, plowing millions of dollars into real estate. In 1958, the year of the First Investors takeover, he and Eivor moved their still-growing family (six in hand, with two still to come) to a house on Saskatchewan Drive, across the university campus from his father George's residence. Within a couple of years, he was developing Cormie Ranch. George Cormie must have been pleased to see his son deepening drainage trenches, installing fences, putting up buildings, buying cattle and applying the breeding theories he had learned in childhood on the Jasper Place poultry farm. Whether George knew that Donald was financing the improvements with the assistance of corporate funds is impossible to say.

George officially retired from his feed mill in 1955. Even so, he continued for years to go into the office each morning to check up on plant management. The mill had flourished over the years and its value had multiplied many times; a report to the corporate registrar in 1965 placed the company's gross asset value at almost $375,000. Two years later—the year after Donald Cormie incorporated Principal

Group—George sold North West Mill to his son, and the next year the mill was merged with Cormie Ranch Ltd.[2] Step-mother Emilie died in 1970, and George followed her in 1971.

In 1975, Donald Cormie moved his family again, this time to a mansion on Grandview Drive, a neighbourhood favoured by lawyers, judges and influential businessmen. The house, now worth several hundred thousand dollars, stands at the edge of a cluster of streets in the middle of Edmonton, magically surrounded by fields and wilderness. To the east is the university farm; to the west is Whitemud Park. The house backs onto a wooded ravine that winds down past the Fox Drive freeway to the river.

There were other properties as well. In the late 1960s, Cormie acquired an elegant cottage hideaway near Stony Plain, 20 miles northwest of Edmonton.

In 1969 Cormie bought two historic mansions on a 50-acre seaside estate at Brentwood Bay, about 20 miles north of Victoria, B.C. The four-storey main house, Dunmora, was built in 1921 of stone and timbers. Perched on a cliff, it has five bedrooms, five bathrooms, four fireplaces and servants' quarters. The second house, Point Colville, built in 1912 at the water's edge, has six bedrooms.[3] The houses, held through Estate Loan and Finance, were occasionally rented out as movie sets. Each autumn they served as the site of the annual Principal planning conference, where Cormie met with senior executives to evaluate their performance and set goals for the coming year.

In 1982, Jaimie Cormie bought a house in Paradise Valley, an exclusive suburb of Phoenix, Arizona, for $600,000 U.S. The 4,300-square-foot villa, built in Spanish mission style, became home for family members and some Principal executives when they were in town. Its walls, like those at corporate headquarters and other properties, were decorated with pieces from Cormie's extensive art collection.

The purchase of the Arizona house marked a new push into the American market. That same year Principal's near-dormant U.S. head office was moved from Seattle to Scottsdale, near Paradise Valley. In January 1983, a new company was activated as the investment advisor to all the Cormie-owned U.S. mutual fund companies. This company, Principal Management Inc., was launched with $35,000, loaned by upstairs company County Investments to Ken Marlin and the three Cormies, who in turn loaned it to their Edmonton-based holding company Principal Management Ltd. (PML), which used the money to capitalize the new Scottsdale subsidiary. Principal Group originally owned PML, used to facilitate the movement of dividends from the U.S. into Canada. That changed in mid-1982, when ownership was transferred directly to Jaimie Cormie (81.5%), Ken Marlin (10.5%) and Donald and John Cormie (4% each).

After this transfer the only connection between the U.S. companies and the Principal Group operation in Canada was common ownership. Nonetheless, much of the expansion into the U.S. and the companies' subsequent operation costs were funded through Principal Group. When the conglomerate collapsed in mid-1987, the U.S. companies owed Principal Group $2.1 million.

In 1983, Cormie became a founding member of the Dean's Council of 100 at Arizona State University, an honourary position shared with such luminaries as former U.S. president Gerald Ford and former U.S. Secretary of State Henry Kissinger. The appointment capped a glittering list of honours which fed Cormie's image, improved his business and political contacts and ultimately fueled the Principal sales campaign. Cormie took on a variety of high-profile community service positions, including director of Alberta's Banff School of Advanced Management between 1968 and 1971; founding member in 1979 of the Business Advisory Council at the University of Alberta; member of the board of directors of Edmonton's Citadel Theatre between 1968 and 1970; and fundraiser for the 1983 Universiade games. He contributed to such causes as the Northern Alberta Children's Hospital Foundation, the Tri-Bach Festival and the University of Alberta's School of Business. All these good works were favoured by the Alberta elite and admired by the investment-buying public. Some brought Cormie business, as well. Principal Group's records show a 90-day promissory note purchased by "Universiade 83" for $200,000 on December 16, 1982.

An in-house Principal publication called the *Crusader*, distributed to the sales staff, routinely featured articles on Cormie's community involvements. Good copy, for example, emerged from Principal Group's annual sponsorship of the Masters Tournament at the Spruce Meadows equestrian centre south of Calgary. Spruce Meadows is an internationally-renowned horse-jumping facility, and founders Marg and Ron Southern are among the most prominent of the Calgary upper crust. The September/October 1985 issue of the *Crusader* featured two photos of Donald and Eivor Cormie at the 1985 Masters Tournament, standing beside the Principal Group Challenge Cup; in one photo they are accompanied by Marg Southern. The article quoted Cormie:

> "I feel some of our best, high-level exposure in the Calgary area is coming from our Spruce Meadows sponsorship," said President Donald M. Cormie...
>
> The Calgary and Foothills salespeople participated with a hospitality booth on the grounds. [Salesman] Arney Faulkner reported that it was a real success and is confident that the leads they obtained will be developed into future Principal clients.

Cormie's involvement in the legal community also enhanced his reputation. During the 1950s and 1960s, he was very active in the Canadian Bar Association. Between 1963 and 1965, he was chairman of its administrative law section; in 1968-69, he was vice-president of the Alberta chapter; and for several years he was chairman of the research committee of the association's Foundation for Legal Research. In 1964, at the age of 42, he was appointed Queen's Counsel, enabling him to add the coveted initials "Q.C." to his correspondence, identifying him as a senior and esteemed member of the Alberta bar.

In August 1965, Cormie represented the Canadian Bar Association at a meeting in Australia of the Commonwealth Law Society. He took the opportunity to enjoy a three-month tour of China, Japan and the South Pacific with Eivor and the five eldest children. After their return, the tour was reported in *The Edmonton Journal* on the women's page. The article featured several photos, including one of the children happily studying chopsticks and a noodle bowl.

Cormie's paper, presented in Sydney, deplored the recent proliferation of government boards, agencies and tribunals which he said increasingly oppressed Canadian society. "There can be few countries where so many citizens sit in judgment on so few fellow citizens as in Canada," he complained, adding that during the previous 25 years the number of Alberta government agencies and employees had increased 4.5 times.

The speech took place when Cormie was planning the incorporation of Principal Group and an ever more complicated corporate structure. It was one of the first occasions, but certainly not the last, that he would criticize "over-regulation" and burgeoning bureaucracy.

At the Code inquiry, Cormie testified that until 1970 he spent most of his time at his law practice, with about a day a week on Principal business. (Those were the years when he consolidated his control over the companies, incorporated Collective Securities and Principal Group, and implemented his functional management system.) Over the next eight years, he said, he phased himself out of the law practice, and in 1978 moved over full time to Principal Group. But his name remained on the masthead of Cormie Kennedy, and he held a nominal 1% of the firm. He kept a supply of law firm stationary in his Principal Group office, and the "Q.C." appeared on certain business correspondence, including his chairman's message in the Principal Group annual reports.

About this time Cormie started using the royal "We." (We expect this change in the economy; We'll increase the emphasis on that product; We've decided to appoint...) In business settings he tended to be stiff, rather formal, more inclined to pronouncement than discussion. "You're a hell of a lot better at broadcasting than receiving, Don," Ken Marlin joked after Cormie had monologued his way through a committee meeting.

Some of his society friends remember him as clever and amusing, an amiable host and fascinating conversationalist. Others—including some employees—describe him as arrogant and heavy-handed. There's a mean streak in him, or perhaps it's out-of-control impatience. Many a humiliated executive has wept on Marlin's shoulder after a dressing down by Cormie in front of colleagues.

Cormie liked to "challenge" his employees and his children, sometimes assigning unlikely goals, then watching them struggle to succeed. One of his maxims was the oft-quoted "Cull the bottom third," based on genetic improvement programs employed at Cormie Ranch, which accounted for the high turnover throughout the Principal machine. Some employees thrived on challenge; many fell by the wayside. You can't cull children, however, and Cormie family members were slotted according to their ability and Dad's need. To a certain extent the family was managed functionally as well. Those with aptitude or interest were given places in the business; there was also a family academic (Allison), a family rancher/politician (Bruce), a family lawyer-in-training (young Robert) and, after the collapse, a family "spokesman" (Neil).

John, the eldest, was something of a disappointment. He didn't always think before he spoke, but he was good-natured, possibly the warmest of the Cormies, besides his mother Eivor. John is the son most like his father in appearance; his face is a little wider, his eyes kinder, but the resemblance is remarkable.

John didn't shine academically, and Cormie decided to have him polished at St. Andrew's College in Aurora, Ontario, about 20 miles north of Toronto. St. Andrew's, an exclusive private boys' school, was the alma mater of Cormie's law partner Jack Kennedy. "The ideal of work is consistently held up to the boys at St. Andrew's as being of vital importance in their preparation for life," school literature advised. "The school's philosophy encourages independent critical thought among its students without necessarily giving them the final right of decision." Perfect training for a Principal executive.

John's biography in *Who's Who in Canada* listed a Bachelor of Arts degree from Simon Fraser University in Vancouver, but that wasn't true. He started university in Edmonton, then transferred to Simon Fraser, taking economics and math courses. Then he went home to work for his father. A call to the registrar's office in early 1993 confirmed that "His degree has not been awarded as yet."

In 1969, John became a director and officer of Collective Securities, replacing Ralph Forster. John had just turned 21: the same age Donald had been when he joined his father as director of the Edmonton mill. In December 1970, Cormie hired John as his executive assistant-cum-securities analyst and put him on the Principal Group sales and investment committees. A year later the directorships picked up steam: first with one of the U.S. operations; then with Principal Group, the trust company, the life insurance company and a couple of mutual funds. By the time of the 1987 collapse, John was on the board of about a dozen companies.

In 1976, John went to London, England, for half a year to work for N.M. Rothschilds and Sons in the domestic credits department. When he returned, he was promoted to vice-president of Principal Trust; later that same year, at just 30 years of age, he was handed the keys to the trust company.

As trust company president, John was paid about $145,000 a year, as well as receiving company loans and dividends. He joined the local tennis and yacht clubs and, following his father's example, got himself appointed to the boards of prestigious community organizations, including the Northern Alberta Childrens Hospital Foundation, the Alberta Ballet Company and the Citadel Theatre.

Donald Cormie described John as "an excellent people person. He liked dealing with the people and got along well with people, so his skills were largely in analyzing the detail of an operation and then working with the people to try and make it better." Unfortunately, John wasn't "quite aggressive enough," according to Cormie. "We felt that he needed a little more action-oriented help. So he suggested that he hire somebody else, and I interviewed, as well, the people that he interviewed, and finally selected George Aboussafy to come in as general manager. But I was always satisfied with what [John] did. I think he and I both agree that sometimes I felt he wasn't quite aggressive enough, but then with George Aboussafy, who was the reverse, it made a good combination."

John's younger brother Jaimie, on the other hand, was sufficiently aggressive. He was sharp, he was focused and he was a whiz in stock market and securities analysis. Photos portray a stereotypical egghead: scrawny, with bottle-thick glasses and dishevelled hair. Jaimie, like his father, was the third son in a large family, and took after him in other ways. Jaimie buzzed through the University of Alberta in three years, receiving his Bachelor of Arts in economics in 1971 at the age of 20. He then attended the Master of Business Administration program and completed the courses, but left in 1973 before finishing his thesis.

While at university Jaimie worked for Principal Group as a junior securities analyst. Then in 1974 he joined full time and rose to portfolio manager. Two years later, at the age of 25, he became manager of the entire stock and bond department. In mid-1975, Jaimie was also appointed director of Cormie Ranch Ltd., a position which, among others, eluded John. In 1978, Jaimie became Principal Group vice-president of investment, in charge of the stock, bond and securities portfolios of Principal Group, Collective Securities and the various subsidiaries.

Unlike John, Jaimie wielded some real power in the organization. Over time he became his father's number-two man, with a better understanding than anyone else of Cormie's overall operation, identified in memos as the person to contact if Cormie was unavailable. Jaimie was the only person, other than his father, who had sole signing authority on cheques issued for Principal Group or Collective Securities. Nonetheless, it was his father who chaired the investment committee meetings, where overall objectives and investment strategies for each of the Principal companies were set. Then Cormie would withdraw while Jaimie and his team of portfolio managers, brokers and analysts proceeded as directed.

In February 1982, while most Alberta companies were struggling in the recession, Cormie moved the Principal Group head office to a brand-new downtown tower sheathed in money-green tinted glass. Principal Plaza stood as the ultimate monument to his success. Its mahogany staircase was perhaps a silent salute to his great-grandfather John Cormie Sr., the master carpenter, who had built several staircases still renowned in southern Ontario. The Plaza, then Edmonton's tallest building, had been built by Campeau Corporation and other partners. Principal Group, as major tenant, was favoured with its name on the building, but many Principal clients imagined that the tower was one of the Principal-held assets they'd been told about. The grandeur of the building and the opulence of Principal's offices were taken as evidence of the quality and security of the customers' investments.

Cormie filled the southeast corner of the penthouse floor with heavy mahogany furniture, expensive art, top-of-the-line video equipment and an enormous fridge with an ice-maker. His suite included an adjoining study, a walk-in vault, a shower and washroom with gold-plated fixtures. From the corner windows he could observe the North Saskatchewan River. In the evenings, out beyond the river valley, the lights of the city shimmered on for miles.

Cormie's desk was placed in the niche in front of the corner windows. He sat with his back to the view, facing the door at the other end of the room. To his right was a shredding machine; to his left a huge credenza, mounted with electronic equipment and video screens. This was control-central, giving him direct access to the corporate computer system and the extensive network of security monitors located throughout the building. With a flick of a switch he could see what was happening anywhere on the premises: in the accounting offices and the investment department; along the corridors; around his car in the parking garage; even inside the vault in his own office. Two cameras faced the 30th floor elevators, and one pointed at the reception area directly outside his door, so that he always knew who was approaching his office.

A security firm monitored the rest of the building, but its staff weren't allowed on the top three floors unless there was an emergency. Cormie had his own people install electronic locks and monitors—his son Neil supervised this work—and patrol the upper sanctum.

Next to Cormie's credenza was a wall-hanging, covering a secret passageway that led outside the office to the mahogany staircase. (The other side of the passage was covered by another hanging; the door was fitted so tightly that the only telltale sign was a tiny keyhole.) If an unwelcome visitor was waiting at the secretary's desk in front of Cormie's office door (or if he simply didn't want his secretary to witness his departure), Cormie could make an unseen getaway through the passage and down the stairs.

There was a second passageway behind a bookshelf in the private study. This one led to the secretary's area, then along a corridor to the offices of his personal bookkeeper, several personal assistants and the suite of Christa Petracca, vice-president of corporate development.

From this richly-appointed aerie Cormie ruled his empire like a personal fiefdom, deciding the fate of every dime eager investors placed in the hands of his evangelizing salesmen. He set budgets, hired and fired, set sales quotas and assigned employees their parking spots. Sequestered in his penthouse suite, glued to his phone and computer and video security screens, he emerged occasionally for a well-staged appearance at a benefit, a celebration or a lecture.

During the autumn of 1983, for example, Cormie gave a series of Principal-sponsored luncheon speeches in several North American cities. One such speech, made before 250 investors at a $16-dollar-a-plate luncheon at the Calgary Convention Centre, was video taped; the tape became evidence at the Code inquiry. The speech provides insight into the workings of Cormie's mind. After dropping names and pumping the cycle theory, Cormie repeatedly pitched Principal's various mutual funds while offering his listeners tips on ways to beat the system, manipulate wealth and avoid regulatory interference in their affairs.

Spread your money around so the government will have a harder time getting hold of it, he suggested: "I'm a great believer in putting a little bit in the U.S. and London, just spread it around in case a government decides that they should tighten up in some way that you don't believe is fair." When you move in the stock market, consider buying outside of Canada: "If you have a share of IBM, you can hold it in Florida, you can hold it in Germany, you can hold it in Japan, you can hold it in Australia, South Africa, and it's—really nobody knows you have it, and you pay your tax when you pick your time."

If you own a house, lease it to yourself to protect against property taxes. Better still, try a modest tax-avoidance scheme:

> If you can show that the proceeds from the mortgage were used to buy an investment for an investment portfolio, then all of your mortgage interest is deductible before you pay your income tax off your salary; because the purpose is it isn't what you secure it with, it's what you use the money for. So the skill is to go to the bank and get the loan to buy the house, wait a couple of months so it's not related, go out and mortgage the house, run it over into an investment portfolio, take the portfolio back to the bank and pledge it as security to the bank...
>
> I've had friends come to me and say, 'I've paid off our mortgage, I've got the house in my wife's name and she's set for life.' I said, 'Gee, what a dirty trick to pay on that poor wife, because they can take all her assets [for taxes] and you're going to be scot-free.' But generally, the strategy on that is usually to make sure that the house—if it's a big house, it is going to be disproportionately taxed... It should be held in a personal holding company with no other assets and you take short-term leases back. Now, you've got some problems with the capital gains taxes under the federal *Income Tax Act*, but you have to balance all of the ins and outs. The question is, really, is that the protection of the personal assets so everyone isn't tied in together, is an important investment strategy.
>
> As you know, when you're in business everybody wants you to guarantee everything and the smart businessmen don't guarantee anything, and certainly never a friend's loan.

That's Donald Cormie: hide the assets, avoid taxes, don't personally guarantee and most important: *Pay Yourself First.*

Part II

Insolvent

5

Basically Flat

April 2, 1984

THEY CAN'T DO THAT!" Reg Pointe protested silently as he read the letter. He slapped it down on his desk and reached for the phone. "Hi, this is Reg. Listen, you know what they've done over at Principal?" he asked. "Remember the CDIC letter last month, complaining about all the bad mortgages and real estate in the trust company? Well, they've fixed it, alright. They sold it to the contract companies. Twenty-three million dollars worth. Do you believe that?"

It was Pointe's job, as Director of Trust Companies in Alberta's Department of Consumer and Corporate Affairs (hereafter referred to as Consumer Affairs), to oversee the activities of five provincially-incorporated trust companies. His department shared overlapping jurisdiction with the federal Department of Insurance, which conducted inspections of financial institutions on behalf of the Canada Deposit Insurance Corporation.

The federal regulators' letter to Principal Trust, demanding improvements in the company's finances, had been forwarded via Pointe on February 24. The feds had been locking horns with Principal Trust for years but this extraordinary letter, this nightmare of a letter, contained unprecedented threats to its continuing existence.

The feds had discovered that the trust company's mortgage arrears had reached an alarming level, with 183 loans worth $36.8 million—three-quarters of the mortgage portfolio—behind in their payments. More than two-thirds of the mortgages were in arrears by three months or more, and half of those were under foreclosure proceedings. The company had already foreclosed on 36 properties valued on the company books at $8 million. But Alberta's real estate market was so soft that many "could not be sold even at distress prices," said the letter, signed by Dick Page, director of the trust, loan and investment companies division of the federal Department of Insurance.

Page also criticized the company's investment, borrowing and accounting strategies. The company books recorded accrued interest payments on mortgage loans, even though the loans were actually in arrears: in effect, claiming fantasy profits. (This accounting strategy is based on the premise that mortgage holders will catch up on their payments. If they don't, earnings have been unrealistically inflated, resulting in an unrealistic picture of the company's financial health. As far as the CDIC was concerned, Principal Trust didn't have a prayer of recouping the lost revenue, and was going to fall further and further behind.)

Trust company investments were supposed to be matched, by term and by interest rate, to liabilities coming due. Otherwise, the company could find itself unable to pay maturing term deposits, or could expose itself to a negative "spread"—paying more for money than it earned from it. Principal Trust, Page found, had borrowed a great deal of money on short terms, then invested in risky long-term Canada bonds, leaving it heavily mismatched and vulnerable to interest rate swings. (The Government of Canada issues high denomination marketable bonds—not to be confused with low-risk Canada Savings Bonds—whose value drops as interest rates rise.)

The CDIC had imposed a borrowing-to-capital ratio of 15:1 on Principal Trust in 1982. This means that for each dollar the shareholders put into the company, they could borrow $15 from the public: as deposits in savings accounts or term certificates, for example. But the ratio at Principal Trust was way out of whack, Page said. If proper reserves were set up on the company books—if the required cash was removed from the capital base and put aside to cover possible losses in the value of real estate and bad mortgage loans—the borrowing-to-capital ratio would have been 41.8 to 1. If the securities portfolio was also revalued to market, the ratio would deteriorate to 92:1, posing an incredibly hazardous and unacceptable risk.

At the end of 1983, Principal Trust had a borrowing base of $12.1 million. Half of that capital, however, had been borrowed from the parent company, Principal Group Ltd., and was secured by $6-million worth of subordinated promissory notes. The trust company was paying interest on the notes at the horrific rate of 21.5% per year, a major drain on earnings. Since 1982 the CDIC had been requesting, without success, to have that interest rate reduced and a portion of the notes converted to permanent capital, in exchange for the issuance of shares.

"If the company does not respond to the concerns expressed in this letter within a reasonable time period, it is likely that CDIC will send a formal report to the company, pursuant to Section 25 of the [Canada Deposit Insurance Corporation Act], summarizing its unsound business and financial practices," Page's letter said. Once such a report was made, the CDIC could cancel the company's deposit insurance. If Principal Trust didn't want the CDIC to start the ball rolling, four actions were required: Principal's shareholders were to inject $2 million in additional capital; the $6 million shareholders' loan was to be converted into permanent capital; and a plan was to be developed for disposing of the trust company's long-term bonds. As well, the Department of Insurance wanted the trust company to establish a minimum $9.5-million reserve on the company books: $1.5

million for real estate losses and $8 million for mortgage losses. If the company did not agree with this conclusion, it was invited to submit updated property appraisals to support its position. In the meantime, at least $5 million in reserves was to be deducted from the company's borrowing base.

Funds which have been reserved are subtracted from the company's capital base, affecting its ability to accept funds from the public. With a strictly enforced borrowing-to-capital ratio of 15:1, every $1 million in cash or assets added to the capital base permits an additional $15 million in public deposits in the institution. A reserve of $5 million would have meant the trust company would have had to reduce its borrowing from the public by $75 million—to less than half of the $134.5 million borrowed as of the end of 1983. A reserve of $9.5 million would have effectively wiped the company out.

Trust company president John Cormie met with Reg Pointe the week after Page's bombshell was delivered. Principal Trust's board of directors was willing to inject an additional $2 million in share capital, John said. But there was silence regarding the other demands, and Pointe had to phone him in late March to remind him of the CDIC's looming deadline. "The CDIC won't hesitate to drop your insurance, John," Pointe warned on March 26. "You're going to have to address all their concerns thoroughly, and I need to have your reply by the end of the week."

Nothing could be worse than the Section 25 notice threatened by the feds. Losing CDIC coverage was tantamount to shutting down the trust company, when it was crucial that the reputation of Principal Trust, the corporate flagship, remain spotless. The trust company was the only member of the conglomerate with CDIC coverage and customers—sometimes confused by the CDIC decal on the door—often ended up buying Principal's other, more risky financial products. Without those customers, everything could collapse.

John discussed the situation with his father. The next day Donald Cormie summoned Principal Group mortgage manager Bill Green and asked for a list of the trust company's most worrisome holdings held in common with its sister contract companies, First Investors and Associated Investors. Green responded the following day with a memo to Cormie headed *RE: SHARED MORTGAGES FIC, AIC AND PST:*

> Pursuant to our discussions whereby you have indicated your desire to have the trust company divest itself of its portion of the shared mortgages, we have prepared, for your review, a list of subject mortgages and same is enclosed herewith. All of the mortgages are in default. We expect most of them will become Owned Property in due course... By copy of this letter, we are asking our Legal Department to advise what the regulatory and legal requirements for a transaction of this nature would be. Upon receipt of their opinion we will pursue the matter further.

Green doesn't seem to have received a reply to his request. Instead, that Friday,

Cormie drafted a letter for John to send to Reg Pointe, reminding him that trust company shareholders had injected an additional $2 million in capital three weeks earlier. Then it said:

> The Board of Directors of Principal Trust generally concurs with the view of Mr. Page that the long-term strategy required to successfully market or develop a real estate portfolio is incompatible with the demand deposit-taking institution. As a consequence, Principal's joint mortgage partners have paid out Principal Trust's large joint mortgages and real estate holdings.

Cormie was talking about the trust company's $23-million sale to the investment contract companies, although he didn't say so. The transaction had been worked out over the past couple of days, but the letter claimed the payout had occurred a week before.

The letter appeared on Pointe's desk on Monday, April 2. Pointe, aware that the trust company's "joint mortgage partners" were First Investors and Associated Investors, began ringing regulatory alarm bells.

In the past few years, the trust company and the contract companies had acquired 23 jointly-held mortgages worth a total book value of $65,773,841. Four of those mortgages were so far behind in their payments that the companies had been forced to foreclose, and now jointly owned them as real estate holdings. The remaining 19 mortgages were all in default, and at least a couple would be foreclosed within days. The trust company's share of this pathetic portfolio amounted to about a third of the holdings, with a book value of $23,245,129. This trash had been dumped, at full value, into the contract companies.

The deal was a travesty, a violent abuse of the contract companies and the thousands of investors who had purchased the companies' investment contracts. The sale crippled the companies with non-producing assets and stripped them of more than $23 million in desperately needed cash. It was commercial rape.

THE CONTRACT COMPANIES HAD OTHER problems as well. Alberta Consumer Affairs auditors had acquired appraisals on a few Principal properties during the winter, and their findings revealed a devastating situation. The market value of all but one of the properties' book values was far below book value—about a third of the values claimed in the companies' books—requiring an average write-down of 65%. The appraisals included those on some of the jointly-held properties subsequently dumped by Principal Trust into the contract companies.

Those appraisals were just the most recent confirmation to Consumer Affairs that the contract companies were in serious trouble; the audit staff had been filing reports about their deteriorating financial situation for the past two years.

Department auditors had watched the mortgage holdings in the contract companies' investment portfolios quadruple between 1979 and 1982—the result of a frantic scurry to absorb unprecedented amounts of deposits from the public. Those were the years of soaring inflation and interest rates, and the Principal companies' competitive rates, backed by an aggressive marketing strategy, attracted interest-hungry investors in record numbers. Much of the customers' money had been steered by the Principal sales force away from the trust company and into the contract companies. First Investors and Associated Investors offered an average half a percentage point more in interest than did the trust company, making that money significantly more expensive to the conglomerate. But with the restrictive borrowing-to-capital ratio imposed by the CDIC, Principal Trust was severely limited in the amount of deposits it could accept, unless the Cormies were willing to inject more capital.

The contract companies, however, were free under the *Investment Contracts Act* to accept deposits without restriction. Rather than increase the trust company's ratio by injecting precious cash, it was preferable that the sales force channel deposits into the contract companies.

During the 1970s, a fundamental change occurred in the product sold by the contract companies. By mid-decade, as interest rates climbed, investment contracts were replaced by "single pay" or "term certificates." Clients no longer purchased contracts and made payments over time; instead, they paid a lump sum and received the sum, plus interest, back at the end of the term. By the end of the decade, sales of this new product comprised almost the entire business of the contract companies. The single-pay certificates were not "investment contracts" as defined in the *Investment Contracts Act*, but rather were comparable to the guaranteed investment certificates (GICs) sold by banks and trust companies. Nonetheless, the contract companies continued to be regulated under inadequate provincial legislation, unrestrained by the stringent capital base and capital ratio requirements imposed on other financial institutions.

There was another crucial difference between single-pay certificates and GICs. Interest on the contract companies' certificates was still calculated on an investment contract basis: the company would pay a "guaranteed" interest of 4%, plus "additional credits" payable at the discretion of company directors. The interest plus additional credits added up to a rate slightly higher than the interest rate offered by banks and trust companies. In later years, the contracts were promoted as paying the total rate, when only the 4% was guaranteed in the contract. The rates were highly competitive and customers flocked, cash in hand, to the Principal salesmen.

Certificate sales in the two contract companies climbed from an average $60 million during the mid-1970s to $170 million in 1980. Sales climbed again to $218 million in 1981; to $298 million in 1982; and to $329 million in 1983.

All that money had to be invested somewhere, and mortgage lending sky-rocketed as the Principal investment department worked feverishly to place the windfall cash. Mortgage staff came under more and more pressure to place more and more mortgage money at ever higher rates. The rates, and the amount of money to be placed, were set by Donald or Jaimie Cormie.

A large pool of money went into the companies through certificate sales just before the prime rate peaked in August 1981 at 22.75%. Caught with their pants down, the Cormies desperately scrambled to invest the money as rates began to tumble. They had borrowed money at the top of the scale, and it was an Herculean task to find investments with sufficient return to cover the interest that fell due when the certificates matured a few months or years down the road. A directive went out to the mortgage department to place the money as soon as possible.

Even before this crisis, the Principal contract companies had never been conventional lenders, had never offered prime-rate loans to well-secured borrowers. Their market was the customer who could not persuade conventional lenders to take his business. Their higher lending rates, generally a couple of percentage points above prime, reflected higher risk. In earlier years, however, they had attempted to control the risk by proceeding cautiously, screening applicants to identify the least dangerous prospects. The companies used to carry a fairly well-balanced portfolio, with more than half their mortgages in residential properties.

But the mortgage-lending market became increasingly competitive when the 1967 *Bank Act* revision allowed chartered banks to move into mortgages for the first time. By the mid-1970s, banks had forced companies like Principal out of first mortgages and into riskier loans, such as real estate investment lending and second mortgages. When the interest squeeze pushed the Principal companies more aggressively than ever before into the mortgage market, they abandoned their practice of combing the files for promising clients. Loans which would once have been rejected hands down were suddenly acceptable.

Wayne Fuhr, Principal's mortgage manager during this period, testified that the companies found themselves desperately squeezed. "At that particular time the mortgage market that we had been tapping, which was the investment real estate market, began to dry up," Fuhr said. "In other words, there was less availability of product, less people buying property and investing in property and it just seemed there was less of it around. But at the same time, we were looking for more homes for the money than we ever had... It appeared that the company had been very aggressive in obtaining money through the sales department, and didn't shut the taps off soon enough and ended up with a pool of money that now was higher than most mortgage investments would allow."

During these years, no company committee examined mortgage applications prior to approval. Instead, authorizations were bicycled around the Principal organization and officials usually signed when asked, often without raising any questions. By the end of 1982, things were moving so fast that authorizations actually piled up in the mortgage department after the loans had been issued. Minutes of the companies' board meetings were issued after the fact, ratifying all transactions in the past quarter year.

As Fuhr testified, the most dangerous loans were assigned to the contract companies, rather than Principal Trust, to avoid attracting the ire of federal regulators. "When I originally joined the company I think I picked up that philosophy by osmosis, that we tried to keep the trust company much more clean, with better types of property and better types of investments, partly because it was regulated more strongly." The interest rate charged by the contract companies between 1979 and 1982 exceeded the rate charged by the chartered banks by 2% to 6%—at rates sometimes as high as 25%.

By the end of 1982, the lending orgy had resulted in $59.6 million loaned to buyers of development land, representing 38% of the $156.6 million mortgage portfolio held by the contract companies. Another 12% of the portfolio was in equally risky loans for hobby farms and other rural acreages.

Alberta's real estate collapse began in the last quarter of 1981 and was evident to all by early 1982. But as late as May 1982, Cormie issued a memo to the Principal sales committee calling for the placement of another $25 million "in specialty situations at 22% plus two points while rates are high." A half a year later Cormie was attacking his staff for the enthusiasm with which they handled the assignment. "I notice a Minute dated the 17th of November 1982 purporting to ratify and approve all of the mortgage placements for the third quarter of 1982," Cormie said in a November 30 memo to an official in the Principal legal department. "As you know, there appears to have been considerable slackness on the part of the signing officers with regard to a number of these mortgages, particularly situations where it appears that the mortgages were not properly or adequately reviewed at all by the officers signing."

A couple of months later, as the full extent of the lending folly became apparent, Cormie's criticism was even sharper. In a January 31, 1983, memo to Fuhr, copied to all Principal vice-presidents, Cormie said:

> There are a number of mortgages approved by Officers of the Company that appear to be very inadvisable mortgage investments; particularly the large ones relating to land development. In many cases I notice that several VPs have signed the mortgage but obviously, in talking with them, did not go into the transaction thoroughly enough to satisfy themselves that the money was 100% recoverable and safe.

The memo went on to say that in the future mortgage approvals should be restricted to five people: Cormie, his sons Jaimie and John, Ken Marlin and vice-president of corporate development Christa Petracca. Three days later, the directors of Principal Trust, First Investors and Associated Investors each signed resolutions to that effect.

Despite Cormie's angry memos, Fuhr said, Donald and Jaimie were in fact involved in approving many of the "scary opportunity" loans. The deals were discussed at investment committee meetings and one of the two Cormies would make the final decisions, even though others ended up signing the formal loan approval documents. In those cases, Fuhr said, signers were advised that Cormie or his son had agreed to the loan, after which they usually reached for a pen.

During this period Cormie held a number of harshly critical meetings with staff, assigning blame for the deepening mortgage crisis. "I think we all got kind of raked over the coals, if that's the phrase, a little bit," said Jaimie, who came in for his share of the roasting. "I think he just basically went through as to what cross-checks or what I would look at, what I would be asking the mortgage placement officers, and then also went through various other questions that should definitely be asked on the properties, in his mind, which, I believe, I then started to do from then on.

"Typically what I would do is go through the value of the property and try and get a feel for the covenant and the personal guarantees. At that time, I think every mortgage we did had personal guarantees on them. I would not necessarily, though, go back in and say, this individual, how leveraged is this individual in the real estate market at this point in time outside of our own loans? Let's say, although there would be a credit check on the individual to see whether or not he had paid his mortgages at another institution, we didn't try and get a full, necessarily, financial picture on the individual across all properties... So it was more questions along those lines that I was not, I guess, an expert at."

Assessment of a borrower's creditworthiness and his cash flow situation are key to prudent lending; Jaimie failed to ask the essential questions before handing out the money.

Wayne Fuhr, also a target for Cormie's ire, ended up in shouting matches with his employer. "[He said] that it was totally my fault that we had made these bad investments," Fuhr said. As far as he was concerned, the fault was Cormie's. The boss, of course, had the final word. Fuhr was replaced as mortgage manager in mid-1983, and left the company a year later. "It was apparent to me that the company no longer wished me to be there and I decided to resign," he said.

Fuhr had made several requests over the years for the creation of a more formal mortgage committee structure to supervise lending. The committee was finally established in early 1983, long after the damage was done. There were few loans approved over the next several months, and in October 1983 Cormie sent a confidential memo to Bill Green (who had replaced Fuhr as mortgage manager) and copied to all vice-presidents, announcing his decision to retire completely from the mortgage placement business "for the time being."

> It is our view that the real estate market will be basically flat and, as a result, there will be considerable rush in placing mortgages without a rising market to cure all our mistakes. In addition, we feel that in 5 to 8 years, the price of real estate will start to decline and money will become tight which would cause a considerable number of defaults on mortgages. Consequently, our strategy would call for us to be completely out of the mortgage business in approximately 5 to 8 years.

The worst of the damage could have been prevented if the companies had followed lending guidelines forwarded by the Alberta regulators in 1978. Jim Darwish (who had been Superintendent of Insurance and the companies' primary regulator for a decade) believed he had a "gentleman's agreement" with Ken Marlin, president of the contract companies, to comply with the guidelines, which limited the kind and maximum amount of loans. But little effort was made, and over the next three years provincial auditors repeatedly protested the companies' failure to abide by the guidelines.

In 1980, when company and government officials were locked in combat over Principal's lending practices, Jaimie Cormie was publicly promoting the company as a cautious, conservative mortgage lender. In an article which appeared in a company publication, he said: "The Mortgage Department is, year in and year out, doing an absolutely fantastic job of placing a substantial amount of mortgage money in very well-thought-out investments." Jaimie also said the company always looked for the highest rate of return for the least risk. "Our strategy is not to invest in situations that we consider ultra-risky, even if there's substantial gain potential. We're interested in protection first, gain second," he said. "I don't know how you describe it, this mixture of conservatism and bullishness. I guess I'm sort of the reluctant or cautious bull in the organization."

The contract companies were not supposed to be in the development business, and were not permitted under the *Investment Contracts Act* to hold real estate except under very stringent conditions. But, forced into foreclosures, they entered the development business through the back door. Their real estate holdings climbed from almost nothing in 1978 to an astonishing $125 million by 1986. As mortgages were foreclosed and the real estate portfolio skyrocketed, the mortgage portfolio declined, from a peak of $173 million in 1982, to $68 million in 1986. But the contract companies' combined mortgage and real estate portfolios continued to climb until 1984—boosted in that year by the $23-million transfer from the trust company—when the total peaked at $207 million and began a small decline.

Provincial regulators knew in October 1981, before the worst of the lending had occurred, that there were problems in the contract companies' mortgage portfolios. A report prepared at that time by Consumer Affairs auditor Burt Eldridge warned that First Investors had 64 mortgages three or more months in arrears totalling $12.3 million, and that it wasn't abiding by the agreed lending guidelines. Ten months later, he filed a report showing significant deterioration. Rather than having unimpaired capital of $500,000, First Investors had a deficit of $28,601,770, Eldridge reported in August 1982; Associated Investor had a deficit of $7,857,261. Eldridge also noted that administrative and sales fees owed by the companies to their parent Principal Group had not been recorded in their financial statements. If the debt had been shown, the figures would have been much worse. "This is a most serious matter and results in the department being misled," Eldridge wrote.

An October 1983 report prepared by Consumer Affairs auditor Al Hutchison showed further deterioration in the contract companies. An update memo in January 1984 said that First Investors' foreclosures had tripled during the previous year.

Finally, Tewfik Saleh, who had replaced Jim Darwish as Superintendent of Insurance, wrote a sharp letter to Ken Marlin. This letter, dated January 12, 1984, said that First Investors had a capital impairment of $35.3 million, placing it in contravention of the minimum capital requirement stipulated by the *Investment Contracts Act*. "In view of the seriousness of FIC's financial situation," Saleh wanted a meeting with Marlin and the Principal accountants.

Marlin's reply of January 16 rejected all Saleh's concerns: "We are of the opinion that your findings are false and that we did comply with all provisions of the *Investment Contracts Act* as at December 31, 1982, and have continued to do so up to the date of this letter."

Saleh wrote back two days later. "While you may disagree with my findings they are far from being 'false' as you suggest in your letter. My findings are based on facts presented to me in my auditors' report of their examination of your company." A meeting was set for the afternoon of January 25.

TEWFIK SALEH, IN CHARGE OF regulating the Principal contract companies, called the January 25 meeting with Principal officials. But it was his boss, Deputy Minister Barry Martin, who ran the show. "Alright," Martin told Consumer Affairs staff before the Principal people arrived, "I want you to just listen to what they have to say. Don't get into any discussions with them. Is that understood?"

They looked around the table at one another—Saleh and his assistant Bernard Rodrigues, Deputy Superintendent of Insurance; Jim Darwish, former Superintendent and now assistant deputy minister in charge of audits; Burt Eldridge, senior auditor—and they slowly nodded.

It was a long and painful session. Although company officials had been called on the carpet to discuss First Investor's capital impairment of $35.3 million, no one demanded that they inject more money. Nor did Principal officials suggest they were willing to do so. There might be some temporary difficulty, they insisted, but it would soon be straightened out. "Okay, there was a loss in 1982, but everything's a lot better now," Ken Marlin argued. "Wait until you see the 1983 statements. This is, what, January? We'll be done the statements in a couple of months and then you can see for yourself."

Marlin said several times that one way to solve a capital shortage, if it became necessary, was to eliminate the payment of additional credits to investment contract holders. That suggestion, that only the initial 4% should be paid out, was preposterous, and the regulators thought he was kidding.

When asked about First Investors' recent repayment of $2 million worth of promissory notes to the parent company, Marlin said the money had been put in to cover a decline in market securities and the decline had been eliminated. Therefore, he said, the $2 million was no longer needed in the company. He ignored the fact there had been an even greater decline in mortgages and real estate. As instructed by Martin, none of the regulators challenged him on the point, despite the fact that the repayment had been made without the consent of the Superintendent. (Nor did anyone note that the $2 million paid by First Investors to Principal Group was the exact sum injected by Principal into the trust company around the same time.)

On February 16, three weeks later, Saleh and Martin met with Christa Petracca for another chat about the mortgage problem. The meeting ended with Martin's request for a plan of action to deal with the companies' woes. No such plan ever appeared.

Twelve days later, the three met again, this time for lunch in the dining room atop the Principal tower. A company memo detailed the guest list: Martin, Saleh, "one other regulatory person," local lawyer Peter Owen, Terry Norman of the Royal Bank of Canada (which served as a depository for contract company assets) and George Mitchell, of Touche Ross & Co., Principal's external auditor. The memo, forwarded by Donald Cormie's secretary to Marlin, Jaimie and John Cormie, Petracca and in-house lawyer Lynn Patrick, said: "The purpose of the luncheon is to discuss the depository regulations affecting Principal." The contract companies had about $30 million in assets in a depository in a New York City branch of the Royal Bank. The regulators believed that under the *Investment Contracts Act* those assets should be held in Canada, and had been demanding their return for years. The companies continued to resist. Owen had issued a legal opinion in 1981 supporting the companies' position, and was included at the lunch to help argue the point.

Martin denies he was influenced during the Principal luncheon. The meeting was a friendly one, "somewhat of a show and tell," and there was no discussion of company problems, he testified. "The company walked us around, particularly showed us their computer situation and how they manage their portfolios and their computer system and that. The meeting tended to be not very much directed to business." Conversation with Donald Cormie, he said, was limited to a "strictly hello sort of situation."

The date was February 28, 1984, and the time was noon—within hours of the delivery of the letter from the Department of Insurance to John Cormie, threatening to shut down the trust company.

February 29, 1984

THE BIG NEWS IN CANADA the next day was the Prime Minister's conclusion, reached during a solitary walk in the snow, that after 16 long years he was ready to resign. Edmontonians greeted his decision with rapture. Like most Albertans, they blamed Pierre Trudeau for the 1980 National Energy Program and the consequential disintegration of the western economy. The next day's Edmonton *Journal* was filled with the story.

The big news in the executive suite at Principal Plaza was the federal regulators' threat to shut down the trust company. "They're just picking on us, Dad," John Cormie said.

The big news in the offices of the provincial auditors was that day's memo from Barry Martin to Jim Darwish prohibiting any further appraisals of the Principal companies' mortgages and real estate. Darwish wanted appraisals of every property in the Principal portfolio, but Martin had limited the budget to $20,000, enough to examine 16 of them. When he'd finished, Darwish resumed his campaign: if not the entire portfolio, then how about another three dozen or so? The cost would be under $40,000. Martin's February 29 memo made it clear Darwish was to forget it.

> I have authorized the allocation of funds for the audit unit to conduct certain appraisals of real property owned or held as security by certain financial institutions. I am given to understand that these appraisals have confirmed what is already common knowledge of the highly depressed market values of real property in Alberta and in other parts of the country. In view of the important role that the various financial institutions play in the economy of our province and the unusual economic hardships most of them are experiencing as a result of unduly depressed market values of real estate, I will be discussing the situation with the Minister. In the meantime I would ask that no further appraisals of this nature be conducted until further notice from my office to you.

It was an unnerving memo, distant and cold, and Darwish felt the chill. It was the first time in all his years with the province that he had ever had trouble getting money to do something important. "I have to say that I was really taken aback when I got this memorandum," Darwish testified. "I had no idea that this was going to happen. The appraisals that we had been getting to date were showing that the company did not have the value to support their real estate and their mortgages. That was important to know from the point of view of protection of the investment contract holders."

Darwish couldn't understand why Martin was talking here about the importance of Alberta's financial institutions. The department, through the Superintendent of Insurance, had a responsibility to protect the contract holders. "It may be that the Deputy Minister has some role to be concerned about the role that the financial institutions play," Darwish testified. "But by taking away the right to do these appraisals, to me, he was interfering with the role of the Superintendent to carry out his duty."

Three weeks later he tried again. "I have your memorandum," Darwish said in a March 20 memo of appeal to Martin.

> I do not believe that the situation at First Investors is the same as the situation with other financial institutions that are faced with highly depressed market values of real property. Burt Eldridge and Al Hutchison both recommend that we continue to get appraisals and I agree... It is absolutely essential that funds be provided in some way to have appraisals done on all of the properties, not just a few.

Darwish noted that Martin had said in his memo that he would be discussing the situation with Consumer Affairs Minister Connie Osterman. "I respectfully request that I be allowed to attend at such a meeting, perhaps along with one of my auditors, to discuss what is considered a serious situation with First Investors." He was still awaiting a reply when he heard a couple of weeks later about Principal Trust's $23-million sale of assets to the contract companies.

DIRECTOR OF TRUST COMPANIES Reg Pointe was astonished by the audacity of the trade. Yes, the deal did wonders for the trust company's books, but the $23-million sale was an atrocious abuse of its sister companies and surely contravened Section 138(1) of the *Trust Companies Act*, which prohibited trust companies from selling mortgages or real estate to any affiliated company.

Pointe raised this issue with John Cormie during a phone call soon after learning about the deal. "That wasn't a sale, it's a tender," John coolly replied.

"A tender?" Pointe said, dumbfounded.

"Sure, a tender. It's perfectly legal, we've had a lawyer look into it."

John said the contract companies (or more specifically, their president Ken Marlin) had wanted the transaction, not the trust company. He said the contract companies were worried that the mortgages and real estate would lose value if Principal Trust continued to hold its share. Under a long-standing corporate policy, when any one of the companies wished to buy out the other's interest, provided it tendered the book value, the other party had to sell. By this perverted logic, the trust company had been forced against its will to accept more than $23 million for assets that were certainly worth less than half that amount.

Meanwhile, federal officials in Ottawa were up in arms. CDIC chairman Robert De Coster considered the trust company's situation so urgent that on April 12 he sent a telegram to John Cormie. The trust company's $23-million sale to "associated companies," apparently in response to the CDIC's earlier letter, did not eliminate the CDIC's concern. Significant reserves might still be required. "The Board of Directors is very concerned that no action appears to be contemplated in response to the first three of Mr. Page's recommendations," the telegram said, concluding:

> I want to emphasize that the board of directors view this situation as being very serious. The issuance of a report similar to a report of the type mentioned in Section 24 of the *Canada Deposit Insurance Corporation Act* is a serious matter and I urge you to review the provisions of Sections 24 and 25 so that you are aware of the potential ramifications.

This telegram was followed almost immediately by a second, establishing a deadline of July 11, 1984, for disposal of most of the long-term bonds.

Reg Pointe learned about the telegrams on April 13 and immediately called a meeting with Principal officials. Ken Marlin, this time acting in his capacity as a director of the trust company, advised that Principal Trust would immediately convert the $6 million of notes into permanent share capital, as requested by the CDIC. But the company didn't want to dispose of the long-term bonds, and he would try to take that up in a meeting with De Coster. "I questioned Principal

Savings and Trust Company's right to sell its mortgage interest to First Investors Corporation Ltd. in view of the prohibition in Section 138," Pointe said later in a memo to file about the meeting.

> Ken Marlin advised that they had reviewed the transaction and it was considered a payout of the mortgages by FIC, which FIC had the legal right to do to protect its position. [Principal vice-president of finance] Archie Campbell advised that they had memorandum from their legal section permitting the transaction and the company's auditors were also reviewing it. I told Archie Campbell that I would require a proper legal opinion from their solicitors.

When Donald Cormie heard about Pointe's demand, he asked in-house lawyer Lynn Patrick for a legal opinion to support the tendering policy. It seemed that none existed at that time. During the Code inquiry, Cormie also couldn't recall when the tendering strategy had ever been used before. "I thought it was written down, but...nobody has found it," Cormie testified. He assigned Christa Petracca to comb the files, and "she couldn't find it. So I suggested then she should get new legal opinions."

During the meeting with Patrick, also attended by Petracca and Jaimie Cormie, Donald Cormie explained the legal opinion needed to support the $23-million transaction. Afterward, Patrick testified, "I said that I would put down in a memo from my notes what I understood that they were looking for, and then I would look into the matter of an opinion." Patrick transcribed his notes of the meeting into a memo, concluding: "The earmarks at law of a 'sale' are not present and this transaction would not in my opinion be viewed as a 'sale.' " He also said that the transaction could not be reversed by the regulators "because there is no jurisdiction to do so."

Despite this memo, Patrick testified that he believed that the transaction was indeed a sale and that he had advised Cormie and Petracca he could not give the opinion outlined in the memo. Patrick said he sent the memo to determine whether he had correctly interpreted the corporate position. What actually was said among the three remains unclear. The fact that a search continued for a favourable legal opinion supports Patrick's version of events. However, a memo to file written by provincial auditor Burt Eldridge several weeks later advises that he discussed the three legal opinions obtained, including Patrick's, with Patrick and John Cormie. There is no indication that Patrick advised at that time that he did not support the opinion outlined in his memo. (In his report, Inspector Bill Code found that "on the balance of probabilities" Cormie and Petracca knew that Patrick considered the transaction a sale.)

In any case, Patrick says he offered to submit the question to outside counsel. He contacted Peter Owen, Q.C., of Field and Field, who had previously provided Principal with a supporting opinion in the U.S. depository debate. This time, however, Owen was unable to oblige.

On April 16, despite Owen's negative response—and despite the protests of

both provincial and federal regulators—contract company directors Ken Marlin and
Eric Espenberg signed documents ratifying the $23-million transaction.

The next day Petracca contacted Owen herself. In her letter to the lawyer,
Petracca requested his opinion on the transaction and enclosed Patrick's memo,
which she represented as Patrick's view of the matter. "I would very much
appreciate your providing us with a legal opinion concerning the above matters,
hopefully concurring with our in-house interpretation of the same," Petracca's letter
said. After an extensive review of the larger mortgages in the trust and contract
companies' portfolios, "and the assurance of the complete co-operation and a
significantly different attitude by the Alberta Superintendent of Insurance with
respect to Alberta-held mortgages," Principal decided to tender the contract
companies' interest in the joint mortgages to Principal Trust at book value "due to
the perceived threat to First Investor's and Associated Investor's ability to
successfully deal with the mortgage securities in their best interests."

Owen replied April 25 with the same opinion he'd given Lynn Patrick a week
before: the transaction was a sale, prohibited by the *Trust Companies Act.*

Petracca tried one more time, and finally hit the jackpot. A tendering policy had
been written—with the help of Cormie or Patrick, Petracca said she wasn't sure
which—and had been executed by Marlin and Espenberg on behalf of the contract
companies. Undated, the policy stated that in the event that Principal Trust took any
action or refused to take any action on security granted to it by a borrower which, in
the opinion of the contract companies might adversely affect the security granted to
them by the borrower, the companies would be entitled to pay out the balance owing
by the borrower to the trust company.

This policy was sent off to C.R. Henning of Parlee, Irving, Henning, Mustard
and Rodney. Henning wrote back May 7, 1984, rendering his opinion that the
exercise by First Investors of its rights under a certain policy should *not* be
characterized as a purchase and sale of security interests.

Mission accomplished.

April 12, 1984

THE DAY THAT ROBERT DE COSTER sent his telegram, warning for the
second time that the CDIC might pull Principal Trust's insurance, the Cormies got
other bad news. In mid-March, two weeks after the CDIC's first warning letter,
Donald Cormie had launched one of his sons into federal politics. Bruce Cormie
announced his candidacy for the Conservative nomination in the federal riding of
Edmonton South. Bruce, responsible for Cormie Ranch and its cattle breeding
operation, left the bull semen in other able hands and went to the city to get himself
elected. His brother John, president of the trust company, found time during this
desperate period to help with the campaign—as did general manager George
Aboussafy and other Principal Trust employees.

Despite his best efforts and his father's ample resources (transaction records
show that Cormie borrowed $20,000 from unwitting Principal Group promissory

noteholders on March 20, 1984, to help finance the campaign), Bruce was trounced by broadcaster Jim Edwards, who went on to be elected to the House of Commons.

Before the nomination meeting, Edwards made a point of meeting each of his opponents, and he later remembered Bruce as singularly disinterested in the political process. When Edwards met with Bruce, John and a campaign aide, John and the assistant discussed political matters while Bruce's mind seemed to be elsewhere. "So I engaged him in a discussion," Edwards told me. "I asked him if [Cormie Ranch's] frozen embryos were fertilized *in vivo* or *in vitro*, and we got off on a very interesting discussion about frozen embryo exports. A couple of years later, after I was on a mission to the Philippines, I gave him a lead on what I thought might be a market [there]. I don't know whether that ever led to anything."

6

"My favourite nit-picking accountant"

I think you have to expect that people being administered by civil servants sometimes get a little impatient.

Jim Darwish in testimony at the Code inquiry

JIM DARWISH WAS FRANTIC. It had been two weeks since he'd asked for a meeting with Connie Osterman to discuss the need for more appraisals—then he learned about Principal Trust's sale of $23-million worth of junk to the contract companies. Since then he'd waited for someone in the department to slam the window on Cormie's fingers, prayed for a summons to Osterman's office so he could explain to the minister how serious the situation was.

During his career Darwish had been involved with the failure and wind-down of several financial institutions. Battleford Mortgage, Dial Mortgage, Tower Mortgage, Cosmopolitan Life Assurance Company, Rocky Mountain Life Insurance, Paramount Life Insurance Company, all in Alberta; Crown Trust in Ontario; Commonwealth Savings Plan in British Columbia—he'd watched them all go down, and over the years he'd noticed a pattern. "I used to talk to Reg Pointe about it," Darwish testified. "What we would often find was that companies were having trouble with their accounting records... The excuse would be given that 'There is a tremendous workload' or 'We have got staff problems.' The next thing we would note that the financial statements would be coming in late. Then we would note that there were financial transactions that they normally wouldn't do. They were, quite a bit, window dressing because they were in bad financial shape.

"When we would start to look into those matters we would get the promoters of the company agitated, which is understandable because it is a traumatic experience... and they would often complain to the government. The final step would be that some of these people would take steps that they ordinarily wouldn't, desperate steps, sometimes even illegal steps. So there was a pattern there."

The pattern was clear with the Principal companies. They were in trouble and operating in desperation mode—and Darwish couldn't understand why Consumer Affairs was standing by.

Finally, he felt he had to act. He had already prepared a briefing note arguing for more appraisals, and on April 24, he wrote a second memo focusing on the $23-million dump. That memo, stamped *URGENT* and *PRIVATE*, urged that the transaction be immediately reversed and that consideration be given to immediately cancelling the contract companies' licences.

The memos were the toughest in Darwish's career, and he expected Osterman and her department to respond. "My reputation was on the line when I wrote my memo. I assumed that it would be potent enough to have the minister and the deputy minister hire consultants... If I was wrong, my credibility would have been destroyed, probably, but I felt that I wasn't."

Jim DARWISH JOINED THE ALBERTA government as a messenger in 1949, carrying documents to and fro among officials in the Department of Public Welfare. He was fast and efficient and demonstrated a head for numbers, so he was taken on as a bookkeeper. Encouraged by his supervisors, he took accounting courses at night, articled with the Provincial Auditor for five years and became a chartered accountant in 1956. Darwish spent two years with the federal income tax department, then joined the Alberta Securities Commission in 1959 as an auditor.

Over the next two and a half decades, Darwish met Donald Cormie fewer than a dozen times, but it seemed as if patrolling the man's companies had become his destiny. For several years, Darwish conducted annual inspections of the Principal contract companies' books; later, as a senior auditor, he supervised the work of others. In June 1972, when he transferred to Consumer Affairs as the province's Superintendent of Insurance and Real Estate, it appeared that he had seen the last of Principal. The next year, however, responsibility for the *Investment Contracts Act* was transferred from the Alberta Securities Commission to the office of the Superintendent of Insurance, and Darwish found himself chin-to-chin with the Cormie companies again.

As we have seen, regulators battled Cormie for decades. As early as 1959, Darwish was writing memos about "well-watered" stock transactions among the Cormie companies. His warnings continued for 25 years, but despite the memos— and despite outside consultants' reports which supported his views—Darwish was frustrated from ever forcing full compliance. He didn't understand why, but whenever a crisis loomed, there was inevitably a hard political tug on his leash.

Investigations would be cancelled or reduced in scope, unfavourable reports would be followed by further studies, proposed legislation would never materialize. More time would pass.

Cormie's companies had always enjoyed a friendly relationship with Alberta politicians. During the Social Credit regime it had been Cormie's partner, the well-connected Ralph Forster, who minded the political store. In a letter written in 1973, Cormie said that Forster "had between 20 and 30 separate interviews with appropriate Cabinet ministers...on the matter of Associated Investors. He advised of an informal understanding that if the shareholders were satisfied that they could continue to support the company, and were making steady progress in improving its position, that they would be given all the time required."

By the early 1960s, Cormie was also at home in the corridors of power. According to his testimony, he sometimes attended meetings of a high-level Cabinet committee in the Ernest Manning administration. In 1964, at one of these meetings, Cormie verbally attacked the provincial regulators after they criticized his companies' sales practices.

Cormie followed this pattern throughout his career. As pressure increased, he would appeal to political figures for relief from what he would portray as unreasonable demands on the part of hostile public servants. He would play on the politicians' natural pride in a home-grown institution and remind them of shared Alberta roots. Then he would warn of dire consequences to the province's entire financial industry if his companies were hurt. This strategy didn't give Cormie *carte blanche*, but the regulators found it difficult to keep his companies pinned down. And there was a frustrating side-effect: a nagging undercurrent of doubt about the regulators' reliability. In times of crisis, their political masters tended to hedge by bringing in outside consultants to double-check their work.

During his years with the securities commission, Jim Darwish worked under commission chairman Harry Rose. In October 1965 Darwish submitted an alarming report to Rose, following his examination of Associated Investors' 1964 financial statements. Rose forwarded a copy to L.J. Beaudry, then-deputy provincial secretary of Saskatchewan, who commissioned an examination of the contractcompanies by Peat Marwick and Mitchell and Co. The accounting firm identified a number of problems: capital impairment, over-valuation of assets, improper intercompany transfers and excessive dividends and management fees.

Saskatchewan, prepared to act, was circumvented when the companies let their licences lapse at the end of 1965. Instead, they became licenced (in Saskatchewan only) as trust fund companies under the *Companies Licencing and Inspection Act*. As such they could not legally sell further investment contracts in Saskatchewan, although they could service existing ones. (The two companies were eventually reinstated in Saskatchewan as investment contract companies: Associated Investors in May 1978 and First Investors in April 1981.)

In May 1966, Darwish wrote a memo to Rose detailing demands he wanted to make: the immediate introduction of acceptable qualified assets; a justification of dividends and management fees; independent appraisals of mortgages; and rejection of investments made in affiliate Alberta Mortgage Exchange. If the appraisals indicated possible losses, Darwish said, allowances should be set up in the company books. The company should stop creating profits and inflating assets; mortgage discounts should be recomputed; audited consolidated financial statements should be prepared; and income and expenses on foreclosed properties should be handled in an acceptable accounting manner. Darwish also prepared the report, discussed in Chapter 3, which advised that the contract companies were paying millions of dollars in dividends to the shareholders out of paper profits. Afterward Rose forced the return of $300,000 in fees paid by Associated Investors and squeezed a promise from Cormie to end intercorporate transactions.

That autumn Rose, a lawyer, wrote a memo to John Hart, Q.C., Premier Manning's Deputy Attorney General, complaining that Cormie was taking his problems with the regulators directly to the Premier's office. "As you know from Mr. Darwish's reports, there is evidence of manipulative practices designed to create a false picture of the status of these companies. As you also know, the two companies have been bled by the payment of exorbitant management fees and dividends." He noted that Cormie had been writing letters to Hart and Manning:

> I am sure you will recognize that these letters are vague general complaints and they do not constitute any acknowledgement by Mr. Cormie of what I consider totally improper conduct in operating these two companies. Perhaps he thinks the best defence is an offence. In any event, what he is certainly attempting to do is divert attention from the plight of his companies to alleged inadequacies of myself and Mr. Darwish. Not only are these matters being raised by him irritating and disturbing, they are also time consuming. Week before last Mr. Darwish spent the better part of Saturday and Sunday analyzing statements and figures which he submitted to the Premier...
>
> I feel that this present exercise with Mr. Cormie can do nothing but undermine my position not only with the Premier and yourself, but with my own staff if it is allowed to continue. As you know, I have asked before that if there is any doubt in the minds of yourself and the Premier about our procedures in this office or the accounting methods used by Mr. Darwish, I would more than welcome you referring it to outside advice. In any event, I think that I am entitled to either this procedure or some acknowledgement from you that the department supports my administration. In a complicated industry controlled by legislation, I don't know how policy can be fixed at one level of government and administration carried on at another. Mr. Cormie is obviously trying to tie my hands and harness any discretion or scare me off by a political approach.

Hart went to work for Cormie after retiring from government service a few years later. "He came over to Principal Group as general counsel," Cormie testified, "and at the time, he told me that, 'Look,' he says, 'You seem to be highly regarded at the Cabinet level, but you are terribly regarded at the regulatory level.' He said, 'You have obviously got a serious personality conflict with Jim Darwish and Harry Rose, and my advice to you is get off those companies and stay off them.' " (Years later Hart's son Barry joined the company as a salesman, and was called to testify during the Code inquiry.)

In late 1966, the Alberta Securities Commission found that the contract companies did not meet the capital requirements of the *Investment Contracts Act* and considered suspending their licences and putting them out of business. It went for the alternative, to "impose such requirements as were feasible and give the companies time to work out of a rather desperate situation," Rose explained in a November 1966 letter to Saskatchewan Secretary Darrel Heald:

> In view of the evidence of good faith on the part of the officials of the company with whom we have been dealing, I adopted the view that suspension of registration would do more harm than good. The result is that the companies have been given a breathing space during which they will have to put their house in order... I can assure you that this Commission is going to make certain that... the malpractice which we have uncovered [won't be] permitted to continue. We will keep both companies under pressure until they have re-established a sound position.

"Good faith on the part of the officials of the company"—quite a different tune than he had sung a month before to the office of Alberta's Attorney General!

The next year Rose refused to accept certain investments as qualified assets under the *Investment Contracts Act*. He notified the company of his decision, stating that the written notice constituted a formal ruling under the Act. The approach was effective, Alberta Ombudsman Aleck Trawick observed in his report. The company had the right to appeal the ruling to the full commission and to the Court of Appeal, but chose not to. Trawick said: "It is unfortunate this procedure was never used again by Alberta regulators prior to [First Investors and Associated Investors] ceasing business."

That autumn the companies again hit the lobby trail. Ralph Forster's diary recorded meetings at the Legislature on the 18th, 19th and 20th of September 1967. On the 19th he lunched with Hart.

Wrangling continued, with annual protests from regulators about dividends and loans from the contract companies to related companies. In 1970, a government auditor advised that First Investors and Associated Investors should ultimately be solvent, but on an immediate breakup basis both were bankrupt. The next year, Associated Investors was deleted as an approved corporation under Alberta's *Trustee Act* because of its serious financial situation.

In mid-1971 Rose, fed up with continual complaints to the politicians, went to then-Attorney General Edgar Gerhart for permission to engage outside accountants to prepare an independent report on the contract companies. Rose engaged Gordon Burton, FCA, of Peat Marwick Mitchell and Co., who delivered his report in June

1971. Burton backed the commission staff and their conclusions about the contract companies. He was critical of interest-free advances made by the companies to Principal Group, and noted that the effect of intercompany transactions within the Principal Group was to splinter regulatory control. He suggested that the government think about appointing one body with the power to measure the entire conglomerate's solvency, and emphasized that amendment of the *Investment Contracts Act* was essential if the companies were to be kept under proper control.

A similar conclusion had been reached in 1969 by a joint federal/provincial study into the investment contracts industry. After three years of deliberation, a committee representing all provincial governments concluded the contracts were not only a poor investment, but risky as well. More than half of all Canadian contracts went into default; much or all of the money already paid toward them was forfeited by the contract holders. The report warned of possible conflicts of interest when the companies were involved in non-arm's-length investments with affiliated companies, and called for full public disclosure of a company's affairs.

There would be repeated recommendations and various attempts to improve the *Investment Contracts Act* over the next decade and a half. But there was only one significant change: in mid-1972, the Act was amended to authorize the securities commission—if concerned the company did not comply with the Act or was behaving in a way prejudicial to contract holders—to make a Special Report to the Attorney General, who could recommend to Cabinet the appointment of a receiver/manager. The change—enacted by Peter Lougheed's government the year after his Progressive Conservative party won a landslide victory in Alberta—pushed ultimate authority for contract companies firmly into the political arena.

During this period, British Columbia regulators were also watching the contract companies. Bill Irwin, the province's Superintendent of Brokers, had been in touch with Harry Rose since mid-1970, when Irwin wrote to Rose asking whether Alberta had sufficient financial information to determine to what degree each of the Principal Group conglomerate members "leans on the other." Rose replied that he had long felt "spooky" about the Principal contract companies and would forward Irwin's letter to Jim Darwish for response.

The two provinces exchanged information for several months, then peppered the companies with questions. Irwin was particularly concerned about a loan of some $7 million on a project for which the total cost was $4.3 million; he also asked about intercompany share purchases and mortgage valuations.

In March 1972, Irwin wrote the companies. He noted that neither would be able to pay off its contracts as they matured, and asked them to show cause why their registrations should not be suspended. A hearing in Victoria on March 23, 1972, inexplicably culminated in renewal of the companies' registrations that same day. The records of those events are no longer available.

A couple of months later, B.C. teamed up with Alberta to retain an independent appraiser to scrutinize apparently over-valued assets. B.C. government accountant L.G. Smallacombe hired the appraiser and forced Associated Investors to pay the bill. He analyzed the findings and provided a detailed report in October 1972—copied to the Alberta regulators—which described First Investors and Associated Investors as "far from being solvent" and discussed deficiencies caused by the actions of related companies. The contract companies' assets were grossly over-valued because of unrealistic appraisals of questionable assets, Smallacombe said. They were financially dependent on Principal Group and Collective Securities "and would be in dangerous condition" if the parent companies had financial difficulties.

In March 1973, as the time for registration renewal approached, B.C. Superintendent Irwin advised the companies that their licences would not be renewed in his province unless the deficiencies identified by Smallacombe ($1,722,147 for First Investors and $2,058,676 for Associated Investors) were rectified. A hearing took place in late March. First Investors' registration was renewed, but Associated Investors—aware the province would refuse to renew its licence—withdrew its application. Both contract companies had their registrations as mutual fund brokers discontinued. (Associated Investors was re-registered as a contract company in B.C. in 1978.)

On March 21, 1973, Harry Rose wrote a letter to Donald Cormie: "I am addressing this letter to you personally, as the individual who has effective control of the two above companies, with a copy to the president of each company." Rose noted a serious deficiency in the companies' qualified assets, which was likely to result in suspension of licences in B.C., and warned that the loss of registration there would "precipitate a crisis in Alberta and immediate reaction by the full Commission here." Cormie replied that for the past several years "I have scrupulously avoided exercising any control over, or being involved in any decisions" regarding the contract companies. He insisted they were being run by an independent, "professionally trained" board of directors, "and there is no basis on which I would or could interfere." He then discussed in detail the companies' affairs, "personally" wondering why the commission would not permit a reserve rate for contracts more favourable to the companies. (The issue of reserve rates is detailed in Chapter 9.) Then:

I personally feel most frustrated that these highly qualified Directors and managers can't work these things out faster so that the Principal Group doesn't suffer any further loss on its investment in Associated Investors. I know you feel the same way. We are simply stockholders in these companies with a very huge investment, and we consider it absolutely essential that the investments in these companies are all properly qualified and solid, and I don't know what else we can do but follow the recommendations of the management and directors who are, in effect, trustees for both the certificate holders and ourselves as stockholders.

Rose, incredulous, decided it was time to act. The steps he took brought the contract companies the closest they ever came to shut-down—until outside pressures forced Alberta to act 14 years later—and the outcome is a dramatic illustration of how firmly lodged in the political arena Cormie's companies were at that time.

These events in the spring of 1973 unfolded during a period of tremendous national drama. Canada's four western premiers were preparing to meet with Prime Minister Pierre Trudeau to discuss "a full role in Confederation" for their alienated provinces. Shortly before the July 1973 conference, hosted by Peter Lougheed in Calgary, the premiers released four papers on western economic development. One emphasized the importance of locally-owned financial institutions.

The Principal Group of Companies was well-positioned to lead the parade, and it wasn't in the cards for the Alberta government to take any steps that could embarrass it.

Rose's first step was to quickly convene a Alberta Securities Commission hearing to consider the renewal of Associated Investors' registration. The result of the hearing, held on March 30, 1973, before Rose and vice-chairman (retired Chief Judge) Nelles V. Buchanan, was a commission decision to renew Associated's licence but to recommend the appointment of a receiver/manager to take over its affairs.

That recommendation appeared in a Special Report dated April 26, 1973, to Merv Leitch, Alberta's Attorney General in the Lougheed government. Leitch, a University of Alberta law school graduate who had studied under Cormie, was now responsible for the Alberta Securities Commission and the investment contract companies.

The Special Report, prepared by Rose and Buchanan, highlighted Cormie's hypocritical denial of involvement with the contract companies.

> Mr. Cormie's reply to my letter is typical of his responses over the years. You will note that he discusses First Investors Corporation Ltd., for the most part, although that Company's affairs are not in issue. Mr. Cormie deals in half-truths and insists on keeping up the fiction that others run these two investment contract companies... [Over the years] the Securities Commission has been faced with one problem after another, created by unethical and, in some cases, unacceptable methods of doing business which, I believe, can be traced back to Mr Cormie.

The Report listed a number of "perennial problems," including investments, usually involving related company transactions, which the commission considered illegal, and a "legalistic" approach by Cormie to compliance with the *Investment Contracts Act*.

Cormie did not attend the March commission hearing, the Report said. Instead, three company directors appeared. During the week between Cormie's letter and the hearing, Associated's president Brian Sopp had disappeared from the roster, to be replaced by Grant Patrick, a young Edmonton lawyer. Patrick, who also served as director of both contract companies for several months, resigned all posts soon after the hearing ended. (Patrick is the son of The Hon. Allen Russell Patrick, a key member of the provincial Cabinet in the Social Credit governments of Ernest Manning and Harry Strom—and a friend of Ralph Forster's. Elected to the Legislature in 1952, he became Minister of Economic Affairs in 1955; during the 1960s he was the Minister of Industry and Development and Minister of Mines and Minerals. His eldest son Lynn was a partner in Cormie Kennedy during the 1960s and 1970s, then joined Principal Group as in-house counsel in 1983.)

Grant Patrick had appeared at the hearing with fellow directors Gerrard Frey and Robert Caithness, the Report said. "These three had little or no knowledge of the Company's affairs." Patrick had practised law for four or five years following his graduation "and has no experience running a financial institution." Caithness had come on board only the previous November. Frey was also brand new, and would soon be appointed to replace Patrick as Associated Investors president, although he too resigned a few months later. The three men were ignorant of one of the most questionable land deals of concern to the commission, Rose said, "other than to half-heartedly say that this land was acquired upon the redemption of a mortgage."

The Special Report's recommendation that a receiver/manager be appointed was qualified with the comment that Associated's assets did have considerable value and might appreciate. It also observed that appointment of a receiver/manager might precipitate a run not only on Associated, but on First Investors and the trust company as well, causing a chain reaction disastrous to "this very substantial financial group."

Three weeks later, Rose backed away from the recommendation to appoint a receiver/manager. In a May 16, 1973, memo to Leitch, Rose said that Associated planned a number of steps to improve its situation, and because of dire consequences likely to ensue if a receiver/manager were appointed, he felt the government should give the company time to carry out its plans. Rose also urged amendment of the *Investment Contracts Act*, and suggested negotiations with the federal government to get the companies insured by the CDIC. These steps were never taken.

That month, responsibility for the contract companies left Rose's hands. The government transferred administration of the *Investment Contracts Act* from the securities commission to the Superintendent of Insurance, appointed under the *Insurance Act* and part of the Department of Consumer Affairs. Jim Darwish, Rose's assistant for many years, had become Superintendent the year before and was now in charge.

On June 6, Leitch wrote a memo to Premier Lougheed discussing long-standing problems with the Principal Group conglomerate.

Both the Alberta Securities Commission and the Superintendent of Insurance have been alarmed for years over the operation of these companies. That alarm is not lessening. I am convinced that we should do everything possible to head off a possible collapse of these companies. I expect that will involve some discussions with Mr. Cormie in which the government will have to take a firm stand.

Leitch suggested immediately requesting reports from Rose and Darwish, then retaining an accountant/lawyer team from outside the government to analyze and audit the entire operation. He concluded with a request for a meeting with Lougheed and then-Consumer Affairs Minister Dowling to discuss the matter: "The sooner it can be held, the better."

On July 19, Rose and Darwish teamed up to write a memo to Leitch summarizing problems with the Principal companies. They advised that since the commission hearing in March, Associated Investors had implemented certain proposed corrections but still had "significant deficiencies." First and Associated were described respectively as "borderline" and "deficient" in their capital requirements. The securities commission had considered cancelling their licences, they said, but it was concluded "that such drastic action might have serious financial repercussions not only on the certificate holders, but on the Province as well; which at that time, had a general reputation of financial stability."

The memo—written five days before the western premiers' conference—explained the connections among the Principal companies, noting that Collective Securities, at the top of the pyramid, was a private company controlled by Donald Cormie. It detailed a number of transactions in which the affairs of Collective, Principal Group, the contract companies, the trust company and other affiliates were intermingled in amounts totalling several million dollars.

Rose and Darwish reminded Leitch of consultant Gordon Burton's 1971 recommendation that a single regulatory body somehow oversee the entire group of companies. It was important, they said, that Collective Securities, Principal Group, Principal Trust and the contract companies be collectively examined. Because there was no jurisdiction under Alberta's *Securities Act* for such an examination, "another method must be sought…

> It is our recommendation that an outside firm of chartered accountants and a first-class corporate lawyer should be retained to conduct a thorough examination of their affairs provided, of course, that they should be authorized to trace something into any one of the other subsidiaries of the conglomerate, should it be necessary for them to do so.
>
> We believe that Mr. Cormie should be notified that the Government at the Cabinet level is concerned with the outstanding recommendation for the appointment of a receiver/manager for Associated; it is also concerned that First Investors is operating so close to the borderline, as is also the Principal Savings and Trust Company… The government should ask Mr. Cormie to authorize the various companies to open their books and accounts to the selected persons, on a confidential basis. By proceeding in this manner, the publicity which would be attendant upon the establishment of a public inquiry may be avoided.

During the summer, Leitch and Consumer Affairs Minister Dowling met with Cormie, who beat the drum of western pride. By the time the outside consultants were engaged, their assignment was much abridged: not the definitive examination of the conglomerate urged by Leitch and the regulators, but a study limited to Associated Investors. Superintendent of Insurance Darwish—Rose was now well out of the picture—was summoned to Dowling's office to hear the decision. His memo to file, dated September 13, 1973, summarized the meeting:

> On this date, I attended a meeting in Mr. Dowling's office with Mr. Leitch also in attendance. They advised me that they had a couple of meetings with Mr. D. Cormie, and that Mr. Cormie felt that any investigation into the affairs of his various companies should at this time be limited to Associated Investors only. Mr. Cormie indicated his concern that, if all the companies were being investigated, word would soon get out onto the street and it would also have a demoralizing effect on his employees.
>
> Messrs. Leitch and Dowling wondered if there would be any objection to limiting the audit at this stage to Associated Investors providing that it be made perfectly clear to Mr. Cormie that if it became necessary, other companies would be looked at.

Darwish agreed the "first audit" could be limited to the one company. "I did point out the fact," he wrote, "that by doing one audit at a time, it would be conceivable if there was a shortage in assets that assets could be moved from one company to the other as they were being audited. I did go on to say, however, that I really did not think that this type of situation existed with the companies."

Documents uncovered by the *Calgary Herald* show that the Lougheed Cabinet was involved in deciding the course of events. Reporter Howard Solomon dug into Edmonton's provincial archives and came up with Cabinet correspondence that included the June 6 memo from Leitch to Lougheed. (There was a handwritten note at the bottom of the letter: "Letter from Mr. Cormie to the Premier." That letter has not been made public.) Leitch told the *Herald* he remembered nothing of the requested meeting with Lougheed and Dowling, but noted that Lougheed was very much a hands-on premier. "He liked to be kept aware of what you were doing and what was happening."[1]

Gordon Miniely, Alberta Treasurer between September 1971 and April 1975, confirmed in an interview that the Lougheed Cabinet discussed Principal Group's financial problems during his tenure.[2]

Another note found among Leitch's papers in the archives, signed "Merv," named a lawyer being considered to help prepare a report on Principal. The handwritten note, perhaps passed between ministers during a legislature session or a Cabinet meeting, was addressed to "Neil and Lou"—likely Lou Hyndman, then-house leader, and Neil Crawford, at that time Minister of Health. The note advised that "MacDonell (sic) of Miler (sic) Steer is not available," and suggested an alternate. This is a likely reference to Edmonton lawyer Peter MacDonnell, a long-time Tory fundraiser and member of Peter Lougheed's original leadership campaign team, who has been described as "perhaps Lougheed's most constant friend and adviser outside the government."[3]

There were two replies, in different handwriting, on the back of Leitch's note. One approved the alternate candidate as "a good political choice." The other cautioned: "He may severely criticize the government's position—calls a spade a spade." He didn't get the job.

In the end Robert Black, Q.C., another long-time Conservative, was chosen to work with the accounting firm Ernst & Ernst in examining the Principal companies. An October 1973 letter from Dowling to Cormie, confirming the appointments, was marked "Confidential" and copied to Lougheed and Leitch. The letter said that while the government felt it ought to have similar reports on all the companies, it would wait for the report on Associated and then decide about subsequent studies. So much for a thorough examination of the financial interdependence of the Principal Group companies, as originally recommended by Leitch and Rose.

This was the closest the province ever came to conducting a comprehensive audit. Despite overwhelming evidence of self-dealing, it would take another decade and a half for the full extent of Cormie's perfidy to be revealed.

It was a neat play by Leitch, who made a 180-degree swing in strategy after meeting with Cormie. With Rose gone, the new and then-inexperienced Superintendent of Insurance Jim Darwish was soft-soaped into agreeing that a pair of Cabinet-selected consultants should examine only one contract company. The other contract company was eventually looked at as well, and that was all: detailed investigation painlessly aborted.

In November 1973—about three weeks after Darwish learned that Leitch and Dowling wanted to reduce the scope of the Principal investigation—Cormie wrote to Dowling, complaining again about the securities commission:

> We would like to add that since Mr. Manning retired as Attorney General there has been a most vicious attack by a number of Officials associated with the Securities Commission, not upon the Directors or even the President and officers over the years of the company, but upon the shareholders, who are the very people that the Commission has a statutory obligation to protect...
>
> Consequently, I would again like to reiterate our most vigorous objections to any of the information originated being made available either directly or indirectly to any of the officials connected with the Alberta Securities Commission in 1962,[4] until the consequence of that matter is determined. We also feel that it would not be proper for any of these officials to sit in judgment on the consequences of their own actions, to be responsible in any way for originating any type of "fishing expedition" so as to embarrass or discredit the shareholders in an attempt to reduce their possible personal liability...
>
> I would again like to point out in passing that there are still a tremendous number of "leaks" coming out from various officials working at the Alberta

Securities Commission, as well as some extremely hostile statements made to various employees and other government officials outside the province. This is causing tremendous damage to the companies, running into the hundreds of thousands of dollars. We would like to request that if you have any urgent complaints that you let us have them immediately and directly so that the particular company can deal with the problem immediately.

We would also like to request that you review with us or with the appropriate officers or directors of the particular companies any report being made by the Department to you, since we had no idea that there was such a difference between the apparent attitude at the Cabinet level and the attitude at the administrative level toward the progress made in straightening up this company...

I would like to express my appreciation for the careful manner in which these questions are being handled by you...

Ernst & Ernst commenced its audit of Associated Investors in February 1974 and completed it that July. A half-year later, First Investors was also audited. The two reports indicated deficiencies in qualified assets of approximately $1.1 million for Associated Investors, and $2.2 million for First Investors. Like others, they urged amendment of the *Investment Contracts Act.*

Ernst & Ernst said that it was evident the contract companies were not being operated in a prudent manner and that shareholders were using every tactic possible to circumvent the provisions of the Act. The reports identified several areas in which the companies had contravened the Act, including many already noted in the regulatory files: a deficiency in qualified assets; intercompany transactions; unduly large holdings of real estate obtained in satisfaction of debts; transactions with shareholders and affiliates; inadequate control over assets on deposit; administration charges by the parent; deficiency in unimpaired capital and reserves; over-valuation of real estate; lack of continuity of management; and the failure to match assets with liabilities. As well, First Investors held a debenture and two promissory notes from the parent company worth $1.3 million. As security for the loans, Principal Group pledged vacant land which, according to appraisals obtained by Ernst & Ernst, was worth only about half that amount.

Meanwhile, in the months since Associated Investors had abandoned its licence in British Columbia, that province's regulators had continued to make life difficult for First Investors, the remaining company. In the spring of 1974, B.C. Super-intendent Bill Irwin held up First's registration until certain information was provided and a promissory note from Principal Group was amended to his satisfaction. A few months later, Irwin threatened to pull the company's licence unless another $1 million was injected over a three-month period. Faced with this unaccustomed firmness, Principal Group did what it was told.

On September 13, 1974, a week after the B.C. demand, Jim Darwish recommended similar action to Minister Dowling. He also took the extreme step of suggesting—as had his predecessor 18 months earlier—that if Cormie didn't co-operate in injecting additional assets, a receiver/manager should be appointed. And, he said, Attorney-General Leitch should review the Ernst & Ernst report for possible charges against the companies for not complying with the *Investment Contracts Act.*

The recommendation to appoint a receiver/manager was put on hold because Jack Lyndon, the new deputy minister in the Consumer Affairs department, decided he needed more information. Lyndon commissioned Edmonton lawyer Jack Shortreed and Vancouver accountant Don Gardner of Clarkson Gordon & Co. to review the Ernst & Ernst reports and write reports of their own. This they did, completing their work in December 1974. They, too, recommended far-reaching amendments to the *Investment Contracts Act.* Their detailed reports, one for each of the contract companies, concluded that First Investors and Associated Investors had failed all three Section 8 financial tests and were in flagrant violation of the Act. A state of affairs existed which could be prejudicial to the contract holders. Shortreed and Gardner criticized the profits taken by Principal Group for the management of the companies and urged the immediate termination of intercompany transactions. However, they said, while the departures from the Act were serious, the contract holders were not in immediate jeopardy and the risk could be eliminated if the companies were forced to conform with the Act on the strict timetable they recommended.

Cormie, alerted that the regulators were primed to pull the contract companies' licences, hit the lobby trail again. During meetings with Leitch and Dowling, he argued that there were errors in the consultants' reports. In any case, he said, it would be a black mark on Alberta and its financial industry if his companies went down. "I'm sure I discussed the importance of supporting and developing the financial industry," Cormie testified.

On March 25, 1975—Sunday, and the day before a provincial election—Dowling, Lyndon, Darwish and Shortreed met with Leitch to review the situation. Lyndon recommended that a letter be sent to the contract companies the following Tuesday setting out the department's demands. Darwish wrote a memo to file: "After some discussion, it was agreed that because there would probably be a new minister appointed shortly after the election that no letter should be sent to each of the companies until the new minister had a chance to review the files."

Lougheed's Conservatives won the election handily. The next day, March 27, Darwish put his concerns on record with Special Reports to Dowling. He pointed out that if the contract holders were not "in immediate jeopardy," as Shortreed and Gardner had said, it was mostly because cash was continually flowing into the companies in the form of new contract sales. "A company such as this could conceivably limp along for many years using this cash flow," he warned. He again recommended sending both the Ernst & Ernst and Shortreed/Gardner reports to the Attorney General "with a view to ascertaining if there has been a breach of trust or other criminal code violations." (Again, this did not happen.) Darwish's reports concluded:

This company has been a constant source of problems to my office and previously to the Securities Commission. Assets have been drained out of the company by way of dividends, management fees and other questionable transactions that benefit the parent companies to the detriment of the investment contract holders. Except when required to do so, no attempt has been made to increase the equity base of First Investors/Associated Investors as its liability to contract holders increased. For this reason, I feel that the timetable for bringing unimpaired capital up to $500,000 be strict, but not unreasonable. We're simply asking that assets previously taken from First Investors/Associated Investors be returned.

Four days later—despite the companies' capital deficiencies—Darwish delivered their renewed licences to Ken Marlin. These were accompanied by a letter stating that although he was providing the licences, "As you know, there is authority in Section 10 of the *Investment Contracts Act* to take action on the registration of any issuer." This was a not-so-veiled threat: Section 10 allowed Darwish to suspend the companies' registrations if it appeared that their finances were not in order. Darwish testified that he felt comfortable with this course of action, because Deputy Minister Lyndon and Minister Dowling knew the situation.

On April 3, MLA Graham Harle replaced Dowling in the Consumer Affairs portfolio, and a week later Darwish forwarded him a detailed briefing package.

A month after that, following discussions with Harle and Lyndon, Darwish finally wrote his compliance letter to the contract companies. Dated May 12, 1975, it did not act on his earlier threat to suspend the licences, but set out directions and a timetable for resolving their financial deficiencies and management flaws.[5] Administration fees were to be thoroughly reviewed by a consultant appointed by Darwish, the cost to be paid by Principal Group.

Lyndon says he took it on himself to press for Cormie's compliance with Darwish's conditions. "We forced some sales of properties, and forced some money to be put aside," he told me in 1990. Lyndon, another Alberta-bred lawyer, travelled in Cormie's social circles, and during this period the two men met at a dinner party. "He just screamed at me," Lyndon told me. "He was saying I was, you know: 'How can you grind a company down? How can you be so difficult?' He was saying we were being too hard on his fine Alberta company. Eivor, his wife, came to me and said: 'Why would Donald—what have you done to him? I've never seen him quite like this. You must have done something terrible.'

"I just said, 'It's not a big deal. He's obviously had a bad day.' "

It was brutally frustrating dealing with Cormie, Lyndon said. "Every time Darwish did something, Cormie found another loophole or he shifted things."

First Investors and Associated Investors agreed to abide by the conditions set in Darwish's May 12 letter. Eventually most of the promises were broken.

Darwish and Lyndon turned their attention to a legislative solution. Amendments were drafted to the *Investment Contracts Act* and were sent to interested parties for comment in the summer of 1975. The amendments, which would block loopholes permitting exploitation of the contract companies, were based on a draft uniform act prepared by regulators in Alberta, B.C., Saskatchewan, Manitoba and Ontario. There were several important features: the legislation imposed a borrowing-to-capital ratio of 20:1, providing a cushion of protection for contract holders; it prohibited non-arms-length transactions; it required a minimum capital base of $1 million and publicly available audited financial statements; it prevented shareholders from drawing dividends from a contract company while the capital was impaired or if the draw would impair the capital; and it stopped the payment of dividends until additional credits had been paid to contract holders.

The amendments would also have added regulatory teeth. As matters stood, the Superintendent of Insurance had only two alternatives for dealing with a problem company: he could refuse to issue a licence, or he could recommend appointment of a receiver/manager. Both were extreme steps that regulators were reluctant to take. The new Act provided for the issuing of conditional licences, and allowed the Superintendent to take temporary control of assets.

It was a good piece of legislation. Harle liked it, his deputy minister liked it, Darwish liked it. "It was on the verge of being introduced," he testified. "I was told by Mr. Harle—and he was proud of it—that he was told by the premier, I think, that this was to be one of the most important pieces of legislation that year, if not the most important piece..."

Donald Cormie, however, hadn't liked it at all, and he wrote to Peter Lougheed. In his letter, dated September 19, 1975, Cormie declared himself "stunned and dismayed to see the radical provisions in this Act" and warned that "the existing Alberta companies"—First and Associated—could not operate under the new legislation. "I would appreciate it if you could advise when the statute will be proposed to the Legislature and who in the political area in Alberta" would be prepared to hear representations from Principal, Cormie concluded. He dashed off this six-page message on his way to Spain for two weeks to attend a meeting of the World Business Council.

According to Ken Marlin, Cormie had met with Lougheed earlier that year, around the time that the contract companies' licences were threatened. (Marlin's lawyer told the Code inquiry his client knew of a meeting in 1975, although he didn't know what Cormie and Lougheed talked about.) Cormie testified that a meeting may have taken place, although he didn't recall it. Then he added: "I generally tried to avoid meeting with the Premier, but it is possible I did at this time to see if it was critical." No one asked him to explain this bizarre statement. What possible reason could there be for avoiding the most powerful man in the province? Cormie certainly didn't shy away from meeting anyone else who might be useful.

In a 1989 interview with the *Calgary Herald*, Cormie said he considered Lougheed a friend, "but I never asked him for anything."[6] We will have to take Cormie's word on the friendship, as Lougheed declines all comment. As for Cormie's claim that he never asked Lougheed for anything—that, we have just seen, is not true.

(There are striking similarities in the two men's management styles, attributable in part to their similar university backgrounds. Lougheed was a law student at the University of Alberta between 1948 and 1952, during the period Cormie taught law there. Then he followed his path to Harvard University, earning a Master of Business Administration degree in 1954. The politically-minded Lougheed, concerned about appearing elitist, would downplay his prestigious degree. Cormie milked his for all it was worth. Both became charismatic leaders—charming but intimidating, tough, strong-willed and absorbed with detail, hands-on managers with a similar strategy: recruit efficient lieutenants, send them into the fray, but keep a tight rein. Both built empires which have been described as "personal fiefdoms."[7] As Lougheed biographer Allan Hustak remarked: "Harvard men have always believed, and quite rightly, that they are chosen to lead.")

A week after Cormie wrote his letter to Lougheed, the premier's personal secretary Wylla Walker sent Cormie a letter of acknowledgement:

> Premier Lougheed has taken note of the comments contained in your letter and has asked me to forward a copy of your letter to the Honourable Graham Harle, Minister of Consumer and Corporate Affairs, in order that he may respond directly to you with regard to your concerns. You will, no doubt, be hearing from Mr. Harle as soon as he has had an opportunity to carefully consider the contents of your letter.

Within a couple of weeks of Cormie's return from Europe, plans to table the amendments were killed. On October 17, Harle sent a memo to Lou Hyndman, government house leader, which said:

> Fall Legislation—amendments to the *Investment Contracts Act*. I do not believe it will be appropriate to proceed with the amendments to the *Investment Contracts Act* at the fall session of the legislature, this year. If you wish to telephone me, I will outline the reasons for the delay.

Jim Darwish doesn't remember asking Harle what happened. "I was very disappointed and I was embarrassed a bit to ask Mr. Harle why it didn't go through because I thought it might have been a bit of an embarrassment to him." The amendment was dropped, not just from the fall session, but permanently. Darwish, who suspected that Cormie had somehow made the legislation disappear, deemed it unwise to pursue the amendments. "From my own personal point of view, I guess I felt that maybe it wouldn't be timely to do that." It was several years before he tried again.

Harle did not testify at the Code inquiry, but was interviewed afterward by Alberta Ombudsman Aleck Trawick. In his report, Trawick said that at the time the amendments were being considered Harle (who had been minister only five months) learned that regulators were considering recommending the removal of the contract companies' licences: "He did not want to proceed with the new legislation until the current matters under the Act were settled." Harle said he later asked Deputy

Minister Lyndon if there were any further problems; it appeared that the problems had been resolved and there was no subsequent request to him to re-introduce the new Act.

The administration fee study ordered by Darwish in May 1975 did go ahead, but it took two years to complete. In December 1977, Clarkson Gordon & Co. delivered a report which advised that Principal Group Ltd. and Principal Consultants Ltd. (the sales arm of the conglomerate) charged a number of fees to the trust company and the contract companies which "appear to bear no relationship to the actual expenses of Principal Group Ltd." The firm was unable to access all of Principal Group's records, but based on data obtained, concluded—no surprise—that the fees were excessive and inappropriate. Six months later, Darwish wrote to Cormie and Marlin, ordering that all intercompany charges should bear some "logical relationship" to the related expenses. According to the Code report: "It would appear that nothing came of this. The regulators took no other action with respect to changing the basis of the intercompany charges."

Leitch would maintain a decade and a half later that the right calls were made in the 1970s. "It turned out that was a sound decision because by the late '70s they were back in a sound position... We weighed all the alternatives but decided we couldn't" pull the licences, he told the *Calgary Herald* in 1989.[8]

He was wrong. The decisions made in those years were not sound, and the kindest explanation is that Leitch and other politicians were distracted by the overwhelming Donald Cormie. Cormie was taking advantage of investors, using money he had no right to, and for most of the years of their existence his contract companies operated outside the laughably minimal capital requirements of the *Investment Contracts Act*. A thorough examination of the Principal conglomerate would have revealed information essential to protecting the public interest. Jim Darwish recommended that Leitch, as Attorney General, be asked to investigate possible breaches of the Act. This didn't happen. The government was asked to strengthen the legislation. That didn't happen. Cormie's companies promised to mend their ways, and that didn't happen either.

In February 1982, Cormie contacted Leitch again. His cordial letter included a copy of a company memo on regulatory requirements for financial institutions, with a request for copies of any government studies on the matter. Similar letters were sent to Neil Crawford and to then-Consumer Affairs Minister Julian Koziak. At that time, Crawford was the Attorney General, responsible for law enforcement, and Leitch was Minister of Energy; the two men were addressed by their first names. The letter to Leitch began: "Dear Merv: I know you are long since out of the more mundane governmental departments, however I thought you still might be interested in the attached internal memorandum..."

Throughout the late 1970s, hyper-inflation and a rising market cured all ills, and the finances of the Principal companies seemed to improve. During this time regulators focused on negotiating mortgage lending guidelines and a reasonable borrowing-to-capital ratio. Jim Darwish thought he had reached an agreement with

Ken Marlin on both points, but as we have seen, the companies borrowed wildly and invested recklessly. (Alberta Ombudsman Aleck Trawick had only two criticisms of Darwish's performance over 25 years: that he relied on these gentleman's agreements with Marlin in the late 1970s, and that he did not continue to push for amendment of the *Investment Contracts Act* after being blocked in 1975.)

By the early 1980s, it was clear the companies' prosperity was an illusion, attributable to stock market gains, the result of a boom market and increasingly risky mortgage lending. High rates of interest paid to investors continued, as did excessive administration and selling fees. By 1980, auditors were reporting renewed financial difficulty, and the problems escalated rapidly from that point.

April 24, 1984

J IM DARWISH WASN'T SURE what to do with his firecracker memos, now that he'd written them. He wanted Connie Osterman to read them—was desperate to have the Consumer Affairs minister thoroughly briefed on the Principal crisis—but knew there'd be big trouble if he handed them to her directly.

Protocol required that he follow the lines of authority, that he report to Osterman through Barry Martin, the deputy minister. Osterman had made it clear that was the way she wanted it. Actually, she'd made other points clear as well. Darwish hadn't been Superintendent of Insurance for three years—he was responsible now only for the production of audit reports—and Osterman wanted him to keep his nose out of follow-up and compliance issues.

Things had started to go downhill for Darwish soon after Martin replaced Jack Lyndon in early 1979. Darwish and Lyndon had worked well together, and Lyndon recalls him with admiration and affection. "My term of endearment for Jim Darwish was 'my God-damn favourite nit-picking accountant,'" Lyndon told me in 1990. "He and I had a delightful relationship of dynamic tension. We didn't always agree on things, but I did give him his head. And often, when he had a problem, I said, 'Take it to the minister, and if you two can't agree, I will come.'"

Martin found Darwish somewhat less endearing, and relations quickly deteriorated. "I told Barry at one stage of the game, 'I'm sorry if Darwish is a problem, he's the best man you have on your staff,'" Lyndon said. "And Barry said, 'Oh my God, Jack, how would you ever make an assessment like that?'

"I said, 'Because he's an honest, very hard-working son-of-a-bitch.'" That's the ideal temperament for a regulator.

Lyndon left the department in mid-1978, and Darwish served briefly as acting deputy minister. Then on January 1, 1979, Martin was parachuted into the top job from outside government circles.

Martin, born in 1931, began his career as a small-town Manitoba lawyer, specializing in commercial and financial law. In 1963, he moved to Calgary, joining the federal government's Industrial Development Bank as in-house counsel. Four years later, he joined Pacific Petroleums Ltd., one of western Canada's most prominent oil exploration companies, as a financial lawyer. As such, he assisted in obtaining financing for major capital projects. Suddenly in 1968, at 37, Martin abandoned the practice of law to join the Southern Alberta Institute of Technology as an instructor in the business department. Within a few months, he was appointed SAIT's academic director, a position he held for nine years. While in that post, he represented the institute in bitter labour negotiations.

Premier Peter Lougheed approved Martin's appointment as deputy minister in the Consumer Affairs department, as he did appointments to all sensitive positions. The screening process, including interviews with the then-minister and other officials, went well, Martin says, but the actual job offer came only after Lougheed's personal inspection. "The next day I got a phone call from [James Dixon, Public Service Commissioner] to advise me that I had passed the scrutiny of all the three groups involved, including the premier, and I was offered the position." During his nine years in harness, Martin never saw a job description. "Mr. Lougheed asked me in the interview I had with him, what I perceived the role of a deputy minister to be. I endeavoured to describe [it] to him. I can assure you it was right off the top of my head; I wasn't sure."

Martin's new job, he learned over time, had two facets. On the administrative side was a staff of up to 500 people serving in 11 programs, with more than 30 pieces of legislation to oversee. "The other side of the function, as I saw it, was in the political area, not in the sense of politics, but in the sense of interpreting the aspirations of the politicians with respect to their assigned programs and endeavouring to develop programs that would meet those aspirations." The job required "political awareness," Martin said. "I was the one who would be charged with interpreting that policy to my colleagues in the department so they could carry on their jobs in the light of that policy."

Within a couple of months of Martin's arrival, the department also had a new minister. Edmonton MLA Julian Koziak, a 38-year-old lawyer, had first been elected to the Legislature in the Lougheed sweep of 1971. He had been Minister of Education since 1975, and after the 1979 election replaced Graham Harle at Consumer Affairs.

When Martin became deputy minister, Darwish returned to his duties as Superintendent of Insurance and Real Estate, the job he'd held since 1972. It wasn't a bad job, really. It kept him in the action, with some power and a sizable staff. He was responsible for supervising Alberta's insurance, real estate and trust companies, as well as the contract companies regulated under the *Investment Contracts Act*. The entire audit section reported to him as well.

But the arrival of Martin and Koziak heralded a new attitude in the department, and things were never quite the same again. Consumer Affairs had traditionally focused its efforts on consumer protection, but within a year the buzzword was "de-regulation." Martin took it upon himself to meet with company representatives, sometimes advocating their positions to his regulatory staff. Darwish sensed that Martin favoured the companies, to the possible detriment of consumers. This perceived shift in priorities resulted in mounting tension throughout the department.

In an interview, Martin described "de-regulation" as "putting more self-policing and self-governance within the industry," and he added: "It was all across North America at that time." Quite right. "De-regulation" had swept north—hitting free-enterprise Alberta with gale force—from the United States, where Ronald Reagan's White House was cutting loose the American savings and loan industry, meanwhile gutting the regulatory agencies of staff. The real estate speculation, political corruption and fraud which followed resulted in a $500-billion (U.S.) collapse.[9]

In early 1981, a couple of years after taking charge of the department, Martin presented Koziak with a proposal for major reorganization; Koziak approved and the plan was implemented. Consumer Affairs was divided into three functional divisions: program support, program development and regional delivery. Each division was headed by an assistant deputy minister (ADM), who reported through Martin to the minister. Darwish's position of Superintendent of Insurance and Real Estate was split in two. Previously, the Superintendent had reported directly to Martin; now Ron Kaiser, the newly-appointed Superintendent of Insurance, reported to Tewfik Saleh, the newly-appointed executive director of program development. Saleh, who had been Darwish's second deputy superintendent, now reported to the ADM, program development.

The reorganization was a disaster for Darwish. Stripped of the regulatory duties from which he took such satisfaction, he was kicked upstairs to a post unsuited to his training and temperament. Darwish was given one of the three assistant deputy minister positions: not as ADM for program development, responsible for regulatory functions, but as ADM for program support. This division handled much of the administration—the paper-shuffling duties—of the department, and included the record systems and the planning and research unit.

Prior to reorganization the audit staff reported directly to the Superintendent of Insurance. Now a newly-created audit section was available on an as-needed basis to the entire department. Darwish's former assistant Reg Pointe became director of this new audit section, reporting to Darwish.

In testimony, Martin described Darwish as capable, meticulous, knowledgeable, tenacious and thorough. He couldn't explain why Darwish was so thoroughly emasculated at what should have been the peak of an honourable career. Was Darwish sidelined because he was *too* capable and tenacious, a liability in the present atmosphere of "de-regulation"? Certainly not, Martin answered.

Martin understood that Darwish was devastated by the change. "I had many conversations with Mr. Darwish about his job," he testified. "He was obviously very unhappy being out of the regulatory role and discussed it with me on a number of occasions. He kept referring to it that he didn't have any power anymore... I remember him very distinctly, [saying] 'You've taken away all my power.' "

Darwish wasn't the only unhappy camper. Consultant Bill Barry, brought in to evaluate the reorganization, uncovered bitter frustrations throughout Consumer Affairs. His report,[10] written a year after the shuffle, sharply criticized staffing decisions and poor communication within the department. Having interviewed two dozen staff members, from the ADM level to a filing clerk, he found almost no one satisfied with the way the department was being run. The organization was top-heavy and senior officials had been inappropriately assigned to duties for which they had no experience or interest, the report said. "The Assistant Deputy Minister Development [Del Keowan, with a background in consumer protection] has continued to involve himself in the day to day problems and issues; the Assistant Deputy Minister for Program Delivery [Harold Thomas] has been by-passed and he has searched for other meaningful pursuits; and the Assistant Deputy Minister for Support [Darwish] has been left out of the decision-making process and has theorized on the merits of audit."

The report indicated that morale was abysmal and tensions so high that officials were preoccupied with the traditional cover-your-ass tactics of frightened bureaucrats: "There is an inclination to write a memo on every trivial subject and to protect oneself by disseminating numerous carbon copies." Staff did not level with or understand one another; future planning was inadequate; and there was a very negative response regarding knowledge and understanding of Minister Koziak's philosophy. "There is a prevalent feeling that more questions and concerns than necessary are passed to the Minister," the report said.

In November 1982, after yet another election, Koziak became Minister of Municipal Affairs, and was replaced by Three Hills MLA Connie Osterman. The new minister, 46, a strong-willed farmer's wife with a high-school education, walked into an economic minefield. Alberta was mired in a debilitating recession. By 1982, mortgage companies were going down like dominos, and the province's credit unions were becoming a worry. In January 1983, Ontario's Crown Trust Company failed amid a blaze of scandal. The Ontario government seized more than $2 billion in assets after taking over Crown Trust, Greymac Trust and Seaway Trust, following the controversial $500-million flip of 10,931 Cadillac Fairview apartments in Toronto. Crown Trust had branches in Alberta, and Osterman ended up freezing the company's assets there.

In the midst of this early crisis, Osterman received a briefing from her deputy minister about a morale problem in the department. The 1981 reorganization "was not necessarily working well in terms of personalities," and there was a great deal of frustration and tension, Barry Martin advised her.

One of the problems was Jim Darwish. He was constantly looking over the shoulder of Ron Kaiser, the man who had replaced him as Superintendent, and he was unhappy with what he saw. Company audits and correspondence were on file in the department, and Darwish wasn't shy about inspecting them. They showed that the affairs of several financial companies—including the Principal contract companies—were deteriorating, and Darwish felt it was time to turn up the heat.

Office politics made it difficult to take his worries directly to Kaiser, so Darwish worked through colleagues. In May 1982, he wrote a memo to Tewfik Saleh, Kaiser's supervisor, about the ongoing U.S. depository dispute, arguing—as he had on previous occasions—that it was important that the Principal contract companies' assets being held in New York at that time (totalling about $40 million) be returned to Canada.[11] In February 1983 he wrote a memo to then-director of audits Reg Pointe, asking him to talk to Kaiser about the "innocuous wording" of letters sent to the Principal contract companies.

The next month, Kaiser left the Superintendent's position (for reasons unrelated to the Principal companies) and Saleh replaced him as Acting Superintendent. A month later, Darwish wrote to Saleh about the need for follow-up on unsatisfactory audits coming in on the contract companies. Within a month Saleh had also been persuaded to again raise the U.S. depository matter. The issue had increased in urgency in the wake of the Crown Trust scandal, and Darwish pressed his point in a memo to Deputy Minister Martin dated January 18, 1983:

> On a number of occasions during the Crown Trust affair, I reflected on the problems that could arise with respect to assets that were actually on deposit in Alberta, let alone in other provinces or in another country. We have learned that it's not so simple to deal with assets. I shudder to think of what problems might arise if we had huge liabilities owning to the citizens of Alberta with assets to cover them in another country.

It took another half a year of departmental dithering, but in a June 1983 letter Saleh ordered the return of the securities to Canada.

Principal vice-president Christa Petracca went into action with a series of letters and meetings with Saleh. She kept Barry Martin—whom she considered an ally—apprised of her progress, and in a confidential September 1983 memo to Donald Cormie, Ken Marlin and Jaimie Cormie, after a meeting with Saleh, she advised: "Barry Martin, in particular, is pushing for a more co-operative attitude with us and they are trying to co-operate to the fullest extent..." The memo also said that Saleh had received a second legal opinion on the U.S. depository issue. The Attorney General's office had concluded two years earlier that it was illegal for the contract companies to hold assets in the United States, but this new opinion indicated the Superintendent had discretionary authority over the assets.

Meanwhile, tension continued to mount in the department. Officials plotted and schemed against one another, distracting themselves with whispering campaigns and endless flows of memos. At least one shoving match took place in a corridor.

Osterman was aware of the poisoned atmosphere. The continual criticism was very distracting, and was creating "negative energy," affecting the department's ability to function, she testified. In the summer of 1983, Osterman shipped off much of her staff—crackling with negativity—to a soul-baring rural retreat. Cloistered away at a wooded Kananaskis resort in the Rocky Mountain foothills, the department's senior officials protested the reorganization imposed on them two years earlier. Some were concerned about a slack attitude toward languishing financial institutions. They wanted the department reorganized again, so as to place all the reins in one firm hand. Afterward, five of the six senior managers (Del Keowan, Jim Darwish, Harold Thomas, George Blochert and Steve Stephens—the exception was

Tewfik Saleh) collaborated on a memo to Osterman proposing changes that would have put all financial institutions, and the audit staff, under a single ADM.

Osterman and Martin looked at the suggestions, and in October responded with a plan of their own. It involved a new post—executive director, financial institutions—with responsibility for all financial institutions: trust companies, insurance companies, credit unions and the contract companies. This position was to be filled by Saleh—the only senior official who hadn't signed the protest memo—who would report directly to Martin. (Martin told me Saleh was "a good friend of mine" and the friendship dated back to Martin's earliest days as deputy minister. "When I went into the office I recognized him as a very capable and conscientious man.")

Osterman's memo announcing the appointment advised that "financial difficulties brought about by the current economic climate make it imperative that we be able to have closer control of these areas." Saleh, Acting Superintendent of Insurance for several months, was also confirmed as Superintendent. This restructuring consolidated all authority over financial institutions—including the Principal companies—in the hands of Saleh, Martin and, ultimately, Osterman. It also catapulted Saleh over his superiors, removing him completely from the line of fire of the three ADMs, particularly Jim Darwish.

Tewfik Saleh, 59 at the time of the second reorganization, came from Egypt. He had earned a law degree there in 1949 and practised law until 1964. The next year he emigrated to Montreal, where he worked for 12 years with an insurance company, drafting contracts and supervising the claims department. In 1976, on Darwish's recommendation, he was hired as Deputy Superintendent of Insurance, a position he held until the first reorganization in 1981. During those years, he was not involved in regulation of the investment contract companies. Darwish and his other deputy, Reg Pointe, handled that.

Darwish testified that Saleh was hired to provide a legal perspective. Unfortunately, his degree was in Egyptian civil law. He had no background in accounting and little experience in the often confrontational duties of a regulator. Nonetheless, he was now responsible for ensuring that the contract companies complied with the *Investment Contracts Act*, as well as supervising all the province's other financial institutions. Saleh liked his new title and in the coming years would vigorously defend his departmental turf from intrusion by Darwish and others; but he would prove utterly inadequate to the pressures of his office.

The second reorganization left Darwish's situation marginally improved. He became the ADM for support and services, with responsibility in three areas: regional services, support services and the audit section.

A couple of weeks after the shuffle, a disturbing audit of Paramount Life Insurance crossed Darwish's desk. The audit made it clear that the Calgary-based company was in serious trouble. Darwish wrote a memo to Saleh recommending that he consider appointment of a receiver/manager.

The memo quickly made its way to the minister. Just as quickly, Darwish received a phone call summoning him to Connie Osterman's office. After the meeting, he wrote a memo to file, dated November 7, 1983:

> I received a call to go to the Minister's office ASAP (approx 10 A.M.) Shortly after I arrived I was told I could go into the Minister's office. I had assumed that the item for discussion would be Credit Unions but was surprised when the Deputy [Barry Martin] left and I was meeting with the Minister alone. The Minister began by saying that she was concerned about a memo that I had written to Tewfik. She had a paper in her hand. I asked her what memo and she said the one I had written to him on Paramount and she quoted the last sentence to me. She said that I shouldn't be writing this type of memo to Tewfik Saleh. She said that she had been shown it this morning, that she wanted a stop to this type of memo. She said that with the new reorganization that I should limit myself to audit material and other material that I had authority over, but not insurance.

Osterman told Darwish he was to leave Saleh and the other regulators alone. If he saw something amiss he should report to Martin. "She said she wanted Tewfik Saleh and the new group to do things themselves, that she wanted to see how they operated, and that if she got burned then it was her problem."

Darwish told Osterman he didn't feel it was appropriate to go over colleagues' heads. He considered it an auditor's duty to follow up on his findings. "I had said to Mrs. Osterman that the Auditor General, for example, didn't simply do an audit on the department and find, perhaps, things wrong and not follow up on it," Darwish testified. But Osterman insisted and in the end, "I told her that it would be like operating with blinders on, that I was a keen person and that I didn't normally do business that way, but that I would give it a try."

Osterman's anger with Darwish was fueled, in part, by Martin's animosity, but it also reflected the sentiments of her Cabinet colleagues. Donald Cormie's lobbying (and similar efforts by other business interests) had made an impact. The Consumer Affairs department was viewed in Cabinet circles as a nest of intrusive, over-zealous rule-book thumpers, with Darwish the worst of a bad lot. Osterman told me that Cabinet colleagues often fielded complaints from business community constituents about their frustration with Consumer Affairs officials. When she took over the department, several ministers made it clear they would like to see her restrain her staff. "There were some people [in Cabinet] who were sceptical about the amount of regulations, and how they were being enforced by the department," she told me. "But I was already accustomed to knowing that some people believed in a freer market place."

Jim Darwish, in particular, "had a very bad reputation in the business community of everything being black and white," Osterman said. When he drew attention to the Paramount Life Insurance audit, resentment was automatic.

Cabinet members weren't happy to hear about regulatory pressure on the insurance company, Osterman told me. "I had resistance, boy did I have resistance," she said. "People were saying, 'Lookit, you've got a zealous bureaucracy here...' And so we obviously took great pains, and took a long period of time, to put our case together, before I got support to move on them."[12]

Amid this testy atmosphere, government auditor Al Hutchison delivered his alarming report on First Investors in October 1983. It said that almost two-thirds of First Investors' mortgages were over three months in arrears, or in foreclosure. The paltry capital requirements of the *Investment Contracts Act* allowed the company to operate with a borrowing-to-capital ratio of 460:1. Mortgages were being valued by capitalizing interest that hadn't actually been paid; if those arrears were deducted rather than added to the value of the mortgages, the year's losses would have increased by a "staggering" $12 million.

Hutchison recommended appraisals on all property six months or more in arrears, and urged that the companies be made to comply with the *Investment Contract Act's* minimum capital test. Failing that, he said, Superintendent Saleh should consider making a Special Report to the minister requiring action under the Act. Hutchison's supervisor Burt Eldridge backed these recommendations and said in a separate memo that action on Saleh's part was clearly required. That memo went to Saleh on November 7, the same day as Darwish's memo on Paramount Insurance—and the same day that Osterman scolded Darwish for interfering in the Paramount affair.

Weeks passed before any action was taken on the audit team's recommendations. Finally, on January 12, 1984, Saleh sent the letter to Ken Marlin, seen in Chapter 5, which summoned Principal officials to discuss the contract companies' problems. Darwish, Hutchison and Eldridge spent many days with Saleh helping him write as aggressive a compliance letter as possible; Darwish took the precaution of writing a separate memo to Saleh noting that their assistance was at Saleh's own request.

The compliance letter in its final form was a watered-down version of the drafts proposed by Darwish and the auditors. It noted a capital impairment of $35.3 million and the deteriorating mortgage portfolio, but a demand for the immediate injection of $7 million in permanent capital was eliminated.

The day the letter was sent, Martin received a protest memo from senior department staff. The same five officials who had requested the reorganization the year before were so fed up they requested a "private meeting" with Martin to discuss "matters which we deem to be of an urgent and important nature pertaining to the operation of the department."

Soon afterward, a meeting room was booked at the downtown Chateau Lacombe. Martin and Saleh arrived in the company of Connie Osterman. Her attendance had not been requested, but she showed up anyway.

Steve Stephens made introductory remarks, then George Blochert took the lead. Blochert, responsible for administration of the department's regional offices, complained that Saleh and Martin were failing to take action with respect to troubled financial institutions. The Principal companies *per se* were not at issue, but Blochert considered that problems with the credit unions and other institutions were being handled in a clandestine and inappropriate manner. Blochert was very blunt: Martin and Saleh were sitting on a powder-keg and his staff, who dealt daily with the public, weren't getting any information or guidelines.

"I realized when I spoke," Blochert told me, "that I was all alone." He had expected his colleagues to back him up, but they "were busy looking at their toes... I had the feeling that something had gone terribly awry. Maybe I should have kept my mouth shut, but you have to look at yourself when you're shaving... Afterward, Barry Martin shook his finger at me in his office, and he said: 'For 30 minutes you lectured me. Don't think I'll ever forget that.' " (Martin has denied this conversation occurred.)

Several days later, the January 25 meeting between provincial and Principal officials took place. This was the meeting at which Martin instructed the regulators to shut up and listen. That was a Wednesday. The next Monday, Osterman abruptly cancelled recently revived plans to amend the *Investment Contracts Act*. Osterman's order to drop the amendments was reiterated in an urgent memo February 16 to Martin from Osterman's executive assistant Doug Cameron: "As per your discussion with the Minister this morning, this is to remind you that she would like the amendments, relative to the increase in capitalization, held until further notice." This memo came the day after Osterman, in the company of Cabinet colleague Mary LeMessurier (then-Minister of Culture), joined Donald Cormie and some of his vice-presidents for lunch at Principal Plaza.

February 16 was also the day that Martin and Saleh met with Christa Petracca to talk about Principal's mortgage problems. Petracca later wrote a memo about the meeting:

> It was indicated that the largest problem they had was the fact that their own internal auditors were "throwing appraisals on Mr. Saleh's desk," which indicated that there was no value in some of the properties that they had appraised. He agreed to provide me with a list of the properties... Mr. Saleh is looking for sufficient information and back-up, in particular, assistance from our external auditors so that, in effect, we will be allowed the time to work out of these problems without regulatory interference.

Martin and Saleh had their turn for lunch at Principal Plaza two weeks later. The next day, on February 29, Martin sent his chilly memo rejecting Darwish's request for further appraisals on Principal properties. In mid-March, Darwish wrote his letter of appeal, asking for a meeting with Osterman to explain the urgency of the appraisals. On April 24, after learning that Cormie had dumped $23 million worth of trash from Principal Trust into the contract companies, he wrote the memo of his life. These explosive documents accurately predicted the tragic course of events of the next three years and are reproduced at length here:

FROM: J.O. Darwish, C.A., Assistant Deputy Minister
TO: J. Barry Martin, Deputy Minister

Please find attached a summary relating to [First Investors and Associated Investors] that I intended to use as briefing notes in anticipation of a meeting with the Minister relating to appraisals of real estate. In my memorandum of March 20, 1984, I requested to attend that meeting. I have not received a reply to my memorandum.

Another very serious matter has now been brought to my attention. As I understand it, on or about March 30, 1984, Principal Trust advised the department that it transferred, either by sale or payout, real estate or mortgages in which FIC and AIC had an interest to AIC and FIC. I assume this was done for cash. The total amount involved is approximately $23 million. This transfer includes the properties on which we have obtained appraisals to date, with a book value of approximately $7.2 million and an appraised value of $2.5 million, for a $4.7-million write-down.

I assume Principal Trust has responded in this way so as to put their house in order for the [CDIC]. By doing so, they have abused the provincial investment contract companies, presumably because this was the path of least resistance.

Apparently, Reg Pointe has been making some enquiries from the point of view of the *Trust Companies Act*. It is not Principal Trust, however, that has been jeopardized by this transaction, it is FIC and AIC. Immediate action must be taken to protect the contract holders. I recommend the following steps be taken:

1. Emergency meeting with the Attorney General's Department so as to get their legal opinion on the transaction in relation to the *Investment Contracts Act* and any other Act that might apply.

2. All three companies be immediately advised in writing that the transaction is not acceptable and it must be reversed immediately.

3. FIC and AIC be immediately advised of the minimum amount of capital that is necessary for them to be allowed to continue in operation under *The Investment Contracts Act*.

4. Should FIC and AIC fail to fulfil conditions #2 and #3 above, it is my opinion that a Special Report should be written to the Minister from the Superintendent under Section 37 of the *Investment Contracts Act* recommending the appointment of a receiver and manager. In particular, Section 37(d) should be mentioned but there are other sections that could also be used.

Serious consideration should also be given to an immediate curtailment of FIC's and AIC's licences.

5. I am now most concerned about the assets in the United States as they are out of our jurisdiction. We better ensure that we get them back fast.

6. To the best of my knowledge, FIC and AIC have yet to file their financial statements with us. They were required by March 31, 1984, in accordance with Section 27(1) of the *Investment Contracts Act.*

If we have not already received copies of the various agreements and documents relating to the transfer of these assets, I recommend that the auditors be sent in to obtain them. If these documents are in hand, I would ask that they be given to the auditors for review.

In my opinion, Principal Trust has transferred, to use the terminology of the Crown Trust affair, its soft assets to FIC and AIC. We thus have a serious and emergency situation with respect to these companies. It is of such importance that I feel the Minister should be immediately advised and would suggest in this regard that you send her a copy of this memorandum and attachments.

Attached to this memo were the briefing notes dated March 2, 1984:

1. The company completely ignored guidelines sent to them setting out limitations on the size of investments. They proceeded to make huge investments without any regard whatsoever to the amount of capital they had and the discussions that were taking place between them and our department at the time.

2. They placed huge mortgages on undeveloped, speculative real estate.

3. They consistently pay higher interest rates to attract deposits than do other companies and therefore have to invest in more speculative types of mortgages and real estate in order to earn for themselves sufficient income to pay these high rates.

4. The present condition of their foreclosed real estate and mortgage portfolio is one of the worst, if not the worst, that the Audit Unit has examined.

5. The company continues to accrue interest on mortgages that haven't received a payment, in some cases, for over two years.

6. At the same time as accruing the above-voted interest, the company sets up grossly inadequate allowances for bad debts. Thus, the combination of item #5 above and this item overstates the company's profits. (See item #18 following.)

7. At the same time when the company seriously needed permanent capital, they had the effrontery to withdraw $2 million from their company to pay off a "so-called" subordinated note to their parent company thus further exposing investment contract-holders (the public) but at the same time protecting their own interests in the parent company.

I use the word "effrontery" because at the meeting that we held with company officials, they stated that the $2 million was only put up during a time of depression in the securities market and now that this depression was gone, they felt entitled to withdraw the $2 million. They did not even mention the fact that their mortgage and real estate portfolio was many times worse than any drop in the securities market.

In essence, we have a serious need for capital because of bad investments coupled with the withdrawal of capital which, of course, makes the situation far worse than it was.

8. Because of the high interest rates that the company offers, it attracts many thousands of Albertans as investors but unfortunately, these investors do not have the protection of the [CDIC]. Should this company fail, the effect on the confidence in financial institutions in Alberta would be serious.

9. I was shocked at the meeting with company officials when they indicated on a number of occasions that one way in which they could solve their financial problems would be to pay their contract holders only the guaranteed amount (4%) and not pay them the additional credits that had been held out to them, but not guaranteed, in the amount of 7% or 8%. They pointed out that if they did this, they would immediately generate a substantial amount of capital. That they even contemplate such a move is irresponsible.

10. The appraisals to date reveal that this company is not simply faced with an unfortunate situation relating to investments in mortgages at a time when the economy is depressed and real estate values have been weakened, but that imprudent and speculative investments have been made which reflect unfavorably on management.

11. Other companies in the mortgage and real estate business, such as Daon, Carma and Nu-West, must value their properties at market. This has caused all these companies to default on various debentures and notes. In order to obtain financing, they must deal with their bankers or the public marketplace. No banker or investment dealer would lend funds on the basis of inflated values for assets. Thus, there is a third party balance to financing these companies. They are not blessed with unlimited cash flow.

It is for this reason that administrators of Acts relating to financial institutions must ensure that proper valuations are used. Failing this, more and more investors place money with the company when they shouldn't. There is a heavy duty placed on an administrator. That is why Provincial and Federal Governments have auditors to analyze the financial statements from the point of view of the investing public, not the shareholders...

14. I have referred to other companies in the Principal group because they are all linked together, they are owned by the same person, and many of the appraisals done to date are on properties in which the two investment contract companies and the trust company all have a share in the investment. Thus, the appraisal deficiencies affect all three companies and in a material way. Should one of these companies fail, because they are part of a pyramid, it is conceivable that all will fail or be seriously affected.

15. On January 4, 1984, the Superintendent wrote a letter to First Investors based on the auditor's report. This was followed by a meeting with company officials, at which department officials were instructed not to discuss items but to listen only. As far as I know, nothing further has been done. I am concerned

that a situation similar to what developed with Paramount appears to be developing with FIC. We should be careful we don't repeat this scenario.

16. This company's problems are more far-reaching than simply the sale of investment contracts. The company's contracts are deemed under the *Trustee Act* to be an acceptable investment for a trustee. Before the company can comply as a trustee investment, however, it must be approved by the Securities Commission. In my opinion, this company should not be allowed to continue as a trustee investment. This decision is, however, up to the Securities Commission. Thus, we should advise the Commission of our concern about the financial stability of First Investors.

17. The financial statements of FIC state that "Real estate obtained in satisfaction of debts," in the amount of $9,219,518, is valued at the lower of cost or net realizable value. The appraisals obtained to date indicate this is not correct.

18. The following is a calculation of First Investors unimpaired capital as at November 30, 1983:

Unimpaired capital as calculated by First Investors	$2,910,000
Deduct: Differences between book value of mortgages ($7,900,000) and appraised value of underlying security ($2,700,000)	
	$5,200,000
Deduct: Differences between book value of real estate ($5,000,000) and appraised value of real estate ($2,100,000)	
	$2,900,000
Impaired Capital	$5,190,000

As may be seen, First Investors is in a seriously impaired position. The above calculation only gives effect to appraisals that have been completed and I think that it is safe to say that other appraisals will also result in substantial reductions in values with attendant increase in capital impairment.

19. The company continues to accrue interest on mortgages in arrears...

20. Accepting the company's unimpaired capital of $2,910,000, the ratio of capital to liabilities would be approximately 77 to 1. A ratio such as this for a company that essential sells instruments similar to a trust company GIC is very serious in itself. Making adjustments for the overstatement of the value of assets makes the situation completely unacceptable.

In my view, the company does not meet the capital requirements under the *Investment Contracts Act* and there exists a state of affairs that is or may be prejudicial to the interests of its investment contract-holders.

We should, therefore, ask the company to immediately rectify the capital impairment, consider taking such other steps as may be necessary such as curtailing or stopping the sale of investment contracts to the public, and discuss the need for the appointment of an administrator. The Securities Commission should also be advised of our concern with our recommendation that FIC and AIC be dropped as "trustee investments" under the *Trustee Act*.

Darwish knew that if he took the memo directly to Osterman, she would likely slam the door in his interfering face. So Barry Martin was the only possible recipient. "Before I sent it to him, because of all of the confusion and problems with the organization, I wasn't exactly sure how I should do this," Darwish testified. "So I didn't know if I should do a memorandum to him with a copy to the minister, or whether I should do two copies and give them both to him and ask that he send one to the minister. I wanted to do it right. So I went and talked to him. I brought in a draft. We decided that I would give him both copies, and he would send one down to the minister. I implored him that it be followed up, and he patted me on the back as I went out of the office and thanked me for it, and he told me that they would be knocking my door down just as soon as possible to discuss this memorandum... He said something to the effect, 'I didn't realize it was so serious.' "[13]

But Martin didn't take Darwish's memo directly to the minister. Instead, he walked around the corner to Tewfik Saleh's office. "Look what we've got here," Martin said to his hand-picked Superintendent, and handed over the memo.

Saleh took one look and exploded. "Will he never stop interfering? Why does he keep poking his nose into matters that are none of his concern?"

"Yes, indeed," Martin said, looking thoughtfully at the incendiary pages.

(Martin described Saleh's reaction to Darwish's memo during testimony at the Code inquiry. Saleh denied being upset at Darwish's interference, and testified that he did not remember seeing the memo. But Saleh's memory blanked repeatedly during questioning in sensitive areas. He did not recall the Chateau Lacombe meeting, although three other participants agree that he was there; and he could not recall what transpired at several other meetings, including the April 30 gathering in Osterman's office detailed below.)

It took a week for Darwish's memo to make its way from Martin's hands to Osterman's.

April 30, 1984

SIX PEOPLE SAT AROUND the coffee table during the early Monday morning meeting in Connie Osterman's office. Barry Martin was there, as were Tewfik Saleh, Robert Edgar (Martin's executive assistant), Doug Cameron (Osterman's assistant) and director of communications Mark Gregory. When discussion turned to the Principal contract companies, Martin handed Darwish's memo to the minister. "Connie, this is from Jim Darwish. Once again he wants you to have information directly."

"Don't tell me that."

"Well, have a look."

Osterman looked, flushed, and got to her feet. She walked across the room to her desk, sat in her swivel chair, then swung around and picked up the telephone behind her.

"Get me Jim Darwish. I want to speak to him right now." She stabbed the speaker phone button with her finger and slammed the receiver down.

"Jim, this is Connie Osterman," she said a few seconds later. "I have a copy of your memo on FIC."

"Yes, Mrs. Osterman," Darwish said anxiously. His voice, broadcast on the speaker, could be heard by every person in the room.[14]

Darwish remembers it this way: "Well, I received a phone call from the minister. She was agitated. As a matter of fact, she was yelling at me. She told me she had a copy of the memo on FIC and she wasn't happy about it. She said she didn't want to see another memo where I made recommendations, that I was only to provide the figures." Darwish, who told this story at the Code inquiry, struggled to hold back tears during his testimony.

"Mrs. Osterman, I'm sorry," Darwish told the minister. "The situation with FIC is one of the worst I've ever encountered and I felt you had to be advised."

"Listen Jim, this is it," Osterman said furiously. "I don't want any more recommendations from you. I've told you that before, and if I have to rewrite your job description, I will. You're interfering with other people's jobs here, and I'm sick of it. If they fall flat on their faces that's their problem. You leave the contract companies to Tewfik, and mind your own garden. If you keep making these recommendations, you're going to have to make a career decision."

She was threatening to fire him! "What are you talking about?" Darwish sputtered. "I understand my job description perfectly well. I don't appreciate hearing this sort of thing on the phone, you know. We're into a very serious situation here and I want everybody to realize it."

"You're on the outside looking in, Jim. There have been discussions with company officials, and you don't have a clue about the other side of this."

"Well, that's part of the problem, there's no communication."

"You're up for retirement in the fall, and I want you to keep in mind what I've said here. You have selective hearing. I've told you this before."

"I have no intention of retiring," Darwish said, "and I don't appreciate hearing about it on the phone."

"Just think about it," she shot back. "You have a career decision to make and if you don't like what I'm saying, think about it over the next few days and maybe we should meet." Osterman punched the button off, then slowly swung her chair around to face her silent staff.

At the Code inquiry, Osterman described her reaction to Darwish's memo as "reasonably negative." For months she had been trying to curb him, and she'd had enough. "From the time of the reorganization," she testified, "I had to discuss with Mr. Darwish his role in matters and the perception that he was looking over everybody's shoulder... And I had expressed very clearly to Mr. Darwish that I believed the people who were directly responsible [should be left alone to do their own work]. This did not mean that he wouldn't be involved in discussing matters with them, but he had a role in making sure that department support services ran smoothly, and it was my belief that he was very busy looking over a lot of people's shoulders that had specific jobs, and he was not addressing himself to the overall area of department support services."

Osterman was also tired of Darwish's desire to communicate directly with her, instead of through the chain of command. "If I did not respond back to Mr. Darwish or get into a conversation with him, I think his feelings were very hurt," she said. "As minister I had the chain of command through the deputy minister and of course Mr. Saleh in his special role, and I did not want to be talking about policy with a whole bunch of other people in the department. I felt that it should be worked through the chain of command. If I did not respond to Mr. Darwish directly then I would probably be subject to another comment at some meeting somewhere—didn't I know that, or hadn't I, or wasn't I going to—and I believed that he had to stick to his role."

Osterman testified that she was so angry with Darwish she didn't finish reading his memo. To this day, she insists that she only glanced at the memo, and therefore wasn't aware it included a recommendation to consider pulling the contract companies' licences. Barry Martin testified that he couldn't remember if she "glanced at it or read it." Tewfik Saleh couldn't remember he'd been in the room. But Mark Gregory, who wasn't called to testify, told me later he watched Osterman read the document. "Oh, yes, she read the memo. She didn't just read the first couple of sentences and then dash behind the desk to hit the phone."

After he hung up the telephone, Darwish realized he'd forgotten to tell Osterman that he had first taken his memo to Martin, on whose advice he prepared a copy for the minister. "I forgot to tell her that. I think it might have been important to do, but in the heat of the moment, I forgot. So I phoned the minister the next day, I think, and told her that I had forgotten to mention to her that I had cleared this with the Deputy before, and asked for a meeting. As I recall it, she wanted to know, 'Do we need a meeting?' sort of thing, and I said, 'Well, yes, I do want a meeting.' So she said she would get back to me."

7

Hopes and prayers

PETER LOUGHEED WANTED A BOOMING financial services industry in Alberta. He wanted banks and trust companies and flourishing credit unions that would finally give those eastern bastards a run for their money. Everybody knew it, and everybody knew he wasn't very pleased with all the bad news lately.

The mortgage and trust companies had started going down in 1981. Now Paramount Life Insurance and the credit unions were in big trouble and it looked as if the province was going to have to step in.

The problem was Alberta's real estate market. People were actually walking away from their properties—selling their mortgages for a dollar, and packing it in. Values had decayed so badly that home owners who had made 20%, 30% or even 40% downpayments had lost all their equity, and were forced to sign their mortgages away to escape the choking interest payments. "Dollar-dealers" collected rent on the houses for a few months, made no mortgage payments, and eventually forced the lenders to foreclose. Close to 5,000 homes had been foreclosed on in 1982 and 1983 alone.

This wasn't the way it was supposed to happen. When the Conservatives swept into power in August 1971, one of Lougheed's first initiatives was to announce plans for the development of regionally-owned and managed financial institutions. Two years later he hosted the Western Economic Opportunities Conference, where the four western premiers blamed the prejudice of central Canadian banks for stifling western enterprise. The West wanted financial institutions of its own—wanted to prove it could prosper without the endless condescension that came with eastern cash.

The Lougheed government's protective attitude toward local institutions was evident soon after taking power, when it arranged a bailout of Rocky Mountain Life Insurance Company. At first it tried to find a buyer for the seriously under-capitalized company but was unsuccessful—eastern Canadian "indifference" was blamed—so in June 1972, the Attorney General's department cancelled its licence, guaranteed all benefits promised to 11,000 policyholders and assumed control.[1] This decision, the precursor of several such bailouts in later years, cost the province an estimated $28 million.

Alberta legend has it that Lougheed—like many other westerners—grew up hating eastern bankers. Journalist Allan Hustak enshrined the tale in his biography *Peter Lougheed*: As a small boy, Lougheed had watched the contents of the family mansion in southwest Calgary sold at public auction, when the house, built by Lougheed's millionaire grandfather, Conservative Senator James Lougheed, was seized in 1938 for tax arrears. Humiliated by this experience, Peter took to heart his father Edgar's complaints that the family was "brought to its heels by the callous money lenders from the East." After his election victory, Lougheed vowed revenge in the form of Alberta's economic liberation.

Alberta separatist sentiment, simmering for years, came to a boil during Lougheed's energy wars with the federal Liberal government of Prime Minister Pierre Trudeau. Lougheed struck first, assuming control of resource pricing and establishing a provincial commission to market Alberta oil and gas. Federally-set royalty limits were dumped, and the oil companies poured more and more cash into provincial coffers.

Albertans were right behind him. They knew that eastern Canadians saw them as greedy, selfish and pig-headed, but for the most part they didn't care. If Trudeau could give voters the finger, Albertans could give it back, along with bumper stickers proclaiming: "Let the eastern bastards freeze in the dark."

During those years, world conditions transformed the value of Alberta's energy resources. The Arab oil embargo of 1973 pushed the price of a barrel of oil from $3.87 to $10.37 in a year. In 1978-79, during the Iranian revolution, the price climbed from $14.85 to $22.40 a barrel, peaking in 1980 at $37.

Those were the days of the Alberta boom, and it made the earlier post-war boom seem like a tiny blip on the economic chart. Between 1974 and 1980, Albertans' average personal income was the highest in the country. Money spilled from briefcases, dripped off teletypes, stuck to the two-inch-heeled, designer-stitched, gen-u-ine alligator and suede cowboy boots that peeked from below the cuffs of thousand-dollar suits. There were paper millionaires everywhere, *nouveau riche* with gold-plated water faucets and toilet fittings.

House values climbed so fast people were living for free. Mid-level executives bought $300,000 and $400,000 homes for investment purposes; political assistants borrowed fortunes to play the stock market; and every businessman worthy of the name had his own executive jet, or at least a turboprop. Things were moving fast— *Wanna nother steak, man? Nother shooter? Hey this one's got grand mariner innit, an'a layer of the green stuff, y'ever have that one before? Hell, take my Corvette, man, or maybe the wife's Cadillac*—and you didn't want to be left behind.

After 1973, Alberta's gross domestic product exceeded that of any other province. Oil drilling and construction skyrocketed; the number of construction workers, approximately 60,000 in the early 1970s, had more than doubled by 1981. That year, a quarter of all Canadian construction, $10.6-billion worth, occurred in Alberta. Office towers transformed the city skylines. In Calgary, epicentre of the boom, people joked that construction cranes, those towering steel birds, were the new provincial mascot.

Suburbs spread like crabgrass, expanding the urban boundaries. The crocus-covered foothills of Calgary's western outskirts were dotted overnight by earth-tone colour-co-ordinated housing developments with two cars in every garage. Suddenly Calgary had freeways everywhere. Folks who had driven their entire lives at a careful 30 or 35 miles an hour were forced quivering and wretched to the curb of the six-lane Crowchild Trail, while the Mercedes and four-wheel-drive pickup trucks streaked by at what seemed the speed of sound.

The streets, like the bathroom taps, might as well have been coated with gold. Swaggering Albertans believed it was true, so it was hard to persuade outsiders otherwise. They poured in from all directions, seeking their fortunes on the frontier. The province's population increased by almost a third, to more than 2.2 million, during the decade following Lougheed's election in 1971.[2]

It ended even more suddenly than it had begun. On October 28, 1980, the federal government unveiled its National Energy Program, and the over-heated Alberta economy dissolved. Intended, the feds said, to make Canada less reliant on foreign sources, the abhorrent NEP forced Alberta producers to sell their gas and oil in Canada at up to 30% less than world prices, removed a number of corporate write-offs and tax deductions and established several new heavy taxes.

Alberta's enthusiastic investment atmosphere evaporated. Drilling plummeted; exploration expenditures dropped from $3.3 billion in 1980, to $2.6 billion in 1981, to $1.9 billion in 1982. Megaprojects were cancelled or put on hold, and the effects reverberated through every sector of the economy. Starting in 1981, the province experienced a dramatic increase in vacancy rates, and house values crashed: smaller ones by 20% to 30%, more expensive ones by as much as half. The construction industry, naturally, also crashed. The number of construction workers dwindled by nearly a third in the next two years, and by 1985 had dropped to almost pre-boom level.[3] With the collapse—much worse than the brief recession endured by eastern Canadians—thousands of Albertans found themselves unemployed. Bankruptcies accelerated, and the new poor lined up at understocked food banks.

Alberta's financial institutions, precariously balanced on speculative portfolios of prairie real estate and petroleum investments, were immediately hard hit. Lougheed, like most Albertans, railed against the dastardly East, but he should have looked closer to home. During the good years his government—faithful in its promise to support local enterprise—had ignored a series of irregularities that would prove fatal when boom turned to bust.

The first three companies to fail had all been in trouble well before their collapses in 1981.

Battleford Mortgage Company Ltd. was run by a group of Edmonton lawyers led by Herbert Michael Liknaitzky, who pled guilty to criminal charges after the collapse and eventually went to prison. Battleford was insolvent in the 1960s, when an Alberta Securities Commission auditor reported improper accounting practices, deceitful financial statements, irresponsible actions on the part of the directors, questionable transactions with interrelated companies and loans to the shareholders for personal purposes. The province dumped the mess in the lap of the Law Society of Alberta, and took no further regulatory steps. Battleford continued to operate until June 1981, when the lawyers and the company defaulted on their obligations to the investors.[4]

When Dial Mortgage Corp. Ltd. went into receivership, 700 creditors were hung out to dry for about $12 million—small potatoes when compared to other failures, but dramatic at the time. Eight years later the Alberta Securities Commission ruled that three company executives had misled Dial investors in a 1979 prospectus which hid financial problems. The executives were barred from trading securities in Alberta for periods of up to five years. During an inquiry, the commission heard that Consumer Affairs auditors knew by late 1979 that Dial was violating regulations, but didn't share the information with the commission. The commission approved Dial's prospectus in November 1979 without seeing the mid-1979 financial statement—already in the hands of the insurance and real estate branch of Consumer Affairs—that would have revealed a cash shortage. On January 27, 1981, Superintendent of Insurance and Real Estate Jim Darwish issued stop orders freezing Dial's funds; a week later a creditor pushed the company into receivership.

The month after that the Consumer Affairs department was reorganized, and Darwish stripped of his regulatory authority.[5]

The Dial affair was highly controversial because vice-president George de Rappard (barred from trading for two years) had been Lougheed's top aide prior to joining the company in mid-1979. He left Dial in 1980, five months before its collapse, returning to the Alberta government as deputy minister to the Lougheed Cabinet and mastermind of the Conservatives' 1982 election campaign. (He subsequently became deputy minister for economic development.) In 1983, the RCMP recommended that criminal fraud charges be filed against the "Dial Five"— de Rappard and four others. In January 1984 crown prosecutor John Faulkner was fired by the government after confirming to the *Calgary Herald* that Dial's officers were under investigation. Soon afterward Attorney General Neil Crawford decided there wasn't enough evidence to proceed with the charges. Demands for a public inquiry were rejected by Lougheed.

In June 1984, the securities commission commenced prosecution of the Dial Five under the *Securities Act* for filing a false prospectus, but the court ruled the next year that the commission had waited too long and the charges were thrown out. When the commission decided to conduct its own inquiry, one of the defendants fought its right to do so all the way to the Supreme Court. When he lost, the way was opened for the inquiry which led to the 1989 trading bans.

Calgary real estate investment firm Abacus Cities Ltd. went into receivership in May 1979, then struggled to stay afloat until its April 1981 bankruptcy. Creditors sued for about $1.4 billion, but have seen little of their money returned. After a lengthy government investigation, costing about $3.5 million, four men, including Abacus president Dr. Ken Rogers and his brother William, a company director,were charged with 10 counts of breaching provincial securities laws. A trial had been scheduled when independent counsel hired by the Alberta government decided to drop the charges in 1985. In 1987, the securities commission imposed a one-day trading ban against the brothers.[6]

By the beginning of 1982, other companies were going down. The number of mortgage brokers licenced to operate in Alberta dropped by more than 20%, and continued to decline. Ram Mortgage Corporation Ltd., which had bought Merit Mortgage Group Ltd.'s $25-million mortgage portfolio the year before, was forced into receivership in March. Vista Mortgage folded a month later, and Merit subsequently closed its doors as well.

In June 1983, Peter Pocklington's Fidelity Trust collapsed, about the time its owner made his unsuccessful bid for the leadership of the federal Progressive Conservatives. Pocklington, once-owner of meat-packing company Gainers Ltd., Palm Dairies and the Edmonton Oilers hockey club—and subsequent vendor of Wayne Gretzky's personal services contract to the Los Angeles Kings—had rolled his real estate development company, Patrician Land Corp., loaded with speculative properties, into the trust company as a subsidiary. When the real estate went sour, so did Fidelity. The collapse cost the CDIC $359 million.[7]

In October 1983, Tower Mortgage Ltd. went into receivership owing $25 million to 2,500 investors. That November, Signature Finance Ltd.'s bank froze its line of credit. After an Alberta Securities Commission hearing, the company consented to a 65-day cease-trading order of its securities. Two months later, Signature was history, owing $4 million to its noteholders.

And then there was Paramount Life Insurance Company. Since late 1983 provincial regulators had been pressing for a capital injection. In January 1984, after Jim Darwish's infuriating nudge, Consumer Affairs Minister Connie Osterman allowed Tewfik Saleh to put the company under a limited licence, blocking further sales. The following June she appointed an administrator.

It was a godawful mess, but the worst was yet to come.

In the spring of 1984, as Osterman prepared to take over Paramount Life, she reported to her Cabinet colleagues on the continuing deterioration of the province's financial institutions. The matter went before Cabinet's priorities, finance and co-ordination committee (or, simply, the priorities committee), chaired by Lougheed himself and attended by his most trusted ministers. On May 24, 1984, the committee established a task force "to review the impairment facing financial institutions governed by provincial statutes and bring forward a plan of action." The task force, chaired by Osterman, included three other Cabinet ministers: Provincial Treasurer Lou Hyndman, Attorney General Neil Crawford and Minister of Municipal Affairs Julian Koziak (Osterman's predecessor as Consumer Affairs Minister)—all key members of Lougheed's priorities committee. Also on the committee were Hyndman's and Osterman's most senior officials: Deputy Provincial Treasurer (finance and revenue) Allister McPherson and Consumer Affairs Deputy Minister Barry Martin.

The new task force focused on the province's 132 credit unions, serving 500,000 depositors in a $2.6-billion financial system beset by a record number of bad property loans. Three weeks before the task force was formed, management of six of the largest credit unions had been taken over by the Credit Union Stabilization Corporation, a body established and funded by the credit unions themselves to help members with financial problems. A total of 42 credit unions, operating at a total deficit of $92 million, were under its supervision.[8]

In September 1984, on the recommendation of the task force, the province announced it would shore up the credit unions by backstopping the stabilization corporation's financial guarantees to credit union depositors. This promise put taxpayers on the line for up to $40 million. The next March, Osterman announced a restructuring plan that would bury $325 million worth of unprofitable real estate owned by the credit unions in a newly created shell company, to be operated as a subsidiary of the stabilization corporation. In exchange the credit unions would receive interest-earning debentures from the shell company, with the interest to be guaranteed by the provincial government. The value of the real estate being transferred, about 1,500 properties obtained through foreclosure, had been written down from $425 million to $325 million: a loss of $100 million.

In June 1985, Osterman announced another injection, in the form of a $35-million interest-free loan to specific credit unions, and another $35-million short-term deposit with the stabilization corporation to provide interim liquidity to the system. In late 1986, the province put together a bailout package for 49 still-distressed credit unions. The following March, the province forced the amalgamation of nine Calgary credit unions, followed in May 1987 by the forced amalgamation of eight credit unions in Edmonton. By the end of the clean-up, help to the credit unions totalled about $186 million.

Meanwhile, in late April 1985, Osterman wrote a memo to the priorities committee outlining the growing crisis with Alberta trust companies. She discussed the five provincially regulated companies, describing Heritage Savings and Trust Company and North West Trust Company as in the worst shape, and Principal Trust the next in line. ("Profitable in 1984, but losses in 1985.") On April 29, 1985, the priorities committee created a second, parallel task force for "the purposes of monitoring the financial position of Provincial Trust Companies." The first task force seems to have been folded into the second, with one important difference: Treasurer Lou Hyndman, a key Lougheed lieutenant for 18 years, replaced Osterman as chairman. Its membership mirrored that of the first—Osterman, Hyndman,

Crawford, Martin and MacPherson—except for Koziak, whose involvement with Heritage Trust prohibited his participation.

Heritage Trust and North West Trust had been in trouble since at least 1983— the CDIC, which insured them, was watching them closely—and in 1985 both delayed delivering their financial statements.[9] In 1984, North West was forced to write down its real estate and mortgage holdings, and shareholdings in two troubled western-based banks,[10] by $23 million. In 1984 and 1985, the Alberta Treasury Branches, the provincial quasi-bank which reported to Treasurer Hyndman,[11] guaranteed a total of $85 million in preferred shares for North West's parent company, which turned around and injected fresh cash into the trust company. The Treasury Branches also injected $19 million into North West in the form of loans backed by subordinated notes.

In October 1985, the smaller Heritage Trust, which specialized in loans to Edmonton's Ukrainian community, also got help. Osterman announced the province would fully guarantee the trust's deposits past the $60,000 limit insured by the CDIC—a guarantee worth several million dollars—and revealed plans to take $10 million worth of unproductive real estate and mortgages off the company's hands. The following year, the Treasury Branches quietly provided liquidity support by depositing cash (interest to be paid at bank prime); deposits totalled $12.7 million at the end of 1986.

In November 1985, the Hyndman/Osterman task forces were disbanded by Don Getty when he replaced Lougheed as premier, but the rescue work continued through the Treasury department. In February 1987, the province forced Heritage and North West to merge under the name North West Trust, then took them over. As with the credit unions, a shell was created, jointly owned by the Alberta government and the Treasury Branches, to take over the trust companies' $293 million worth of junk real estate and bad mortgage loans. The CDIC contributed $275 million to the rehabilitation package.

Meanwhile, Principal presented another difficult challenge. This was a massive conglomerate of companies whose affairs were thoroughly entangled. Action against one company would affect them all, and they were run by a well-connected, combative individual who wasn't going to take direction without a fight. The CDIC was giving the trust company a hard time, but the rest of the conglomerate faced little outside pressure to resolve its problems. Principal Group's contract companies—and their parent—were under sole provincial jurisdiction. Their problems, it was decided, could wait. Cormie's companies were permitted to limp on unimpeded for another three and a half years.

Government officials have offered conflicting stories to explain the province's inaction. Connie Osterman and Lou Hyndman testified that they didn't understand how desperate the situation was. Sure, they headed task forces charged with redeeming Alberta's financial industry, and sure they heard passing mention of disputes between the contract companies and government auditors—but there was nothing to make them particularly uneasy.

Osterman testified that any concerns she may have had about the Principal Group companies were pushed to the back burner because other problems—the credit unions and trust companies—loomed so much larger. Her years as Minister of Consumer and Corporate Affairs, 1982 to 1986, were "one crisis after another," she testified. "I think that it is fair to say that there were times when I felt that I was standing in the middle of a financial battlefield and trying to priorize the patient that we would minister to first."

Osterman also insisted that attention to the Principal companies was delayed because the real estate market was so unstable that she could not rely on property appraisals. She made this claim despite the fact that, during the same period, appraisals were taken, consultants engaged and solutions found to the problems of Paramount, the credit unions and the trust companies.

In any case, Treasurer Hyndman testified, the companies were within Osterman's jurisdiction. He had no right or responsibility to intervene unless asked. He says he wasn't asked; therefore, any blame is Osterman's.

Osterman's deputy minister Barry Martin tells a different story. He knew by 1983 that the Principal companies were in big trouble. He understood they did not meet the capital requirements of the *Investment Contracts Act*, and were therefore operating outside the law. He testified that he shared that information with his minister and with the task force.

For two long years, Martin and Osterman worked hard to protect the Principal companies. They muzzled staff, blocked investigations and suppressed information, thereby allowing the public to be deceived. Auditors wrote scathing reports that ended up in the department's dead-end files; consumers got the brush-off. Martin denied none of this, but insisted he was only following policy. The mandate of the Cabinet task force, he testified, was to avoid further failures and find ways to help institutions resolve their problems. When the credit union crisis emerged in 1984, "the policy position that I perceived the Government of Alberta to be taking was one of the long term; in other words, looking toward a work-out."

The policy, Martin said, was to delay action against wobbly financial institutions, including the Principal contract companies, until their backs were pressed against the wall. "It was the policy of the government of Alberta to, if at all possible, maintain the viability of the financial institutions as long as it was feasibly and humanly possible." In the case of the contract companies, no projections were prepared to determine whether the companies could in fact recover, even if real estate prices miraculously improved. The policy was based on "a hell of a lot— excuse me—a great deal of hope and prayer."

Despite repeated pleas from regulators and consultants, the horribly inadequate *Investment Contracts Act* remained fundamentally unaltered after its passage in 1957. Early in her ministry Osterman attempted to clean up the legislation; as we have seen, in January 1984 she received approval in principle from Cabinet for amendments to the legislation that would have increased the minimum capitalization requirement to a million dollars and imposed a borrowing-to-capital ratio of 25:1.

Two weeks later, the proposal was killed. Osterman testified that she wanted to await development of a more comprehensive bill, and that she changed her mind about the legislation after discussions with "various people." She couldn't remember who these people were, describing them only as "interested individuals."

Martin testified that he understood it was a Cabinet decision "on the basis that they may tend to draw unnecessary attention to these investment contract companies and may create a situation that could get out of, I guess—and these are my words—could get out of control, resulting in runs on the company and a danger to the financial institutions in the province. That was my understanding."

Martin said that the decision to delay the amendments was part of a hands-off policy motivated by a desire on the part of Peter Lougheed and his Cabinet to maintain Alberta's reputation as a reliable place to do business. He said the policy was relayed by Cabinet members on the task force—he could not identify which ones—and reinforced "by listening to the public comments that the Honourable Mr. Lougheed was making in speeches around this province, and by just a general awareness of what initiatives the government was taking." He emphasized that Lougheed did not communicate such policy directly to him. "One had to be, and I think I used the word earlier, politically aware. One had to be sort of tuned in or attempt to be tuned in to what was going on in the province and what the politicians were saying and what actions and initiatives the politicians—it was not a clearly defined written-down-in-the-book policy."

Hyndman denied the existence of such a hands-off policy. The policy, he testified, "was to take whatever steps could be, to try to, firstly, hold or ensure that the confidence of business and consumers didn't drop too far, and also to suggest that there were some basic long-term strengths in the Alberta economy, and that everyone should be aware of that, and that we had a future." Problems would be dealt with as they arose, when recommendations came from the responsible ministers. "The policy was to not act prematurely, but to monitor, on an astute basis, the financial institutions under which the minister had responsibility, and to then bring forward, if, as and when necessary in the judgment of the minister, to the task force those problems that appeared to be reaching a very urgent stage." Once the problem was seen as urgent, "then the task force would have to get to work, roll up its sleeves, and it would do that whether there was one, two, five or however many problems in front of it... It was not a question of simply letting matters drift."

Actually, there isn't much difference in Martin's and Hyndman's versions. Both amount to leaving the companies alone until it's decided that action absolutely must be taken. But who was watching the companies, and who would decide when the situation had become "very urgent"?

Hyndman says Osterman and her department were watching, and no one else knew about serious problems. The task force would supervise the surgery, but the choice of patient was Osterman's alone.

Martin, however, says the entire task force was watching, and would jointly make decisions. "We were reporting breaches of their statutory obligations," he testified. "We were reporting a declining state of affairs with these companies. The information was being accepted by members of the Cabinet committee, and we were receiving no direct instructions that it was now time to move on these companies and to commence procedures for take-down."

Two versions of events: If we believe Hyndman, then we must accept that Peter Lougheed—a premier renowned for his hands-on management style—left Osterman, a junior minister, to make decisions alone in what had become a crucial portfolio. We must accept that officials in the Consumer Affairs department—at the same time they were working closely with Hyndman's task force and his Treasury officials to salvage other institutions—were hoarding the bad news about the Principal companies among themselves; that they did not seek guidance or support from senior government colleagues.

On the other hand, if we believe Martin, then we must accept that the Alberta government watched in silence for three years, blindly hoping that Donald Cormie would somehow return First Investors and Associated Investors to financial health, while those insolvent companies borrowed millions of dollars from the public without the means to pay it all back. We must accept that a reckless wait-and-see policy pursued at the expense of unknowing investors originated in the highest echelons of the provincial government.

The official record is sketchy. No minutes were taken of the deliberations of the task force. The four ministers and two deputy ministers—unaccompanied by staff—met every week or so during the lunch hour for what Martin described as "soup-and-sandwich" sessions. Notes taken by the participants have since been destroyed, and the memories of all task force members who testified at the Code inquiry—with the stark exception of Barry Martin—failed them on occasion. Unfortunately, two of the task force members—Crawford and Koziak—were not called as witnesses. (Crawford died in 1992. Koziak told me that he only remembered task force discussions concerning credit unions and that he had excused himself from meetings where trust companies were mentioned.)

Osterman testified that she provided several overviews of the contract companies' problems—including information about capital deficiencies identified by department auditors—to the task force. She said she made it clear in her reports that the contract companies were deteriorating over time.

Hyndman confirmed that Osterman made occasional reports, but insisted they were very brief, presented orally and contained no alarming information. Hyndman categorically denied ever seeing any written reports, or hearing about capital deficiencies, during the task force meetings. He testified that he had no specific recollection regarding what Osterman said about the contract companies, except for what *wasn't* said: It was his firm conviction that no numbers were provided and no recommendations for action made. "I would deny those suggestions that there were documents detailing the financial health of FIC/AIC presented by Mr. Martin or by the minister to the task force. That did not occur," Hyndman testified. "The reports were all—and the information on FIC/AIC—all came via verbal reports from the minister." Hyndman said he had no understanding, based on what Osterman said, that the companies were either insolvent or operating outside the law.

He did, however, know of an ongoing debate between the department and the contract companies as to "the adequacy of compliance." Hyndman said Osterman's briefings on the companies, usually delivered at the end of the task force meetings, "left the impression to me that they were being watched, and that there were some differences with respect to legal opinions, differences with respect to the opinions of auditors, differences with respect to appraisal of real property. And that she was monitoring [the situation] and would come forward if, as and when necessary with the recommendation, but she did not... She might have indicated that there were difficulties, and these difficulties were moving in one direction or another. But that she was monitoring the situation, watching over it, and if that situation changed, [she] would come to the task force as the matter became urgent." He said that Osterman indicated some frustration with the differences in opinion regarding audit problems, "but didn't indicate what she was doing."

Allister McPherson, Hyndman's second in command, remembered more. He recalled hearing during a 1984 task force meeting "a brief report saying that there had been a transaction between Principal Savings & Trust and one or both of the contract companies, I don't recall, and that Consumer and Corporate Affairs were concerned about that transaction. They were in discussions with the companies, and it either asked or capital was being put in, I guess to the contract companies, to alleviate the problem." Further, from comments Osterman made, McPherson had the impression there were questions about whether the companies were viable, "whether they were meeting the tests under the [*Investment Contracts Act*]." This contradicts the evidence of Hyndman, who insisted nothing was ever said to suggest either that the companies weren't viable or that they were operating outside the requirements of the Act.

Inspector Bill Code and Alberta Ombudsman Aleck Trawick weighed the meagre evidence and pinned the blame on Osterman and her senior officials. "The evidence tends to show," Code said in his report, "that [Consumer Affairs] recognized by the summer of 1984 that [First Investors] and [Associated Investors] were no longer viable... The evidence shows that the regulators allowed FIC and AIC to continue to operate when there was no hope for recovery." Code labelled Osterman naive, "neglectful, misguided or even reckless." The hands-off policy, "which I find was her policy," Code said, "derived from her perception of a general Government desire to preserve Alberta-based financial institutions and public confidence in them.

> The evidence tends to show that she knew the companies did not meet the requirements of the *Investment Contracts Act*. She took a conscious decision to simply wait and hope for an improvement in the economy, in accordance with her policy of attempting to preserve Alberta-based financial institutions, a consideration irrelevant to the purpose and objects of the [Act]. In the meantime, she prepared no plan of action to deal with the companies. The

effective result of Osterman's conduct was that administration and enforcement of the [Act] and regulation of [First Investors and Associated Investors] were suspended. This was in breach of her public duty to carry out the purpose and objects of the [Act].

Osterman was prepared to allow the public to continue to invest in FIC and AIC when she had no idea whether the companies would be able to honour maturing obligations, because of what she perceived to be a greater public good. In the end, it was the investors who bore the risks of her decision and her policy and her hope that economic conditions would improve.

Code noted that governments have no legal obligation to pass or amend legislation. Having legislated, however, there is a duty to administer the law.[12]

Trawick criticized Osterman's "circular reasoning":

She states she could not take action until and unless her regulators could be unequivocal about the shortfalls of the companies. However, she was not prepared to allow them the only tools available to them under the [*Investment Contracts Act*]... There were to be no appraisals, because she believed them to be unreliable based on her general experience. There was to be no investigation of sales practices, because that might focus attention on the companies. There was to be no independent investigator, because that might do the same... The main administrative shortfall is that Osterman may have conveyed, and Martin and Saleh may have perceived, a policy that nothing was to be done concerning FIC and AIC no matter what.

Osterman followed a principle of the "greater public good," Trawick said, a principle directly contrary to the purpose of the *Investment Contracts Act*, which was intended to protect individual investors. There was, he found, a fundamental difference between the Principal contract companies and other provincial deposit-taking institutions protected by the "greater good" policy: by mid-1984 only First Investors and Associated Investors operated without some form of federal and/or provincial protection or guarantee for depositors. "To use the depositors' retirement savings to bolster up institutions that the government was already guaranteeing," Trawick said, "was to in effect gamble with those savings to partially benefit the government itself." Trawick found that by mid-1984 there was "a serious administrative error" in the regulation of the contract companies by the Consumer Affairs department. A decision had been taken "to completely abdicate rather than merely suspend" the regulatory duties imposed by the *Investment Contracts Act*, he said.

Both Code and Trawick found that Superintendent of Insurance Tewfik Saleh had failed in his duty to enforce compliance with the *Investment Contracts Act*. Code, however, let him off easy, saying he was not allowed to enforce the Act and had been "put in an impossible situation." Trawick was much harsher:

It should be noted that under the [*Investment Contracts Act*], virtually all responsibilities of regulation with the exception of causing receivership and liquidation of a company lie with the Superintendent of Insurance...

I conclude, therefore, that the Superintendent's duty to recommend and advise, and to act, was, for the limited and specific purposes required by the [Act], at least as high as that of a Deputy Minister...

In my opinion, Saleh did not possess or obtain the necessary knowledge to oversee regulation of FIC and AIC, or to communicate his views regarding the regulation to his superiors, the Deputy Minister and Minister.

By mid-1984, Trawick said, Saleh should have been advising Osterman and Martin that action had to be taken, and "probably should have been considering at that point whether he could continue"—whether he should resign—"and making that part of his recommendations." Instead, refused permission to appoint an independent investigator, he continued to operate without protest, making ineffectual threats to the companies "which of course were not backed up by any action."

The brunt of Trawick's criticism, however, fell on Barry Martin—who received little attention from Code. Trawick said Martin had betrayed a deputy minister's most essential duty: to confront his Minister with the consequences of ill-considered policy, whatever the political environment. Advice and recommendations "must be given to the Minister if action is necessary or legally required, no matter the Minister's viewpoint," Trawick said.

As for the Cabinet policy which Martin believed existed, he should have been relying on more than perceptions and impressions, Trawick said. Martin should have been able to testify or show through documentation "that he specifically and forcefully made the Minister and the Cabinet committee aware" of (1) the difficulties; (2) the serious nature of the duties and responsibilities under the *Investment Contracts Act*; and (3) the ramifications of the decision not to take any action, "the effect of which was to grant carte blanche to those companies to embark on an intensive selling campaign of investment contracts" which Consumer Affairs auditors had warned could never be redeemed. Then he should have sought specific instructions.

Trawick concluded that information about the contract companies had come to the attention of the priorities committee but did not indicate an urgent situation. Code accepted that both task forces and the priorities committee "had little specific knowledge" of the contract companies' problems in 1984 and 1985. "They would not become involved unless and until the Minister of [Consumer Affairs] brought forward a recommendation and plan of action. That never happened."

After these reports were completed—almost silent on the subject of Principal's lobbying efforts over more than two decades—Code inquiry counsel Neil Wittmann told me that the decision to accept Hyndman's version of events came down to credibility. "I believe those guys when they say the problems in the trust companies and the credit companies were so huge they did not turn the investment contract companies under any particular scrutiny," Wittmann said. "Lou Hyndman, that I've known for years professionally and personally, I believe him."

As for Peter Lougheed, Wittmann met privately with him in 1988 during the Code investigation. He "chose not to tell" reporters what Lougheed had said to him about government policy regarding problem financial institutions. Lougheed's testimony would not be required, Wittmann said, because the former premier didn't know anything that would assist the inquiry; Lougheed had said he could not recall having been involved in any decisions regarding either of the Principal contract companies, and he denied meeting with Cormie during his years as premier. He was not called to testify. (Shortly afterward, the *Calgary Herald* broke the story of the 1973 events discussed in the previous chapter.) Lougheed, through his secretary, refused to be interviewed for this book.

Wittmann told me he was convinced that Lougheed knew nothing about the Principal problems. "When a guy tells me he didn't know there was difficulty, my experience as a lawyer tells me if a guy's not telling you the truth and he's in a group situation, with many participants and memoranda, [there will be evidence to contradict him]," Wittmann said. "But if there's no paper trail, no evidence of his involvement—probably he's telling the truth. I've seen the Cabinet minutes. There were no documents or any other evidence independent of [Lougheed] linking him to even a passing knowledge of it in the 1980s."

That's odd, because Lougheed ought to have known, at the very least, that the companies were in conflict with Consumer Affairs. Osterman give occasional updates to the priorities committee and to Cabinet—chaired by Lougheed—as Hyndman testified: "In perhaps a 10- or 15-minute overview of financial institutions, most of it would deal with credit unions, North West Trust, Heritage Trust. And then she might say, as I recall, something to the effect that there are some ongoing problems with respect to Principal Trust, [Associated Investors and First Investors], which I am watching and I have no recommendation to make at this time."

The task force heard more than this. As Hyndman testified, Osterman gave the impression that there were disputes regarding legal opinions, auditors' opinions and appraisals. Each of these are significant red flags, clear indications the companies were in difficulty—you don't fight with auditors or the government when things are going well.

We should note that each of the three lawyers on the task force had knowledge of previous problems with the Principal companies. Julian Koziak, Consumer Affairs minister between 1979 and 1982, received a four-page memo from Jim Darwish in 1980 summarizing the department's turbulent history with the contract companies. Hyndman and Neil Crawford had been members of Cabinet during the 1970s when consultants were engaged to look into the companies. (Crawford knew Donald Cormie for decades. He joined the Cormie Kennedy law firm in 1957 and served as counsel for Associated Investors during the 1960s.[13])

As for paper trails, few records were kept at meetings during Lougheed's administration unless decisions were made. But decisions are often made outside the committee room. Issues are discussed over coffee or a scotch, leaning against corridor walls, on the golf green, in clubs or private homes. Minutes are never kept of such conversations, even though policy is formed there.

Code's report noted that Cormie wrote to Lougheed in 1975 protesting proposed amendments to the *Investment Contracts Act*, which were subsequently withdrawn. Code concluded that "the evidence did not tend to show and I make no finding as to why the amendments were withdrawn or what, if any, impact Donald Cormie's letter had on that decision."

Of course, if Lougheed and others involved in the incident had testified, we would have an answer to that—and to other troubling questions. Since the Principal collapse Lougheed has made little comment, with the exception of a September 1987 interview with the *Calgary Herald* in which he blamed the collapse on those inevitable bogey-men, Ontario and the National Energy Program. The NEP prevented Principal and other companies in the province's financial industry from having time to attain "adequate maturity," Lougheed said. The article continued: "The institutions were unable to become 'broadly based,' Lougheed said, adding they couldn't diversify their portfolios to protect themselves from a collapse of the commodity and real estate markets. 'There just was not enough time.' "

The former premier's subsequent silence is most disappointing, and leaves an unfortunate gap in our understanding of events. Was there a desire to let financial institutions survive at any cost? What about the friendship Cormie claims to have shared with the former premier? What about Lougheed's role—if any—in the decision to water down the investigation of the Principal conglomerate during the 1970s? If Lougheed knew nothing about problems with Principal he was morally-bound to share that with the public. Instead, like his successor Don Getty, he continues to hide behind the skirts of junior minister Connie Osterman.

Those familiar with Lougheed's hands-on management style find the suggestion that Osterman was left to make the calls—without the input of colleagues, without the knowledge of the boss—incomprehensible: that wasn't the way the premier operated. And why, with a wealth of sophisticated talent to chose from, did Lougheed hand Osterman this job in the first place?

Osterman had little understanding of finance or accounting, little awareness of the law or comprehension of the regulatory obligations of government. She hated to read. She avoided reports, preferring to have staff provide oral briefings. She didn't like numbers and she disdained "number crunchers." What she did have, however, was folks smarts. She was popular with the public, capable of taking a lot of heat and deeply loyal to the premier. (Her first assignment after her election in 1979 was as party whip, responsible for maintaining discipline in the Progressive Conservative caucus.) Excellent political credentials, but hardly sufficient for someone, as Osterman said, in a "financial battlefield." In November 1982, when Lougheed appointed Osterman to Consumer Affairs, Dial, Battleford, Abacus, Ram, Merit and Vista had gone down, and the province's mortgage brokers were disappearing one by one. Lougheed had to know that Osterman was in for a very rough ride.

NOTWITHSTANDING THEIR FINDINGS, Inspector Bill Code and Ombudsman Aleck Trawick heard several curious pieces of evidence which seem to take knowledge of the Principal crisis well beyond the Consumer Affairs department into the offices of the provincial Treasurer, the Attorney General and Cabinet, as well as the Alberta Securities Commission, under Connie Osterman's jurisdiction but not her authority.

Documents entered into evidence at the Code inquiry show that Treasury officials were keeping their own eye on the Principal companies, and that their observation started within weeks of the creation of the first task force in mid-1984.

Treasury official George Kinsman was director of the loans and guarantees section of the Treasury department—head of the nine-person team, responsible for reviewing requests for government guarantees on various types of financings, which spearheaded the province's rescue of its financial institutions. His staff specialized in financial analysis, and was responsible for developing the multi-million-dollar recovery programs which pulled the credit unions and trust companies back from oblivion. In 1987, Kinsman became involved in bailout negotiations and ultimately the take-down of the Principal contract companies.

Much to his embarrassment, it was revealed during the inquiry that Kinsman had been watching the contract companies for at least a couple of years before he became officially involved. In August 1984, Tewfik Saleh sent him several documents relating to the contract companies, including a department auditor's annual examination which concluded that they were "virtually insolvent" in early 1984. (We will return to this report in Chapter 12.)

Kinsman's testimony on his early interest in the companies was confusing and contradictory. He said he had no recollection of asking for the highly confidential material in 1984, and couldn't explain why Saleh sent it to him. Nonetheless, Kinsman said, he read the reports to gain information on the issue of valuation of real estate and mortgages, as background for work being done on the credit unions. Incredibly, he said he stopped *one page short* of the reports' final sections, and thus never saw the auditor's conclusion that both companies were "virtually insolvent." Kinsman's memory failed him on many occasions, but he recalled this point with "absolute certainly." When pressed, he admitted he had read the test sections of the reports, and thus saw that First Investors had a capital deficiency of $84 million and a $130-million deficiency in qualified assets. Then Kinsman, a financial analyst, said the material was very complicated, and he hadn't understood it. Whatever his under-standing, Kinsman insisted he never discussed the companies, or their prospects for survival, until the Treasury takeover in 1986. Why? Because his department wasn't looking at the question of First Investors and Associated Investors at that time.

Kinsman also testified: "My recollection is that we [the Treasury Department] were very closely involved with several officials in Consumer and Corporate Affairs with respect to credit unions. We were having frequent meetings and we shared information on credit unions very liberally." As far as he was concerned, he said, the material sent by Saleh was just more information on credit unions. He then admitted that the Principal contract companies had come up in conversation with Saleh during meetings on the credit unions: "I gained the impression that FIC and AIC were in financial difficulty. However, I had no real measure of the extent of the problem... I believe on more than one occasion some remark was made in discussions with Mr. Saleh that there were other financial institutions that were experiencing difficulty, among which were FIC and AIC." Kinsman said he never discussed the companies with Barry Martin. However, "Mr. Martin may have been sitting at the table at the time that Mr. Saleh and I were—I was listening and Mr. Saleh was talking." Did Martin ever say anything about these companies? "I don't recall."

Kinsman conceded that he knew the companies had financial problems and might "come up for future work on my behalf, yes... At the time, I would say that the word 'next' was not in my thinking, but possible future was in my thinking."

What does all this add up to? Tewfik Saleh, deeply disturbed about the contract companies but blocked by Martin and Osterman from taking action, discusses the problem with Kinsman, the Treasury specialist in institutional rescues; Saleh forwards company audits to Kinsman showing how badly off the companies really were; and Kinsman acknowledges that he anticipated they might some day end up on his dissecting table.

Let's bring Kinsman's superior Allister McPherson into the picture. McPherson, whose memory also failed him from time to time at the Code inquiry, offered a somewhat different explanation of his department's early interest in the contract companies. Treasury had no involvement with them in 1984, and neither did he: "Not directly," he testified. What did that mean? "Well, only indirectly in the sense that I recall a brief discussion at one of the task forces" about a transaction between Principal Trust and the contract companies. "I believe it came up in the context of discussion on trust companies."

By mid-1984, Kinsman had begun assembling a file on the contract companies. By mid-1985—when Treasurer Hyndman, Kinsman's minister, became chairman of the second task force—it included First Investors' and Associated Investors' 1983 and 1984 financial statements and an analysis of assets and liabilities.

In May 1985, shortly after the creation of Hyndman's task force, his deputy minister McPherson requested financial information from Saleh on the contract companies, and sent it on to Kinsman when it arrived. This material included up-to-date unaudited financial statements and a memo advising that the companies could not generate sufficient income from assets to meet their contractual obligations. Kinsman says that McPherson passed the material to him without instruction or discussion, and that, again, he simply read it and filed it.

The same day, Kinsman requested and received information on Principal Trust from Director of Trust Companies Reg Pointe. That material included the trust company's audited financial statements from 1980 to 1984.

McPherson testified he had no "specific" memory of discussions about the contract companies, but said they "would have likely come up in the course of discussion on trust companies or credit unions, in that context." But why, at that time, was he seeking information on the contract companies? "Well, I think I was, at that point, not really familiar with the companies, and I was just looking for some basic information, the size of the companies, what they were doing and that sort of thing." Was that because the second task force was looking at First Investors and Associated, as well as the trust companies? "There may have been a discussion at that point, but I don't recall specifically." And why was Kinsman seeking information on Principal Trust at this time? Was it at McPherson's request? "Not that I recall specifically, but I think at this time we were certainly, from Treasury's point of view, trying to get up to speed on the various trust companies." Was Treasury doing this, or the task force? "Well, I think, as I would understand it, Consumer and Corporate Affairs were the regulators. The task force was not replacing that responsibility, but it was set up to receive reports, monitor and to consider requests that might have come to the government from trust companies for assistance."

All this fact-finding followed Connie Osterman's April 1985 report to the priorities committee that several provincial trust companies were in trouble. The portion of her memo dealing with Principal Trust advised:

> Capital has been provided as necessary to the trust company by the parent company, Principal Group Ltd. The continued ability of the parent to provide capital is doubtful, as another subsidiary of the parent is preparing a preferred share offering to the public. However, it does not appear, at this time, that government assistance will be requested.

The same month the information was passed from Consumer Affairs to Treasury, the Alberta Securities Commission was taking a hard look at the contract companies. We will explore these events in greater detail in Chapter 14. Briefly, however: First Investors came under the scrutiny of the securities commission in April 1985 when Principal vice-president Christa Petracca sought commission approval of a preliminary prospectus offering to sell $50 million worth of newly issued preferred shares to the public. By the end of June, the commission had decided that First Investors' finances were so inadequate that not only should it not go public, it no longer qualified as an approved corporation under the province's *Trustee Act*.[14]

Instead of cancelling this designation, the commission suggested on July 5 that First Investors write directly to Cabinet, requesting an order revoking its designation. First Investors did so on July 8. Mysteriously, the request was never acted upon.

However, on July 9, Principal in-house lawyer Lynn Patrick wrote to Douglas Rae, assistant deputy minister in the Attorney General's department, to say: "I have spoken with Mr. George de Rappard at the Executive Council and he indicates that in all likelihood the matter will be before the next Cabinet meeting for an appropriate Order in Council." At this time de Rappard was deputy minister to the

Cabinet and a member of its priorities committee. In 1989, reporters asked de Rappard what had happened to the First Investors request in 1985: "I'm not familiar with that at all. I can't help you," he said.[15]

A note-to-file written July 12, 1985, by Marguerite Childs, deputy director of the commission, said that Cabinet might choose not to revoke the company's designation under the *Trustee Act* "since the publicity may be fatally damaging to the company. There is no need to advise the Lieutenant Governor in Council"— Cabinet—"of the financial standing of this company since they are fully aware."

On October 1, 1985, D.W. Axler, a lawyer in the Attorney General's office, wrote to his superior Rae: "Allister McPherson advised by telephone that the Attorney General [Neil Crawford] was absent at the last meeting of the Committee looking into the financial affairs of institutions. At that meeting it was decided that the request by First Investors for deletion from the *Trustee Act* list of approved corporations be placed on hold pending a further review of the possible problems on related matters of the Principal Group."

Axler went on to say that he had asked Martin about that review, and Martin had "indicated to me that he has been very busy, occupied with other urgent matters and has to date been unable to organize a time line in completing the above requested review. He indicated it could take quite some time, *possibly years*." (Italics added.) At the Code inquiry, Martin couldn't remember such a conversation with Axler, but didn't deny it occurred. McPherson was not questioned on this matter.

Ombudsman Aleck Trawick concluded that First Investors' request for revocation of its status under the *Trustee Act*:

> ...was not acted upon because the Cabinet, at that time, was reluctant to make any change to the status of FIC given the concern...that any information that became public concerning the financial situation of the investment contract companies would be harmful... The expressed reason was that Cabinet was awaiting a report by [Consumer Affairs]; the real reason was clearly the fear of an adverse reaction on the affairs of the company.

(Trawick found that the issue of First Investors' *Trustee Act* status was a perennial problem going back decades. The company failed to satisfy the *Trustee Act's* capital requirements in 1965 and 1966, from 1971 to 1975, and in 1984 and 1985. Marc Lemay—then deputy director, filings, of the Alberta Securities Commission and later its director—met with Ken Marlin in 1974 to discuss that year's financial deficiency. Marlin disputed the commission's capital calculations, then persuaded Lemay not to report to Cabinet in exchange for an agreement that First Investors would not accept trust funds. This was done, Trawick reported, "on the basis that the adverse publicity of withdrawing the approval would have harmful effects on the business of FIC." For the next decade, no report regarding First Investors' *Trustee Act* status was made by the commission. Marlin, asked by Childs about the situation in 1985, replied that his agreement the decade before not to accept trust funds had only applied to the year he made the promise.)

On July 29, 1985—less than three weeks after First Investors' request for deletion under the *Trustee Act* bounced from the Cabinet office into oblivion—Kinsman's staff completed work on an organizational chart of the Principal companies. It showed the relationship among the contract companies and Principal Trust, their parent Principal Group and their grandparent Collective Securities. Kinsman explained his interest this way: "Well, at that time, we were interested in the trust company... We just wanted to see how the trust company integrated and related to the other corporations as part of the Principal Group of Companies."

In October 1985, Kinsman added an *Alberta Business* cover story on Donald Cormie to his file on the contract companies. "I ripped this out of a magazine because I thought it made good reading... it was fascinating to me," he explained. The article repeated several Cormie myths and included this remark: "Aside from the tremendous technological innovation that infiltrates the Principal Group, the economic foresight of Donald Cormie has kept the company's investors in the money."[16] Fascinating indeed.

Another illuminating incident occurred during the autumn of 1985 when three senior Consumer Affairs officials—Superintendent of Insurance Tewfik Saleh, Director of Trust Companies Reg Pointe and senior auditor Burt Eldridge—were summoned before the financial institutions task force during a discussion of the Principal contract companies. None of the participants who testified (Osterman, Hyndman, Martin, Pointe, Saleh or Eldridge) recall the discussion in any detail. But Eldridge testified that Hyndman asked: "Do you see any light at the end of the tunnel?"

Eldridge also remembered his answer: "No."

No one else can confirm or deny this exchange, even Hyndman: "I don't specifically recall the question or the answer... He could have said it, but I don't recollect." If we accept Eldridge's account—and he was very firm in his recollection—then we have Lou Hyndman, in the autumn of 1985, sufficiently aware of the urgency of the contract companies' situation to be seeking assurance of a light at the end of the tunnel. And we have a government auditor, intimately familiar with the companies' dire circumstances, offering not a glimmer of hope.

The exact date of this meeting was not pinpointed, but it was during the period that Peter Lougheed was entering retirement after 14 years as premier. In mid-November—a couple of weeks after Don Getty took over—Hyndman forwarded a memo to Getty and the priorities committee entitled "Alberta Financial Institutions" which discussed the shaky state of the province's financial services industry. This memo included the fact that half of Principal Trust's mortgage portfolio was in arrears by six months or more. Attached to the memo was a separate two-page report on the contract companies, prepared by Barry Martin and Connie Osterman. It advised that the companies were several million dollars in the red and that they might be forced into receivership or liquidation if the real estate market did not improve. (See Chapter 15 for more on this memo.) Under the *Investment Contracts Act*, the companies could not do business without an adequate capital and asset base: if they were in the red, they were operating illegally. Despite this shocking revelation, it would be another 19 months before they were shut down.

Three years later, in lieu of testifying at the Code inquiry, Getty signed a declaration that he had no knowledge of any financial difficulties of the Principal Group of Companies, including First Investors and Associated Investors, until shortly before their collapse in 1987. Later, after aggressive questioning in the Legislature, Getty admitted reading the November 1985 report. He said it indicated that there was a dispute between Consumer Affairs and the two Principal subsidiaries. He said he took no action because none was called for.

A copy of Hyndman's November 1985 memo went into George Kinsman's now overflowing file on the contract companies. The same day the memo went to Getty, Kinsman had his staff prepare a consolidated balance sheet on First Investors and Associated Investors, "just to have a look at what these companies are doing," he testified. This too, he said, was "background" for his work on credit unions and trust companies.

In June 1986—a couple of weeks after Dick Johnston replaced Hyndman as Treasurer—responsibility for the contract companies was transferred from Consumer Affairs to Treasury. Conveniently, Kinsman already had a thick file on the companies, and he immediately asked his staff to prepare a detailed analysis of their finances. Within a month, this report was in the hands of his immediate supervisor, Jim Drinkwater, Assistant Deputy Provincial Treasurer (finance). It revealed, among other things, that the companies had a negative spread of 2.5%: that they lost $25 every time they sold a $1,000 contract.

Kinsman testified that he never told his superiors that he already had a file on the companies. Drinkwater, however, already "knew the files I had." (Drinkwater, who reported to Deputy Provincial Treasurer McPherson, was not called to testify at the Code inquiry. He refused to be interviewed for this book.)

The companies were actually losing a lot more than Kinsman's analysis showed. He had based it on the Consumer Affairs annual examination of the companies for 1984, completed in mid-1985. That audit had "recalculated" their capital deficiencies, using a method which disallowed the massive mortgage and real estate write-downs of the year before. The December 1983 examination of First Investors showed a capital deficiency of $62.5 million; a follow-up examination in April 1984 found the deficiency had climbed to $84 million. But the December 1984 examination, using the restated figures, showed a deficiency of only $1.4 million. (This change in capital calculations will be discussed in more detail in Chapter 15.)

Kinsman said he used the more positive numbers in his analysis, and never looked at the 1983 examination reports again. Trends are essential in Kinsman's profession, yet he testified he never brought those earlier reports, nor any of the other documents he had accumulated, to the attention of the Treasury officials now responsible for the contract companies.

Nor did he tell them what he had learned about the desperate straits of those companies while assembling his file.

Why? Because he didn't need to. He could remember nothing more.

INFLUENCE IS A SUBTLE GAME. It's not always bought and sold, not always bartered for favours. Sometimes it's exercised simply by keeping silent, giving a pal a chance to do his stuff. It can be calculated and self-serving, or motivated simply by the reluctance of one person to believe the worst about another.

Donald Cormie has an interesting view of how this process works. During a presentation to the House of Commons finance committee in September 1985, he described it as "big round robins." Cormie was commenting on conflict of interest in Ontario financial institutions, but his observations are applicable in a wider context:

> What I am really saying is that one of the problems you have is where does the interlocking occur in conflicts of interest and things? It does not occur in the biological family... as I have pointed out in the briefs. You have what we call the "old boy network" in Ontario. It works. You have people interlocking who went to school together. They work together. You have religious and cultural groups that interlock and work together; they help each other. I think you have to recognize that. So when you talk about conflict of interest being narrow little interests, that is not the way it works. It is big round robins. Unless you recognize that, a person is not going to see it.

What Cormie didn't add was that Alberta has its own old boy network: a tight-knit moneyed gentry that drives both the provincial government and Edmonton society. The circle is dominated by a small number of families, some of whom go back together through several generations. Despite the oil boom, Alberta's aristocracy remains very small-town. Its members share lunch in one another's boardrooms, consume steaks and scotch over one another's barbecues, play golf at one another's clubs and watch the Oilers on one another's televisions. Lawyers' sons marry businessmen's daughters. The fathers attended the same high schools and universities, cheered the same football teams, joined the same fraternities and campaigned in the same elections.

Cormie and his family were an integral part of this community. He was head of a prominent law firm and ran a renowned investment business controlling hundreds of millions of dollars. His wife Eivor was a warm woman who graced any social gathering. Their Christmas party was the talk of the town, a coveted invitation. Everyone who was anyone—lawyers, millionaires, judges and Cabinet ministers—was there. Cormie attended Law Society events, spent time at upper-crust watering holes and involved himself in prestigious local causes.

After the Code report was delivered, Cormie lamented that he had failed to cultivate the right connections.[17] "I never did pay attention to politics," he told the

Calgary Herald in May 1989. "I regret that I didn't have a better handle on political thinking," he told the *Financial Post* a half year later. In February 1990 he told the *Edmonton Sun* he was never a government insider, never wanted to be, and that refusing to be one of the "good ol' boys" cost him dearly. "We never got a penny from government. I'm glad because we've always believed in being independent."

Actually, Cormie got quite a few pennies, in the form of grants for different companies. But more important, he received gifts without price: he got time to manoeuvre, and he kept control.

It's true that Cormie didn't have an adequate grip on political thinking, and that failure cost him dearly in Principal's final days. But if Cormie wasn't sufficiently connected to save his companies from take-down in 1987, it wasn't from lack of trying. For many years, he was remarkably successful at playing regulators off against politicians; in the hands of a less determined and influential man, Principal might well have gone under far earlier.

For three decades, Cormie did his best to maintain agreeable relations with political figures. In recent years, he testified, it was "a regular practice" to try to include Cabinet ministers at weekly lunches at Principal Plaza. They were usually invited in pairs so they'd feel more comfortable. Cormie saw such get-togethers as an effective way of cultivating valuable contacts. In a memo written February 20, 1984—the week after Consumer Affairs Minister Connie Osterman was a lunch guest—Cormie instructed in-house lawyer Lynn Patrick to draft a strategy for lobbying government officials. "To some extent we have been doing this through the luncheons in the dining room and also by the public talks which I have been giving in various locations where it gives me an opportunity to meet and influence some of the more prominent people in those communities."

Cormie was asked at the Code inquiry about his efforts to undermine regulatory officials, and about meetings with provincial Cabinet ministers for that purpose. He said: "You know, when you're in a city like Edmonton, you're running into them at various events all the time, so if I talked to one or the other, I would just chat with them. I don't know that I—normally I wouldn't raise specific problems with a Cabinet minister under those circumstances, I would just make some general comments that I thought the financial services industry needed a different sort of a focus. Instead of confrontational, I thought it should be supportive... If I would run into one [Cabinet minister] that I would talk to at some social event or I would be sitting next to them at some dinner...we would chat about the companies. But I always avoided specifics."

Cormie occasionally ran into officials like Consumer Affairs Deputy Minister Barry Martin and his predecessor Jack Lyndon on the social circuit. Martin testified that he met Cormie only once in a business setting, during his lunch at Principal Plaza two weeks after Osterman was there. But "I had run into him on other occasions at social events and, you know, the usual Christmas party routine that goes on in this city." Martin told me that his conversations with Cormie on such occasions consisted of discussions of "the state of Wayne Gretzky," and that he never allowed himself to be "lobbied" at social events. He described Cormie as a "highly visible and very vocal Edmonton businessman." He also said: "I believed him to be an ardent [Conservative] party supporter."

Cormie attended big-ticket party fundraisers (tables at the premier's annual dinners were $2,500 each) and authorized regular corporate donations to politicians. This had been happening, he testified, since Social Credit was in power. Between 1984 and 1987, "my recollection is we made a substantial contribution to the Liberals and to the Conservatives and we also contributed to certain specific candidates running where some manager felt that they had to give special support in his particular district or it was desirable to do so."[18]

The largest known donation was $20,000, contributed by Principal Group to Don Getty's leadership campaign in 1985. The money was solicited by Bill Comrie, owner of The Brick Warehouse Ltd., and lawyer Gary Campbell, a former Cormie Kennedy partner. (Campbell joined Cormie Kennedy during the 1960s, served as managing partner for several years, then in 1981 became president and chief executive officer of Churchill Development Corporation Ltd., later renamed The Churchill Corporation. He acted during this period as Cormie Kennedy legal counsel. During his early years, Campbell served as a director of Cormie's "upstairs" companies: between 1966 and 1970, he was director and secretary of County Investments Ltd. Between 1963 and 1969, he was also a director of Estate Loan and Finance and Cormie Ranch.)

Principal Group vice-president of finance Bill Johnson well remembers the day that Campbell and Comrie came to call for the $20,000. "There was a luncheon on the 30th floor one day and those guys were there and that's when that whole thing came up," he told me. "Right at that luncheon Cormie agreed to contribute $20,000. Most of the conversation at the luncheon was just a general discussion of the Alberta economy in general—the financial services business—and one of those guys got into: 'Well, you realize that Don Getty's running for the leadership,' and etcetera, 'and if you can see your way to contributing some funds to his leadership campaign, we'd be happy about it.' That kind of thing."

Campbell was a founding member of the Edmonton South Federal Progressive Conservative Association when the riding was established in 1976, and served as its president for many years. Later, he became provincial party treasurer, and was well known as one of Getty's most valued advisors. In 1984, the Lougheed goverment appointed Campbell to a committee established to help with the work-out of Alberta's credit unions. In 1987, Getty's government appointed him to head the board of directors of the newly formed crown corporation, North West Trust (built on the ashes of North West and Heritage trusts).

Campbell's company, The Churchill Corporation, was founded in 1981 by an assortment of Tory bagmen, Cormie Kennedy partners and members of the local entrepreneurial elite—several of them with important ties to Donald Cormie and his companies. Builder Allan Olson, head of Stuart Olson Construction Ltd. (a Lougheed fundraiser and co-chairman of Getty's 1985 leadership campaign) made a call to the provincial Treasurer on Cormie's behalf a couple of days before the contract companies went down; Cormie Kennedy partner Jack Agrios (also on the Getty leadership team) represented Cormie during bailout negotiations with the Alberta government in 1987; and developer Jim Hunter co-operated in a number of questionable Principal deals, including the scandalous Derrick Plaza flip in 1986. (See Chapter 19.) Also involved was Cormie Kennedy founding partner Jack Kennedy, an extremely well-connected Tory who raised funds for Peter Lougheed. (According to a lawyer close to the scene, every time there was an election, Kennedy pulled out an exclusive list of about a dozen prominent people and tapped them for contributions.) Kennedy was rewarded in July 1985 with the post of Alberta's agent general in Hong Kong, a plum appointment made shortly before Lougheed's retirement from politics.[19]

During the Code inquiry, lawyer Jack Major, acting for the Alberta government, questioned Cormie about political favours. Here's the exchange:

Q: Now, in return for any political donations you may have made,
were you promised anything?
A: No, not a thing. We didn't discuss that at all.
Q: Did you feel that you had access to members of the Cabinet beyond
access that any businessman of your stature would have?
A: No, I didn't.

Of course, in pro-business Alberta, many prominent businessmen have access to government ministers. Cormie was just one more.

Among the pipelines providing Cormie access to politicians was his membership in a secretive organization called the Young Presidents Organization. The Texas-based YPO has some 6,000 members around the world, including about 50 in Alberta. Members must be president or chief executive officer of a company with gross annual revenue of at least $4 million or average assets of $80 million, and they must have reached their position before turning 40.[20] Cormie joined the YPO in 1958, at the age of 36, after replacing Stan Melton as president of First Investors. He was vice-president of the Alberta chapter for a while, and later became regional vice-president for the Pacific Northwest, including all chapters as far east as Japan. The YPO was an important part of Cormie's life, and many local members formed the basis of his blue-ribbon guest list.

By charter, the YPO is not politically affiliated. Nonetheless, its profit-motivated members are understandably right-of-centre and free-enterprise-oriented. They routinely meet with politicians, for what is described as an exchange of views, in many cities around the world, including Edmonton. Both Connie Osterman and Julian Koziak remember attending Cabinet meetings with the Alberta chapter, and they recall seeing Cormie there. "Some members of the Cabinet would meet with them, talk about the economy, any number of things, in sort of a big picture way," Osterman told me. "We do this with major organizations, for example the Alberta Chamber of Commerce meets with us." Cabinet members met with the

YPO at least once a year, Osterman said, at a formal dinner meeting which focused on corporate Alberta's views of the provincial government's activities.

A letter written to Lougheed in September 1984 further illustrates Cormie's lobbying tactics. His eight-page letter, a response to Connie Osterman's new white paper on the financial services industry, argued for extensive deregulation and more provincial boosterism. Written on Cormie Kennedy letterhead, the letter reminded Lougheed that in 1963 Cormie had chaired a special section of the Canadian Bar Association that prepared an extensive brief to the Manning regime about the administrative problems of the Alberta government. Then he dropped the names of several Cabinet ministers:

> I was at dinner the other night with the Hon. Lou Hyndman, the Hon. John Zoazirny, the Hon. Neil Neil Webber[21] and the Hon. Don Sparrow, along with six local businessmen where there was a very close and informative exchange of ideas and concerns. They stressed the importance of bringing some of our views forward.
>
> We pointed out that in this environment the pressures on Alberta business are so heavy that it is very difficult to free up the senior people to conduct a proper liaison with the government in Alberta and particularly the government in Ottawa. However, Mr. Hyndman suggested that we are better to put comments and suggestions in piece-meal than not to get them in at all...

This was followed by three recommendations: deregulation ("I can honestly say that in 30 years in this industry I have seen very few detailed regulations that accomplish a positive, useful purpose"); deposit insurance for Alberta companies; and the appointment of a senior government officer to promote the financial services industry in Alberta. He complained that Consumer Affairs was overly preoccupied with consumer protection:

> This leads to reports on companies that are always negative, and complaining, and these reports are produced and widely circulated... A program is needed to gradually substitute forward thinking and positive personalities in dealing with these areas for a number of the negative thinking and consumer protective personalities that presently dominate the department.

Hyndman—appointed, we will recall, to the financial institutions task force just four months before Cormie's letter was written—testified that during his dinner with Cormie, Cormie argued that Alberta was "too overly-rigorous from the point of view of the potential health of provincial financial institutions." Hyndman described the setting as "a dinner where there was to be provided an opportunity to exchange views, to listen to what local businessmen felt was going right and going wrong, to get advice and to be in a listening posture—to have ministers of the Crown there to listen to what they had to say."

The 1984 white paper was the government's final attempt at tightening up the *Investment Contracts Act*. It was abandoned.

8

Going-concern

May 7, 1984

"THIS IS DONALD CORMIE SPEAKING."

Bruce Pennock clutched the telephone tighter. "Why, yes, Mr. Cormie. What can I do for you?"

"What's this I hear about a going-concern note in the audit, Mr. Pennock? That doesn't sound very satisfactory."

It was May 7, a Monday night, and Pennock was working late, wrapping up the 1983 audits of the Principal contract companies. Pennock, a partner with the chartered accounting firm Touch Ross & Co., had had trouble completing the assignment. The mortgage portfolios held by First Investors and Associated Investors were a disaster, and it seemed unlikely to him that things were going to improve. He therefore felt obliged to include a "going-concern" note in the audit, to warn readers that the companies might not survive another year. Pennock had sent a draft of the note to the Principal offices, and now the corporate president was calling him on it.

"Touche Ross seems determined to have these companies reflect a loss," Cormie said grimly.

"Now that's not fair, Mr. Cormie. We're just doing our job here."

"We're having some problems with foreclosures right now, I know," Cormie said. "But we can move about 20% of them out for sale a year, and we'll have the real estate problem all cleaned up in about five years... Those notes will just perpetuate the problems everyone is trying to avoid."

Financial statements are prepared by company management, then go to the external auditor for inspection. The auditor's responsibility is not to management, which pays him, but to the shareholders, who appoint him. In the case of the Principal companies, both management and shareholders were the same—Cormie, his family and employees. This gave Cormie extra muscle in dealing with Pennock, but the auditor had other responsibilities—specifically to the regulators, and the investors they represented, who relied on him to ensure that the accounting and reporting were accurate and fair.

If everything is correct, an auditor provides a "clear audit," issuing a report which appears on a certificate at the front of the statement. During the 1980s, a typical report had two paragraphs. The first described the scope of the examination; the second advised that the statements presented fairly the company's financial position on the date the audit was completed. (These days there's also a reminder that responsibility for the statement rests with management.)

If a statement isn't accurate—if losses have been hidden, or profits over-estimated, or improper accounting methods used to disguise bad news—the auditor must say so. There are several ways of doing this, among them refusing an opinion ("...we are unable to express an opinion..."), or by issuing a qualified opinion, identifying the dubious items. The auditor is entitled in the first instance to assume that management is ethical, but if he suspects misrepresentation, he must delve into the company's records until he is confident of the truth, and then reveal it, whatever the consequences. The Hon. Willard Estey, in his report on the collapse of two Alberta banks, calls this the auditor's "grave and lonely duty."

Cormie's staff had prepared statements for First Investors and Associated Investors which, Pennock believed, grossly underestimated the impact of the real estate downturn. The proper response to the companies' losses would have been to "write down" the loans, establishing "provisions" for the losses and recording them as an expense in the statement. But, as Cormie often said, he had never lost money on a mortgage and he had no intention of starting now. Pennock had pressed his point, and had persuaded Cormie to book a provision of $2,090,000 million for First Investors (on top of $800,000 the year before) and $624,000 for Associated Investors (up from $250,000).

Obviously this didn't go far enough. In Pennock's view, the companies faced millions more in losses. If they materialized it would endanger the companies' existence, and that had to be acknowledged in the statements. Cormie wouldn't agree to increased provisions, but was desperate for an unqualified audit—anything else would mean the companies could not continue under the *Investment Contracts Act*. Eventually, Pennock decided that he would be satisfied if his reservations were recorded in notes to appear in the back of the financial statements, and the notes were drafted:

> These financial statement have been prepared in accordance with accounting principles generally accepted in Canada, *and have been presented on a going concern basis*, which should be considered in relation to Note 9, which contemplates the realization of assets and the satisfaction of liabilities in the normal course of business. [Italics added.]

Despite the dry language, this was a clear warning to an experienced reader that a company is in bad shape and may not last the year. Note 9 advised that the contract companies faced additional exposures (estimated at $10 million for First Investors and $2.95 million for Associated Investors) if the depressed real estate market levels turned out to be permanent, rather than temporary. Another note, titled "Subsequent events," concerned the $23-million "tender" to redeem jointly-held assets from Principal Trust, three months after the 1983 audit period. Note 9 warned that this transaction had increased First Investors' exposure to loss by a further $4.6 million.

This is a standard means of presenting a warning—not as dire as including it in the body of the auditor's report, not as solid as booking provisions, but a clear indication of impending trouble. A financial statement's notes contain most of the real news, and that's where experienced readers look first.

Cormie was furious about the notes, and argued for a while longer on the telephone. It's a situation familiar to any accountant who's handled a problem audit. The more difficult the circumstances, the more aggressive the client. If he gets upset enough, the firm risks losing a lucrative account. That can make it tough to keep a grip on your professional ethics.

The next morning, Cormie showed up unannounced at Pennock's office, accompanied by several of his vice-presidents. Ushered into the Touche Ross boardroom, they went through it all one more time. Despite the pressure, Pennock held firm: if Cormie refused to include the notes, he wouldn't sign off on the statements. That was that, and Cormie acknowledged defeat.

Pennock and company directors Ken Marlin and Eric Espenberg signed off on the statements, and Marlin immediately sent them to Superintendent of Insurance Tewfik Saleh. In his covering letter, Marlin promised that a second set of statements, providing information required under the *Investment Contracts Act*, would be forwarded the next day.

The statements just completed by Pennock were known as "GAAP statements," prepared according to "generally accepted accounting principles" detailed in the inches-thick handbook issued by the Canadian Institute of Chartered Accountants. The second set of statements, known as the "statutory" or "regulatory statements"— reports detailing the companies' assets and liabilities, to determine whether they met the Section 8 financial tests in the *Investment Contracts Act*—were also supposed to be audited. Those forwarded by Marlin two days later were not.

There's a mystery here. The second set of statements were presented to Pennock and he—employing the most severe weapon in an auditor's arsenal—refused an opinion on them. The set forwarded to Saleh were prepared by an unidentified person in the Principal organization.[1] Marlin testified that he didn't realize the second set of statements were unaudited, and says that they came to him, via his secretary, from someone else in the company.

A second mystery: the audited GAAP statements received by Saleh's office were immediately shared with government auditors. But the unaudited regulatory statements disappeared, and weren't forwarded to the government auditors for three weeks. On May 17, Burt Eldridge, unaware they had arrived a week before, sent a memo to Saleh's assistant Bernard Rodrigues asking him to obtain them from the company; Rodrigues didn't reply until May 28. When Eldridge finally got the statements he saw they were faked, and wrote a memo to Saleh:

> Would you please point out to the company that we cannot accept the unaudited statement of assets and instruct the companies to file an audited Statement of Assets without delay. These statements, with the attached notes on the auditors' letterhead, unless in fact they have been authorized or approved by the auditors, are misleading. We should ascertain the position of the auditors and if they have not authorized the use of the statements in this form we should inform the company we consider this submission misleading or improper.

Saleh testified he couldn't remember receiving the memo.[2]

May 2, 1984

THE CDIC LEARNED ABOUT the $23-million transaction in mid-April when Bruce Pennock's audit of Principal Trust was delivered. Pennock had completed it three weeks before his audit of the contract companies, and had insisted on including a similar "Subsequent Events" note reporting the $23million transfer. The note advised that if the trust company had held onto its share of the portfolio it would have been exposed to a loss of $5.1 million; the transfer had reduced its risk to $585,000.

Federal auditors didn't like the sound of that, and phoned Reg Pointe, Alberta Director of Trust Companies. The CDIC was already upset with Principal Trust and didn't think a loony deal like this one was going to solve anything. First, it was illegal under provincial legislation. Second, if it wasn't reversed, surely the contract companies would come after Principal Trust for compensation.

Pointe was under pressure from another direction as well. After completing his audit of the trust company on April 19, Pennock had written a letter to Pointe, reporting that the $23-million transaction was a possible violation of the province's *Trust Companies Act*. Pointe knew that already, but receiving such correspondence from an auditor really turned the heat up. Pointe passed the grim news on to Saleh the same day, and over the next few days the whole sad mess was discussed with Deputy Minister Barry Martin and with the Minister, Connie Osterman.

On May 1 (Tuesday, the day after Jim Darwish's alarming memo was delivered to Osterman during the staff meeting in her office) Saleh drafted a letter to the Principal companies protesting the $23-million transaction. He sent a copy to the audit department, advising that it had been approved by Osterman and Martin, and asking for reaction. This request landed, of course, on the desk of Jim Darwish, as head of audit staff. Darwish was still stinging from Osterman's tongue-lashing the day before, and had spent the evening with his wife Elvera trying to decide how to respond. Osterman had ordered him to keep his nose out of other people's jurisdictions; but now here was Saleh, writing what amounted to an engraved invitation to interfere.

Darwish jumped in with both feet.

Saleh met Thursday with the audit staff, and Darwish pulled no punches. Saleh's draft letter was weaker than his letter of January 12, and had to be toughened up. Over the next several days, the group worked on it together. Darwish and Pointe argued the transaction had to be reversed because it contravened the *Trust Companies Act*, and auditor Al Hutchison provided several shocking numbers. His best estimate of the overall shortfall in the two companies was a total of $72 million ($52 million for First Investors and $20 million for Associated Investors).

The long-awaited audited GAAP statements arrived in the government offices the same day and provided further ammunition. Despite repeated promises, the contract companies' financial situation had not improved; even their auditor thought there was a problem with the mortgage holdings. (Pennock's estimate of the shortfall was significantly less than Hutchison had reached using government-obtained appraisals, but his numbers still reflected a serious problem.)

On Friday, May 11, Saleh's letter was finally couriered to Principal. Darwish and his colleagues had prevailed; it was aggressive and thorough, and demanded immediate injections of cash to shore up the contract companies. A key passage follows:

> We are very concerned that despite your expressed anxiety about the status of the mortgage and real estate portfolio of FIC and AIC, they have nevertheless purchased [Principal Trust's] share of the seriously troubled and overvalued portfolio. In our opinion, this transaction is prejudicial to the interest of FIC and AIC contract holders... *Accordingly this transaction should be immediately reversed.* [Italics added.]

The five-page letter also fired a shot in Pennock's direction:

> Of particular concern to us is the $10-million additional exposure referred to in FIC's 1983 audited financial statements. We would like to discuss with you and your external auditors the method by which this exposure was assessed without obtaining current appraisals. Based on the percentages of write down according to the appraisals we obtained, the overall shortfall is estimated by our auditors to be approximately $52 million for FIC and $20 million for AIC. It is pointed out that this shortfall does not include the $23-million transfer from [Principal Trust] which would of course increase it.

If the companies disagreed with the regulators' assessment, the letter continued, they were welcome to acquire independent appraisals. Nonetheless, an immediate injection of share capital was required, $25 million for First Investors and $10 million for Associated Investors, "as an interim measure to provide protection to contract holders while additional appraisals are being obtained." The injection was to be in the form of cash or marketable securities.

Much of the companies' existing capitalization was in the form of "subordinated notes," high-interest loans from the parent company whose repayment was subordinated to (ranked behind) other forms of debt. Saleh ordered that all these notes ($8.2 million for First Investors and $1.7 million for Associated Investors) be immediately converted into permanent capital.

Although it was not revealed in the financial statements, the contract companies, like Principal Trust, were accruing interest on mortgage loans in arrears and claiming the unpaid and largely uncollectible interest as income. (The accrued interest capitalized by the two companies amounted to $57.9 million between 1983 and 1985.) "This practice artificially inflates earnings and should cease," Saleh said in his letter. He wanted accrued interest on loans delinquent for 90 days to be covered in an allowance for bad debts, a step which would have considerably darkened the statements' bottom lines.

Finally, he invited the companies' representatives and auditors to a meeting in the regulators' offices at the end of the month to discuss the steps necessary to "rectify the existing serious situation."

It was a tough letter and a job well done, but the orders would never be enforced.

A couple of weeks later, the head of the CDIC wrote to the top official in Connie Osterman's department about the Principal companies. In a nine-page letter to Barry Martin, CDIC chairman Robert De Coster said it seemed likely that the $23-million transaction would be reversed, and he had therefore decided that Principal Trust must reduce its borrowing base by the $6.3 million that would have been required if the deal had not taken place. However:

> ...we are concerned that if we put pressure on the owners of the company to correct the situation without doing so in concert with the Alberta authorities, action may be taken to improve the position of the trust company that will disadvantage investors in associated companies supervised by Alberta but over which CDIC has no jurisdiction. This appears to have been the case with the sale of the $22.6 million of mortgages at book value to the investment contract companies.

De Coster also took note of something which, to the very end, would never be of great concern to provincial officials: the parent company Principal Group did not seem to be very well capitalized, and most of its financing was obtained in the form of promissory notes from Alberta investors.

> All of these things lead CDIC to believe that independent action on its part to put additional pressure on the trust company may result in some improvement in the position of the trust company but at the expense of small investors in Alberta and elsewhere. It is for this reason that I am writing to suggest that CDIC and the Alberta Department of Consumer and Corporate Affairs work together in dealing with this situation. The Board of Directors of CDIC considers that it is urgent to take action... In the absence of concerted action, CDIC will be forced to act on its own.

Martin testified that he held discussions with De Coster, and "we indicated that wherever possible, the Province of Alberta would like to work and co-operate with them in whatever resolution we could come up with relative to these problems." But he rejected the proposal of a joint effort to straighten out the Principal companies, considering the move "premature" at that time. He would make the same decision a year and a half later.

The contract companies were Alberta's jurisdiction, and Martin didn't care for interfering feds. "Secondly," he testified, "I was also concerned with my ongoing apprehension about commencing these large investigations in these companies which might have consequences."

In early May the legal opinions obtained by Christa Petracca, regarding the "tender" concept of the $23-million transaction, had been received at the government offices. Jim Darwish had noted the oddity of seeking three opinions on a single issue, and suggested they be passed on to the Attorney General's office. That request went to government lawyer Stan Franklin, who, on May 28, delivered his opinion that the deal was prohibited under the *Trust Companies Act*, but that Reg Pointe, Director of Trust Companies, didn't have the power to reverse the deal; he could only impose a penalty.

Pointe talked it over with Saleh. Franklin's opinion closed the door on reversing the sale under trust company legislation, but there was still the *Investment Contracts Act*.

May 8, 1984

CONTRACT COMPANIES DIRECTOR ERIC ESPENBERG remembers the day the resolution crossed his desk. This one seemed odd: it was a decision to suspend the additional credits on some of the investment contracts. "The first I heard of it was when I received it for signature," he testified. He never asked anyone why such a thing was happening—just signed it, and tossed it back into the inter-office mail basket.

May 10, 1984

"I HAPPENED TO BE DOWN WITH the auditors," Jim Darwish testified, "and there was an ad in the [Edmonton] *Sun* advertising interest rates of various trust companies. It was under the heading Principal Group, and I said, 'Now, whose rates are those? Are those the trust company's or the investment contract companies'?' " By that time First Investors and Associated Investors were, in Darwish's classic understatement, "a pretty major topic of conversation" among the audit unit.

Darwish dialled Principal Trust and, without identifying himself, asked for the trust company's interest rates. He was quoted a quarter of a percentage point higher than the advertised rate. "Is that the trust company rate?"

No, he was told, that was the First Investors rate. "Then he asked me if I knew the difference between First Investors and the trust company, and I told him, 'No.' He told me that First Investors was like an insurance company, and I asked him what the interest rates were for the trust company. He quoted me the rates that were the same as those appearing in the paper, which were a quarter percent lower than First Investors. So I asked him why the trust company rates were lower than the investment contract company rates, and he told me that that was because you have got CDIC coverage with the trust company and that you have to pay for that. And that is why your return was a quarter percent less.

"I said to him, 'I suppose a person should pay the quarter of a percent in order to get the CDIC coverage?'

"He said, 'Well, if you think that First Investors is going to go bankrupt, then you should invest in the trust company.' But he went on to say that First Investors is 100% secure, that it is secured the same way as any insurance company.

"He said that all the assets are deposited with the Royal Bank and that if First Investors had a problem, the Royal Bank would pay me out. He said the Royal Bank is the trustee for all of the money. If there is a problem, they take over and distribute out the money.

"He said that First Investors' money is not 100% secured, but it is insured, while the trust company's money is 100% secured. And unless you had $1 million to invest, then you are secured only to $60,000, and in that case, you should put your money in First Investors to get the extra quarter percent."

This presentation, Darwish knew, was almost entirely false. First Investors was *not* "secured the same way as any insurance company." Insurance companies were regulated under entirely different legislation; the *Investment Contracts Act* specifically noted that the contracts weren't contracts "within the meaning of the *Insurance Act*." The only connection between investment contracts and insurance was that the *Investment Contracts Act* required that the "qualified assets" of contract companies' investments be the same sort of investments authorized for insurance companies under the *Canadian and British Insurance Companies Act*.

There were other errors. First Investors' money was *not* insured. The trust company's rate wasn't lower because of the cost of the CDIC insurance; it was lower because it was a less risky investment. All the assets were *not* deposited with the Royal Bank, and if First Investors had problems the bank would *not* pay out investors. The Royal Bank was *not* the trustee for all the money, and if there was a problem it would *not* take over and distribute out the money. First Investors and Associated Investors did have depositories at the Canadian Imperial Bank of Commerce and the Royal Bank respectively, where documents evidencing title to their assets were held. But not even the investors' principal, nor assets equal to that value—let alone principal plus 4%—were on deposit.

If Darwish hadn't specified twice he wanted the trust company's rate, he might never have been told he had originally been quoted the contract company's higher rate. Or that the interest offered by the contract company consisted of a guaranteed 4% and additional credits.

There was one correct statement: First Investors' money was *not* 100% secured. The contracts were backed by nothing more than the company's guarantee. As Darwish well knew, that guarantee left something to be desired.

Darwish wrote a memo summarizing this exchange, then asked George Blochert to look into it. Blochert, executive director of regional services under Darwish, was responsible for the consumer investigations team which probed complaints of misleading advertising. On May 16, he wrote a memo ordering an investigation, first in the Edmonton area and then, depending on what was found, elsewhere. Both Darwish's memo to Blochert, and Blochert's memo to staff, were copied to Reg Pointe and Tewfik Saleh. When Saleh received his copy of Blochert's memo he flew with it, enraged, to Barry Martin's office. That same day Martin wrote to Blochert:

> It has just come to my attention that inquiries are going to be initiated at the regional level into the sales practices of the above companies. Inasmuch as the financial status of these companies is now receiving my attention, and that of the Minister, I would request that your instruction of May 16, 1984, be immediately withdrawn and no further action be taken on this matter unless under my specific instruction.

This was one of the few times where Saleh, on the witness stand, could recall what he did, as follows: "My discussion with Mr. Martin was that a complaint came from a telephone call from one of our staff members of the department. We didn't have a complaint from the public, from any member of the public at that time. We didn't even have the name of the person to whom Mr. Darwish spoke. So it was my opinion that that doesn't really warrant a full-blown investigation."

Instead, Saleh went to one of the people who should have been under investigation—Ken Marlin, the man responsible for the Principal sales staff—and tipped him off. "He assured me that this could happen from time to time," Saleh said. "A zealous employee or new employee could possibly give false information or untrue information, or is very zealous in his way of, you know, providing the information. And that he would do everything possible to prevent a recurrence." Saleh's behaviour was most inappropriate. If normal procedure were followed, Saleh, at a bare minimum, should have followed up his discussion with Marlin with a letter; the department should also have checked back to determine that the misleading practices had stopped. These things didn't happen.

During a subsequent meeting with Pointe, Saleh and others, Barry Martin made it clear there was to be no investigation into the Principal companies because it could draw publicity and endanger their survival. Martin testified that he was afraid that an investigation might cost the companies their licences if it uncovered widespread misleading sales practices. "My reason for doing that was similar to the reason that we didn't do a legislative initiative," Martin said, referring to the 1984 abandonment of amendments to the *Investment Contracts Act*. "If we had started an investigation into this company or into the affairs of this company, it would undoubtedly become a focus of attention, and it would likely lead to a further erosion of the companies' position."

What about consumers who might be lured into buying investment contracts because of false representations made by the salesmen? "Well, I don't think I gave any consideration, in making the decision, to future purchasers," Martin said. "I was more concerned about the ongoing existence of the company."

There was no discussion with either Martin's staff, or with Minister Connie Osterman, about the department's legislated responsibility to protect consumers. "I recall simply advising her that for various reasons the—I had asked the investigators to curtail their investigation," Martin said.

As for Saleh's claim there had been no complaint from "any member of the public," that wasn't true. As we shall see in the next chapter, investors and regulators in several provinces had been complaining for two decades about Principal's sales practices. The month before Blochert's investigation was blocked, Saleh had personally corresponded with British Columbia investor Lloyd Robbins, who complained that he had been misled about the security behind an Associated Investors certificate. As well, Reg Pointe had written John Cormie less than three months earlier, noting complaints from B.C. and Saskatchewan. He had sent a copy of his letter to Saleh.

May 23, 1984

JIM DARWISH WAITED ALMOST A MONTH for his promised meeting with Connie Osterman. Finally, a week after Barry Martin had killed the investigation into Principal sales practices, she called him in. He'd had 24 days to think about his verbal thrashing, and he went prepared for a fight.

"Before I went into the meeting," Darwish said, "it was my intention to either have Mrs. Osterman withdraw her comments, and if she wouldn't, [then] I was going to tell her that I considered that she had effectively fired me and I was going to leave. I took along an agenda and part of that agenda was to discuss the First Investors/Associated Investors situation." Darwish had found his April 24 memo buried in the department files. Martin had marked it "Referred to the Minister" and "No action required." Darwish wanted to talk to her about that.

He went into her office, sat down, and suddenly they were talking about a severance package. "I just can't work with you, Jim," Osterman said. There was no discussion of Principal's financial situation.

"When we met in the morning she was very sweet-voiced and pleasant, and... we never did discuss those items," Darwish said. "I asked her two or three times if she wanted to, because we started to talk about leaving and a package, and that sort of thing. I guess maybe I didn't want to necessarily disrupt that flow, but I was still prepared to because I told her a couple of times I had this agenda and did she want to talk about it, and she didn't."

Darwish, a lifer with the province, was eligible for early retirement. It was decided that he would leave in November, when he turned 55. A severance package was worked out over the next few days.

Martin had completed his 1984 review of Darwish's work on April 17, a couple of weeks before the blowup over Darwish's memo. Martin told Darwish that his performance "was fully satisfactory and you made a very positive contribution to the development and implementation of our strategic planning process and fully supported the implementation of the government's restraint policy." Then why was Darwish squeezed out? Martin testified that he found him skilled, knowledgeable and effective. But Darwish was applying "pressure" to Reg Pointe and Tewfik Saleh, his former assistants. Martin didn't like it.

June 11, 1984

MEMO FROM CONSUMER AFFAIRS AUDITOR Al Hutchison to Burt Eldridge, senior auditor, regarding the $23-million transaction:

> Christa Petracca, C.A., V.P. of Corporate Development informed me that this transfer was made as CDIC was completely unreasonable in regards to the amount of reserves on real estate and mortgages which were required (as they were from Ottawa and didn't understand the situation in Alberta) and as a result they had to transfer these mortgages and real estate to FIC and AIC...
>
> Mrs. Petracca indicated that the Superintendent of Insurance was much more reasonable and understood much better than CDIC the situation in Alberta and as a result could not see any problem with this sale...
>
> I am finding the staff of FIC and AIC (C. Petracca, L. Patrick, John Cormie and A. Campbell) increasingly more difficult to contact and obtain answers to my questions. Either they are very busy or they are reluctant to discuss this transfer.

June 15, 1984

WHILE THE REST OF CANADA tuned in to Ottawa, where Liberals were convening to chose a new national leader, federal regulators climbed on a plane and headed west.

Tewfik Saleh, in his May compliance letter, had called for a meeting with Principal Group officials. The CDIC, hot for a confrontation, decided to attend. It was a high-powered group: Charles de Léry, the CDIC's new chief executive officer; CDIC chief operating officer Jean Pierre Sabourin; Robert Hammond, the federal Superintendent of Insurance; and Denis Sicotte, senior investigations officer in the Department of Insurance.

Hammond, the effective head of the delegation, had been Superintendent for two years. "I'd just come in [in 1982] and the roof fell in," he laughed during an Ottawa interview. Within a few months, the Crown Trust debacle began to unfold, ending in Ontario's seizure of Crown, Greymac and Seaway Trusts in January 1983. The once-lethargic CDIC took a pounding, and emerged battered but grimly determined: no more Mr. Nice Guy. "I've learned a couple of things in my years here," Hammond told me in 1990. "When you think there's a problem with a financial institution you're always right, and the problem usually turns out to be worse than you expected. And the second lesson is that problems don't go away, they just get bigger."

At that time Hammond had a staff of about 30 people responsible for supervising insurance, trust and loans companies and pension plans across the country. The tiny Department of Insurance team, which acted as agent for the CDIC, was woefully inadequate for the amount of work necessary to supervise the dozens of companies under their jurisdiction. (The CDIC, which they served, had only four clerks and a part-time chairman to administer the deposit insurance program.) The fact that four officials took the time to go to Edmonton was a measure of their concern about Principal Trust.

The company was well known to federal regulators. It had quarreled with the CDIC for years, and Chairman de Coster and Sabourin had advised Barry Martin, Tewfik Saleh and Reg Pointe in 1983 that Principal Trust was one of two Alberta trust companies that caused them grave concern. (The other was North West Trust.) The CDIC had imposed a borrowing-to-capital ratio of 15:1 on Principal Trust several years before, and refused repeated requests for an increase because it didn't trust the Cormies.[3]

The day began with an 8 a.m. meeting between federal and provincial officials. Hammond led: First, Ottawa wanted assurances that Alberta wasn't going to force the return of the properties sold by the trust company to First Investors. Failing that, it wanted the trust company to put up $6.3 million to cover the estimated shortfall that would occur if the assets were returned. Second, they were very concerned about Principal Trust's failure to match assets to liabilities.

Hammond passed out copies of the CDIC's most recent report and explained his determination to keep Principal in line. Between 1980 and mid-1984 the CDIC had poured more than a billion dollars into nine failed companies, and it didn't want to cover any more bad debts. If Principal Trust's hazardous investment strategies were successful, its owners would profit, Hammond said. If they failed, the CDIC would be left holding the bag. "And in the end it's the other institutions who finance us who end up paying the bill," he said.

"I know these investment contract companies are outside our jurisdiction," Hammond continued. "But if they fail it's going to impact on Principal Trust, and the CDIC will be on the hook. However, we don't want to do anything that would affect an Alberta financial institution without letting your government know so that if they wish to do so, they can take some action on their own... We want to be sure that your government is aware of what's happening with these companies."

"Our Minister is informed," Martin nodded.

Hammond described the Principal organization as a pyramid, "and if one company goes down, the others will probably be right behind." Darwish commented that parent company Principal Group also appeared in bad financial shape. Exactly,

Hammond said. The situation reminded him of Re-Mor Investment Corp., which went down in Ontario in 1980: the public dealt with one office but their investments were channelled elsewhere, and bad assets were sold between companies to protect the favoured entity. Hammond advised that time was running out for Principal Trust, and that the CDIC would issue a Section 25 notice if matters didn't improve.

The group broke for lunch, then reconvened with the provincial officials, Hammond and Principal in attendance. Donald Cormie wasn't there, but Ken Marlin appeared, accompanied by Christa Petracca, lawyer Lynn Patrick and Cormie's sons John and Jaimie. It was a tense meeting, with voices raised and fists pounded on the table. Marlin launched an offensive: Tewfik Saleh's May 11 letter was based on unreliable appraisals—"Appraisals don't mean a thing in a dead market like this!"—and could create panic among Principal's clients. "You don't want to give us grounds to sue you, do you?" Marlin asked a wide-eyed Saleh. "Financial institutions need public confidence to survive, and a letter like that could do us a lot of harm."

Marlin admitted there were some problems with the mortgage portfolio, "but we'll be able to work it out if you just give us some time." Then Jaimie spoke up: the company was working on a confidential transaction with Carma Ltd., a Calgary real estate development company. The deal had something to do with a bank in the Carribean, and was going to solve a lot of problems. His explanation was vague and rambling; the Alberta regulators couldn't understand what he was talking about. Then Petracca tossed a bombshell. More than a month earlier, without advising the province, the contract companies had stopped declaring additional credits on some of the investment contracts. "It's going to save us about $12 million," she said cheerfully.

"What the hell!" Darwish gasped.

"We're well within our rights to do this," Marlin said. "Credits are declared at the discretion of the board of directors. If we can't afford the credits, we don't have to pay them."

"Have you told the contract holders the credits aren't being declared?"

"Well, no."

On May 8, the additional credits for all certificates maturing after April 1, 1985, had been retroactively cancelled from the beginning of 1984. The maturity date was distant enough that investors wouldn't learn about the cancellation for at least a year. Credits on earlier-maturing certificates continued to be declared, and new purchasers continued to be told they would get additional credits when their contracts matured.

"This isn't right!" Darwish sputtered. "What's going to happen to FIC when the public finds out? You're talking about public confidence and then you do a thing like this?"

"Relax, we're going to pay them eventually."

Several times, Saleh asked Marlin how much capital Principal was willing to put in to support the contract companies. "None at all," was the answer. That's how it was left: no threat to pull the licences if capital wasn't injected, no pressure to correct the $72-million shortfall identified in Saleh's May 11 letter.

At the end of the day, the provincial and federal officials reconvened, *sans* Principal. The feds repeated the point they'd made that morning. They wanted to be protected, one way or another, from the consequences of the property transfer, and they wanted the trust company's other problems addressed. Then they rushed to the airport and caught a plane back to Ottawa.

On Monday, the CDIC couriered a letter to John Cormie, calling for a $2-million reserve on mortgages remaining in the trust company, and another $6.4-million reserve to cover the assets it had transferred to the contract companies. Marlin immediately phoned Hammond to say that Principal Group was willing to put up $6 million while the property transfer was being resolved.

In the Alberta government offices, Darwish was still seething about the Friday meeting. He vented his frustration in a memo to Martin, copied to Saleh:

> They had no written reply to the letter and simply discussed, in a vague way, a number of transactions that might be taking place that they assumed would satisfy us... In my opinion, this method of selectively deciding which investment contract will receive an additional credit is aimed at ensuring that the public does not find out that the company is no longer able to declare additional credits for all investment contracts. It was estimated at the meeting that there are approximately $100 million worth of such contracts. Company officials admitted they have not advised any contract holders of the new policy. The reason for the new policy is that there is not sufficient income to pay the expense of the additional credits.
>
> The company takes the position that while they are not declaring additional credits, it is still their intention to pay them. This, of course, is sheer speculation. The company knows about this change. Our department now knows about the change. The only people who do not know are those who are affected, namely, the investment contract holders.
>
> While the company took the position that knowledge of the failure to declare additional credits would not seriously affect their operation, I find this hard to believe. Even so, I don't think that it is proper for the company to continue to operate on this basis and I believe it should not be allowed to sell contracts on the basis that they will pay additional contracts when they are not doing so for all contracts. I also believe that company officials should be advised they must inform all contract holders, that they are not having additional credits declared.

Hammond called Darwish that day from Ottawa to tell him that Marlin had agreed to put up the $6 million. "You'll want to know the exact source of funds," Hammond advised. "You want to be sure that they aren't directly or indirectly coming from the investment contract companies." Darwish made several unsuccessful attempts during the day to see Martin and pass on the news. The following morning he sent a hand-written note down the hall.

That afternoon, a Tuesday, Alberta continued to meet with Principal. This time only Ken Marlin and Jaimie Cormie showed up; but Marlin, finally, delivered a formal reply to Saleh's letter of May 11. Largely written by Donald Cormie, it made the same points covered on Friday. Saleh, it claimed, had made a dreadful mistake with his May demands, which were based on false assumptions and overly conservative property appraisals. He was "erroneously" treating the contract companies as if they were deposit-taking institutions (such as trust companies), when they were more like life insurance firms. Thus, Saleh was in error in establishing a borrowing-to-capital ratio at all. There was a vague reference to a just-completed deal "with a benefit of several million dollars to First Investors. To reverse the tendering transaction at this time would not, in our opinion, serve any good purpose and it is questionable if it would in fact be legally possible in any event, since some of the properties are now gone."

The letter also addressed demands that subordinated notes be converted to permanent capital: "[This] requires serious consideration. Locking the funds in as capital will automatically make it more difficult to attract further funds. It is our understanding that shareholders' subordinated loans are an acceptable form of capital and are used by other financial institutions."

This is delightful bafflegab. "Further funds" would of course come from the shareholders—the Cormies and Marlin—so this passage translates as: "Locking the funds in as capital will automatically make us more reluctant to give these companies any more money." (In the case of a note, it was always possible to have the company pay back the loan, freeing the cash for use elsewhere. As capital, it was there permanently—and earning no interest.) The passage was a veiled threat: *We put the money in our way, by subordinated note, or the companies get nothing from us.*

During the Tuesday afternoon meeting, Marlin indicated that Principal Group was prepared to put up a $4.5-million subordinated note to First Investors as security against any lawsuits contract holders might bring against the company as a result of the $23-million property transfer.

About this time, the Alberta officials met separately to discuss the legality of the $23-million transaction. During the Friday morning meeting with federal officials, Saleh had said he wanted the deal reversed. During the private provincial meeting, he took a different line: it was his opinion that the sale could not be reversed, based on the opinion received from the Attorney General's office. This comes from a memo to file written by Darwish, which continues:

I asked Mr. Saleh if he had confirmed his legal opinion with the Attorney General's Department as it related to FIC and he stated that he had not done so because he was satisfied.

I emphasized that he should be very careful about this matter because if it should turn out that he was wrong and there were Statements of Claim filed by disgruntled investment contract holders, that the government could be subject to large losses. Eventually, Mr. Saleh and Mr. Martin left the meeting and returned to state that they had phoned [Sydney] Bercov of Emery Jamieson and that they were going to get his opinion as to whether the transaction could be reversed or not.

There was a final meeting with the company on Wednesday, attended by auditor Bruce Pennock. Challenged by provincial auditors on the mortgage reserve figures he had established for First Investors and Associated Investors, Pennock said he had obtained appraisals on a dozen properties and retained A.E. LePage to do a "verbal evaluation." He had not received anything in writing from the real estate company. (The auditors were aghast: a verbal appraisal isn't worth the paper it's not written on. As for written appraisals, they depended on what instructions the appraiser had been given. This dispute would continue for months.)

During the meeting it was agreed, after a phone call to Ottawa, that Principal Group would inject $6.3 million in additional capital into the trust company in the form of, yes, subordinated notes, "to appease CDIC"[4] in the event the $23-million transaction was reversed.

The next afternoon Saleh met with Sydney Bercov and dumped his worries into the Edmonton lawyer's lap. Bercov agreed to consider the legality of the $23-million transfer, as well as the conflicting valuations of mortgages and real estate, and said he'd get back to Saleh in a couple of weeks. It would take four months.

June 29, 1984: Section 25

UNLIKE THEIR ALBERTA COUNTERPARTS, the federal regulators could not be put off by complaints, demands and specious arguments. A week and a half after their visit to Edmonton, they issued the Section 25 notice. CDIC chief Charles de Léry wrote that Principal's argumentative response to the severe mismatch situation and to the CDIC's objection to the capitalization of interest on mortgages in arrears was unacceptable. After several deductions and adjustments to the borrowing base, "we estimate the company's borrowings of approximately $145.2 million represent 43.8 times its adjusted borrowing base." As for the $23-million transfer of properties to the contract companies, de Léry ordered the trust company's borrowing base by reduced by the $6.3-million reserve which would have been required if the transaction had not taken place. The company had 30 days to correct its "unsound business and financial practices."

The clock was running.

9

Under the Principal umbrella

B Y THE MID-1980s, SALESMAN DON SLATER had grown weary of incessant phone calls from fuss-budget clients worried about the safety of their investments. Some called again and again, drawn by Principal's extraordinary interest rates, but confused about the guarantees Slater insisted made the investments as safe as the Rock of Gibraltar, as secure as the Government of Canada.

Impatient at the drain on his time, Slater nonetheless did his best to ease his clients' minds. In kitchens and living rooms throughout southern Alberta he cited the prosperous history of Principal's contract companies, preached the Principal concept of thrift and extolled the financial prescience of Donald Cormie.

The investment contracts, backed by the entire $1-billion Principal conglomerate, were safer than federally-insured RRSPs, Slater explained. The CDIC only covered deposits up to $60,000 and was going bankrupt anyway, he claimed, waving newspaper articles which detailed the CDIC's difficulties. But the investment contracts, Slater said, were regulated separately under Alberta's *Investment Contracts Act*, and were guaranteed 104% no matter what the sum.

"He used to become agitated with me, and say: 'Marjorie, how many times do I have to tell you your money is safe?'" testified retired Calgary nurse Marjorie Given. "I think he was quite annoyed with us wanting all this assurance. He said: 'You won't get anyone more conservative than the Hutterites, and they have $50 million with us.' And I thought, well, that sounds pretty good."

Alarmed at the collapse of several Alberta financial institutions during the early 1980s, Marjorie and her husband William queried Slater repeatedly about Principal's involvement in the province's real estate market. Slater flourished company literature and fawning media reports, assuring them that "Mr. Cormie, 'in all his great wisdom'—and that's a quote—had got out of all real estate holdings in 1980 and 81." It all sounded, Marjorie said, pretty good.

Gerald Heffernan, a retired railroad conductor, had been dealing with Slater since 1979. In all those years, he testified, he was never told he had the option of purchasing a CDIC-insured term deposit from Principal's trust company. Early in 1984, as a maturing investment contract came due, Heffernan visited the Principal Trust office in downtown Calgary to talk with Slater. "I asked Don how safe my investments with Principal were, and I mentioned to him that Crown Trust was having trouble. He said, 'I see you are reading the paper again, Gerry.' And I says, 'Well, I am getting a little too much money in here...to feel real comfortable when I read things like this.' And he says, 'Well, you haven't got a worry in the world, your investments are absolutely secure.'

"He agreed with me that, no, I wasn't covered under the CDIC, but he says, 'You are covered.'

"And I says, 'Am I? If so, how?'

"And he says, 'You are covered under the *Canadian and British Insurance Companies Act*. And furthermore, you are doubly covered because we have to have assets on deposit with the government equal to the assets that you hold with us.' He mentioned something about matching dollar for dollar with my investments, along with the government. He says, 'My God, Gerry, you know we are worth close to a billion dollars, our firm.' "

Listening to the evening news in June 1987, the Givens learned to their horror that Principal's contract companies had collapsed. They checked their certificates: $86,000 in First Investors and Associated Investors. In the Heffernan home, a scramble through the records also confirmed the worst: Heffernan and his wife Marguerite had invested $81,500.

Six weeks later, most of the rest of the Principal conglomerate went down. The Givens, persuaded by Slater that the contract companies' failure was an isolated event with no impact on the rest of the empire, had another $125,000 (the proceeds of the sale of their family home) in a Principal Group promissory note. The couple now expect to receive only about $130,000 of the total $211,000 they entrusted to Principal.

"We had all the faith in the world in Mr. Slater," Marjorie said. "We were dealing with a financial expert and he knew we were nervous investors. We thought if there was any risk in this...he would surely, surely tell us."

ONE-STOP SHOPPING: an inspired concept. Run an ad for the trust company—fail-safe and "CDIC-insured." Then, when they're through the door, spread out the rest of the wares. Sell them an investment certificate, a promissory note, mutual funds, savings and chequing accounts. Lend them money through the trust company to buy the mutual funds; that way there's interest on the loan as well as administration fees. It was a financial supermarket for the unsophisticated: Just toss their purchases into a basket and steer them to the cash register. Keep it as simple as they'll let you; a confused client is a lost sale. If they don't ask, why would you want to tell them?

On February 28, 1984, Richard Duma arrived at Principal Plaza, newspaper ad in hand, to purchase a $5,500 CDIC-insured RRSP with Principal Trust. He came out with a First Investors term certificate for 11.75%—a quarter of a percentage point higher than the rate that had attracted him. His wife Marilyn made the same journey, with the same result, later the same day. Each was referred by a receptionist to an "investment consultant."

"I told him I wanted to take out an RRSP and showed him the ad and told him that's what I wanted," Marilyn said. "I told him I don't want to gamble. I'm not a gambler." The Dumas, who owned a small construction firm, never realized they'd bought investment contracts. They continued to purchase certificates for the next three years, and had a total of $20,000 locked in when First Investors went down. They didn't learn until the collapse that their investments were uninsured. They never knew the additional credits on their certificates were cancelled in May 1984— three months after they signed their first contracts.

Robert Wheaton, a building contractor from Victoria, B.C., knew he wasn't getting a CDIC-insured investment, but believed a salesman who told him there were sufficient funds "in the vault" at the Royal Bank to cover every dollar placed in the investment contract. Wheaton had bought two Principal Trust RRSPs in previous years, then was persuaded to invest $1,750 in First Investors in February 1987. The salesman said that Alberta legislation required the company to lodge $1.04 in a government-approved institution for every dollar invested.

"He presented me with a brochure which on the front page says 'Principal Term Certificates, Flexibility, Competitive Rates and More!' Down at the bottom it says 'Offered by First Investors Corporation and Associated Investors of Canada.' And I don't think at the time I paid very much attention to the names of these companies, they meant nothing to me. All I knew was that I was talking about a Principal term certificate.

"He then opened the brochure and laid it in front of me. And under the panel that is headed with the word 'Security,' he explained to me that this particular investment format was controlled by government regulation, it was the same type of fund that the life insurance companies of Canada used from one side of the country to the other, that the funds were deposited with a government approved custodian. And he said, 'In our case, we use the Royal Bank of Canada.' And he said, 'We are required by law to deposit dollar for dollar the amount that you invest with us. Now,' he said, 'we improve on that.'

"He said, 'We deposit a dollar four for every dollar that you invest with us.' He said, 'It is completely guaranteed.' He said, 'The money is in the Royal Bank.' He said, 'It's in the vault. You can look at it any time you want.'

"He reached over with his pen and underlined the word 'must.' He said, 'We are required to keep that money with the Royal Bank.'

"And so I then proceeded to ask him a few questions about it. I said, 'The rate that you are offering is 10%, and you are telling me that you deposit a dollar four for every dollar that's invested, and what about the other 6%?'

"And he said, 'Well, Bob, you must remember that you are dealing with the Principal Group here.' I can't remember whether he said Principal Group, but he said, 'You are dealing with Principal Trust or the Principal Group,' and he said, 'You know, you don't think that they are ever going to let you down on that 6%.' And I sort of shrugged my shoulders and agreed that probably that wouldn't be a likely situation. He said, 'You know, the bulk of this, the dollar four, is maintained at the Royal Bank of Canada.' And he said, 'You know, they are not likely to fail.' And he said, 'My God, if the Royal Bank fails, we are all in trouble.' And I sort of laughed and said, 'Yes, I guess that's true.' So it was on that basis that I decided to go ahead and put this money into this other plan."

Warehouseman Lawrence Gallucci got a similar story from his Principal salesman in Saskatoon, Saskatchewan. "He told me, his exact words were: 'We don't carry CDIC, but we have something that is far superior. We have a—what we call a dollar for dollar. For every dollar you invest with us, we have to have another dollar on deposit in a bank in Edmonton... We really don't want to do it, but we are forced by Alberta law, government law to do this.'

"And he also mentioned to me that in case of failure, you could always recoup your principal investment. But he also said, the likelihood of Principal ever going bankrupt is very unlikely because all their money is in—the majority of their money is invested in government bonds. Now he didn't mention what type. And he says, 'Credit unions and banks lend money to farmers and businesses, but we don't do that. The majority is in government bonds, so the likelihood of ever coming to this point would be just about never.' "

Gallucci and his wife had $150,000 in First Investors and Associated Investors when the companies went down.

Edmonton fire-protection salesman Hubert Ouimet and his wife had approximately $150,000 in Associated Investors when it collapsed. Ouimet was led to believe that the company was backed by the full resources of the Principal Group. "We were told these [investments] would be placed in different rooms of the same house under the same roof and that in these different rooms our money would be more viable."

Retired Edmonton secretary Edna Pollard and her husband had $52,000 in the contract companies. They were also told the companies were required to deposit their full investment plus 4% "in the form of assets," held by the Royal Bank. "We felt—you know, we were proud to be Albertans and we wanted to put our money in a good Alberta-based company and this is why we chose Principal."

The Pollards were asked to write cheques for their investments to Principal Plans, and therefore believed their money was "under the Principal umbrella." Mrs. Pollard's salesman assured her there were no investments in mortgages or real estate. "'No, no, absolutely not. Donald Cormie is too smart to do that!' he said. 'He would never invest in real estate.' "

Calgarian Ruth Hogue had almost $46,000 in First Investors when it collapsed. In February 1984, when the young widow first invested in the company, a salesman described it as "just a branch of Principal that they put their term deposits in," Hogue said. "He also told me it was insured by the 'British North American Insurance Companies Act'. He told me it was insured by that, and that was an insurance that trust companies and insurance companies belonged to."

In December 1985, Hogue received a letter from Principal Trust:

> Through placing your investments and confidence in Principal, we are pleased to place our confidence in you by providing you with an automatic line of credit of $10,000... No personal guarantees or other collateral is required. Your present investments with us are all you need...
> JUST WRITE A CHEQUE AND IT'S YOURS.
> THAT'S FLEXIBILITY—
> THAT'S SERVICE—
> THAT'S PRINCIPAL.

The letter encouraged her to visit the Principal Trust Office—"Ask for the Trust Manager or any of our Trust Staff, and within minutes, you will enjoy the financial services freedom you deserve..." It was signed by the general manager of Principal Trust, George Aboussafy. At the bottom, in capital letters, were the words: *MEMBER OF CANADA DEPOSIT INSURANCE CORPORATION.*

At that time Hogue's only investment "in Principal" was her contract with First Investors. The letter reinforced her impression that her money was "under the Principal umbrella."

In 1986, when the certificate matured, Hogue intended to transfer her money to another institution. She explained to a Principal salesman that she was concerned about the failures of other financial companies. "So he said to me, 'Well, the reason why those companies ran into trouble was they had too much invested in real estate and oil and gas.' He assured me that they had gotten out of that before the decline in the economy. And so, you know, he went on about it and he told me about how in First Investors, you had the backing of the whole Principal Group of Companies. And he said, 'The whole world would have to turn upside-down before anything would happen to your investment.' ... He also said that after they pulled out of the real estate when they did, they put their money into government bonds and blue chip stocks and secured investments."

Hogue, too, was told that *Investment Contracts Act* guarantee was better than CDIC insurance, "and he also mentioned that CDIC was in debt by billions of dollars and who was to say that CDIC wouldn't go bankrupt, you know, any time." Impressed by the pitch, she rolled her money back in for another two years.

Parminder Dhillon, a partsman in the oil industry from Medicine Hat, Alberta, was also told his money was going into the Royal Bank. "I asked him, 'Well, what do they do with it?' He said, 'All your money is kept in a vault, like in a bag with your name on it.' And I says, 'What happens if the company goes under?' He says, 'Well, you don't have to worry, your money is there.' He says, 'Plus, you got the certificate saying that it's guaranteed by the government.' "

Dhillon and his brother Gurdev had about $24,000 in the contract companies, including $17,000 invested just three weeks before the collapse.

In St. John's, Newfoundland, provincial engineer Morgan Hinchey was drawn to the Principal Trust office in 1982 by an ad in the local *Evening Telegram*. That year, and in 1983, he bought term deposits with Principal Trust, but by late 1983, as the original investments matured, they were rolled over into First Investors. "First Investors to me, until they went into liquidation, was just an investment arm, so far as I was concerned, of Principal," Hinchey testified. "Principal is the people we were dealing with, as far as I was concerned."

By 1985, Hinchey's stake in First Investors had grown to $78,000. Concerned he had passed the CDIC's $60,000 insurance limit, he asked his Principal "consultant" about putting half the money in another institution. The salesman protested, and Hinchey learned his money wasn't protected by the CDIC at all. "He said your investments are covered 100%, we have got them covered under insurance in Alberta, under the *Investment Contracts Act*," Hinchey said.

Hinchey and his wife Barbara had about $58,000 with First Investors in mid-June 1987 when another term deposit for about $10,000 came due. Pressured by their salesman, they rolled it over into a First Investors certificate as well. A week later the company was dead. "I honestly believed the man knew what he was talking about and that my money was insured," Hinchey said. "You would have to be a lunatic to put money with somebody with no insurance... If it was explained to me, your interest rates will be a little higher, an eighth of a percent or half a percent, but there is no insurance, you have to be out of your mind completely, to give somebody $60,000, $70,000 when she could go bottom up tomorrow and not get a cent back. If somebody had explained that to me in the beginning, he wouldn't have got a cent."

Everywhere that Principal operated the stories were the same. Lies about the safety of the investment contracts, lies about investment and value of the assets, lies that some entity other than the contract companies themselves guaranteed the investments.

In 1987, soon after the Principal collapse, the British Columbia government appointed Lyman Robinson, former dean of the University of Victoria law school, to investigate Principal's sales practices. Robinson conducted formal hearings in several cities, distributed questionnaires, conducted interviews and reached a number of stunning conclusions. Over half the 2,000 people who returned questionnaires were over 60 years of age. They didn't regard themselves as investors but as "savers" looking for a secure place to keep retirement funds. Some of them had transferred money from a chartered bank or other CDIC-insured institution to Principal, Robinson said.

> There were often several reasons why they transferred their funds to Principal. In some cases, there is no doubt they were involved in "interest rate shopping," but this was usually done on the assumption that they were comparing interest rates among financial institutions which offered the same form of security...

The assumption that "Principal" offered the same financial security as other financial institutions was often the product of representations which were made by the Principal consultants or sales personnel.

Almost half of those who replied to Robinson's questionnaire believed their First Investors/Associated Investors certificates were insured by CDIC. Some had been specifically assured of this; others had asked for a CDIC-insured product and naturally assumed their request had been honoured. Some were told the presence of a CDIC decal on the premises meant that all investments sold there were covered. A fifth of the respondents had their investments rolled over from the trust company to one of the contract companies, often after an unenlightening telephone conversation with a salesman, but believed their investment remained CDIC-insured.

Still others, aware that CDIC wasn't in the picture, were told their investments were simply "insured." Some received no details about the nature of that insurance. Over half were told that Principal Group Ltd., "Principal Group" or the "Principal Group of Companies" guaranteed or insured their investment; another quarter were told that it was guaranteed by Principal Trust. A third were told the contracts were insured or guaranteed by a chartered bank, or by the Bank of Canada.

Some were told they were insured or guaranteed by the Alberta government.

Others, confused by a passing reference to the *Canadian and British Insurance Companies Act*—or misled as a result of their salesman's own confusion about its role—believed their certificate was insured under the Act, or under something called the "British North American Insurance Company" or the "International Insurance Fund." Several people were told that First Investors and Associated Investors were the same as an insurance company; or that their investments were as safe as those with an insurance company; or that the companies were governed by the same law as insurance companies.

Some were told that the guarantee offered by the contract companies was as good or better than that offered by the CDIC.

Most appalling, an incredible 38% believed their investment was secure because their funds—104%—were kept *on deposit* with a chartered bank.

Where did all these outrageous stories come from?

For the most part they were delivered by Principal salesmen. But in many cases, Inspector Bill Code concluded, the lies could be traced up the line to sales vice-president Ken Marlin, and ultimately to Donald Cormie. In his report Code identified half a dozen areas of "disinformation," and concluded:

...the evidence tends to show a grand plan to cover up the problems [First Investors], [Associated Investors] and [Principal Group Ltd.] had encountered... both Donald Cormie and Marlin, through their involvement in sales and marketing, perpetuated the "disinformation" that these three companies, and indeed the Group, were not only healthy but facing a bright future...

Code found that the evidence also tended to show that to the knowledge of at least Cormie and Marlin, "the sales force was selling FIC and AIC term certificates to the public when those companies were no longer viable and indeed, were insolvent" and that "deliberately permitted the companies to carry on while he took steps to disguise their true financial situation."

> The evidence tends to show that a deliberate effort was made by Donald Cormie and Marlin to hide the real estate and mortgage crisis facing the Group and lead investors to believe that the Group, including [First Investors] and [Associated Investors], had escaped the effects of the real estate collapse.

Code also concluded that Principal's cross-selling practices amounted in some instances to "bait and switch" tactics: "The effect of the Group's practices was to blur distinctions between the companies in the Group, their products and their features, with the result that some investors did not know which company they contracted with or the nature of the product they purchased."

These distinctions were systematically blurred in several ways.

Clients responding to a Principal Trust ad ended up at a "Principal Financial Centre", a one-stop retail outlet which housed both the trust company and Principal Consultants Ltd., Principal's sales arm. They were routinely handed over to a Principal "consultant," who posed as "the person from Principal." Few clients realized they were no longer dealing with a trust company employee, and salesmen rarely set them straight. There was usually no visible demarcation between the two operations to let a customer know he'd crossed over from the trust company to a sales company. The salesman would complete an application form, ask the investor to sign, then request a cheque payable, usually, to "Principal Plans." When the cancelled cheque was returned from the customer's bank, its markings indicated it had been deposited to the credit of Principal Trust.

Assurances that investments in the contract companies were "guaranteed" and "secure" and "safe" abounded in the corporate literature. Marlin testified that he felt justified in using the word "guarantee"—a "good word" to use with clients— because others in the investment business did so.

Complaints about these assurances went back to at least 1963, when Jim Darwish wrote a memo which concluded:

> The only real claim an investment contract certificate has to a place in one's savings portfolio is that it produces a fixed guaranteed rate of return. This guarantee is, of course, only as good as the company's management, investment policy and supervision by the government over its affairs. The fact that these companies are government supervised and controlled pursuant to the terms of the *Investment Contracts Act* is likely the strongest part of a salesman's pitch. I know this to be true, because of the number of telephone calls received from the public asking the Commission to confirm this representation and to give assurance that an investment is absolutely safe.

The propriety of using the word "guarantee" was debated for many years, without resolution.

In 1978, sales practices became a major issue when Mrs. M. Becze of Edmonton was sold two investment contracts totalling $35,000 on the understanding they were issued by Principal Trust and insured by CDIC. When she complained, branch manager Jack Gelber wrote Becze a letter on trust company letterhead, claiming that Associated Investors complied with "regulations set by the *Investment Contracts Act* and the British North America Insurance Act which protects our investors, in our opinion, to the same extent." There is, of course, no such thing as the British North America Insurance Act. The relevant legislation, called the *Canadian and British Insurance Companies Act (Canada)*, is simply referred to in the *Investment Contracts Act* as the place to look for identification of the sort of securities that contract companies might invest in.

Gelber and Marlin were summoned to the Consumer Affairs office and severely dressed down by Darwish. Marlin assured Darwish (in the company of Reg Pointe, then the department's chief financial analyst), that the mistake was an isolated incident and would not happen again. He promised that investment contracts would not be represented as secured by the *Investment Contracts Act* or the *Canadian and British Insurance Companies Act*. Later that year, Darwish learned from Bill Irwin, B.C.'s Superintendent of Brokers, that he had ordered an investigation into similar complaints there.

In his report Code found that, despite promises to the contrary, Marlin continued to direct the sales force to emphasize the "government protections" required by the *Investment Contracts Act* that made the investment contracts "safe" and "secure." He also continued to encourage his sales team to think of the contract companies as similar to insurance companies. An information sheet on the *Canadian and British Insurance Companies Act* provided by the company to salesmen advises: "This acts as a type of insurance on deposits," and goes on to suggest the Act guarantees 104% of a term certificate "for any amount." Neither claim is accurate.

In February 1979, a few months after the Becze and Irwin incidents, Marlin issued a directive instructing salesmen to tell clients that only First Investors and Associated Investors "guaranteed" the investment certificates. But, he continued, the companies' assets were invested in securities and mortgages that qualified under the *Canadian and British Companies Act*, "the same as any Canadian Life Insurance Company."

> Sometimes too much explanation only leads to confusion and doubts, but it is important to point out that CDIC is only applicable to deposit-accepting companies, like banks and trust companies, and that Life Insurance and Investment Contract companies that accept funds under contract do not have and do not require any outside insurance of guarantee. The capital reserve and custodian requirements, as well as the quality of investments set out in the *Investment Contract Act* makes an investment with First Investors or Associated Investors a conservative safe investment.

Several months later, Grant Mitchell, at that time Marlin's executive assistant, wrote a memo warning that regulatory authorities were "making test calls to determine what explanations are being used" about the guarantee behind the investment contracts. Mitchell instructed sales staff not to discuss the guarantee over the phone, but to "simply emphasize the 'safety' of the investment and ask them to come in to the office for greater clarification." Once in the office, clients should be told the *Investment Contracts Act* regulated the investments "in the same way that Canadian Life Insurance Company investments are regulated."

In subsequent years Marlin issued or approved product information indicating that assets equal to 100% of certificate liabilities were required to be on deposit with a custodian. That claim was prominently displayed on the contract application form, and was instrumental in persuading clients of the investment's safety. Marlin knew that salesmen—and many of their supervisors—understood the claim to mean that principal, or principal plus 4%, was on deposit, and he did not disabuse them.

In fact, there never ever was enough on deposit to match even investors' principal. Under the Section 8 tests of the obsolete *Investment Contracts Act*, a registered company was required, first, to hold on deposit in a Canadian chartered bank "qualified assets" worth at least the amount for which the company "is liable as of that time to pay in cash to the holders of all its investment contracts then outstanding"; second, to maintain "reserves" which, if invested at an assumed rate of interest, would yield the amount owed to the investor at the end of the term; and third, to maintain "unimpaired capital" of $500,000.

The first test, the basis of the claim that the contract companies maintained "qualified assets in excess of 100% of the cash surrender value of all certificates at all times," originated in the era of installment certificates, when customers paid in a sum of money each week or month for a certain number of years. Those certificates indeed had a "cash surrender value"—an early cash-in value in case the client needed his money before the certificate had matured. That value was significantly less than the amount of money the client had actually paid in. However, the term deposits which the investment contract companies had sold since the mid-1970s were locked in; they could not be cashed in early, and thus had no "cash surrender value" whatsoever. Thus the cash surrender value of all those hundreds of millions of dollars of contracts was close to *zero*. The only assets the companies needed to have on hand to exceed "cash surrender value" was enough money to pay out the certificates maturing in the next 30 days.

The second test, the maintenance of reserves, was the only test capable of providing any real protection to contract holders—but it too had been subverted in the 1970s by the movement toward higher and higher interest rates.

The "assumed rate" of the reserve, to be approved by the Superintendent of Insurance, was supposed to be established on the basis of what the company could reasonably be anticipated to earn by investing the assets. From the very early days, the reserve rate used by the Principal investment contract companies was 6%. That rate was established when the market rate was about 4% or 5%—close to the rate "guaranteed" by the contracts. A reserve of 6% assumed that the companies could earn 6% on the money they had borrowed from the public at 4%; thus the companies were given a 1% or 2% advantage, and there was money left over after the required reserves were established to allow the companies to pay sales commissions and other operating costs. As with life insurance companies, the reserves were intended to ensure that a contract company maintained at least the minimum assets necessary to meet its liabilities as they fell due. If the company made extra money, after meeting its own expenses, then profits could be passed on to shareholders and clients: In the case of insurance companies, by declaring dividends; in the case of contract companies, by declaring "additional credits."

These additional credits were intended to be declared by a company when it knew a profit had been made; but by the end of the 1970s, with the market pressure of ever-upwards interest rates, the additional credits were promised when clients purchased the contracts. Their interest was promised in the form of a 4% "guaranteed rate" plus another 6% to 14% in additional credits; but the expected return was the full 10% to 18%.

The companies should logically have been reserving assets sufficient to pay clients the full interest and credits when their certificates matured; and they should logically have been increasing the "guaranteed rate" on their certificates to the full promised interest. But they did neither. They continued to "guarantee" only the 4%.

Let's look at how reserve calculations are made. If a one-year term certificate of $1,000 was sold at an interest rate of, say, 15%, then assets would have to be reserved in an amount which at an assumed rate would yield $1,150 at the end of the year. If the company "reserved flat" at 15%, the entire $1,000 would have to be invested. With a guaranteed rate of 4%, a $1,000 one-year First Investors term certificate would be "guaranteeing" the payment of $1,040 at the end of the year (even though it had promised between $1,100 and $1,200). A calculation using the 6% reserve rate—the rate used by Principal—shows that the sum that must be invested at the beginning of the year at 6% to yield $1,040 is $981.13.

Subtract that $981.13 from the $1,000 originally handed over by the client, and there is a balance of $18.87 which, under the perverted logic of Alberta's *Investment Contracts Act*, the company was free to dispose of as it chose. And it left the company with the insurmountable challenge of generating a profit of more than 17% on the $981.13 worth of reserved assets—at a time when the investment market was in decline and half the Principal contract companies' assets were generating no income at all.

Disaster might have been averted—or at least allayed—if the balance of $18.87 had been left in the companies and also invested, ultimately paying investors their additional credits. It was not. Instead, that money—almost 2% of every dollar invested—was immediately creamed off the top for sales commissions, administration fees and a little something called "term surplus."

The following table shows how that $18.87 was distributed by the contract companies (as detailed in a company submission to the province in June 1987):

Distribution Costs
of a $1,000 one-year Term Certificate

salesman's commission $2.25
sales managers 95
administration fee (Principal Group Ltd.) 5.20
agency (Principal Savings & Trust Ltd.) 10
head sales office (Principal Consultants Ltd.) 50

Subtotal 9.00
"SURPLUS" 9.87

Total $18.87

Thus $9.87 in "surplus funds" was drained from every $1,000 investment contract and poured directly into Principal Group. No good reason has ever been offered for diverting this "surplus," about 1% of every investment contract sold, from the contract companies. Donald Cormie explained at the Code inquiry that the cash went to Principal Group as a matter of "policy," and he tried to justify the payment "because it was just part of the administrative costs going to Principal Group." No satisfactory explanation emerged as to what administrative costs were supposed to be covered, especially given that administration fees were already being paid.

The public was never told anything about reserves, administration fees or surplus. Under the *Investment Contracts Act* the contract application form was supposed to include information about the reserve rate, but it did not.

Despite this situation, contract company brochures declared: "More Benefits... No Fees—All your money goes to work for you!"

The third financial test in the Act—the maintenance of $500,000 in unimpaired capital—was also horridly inadequate.

The $500,000 was intended to act as a cushion, in case of a decline in value of company assets—but with contract obligations worth hundreds of millions of dollars, a decline in value of only a fraction of a percentage point would wipe the cushion out. Nonetheless, Ken Marlin promoted this $500,000 capital requirement as another of the government's protections.

Marlin also told his staff that there was no CDIC protection for the investment contracts because it had not been "considered necessary"—despite the fact that in 1982 he had personally approached the CDIC in hope of obtaining federal insurance for First Investors and Associated Investors. (He was turned down.) Since then sales staff had been routinely provided copies of any newspaper article detailing the CDIC's financial difficulties.

Salesmen's business cards described them as "financial consultants" and "account executives." They were represented by the company as a well-trained professional group "backed by the expertise of our investment, tax and legal departments." In fact, the sales division was a high-pressure boiler-room operation where staff were trained to wring the last dollar possible out of their clients.

Marlin's team carefully sifted through many job applicants to identify the special few who would succeed in the Principal environment. "I used to call them 'winners,'" Marlin testified, "someone who had a high level of energy, who wanted to have money and was highly disciplined with ego and empathy. If you could find that individual, your chances of having a successful salesman were exceptionally good." The candidates were run through a training course which focused not on the products themselves, but on Principal and the Cormie myth: "What the mission of the company was, what it stood for, who was behind it and why it was good for the world," Marlin said. They were taught the big picture, the-world-according-to-Cormie, "and if you couldn't paint or get the big picture accepted, that was the end of the training."

Those who passed the initial indoctrination then received a product orientation "to emphasize what services we made available to the public and how those services, again, made a contribution to society and to the community and to the individual. We found it very important for the potential salesman to believe in the philosophy. In the early stages, many of our salespeople attributed their success not to the product, not to the interest rate, but to the fact that they, themselves, had applied the philosophy, were living what they were preaching. They believed in thrift and they were on a crusade."

The salesmen were trained to "sell Principal," to attract clients by touting the quality and financial strengths of the "Principal Group of Companies." As one area manager testified, they were taught to promote the entire conglomerate: "Everything, right to the ranch." Once the whole was sold, individual products were easily moved.

The company had not strayed far from the manipulative tactics of Ab Coyne's "pots and pan" days: get your foot in the door, stroke like crazy, do a fast psychological/financial assessment of the target, choose your weapon and go in for the kill. *The Richest Man in Babylon* was still an essential part of the sales kit, as was the gospel of "thrift."

Recruits were issued verbatim scripts introducing the three "basic laws" of thrift: A part of all you earn is yours to keep; pay yourself first; there is no better time to starting saving than now. Sample presentations enabled salesmen to overcome client resistance in dozens of situations. "I go through some of the sales material today, and I see those same phrases from 30 years ago still being used," Marlin testified. "We found that was very valuable in controlling how things were explained. And only once they had mastered that could they move on to learn the next step."

To the most obvious question, "How do I know your company is safe?" salesmen were taught to say:

> That's a fair question. But when corporations such as Principal, the banks and the life insurance companies go broke, then the Government will have failed and it won't matter where you have saved.
>
> How do I know the bank will be open tomorrow? How do I know the insurance company will pay my policy? A Principal plan is backed by years of experience and millions of dollars. Besides that, the law in the country protect our client's interests:
>
> 1. In accordance with statutory requirements, the Company can invest only in securities eligible under the *Investment Contracts Act* (Alberta);
>
> 2. These securities are required to be maintained with an approved depository;
>
> 3. The Company has always maintained assets on deposit substantially in excess of its certificate liabilities.
>
> Frankly, if that is not security for your savings and mine, Mr. Prospect, what is good security? If that doesn't constitute sound security, then I say, there is no good security.

"Substantially in excess of its certificate liabilities"—thoroughly cold-blooded, when the certificate "liabilities" were close to zero.

Because they were on a crusade, few salesmen felt any need to question the products they were pushing. They knew little about the financial circumstances of the various Principal companies, and nothing at all about First Investors and Associated Investors, except that the companies were private and not obliged to publicly disclose their books. They were told about the *Investment Contracts Act*, and hyped it constantly, but few ever looked it up. Even fewer checked the *Canadian and British Insurance Companies Act* to find out what investments were qualified under the Act.

Primed with lies and half-truths, and confused about what little information they had, the Principal apostles enthusiastically filled in the blanks in ways most favourable to their cause. Established salesmen helped train new staff, and thus misunderstandings were passed from generation to generation.

Salesmen didn't have to be told to push the much riskier investment contracts and promissory notes as opposed to the federally-insured trust company deposits. The commission structure (and their faith that the products were equally secure) provided all the necessary motivation. Before 1985, a "qualified consultant" received a commission of $1.50 for every $1,000 a client placed in a trust company term deposit; as opposed to $3 for every $1,000 placed in an investment contract or promissory note. A top-selling "account executive" received even more— $3.68 per $1,000 in an investment contract. (This commission structure changed in October 1985; see Chapter 17.) Branch and area managers were rewarded with over-rides tied to their sales force's productivity.

Principal salesmen—like their vacuum cleaner-hustling forebears—met with branch managers every morning to report on their efforts the day before, and to receive fresh assignments. Special achievements were shared, and emphasis given to successful strategies.

Each week, they filled out activity reports accounting for every minute of their time: who they saw, when they saw them, what was said, amount of sales, number of products sold and current volume. These reports were presented at the Tuesday morning sales committee meeting, chaired by Donald Cormie. The review included a salesman-by-salesman, product-by-product scrutiny. Marlin and Cormie also met monthly with area managers and area vice-presidents to evaluate their sales activity. Congratulatory telegrams were often sent to top achievers.

The sales staff was well rewarded for its efforts. There were generous commissions and other perks: diplomas, diamond rings or exotic vacations in Greece and Mexico, Paris and the Far East. There were dinners with Marlin, and if someone were incredibly productive, the most coveted prize of all: Cormie would emerge to lunch with him and shake his hand.

As well, sales achievements were duly reported in Principal's *Crusader*. The February 1987 issue, for example, was replete with photos of a pre-Christmas cruiseship holiday: top-selling Principal Plaza branch manager Jim Gilhooly at the wheel; top-selling account executive Don Slater and his wife Jacquie, shaking the captain's hand; top-selling consultant Cecil Galloway, from Red Deer, receiving a surprise birthday cake. The 86 smiling tourists—winners of a two-year Principal sales campaign and their families—romped through Disneyland and the Universal Studios in Los Angeles, before boarding the good ship *Fairsea* for a nine-day journey down the Mexican coast. The accompanying article described the sun and sights, then continued:

> But there was more to the trip than just sea and sun, fun and food. There was a chance to learn the fabulous new Principal song, written by Janice Fowler, and to be inspired and informed by a trio of great Principal speakers, two of them members of the Twenty Plus Club, recently formed to recognise outstanding achievers with 20 years or more at Principal. Jim Gilhooly, Don Slater and Wally Noble spoke eloquently about their years of experience at Principal, and what it is that motivates them to make such enormous contributions to the company. They emphasized the fact that you don't have to move to Head Office or be a VP to win the Principal way—a member of the sales staff can make as much or more than any VP, with the right attitude and approach.

DON SLATER DEFINITELY HAD THE right attitude. There were plenty of hot salesmen on the Principal team but Slater was among the first, and undoubtedly the very best, to ever pitch an investment contract. He'd been with Principal since March 1959 and had a list of, as he testified, "hundreds and hundreds and hundreds" of clients. Slater was a company role model; his incredible sales volume was routinely extolled in staff publications and Principal Group annual reports, sometimes with a photo or quote. He addressed sales staff gatherings, and occasionally took trainees with him to observe the old master do his stuff.

Slater sold Principal's paper with all the fervour of a religious convert. Half his sales were investment contracts, a product "most dear to my heart," he testified. "We felt so safe and so secure. We were so proud of these certificates." He put his money where his mouth was: at the time of the collapse he had $81,000 in First Investors.

Because he had faith, Slater didn't need information. He testified that in the three decades he worked for Donald Cormie, he never read the *Investment Contracts Act*. Slater didn't know and didn't want to know what assets the contract companies held to back up their guarantees, or what proportion of their portfolios were in mortgages. "No, it wasn't for me to know that," he insisted. "I was licenced by the provincial government to sell AIC/FIC, knowing that they were looking after things. Should I have been phoning them up and saying, 'Here, you better move it over here'? I felt they were looking after it."

During his testimony at the Code inquiry, Slater, wretched and crimson-faced, kept launching into testimonials for Principal. Like a man on automatic pilot, he proclaimed the quality and safety of the contracts he'd pitched for 29 incredibly profitable years.

Years before, Slater had decided that the interest rate difference between the trust company and the investment contract companies had nothing to do with the products' relative safety, but was the result of deducting the cost of the CDIC insurance from the Principal Trust term deposits. He had presented that supposition to clients as fact, and taught it to some of his younger colleagues as well. Unlike some of his customers, Slater understood the distinction between "real estate" (the ownership of property) and "mortgages" (pledging property as security for a loan) and he knew the contract companies had always invested in mortgages. He didn't draw that to the attention of his clients, many of whom had become afraid of any property-related investment since the real estate crash. Instead, he repeatedly assured them that Cormie had taken Principal out of real estate prior to the crash. He made a point of never talking about mortgages.

Half a dozen of Slater's customers appeared at the Code inquiry. Those people (Gerald Heffernan, Marjorie Given, Barry Armstrong and Ronald Wilderman, all of Calgary, and Viola Pearson of nearby Brooks) described him as misleading, confusing, pressing and patronizing. Confronted with their evidence, Slater prefaced his replies to their allegations with the remark that each was "a dear personal friend of mine." He denied little, except their claims that he had never raised the option of buying CDIC-insured term deposits.

For all his "friendship," Slater was quick to denigrate his clients as "interest-rate junkies" who beat a path to his door. "If you sold something at a quarter percent higher interest they'd want it. We didn't force it on them." He had so many long-time clients, he said, that he had to be persuade to take on new ones. Elderly clients were "so impressed and so enthralled, really, with what I was doing for people, they would quite often refer me to their grandchildren, their children, saying, 'For heaven's sakes, go out and help these people to save some money.' "

Slater's stationary and business cards identified him as a member of the "President's Club" and "Holder of the Masters Key." Marjorie Given was impressed by these designations, which increased her trust in his advice. "We assumed he was very knowledgeable in financial matters," she said. She didn't understand, and Slater didn't tell her, that the titles meant simply that he was a fantastically successful huckster. The Masters Key, presented by the Investment Funds Institute of Canada in the late 1970s, honoured his skill at selling mutual funds: more than a million dollars worth in the year he received the award. Slater was president of the Principal Consultants' President's Club by virtue of the flood of investment products he sold year after year.

Slater took inordinate pride in his abilities. In a July 1986 letter to Principal head office, he bragged about talking a sick retired farmer—who had asked for a federally insured investment—into buying $100,000 worth of promissory notes and mutual funds. "I must admit it was one of my finer presentations," the letter said.[1] On a warm and muggy May evening, Slater sat with the farmer—Svend Kargard of Bassano, Alberta—in lawn chairs in the shade of the man's house, and made a three-hour pitch that lasted until 9:30 that night.

Kargard, who had "had a bout with cancer," was passed on to Slater when he phoned the Calgary Principal office in response to a newspaper ad. When he told Slater that he had between $60,000 and $100,000 to invest:

> I suggested to him, that with that amount of money he should receive proper financial counselling, with no obligation... I satisfied him that his funds were perfectly safe without the protection of the Canada Deposit Insurance. After hearing my presentation on thrift, the cycles and the advantage of mutual funds he was truly elated. He was elated even more when I assured him of the comfort and trust he would enjoy investing with Principal. He thanked me for having spent so much time and patience in giving him such valued and vital information.

10

Caribbean hideaway

June 29, 1984

JAIMIE CORMIE HAD HINTED at a deal with Carma Ltd. that would solve a lot of the contract companies' problems. In the two weeks after the meetings with the CDIC and Alberta officials, negotiations with Carma were settled, the paperwork completed and on June 29, the agreement was signed—the same day that the CDIC issued its Section 25 notice to Principal Trust.

At first glace it looked like a good deal. It took $21 million worth of overvalued real estate, and two bad mortgages worth $7.8 million, off the books of First Investors and Associated Investors and transferred them, at book value, into Carma subsidiaries. Another $7.5 million in problematic Carma debentures held by the contract companies went back to Carma. Apparently attractive assets were then traded over to Principal, seeming to improve the contract companies' outlook by at least a couple of million dollars.

As was often the case with Principal, appearances were deceiving.

Carma and Nu-West Group Ltd., which owned close to half of Carma's voting shares, were both in the real estate development business. Each had been devastated by the Alberta crash, and by the spring of 1984 were technically insolvent—unable to pay their debts and dividends—and struggling to survive. Each had announced debt reorganization plans, but needed the support of creditors to proceed. Principal's contract companies held debentures issued by Nu-West and Carma subsidiary Carma Developers Ltd., giving the Cormies a voice in the reorganizations. Creditors had recently approved Carma's plan, but Nu-West's meeting with its creditors was coming up, and Principal held enough Nu-West debentures to give it a chance at killing that reorganization if it chose.

At the same time, the Carma and Nu-West debentures held by the Principal contract companies had become a contentious issue with the provincial auditors, who wanted them written down to 30 cents on the dollar. That would wreak further havoc on the contract companies' books, and the Cormies were keen to have the debentures off their hands.

"So in talking to Jaimie," Ken Marlin testified, "we decided that there has got to be a deal here somewhere, and I agreed that I would call Ralph Scurfield [head of Nu-West] and see if we couldn't explore the possibility of helping each other, which I did. That was the start of the negotiations on Carma." Donald Cormie testified that he and Jaimie worked out the actual deal with Carma Ltd. president Roy Wilson.

Carma was interested in Principal's proposal only if it received assistance in unloading some of its own problem assets. "They suggested that there was a bank in the Cayman Islands that they owned and there were some oil and gas properties they owned," Marlin testified. "And they said that they had been asked by their bank to dispose of those and wondered if we may be interested in putting those into some type of a transaction."

Yes, Principal was interested. Unfortunately, under the *Investment Contracts Act*, First Investors and Associated Investors were prohibited from acquiring the companies that Carma wanted to unload. So a scheme was worked out for getting around the restriction: another Principal company (one that was "legal for life" and therefore a permitted investment under the Act) would acquire the Carma assets. Shares of that company would then be sold to the contract companies. The vehicle chosen to implement this plan was Athabasca Holdings Ltd. (owned by Collective Securities), which we'll recall was used by Cormie in 1959 in a bizarre transaction with First Investors. (See Chapter 4.) Athabasca had been semi-dormant for years, but was dusted off to participate in the Carma deal.

In the end, it took a convoluted five-step transaction to meet all the objectives of both parties. First, Athabasca bought from Allarco Group Ltd. (a Carma subsidiary) all of its shares of Allarco Energy Ltd. (an oil and gas company operating in Alberta) for $17.2 million; all of its shares of North West International Bank and Trust Company in the Grand Cayman Islands for $19.8 million; and half of the shares of Travellers Acceptance Corporation Ltd. for $1 million. Athabasca paid for the assets by issuing from its treasury 36,340,000 preferred shares valued at a dollar each, and by transferring $1.7 million worth of Principal Group Ltd. preferred shares—for a total consideration of $38 million. (See DIAGRAM 3: *The Carma/Allarco Transactions*.)

In the second step, First Investors and Associated Investors purchased the $36,340,000 worth of Athabasca shares from Allarco Group (Carma). The contract companies paid for these shares with the Carma/Nu-West debentures, two problem mortgages and cash. Some of the payment went to Allarco Group, and some to Allarco Group's newly created subsidiary, numbered company 314986 Alberta Ltd., in the following way: the Carma and Nu-West debentures were transferred at their face value of $7.5 million to Allarco Group; two mortgages and related securities on two downtown Calgary properties, known as the Venture Properties Securities,[1] were transferred for $7.8 million (book value) to the numbered company; the numbered company was credited with the sum of $5.84 million to be applied against a purchase of properties executed in the fourth step; and the contract companies paid $15.2 million in cash to Allarco Group.

In the third step, Principal Group bought back the $1.7 million worth of Principal Group preferred shares that had been transferred to Allarco Group in the first step. It paid Allarco Group with another $1.7 million worth of Carma and Nu-West debentures held in the Principal Group portfolio.

In the fourth step, the contract companies sold seven properties, at book value, to the Allarco Group numbered company for $21 million. Among them was some of the trash dumped on the contract companies by Principal Trust three months earlier. The $5.84 million credited to the numbered company in the second step was applied against the sale price of $21 million; the remaining $15.2 million remained outstanding as a debt owed by the Allarco Group numbered company to the contract companies. (The agreement for sale, basically a vendor takeback mortgage, provided for interest of 6% in the first year, 10% in the second year and 14% in the third year. At the end of the third year the balance became due.)

In the fifth step, First Investors loaned $2 million to the Allarco Group numbered company, as a mortgage against the Venture properties; $1.5 million was actually paid to the numbered company, and the final $500,000 went to Principal Group on behalf of the numbered company for deposit in a sinking fund account. (Principal was to use the money from the sinking fund to pay the 14.3% interest owed each year by the numbered company to the contract companies on the $2-million loan.) In return, Principal Group issued a $500,000 promissory note to the numbered company, which was then pledged to the contract companies as security for the loan, along with a mortgage on the Venture Properties Securities.

At the conclusion of the transaction, First Investors and Associated Investors had unloaded the Venture Properties Securities ($7.8 million); the Carma and Nu-West debentures ($7.5 million); $21 million worth of real estate; and it had handed over $17.2 million in cash. In return, it received $36.3 million worth of Athabasca shares, which carried a modest dividend rate of 4% a year (enough to pay investment contract holders their 4% "guaranteed interest," but far short of the 6% to 14% they expected); it was owed $2 million by the Allarco Group numbered company as a result of step five (and had actually loaned the money necessary to pay the interest owed on the loan); and it was owed $15.2 million by the Allarco Group numbered company as a result of the sale of the real estate executed in step four.

In theory, the contract companies came out ahead. They got rid of sour assets at book value, reversed write-offs on the company books and acquired fresh assets. The deal allowed Principal to restructure the contract companies' books in a way that made them appear healthy again. But it had cost First Investors and Associated Investors $17.2 million in cash, and the loss of the potential investment income that money could have earned them. (Mutual funds and stocks, for example, were at an historic yield of 20% to 25% at this time.) Any gain was dependent on the Allarco Group numbered company making good on the $2-million and $15.2-million loans.

It did not.

As soon as the $500,000 sinking fund was exhausted on the $2-million loan, the loan went into default. Little or no interest or principal was ever paid on the $15.2-million loan; the only money to ever come back was a few hundred thousand dollars earned by the properties transferred in the deal. Any capital expenditures, such as taxes and improvements, were made by the contract companies, not by the new "owners" of the properties. Principal had no recourse on the loan except the seven drastically over-valued properties, and in 1986 they began "coming back" to the contract companies.

There is evidence that neither Principal nor Carma ever expected the contract companies to benefit from this transaction. A memo written by Principal Group comptroller Ginny Nicholson summarized a September 1984 meeting with Allarco Group personnel as follows:

1. Allarco says none of the properties will generate a positive profit...
2. Allarco says its understanding of the agreement is [Principal Group] will:
   —absorb and fund operating losses
   —fund improvements

When it was mentioned that we did not see any such clause in the agreement, Allarco indicated that it was in PGL's interest to fund losses and improvements because "it would only be getting the properties back at the end of the three years anyway."

In his report Inspector Bill Code found that this transaction had put First Investors and Associated Investors:

...at extreme risk, if not guaranteed loss. Not only was the security inadequate, but also it is incredible to suggest that that debtor's covenant was of any value where the debtor was a newly-formed numbered company and a wholly-owned subsidiary of a corporation in default on its debentures and in the process of reorganizing itself... That the risk materialized is no surprise...

I find that the transaction was designed to cover up the serious problems in the FIC and AIC mortgage and owned property portfolio (and indeed that of Principal Trust when considered with [the $23-million sale of assets from the trust company to the contract companies]... FIC and AIC were simply throwing away good cash in exchange for financial fantasy and these men knew it.

Other aspects of the Carma transaction are also interesting. The sour real estate and mortgages "purchased" from the contract companies were buried by Carma in a numbered company created expressly for this purpose, and were immediately written down: the real estate by $5.84 million and the Venture Properties Securities by $6.3 million. (The real estate write-down left the properties with a book value of $15.1 million, less than the $15.2 million owed against them. The Venture write-down left that asset with a book value of $1.5 million, less than the $2 million borrowed against it.) The debt for the two loans, $17.2 million borrowed from the contract companies, was assigned to the numbered company, which, as mentioned, never paid it. But anything of value—the Carma/Nu-West debentures and the $15.2 million in cash—went up to the numbered company's parent company, Allarco Group, and was doubtless welcomed by the desperately strapped Carma conglomerate.

Principal Group came out ahead as well. With the help of the contract companies it had managed to dispose of its Carma and Nu-West debentures at face value, significantly improving its balance sheet. Through Athabasca (the directors were Donald Cormie and his vice-president Christa Petracca), Cormie had gained control of two fascinating new companies. The acquisition of Allarco Energy moved Cormie in a big way into the oil and gas business. Best of all, though, was the delightful prospect of one's very own offshore bank, and a bank in the Cayman Islands, no less.

The ostensible lures of the Cayman Islands are non-stop sun and fun, beaches and seafood and golf courses. Their real attraction, however, is their tax-free status. As Montreal money-laundering expert N.T. Naylor[2] has so eloquently put it, they rank with the world's great "peekaboo centres." The Caymans, a British Crown colony located about 500 miles south of Florida are—like Liechtenstein, Switzerland, Hong Kong, Bermuda and the Bahamas—an ideal place to shelter flight capital and escape tax on hidden investments.

Secrecy is a fetish on the Cayman Islands; both financial and personal privacy are considered an inalienable right. In 1964, before entering the tax haven business, the islands had only two domestic banks. By 1983, there were 450. About 250 of them were booking branches of major international banks, 100 were locally incorporated subsidiaries of international banks and 100 were locally chartered "private" operations. There are 18,000 companies registered on three tiny islands with a total population of about 14,000. The official purposes of these companies have been variously identified as investment, sales, trading, shipping, insurance and real estate. Many are actually shell companies whose invisible owners, non-residents all, want to hide money and assets from the tax man back home.[3]

George Town, the capital of Grand Cayman, the main island, was the site of Donald Cormie's offshore bank. It was a modest operation, with a director, a book-keeper and a secretary working out of a rented room on the second floor of an office building. But it had a Class B unrestricted offshore licence, authorizing it to carry on banking and trust company business anywhere in the world (except for local business in the Cayman Islands) on behalf of non-resident clients.

So eager was Cormie to execute the Carma deal that he had no valuation of either Allarco Energy or the bank performed before taking them over. In August, however, Cormie and Petracca escaped the mounting corporate crises in Alberta with an inspection visit to the Caymans. They met with the Caymans' Inspector of Banks, the bank's staff and local board members, and came home pleased with their acquisition—despite the fact that its net book value was almost $4 million less than what they paid for it.

Back in Edmonton, Petracca went to see chartered accountant G. Douglas Carr, managing partner of Peat, Marwick, Mitchell & Co. (the same firm which had helped with the paperwork culminating in the Carma transaction). Petracca wanted him to provide her with a letter of opinion that could go to provincial regulators to prove Principal had gotten good value for its money. Later, she wrote him a memo, attempting to justify the bank's purchase price.

The bank would be "a very valuable member of our group of companies since it will enable us to use the staff complement in the Caymans...to run an offshore Investment Advisor for both our two, new, proposed Canadian funds, as well as offshore funds which we will be offering to our United States clients," she wrote. Most important, the bank would provide a shelter from Canadian tax:

> Due to all the above factors, including the possibility of, through various vehicles, earning approximately $400,000 to $800,000 per year in the Caymans tax sheltered, the Principal Group of Companies concluded that the bank would be well worth the approximately 23% premium paid over the net asset value of the bank.

Carr did his best to work with what Petracca had given him. On September 12, he wrote her a letter advising that, in view of the fact "that a premium is often paid in transactions such as you are contemplating, a price in the range of $18.5 million to $19.5 million [Canadian] does not seem inappropriate." Principal, we'll recall, had paid $19.8 million. Carr quoted much of Petracca's own memo back to her, then laid out several tax advantages, including:

> 3. Assuming it would take six months to create such a vehicle, the purchase of an existing company enables [Principal Group Ltd.] to earn tax-free income six months earlier than would otherwise be the case.
> (a) On the present portfolio, an assumed tax savings of 6%
> on $12.35 million for six months $370,500
> (b) Assumed use of the vehicle to shelter approximately $400,000 annually
> of investment management fees. Savings for 6 months
> of $200,000 x 50% $100,000
> (c) As well, tax savings could be attributed to any additional funds transferred to the vehicle.

Clearly, the bank's new owners were keen to take speedy advantage of the Caymans' tax-free status and fabled secrecy. Exactly what use was made of the bank during the next three years—what corporate and personal investments were handled through it, what transactions conducted, what dividends issued, what service, administrative or consulting fees paid, and what clients, Canadian or otherwise, it served—is not known.[4]

However, its circumstances at the time of the Principal Group bankruptcy in mid-1987 are known, and suggest the bank was little more than a holding company for a wide range of investments. At the time of the crash, there were only 12 depositors (identities not revealed) with a total of $2.5 million in the vault. There was a single loan of $15,000 on the books. But the bank held a $23-million portfolio of highly liquid securities: blue-chip stocks, U.S. government securities and international mutual funds. That portfolio, worth $16.3 million at the time of the acquisition in 1984, had increased by almost $7 million in the intervening three years.

Canadians must pay tax on income earned from overseas investments; however, as long as the Cayman bank assets, and any profits, remained untouched, they were not taxable. Cormie testified that Collective Securities took no money out of the bank. Whether Collective shareholders (Donald, Jaimie and John Cormie and Ken Marlin) ever received dividends or other income or benefits from the bank, or whether they paid tax on such income, is unknown.

Carr's letter to Petracca included the usual disclaimer, a normal part of such evaluation letters if a detailed on-site appraisal had not been conducted:

> You will appreciate that we are not expressing an opinion on the value of the shares of the Bank, nor have we been engaged to carry out such a valuation, but based on our knowledge of the Bank, our discussions with our office in the Cayman Islands and our experience with clients who have established offshore entities we believe the above-noted price range may be appropriate for purposes of your negotiations.

Upon receiving the letter, Petracca called Carr and complained that his disclaimer rendered his letter useless to her. "Please take it out," she asked, and he did. On October 19, the letter was reissued, without qualification.

Carr did so over the objections of a colleague actually based in the Cayman Islands. Four days before Carr issued the second letter, Theo Bullmore, also with Peak Marwick, wrote Carr a memo ridiculing his justification of the bank's purchase price. "The justification of the premium is certainly very ingenious, but I would be uneasy to see it form part of a formal valuation opinion..." Bullmore wrote. "Without wishing to be negative in this matter, I would not wish to have this office's name quoted as a source in a formal valuation along the lines of the [Carr's] letter, without the disclaimer. Unhappily, I am unable to think of any factors not mentioned in the letter which might justify the premium."

June 30, 1984

THE CORMIES NAILED DOWN the Carma transaction on Friday, June 29, then rushed off to Tomahawk to prepare for the semi-annual Ranch Day celebrations. *The Edmonton Journal* society columnist Maureen Hemingway[5] enthusiatically reported the event:

> Despite the ominous clouds hovering over the Cormie Ranch Field Day last Saturday at Tomahawk, the Cormie family and the directors and officers of

Principal Group showed it is still possible to create excitement and drama out of cattle and sheepdogs.

Hay rides leaving every half-hour toured around the 14,000-acre ranch, stopping at the Heritage Farm built in 1915, the computer farm equipment which can instantly release individual animal data and management reports, and the cattle displays of approximately 1,500 head of Charolais, Maine Anjou and Simmental breeds. By the way, Signal, their prize bull, has gone to the happy pastures in the sky but not without leaving around 150,000 descendants...

After the 1,100 guests were introduced to life on the ranch, they were all fed filet mignons while they listened to Dr. Roy Bern, dean of agriculture at the University of Alberta, talking about the Cormie Ranch being the competition to the U of A research program. He said: "That's all to the good because Don Cormie has been a pioneer in many ways and he enjoys the challenge." The man himself confirmed this and explained: "We are learning to breed a leaner beef these days because people's eating habits have changed and we have to respond."

After dinner a hoedown began with the County Line capping off an untypical ranch day....

Not a word was spoken about the nightmare Section 25 notice the Cormies had received from the CDIC the day before. There was no discussion, during filet mignon dinner or evening hoedown, about the $72 million demanded by the Superintendent of Insurance in mid-May to shore up the contract companies.

The following Thursday, July 5, Ken Marlin wrote Tewfik Saleh, advising that the Carma transaction was completed. He promised supporting documentation in the near future, but did not detail the deal's complexities. Several months would pass before its full implications were understood in the government offices.

Saleh had spent the Canada Day long weekend dithering about Principal Trust's $23-million dump of assets into the contract companies. Desperate to rationalize it, Saleh called auditor Bruce Pennock on Tuesday, July 3, and asked for a letter explaining how he and Principal had determined the value of the mortgages before signing off on the contract companies' financial statements. Such a letter, Saleh hoped, might help resolve the dispute between Principal and government auditors on the valuation issue. The situation was increasingly "serious," Saleh confided, "and I don't think I can accept the [$23-million] transaction."

The next day, copies of the CDIC's Section 25 notice to Principal Trust arrived in the Alberta government offices, causing Saleh further unease. He was still waiting for an opinion from lawyer Sydney Bercov on the legality of the $23-million transfer, but time was running out. Something had to be done; the trust company was going to lose its CDIC insurance if matters weren't straightened out by the end of July to the satisfaction of the federal regulators.

After yet another agonizing weekend, Saleh wrote a memo to Deputy Minister Barry Martin saying he wanted outside help with the Principal mess. Incapable of untangling himself from the conflicting arguments of Principal representatives and his department's audit staff—and prohibited from doing anything that would focus attention on the sorry state of Principal's affairs—Saleh prayed for a third party to tell him how to handle the situation. His July 9 memo described Principal Trust and the two contract companies as being in a "critical situation," and attributed the problem to a "decline in the underlying value of real estate held as security for loans." This memo is significant because it states that the $23-million asset transfer was an attempt to relieve CDIC pressure on the trust company; Saleh repeatedly testified that he didn't realize this, until confronted with documents proving otherwise.

Saleh also discussed his inability to sort out the real estate appraisal dispute, making it impossible to determine what demands should properly be made of the contract companies.

> Because of the current economic downturn and depressed real estate market experienced by our province and because of the importance of the decision that has to be made, I would request the Minister's permission and yours to solicit outside professional advice from a firm of chartered accountants of the Minister's choice, for an overall assessment of the financial position of FIC and AIC based on proper valuation of their assets and practices and at the companies' expense.

Under the terms of the *Investment Contracts Act* (Section 8) a company could not continue in business if its reserves, qualified assets or unimpaired capital were offside. Despite his clearly defined responsibility, Saleh felt unable to take action without his superiors' approval. Saleh testified that he met with Martin and Consumer Affairs Minister Connie Osterman after writing his memo, and reminded them of Ken Marlin's statement that there would be no new capital injected into the contract companies. But he was denied permission to bring in an independent consultant because it might cause a run, resulting in massive losses for the companies, and, most important, erode public confidence in the province's other financial institutions. He was to maintain pressure on Principal by way of meetings and demands, but he was not to threaten the contract companies' licences because "that would trigger the whole thing."

"Continue to work with the company," Martin told him, and he obeyed.

Tewfik Saleh was 60 years old in 1984, counting down to retirement after a decade of service to the province of Alberta. The last thing he wanted was a confrontation with his superiors. That scene between Jim Darwish and Connie Osterman, witnessed blow by blow courtesy of the Minister's speaker phone, would have put the fear of hellfire into any seasoned bureaucrat.

Saleh, hand-picked by Martin as the province's senior regulator of financial institutions, had a particularly timid nature. He was well known as a man who had trouble making decisions, and was temperamentally and intellectually unsuited to a high-pressure regulatory job. By mid-1984, Saleh should have been telling Martin and Osterman that action *had* to be taken. He should have written a Special Report to Osterman recommending the appointment of a receiver/manager, forcing her to take the issue up in Cabinet. Instead, he expressed his "preference," then bowed to his superiors' will.

Saleh's July 9 memo to Barry Martin was his one inadequate shot at independence; never again would he question Martin's wishes, or argue against the "hands-off" policy. His job, he testified, was to express his views, then to "take instructions." For two and a half more years, Saleh watched in silence the ever-escalating deterioration of the contract companies—until responsibility was finally taken from him in late 1986.

In testimony, Saleh portrayed himself as a man wringing his hands in hopeless frustration, horrified at the crisis but unable to persuade his superiors to act. But a frustrated government official need not remain passive: he can ask to be relieved of his duties, or seek a transfer out of the department. He can threaten to resign and, if necessary, offer his resignation. This is the bureaucrat's final ace in the hole. It seems little enough, but it carries a certain moral—and attention-grabbing—force within government service.

Instead, Saleh remained silent. Stymied in his effort to bring in an outside "judge," he reverted to an earlier plan: he would pass the real estate valuation issue over to lawyer Sydney Bercov, and wait for his opinion.

The week after his request to Martin was rejected, Saleh received a letter from Ken Marlin. It included an "updated progress report" on the contract companies. This letter, dated July 16, was drafted by Christa Petracca and sent to Marlin for signature. It claimed that the Carma transaction two weeks earlier had increased First Investors' capital by $4.4 million and Associated's capital by $1 million. It continued:

> We feel we have utilizing dedicated, concerned and experienced management, taken tight control of the companies' real estate and mortgage assets and realized the maximum potential available in this environment. As previously expressed, it is important that this be recognized explicitly by your department and you assist us in restoring the confidence of the government, the public and the auditors by confirming that:
> (1) The tender at book value of the joint mortgages was in the best interest of the companies...
> (2) It is in everyone's best interest to utilize a long term common sense approach to real estate valuations which gives the company, its management and its client the maximum opportunity to realize the potential inherent in its portfolio without undue pressure on its capital.

The letter was handed to Saleh and Martin during a meeting the next morning (July 17) with Marlin, Petracca and Jaimie Cormie. Saleh told the Principal officials that Bercov was looking into the contract companies' mortgage situation, and all material relating to the $23-million transfer should be forwarded to him. Saleh also wanted more information on the Carma transaction, to be sent to Bercov as well. Then Saleh complained he had not yet received the letter from Pennock requested a week earlier, concerning the methods used to valuate the contract companies' mortgages.

The big issue that day was the preparation of a financial statement for Principal Group Ltd. Auditor Pennock had completed the statements for the trust company, the contract companies and the various mutual funds, but was stalled in the production of a consolidated statement, which would combine the finances of Principal Group and all its subsidiaries into a single report. This statement had been put on hold pending completion of the Carma transaction.

Pennock had been told about the deal in mid-June: Cormie expected it to improve the contract companies' finances and wanted that improvement reflected in Principal's statement. (If the finances of one company are bad, it drags down the combined results of the entire group.) Cormie felt that if some of the contract companies' bad assets had been traded away at book value, as appeared to have happened in the Carma deal, then the contingencies against loss should be reduced and the going-concern note dropped.

With the Carma deal completed, Cormie hoped to see the consolidated statement signed off quickly. But now came another delay: Pennock had learned in late June about Saleh's May 11 letter to Marlin demanding a $72-million capital injection into the contract companies. He considered the letter a further threat to their survival, and unless the issues raised in the letter were resolved, he would be compelled to include further disclosures, including another going-concern note, in the consolidated statement. It was crucial this not happen. Principal's consolidated statement was always released to the public in an annual report, and such a note would be the kiss of death for the conglomerate.

During discussion with the Principal officials, Deputy Minister Martin decided to take a hand. Petracca wrote a memo to file describing the incident:

> Barry Martin put all of the people present on the speaker phone and we phoned Bruce Pennock to clearly indicate to him that the valuation of the assets, and the doubts with respect to the same, was what was causing a request for capital and since we were still discussing the valuation of the assets, the letter of May 11th was not a finite demand for capital in the amounts stated.
>
> Bruce [Pennock] had verbally indicated to me that this is what he needed to be able to assure himself that the letter of May 11th did not require disclosure on a consolidated basis. We were assured again that the Department was "on our side" and was interested in assisting us in stabilizing the companies and giving all of our publics [sic] the confidence based on our good performance and good, competent management of the above companies.

Not a finite demand for capital: the $72-million demand might look pretty serious, but Pennock wasn't to worry about it, Martin implied. It was merely an opening gambit. Some capital might be required, but it would be much less than $72 million; the exact sum was still to be negotiated. Until the issue of property valuation was resolved there really wasn't a demand for capital, and thus no need to mention the letter in the financial statement.

The next day, Pennock wrote Saleh the requested letter regarding his treatment of asset valuation during the contract companies' audits. Pennock took pains to distance himself from Principal: "We conducted extensive audit testing to satisfy ourselves that management was knowledgeable of their portfolios, that they had taken reasonable steps to assess values and that their approach to presenting the information was reasonable. We are not appraisers or valuators." The message was clear: the values claimed in the statements were provided by the companies, and the auditor was not warranting their accuracy. The accounting policies and practices were management's; Pennock's job was to determine the fairness of the report.

On Friday, July 20, Marlin and Petracca handed the letter to Saleh's assistant Bernard Rodrigues. Rodrigues took a fast look and told them the explanation was not adequate: Saleh wanted to know the actual steps taken to arrive at the values reported in the statements. The following Monday, Petracca sent a letter to Pennock's office, for his signature, that she thought would satisfy Saleh.

"She was giving me a document with her point of view of the extent of the work that had been done, that I guess she wanted me to do something with," Pennock testified. "To be honest with you, I completely disregarded the letter... I was not pleased with someone writing me and putting into their words what they wanted me to say to someone else. I believe I had made our intentions pretty clear to the company around the representations that we were willing to make, and that is that we had completed a financial statement and given an audit report, and we were not going to make representations above and beyond that. We completed our engagement and we were satisfied we complied with the requirements of the Act."

Nonetheless, Pennock would remain involved for several months in discussions between Principal and the Alberta regulators about valuation of the contract companies' holdings. A decision on the province's response to the $23-million asset dump would not be made until Christmas.

While delivering Pennock's letter, Marlin had produced one of his own. The Carma transaction had so improved the contract companies' affairs, it announced, they were able to declare and pay additional credits after all. Abracadabra!

All the credits that had been cancelled May 8 were now reinstated, as of a resolution dated June 29, 1984—the same day the Carma deal was pushed through —and duly signed by board members Marlin and Eric Espenberg.

But there was another twist, not made clear in the letter. First Investors and Associated Investors had always declared additional credits quarterly and in advance. For example, credits for the period of April to June 1984 would have been declared on March 31. With the cancellation and redeclaration, however, a new system was implemented: from then on, credits would be declared *at the end of each quarter.*

We'll recall that, as permitted under the *Investment Contracts Act*, the companies only reserved sufficient assets to pay the 4% interest "guaranteed" on the investment contracts. The rest of the interest, promised to clients in the form of additional credits, didn't officially exist and wasn't recorded as an expense in the companies' financial records—until the credits were declared at the beginning of each quarter. With the new system, the companies were even further behind, with the debt unreflected on the books until after the end of each quarter.

It was clever accounting sleight of hand, the equivalent of paying your June rent with your July paycheque. The third quarter's credits weren't declared until October, and the fourth quarter's credits weren't declared until January 1985. Thus the fourth quarter's credits, for the first time, *weren't recorded as an expense in that year's financial statements.* The effect was to defer to 1985 the recording of 1984 additional credits totalling $2,538,000 for First Investors and $803,000 for Associated Investors. The strategy concealed a debt incurred in 1984 and improved the appearance of the contract companies' books—and the consolidated statement of their parent Principal Group—by a total of $3,341,000.

July 23, 1984

TEWFIK SALEH TAPPED ON JIM DARWISH'S door, and stepped inside. He looked shaken, and must have been, to go to Darwish for advice after everything that had happened in recent weeks.

"His background isn't in accounting," Darwish testified, "and he asked me during the short conversation if I knew that Mr. Cormie was quite a powerful person in the Conservative Party, or words to that effect. He seemed genuinely concerned about it, and I said to him, 'Well, he may be, so what?' "[6]

Saleh went back to his office and drafted a memo summarizing his dilemma regarding the contract companies and asking for yet more analysis on the valuation debate. Saleh had Bernard Rodrigues sign it and send it over to Darwish:

> While the values determined by CDIC, Touche Ross & Co. and ourselves are all a matter of opinion, I am now advised by the companies that they have since disposed of some of the properties in question and have actually made a profit where we were projecting a loss.
>
> I am concerned that the basis we used to determine the value of the mortgages in arrears and foreclosed real estate may now appear to be unreasonable and unrealistic in view of the circumstances. If we pursue the company on such basis we may expose the department to civil liability and the possibility of being accused of acting irresponsibly.
>
> Because of the current general downturn in the economy of Alberta it would appear that appraisers are not the appropriate method of valuing the mortgages in arrears and foreclosed real estate, I therefore feel that the [provincial] auditors should closely examine the bases used by Touche Ross & Co. and CDIC, discuss it with them and provide me with their comments.

While reviewing the valuation methods used by Touche Ross & Co. and CDIC, I would ask that the auditors report on any sales subsequent to December 31, 1983, of foreclosed real estate and repayment of mortgages in arrears to determine whether or not a profit was actually made as the companies claim. In this regard I would require a complete examination of the details of the purported transaction with Carma and its pertinent documents.

Darwish replied with a memo providing answers to each of the issues raised, while pointing out that Saleh already had most of the information requested on the valuation issue. It was no surprise that Principal officials would dispute the government auditors' analysis of their financial situation, he said. At the same time, the company's explanations of the higher values they attributed to their mortgages and real estate:

> were not found to be of real substance and were nothing more than general long-winded explanations, completely unsupported by appraisals, memorandum or anything else. You will recall at our meeting with the CDIC people that they pointed out to us that they too encountered this type of presentation from another member of the group, namely [Principal Trust]. They finally took the position that if the company could not come up with some documented proof that the value of their properties was higher than estimated by CDIC, the only alternative was to put in new capital which is, of course, what the trust company did.

Principal's external auditor Bruce Pennock had attended a meeting between the company and the regulators, and briefly discussed their valuation method, Darwish said. "We were not particularly impressed with the method used"—including reliance on verbal reports from a real estate company representative without supporting documentation. He reminded Saleh of his May 11 letter to Principal which said that if the company disagreed with the provincial auditors' assessment, they were invited to support their arguments with appraisals. "As stated above, in 2 1/2 months, they have provided us with nothing but lengthy verbal explanations and a couple of paragraphs in their letter of June 19, 1984, none of which are supported by appraisals or other documentation to show that our figures require amending."

As for the Carma transaction, the company had sent a "most incomplete" letter on July 5 advising of the transfer's completion.

> They gave us no supporting documents. Furthermore, they stated that they had explained the transaction to you at our meeting in mid-June. This is not correct and I regret that it has gone unchallenged... Essentially what we're looking at with respect to this transaction wherein a profit was apparently generated, is a swap.

Based on our experience with respect to Tower Mortgage, Paramount Life and the credit union movement, the likelihood of a swap being done at book value, let alone at a profit, during the present economic times, would be unusual to say the very least.

Darwish pointed out that while continuing to debate real estate values, "the company continues to raise money from the public at a time when their financial position is serious." Saleh knew he was right on every count, but acted on none of his advice.

July 19, 1984

THE CLOCK WAS STILL RUNNING on the Section 25 notice to the trust company. Principal Trust had until the end of July to satisfy the CDIC's demands, and John Cormie was in constant touch with federal regulators, working out the steps necessary to stop Ottawa from yanking his insurance.

On July 19, John wrote the federal Department of Insurance, advising that the requested $6.3 million had been injected into the trust company in the form of subordinated shareholder notes. The difference in tone in his letters to the CDIC, compared to Principal's correspondence with Alberta regulators, was striking. The former were detailed and courteous; the latter, evasive and demanding.

John's formal reply to the Section 25 notice, sent on July 24, proposed measures to eliminate long-term mismatching and reduce the company's portfolio of long-term Government of Canada bonds. This was accompanied by another complaint about the CDIC's demand that the trust company sell the long-term bonds, since their early liquidation could result in a $15-million loss. Lastly, John requested relaxation of the required borrowing-to-capital ratio from the existing 15:1 to 18:1 until at least year end. This letter was copied to both Consumer Affairs minister Connie Osterman and her deputy minister Barry Martin. "We just wanted to make sure that the Minister was aware of the situation," John testified.

The clock was temporarily stopped by receipt of the letter. CDIC chief executive officer Charles de Léry replied on August 10, well after the 30-day deadline, observing that John's response "appears to have the elements of an acceptable plan of action," pending clarification of several points. There would be no relaxation of the 15:1 capital ratio; accrual or capitalization of interest on mortgage loans would cease on any loan more than three months in arrears; the long-term mismatch attributable to the long-term bonds would be eliminated over the coming year; and in the meantime a reserve would be established against the possibility the company was unable to meet its matching objectives. The reserve would be adjusted monthly and deducted from the company's borrowing base. As well, de Léry said, when the bonds were sold there would be capital to be reinvested. He wanted to know what Principal Trust intended to do with it. He also wanted to know the "ultimate source" of the $6.3-million injection.

John wrote back two weeks later, agreeing to everything. Proceeds from sale of the long-term bonds "will be directed to those areas that will alleviate the company's short-term mismatched situation as seen by you," and would include demand loans to the public. As for the capital injection, John said the money came by way of shareholder loans from Principal Group Ltd. No mention was made of the promissory notes being sold to the public by Principal Group.

There were a couple more letters back and forth—the CDIC wanted assurance that the new demand loans would not in any way involve the investment contract companies. Then, on September 27, the Section 25 notice was withdrawn.

July 27, 1984

MEANWHILE, BRUCE PENNOCK was taking a close look at the Carma transaction. On July 27 he concluded, to Donald Cormie's great chagrin, that the deal did not truly improve the financial situation of either the contract companies or Principal Group. The companies faced the same exposure to loss from their dismal mortgage and owned properties portfolios as they had before the deal.

Pennock drafted two notes to be included in Principal's consolidated statements. The first advised that three subsidiaries which had been consolidated into the statement (First Investors, Associated Investors and Principal Trust) invested in mortgages as part of their business, and that a cumulative allowance of $5,326,000 for anticipated losses had been provided for in their accounts. But, it continued, "these companies in total may have an additional exposure to loss of $18,200,000 if the current market levels represent a permanent rather than a temporary decline in value." Cormie had expected to see the $5-million allowance eliminated or reduced; instead, Pennock wanted to increase it by another $18 million! (The exposure was much less than the provincial auditors were predicting, but still a disaster.) The second note was even grimmer:

> Subsequent to the year-end, these subsidiaries received communications from government regulatory authorities requesting information and advising them that additional capital must be raised. Senior officials are presently in the process of dealing with requests. In satisfying the capital requests relating to one of the subsidiaries [Principal Trust], the parent company has invested $8,300,000 into capital stock and subordinated notes subsequent to year-end. At the date of preparation of financial statements, the other matters have not been resolved.

At least Pennock hadn't included the specific amount, the $72 million demanded by the Alberta Superintendent for the contract companies. But any mention of demands from regulatory bodies would be a major red flag to anyone considering investing with Principal. Cormie wanted the note eliminated; the consolidated statement was again put on hold while Principal attempted to settle the capital demand issue with Tewfik Saleh so the note could be dropped.

It would not be signed off for another half year.

Pennock also had questions about the $36-million worth of Athabasca Holdings preferred shares that had gone to the contract companies during the Carma transaction. Were they qualified assets under the *Investment Contracts Act*? Could Cormie take companies which were prohibited investments, put them into Athabasca, and then legally sell Athabasca shares to the contract companies? Pennock referred this question to his firm's lawyer. "They just said that, quite correctly, there was some serious questions around it and we terminated their services at that time, just from the point of view that we didn't want them to continue with it," Pennock testified. "Our strategy then was to go back to management and ask them to clarify it for us."

This request sent Principal officials scurrying for a satisfactory legal opinion, and for appraisals supporting the prices paid for the companies acquired in the Carma deal—witness Christa Petracca's search for a favourable valuation of the Cayman Islands bank, described earlier in this chapter.

Petracca also went to Keith Ferguson, a lawyer with Parlee, Henning, Mustard & Rodney, which had handled the Carma transaction. In May, Ferguson's colleague C.R. Henning had provided an opinion that the $23-million asset dump was not a sale. Now she asked Ferguson for an opinion that Athabasca was a "legal for life" company, and therefore a qualified investment for the contract companies under the *Investment Contracts Act*. Drafts of the opinion floated back and forth among Ferguson, Pennock and Petracca throughout July and August, and a favourable opinion was finally issued on August 27, 1984. The letter satisfied Pennock, but not the provincial auditors, who continued to ask questions for several months.

During July, Pennock twice asked Donald Cormie whether the CDIC had followed up on its earlier threats to Principal Trust. Both times Cormie told him, "No." Pennock eventually learned about the Section 25 notice from John Cormie, who was, Pennock said, "pretty sensitive about giving me the letter because of some concerns his father might have." Donald Cormie apparently intended that Pennock should not know about the Section 25 threat until after Principal's consolidated statement had been signed off. If Pennock wasn't aware of it, he couldn't report it in the statement.

Several months later, Pennock wrote a memo to file on his dealings with Principal Group: "During the course of events D.M. Cormie twice denied having received a letter from CDIC that was clearly issued and delivered to PS&T prior to our asking if such a letter had been received. This significantly contributed to the ensuing breakdown of communications and also brought the questions of management integrity into focus in our minds."

On July 16—the day before his telephone speaker conversation with Deputy Minister Barry Martin—Pennock wrote to Cormie recommending several improvements to Principal's accounting and management practices. Cormie ignored Pennock's suggestion that Principal should be more conservative in its accounting practices. Aggressive accounting was all that separated Principal from bankruptcy, and things were going to get worse, not better. But he did act on Pennock's personnel advice; he would search for, and three months later hire, a talented vice-president of finance. (We'll meet Bill Johnson later.) And he would assign Christa Petracca to head a "SWAT team" to concentrate on the "recovery of value" of a couple of dozen of Principal's shakiest properties.

ABOVE: Edmonton's Victoria High School Students' Union 1938-1939. Room Rep Donald Mercer Cormie, 17, is in the centre.

Photo: The Edmonton Journal

ABOVE: From *The Edmonton Journal* archives: George Cormie was provincial poultry inspector until losing his job during the Depression. He soon found work at the North West Mill and five years later bought the company. In 1963 George had the great satisfaction of telling the *Journal* that getting fired from his government job at 47 was the best thing that could have happened to him.

RIGHT: Donald was always George Cormie's golden boy. At 21, while still at the University of Alberta, he became secretary-treasurer of his father's feed mill. After Harvard he articled with the prominent Edmonton lawyer who handled the mill's legal work.

Evergreen & Gold, University of Alberta

City Man to Wed in Massachusetts

Engagement of Miss Elver Elizabeth Ekstrom, of West Somerville, Mass., shown above with her fiance, Mr. Donald Mercer Cormie, son of Mr. and Mrs. G. M. Cormie, of Garneau, was announced recently by the bride-elect's parents, Mr. and Mrs. John E. Ekstrom of West Somerville. Miss Ekstrom was born in Sweden and received her education in the United States, where she has been active in international student activities. Mr. Cormie was graduated from the University of Alberta in law, and is a former editor of The Gateway, the university newspaper. He received the Judge Green Silver Medal in law and a scholarship under the Viscount Bennett Trust fund. Mr. Cormie was a purser with the Canada Steamship Lines before taking post-graduate

ABOVE: (L) This announcement of Cormie's 1946 engagement created an indignant stir among some of his war-fevered set back home. The uniform looked military, but came from a summer job aboard the luxury liner *S.S. Noronic*. Edmonton chums knew the closest Cormie got to the war was compulsory training on the University of Alberta campus. (R) This U of A yearbook photo was captioned "Cormie on guard."

In 1953 Ralph P. Forster pitched his idea of a western-based financial institution to realtor Stan Melton, then brought in the vacuum salesmen who applied their hard-sell tactics to investment contracts. DMC, Melton's lawyer, got in on the ground floor and four years later took over the company. LEFT: During WWII Forster did P.R. for the British. Here he chats with U.S. president Harry S. Truman.

Principal's Professionals

We Pay These Men . . .
To Work For You

They do their work well — how well?
Example: a 62% increase in net asset value
on the Principal Growth Fund. Single year
increase from $3.00 — February 1, 1967
to $4.85 — December 31, 1967. Principal
Growth Fund is just one of the many
specialized investment services offered as part
of the Principal "performance portfolio".
Put the "Professionals" to work for you.
You owe it to yourself. Mail the reply card
now — and get the full story on
Principal's Professionals.

PRINCIPAL
SAVINGS & TRUST COMPANY

A MEMBER OF THE PRINCIPAL GROUP

Head Office: THE FINANCIAL BUILDING, EDMONTON, ALBERTA — Phone 429-5361
offices across Canada

*The largest Alberta-based, All-Canadian financial institution
with over $76 million assets under administration.*

Flier circa 1969.
DMC is flanked
by Ralph Forster,
seated left, and
sales maestro
Ken Marlin,
standing right.
Note the crest
with the P on
the knight's
shield. That's St.
George, battling
the fire-breathing
dragon of "fear,
doubt and want."
Also note the
reassuring CDIC
decal in the lower
left corner. The
pitch here is for a
mutual fund
which is not
CDIC-insured.

LEFT: From the *Babylon Course in Financial Success:* Every gold piece you save is a slave to work for you. Packaged in simulated parchment, the booklets were written in quasi-Biblical jargon that rang all the emotional bells of Principal's working class prairie clientele. Salesmen were taught to pitch the *"three laws of thrift"*:

- *A part of all you earn is yours to keep*
- *Pay yourself first*
- *There's no better time to start saving than now.*

BELOW: In 1965 DMC took his family to China. L TO R: Neil, 11; John, 18; Allison, 15; Donnie, 17; Jaimie, 13. John became president of Principal Savings & Trust. Jaimie took charge of securities trading. In 1986-87 Principal paid Allison, an archaeology student, $120,000 for her research into the carbon dating of ancient deer bones. DMC claimed the data was required for his cyclical analysis of the economy.

ABOVE: In the boardroom: DMC at the head of the table, with Jaimie and Ken Marlin to his right and Christa Petracca and John left.

LEFT: DMC felt son John "wasn't aggressive enough" and hired George Aboussafy as Principal Trust general manager. Here Aboussafy drums up support for Bruce Cormie during his 1984 bid for a federal Tory nomination.

BELOW: Super salesman Ken Marlin was a railroader and vacuum salesman when he joined Principal in 1954.

Photo: Ken Orr, *The Edmonton Journal*   Photo: Ray Guigere

Photo: Brian Gavriloff, *The Edmonton Journal*

ABOVE: In 1983 the Cormie Ranch auctioned prime heifers in the Principal Plaza penthouse. Ranch-hands stood by with brooms at the ready to eliminate any indiscretions. BELOW: In 1987 the auction was at the West Edmonton Mall ice arena. Here DMC and wife Eivor proudly display an award applauding their bulls' power-packed bloodlines. The cutline for this photo, published in Principal's *Crusader*, quoted DMC's favourite motto: *"Make no small plans for they have no magic to stir men's souls."*

The Principal *Crusader*, April 1987.

ABOVE: Diane Stefanski was bookkeeper for the mysterious Department 8, which secretly chanelled Principal Group funds to Cormie's privately-controlled companies as low- and no-interest loans. At the time of the collapse the debt amounted to $64.4 million. Stefanski's testimony was crucial to comprehending the byzantine Principal structure and the flow of cash to the "upstairs" companies.
RIGHT: Principal Plaza in downtown Edmonton. In 1982 Principal leased the top three storeys of the tower, but many investors believed the company owned the building.

Principal Group Ltd. 1984 Annual Report

ABOVE: Eric Espenberg, member of the investment contract companies' boards of directors— the "human pencil." His duties: "Just put my signature on various documents."
RIGHT: Nor did Jude Halvorson, DMC's secretary, ask questions when he suggested she buy shares of County Investments Ltd., one of the Department 8 companies. During the collapse Cormie's lawyers stunned her with a request to sign an affidavit acknowledging County's debt of $6.9 million.

Photos: The Principal *Crusader*, September 1985 and February 1987

Principal salesmen were portrayed as professionals "backed by the expertise of our investment, tax and legal departments." In fact they were part of a high-pressure operation, trained to wring the last dollar possible out of their clients. They earned high commissions, diamond rings and exotic vacations for selling risky investment contracts, mutual funds and promissory notes.

ABOVE: In 1985 Field Supervisor Jay Moulton and and General Sales Manager Wally Noble "fight over the purse"—a trip to Greece.

LEFT: In December 1986 sales campaign winners cruised down the Mexican coast. Top-selling Principal Plaza branch manager Jim Golhooly is at the captain's wheel.

RIGHT: Don Slater, Principal's hottest salesman, and his wife Jacquie meet the ship's captain.

Photo: Mike Pinder, *The Edmonton Journal*

ABOVE: Hutterites were essential customers from Principal's earliest days. Colonies held $30 million in Principal Group promissory notes when the company collapsed and will receive less than half their money back.

ABOVE: DMC and Christa Petracca, Principal Group VP, emerge from the Café Select, one of their favourite Edmonton haunts during the Code inquiry. Petracca, Cormie's close friend, nagged him in the days before the collapse for delivery of a $120,000 bonus.
BELOW: For 25 years Alberta regulator Jim Darwish (L) wrote reports criticizing the operation of the Principal investment contract companies. In 1984 he lost his job after warning Consumer Affairs Minister Connie Osterman that the companies' finances were desperate and dangerous to investors. Osterman's deputy minister Barry Martin (CENTRE) knew the Principal companies were in big trouble—but he believed he was following the policy of the Conservative government when he stopped regulators from conducting investigations or making any demands which could threaten their survival. Superintendent of Insurance Tewfik Saleh (R) was supposed to refuse the companies licences if they weren't solvent. He testified that Martin and Osterman stopped him from doing his job.

Photo: Jim Wells, *Calgary Sun*

ABOVE: Fifty years of Alberta free enterprise: Premiers Ernest Manning, Don Getty and Peter Lougheed. When Lougheed took office in 1971 he declared his support for western-based financial institutions. Dozens of financial companies thrived during his regime, before collapsing in the 1980s. RIGHT: In 1973 Attorney General Merv Leitch wrote a memo to Lougheed warning that regulators had been alarmed for years about Principal. "I am convinced we should do everything possible to head off a possible collapse of these companies," Leitch said. BELOW: Treasurer Lou Hyndman (L), head of a Cabinet committee (1984-86) dealing with financial companies' problems, testified he had no idea the Principal companies were insolvent. (CENTRE) Allberta only became aggressive with Principal after pressure from British Columbia regulators. Bill Smith was B.C.'s Superintendent of Brokers in 1986 when he discovered the contract companies' insolvency and demanded a solution. (R) In June 1987 then-Treasurer Dick Johnston pressed Donald Cormie to throw in more money. When he refused, there was no choice but to cancel their licences.

Photo: *The Edmonton Journal*

Photo: *The Edmonton Journal*   Photo: Ray Giguere   Bruce Edwards, *The Edmonton Journal*

Signs visible in photo:
PRINCIPAL'S GAINS ARE FIC. + A.I.C. LOSSES
STRIP! CORRIE OF OUR MONEY
MAY BE UNSOPHISTICATED BUT NOT STUPID
WE WANT NO HANDOUTS JUST OUR OWN MONEY BACK NOW
THE RAT PACK ALBERTA B.C. AND
E E WASUIK I AM A PRINCIPAL INVESTOR

ABOVE: Six weeks after Alberta cancelled the contract companies' licences, the rest of the Principal house of cards collapsed. Unprecedented public protest forced Alberta into a public inquiry.   BELOW: Inspector Bill Code with transcripts of testimony taken during his two-year inquiry. Six years after the collapse the RCMP continues to investigate.

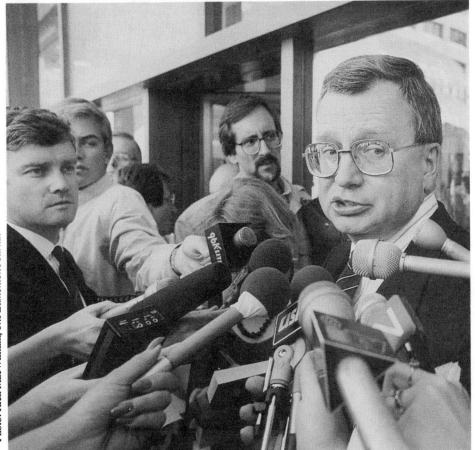

Photo: Rick MacWilliam, *The Edmonton Journal*

Photo: Larry Arbour

ABOVE: Lawyer Robert White is swarmed by reporters after release of the Code report. White, court-appointed investors' counsel, persuaded Inspector Code there was "evidence tending to prove" fraud, theft, tax evasion, false advertising and stock market manupulation.

LEFT: White's co-counsel John McNiven focused on government involvement, arguing that Alberta was negligent in its regulation of Principal's contract companies. Code laid the political blame on Consumer Affairs Minister Connie Osterman, a junior minister in the Lougheed and Getty Cabinets. In a 1991 interview McNiven said he backed off pursuing senior politicians' involvement because he didn't want to embarrass the people who could authorize compensation to his clients. He said of Osterman: "Can you think of a better fall-guy?"

OVER: Osterman leaves the Alberta Legislature in 1989 after Premier Getty fired her from Cabinet.

11

Donald and the Cupcake

And I want to tell all the women in this room that this is one company where women have tremendous opportunity. You can go right to the top just as fast as you can move.

Donald Cormie in a speech to Principal employees in 1983

PRINCIPAL STAFF CALLED HER "Cupcake." The *CUP* were her initials—Christa Ute Petracca—which appeared on office memos. She was a gorgeous blonde and she was Donald Cormie's very special friend.

Petracca, vice-president of corporate development, was an important force within the Principal Group of Companies. She was one of only a handful of people aware of Principal's financial problems, and Cormie used her as his "trouble-shooter," assigning her to several particularly sticky problems. Sometimes she joined him on lobbying visits to powerful political figures; other times she cultivated her own personal contacts. In her capacity as director or executive of various Cormie companies, Petracca put her signature to several questionable transactions. A few times, she signed on both sides of a deal.

After 1982, Petracca assisted Cormie in his push into the U.S. market. She was vice-president and chief executive officer of most of the U.S.-based investment companies and was frequently in Arizona to oversee operations there. After 1984, as Cormie's co-director of Athabasca Holdings, she shared control over the Cayman Islands bank and joined him on visits to the island. In 1985, Cormie assigned her to head the three-person "SWAT" team established to deal with the conglomerate's massively overvalued real estate portfolio. In that capacity, Petracca handled several costly controversial projects.

Petracca's friendship with Cormie was one of the untold stories at the Code inquiry. None of the lawyers cared to raise the issue in front of the television cameras recording the hearings. When the microphones were off, the Cupcake jokes were unstoppable—and largely unrepeatable.

In Cormie's penthouse office, a small Picasso drawing used to hang above the toilet. Cormie took the drawing with him when he departed in 1987. A member of the Principal Group bankruptcy trustee's team, which occupied the office during part of the Code hearings, gleefully thumbtacked a photo of Petracca in place of the Picasso.

Cormie and Petracca were close companions. Cormie spent time at Petracca's home, and was sometimes seen jogging or bicycling in her neighbourhood. They lunched together, dined together, travelled together and appeared together socially. Petracca glowed in Cormie's reflected glory, and often wrote memos or made comments to employees and associates which made it clear she operated with his complete confidence and support.

Petracca was sometimes described in news reports as a "family friend," but the only Cormie close to her was Donald. His wife Eivor maintained a dignified public silence. She remained in the house on Grandview Drive and tried to keep up appearances at parties and company functions. One Principal employee remembers seeing Cormie dancing with Petracca at the Cormie Ranch Day hoedown, while Eivor looked on. Another remembers the Christmas parties where Cormie sat, ignoring Eivor on his right, while absorbed in conversation with Petracca to his left. Mortified family members sometimes summoned up courage to ask Cormie to drop the relationship, but got a chilly brush-off.

The friendship was the talk of moneyed Edmonton. Lawyers, accountants and their business clients chortled together during rounds of golf and expense-account lunches. Their wives whispered over bridge games and afternoon coffee. "He just flaunted her," one city matron muttered.

While reporting on the Code hearings, I invited Neil and John Cormie for coffee, and asked them about the relationship between Petracca and their father. John dismissed the question as irrelevant. "My God, if you dug up all the flings and affairs between people in every big company, you wouldn't have time to do anything else," he said. Neil elbowed him, and he would say nothing more.

As the family rift deepened, Neil grew more forthcoming. In a mid-1989 interview with the *Calgary Herald*,[1] he said his mother had been "deeply hurt" by the publicity surrounding Cormie's friendship with Petracca. "My father works very well with Christa," he said. "I do not, nor do any other members of my family." He added that Eivor, despite the hurt she felt, had been invaluable in "keeping everyone's spirits up" during the Code inquiry.

A wonderfully telling photograph appears in Principal Group's 1985 annual review. Several Principal executives are seated around a mahogany boardroom table. At its head, papers in hand and clearly in charge, is Donald Cormie. Jaimie is to Cormie's right; to his left is Petracca. Further down the table, to Jaimie's right, is

Ken Marlin, Cormie's partner of 25 years. Below Petracca is John. How mortifying for him, the eldest son, to be upstaged both by a younger brother and Petracca. Over coffee, he denied that Petracca held power in the corporation. "She was just involved in a few of the glamour projects—some of the more interesting real estate developments—and people are so jealous," he told me. "She really didn't have a lot of say elsewhere."

In fact, Petracca was active in many areas, including the trust company, John's personal turf. In early 1987, when George Aboussafy quit his job as general manager of Principal Trust, things were going badly for the company. But Aboussafy also blamed his departure on frustration at Cormie's favouritism toward family members and his female vice-president. "I was concerned with Ms. Petracca's influence, yes," Aboussafy testified. "She was becoming involved in sales, marketing and real estate, and I felt she didn't have the [necessary] background. I know Christa certainly didn't understand real estate."

While clearly a clever and hard-working woman, Petracca had little business experience. She had worked one year as an accountant when Cormie hired her in 1978 as his executive assistant. Two years later he appointed her vice-president of corporate development, a position he created just for her.

During the Code inquiry Petracca was asked what qualifications justified her control over a multi-million-dollar real estate portfolio. Here's her reply: "I have a Bachelor of Commerce with distinction from the University of Calgary. I have an MBA, I'm a chartered accountant. At the time I was asked by senior management to take over the executive, really, direction of managing this task force on the real estate, I had been with the company for eight years and, I believe, Mr. Cormie had confidence in my judgment, I gather, and felt that I was obviously the most—one of the most familiar people with the real estate portfolio, at the executive level, certainly."

SHE WAS BORN CHRISTA UTE LASER in Neuwied, a town in the West German Rheinland, in December 1947—six months after Eivor Cormie gave birth to John. Thirty-one years later she was interviewed for a job by Ken Marlin, who referred her to John, who referred her to his father. By four o'clock that day, Donald Cormie, then 56, announced that he'd hired a new executive assistant. Before long, company executives were speculating about their relationship.

In 1978, when Petracca joined Principal, she was involved with millionaire Robert Wekherlien, whose wife Helene described to me the genesis of the affair. Petracca met Wekherlien, a real estate developer, while doing accounting work for his partner. "And then it started," Helene said. Suddenly Wekherlien was always late, he had to go out of town on weekends, "and you never knew if he would come home or not." The phone would ring, Helene would answer it, and no-one would speak. When Petracca was on the road she would call collect, "and she would want to speak to my husband. She was a pest, an absolute pest."

That was in the spring of 1976. Wekherlien was 53 and Helene was 47; they had been married for 18 years. Petracca was 29. The Wekherliens quarrelled violently after Helene learned her husband had co-signed Petracca's loan application for a $60,000 mortgage to build a house. "I guess he was absolutely taken with her," Helene told me. "He said, 'I like her. She showed me how to live.' " Thanks to the Alberta real estate boom, Wekherlien's income had increased dramatically just before he met Petracca. For the first time in his life he was in a position to be extravagant, and he showered Petracca with gifts and very good times.

Helene endured a barrage of physical and verbal abuse, then, in mid-1978, Wekherlien abandoned her with no other support than the couple's charge card at Woodwards Department Store, where Helene worked as a part-time clerk. That December she filed for divorce. The action dragged on for years.

Wekherlien bought a house on Patricia Drive and moved in with Petracca, after transferring joint ownership to her name. In 1979, Petracca had a baby girl and Wekherlien gave the infant, Shauna, his last name. He decided to provide for the little girl's future and endured an intensive medical examination, passing with flying colours. The Mony Life Insurance Company of Canada issued him a $500,000 policy naming "Christa Petracca Wekherlien, Wife" as beneficiary in trust for Shauna.

Three years later, Petracca publicly declared her regard for Donald Cormie in an *Edmonton Journal* society column which occasionally featured prominent local women. "Christa loves Beethoven and Haydn and most admires Don Cormie, Henry Ford and Leonardo da Vinci," it said. The July 1982 column, which described Petracca as a vivacious blonde, said her "likes" included "her three-year-old daughter, travelling, speaking engagements, intelligent people, people who are doing interesting things, business people, bankers, exercising and swimming. She dislikes uninformed or egocentric people and those who absolutely know everything about everything even when they don't." Her favourite books were *Great Expectations* and *The Covenant*.

Two months later Wekherlien and Petracca broke up. In September 1982, they signed over the Patricia Drive house to Wekherlien's real estate company for $25,000. He continued to live in there, and until his death paid all Shauna's expenses, including a nanny's salary. He kept a room for the little girl in his home, where she was always welcome.

The same month that Petracca released her interest in Wekherlien's house she bought an elegant condominium in the exclusive neighbourhood of Wolf Willow. It was purchased with a $200,000 interest-free mortgage from Principal Group Ltd., personally approved by Cormie. Principal got the money for the loan by borrowing $200,000 at market rates from the Canadian Imperial Bank of Commerce down the street. This was an extraordinary deal for Petracca. Cormie's partner Ken Marlin, in contrast, was charged 20% interest on a business loan. Marlin's $97,000 mortgage was taken with National Trust Company at 10% because, he was told, company policy prohibited doing business with shareholders or employees.

Petracca's mortgage came with strings attached: she had to live in the condo as her principal residence, and had to be employed full time by Principal. If not, the entire loan and retroactive interest became payable in full. As well, the mortgage said, "the Mortgagee [Cormie] shall always have the sole right to determine that the Mortgagor [Petracca] has ceased to be employed as provided above and/or has ceased to live in the premises as her principal residence, and thereupon, without notice, to declare this mortgage for all purposes, immediately due and payable." It was a sweetheart leash, giving Cormie almost absolute control over Petracca's personal life. If Cormie fired her, or if she chose to work or live elsewhere, she lost her home—unless she could find a similarly generous deal.

In December 1983, Wekherlien was stricken with cancer. He underwent surgery in January 1984, but continued to weaken and died that September. Helene Wekherlien reconciled with him and nursed him during his final months. When Shauna stayed at the house—Petracca was often out of town on business—Helene took care of her as well.

When Wekherlien died, his estate was a shambles. The 1982 real estate crash had severely reduced the value of his property holdings, which were heavily mortgaged by several banks and trust companies. The assets disappeared into a pit of unpayable debts and when the estate was dismantled a year later, $1,676,457.55 was left owing. Wekherlien made a deathbed effort to put his affairs in order, according to court documents filed by lawyers acting for the executors of the estate (including his son Rainer, from a previous marriage). The will was rewritten, creating a trust agreement which would have used a portion of the $500,000 insurance policy to deal with persistent creditors, thereby buying time for his executors to bring the estate to a better financial position.

Petracca challenged the changes, arguing they were "procured through undue influence," and that Wekherlien was under heavy sedation and thus mentally incompetent. "There was an oral understanding between myself and the deceased," Petracca said in an affidavit filed in August 1985, "that the deceased would provide for Shauna Wekherlien by naming her as the beneficiary of a life insurance policy in the amount of $500,000 and that the income from the insurance policy was to be used by myself to support Shauna Wekherlien."

The battle continued for 11 months. Finally, Wekherlien's creditors commenced foreclosure actions against his properties. At that point, Wekherlien's executors dismantled the estate.

Soon after, Petracca won control of the $500,000. A court order issued in September 1985 instructed that she be paid $2,500 a month from the fund to support Shauna, then six. As well, she was to control investment of the money, reporting annually to the province's public trustee about its administration.

A report filed by Petracca that year detailed an impressive assortment of expenses. The nanny's salary and miscellaneous child care expenses came to $1,400 a month. As well, Petracca spent $145 a month for various classes (swimming, ballet, skiing, skating, music, gymnastics and crafts); $155 for clothing and shoes;

$300 for food for Shauna and the nanny; $295 for transportation, "including gas"; $275 for family vacation and outings; $145 for video rental and entertainment; and $85 for books, toys and miscellaneous. "In addition," Petracca said, "I pay the sum of $2,000 per month for housing, a portion of which is for the benefit of Shauna Wekherlien."

In early 1986, Petracca gave birth to a second daughter. She has never said who fathered the child.

Petracca's lifestyle during those years was a far cry from the more modest circumstances Petracca knew when she first came to Canada. When she emigrated here in 1964 at 16, she spoke little English and had no money. Within a day of her arrival, she married fellow German immigrant Frederick Widmann, a 32-year-old engineer working at a gold mine near Yellowknife, North West Territories, and set up housekeeping in a trailer park.

Petracca likes to talk about her first job in the Canadian north—tagging clothes in the basement of Yellowknife's Hudson's Bay store for $150 a month. But she didn't stay there for long. Over the next five years, she moved through a string of clerical and secretarial positions in the construction, mining and petroleum industries—including a stint as secretary to the Clerk of the Supreme Court in the Yellowknife court house. She's remembered as flamboyant and well-dressed, "a man's woman," with few female friends. She liked the company of married men, especially older married men, and was popular grist for the local rumour mill. "I remember what stuck in my mind," one female court worker told me. "That people talked about her all the time, that she created a stir because she was young and glamorous and married to an older man." Another former co-worker, a man, recalls: "We used to call her the Blonde Bomber."

Widmann, long-divorced from Petracca, confirms his young bride's notoriety in the mining town, but writes it off as predictable jealousy on the part of less dazzling women. "She had brains besides looks," Widmann told me in 1990. "This is a combination that is terrible. You don't want a woman like that anywhere around your husband." At the same time, he agreed that Petracca was primarily interested in the conversation and company of men. "Of course, because she probably perceived that most women were not her equal," Widmann said. "This is the feeling that I had, and…she was perfectly right. I mean, why talk to people, when you say 'Hi' to them they're stuck for an answer?" Widmann described Petracca as "very condescending… She tolerated people. She never considered another woman a threat to her. She probably perceived herself as a cut above, and 90% of the time she was right."

This attitude can be traced partly to the pair's elitist backgrounds in Germany, where Widmann met Petracca at a wine festival. She was a beautiful, convent-educated girl with highbrow tastes in literature and music. Her well-to-do family had made its fortune in the chemical-pharmaceutical industry. Her mother's family—Widmann described them as "very refined people"—had been wealthy before World War II, and ended up afterward in reduced but comfortable circumstances.

There was, however, tension in the household. "Her mother and her grandparents, they were old money," but her father—to whom Petracca was devoted, "just married into that... He struck me as the kind of chap who did not fit into the old-time family album. He came from a different social sphere." Widmann remained in Germany for about half a year after his chance meeting with Petracca (she would have been 15 when they connected at the wine festival) before returning to Canada. Seven or eight months later, he arranged to have her join him. They married immediately, as required by Canadian immigration law.

Two decades after their parting Widmann remembers Petracca fondly and a little wistfully. Because of the difference in their ages, "you function more as a mentor than anything else," he said. It didn't seem odd to him that a 16-year-old girl would marry a man twice her age. "Probably it's better for a young girl to get on to an older man, because older men are a little more gentle you know, less selfish than their younger counterparts," he said. "We had a good understanding, she learned quickly. While she was married, she was always the perfect wife, the perfect hostess. She was terrific. She could entertain people, even at that age, she could draw out men, professionals, talk with people almost at a level with them."

At the same time, "where men were concerned, she reminded me of a little boy in front of an anthill. He pushes the stick in to see what the ants will do."

In the end, Petracca grew tired of life with Widmann. "As it turned out she really wasn't cut out for marriage, period," he said. "I thought perhaps for some time in our marriage, well maybe she might get over it and settle down, but then I realized it was not to be. One day she said, 'I can't go on like this. I'm going to strike out on my own.' "

They had been married about four and a half years, and parted, Widmann said, "on excellent terms." He divorced Petracca in 1969; a local lawyer was named as correspondent. Afterward they remained friends, and Petracca sometimes came to him for advice. "I advised her to seek out higher education. I always instilled that in her."

Both Widmann and Petracca left Yellowknife. Petracca ended up in Calgary, where she completed correspondence courses leading to her high school matriculation in 1970 at the age of 23. She became a Canadian citizen that year.

In 1970 she also met and married Antonino Petracca, an Italian immigrant 10 years her senior. Nino, as he was known, worked as a geologist with a large Calgary oil firm. During their marriage Christa attended classes at the University of Calgary, earning a Bachelor of Commerce degree in 1974.

Petracca attended most of high school and university part-time, working variously at an oil firm, with National Parks and briefly for a small publishing company. During the last few months at university, she studied full-time and Nino supported her. "She was extremely ambitious and determined. She worked hard to do what she wanted to do and get what she wanted to get," he told me in 1988. Petracca launched a vigorous campaign during her university years to gain entrée to the privileged elements of society. "She would meet people at various clubs, tennis clubs and that kind of thing, and befriend people to get certain things—to get perhaps a job, perhaps to be able to say: 'I'm a friend of so-and-so.' "

Nino knew little about Petracca's early years in Canada. By the time they met her English was excellent, and she had little interest in dwelling on the past. "She didn't talk a lot about much of her past, no," Nino says. "She had an unhappy marriage. She was married to the wrong person, she said. All I know, she said she left Yellowknife because she wasn't happy being with the man she was married to. As a matter of fact, she left with $50 in her pocket."

When Petracca became disillusioned with her second marriage, she went to her first husband for advice. By that time Widmann was working in Kimberly, across the border in British Columbia, and the pair rendezvoused in Banff. "I always tried to keep my advice on the level of utmost practicality," Widmann said. "I said, 'Look, Christa, you just hang in there—you just go to school. You might as well have the security. The main thing is you finish your schooling, period, and it is most expedient to do that in the auspices of Mr. Petracca.' Probably she saw it my way, and that's exactly what she did."

Christa's marriage to Nino broke up shortly after her graduation. The couple signed a separation agreement in September 1974 and she moved to Edmonton to study for an MBA degree at the University of Alberta. At Petracca's request Nino filed for divorce in 1976. "We agreed between ourselves the grounds was adultery, and she was the adulterer," Nino says. "It was very easy. The judge said did you commit adultery and she said, 'Yes.' " The divorce was granted in 1977, and that was the last Nino heard of her. In 1981, he moved to California and became a real estate salesman.

Nino told me the marriage ended because of philosophical differences. "I didn't agree with her that the important principles in life were money and power, no matter how you got it. We were not compatible at all. I might be ambitious, but not to the point where I don't care about other people in order to make money. She used people...you can use people for a while, but eventually it's going to catch up with you."

Petracca continued to use her married name after moving to Edmonton. She earned her MBA in one year, then articled with the firm of Thorne Riddell, becoming a chartered accountant in 1978. In 1977, she incorporated Laser Management Ltd. (using her maiden name Laser), and for a year operated an accounting and consulting business. Then she went to work for Donald Cormie.

It was a match made elsewhere than heaven: two clever, manipulative, greedy individuals, "goal-oriented," and happy in their work. Petracca lied, bullied and flirted whenever it might help the cause.

Petracca wasn't shy about using her good looks to advantage in a business setting. One government regulator felt the steam so strongly during a particularly difficult meeting that he told his wife about it when he returned home. "Christa is bright and very impressive but I had a feeling she was dangerous as well," he told me. "I had the sense that you had to be careful not to get swept in. If one were susceptible to guile and charm, you know, that she would be an expert at doing it. Christa was not beyond using her charm to manipulate people."

The official remembers being invited by Christa to step out into the corridor for a quiet chat. "She wanted to talk person-to-person, you know: 'I think I can talk to you, you would understand. If you and I did talk about it, I'm sure we could make each other understand.' In my years of business experience, I have never run into business women who were using guile and charm to get what they want. You hear stories about that kind of thing but I had never before experienced that. I remember another thing about Christa. She would talk to you close up. I did find it disconcerting... North Americans tend to stand apart, but I remember reading that Europeans seem to need less personal space than we do. Christa did not stand apart. It was close enough for me to notice it."

Despite the discomfort, he doesn't recall backing away during their tete-a-tete. "I probably just stood there. She was a very impressive woman."

In August 1986, Petracca wanted a property evaluator to provide a favourable valuation of the Rimrock Inn, a Banff hotel owned by the contract companies. Peter Walsh, a partner with Pannell Kerr Forster Management Consultants, had estimated the hotel's market value at about $12 million. Petracca wrote Walsh a letter asking him for "an 'audit' opinion of value closer to the $15 million for internal purposes." She said she needed the opinion "for mortgage purposes as soon as possible" and playfully promised to pay his consulting bill "on receiving two opinions of value together with one free lunch and champagne of your choice." The second opinion estimated a value in the range of $13.8 million to $15 million. About the lunch? "We didn't have champagne and, yes, we had lunch," she testified.

The next year, Petracca got into trouble with Walsh's firm when she claimed in an offering memorandum that Pannell Kerr had "appraised" the Rimrock at $14.6 million. This document announced Principal's plan to raise money from Hong Kong investors to develop the Rimrock. Jim Devonshire, Pannell Kerr's professional standards partner, wrote Petracca furious letters in February and April 1987 demanding correction of her "false and misleading" claim. No specific value of $14.6 million had been determined, he said. The opinion was not an appraisal, and had been given to assist in arranging mortgage financing, not for publication. It took Petracca weeks to reply, with an abusive letter to Devonshire that basically told him to keep his nose out of her dealings with Walsh.

The $14.6 million figure was used in the memorandum, Petracca told Devonshire, because a detailed range of values "did not appear relevant to us at the time since this was mainly for additional information purposes and not for project valuation purposes." This is nonsense. The memorandum went to the Hong Kong Securities Commission and was designed for circulation to potential investors, who would rely on the information provided to decide whether to put money into the hotel. Finally, in mid-May, she forwarded an amendment to Hong Kong addressing Devonshire's concerns.

Devonshire recalls Petracca as a client who "leaned" on members of his firm.

He told me in 1990 he hadn't dealt with her directly, but had heard about her tactics from colleagues. "She is a very intelligent and I think very versatile lady in that regard," he said. "She's no dummy. I think if cajoling and persuasion don't work, she'll try threats. There's more than one arrow to her bow." Devonshire said that he and Walsh worked out a good cop/bad cop strategy in an effort to cope. "Peter liked the combination. He'd be the good guy and get the work. I'd be the bad guy and keep them in line," Devonshire said. "He wasn't under any particular illusions about her. I think he just found it helpful to have someone like me as back-up when Christa sort of got aggressive about things."

Petracca had little credibility with accounting colleagues. Provincial auditor Al Hutchison testified the financial information she supplied "was misleading at best and very unacceptable," and that she had a serious "attitude problem." Petracca was constantly evading important questions, he said. "It seemed like everything she told me was like a total snow job. After a while I distrusted her completely."

There were also quarrels with Bill Johnson, who joined Principal as vice-president of finance in late 1984. Once Petracca so exasperated him that he hung up the phone on her. Petracca backed Cormie in his demands that dozens of properties be recorded in financial statements at values sometimes several times their real worth, and told members of Johnson's accounting staff that he "didn't know what he was talking about" when he argued the properties should be written down to a more realistic value.

Petracca's behaviour has cost her her registration as a chartered accountant in Alberta. In July 1992, the Institute of Chartered Accountants of Alberta cancelled her registration after finding her guilty of unprofessional conduct. The announcement issued by the institute said Petracca had (1) associated herself with misleading real estate asset values in financial statements; (2) associated herself with statements or representations in Special Bulletins (See Chapter 14) and the 1985 Annual Review (See Chapter 17) which were provided to investors when she knew—or should have known—statements related to the nature of the company's investments were false or misleading; and (3) associated herself with misleading financial information through the structuring of transactions.

During the Code inquiry, Cormie described Petracca as an excellent employee. "My only complaint was that she would sometimes run off in a direction that wasn't clear what the end result was. So I felt that I needed a better reporting system from her on a short-term basis." Petracca co-operated in spades, pouring a steady stream of memos and copies of correspondence in Cormie's direction. Unfortunately, she liked to let others know the boss was in the know, by way of the notation: "CC:DMC" (Carbon Copy: Donald Mercer Cormie). It gave her extra muscle. When instructing colleagues or requesting something from them, Petracca also liked to advise that Cormie had approved the action.

Cormie tried hard, but with limited success, to break her of these habits. In September 1985 Cormie wrote Petracca a memo: "I have indicated numerous times you are not to refer to my name on your correspondence and particularly that you have sent copies of correspondence to me. Would you please discontinue the practice and make sure that they are silent copies only."

Cormie took good care of his only female executive. Petracca collected almost $1 million in salary, bonuses and loans during the two and a half years before the Principal collapse. In June 1985 Cormie rewrote her employment letter, increasing her salary to $100,000 plus an annual bonus based on Principal Group profits. Petracca's salary jumped to approximately $125,000, then to $180,000 at the end of 1986.

Those in the know laughed themselves sick when they read Petracca's comments in an *Edmonton Journal* article, titled "Management climbing tips," part of a series on women and the work force. It advised ambitious women to find a "mentor" to speed their progress up the corporate ladder. "It's very important having someone helping, someone with your best interests at heart who looks at you not as a threat, but is older, experienced and secure in their position," Petracca said in October 1986. "But I've never seen an attractive woman yet that somebody didn't say: 'It can't be because she's capable, she must have slept her way to the top.' Eventually, they'll look at your work record and see that you're competent."

Petracca told the newspaper that Cormie "tells me people sometimes say to him: 'Gee, I saw you out with your pretty blonde secretary the other day.' He sort of smiles and tells them that's not his secretary, that's his vice-president of corporate development. People just aren't used to looking at a woman and saying 'There goes a senior executive.' It just takes time."

Petracca was represented by Cormie's lawyers during the early part of the Code inquiry. A few months into the hearings, when Petracca realized that Cormie intended to defend himself by denying responsibility, by insisting that the sleazy deals that littered the corporate books were the work of his underlings (including his sons and Petracca), she engaged her own lawyer, Sharon Harper. In a submission at the close of the inquiry, Harper said Petracca "had no knowledge of an intent to defraud" and was acting under Cormie's direction.

Petracca's memory often proved unreliable during her testimony. She could recall some incidents and details with crystal clarity, but many of the most difficult questions were answered by: "I can't recall." Sometimes she qualified her responses with: "to the best of my recollection." But she survived several days of questioning largely unscathed until confronted by investors' lawyer Robert White, who grilled her for hours before accusing her outright of participating in a cover-up. "Mrs. Petracca, there was, was there not, a practice in the Principal Group to conceal or obscure facts? You knew of that practice and you participated in it, didn't you?"

"No, Mr. White, I think that is inaccurate," Petracca protested. Then she burst into tears, a package of tissues at the ready. "Can I get a break, please?" she asked Inspector Code, then left the room weeping. She returned five minutes later. White declined to apologize for his aggressive questioning, saying only: "Mrs. Petracca, I am sorry about your feelings. There are a lot of people whose feelings have been hurt in this case and I act for a great number of them." Then, for the 15 minutes remaining, he continued his unrelenting cross-examination. Here's what happened next, as recounted in *Alberta Report*:[2]

> But instead of leaving, the normally publicity-shy Miss Petracca headed for a waiting CFRN television news camera. Her tears flowed afresh for the late-night news, and she accused Mr. White of "badgering" her. John Cormie just happened to be present. He decried Mr. White's tactics...
>
> But by then a seething Mr. White was demanding a retraction, and refusing to apologize for "doing his duty." Cross-examination may be tough, he said, but is "a device we need to test truth." John Cormie, notwithstanding his immediate instinct to back off, in the end refused to withdraw his statements. Mr. White, saying he would not be sidetracked by personal attacks, vowed to press on with the inquiry.

During the hearings, I called Petracca's office several times seeking an interview with her, but was always refused. Finally, I waylaid her in an elevator, and on the way down tried to persuade her to tell me her side of the story. She was clearly proud of her achievements since coming to Canada, and agreed it had been tough during the first years. Then her lawyer intervened, planting herself between us to end the conversation.

Asked for a photograph, Petracca refused. "A picture in the paper is the last thing I want. I want to preserve my family life," Petracca said softly over the lawyer's shoulder, a mere whisper of the German left in her accent. She looked me straight in the eye, an appeal from one woman to another. "Do you understand?" she asked, as the lawyer led her away.

12

Virtually insolvent

PROVINCIAL AUDITOR AL HUTCHISON had the unhappy task of analyzing the Principal companies' financial reports. Bruce Pennock's audit of the 1983 statements had been delivered in mid-May 1984 and landed on Hutchison's desk a few weeks later. He looked at them during the summer, went over to Principal Plaza to conduct his field examination, and in mid-August completed his annual reports on the companies. The reports employed the bluntest and strongest language available to an auditor, in the futile hope of prodding Tewfik Saleh into action. The "Conclusion and Recommendations" section of the 58-page analysis of First Investors began:

> FIC is virtually insolvent, has a severe capital shortage, is losing approximately $1 million a month from operations and is dependent on new customers' deposits to pay off existing customer deposits and to subsidize the company's losses.
>
> In addition FIC is reluctant to put additional capital into the company, does not follow direction from the Superintendent's office and is entering into large transactions with non-arms length companies [without advising the department] that are prejudicial to contract holders.
>
> It is my belief that if a large amount of additional capital is not injected into the company immediately they could incur severe cash flow problems once the public learns that their 10% to 18% certificates are only earning 4%...
>
> The cash flow problems and lack of capital is what caused the demise of our Provincially licensed mortgage brokers and it is my belief that this company is headed in this same direction and the crunch could be near.

The parallel report for Associated Investors advised that it was losing money at the rate of $360,000 a month. That totalled $1.36 million a month for the two companies, a combined operating loss (despite some window dressing to make them appear more profitable than they were) of $16.32 million a year.

Contrary to Ken Marlin's promise that spring, Hutchison's analysis revealed a continuing deterioration of both companies. The Section 8 financial tests showed that First Investors' deficit in unimpaired capital had increased from $62.5 million at the end of 1983 to $80 million on April 30, 1984. Its reserves were deficient by $76 million, and it needed to increase its qualified assets on deposit by another $130 million.[1] Associated Investors' unimpaired capital was deficient by $24 million. It showed a $21 million deficiency in reserves and a $33 million deficiency in qualified assets.

Using the company's own figures, First Investors' debt-to-equity ratio was a "staggering" 376:1 on April 30, 1984—up from 250:1 at the end of 1983. Three-quarters of the two companies' mortgages were now in arrears by three or more months. Hutchison estimated their book value was overstated by $67.9 million. For the first time, the break-up value of the two companies was calculated. Hutchison reported that First Investors had assets of $212.5 million and liabilities of $286 million. If it were liquidated, there would be a shortfall of $73.5 million. Associated Investors' shortfall was $21 million. And there was another problem:

> The co-operation from upper management during the current audit was very poor. e.g. phone messages were not returned, management was not always available to discuss items, information was not provided when promised and incorrect information in some cases was provided. As a result the audit took longer than usual and information requested at the time of our audit is still outstanding. I think the company's senior employees are beginning to recognize the serious situation facing FIC.

Hutchison made a number of recommendations: the contract companies should be held to a reasonable borrowing-to-capital ratio; the falsified Statement of Assets delivered in May by the company should be correctly prepared and audited; and, as others had advised, the $23-million transfer of properties from the trust company should be reversed. None of these things ever happened.

Hutchison's reports went first to his supervisor Burt Eldridge, who wrote a covering memo supporting all Hutchison's comments. He compared First Investors' situation to that of Alberta's devastated credit unions. Then he sent the reports, urging immediate remedial action, up the line to Superintendent of Insurance Tewfik Saleh.

Saleh read the reports in a panic—then went down the hall to show them to Barry Martin.

A couple of weeks later, Saleh also sent copies of the reports to George Kinsman, over in the Treasury department. The Cabinet's financial institutions task force had been established a couple of months earlier, and Kinsman was the Treasury official in charge of the Loans and Guarantees section, where the provincial bailouts of the Alberta financial institutions were worked out. Kinsman testified he didn't recall either asking for or receiving the reports. Nonetheless he read at least the first half of each one, making notes on the pages as he went.

Curiously, Saleh also sent Kinsman a sample copy of Principal's investment contract application form. Herein lies a tale.

That application form had arrived in Saleh's mail two months earlier, in early July, a couple of days before Saleh went to Martin with his appeal for an outside consultant. Addy Smith, a Cormie employee since the 1950s, was now a paralegal with Principal.

One of her duties was confirming that Principal had the approval required under the *Investment Contracts Act* for promotional materials issued by the contract companies. Going through the files, she had found no record of provincial approval for the application form—so she wrote to Saleh, resubmitting it for what must have seemed to her a rubber stamp.

Saleh was horrified at what he read. On the back of the form, up at the top, were the "Terms of the Contract," including:

> First Investors Corporation Ltd. and Associated Investors of Canada Ltd. are registered under the *Investment Contracts Act (Alberta)*. Assets equal to 100% of certificate liabilities are maintained on deposit with a Canadian Chartered bank. Assets are in qualified investments of the type permitted to Canadian incorporated life insurance companies.

The second sentence leapt to Saleh's eye. The companies were millions of dollars in the hole, and there was no way they could be allowed to claim they maintained enough assets to pay off all the certificates. Saleh sent the matter on to his assistant Bernard Rodrigues with a request for advice on how to handle it. In mid-July, Rodrigues contacted audit director Burt Eldridge, who responded on July 27 with a memo recommending the Superintendent consider stopping the contract companies from selling their certificates—period.

Eldridge, like Jim Darwish, had been fuming for years about the inadequacies of the *Investment Contracts Act*. He had joined the department as an auditor in 1976, and soon began to warn of the consequences of the inadequate 6% reserve and the drainage of "surplus" funds from the companies. In 1982, a government lawyer had supported this view, and in 1983 a letter sent by the Superintendent's office to First Investors directed that if the reserve rate was not specified in a contract, it would be assumed to be the guaranteed rate of 4%. First Investors ignored the directive, continuing to reserve at 6% and to drain the 2% "surplus" upwards.

The matter had continued to be raised periodically with the companies, most recently in January 1984 during the exchange of correspondence between Saleh and Ken Marlin. At that time, Marlin argued that the public would be "confused" if the 6% reserve rate were put on the contracts.

Now, in his memo to Saleh, Eldridge pointed out that additional credits were no longer being declared quarterly, as claimed on the application form. Given the companies' "present serious financial position," he recommended the Superintendent consider refusing approval for the companies to issue certificates with additional credits. He also remarked that the claim that "assets equal to 100% of certificate liabilities are maintained on deposit with a Canadian Chartered bank" was inaccurate because millions of dollars worth of assets were held in a bank in the U.S. As well, the reference to "life insurance" should be deleted, he said, because it created an illusion of security. Taking one final shot at the reserve system, he noted two additional shortcomings in the form:

> (a) The reserve rate is not stated (Section 30(b) of the *Investment Contracts Act*). The company uses 6% and this amount should be stated in the contract.
>
> (b) The definition of an investment contract states cash surrender or loan values must be included in the contract. This statement is not included.

Saleh, typically, went looking for another opinion. This time he asked Syed Zaf Bokhari, an accountant attached to the Superintendent's office, who replied on August 21 with a memo indicating he agreed with Eldridge on several points. The reference to life insurances companies should be dropped and the reserve rate should be stated in the contract, Bokhari said. He also recommended that the statement "Assets equal to 100 percent of the certificate liabilities are maintained on deposit with a Canadian chartered bank" be deleted.

A horrible dilemma for Saleh: that passage was the Principal sales force's single most effective tool. The next week, on August 29, Saleh told Rodrigues he had decided to ask Principal for a wording change on the contract application. Rodrigues summarized the discussion in a memo back to Saleh.

> The application form states that the company has on deposit assets equal to 100 percent of its liabilities with a Canadian chartered bank. Under the present financial circumstances we do not agree with this statement. It should be that the company is <u>required</u> to hold on deposit. In addition, the company should not compare itself to a life insurance company which falls under different legislation.

"Required" was underlined in the memo.

That was the solution. It was a lie to tell people that the companies had assets equal to their obligations when they didn't. Instead, the companies would now say that they were *supposed to have those assets*—without any indication that in fact they did not, and were jointly $163 million in the hole.

Grilled on this point at the Code inquiry, Saleh testified that he didn't consider the change to be misleading. If the passage referring to assets was deleted, "the person who would take it [the application form] would know nothing about it," he said. "But if I put the requirement of the legislation, I would give them a flag... The normal question would be, "Are they meeting this requirement or not?" Saleh offered this pathetic explanation even though he was aware at the time of his decision that the contract companies' financial records were a closely guarded secret, and that the only assurance the public could possibly seek would be from his department—which was determined to protect the companies.

Another decision was summarized in Rodrigues' memo:

While the *Investment Contracts Act* states that the assumed rate [reserve rate] be shown in the contract, it was concluded that it could possibly mislead the public. It was decided that the company determine the reserve rate for each class of contract and have the rate approved by the Superintendent when the contract is submitted for approval. It was concluded that the purpose of... the Act is for the Superintendent to regulate the reserving formula used by an issuer and not for disclosure to the contract holder.

This was Saleh's decision: investors, who had never had a hint about the use of an "assumed rate" of reserves, were not to be given the information for fear it might "mislead" them.

As Eldridge pointed out in his memo, the companies were required under the *Investment Contracts Act* to include the assumed rate in the contracts. But they never had, and Saleh had decided they never would. Who Saleh might have consulted with on this matter isn't known. He claims responsibility for the decision, but it is difficult to imagine that he took this step without discussing it with someone in authority. In one of those situations too remarkable to be a coincidence, Saleh had passed these decisions on to Rodrigues on August 29—the same day that Saleh had forwarded, to Treasury official George Kinsman, Hutchison's damning examination reports of the contract companies and a copy of the contentious application form.

Asked at the Code inquiry whether the application form had been sent to the Treasury Department because it "was also involved in connection with what should go on the form," Saleh answered: "Correct." Then he backtracked: "I didn't mention that they were involved in the approval of the form. I didn't mention that." Kinsman wasn't asked if he had anything to do with the decision to re-word the form. There was no point: Kinsman testified that he couldn't recall receiving or looking at the form. Nor did he remember asking for it, but conceded, "it is possible that I did." And, he volunteered: "I would have no interest in the contract."

There is evidence to the contrary. In the examination reports forwarded to Kinsman with the application form, there are a number of markings which Kinsman testified were indications of passages of particular interest to him. Among those passages were references to the reserve rate, including the following: "Our legal opinion obtained from the Attorney General's Department pursuant to Section 30 of the Act states that accumulations of interest at an assumed rate provided in the contracts relating to the reserves must be stated in the contracts. The assumed rate is not stated." This passage was boxed and marked "NB." Confronted with this, Kinsman testified that the passages were marked out of "idle curiosity," not any particular interest in the contracts or the reserve rate. He added that he knew nothing about the surplus being drained from the contract companies.

Meanwhile, Saleh instructed Rodrigues to have a letter drafted informing Principal of the change. Rodrigues passed this chore on Syed Zaf Bokhari, who went back to Saleh and tried to talk him out of it. Changing the words from "are maintained" to "are required to maintain" was really no change at all, he argued: it was itself misleading. Bokhari flourished Al Hutchison's recently completed annual examination reports of the contract companies. "Look here," he said, flipping through the First Investors report. "This company has a $130-million deficiency in its qualified assets on deposit. How can we allow them to tell the public that they have assets on deposit equal to 100% of their certificate liabilities?"

Saleh was on his way out the door for a meeting—with the crises surrounding the credit unions, the Principal companies and everything else, there seemed to be an endless flurry of meetings—and stopped to look at Bokhari. "Well, leave it with me. I'll get back to you."

And that was that.

A couple of weeks later, Bokhari still hadn't produced the requested letter, so Saleh took care of it himself. He handed the draft to Bokhari. "Zaf, I've got a meeting to attend, can you please send this letter in your name," he said, and rushed out. Bokhari typed the letter without modification and signed it. It went out on September 28, addressed to Addy Smith at Principal:

> On the back side of the application form, it is stated that the company has on deposit, assets equal to 100% of its liabilities with a Canadian Chartered Bank. Under the present financial circumstances we do not agree with this statement. However, if you wish, a statement similar to the following may be included: "Company is required under the *Investment Contracts Act* to maintain funds with a Canadian Chartered Bank equal to its liabilities to the holders of its contracts."

The letter went from Smith to the desk of her supervisor, lawyer Lynn Patrick; to the desk of Grant Mitchell, Principal vice-president of operations; then to the desk of advertising manager Barbara Jones. Jones, a university student at the time, had been told by Ken Marlin in July—the same period when the application form became an issue in the Superintendent's office —that she had been assigned the job of assuring that all promotional material complied with regulatory standards. "It was more a matter of, I suppose you could say, segregating the responsibility and narrowing the responsibility," Marlin testified. "My discussion with Barbara Jones was more to get her to realize that we expected her to carry that responsibility personally."

During the Code inquiry there was much debate about whether Mitchell, who would be elected as a Liberal to the Alberta legislature in 1986, had handled or seen the wording change on the contract forms. Mitchell, who had earned the CFA designation (chartered financial analyst) from an American university, acknowledged he had received Bokhari's letter. But he said he didn't remember reading it and didn't notice the significance of the change.

Mitchell did play a minor role in getting the form changed. In October he phoned Bokhari for clarification of another point raised in his September 28 letter, and the two exchanged brief correspondence on that matter. But, Mitchell testified, if he did notice the passage recommending the wording change, he didn't understand its implication. "It didn't strike me that a letter from a lower-echelon bureaucrat in government to a legal secretary would be a place where I would discover some profound difficulty with the company."[2]

Jones, on the other hand no problem figuring it out: "It was my impression that there was a problem."

August 15, 1984

DURING THE SUMMER DONALD CORMIE took a step that improved his personal financial situation tremendously, while pushing Principal Group Ltd. into irretrievable (although unacknowledged) insolvency.[3] At a time when the world was closing in on the Principal tower, Cormie decided to transfer a valuable asset upstairs from parent company Principal Group to grandparent company Collective Securities Ltd. The transaction not only snatched a multi-million dollar asset from Principal's hands, but moved it beyond the reach of the company's promissory noteholders.

The asset, subsidiary Principal Securities Management Ltd., known as PSML, was the money-making stock and bond investment arm of the Cormie conglomerate. At the time of the transfer, PSML was worth at least $15 million and was earning princely management fees for acting as investment advisor to Principal's various mutual funds. Most of the fees flowed to parent company Principal Group Ltd. (whose staff provided the actual investment, accounting and management services), producing approximately $9.3 million in revenue for Principal Group between 1980 and 1983.

Despite this, Principal Group sold PSML to Collective Securities at "book value"—the bargain basement price of $51,485. At the same time it was decided that the fees which PSML had been paying to Principal Group should now go upstairs to Collective Securities, and that Collective would then pay back to Principal Group about 50% of the fees. (Collective Securities, it was rationalized, provided advisory services, while Principal Group did the administrative work. Despite this excuse, investment decisions continued to be made during meetings of the Principal Group investment committee.) The sums diverted in this way totalled $7,496,904 between 1984 and the bankruptcy in 1987.

The transaction—authorized in a Principal Group resolution signed by director/shareholders Donald Cormie, Jaimie Cormie, John Cormie and Ken Marlin—tossed PSML into the hands of a company owned by the same four men who had authorized the transfer.

Over the years, Collective Securities had borrowed aggressively from Principal Group. At the time of the transfer its debt amounted to about $19 million. Prior to August 1984 Principal Group had two significant assets: a valuable company and the loan to Collective Securities. The transfer effectively handed over the first asset, PSML, to Collective Securities, so that it could make good on Principal Group's second asset, the debt of $19 million. (This debt would more than triple over the next three years.)

In his report, Inspector Bill Code noted that the transfer came on the heels of

Tewfik Saleh's May 1984 demand for a capital injection into the contract companies. Principal Group's consolidated financial statements were under the threat of a going-concern note, and the Carma transaction in June had failed to appease auditor Bruce Pennock, as Cormie had hoped. Code concluded:

> The evidence tends to show that Donald Cormie and James Cormie intended to move the asset to protect it from the insolvency of PGL. Transferring it at book value and then taking it public hopefully would allow CSL to pay off its debt, and leave PSML beyond the reach of PGL creditors... The reality is that First Investors, Associated Investors and Principal Group were insolvent by this time and the evidence tends to show that Donald Cormie knew it and that this transfer of PSML at cost to CSL was done in an attempt to enrich CSL and the other upstairs companies when PGL was insolvent or the transfer would make it so.

Over the next three years the Cormies directed massive resources—including Principal Group cash and staff labour—toward developing and promoting PSML and the mutual funds it managed. In 1986, when they attempted to take the company public, PSML was valued by the underwriter, brokerage firm Wood Gundy Inc., at $120 million.

Autumn 1984

DONALD CORMIE HAD BEEN TRYING to get his companies into Ontario for over a year. The sales force had achieved maximum penetration of the western Canadian and Maritime markets, and the East beckoned. Unfortunately for Principal, Ontario regulators stood resolutely in the way. Stung—like their federal counterparts at the CDIC—by criticism of their handling of the recent Crown Trust disaster, Ontario regulators had greatly increased their vigilance. They smelled trouble at Principal, and they weren't about to let it cross their border.

In 1983, Associated Investors had applied to Ontario's Superintendent of Insurance for permission to sell investment contracts there. The province had a look at the company's financial situation, then speedily rejected the plan, saying it was against the public interest. Principal persisted, more letters were exchanged, and in January 1984, Ontario delivered a list of conditions to be met prior to registering Associated Investors in Ontario. A letter from Brian Newton, Senior Actuary in the Superintendent's office, said the company would need a cash injection of at least $4 million, followed by another $2 million within three years.

With that, Associated's application was abandoned. A simultaneous campaign to register Principal Trust in Ontario also met with a chilly response, and was soon abandoned as well.

Meanwhile, Cormie and Ken Marlin had found another way to get their corporate foot in the closing door. In September 1983 they bought into a Toronto-based company which traded on the Toronto Stock Exchange. Principal Group spent

$2.6 million to acquire 78% controlling interest of Bomac Batten Ltd., a computer graphics company, which was reorganized with Marlin as president. The company was intended, among other things, to provide Principal with an entrée into Ontario's financial services industry, so Marlin went shopping for an existing trust company that could be taken over. He and Cormie looked at Dominion, London and Fidelity Trusts. Finally, Executive Trust, a small Toronto-based company, caught their eye. Terms of purchase were negotiated, and in mid-1984 application was made to the Ontario Securities Commission for approval to transfer the shares of Executive Trust to Bomac Batten (by then renamed Principal Neo-Tech Inc.)

"We were quite encouraged that that would happen," Marlin testified. "As it turned out, there was a request for additional information, information on Principal Group, information on Principal Trust. We felt that because Principal Neo-Tech had an independent board and was a public company trading on the Toronto Stock Exchange, that they were probably going beyond what was reasonable in requesting financial information. As a result of, I suppose, saying enough is enough and we provided information to a certain point, they declined our application for the trust company." That rejection came in the autumn of 1984. Marlin launched an appeal, but dropped it the following year.

This was Principal's last stab at entering the trust business in Ontario. Instead, Principal Neo-Tech moved aggressively into graphic arts, buying several businesses in Toronto and Montreal over the next couple of years. It also jumped into the petroleum services industry with the April 1984 acquisition of Neo-Tech Inc. of Denver, Colorado. This company, purchased for $1,210,270 through a preferred share swap with its former owners, was a seismic data firm which conducted geophysical analysis in the American mid-west, then attempted to lease the information to oil exploration firms. It went on a buying binge of its own, picking up Data Acquisition, Inc. in Houston, Texas, a data brokerage company; and Customer Digital Services, Inc., an oil services business operating out of Denver and Houston which specialized in advanced digitizing and plotting of seismic data.

Total count: 17 companies in two busy years. They started out as assets of Principal Group, but they didn't end up that way.

October 11, 1984

PROVINCIAL AUDITOR ALAN HUTCHISON did an update examination on the investment contract companies as of July 1984, then wrote memos recommending that Consumer Affairs consider suspending First Investors and Associated Investors from selling certificates at high interest rates "in order to protect future consumers." The companies were "headed for serious financial disaster," and, by their own admission, were attracting additional capital in order to help carry their non-producing assets. "I suspect that if FIC were borrowing from the bank rather than the unwary consumers that they would have been placed in receivership long ago."

First Investors' borrowing-to-capital ratio had deteriorated to 578:1, Hutchison reported. In order to meet a 25:1 ratio, additional capital of $11.3 million was needed—and that was calculated using the company's unrealistic numbers, which were produced by ignoring the serious write-downs required on its assets. Hutchison said that the public was being intentionally misled about additional credits. "FIC has changed its policy on additional credits three times in 1984 and we have no evidence of the public ever being notified of any of these changes." He then deplored the accounting sleight of hand that had accompanied the reinstatement of the additional credits at the end of June. Hutchison's reports went to Senior Auditor Burt Eldridge, who forwarded them to Tewfik Saleh, an exercise akin to sending them to the Bermuda Triangle. "Yes, it is always frustrating," Eldridge testified. "But it wasn't unusual. I had been there a number of years and had filed many reports [on other matters, as well] on which there has been absolutely no feedback."

October 29, 1984

THE DEBATE ON THE REAL ESTATE valuation issue continued for months. Several meetings between Principal officials, Touche Ross auditors and provincial auditors produced no meeting of minds. Eventually, audit director Burt Eldridge urged that there be major write-downs of contract company assets; at a minimum, the companies should be forced to inject almost $13 million to cover the exposures identified in their financial statements, plus an unidentified amount to compensate for the $23-million trust company transaction and the subsequent Carma deal.

At the end of October, Sydney Bercov, the lawyer engaged to look into the $23-million asset dump, sent Saleh his opinion on the transaction. In Bercov's view it contravened the *Investment Contracts Act*, and in fact may have been an offence under the Act, which Saleh might consider reporting to the Attorney General. The directors of First Investors and Associated Investors who had approved this "improvident transaction" were in breach of their fiduciary duty to the companies, Bercov said. He advised that the Superintendent had no specific authority to require the transaction be reversed, or to make an order requiring an injection of further capital to remedy the transaction. He nonetheless suggested that Saleh might take that position anyway. He pointed out that the Superintendent had the options of suspending or cancelling the companies' registration, or making a Special Report to the minister pursuant to the provisions of the *Investment Contracts Act*. The loss sustained by the contract companies because of the $23-million transaction, Bercov said, was, "depending on various assumptions," in a range between $6.3 million and $11.3 million. "If $11.3 million of capital is contributed it is reasonable to assume that the contract companies will sustain no loss."

Around this time, Eldridge wrote another memo to Saleh which detailed, again, the desperate circumstances of the contract companies. They were increasing their volume of certificate sales at an alarming rate, he said. During an early October meeting Marlin had said that the increase was needed "to provide an increased asset earning base as the company has a significant amount of non-income producing assets." More and more new investors' money was needed to pay off old investors and meet other obligations.

Once again, Eldridge laid out the reserve issue. In order to repay the new certificates, which were then offering interest of around 12%, the contract companies would have to earn 17% on the money invested. "I am not aware," he said, "where the company could place its additional funds to earn the income needed to cover these liabilities." Most of the $54 million taken in by the companies in the past nine-month period was generating hardly any income at all: $23 million had gone to Principal Trust to pay for non-producing mortgages and real estate, and $17 million had gone to the Carma conglomerate in exchange for IOU's and Athabasca Holdings shares producing dividends of only 4%.

Eldridge also reported in detail to Saleh the unsatisfactory outcome of his meetings with the Touche Ross auditors. To resolve their differences, proper appraisals were necessary, Eldridge said. He was confident of the department's approach, but suggested that an independent accounting firm be retained to review what had been produced to date. Saleh would have liked nothing better, and sought Barry Martin's and Connie Osterman's permission to bring in a consultant. "My opinion," Saleh testified, "was that if you want to determine the proper action to be taken against these two companies, you have to have an independent examination to strengthen our position." Again he was refused. "They told me that we have to continue to consider the [consequences] of appointing an independent consultant." The consequences, as usual, were a run on Principal, followed by a domino effect on all the province's financial institutions. "There was always hope that the real estate market would come back, and it always comes back," Saleh said. "It goes into cycles. They might be able to recover."

Osterman was advised of Bercov's opinion that offences had been committed under the *Investment Contracts Act*, but did not refer the matter to the Attorney General. She testified that she did not recall why she did not do so.

October 19, 1984

Memo FROM DEPUTY MINISTER Barry Martin to Consumer Affairs staff, with copies to Jim Darwish and Minister Connie Osterman:

> Effective immediately and continuing until further notice, all the members of the Audit Unit for the department will report through Burton Eldridge as Senior Auditor to the Deputy Minister. This move is necessary to meet program and administrative needs within the department.

Jim Darwish wasn't due to retire until November 15, but Barry Martin couldn't wait to get him out of his hair. In August, Darwish and his wife Elvera went on a three-week driving holiday to attend the Los Angeles summer Olympics. He then returned to the office. Darwish had accumulated another three weeks vacation time, but wanted to work instead and be paid for it. Martin wanted him out, and announced that the department would not make cash pay-outs for unused time.

"I had just come back from three weeks holiday, I had nowhere to go, I was about to go on the biggest holiday of my life, and I could use the money," Darwish told me. He stayed put, continuing to show up each morning despite Martin's objections. On October 19, the deputy minister circulated the memo above, stripping Darwish of his duties and putting Eldridge in his place. After that Darwish just sat in his office, twiddling his thumbs.

Despite 35 years of service, there was no retirement party. Darwish's two fellow-ADMs and their assistants took him to lunch, as did the audit staff. That was it. Darwish took his humiliation home and nursed it silently. He had talked the situation over with Elvera, but they never told the rest of their family what had happened. He didn't even tell his lawyers about the fight over the Principal companies: "I felt I had a duty, because I had a duty to the government [to maintain confidentiality]," he told me.

Three years later, "when the collapse happened I called my family together, including my mother, and told them for the first time that I was forced out. We had told them that I was 55 and I could retire. One of my daughters said she often wondered why there wasn't a big send-off in the department."

After his retirement Darwish occasionally visited his stockbroker's office, coincidentally located in Principal Plaza. "Every time I'd go there I would look up at the Principal sign... I thought the company was going to go down, unless they put in some money," he told me. "A year, then a year and a half, then two years went by, and I thought, 'Well, they made 'er.' Then one day I was driving down Jasper Avenue, when I heard on the radio that the Principal companies had gone under. Well, I grinned and I said, 'I can't wait to tell Elvera!' and I dashed home."

In July 1987, the month the contract companies collapsed, Darwish sued the province for $7,678 in back holiday pay and won. The package he negotiated with Osterman and Martin included approximately a year's salary and full government pension, allowing the Darwishes to ease comfortably into retirement. The former regulator now confronts the Alberta government on environmental issues. Darwish works on a volunteer basis for Edmonton Friends of the North, fighting a province-sanctioned proliferation of pulp mills.

George Blochert, whose investigation into Principal sales practices was blocked by Martin (and who had criticized Martin and Saleh during the departmental meeting at the Chateau Lacombe), has also spoken out. Blochert left government service less than a year after Darwish, having experienced what he considered constructive dismissal at Martin's hands. He sued the province, winning a settlement of half a year's salary. In mid-1989, he wrote a letter to the editor condemning Consumer Affairs' role in the Principal collapse. "No individual or group should be made to suffer just because the taxpayers have to foot the bill," Blochert said. "What seems to be overlooked in this whole debate is that the Department of Consumer and Corporate Affairs was set up to ensure that there is a fair marketplace for all in this province. It is this failure to meet its mandate that requires a much closer scrutiny by the voters and taxpayers of Alberta."

November 13, 1984

AUDITOR BRUCE PENNOCK LEARNED he'd been fired from the Principal account three months after his replacement received the nod. Donald Cormie held back the news from Pennock in hopes that Principal Group's consolidated statement for 1983 would first be completed—but finally told him during a mid-November phone call that the 1984 audit was going to Deloitte Haskins & Sells. "At that time," Cormie testified, "I indicated that if they couldn't complete the consolidation, then what else could we do but get other auditors?"

The 1983 consolidated statement should have been completed in the spring. But here it was, November, and Pennock was still asking questions. He wanted the statement to include the contentious notes drafted months before; he queried the asset swap with Carma, and was considering a going-concern note that went even further than the one included in the contract companies' statements: he wanted it expanded to discuss the effects of a potential business failure.

Cormie decided to drop Touche Ross in mid-August. Around that time, Cormie, Christa Petracca and Ken Marlin took three members of the Deloitte firm to lunch to discuss their takeover of the Principal audits. Don McCutchen, who would be senior auditor, testified the luncheon's purpose "was stated to be that they were considering a change of auditors and they were asking us what our feelings of coming back would be." The firm was, obviously, delighted. During the lunch, McCutchen heard complaints about Pennock's foot-dragging and the disagreement over the valuation of mortgages and properties. "I believe it came out over the lunch that the auditors' [valuations] were lower than management's expectation," McCutchen said. Were they felt out during the lunch on whether they would be more co-operative than Touche Ross had been? "I really don't recall."

McCutchen was already well acquainted with Cormie, Marlin, Petracca and their companies: his firm had been Principal's auditor until 1982, when, on Petracca's advice, Cormie invited bids from all the major national accounting firms. McCutchen's firm charged about $400,000 a year, too rich for Principal's blood. Touche Ross came in considerably lower—$160,000 a year for the audit of Principal Group Ltd., all its subsidiaries and the consolidated financial statement—and won the contract.

Now the work was being returned to McCutchen's firm, for much the same fee as before. Three months later, in a letter dated November 7, 1984, Deloitte Haskins & Sells was officially appointed to the file—a week before Cormie gave Pennock the news. (Petracca had been using Deloitte for at least a month before the engagement letter was sent, and secured from it a letter on October 4 supporting the $17.25 million paid for Allarco Energy during the Carma transaction in June. This letter contradicted the opinion of appraiser Graham Weir, who 10 days earlier had valued Allarco at just $15.68 million.)

During the November 13 phone conversation, Pennock told Cormie he had drafted a letter to him discussing the reasons for his failure to complete the Principal consolidated statement. The letter said that the "pervasive and significant" demands made by regulatory authorities on Principal subsidiaries threatened the future viability of Principal Group. Thus it was not possible, before the demands were resolved, to prepare statements that would fairly present the company's financial position. "As a result, we would be required to deny an opinion on the financial statements if we were asked to report before these matters were resolved."

Pennock testified that Cormie responded by instructing him not to send the letter, but simply to read it to him over the phone. Cormie testified that he had no memory of the letter, nor of any such discussion. "My recollection," Pennock repeated, "is I read it to Mr. Cormie because his response was, 'We don't want any of those kind of letters here, don't send it.' I assumed that if I put it in the mail to him, he wouldn't take delivery of it."

Pennock offered to resign and let the new auditors deal with the situation. It was agreed that he would complete the consolidated statement later, but that it was to be put on hold until the resolution of the capital demands.

The same day that Cormie fired Pennock, Hal Irwin, managing partner of Deloitte Haskins & Sells, wrote Pennock to advise him that Deloitte was taking over. This letter, following the rules of conduct adhered to by chartered accountants, asked why Pennock was being removed and inquired whether anything precluded Deloitte from accepting the engagement. Pennock testified that he received Irwin's letter on November 19 and immediately wrote a response advising that he was awaiting formal notification of his removal. A second letter was sent in February 1985 advising only: "We know of no professional reasons that would preclude you from accepting an appointment as auditors of the above companies other than the high degree of professional risk associated with your involvement with these companies as discussed with your Mr. McCutchen during our mid-December 1984 meeting."

Whatever was said between Pennock and McCutchen during that meeting never made it to paper, and both men's memories are very cloudy. In a subsequent note to file, Pennock said only this:

> We provided Deloittes with access to our files in early December and I met with Don McCutchen in mid-December. Although I did not document the meeting at the time, I answered his questions as directly as I could and attempted to apprize him of our concerns and the risks involved as we saw them of accepting the engagement. They had already spent considerable time on the client by this time and obviously had no intention of not continuing.

Pennock testified that it took a long time to get an explanation from Principal about the reason for his removal. "Ultimately," Pennock testified, "there was a call from Mr. Cormie stating that the reason why he was changing auditors, it had to do with the long-term relationship that he had with Deloittes proved to be invaluable."

November 29, 1984

A MONTH AFTER RECEIVING lawyer Sydney Bercov's advice—that Principal
Trust's asset dump into the contract companies was illegal—Tewfik Saleh, aided by
Burt Eldridge, drafted a letter to the companies demanding that they inject
$24.3 million before the end of the year or face losing their licences. He arrived at
the sum of $24.3 million by following Eldridge's minimal recommendation: the
$13 million would cover the exposure notes in the two companies' financial
statements, plus an additional $11.3 million, the amount identified by Bercov as
necessary to remedy the harm of the trust company transaction. Included in the
letter, addressed to Ken Marlin, was a passage which demonstrates Saleh's acute
awareness that the companies were operating improperly:

> We have done all we can to assist you in resolving the financial problems of
> your companies, however, you have consistently resisted our calls for a capital
> injection to rectify the situation. We do not anticipate that those problems will
> correct themselves in the foreseeable future and therefore additional capital for
> your two companies is urgently needed now, particularly as the companies
> continue to raise money from the public while experiencing substantial capital
> impairment.

But Saleh didn't send the letter. Instead, he took it to a meeting with Connie
Osterman, Barry Martin and department auditors. Saleh told them that the
companies were in serious trouble and had embarked on transactions which
contravened the *Investment Contracts Act*. He then presented Osterman with a
summary of the companies' financial position and Bercov's advice, along with the
letter. Martin intervened, telling Osterman that he had met with Marlin and promised
him one more meeting before Saleh took any action. Osterman then instructed Saleh
to hold off until he and Marlin had reconvened.

They did so on a Friday morning two weeks later. On December 17, the
following Monday, Marlin wrote Saleh confirming what he claimed was the
agreement they had reached: Principal would put up $11.3 million, which would
settle all outstanding items to date. The next day Saleh wrote back, saying that
wasn't what he'd agreed to. He could accept the $11.3 million only as a resolution of
the March transaction between the contract companies and Principal Trust. Then he
handed over the keys. Despite the $72 million capital shortfall identified in the May
11 letter (and repeated in the November summary he gave to Osterman), and despite
his draft letter of two weeks earlier demanding a $24.2 million injection, Saleh
decided to settle, for now, for the $11.3 million:

> If you make the capital injection of $11.3 million above referred to then, in
> view of your assurances that the 1984 results will show much improvement in
> your companies' financial position and as the 1984 year end is rapidly
> approaching, I will agree to forego any action based on the 1983 annual

statements regarding the outstanding items in my letter of May 11, 1984, relating to capital requirements until such time as I have received and reviewed the 1984 annual statements of FIC and AIC.

Saleh made this decision knowing he would not receive the 1984 statements from the contract companies until the spring of 1985. He made the decision knowing that Marlin's earlier promises of improved circumstances had not been reliable, at a time when investors were pouring money into the insolvent companies at the rate of about $7.5 million a month.

On December 17, the same day Marlin wrote to Saleh, Principal Group injected the first half of the promised $11.3 million into First Investors. It came not as permanent capital, but in the form of a $5 million loan backed by a subordinated promissory note with a very generous rate of interest (prime plus 2.5% a year). That same day, much of the $5 million was sucked back up into Principal Group as loans bearing the exact same interest rate. A total of $4,022,821 ($3,519,969 from First Investors and $502,852 from Associated Investors) went to Principal Group in three collateral loans in the names of Donald Cormie, Jaimie Cormie and C. McEwan (the bookkeeper at Cormie Ranch). The money was used to purchase about $5.7 million worth of mutual funds for Principal Group at a margin of 70% (Principal put up 30% and borrowed the final 70%). The profit that might have gone to the contract companies from the investment of that money went instead to Principal Group.

Another $6.3 million, the balance of the injection promised by Marlin, went into First Investors on December 21. This was the result of an agreement between Principal, the Superintendent of Insurance and the CDIC: the $6.3 million which had gone into Principal Trust during the summer to satisfy the CDIC would be redeemed by Principal Group and given to the contract companies. The deal was contingent on Saleh's assurances that he would not demand reversal of the $23-million asset dump of nine months earlier, and he made that commitment in a telex to Ottawa on December 21. The $6.3 million was released by the CDIC, and went into First Investors a week later—like the first $5 million, also as a loan, also at prime plus 2.5%.

In his report, Inspector Bill Code observed that Principal was earning about 20% a year in 1984 in the stock market. Had the $23 million paid by the contract companies to Principal Trust been invested on behalf of First Investors and Associated Investors, it would have earned about $4.6 million a year. Instead, having been loaned $11.3 million at a high rate of interest and saddled with non-producing assets, First Investors lost about $3.2 million in 1984 and about $3.5 million a year commencing in 1985.

There was one more transaction at the end of 1984, this one sparked by questions from provincial auditors about the underlying value of assets acquired by Athabasca Holdings in the June transaction with Carma. The contract companies had wound up with $36 million worth of Athabasca preferred shares during the course of that deal, and by November, Eldridge and Saleh had determined that (despite the legal opinion obtained by Petracca) the shares were a prohibited investment under the *Canadian and British Insurance Companies Act*—because of Donald Cormie's indirect controlling interest in both Athabasca and the contract companies—and therefore in contravention of the *Investment Contracts Act*.

The Athabasca shares carried a dividend rate of 4% a year, but the assets it acquired (the Cayman Islands bank, Allarco Energy and Travellers Acceptance) did not yield sufficient cash flow to support payment of even that amount. Rather than relieve the contract companies of the shares, the Cormies decided to provide Athabasca with an asset which they pretended could generate the required dividends: preferred shares in Athabasca's sister company Principal Group Ltd.

On December 17, Athabasca bought $12.5 million worth of Principal Group preferred shares carrying a dividend rate of 11.6% (a yield of $1,450,000 a year). The rate on these shares, created for the purposes of this transaction, was chosen to yield the same amount of money as the dividend payable on the Athabasca shares owned by the contract companies. Athabasca, of course, didn't have $12.5 million to buy the Principal shares, so another circular transaction was worked out to provide the financing. Principal Group loaned $12.5 million interest-free to its parent Collective Securities, and Collective then loaned that cash to Athabasca at an interest rate of 12.75% a year; Athabasca then used the money, Principal's (or, rather, its promissory noteholders') money, to pay Principal for the shares. (See DIAGRAM 4: *Athabasca Holdings Ltd. Purchase of Principal Group Ltd. Preferred Shares.*)

Having loaned $12.5 million interest-free, Principal also ended up on the hook for dividends to Athabasca of $1,453,600 on the shares. Athabasca incurred a debt of 12.75% interest a year ($1.6 million) on the $12.5 million borrowed from Collective, to acquire an asset (the Principal shares) which offered a dividend of only 11.6% ($1.45 million)—less than the cost of borrowing the money to acquire the asset. And what an asset: preferred shares in a company which, by the end of 1984, was technically insolvent. The Principal Group shares were certainly not worth what had been paid for them, but Athabasca was liable for the full price. To add insult to injury, Athabasca's multi-million debt to Collective now ranked ahead of its obligation to its preferred shareholders, the investment contract companies.

Only Collective—the grandparent company owned by the Cormies and Ken Marlin—came out ahead. It borrowed $12.5 million from Principal Group interest free, then loaned it to Athabasca at 12.75%—generating for itself a profit of $1.6 million a year.

Nice work if you can get it.

13

Department 8

This is normal tax planning.
Donald Cormie in testimony at the Code inquiry

OVER THE YEARS DONALD CORMIE had developed some firm rules regarding the handling of cash. The first, and most important rule, was: *Idle Cash is Wasted Cash.* Cormie loathed the prospect of dollars stagnating in low-interest bank accounts. The function of money is to multiply. Money has to work, to earn its keep.

The second rule, increasingly important as cash became more scarce, was: *Never Use Cash When Something Else Will Do.* Sign a promissory note, move stock, shuffle real estate, swap mortgages, trade favours, make promises, threaten lawsuits... But cash was a resource of last resort, a commodity too precious to waste on meeting debts or capitalizing sagging enterprises.

Unfortunately, some situations demanded cash: taxes, for example. Cormie paid his taxes with cash. So did his kids, his wife and his companies—but not always from their incomes. That was inefficient; Cormie preferred to borrow.

Nor did he pay taxes gladly. An elaborate corporate structure was built and fine-tuned endlessly, distributing income and losses as evenly as possible among its components, minimizing tax across the entire system.

Cormie's third rule was: *Cash Does Its Best Work in the Dark.* It's nobody else's business what you do with your money, or anybody else's money for that matter. Cormie jealously guarded his secrecy, thwarting scrutiny at every turn.

The final rule was: *Cash Must Flow. Preferably Upwards.* Cash rarely followed a direct line in Cormie's complicated world. It journeyed in bizarre, circuitous paths, looping briefly off its route between lender and borrower, to perform errands for Cormie or a relative. Occasionally money appeared in two places at once, simultaneously loaned from A to B as it paid off F's debt to G.

Cormie's book-keeper knew what to do with cash. Diane Stefanski's job was to channel loose cash up and out—often hundreds of thousands of dollars at a time—in loans to a series of companies controlled by her boss. Some of the money, borrowed from trusting investors, was used by the Cormies to purchase houses, paintings, a yacht and mutual funds. Some financed the operations and stock market investments of the chronically unprofitable Cormie Ranch.

Sworn to secrecy by her employer, Stefanski laboured a few steps from Cormie's opulent suite on the 30th floor of Principal Plaza. For six years, she asked no questions, sought no explanations and signed where instructed. She kept her office locked and maintained a chilly distance from curious co-workers. Obedient and silent, she issued cheques and tracked the journey of cash through the Principal labyrinth. Stefanski was gatekeeper of the mysterious cluster of "upstairs" companies known as Department 8, or "the upstairs fund." Few people knew of the existence of Department 8, likely named after Cormie's eight children. Not even Bill Johnson, Principal's vice-president of finance, nor Cormie's partner Ken Marlin, understood what became of the money after it made its way into the stratosphere.

The night before Stefanski appeared at the Code inquiry, Cormie appeared at Inspector Bill Code's office, where Stefanski was about to review her testimony. "I had signed in and was just going up the elevator," Stefanski told me, "and within a minute of getting to [inquiry counsel Neil] Wittmann's office, Cormie and his lawyer Bob Duke and James Cormie showed up. Cormie was unshaven, he barged up, and there was a lot of yelling and screaming. He said they had no right having me testify and he was going to get an injunction. They had put me in the next office and I could hear everything, then I got shuffled into another office further away. I was in there alone for about an hour, then one of the other lawyers came in and I asked him to stay with me. Sure I was afraid. I've heard him yell and scream before, so that wasn't new, but I realized it was very serious. I was basically bursting the bubble of the dream he'd lived for 30 years." Code was not impressed by Cormie's performance, and Stefanski appeared as scheduled.

Stefanski, not a licenced accountant, went to work for Cormie in September 1981. She inherited from her predecessor a number of duties and policies for operating her enigmatic department. Once Cormie was confident she'd grasped the system, she was pretty much on her own. Stefanski says she found nothing odd about her work. "I wasn't paid to think," she joked with me. Then she sighed. "I had chartered accountants coming in every year to audit [the upstairs companies] and they never raised any questions with me."

Over the years, Stefanski moved millions of dollars of investors' money from "downstairs" to "upstairs" companies. In the early days, Cormie had borrowed money directly from corporate subsidiaries, including the investment contract companies, but by the time Stefanski arrived, the tap was attached to Principal Group Ltd. By the end of 1986, Principal Group had borrowed $90 million from promissory noteholders. About three-quarters of that had been loaned upstairs.

Here's how it worked. When a customer purchased a promissory note, the funds were deposited first to a Principal Trust account, then transferred to the "PGN" (Principal Group note fund) account at a branch of the Canadian Imperial Bank of Commerce down the street. Next, it was loaned to Collective Securities, Principal Group's holding company; then Collective loaned it upstairs to a Cormie family company. Some of the money went to Cormie Ranch, but most went to County Investments Ltd., which loaned it to members of the Cormie family. They in turn loaned much of it further upwards, to Estate Loan and Finance, where the yacht, houses and other property were held and family investments administered.

County Investments was incorporated—according to Cormie, as a "tax-planning" vehicle—in December 1955. As would soon be the case with Estate Loan and Finance, Cormie's name appeared on County's corporate records only once—as a director on incorporation day. Then he was immediately replaced by an employee. No Cormie family member was ever a director, officer or owner of the company. Instead, Cormie's employees became the shareholders—the owners of record—and served as County's directors. (See DIAGRAM 5: *Department 8.*)

Cormie's children grew up in the shadow of County Investments. Most parents encourage their kids to save by giving them a piggy bank, or by taking them to a bank branch to open a tiny account. Cormie's offspring dealt with County from the cradle. Jaimie testified that he remembered doing so as early as age six. If he earned money for mowing the lawn, for example, he would put it into an interest-bearing County account.

According to corporate legend, Cormie emulated his father George, whose "big black book" contained the family finances. Twice a year, Cormie liked to say, George gathered everyone together to review the situation. So dear to Cormie's heart were the principles of thrift that he kept well-thumbed notebooks on each boy and girl to make certain they saved a tenth of their earnings.[1] Many a Principal investment was sold by telling that tale. What wasn't revealed was that the notebooks were kept under lock and key in Cormie's executive suite, and that the children's earnings included profits drawn from investing small fortunes loaned to them at low interest by Principal's unwitting customers.

Through the County accounts, Cormie controlled the most intimate details of his family's finances, including the preparation of his children's income tax statements, their purchase of RRSPs and the deposit of their tax refunds. If they wanted cash they came to him, and he authorized its release. Besides ensuring Cormie's domination, the strategy meant that assets acquired in relatives' names were difficult to trace to Cormie, and would be harder to wrestle away in case of a legal dispute or income tax re-assessment.

The Cormies didn't receive an income from County, they received loans. Basically, they made free use of millions of dollars of investors' money, pocketed any profits it generated and returned some of the "borrowed" money briefly at the end of each year. Had these funds been paid by Principal Group as salaries or dividends they would have been taxed. (Dividend income would have had to be shared with partner Ken Marlin on a 10.5% basis.) Had it been known the family controlled the company, the loans would have been taxed as well.

Jude Halvorson, Cormie's personal secretary, was a County shareholder in the years leading up to the Principal collapse. "I didn't know what the business of County Investments Ltd. was," she testified, "but to me, it seemed like it was a bank, a little bank. I knew there were monies on deposit." On Cormie's instructions, Halvorson prepared minutes of directors' meetings and occasionally deposited income tax refund cheques. She says she signed County's financial statements, but never read them, and that she never saw the banking records.

Halvorson had been a legal secretary for an Edmonton law firm[2] before going to work for Cormie in 1981. Two weeks after she was hired, Cormie "indicated to me that it was the practice that his secretaries purchase shares in County Investments Ltd. He also indicated to me that the company would lend me the money to purchase the shares... that it was a way for me to save some money, and that I would be getting dividends on the shares that I had purchased."

Halvorson "bought" 35 of the company's 100 shares. She paid $100 a share, borrowing the $3,500 from County interest-free. She repaid the loan at the rate of $100 a month, with dividends further reducing the loan balance. (The dividends, according to Cormie, amounted to several thousand dollars a year.) In 1984, Halvorson also became a director of Cormie Ranch Ltd. In 1985, Halvorson was asked to acquire another 30 shares of the company "so that I could then receive the larger dividend for County Investments." Heather Lindsay, who became the accountant for Cormie Ranch, acquired the final 35 shares.

At the Code inquiry, Cormie claimed these shareholders effectively ran the company, and he simply advised them what they should do. Code concluded instead that Cormie was the beneficial owner of County, "a sham created to avoid tax." By having outsiders "own" the shares, Cormie attempted to have his family avoid tax by borrowing from a company with which they were not connected. County Investments, Code found, was formed and operated "so that it would appear to be something which it was not... The evidence tends to show that this was done for a fraudulent and dishonest purpose."

The loans were made without security and without regard for the borrowers' ability to pay, and were issued on a demand basis: Cormie lending to Cormie lending to Cormie, with Cormie deciding whether to force Cormie to repay. The interest due on the loans, and some of their principal, was routinely paid to Principal at year's end in a two-step circular transaction known to Stefanski as the "year-end interest adjustment." Principal Group provided not only the loans, but the funds to repay them, and to pay the interest owed. Then the loans were replaced with new ones. Let's have a look at how this worked.

On November 30, 1981, Principal Group loaned $4,635,000 to County Investments. County used the money in three ways: to loan $1,292,000 to Cormie Ranch Ltd., to repay a $73,000 debt to Principal Group and to pay $3,141,829 to Collective Securities ($3,100,989 in principal and $40,840 in interest). Cormie

Ranch used the money to repay a fraction[3] of its debt to Collective ($1,015,948 in interest and $280,056 in principal). Collective combined the sums received from County and Cormie Ranch and sent $4,330,000 to Principal Group to pay the interest and some of the principal it had borrowed over the year. (The sums loaned and repaid in this and other transactions are not exactly equal because some of the money loaned to various companies was not passed along.)

The first half of this transaction left County Investments indebted to Principal Group. The loan had to be eliminated before the year-end audit, so the two companies would appear unrelated. Thus, on December 10, 1981, the money travelled in the opposite direction: Principal Group loaned $6,150,000 to Collective Securities, which loaned the money to County Investments. County, in turn, used the money to repay a $6,134,914 loan and $14,227 accrued interest back to Principal Group. (See DIAGRAM 6: *The Year-End Interest Adjustment, 1981.*) Let's look at the transactions that occurred over the next few days.

On December 15, 1981, Principal Group loaned $50,000 to Collective Securities, which loaned the money to Cormie Ranch.

On December 22, 1981, Principal Group borrowed $290,000 from the Canadian Imperial Bank of Commerce, and loaned $173,700 of that money to Collective Securities. Principal also paid $157,800 in dividends to Athabasca Holdings, which immediately loaned $157,800 to Collective Securities; Collective then paid a $537,000 dividend to County Investments. (The dividend went into three accounts, with cheques made payable to County/Donald Cormie $512,998; County/Jaimie Cormie $24,000; and County/John Cormie 66 cents.) Then County sent $577,000 to Collective as repayment for a loan. With that money, Collective paid $129,555 to the Receiver General in taxes; and another $118,015 in net salaries—to Neil Cormie ($5,000), Bruce Cormie ($12,000), Eivor Jr. ($28,000), 17-year-old Robert Cormie ($30,000) and Mrs Eivor Cormie ($155,000). Collective also loaned another $118,700 to County Investments.

Two days later, County borrowed $409,000 back from Collective Securities. Collective got the money from Principal Group ($328,171 came from the Principal Group promissory note fund, and $81,551 from brokerage firm Merrill Lynch Canada Inc.)

On December 31, Principal Group repaid the CBIC its $290,000, plus another $10,000, receiving $1,227,183 from the Principal note fund (which had just obtained the money from the Elmspring, King's Lake and Sunshine Hutterite colonies). Principal also loaned $935,000 to Collective Securities, which paid $50,844 to the Receiver General for back taxes from 1978. Then Collective loaned another $820,000 to County Investments.

You get the drift: the transactions were convoluted and endless, as befitted Cormie's endlessly convoluted interests. Stefanski kept a pile of cheques for each company and would record each portion of each transaction on a separate cheque, to be sent to Cormie or the appropriate "shareholder" for signing.

That was Department 8.

At first, Stefanski tracked the transactions in a top-secret handwritten ledger, locked in a safe to which only Cormie had a key. In 1985, the records were transferred to a personal computer, independent of the main Principal computer network. Only Cormie, Stefanski and Rob Pearce (hired as Collective Securities vice-president in 1984) had the passwords.

Token interest of 1/8th of 1% was added to the promissory note money borrowed from the public, to make it appear that business was being conducted and profit generated. (If someone purchased a note at 10%, for example, the money would be loaned upstairs to Collective Securities at 10.125%.) It actually cost Principal Group more than that to acquire the money, because salesmen received a commission of .6% on the notes. Thus every dollar loaned upstairs created a loss for Principal Group's investors.

The 1/8% was charged each party as money travelled up the line. So, for example, on April 9, 1984, the Principal Group promissory note fund loaned $100,000 to Principal Group at 11.25%; Principal loaned $112,000 to Collective Securities at 11.375%; Collective loaned the money to County Investments (Donald Cormie's account) at 11.50%; Cormie loaned $115,000 to Estate Loan and Finance at 11.625%; and Estate sent the money to the Toronto Dominion Bank to settle a letter of credit for the purchase of motors for Cormie's yacht.

Only the promissory note money, and money borrowed from banks or other institutions, was subject to the 1/8% notch up. Money originating from other sources, a gain from stock market investments, for example, was borrowed interest-free. Here's an example: on May 11, 1984, Principal Group made a profit of $425,000 U.S. when brokerage firm Merrill Lynch sold some securities. "My instructions from Don Cormie would be to loan any gains on sale of stocks or bonds or options to Collective Securities interest free, since it was surplus cash," Stefanski testified. She borrowed the $425,000 U.S. interest free, added it to $180,000 U.S. borrowed from the Principal Group note fund (30-day money) at 9.625%, and loaned the total $600,000 U.S. ($778,140 Can.) to Collective Securities. Collective loaned the money to Cormie Ranch, which loaned it to Estate Loan and Finance, which used the money to pay off a $600,000-U.S. margin call on American stocks held by Estate Loan in trust for Cormie Ranch.

Cormie played the stock market enthusiastically, on his own behalf and for his family and companies. There were accounts with Merrill Lynch Canada Inc., Dominion Securities Ames, Levesque Beaubien Inc. and Richardson Greenshields—four of Canada's largest brokerage houses at that time. (There is evidence of accounts with brokerages outside Canada, as well.) Stocks and mutual funds in various portfolios were usually margined to their maximum limit. International stock exchange rules impose a margin limit of 50% on stocks selling at over $2.00 (with lower limits for cheaper stocks), so that investors pay cash for half the value of purchase and hold the rest on credit extended by the broker. "Margin" is the difference between the price of the stock and the amount loaned by the stockbroker; if the value of the stock goes down, so will the amount of the loan the broker can extend, and the client will receive an urgent phone call requesting payment of the difference. In the case of the May 11 transaction, it seems that certain stocks held for Cormie Ranch took a dive, and there was a scramble to find cash to cover the loss.

There appears to have been an earlier margin call crisis between mid-April and mid-May 1982. During a five-week period, $2,151,359 in promissory note funds was drained upwards into Merrill Lynch accounts held in the Cormie children's names. The money, much of it borrowed from the Hutterite Brethren of Brant, Cluny and Sunshine (also investor "Corasht"), moved upstairs—from Principal Group to Collective Securities to County Investments into the eight margin accounts—in a series of 19 transactions. The first, the movement of $640,000 into the accounts of the three youngest Cormies, occurred on April 12, when the price of gold dropped on the international market. Over the next few weeks stock market prices plummeted, falling on May 6 to a two-and-a-half year low on the Toronto Stock Exchange.

When Stefanski started work, she routinely used new promissory note money to "pay off" the oldest upstairs loans first, replacing them with new ones. In May 1982, Cormie ordered a change: in future she was to pay off loans with the highest rates first. This came at the time when interest rates, which had been climbing since the late 1970s, began their decline. The effect of Cormie's edict was to replace old loans with high interest rates with new loans at lower interest rates. Over the next year and a half almost four dozen transactions were booked with the sole purpose of reducing interest charged to family members and personal companies. The rate "rolldown" reduced the cost of money to the Cormies, but the promissory notes which funded the original loans remained, and had to be repaid to the public noteholders at the higher rate, further exacerbating Principal Group's financial situation.

Let's look at a couple of the rolldown transactions. On October 14, 1982, Principal Group borrowed $1.1 million at about 14.25% from four promissory note holders ($50,000 from a company called Progressive Construction, $50,000 from investor "Durand," $100,000 from investor "Heinrichs," and $900,000 from the Acadia Hutterian Brethren). Principal loaned the money to Collective Securities at 14.375%, which loaned it to County Investments at 14.50%, which loaned it to Donald Cormie's account at 14.625%. Cormie, now using new money, sent the old money—an identical $1.1 million, borrowed previously at 18.625%—back down through Collective and Principal to pay off the old loan. The effect was to reduce the interest on a $1.1 million loan by 4%—saving Cormie $44,000 a year. (See DIAGRAM 7: *Interest Rate Rolldown, October 14, 1982*).

A second example is more complicated. At five o'clock on the afternoon of January 30, 1984, "Metro Edmonton Hospital" purchased $2.5 million worth of promissory notes at 9.85% interest for 60 days.[4] The next afternoon at 1:57 p.m. Stefanski took that money, added it to smaller amounts borrowed from two other note holders ("Gregg Dis." and investor "Hobbs") and loaned $2,675,000 upstairs: from Principal Group to Collective Securities to County. Most of the money was then allocated to the County accounts of five Cormies. Then it was returned from

County to Collective to Principal, which returned it to the Principal promissory note account at the Royal Bank. The money appears to have gone full circle within a day, but in fact the new money was used to pay off a County loan at 10.125% and to replace it with a new loan at 9.875%—reducing interest by about $6,687.50 a year.

By the beginning of 1984, the upstairs loans had been rolled down as far as they could go—bottoming at around 9% or 10%—and the rolldown program ceased. But several months later, during the same month that mutual fund management company Principal Securities Management Ltd. (PSML) was transferred upstairs from Principal Group to Collective Securities (see Chapter 12), a new program was instituted to make all Cormie Ranch loans interest-free.

After the PSML transfer it was decided that the mutual fund management fee would be paid to Collective Securities, rather than Principal Group; then Collective would pay back half of the fee to Principal. Stefanski was instructed to forward the total PSML fee each month from Collective to Cormie Ranch. Then she returned half the fee to Collective, which sent it to Principal. While that money was with Cormie Ranch it was used to roll down to zero the interest rate on money previously borrowed from Collective.

The first of these transactions occurred at the end of August 1984. By the end of the year, Cormie Ranch's entire debt to Collective (which had increased from $8,691,547.46 in 1983 to $12,084,055.74 in 1984) was interest-free. Challenged by Ken Marlin's lawyer, Ken Chapman, at the Code inquiry about this extraordinary procedure, Cormie remarked: "We had been doing that for 25 years, of financing the other company." Quite right, but careless. The comment permitted Chapman to enter into evidence the bitter letters written by former partners Ralph Forster and Ken Marlin in the 1960s and 1970s, opening a window into Cormie's financial machinations over three decades.

As he had in those early years, Cormie continued to pay generous fees and salaries to upstairs companies and family members, largely through Estate Loan and Finance, up the line from County Investments. The shares of Estate Loan were in the name of his wife Eivor, but Cormie's employees held the shares in trust for his wife (among them Jude Halvorson and Diane Stefanski), so that their names appeared on documents filed at the corporate registry.

Stefanski testified that the share certificates were physically held in the company's minute book and stored in Cormie's office. The paperwork for transferring a share to a new holder, and for transferring it from that person to someone else (left unnamed), were both completed simultaneously, she said. "As soon as they were issued they were signed off. If for any reason a person left employment, just one of those things would be cleaned up already." This arrangement meant that Cormie could remove his employees as shareholders any time they became uncooperative.

As well as signing a Declaration of Trust in favour of Eivor, Halvorson was asked to sign a Power of Attorney, giving Eivor legal control of the company. She understood that this was established practice, and didn't question it.

Between 1982 and 1986 Principal Group paid Estate $1,580,975 in "sales distribution management fees" and $375,000 in "conference fees" for meetings held at Cormie's houses in Victoria and Scottsdale. Asked to explain this practice, Cormie said the fees dated to the original management contract signed in 1956, whereby Estate managed the First Investors sales organization.

But that arrangement was changed in 1973, when Principal Group took over sales. Confronted with this, Cormie said Estate remained responsible for "forward planning, strategic planning," including his cyclical analysis of economic trends. The service supplied by Estate to Principal Group was not committed to paper, he said, but consisted of verbal advice after 1975.

Basically, the service seemed to amount to Cormie's attendance with his wife at dances or parties for the sales group in every sales area twice a year. Code concluded that Estate had done nothing after 1973 to earn its fees, and that it had been paid "for no justifiable or even plausible reason". Any strategic or forward planning undertaken by Cormie or his sons was paid for in their capacity as officers and directors of Principal Group and PSML, not by Estate.

In fact, all investment research and market forecasting—including research into investment decisions for the upstairs companies—was handled by Principal Group's investment department. Cormie, his son Jaimie and department employees gathered information from many sources—brokerage and financial institution reports, "guru" reports (as John Cormie would say), business publications, general economic trends and conditions and commodity prices. Then, like every other market player, they held their breath and shook the dice.

As for "cyclical" analysis, Code's requests for original research material turned up little more than the arcane archaeological studies of Cormie's daughter Allison, a doctoral student at McMaster University, and water level studies of Lake Wabamun, located near the Cormie ranch. Allison's work embraced weather patterns going back a thousand years. She used radio isotope carbon dating to inspect deer bones and other animal remains. Her findings, which weren't delivered to Cormie until after the collapse, may or may not have been good science, but their value in predicting the ups and downs of the modern stock market seems somewhat limited.

Cormie said that support of Allison's research was one reason for Principal Group's payment of fees to Estate, until he was confronted with the fact that this same research was supposed to account for the $120,000 Allison was paid by Principal between August 1986 and August 1987. In the end, Code concluded that her salary was "fraudulent and dishonest."

Cormie gave the game away on the Lake Wabamun study when he remarked that it was prepared "in conjunction with looking at the economics of a ranching venture in that area." The Cormie Ranch was plagued with marshy fields unsuitable for crops. Information on water levels could be useful to a fellow with a damp 14,000-acre ranch, trying to evaluate on-going drainage efforts.

During the 13 months before the Principal Group collapse, Cormie's wife Eivor was paid $275,000 by Collective Securities. Code found that Eivor, who wasn't called to testify, did nothing to earn the money, and called it another "fraudulent and dishonest expense." In 1987 the entire family was on the payroll, and involved—to the extent they let their names be used—in Cormie's borrowing and investment schemes. The family received a total of $2,743,694 in salaries from various companies between 1985 and mid-1987: Cormie himself received $759,800; Eivor the $275,000; Jaimie $352,494; John $359,160; Allison $288,440; Neil $293,133; Bruce $177,000; Eivor Jr. $115,667; and Robert, then a law student, $123,000. Salaries paid by Collective Securities went into their County Investments savings accounts and were used to pay off corporate loans. Other benefits included interest-free housing loans for Jaimie, John, Neil and Eivor Jr.; use of the corporate credit card by Cormie, his wife and four of the children (a total of $297,579.30 was charged by the six between 1985 and 1987—half of that by Cormie, another quarter by John); and dividends paid by a variety of companies.

The only exception was Donald Cormie Jr., the second son. "Donnie" was on the Principal payroll for several years, appearing first in annual reports as a mortgage department employee, then as an analyst in the stock and bond department under his younger brother Jaimie, and later in institutional sales. Suddenly in 1983, at the age of 35, he pulled out and moved to Vancouver, the only family member ever to escape his father's sway. He didn't just abandon his salary, he cut himself out of the entire set-up. County Investments records show that at the end of 1982 Donnie's savings account held $330,418, and his loan account (the money borrowed from downstairs and managed by his father) contained $874,672. The next year-end, his savings account was empty, and his loan account showed a debt of $353,262. By the end of 1984 that account had been cleared as well.

Even Donnie's RRSPs, carefully built up over the years by his father, were liquidated. A cryptic entry in Stefanski's records shows that on August 17, 1984, $80,000 in promissory note money was transferred to Principal Group, of which $78,497 was wired to Donnie. "Then Aug 28/84," the entry continues, "DRC [Donnie] liquidated RRSP to PGL to PGN $78,831."

During the Code inquiry, a curious exchange took place between Donald Cormie and Ken Marlin's lawyer, Ken Chapman, who asked Cormie whether Donnie had ever accused him of laundering money through his name.

CORMIE: I don't think that is a—you know, we have had lots of
discussions about whether or not his salary went into here and he
paid tax on it or not. But he never—I don't like your words, I
don't know where you got those from.
CHAPMAN: Did he ever accuse you of laundering money through
his name?
A: It is possible he might have. I don't recollect him saying that, no.
Q: Do you recall at a meeting between Don Jr. and yourself that Mr. Marlin
was asked to attend by Don Jr. to discuss how you were operating?

A: I think, yes, that Ken and I met with Don Jr. when he wanted to take his money out of these companies, out of some of these investments, and we met with Don and discussed it. If Don said that, then that is something that I don't recollect, but maybe he did.

Q: But you weren't laundering money through his name, were you?

A: Of course not. I mean, we kept perfect records all the time. That's why we sat down and discussed it with him, Ken and I discussed it with Don Jr. because he wanted to come out of the companies, trust company and everything else.

The day after this dialogue was reported in the media, Donnie denied Chapman's allegations. "I want to make it clear the statement attributed to me is absolutely false and totally unsubstantiated," he told *The Globe and Mail*.

Marlin stands by his version of events. In 1991, he told me that Donnie had asked him to mediate a dispute with his father regarding money held in Donnie's name. "In order to pay as little tax as possible, Don was doing what you might call 'income splitting'—he was paying all family members a pre-determined amount that would keep the tax rate as low as possible," Marlin said. "Of course this money was being paid in their name and being credited in County Investments and tax returns being filed on behalf of the various children. And of course those accounts started to build up and there was quite a bit of money in them. Donnie got it in his mind this money was his and of course it was his because he'd paid the tax on it, and he just felt he should be entitled to some of that money."

Cormie didn't, and the two quarrelled bitterly. Finally, there was a showdown, attended by Marlin, in Cormie's office. "That comment, 'You're just using me to launder the money,' that was an expression he actually used in a fit of frustration or anger, about the fact this money was not being used as if it were his money. His Dad still used it, controlled it, spent it, looked after it," Marlin said. In the end, Cormie offered his son a settlement, "and he said, 'That's it, you're off the list,' and he no longer appeared on the payroll or received any money."

Before Donnie liquidated his RRSPs, Donald Cormie embarked on yet another transaction. On August 15, 1984—around the time he was battling auditor Bruce Pennock's plan to include a "going-concern" note in the Principal Group financial statements—$250,000 was transferred from the Principal Group promissory note account to Collective Securities to Cormie Ranch to the brokerage firm Merrill Lynch. The next week, Cormie wrote Merrill Lynch authorizing the wire transfer of $262,300 to the Ottawa bank account of a local yacht dealer who represented the Hong Kong shipbuilding firm responsible for Cormie's 47-foot cabin cruiser the *Anchor Sea*: a luxury yacht registered in Victoria, B.C., in early 1985 under the ownership of Estate Loan.

There wasn't enough money in the promissory note account at the time of the $250,000 transfer, and an overdraft existed for about an hour. Then, $100,000 invested on August 14 by client "Kinash" was combined with money received from clients "Lynn Chee" and "Funk" on the afternoon of August 15 and transferred to cover the overdraft. Still more money invested by "Funk" on August 15 was used in the transfer to Donnie two days later.

Cormie's peculiar use of the promissory note money went undetected by regulatory agencies. Under Alberta's *Securities Act* the notes were exempt from the province's usual prospectus and reporting requirements, and over-worked officials had little time or motivation to dig where duty did not call. In most cases the investing public is protected by regulatory requirements governing registration of people who sell securities, and by the preparation of a prospectus that discloses in detail the business and affairs of a security's issuer so that investors may make a reasoned decision concerning the purchase. The Principal notes, however, slipped between the cracks of the regulatory system. The assumption in Alberta, as in Ontario, is that people who can afford such a large investment are sophisticated enough to fend for themselves, unprotected by legislation. The only requirement was that vendors of exempt securities file a report to the Alberta Securities Commission within 10 days of the trade.

There were two kinds of notes: short-term (less than one year) of an amount not less than $50,000; and medium-term (one to five years) of at least $97,000. The notes, unsecured and uninsured, were simply acknowledgement of money borrowed and a promise to repay by a certain time at a certain rate of interest. The information memoranda used to distribute them said the funds were to be used for "general corporate purposes," and there was no way for investors to determine what those purposes were.

There appear to be only two occasions during the 1980s when regulators came close to asking the right questions. The first was in June 1984 when the CDIC and provincial officials met to discuss problems with Principal Trust and the contract companies. The second was in May 1985 when Alberta Securities Commission officials, hearing rumours that Principal had been barred from buying an Ontario trust company, exchanged memos about the notes. Al Woo, the commission's Deputy Director of Enforcement, sent a memo to Tom Bertling, its consumer relations officer, outlining his concern that some of the noteholders' money was being loaned to Principal insiders at "favourable" rates lower than the rates promised the investors.

> Were it not for the fact that Principal is engaged in some apparently *bona fide* business endeavors, one would be inclined to remark that the issuance of promissory notes with a delay of six to twelve months return of payment of principal and interest smacks of a classical Ponzi scheme where new investors' monies are used to pay old investors out, the key being that there is an appreciable time delay in paying out early investors. We are aware of course that many investors may simply "roll over" their investments upon maturity, giving the issuer the additional funds and time to meet old commitments. We are also aware that Principal has the liberty of channelling funds and assets to meet particular regulatory requirements of certain of its entities, possibly to the deprivation of other unregulated entities. However, the inter-corporate maze

has not been understood and only Don Cormie and Ken Marlin and other selected insiders really know what's going on. This may be a challenge for our Securities section should any new filings in the nature of public offering documents be submitted.

Despite his suspicions, Woo ordered no further investigation into the company. Rather, he told Bertling, "Given that we have detected no violations or mischief in selective review, you may discontinue any active procedures on your part and simply follow the Company's progress." This seems to have been the commission's last involvement with the sale of Principal Group promissory notes until after the collapse.

Woo should have followed his hunch. Two years later Principal went down in flames, and bankruptcy trustee J. Stephens Allan subsequently concluded that the company indeed appeared to be involved in a Ponzi scheme. In a report to the federal Superintendent of Bankruptcy, Allan said that Principal Group was bankrupt in 1984, and probably as early as 1983—one or two years before Woo's memo. Allan testified at the Code inquiry that he told the Superintendent "there was possible fraud involved and I recommended that he postpone any action until such time as the [Code] inquiry was completed because I was aware that the RCMP were monitoring the inquiry."

Ponzi schemes, the oldest and simplest form of swindle, are based on the concept of using new investors' money to pay off old debts. They're named after Charles Ponzi, who operated in Boston shortly after World War I. Ponzi borrowed money from investors at the extraordinary rate of 40% for 45 days, then took money from new investors and used part of it to pay interest on the original deposits. He pocketed $10 million before he was arrested for fraud.

Such schemes, like chain letters and other pyramid sales scams, must continually expand. They work for a while, but ever more investors are needed to keep the system operative until it finally collapses of its own weight. The greedier the con artist, the sooner the catastrophe. Investors who remain in when the scheme topples, usually when the swindler makes a run for it, may end up losing everything.

After the Principal Group collapse, bankruptcy trustee Allan and colleagues investigated the company's operations and concluded that its liabilities grossly exceeded its assets. It was able to meet its obligations as they fell due only by using incoming investors' money. Principal had no cash flow problem while it was able to sell promissory notes. The problem occurred July 17, 1987, when its exemptions were lifted and it couldn't sell any more.

Allan explained to the Code inquiry that Ponzi schemes usually have a gimmick to attract the unsuspecting public. Principal's hooks, he said, were threefold: an aura of respectability, an appearance of stability and a generous interest rate. "It is able to sell promissory notes to people under the guise of a respected financial institution," he said. "It is able to point to parts of the institution that are being regulated by the provincial government, another part that is being regulated by CDIC, backed by the billion dollars of the Principal Group assets, and it is paying a very nice rate of return."

During the years before its collapse—between January 1984 and August 1987—Principal Group sold $293.7 million worth of promissory notes. Almost 90% of that money , totalling $260.8 million, was used to redeem old notes, leaving only $32.9 million in note money to be managed by the company. Another $21.7 million came in through other sources, including the sale of securities, providing a total of $54.6 million in cash received.

Little was invested in ways that would realize a good return. Despite Principal Group's dire circumstances, it continued to loan money, increasingly interest-free, to Collective Securities, which funnelled it upstairs. Collective's debts to Principal Group totalled $64 million at the time of bankruptcy: approximately three-quarters of the total $87 million worth of promissory notes outstanding on that date. About $76 million of those notes were sold after January 1985—after the company was clearly insolvent—including $34 million worth sold to people who had never before invested in the company.

In 1984, the year before Woo's memo, here's what happened with investors' money: there were $85 million worth of promissory notes sold, with $70.5 million used to repay maturing notes. That left a balance of approximately $14.5 million. The money was used, not for investment, but to prop up other parts of the conglomerate and to finance the Cormie lifestyle: $11.3 million was poured into First Investors to remedy the outrageous $23-million asset dump from the trust company, and the remaining $3.5 million was loaned upstairs to Collective.

Conditions worsened in 1985. Despite a vigorous sales campaign to push the promissory notes, only $2 million was cleared after maturing notes were paid off. The only other source of cash (besides intercorporate fees and charges) was $2.6 million from the sale of marketable securities. That year, Principal advanced its total cash balance, $4.6 million, to Collective Securities.

So how did the company meet its operating expenses: advertising, travel, accounting, computer services, staff benefits, commissions, office costs, generous salaries and rental of the Principal Plaza headquarters? It dipped into the pockets of various companies in the Principal conglomerate, returning with cash in the form of administration fees and levies. Between 1979 and 1986, these fees amounted to $54,530,888, including $31,711,074 paid by First Investors and Associated Investors.[5]

The contract companies gave in another way as well. Between 1981 and 1987, a total of $23,207,710 in "surplus" funds was drained from them into Principal Group. They not only lost that cash—$9.87 from every $1,000 certificate sold—but the use of it, and were denied the $15 million or so that the "surplus" could have earned by mid-1987 if properly invested. Had this money been placed in reputable securities it might well have earned between 18% and 22% a year, according to Jaimie Cormie. Compounded, the sum would have grown to approximately $38 million.

Of the many financial products sold by the Principal companies, only the investment contracts generated a "surplus." This came as a nasty surprise to many certificate holders, who believed that their entire investment, plus 4%, was waiting for them in a bank vault. They had no way of learning that their money, invested in one insolvent company, was being used to prop up its insolvent parent, which was in the business of making no-interest loans to the conglomerate's owners.

Much of Cormie's upstairs activity remain a mystery. The books of Cormie Ranch and of Estate Loan and Finance, which would reveal the ultimate destination of the millions of dollars borrowed and invested by them, have yet to be made public. No one knows what salaries and fees were paid, what investments made, what transactions conducted, to move money even further into the mist. However, tantalizing details have filtered through.

In the spring of 1983, Estate Loan submitted an application form[6] to the Alberta Securities Commission, identifying Cormie's wife Eivor as sole beneficial shareholder and Cormie as the person responsible for its management. The application stated that Estate's investment portfolio was worth $1 million to $10 million and was expected to increase in value to $20 million. Total assets amounted to about $1,450,000. The next year's renewal application advised that Estate had assets of about $1,650,000. In April 1986, it reported assets of $2 million. The next application, filed May 28, 1987, said that Estate's total assets were $10,858,037 as of August 31, 1986. The reason for this escalation is unknown, although it appears to reflect activity in the Cormies' highly leveraged mutual fund accounts.

Stefanski's records show that Merrill Lynch advanced $10.2 million toward the purchase of mutual funds for Estate Loan, Collective Securities and Principal Group between March and August 1986. (At a 50% margin that means accounts totalling over $20 million.) Curiously, the three companies' accounts were pooled and cross-collateralized, with Principal Group advancing significantly more than 50% on its holdings. At the time of the July 1987 collapse, the value of mutual funds held by the three companies totalled $23,325,908, with $11,088,661 owed to Merrill Lynch to cover the margin—but Principal Group, which owned half the funds, was margined only 18%, while Estate was margined at 79%. Collective actually had an unheard-of negative margin: it had acquired $2.5 million worth of mutual funds without putting out a penny of its own. Thus Cormie was using Principal's credit to acquire millions of dollars worth of mutual funds for his own companies.

Merrill Lynch was only one of the investment houses Cormie dealt with, and records are spotty on other accounts. We also don't know how much money Cormie might have sent out of the country in the last couple of decades: we don't know where it might have gone, or what became of it once it got there. We do know that Cormie favoured, and recommended, foreign investment as a way of baffling tax-officials, and we know that sums were invested on foreign shores: witness his acquisition of the Cayman Islands bank. There are other hints as well.

On October 19, 1982, Cormie hastened to send money to an overseas branch of the Chemical Bank (Stefanski testified that she believed it was in Switzerland), probably to meet a margin call. Principal Group raised the money by borrowing $150,000 from the CBIC, then loaned it to Collective Securities, which loaned it to County Investments. County wired the money abroad—$50,000 each in the names of Donald Cormie, Eivor and their son Bruce.

Another such activity occurred on March 1, 1984, when Stefanski was hustled off to the Toronto Dominion Bank to wire $900,000 to Europe. "Mr. Cormie just came to me and said, 'It is 10 o'clock, we have to wire some money to Europe. Please write the cheques in this order.' " Meanwhile, Jaimie authorized $1,870,000 to be moved from the downstairs fund into the Principal Group note account during the lunch hour. Three minutes later, it was loaned upstairs to Principal Group, to Collective (loan receivable to Donald Cormie), to County and to Estate, from which $900,000 crossed the Atlantic.

Stefanski said she didn't know where the money was sent. "This transaction was done very quickly," she testified. "I wasn't party to preparing the letter. I was just told to get to the bank because it was urgent to wire because of timing. And I was told not to keep a copy... He told me it was personal."

Part III

Another Outstanding Year

14

A teaspoon of honey

January 4, 1985

THE STORY WAS PLASTERED across the front page of *The Globe and Mail*: four unnamed Canadian trust companies were in big trouble because their financing of a hundred real estate transactions in Western Canada, worth more than $1.5 billion, was based on exaggerated appraisals. The deals involved commercial properties, mainly in Alberta and British Columbia, ranging from shopping centres to apartment and office buildings.

The article, written by Canadian Press reporter Gord McIntosh, quoted an unnamed federal official as saying that appraisers often felt pressured to value a property far above its fair market value—because the client wanted to support either high financing or an inflated purchase price. "In many cases, it's not the appraiser's fault because he is only working from the information the client gave," the official said. Some of the trust companies involved had been ordered to pump additional equity into their treasuries to protect their borrowing bases, or risk losing their CDIC coverage.

McIntosh's article created an uproar coast to coast, and intense speculation about the "group of four." His revelations caused great distress in the Principal tower, where staff were gearing up for the 1985 RRSP sales season. Within hours of the article's appearance, Ken Marlin fired off an "ALL STAFF" memo:

> The recent publicity that has arisen because of the news story released
> concerning western trust companies is unfortunate but should not concern you.
> Principal Savings and Trust Company is not one of the four companies
> included in the comment and has received a clear bill of health from both
> Canada Deposit Insurance Corp. and The Alberta Superintendent of Insurance.

The next day federal Superintendent of Insurance Robert Hammond confirmed to the *Globe* that several trust companies had been hurt by the collapse of Western real estate prices and had been forced to raise additional capital, but he refused to reveal their names. Nonetheless, the story identified three companies whose financial statements indicated that real estate losses had required capital injections: Pioneer Trust, North West Trust and Principal Trust. It continued: "While Principal turned a profit in 1984, it still suffered from the real estate collapse." Marlin, interviewed by the paper, claimed that part of the increased capital raised during the year was not to cover real estate losses, but to finance "additional growth."

Connie Osterman was quick to bolster her province's sagging reputation. In interviews which appeared the next morning in Edmonton's *Sunday Sun* and *The Edmonton Journal*, she insisted that Alberta's trust companies enjoyed excellent health. The *Sun*[1] quoted Osterman as saying that they were "sound as a dollar and in no danger of collapse":

> And she's angered by media reports that suggested the Alberta government is ready to step in to bail out some provincially-based trust companies caught short of cash by declining real estate values. "We're very confident our financial institutions are sound," Osterman said.
>
> "I can unequivocally make the statement that none of our trust companies are in danger. I don't know how much more assurance I can give..."
>
> She called the report a "fiasco." And she added that there is "no risk whatsoever" the provincial government will step in to "backstop" financially-strapped trust companies as it did last spring with cash-starved credit unions.
>
> Osterman agreed at that time to guarantee $200 million to the province's credit unions, which have also taken a severe beating because of slumping credit unions.
>
> The minister's comments were backed by Robert Hammond, superintendent of insurance for the [CDIC], who called the report "unnecessarily alarmist."

As we know, the Alberta Treasury Branches had already poured $10 million into North West Trust, and within weeks of Osterman's comments would indirectly provide another $25 million in assistance. Within four months, Osterman would present a top-secret memo to Premier Peter Lougheed identifying a crisis among the province's trust companies and naming Heritage Trust, North West Trust and Principal Trust as the three most worrisome institutions. Over the next couple of years, the province's tab for bailing out Alberta's credit unions, trust companies and banks would run to hundreds of millions of dollars.

Director of Trust Companies Reg Pointe saw both Osterman's remarks and Marlin's memo to staff. Pointe knew that Marlin's claim of "a clear bill of health" from both the federal and provincial regulators was a lie—that in fact Principal Trust's position remained precarious—and he testified he kept Osterman advised of developments.

The CDIC had dropped its Section 25 notice against Principal Trust in September, but discussions continued regarding the company's improperly escalating borrowing-to-capital ratio, unsolved matching problems and the remainder of its problematic real estate and mortgage portfolio. There had also been a couple of demands for additional capital. But Pointe took no steps to determine whether Marlin's misinformation had been passed on to the public. "I just took it as information and filed it," he testified. Nor did he challenge Osterman's remarks, of which Marlin took immediate advantage. Within a week the two newspaper articles had been distributed to the sales staff, and would remain part of the Principal sales kit until the collapse.

January 8, 1985

BILL JOHNSON WENT TO WORK for Donald Cormie in November 1984, as Principal Group vice-president of finance, responsible for the two dozen accountants who kept the records for Principal and its subsidiaries—the "downstairs" companies.

Johnson was an excellent find: he had been a chartered accountant since 1972, and was an acknowledged expert in the area of business tax accounting. He negotiated a good package for himself: a $200,000 salary and an interest-free $200,000 mortgage. "I interviewed Bill," Cormie testified, "and he seemed ideally suited for the spot, in that I found him to be quick, he had a strong accounting background, as far as I could see, and he seemed to be fairly decisive... I found Bill to be really good, in that he learned the *Investment Contracts Act* faster than anybody I had ever worked with in 20 or 30 years. A person always has difficulty the first few months, as there are lots of chartered accountants who can't find their way through the Act first time around."

Johnson had understood during his interview that he would be supervising the accounting and reporting functions within the Principal Group of Companies, as well as supervising the preparation of management reports, co-ordinating the year-end audit, assisting with budgeting, analyzing acquisition possibilities and preparing public issues—normal duties in a large corporation. Instead, he was amazed to find how much of his time was spent dealing with unhappy regulators and frustrated auditors.

Johnson couldn't believe how long it was taking to wrap up Principal's 1983 consolidated statement. He had been hired after completion of the $23-million "tender," the Carma asset swap and Superintendent Tewfik Saleh's capital demand, but he had to deal with the fallout. Still, given the agreement to inject $11.3 million into the contract companies, Johnson assumed—like Cormie—that the damn thing would be signed off in short order. Instead, Bruce Pennock found new issues to raise. On January 8, Johnson wrote a memo to Cormie:

> Rather than the regulatory issue, Touche Ross now seems to be hung up on the following:
> (1) [Principal Group's] $15 million receivable from [Collective Securities]—collectibility and security.
> (2) Where the $11.3-million injection into [First Investors] came from—ie. the ultimate shareholders vs. note holders of [Principal Group].

As Principal Group's auditor, part of Pennock's job was to examine all receivables on the company's books, to ascertain whether the debts were actually collectible. But, he testified, it was horribly difficult to get information about the collectibility of the upstairs receivables: the millions loaned to parent company Collective Securities.

The network of companies controlled by Cormie was an interconnected, financially interdependent system and, under standard accounting principles, should have been audited as a unit by a single auditor, so that the entire picture could be seen. But Cormie split things up: Touche Ross audited the "downstairs" companies (Principal Group and its subsidiaries); Coopers & Lybrand audited the "upstairs" companies (Collective Securities and the Cormie family companies) on an unconsolidated basis only; and a third firm, Peat Marwick, audited the books of Athabasca Holdings and, after their acquisition in 1984, Allarco Energy and the Cayman Islands bank. As of 1983, Deloitte Haskins & Sells audited Principal Neo-Tech. In 1984, it replaced Touche Ross on the downstairs companies as well.

In June, at Pennock's insistence, one of his colleagues was allowed into the Coopers office to see the Collective financial statement (still in draft form, awaiting the completed Principal Group statement). The major item on Collective's books was a loan to Cormie Ranch for about $9.6 million. As well, Collective owned all the preferred shares of the ranch, valued at $1 million, so that $10.6 million of Collective's assets related to Cormie Ranch. Pennock obtained permission to look at the ranch's financial statement as well, then attempted to put together his own version of a "condensed" consolidated balance sheet for Collective Securities/Cormie Ranch. Pennock's highly simplistic analysis showed approximately $36 million in assets and $36 million in debts. On the face of it, Collective had sufficient equity to support the money owed to Principal Group.

There was the regulatory matter to settle as well. Pennock had been led to believe that the $11.3-million injection into the contract companies had resolved all regulatory demands. The day that Bill Johnson wrote his memo to Cormie, Pennock called auditor Al Hutchison in Consumer Affairs to confirm that fact. Hutchison repeated what had been said in Saleh's December letter: the $11.3 million was compensation only for the transaction with the trust company and the other items were still outstanding, but action had been delayed on these matters until receipt of the 1984 financial statement.

Pennock hung up and called Johnson. "Look, nothing's changed," he said. "I know Cormie wants me to kill that note in the statement that there are still items to be resolved with the Superintendent—but it has to stay. I just talked to Hutchison over in the government office and he says..."

Johnson called Hutchison's supervisor Bert Eldridge to complain. "We can't get involved in this," Eldridge said. "It's a matter between you and your auditors."

Eldridge wrote a memo outlining the situation to Tewfik Saleh, who called Pennock the following week. By the end of their conversation, Pennock testified, he had the impression that the capital demand made in Saleh's May 1984 letter had in fact been satisfied. Three days later, on January 18, the statement was finally released.

It was, however, qualified, rather like the contract companies' had been. The first note advised that it had been prepared "on a going-concern basis" and referred readers to another note which detailed a number of contingencies, among them a vague reference to requests for additional capital. "Based on capital contributed subsequent to the year-end, the regulatory authorities of two of the subsidiaries have agreed to forego any further action regarding additional outstanding items relating to capital requirements until they have received and reviewed the 1984 annual financial statements," the note said.

After all his trouble, that was all Cormie got. The miserable thing was useless as a marketing tool, so it was buried deep in Principal's accounting department, where no other member of the company—or, God forbid, any member of the public— would ever see it. No annual report was ever published for 1983, the first time this had happened since Principal Group began selling promissory notes.

One other outstanding piece of business remained. The contract companies' faked 1983 regulatory statements, sent to the Superintendent's office in May, had never been replaced with properly prepared, audited statements of assets. Government auditors had been after them for months, but in January 1984 Pennock called Hutchison to say that he had no intention of completing them. Instead, he wanted the regulators to wait for the 1984 statements that would soon arrive from the new audit firm.

In accounting jargon, Pennock had—orally, if not in writing—"refused an opinion" on the statements. "I was not comfortable," Pennock diplomatically testified, "signing that particular statement because there were—it was just—there was some interpretations and things that I was not comfortable with." Pressed for detail, Pennock said that "the risks of the business had increased" in the intervening year and, yes, there had been some lessening of confidence in the client.

Pennock's refusal to issue an opinion on the regulatory statements—legally required under the *Investment Contracts Act*—should have set alarm bells ringing up and down government corridors. Instead, it caused barely a ripple within the deeply demoralized department, and the request for the 1983 statements was permanently dropped.

January 29, 1985

PROVINCIAL AUDITOR ALLAN HUTCHISON prepared to follow Jim Darwish out the door. Fed up with life in the poisoned Consumer Affairs department, he decided to go into private practice in Scottsdale, Arizona.

Hutchison had put money in First Investors in 1978, two years before going to work for the province. From his regulatory vantage point, he watched the company digging itself a deeper and deeper hole. By the summer of 1984, he testified, "I knew there was just absolutely no way out unless they could get a huge injection of capital from some source, huge, like millions of dollars, like $70 or $80 million.

I felt they weren't prepared to put any additional money in."

As his investments matured, Hutchison moved his money elsewhere. And—in an ethically questionable move which has fellow chartered accountants hyperventilating—he pulled a number of private investment clients out as well. Hutchison admitted that he "might have indicated [to the clients] that [the companies] were having problems in the mortgages and real estate area," and he agreed that he would have learned this through his work as a government auditor. That's a serious breach of confidentiality, one of the premier canons of accounting, but Hutchison had no doubt that he'd done the right thing.

Hutchison said he was appalled at his superiors' lack of action, and by the accounting games Principal played to distract Tewfik Saleh from the real issue of the contract companies' bankruptcy. "As you can see, for two years I wrote memos and banged my head against the wall trying to get the public aware of this, and nothing happened. So I took it on my own to advise certain clients to pull their money out."[2]

At the end of January 1985, just before leaving public service, Hutchison wrote two wrap-up memos to Burt Eldridge on the contract companies. In the first, he described the Carma swap as a "complete sham." In the second, he pointed out that expenses were being understated by $2.5 million due to the deferral of the declaration of additional credits:

> This is a very significant change in accounting treatment and was only picked up by our review of the fluctuations in additional credit interest expense from month to month on the company's financial statements. It shows again the fact that FIC is deliberately providing the department with misleading financial information which is used to monitor the company...
>
> In addition we are receiving more and more evidence that the company officials can no longer be trusted. eg. Carma sale, PS&T sale, misleading monthly financial statements, misleading mortgage reserves, misleading real estate values, stopping and reinstatement of additional credit interest expense, etc. and it is therefore essential that we obtain quarterly audited financial statements that can be relied on.

Then Hutchison washed his hands of the mess, and headed south.

February 4, 1985

BRUCE PENNOCK WAS BARELY out the door, the 1983 Principal Group audit finally completed, when his replacement Don McCutchen signed off on the contract companies' 1984 financial statements. There was little disagreement between Principal management and its auditors on their contents. The company had recorded its version of events, and McCutchen had simply endorsed it.

Several years later, in mid-1991, the Institute of Chartered Accountants of Alberta condemned McCutchen for signing off on these misleading statements. It found McCutchen "guilty of unprofessional conduct" with respect to his audit of

First Investors' 1984 financial statements; he was fined $25,000, ordered to pay costs of $100,000 and suspended from the association for 30 days.[3]

The 1984 statements were prepared using the most aggressive accounting strategies possible. As noted in the Code report, they were designed "to recognize income as soon as possible and to defer losses as long as possible." A reader would have been left with the impression that the companies' situation was much improved from the year before. Income and earnings were up; the going-concern notes were conspicuous by their absence.

According to GAAP—the generally accepted accounting principles which are an accountant's Bible—a statement should provide full disclosure of all significant balances, transactions and events. (Items are significant if they could affect or influence a reader's assessment of the company's financial condition and operating results.) It should recognize revenues and expenses in the period in which they are considered to have been earned or incurred, whether or not they have been actually paid during that period. As well, auditors must sometimes look beyond the form of a transaction and reflect its substance, to ensure that readers are not misled by superficial appearances.

Chartered accountant Richard Cormier, of the firm Clarkson Gordon, called before the Code inquiry as an expert in auditing issues, prepared a report analyzing the accounting practices in the contract companies' financial statements between 1981 and 1986. Cormier found that, while the 1983 statements approved by Pennock could have been more conservative in writing off mortgage and property losses, the job had been done to a reasonable standard. But, he testified, the statements audited by McCutchen in 1984 included several misapplications of GAAP, were not done to a reasonable standard and did not fairly and accurately describe the financial position of the contract companies.

First Investors and Associated Investors routinely accrued interest on mortgages up to the point of foreclosure, even though a payment might not have been received for months or years. In 1984, the companies claimed mortgage interest revenue totalling $29.2 million—half of their total revenue—even though the vast majority of the mortgages (87%) were in arrears, and only a tenth of the revenue had actually been received. This was not disclosed in the statements. The total provision taken against mortgage and property losses in the two companies' 1984 statements totalled an insignificant $3.5 million, and should have been many millions higher.

McCutchen and Bill Johnson had worked out a strategy for reclassification of owned property that minimized write-downs of the real estate, allowing First Investors and Associated Investors to avoid recognizing an additional $5.4 million in losses.[4]

There were other accounting games. By deferring declaration of the fourth quarter additional credits, the contract companies had deferred interest expense of about $3.3 million. Neither the change in policy nor its effect—nor the fact that the credits had been temporarily cancelled—was disclosed in the statements.

When related companies do business, there is always the possibility that their relationship will result in a disadvantage to one party. GAAP requires that such non-arm's length transactions be disclosed. That disclosure, usually by means of a note, is supposed to detail the nature and extent of the transactions, the nature of the relationship and the amounts due to or from the related parties.

The $23-million asset dump from Principal Trust to the contract companies, and the subsequent shuffle between the Carma and Principal conglomerates, were related party transactions and should have been disclosed. They certainly were discussed in "subsequent event" notes after Pennock's 1983 audit, and similar notes should have appeared in the statements for the years during which the events occurred. They did not. The contingency for loss booked by Pennock because of the $23-million deal was abandoned, as was the note on regulatory demands for the injection of capital. At the same time, a fictional gain of $2.933 million on the Carma swap was recorded by the contract companies.

Another transaction, recorded in a resolution dated the last day of 1984, further improved the look of the contract companies' statements. For several years, the two companies made monthly cash payments to Principal Group for administration services and interest on subordinated notes. The payments had been made throughout 1984, but at year's end had been partly "forgiven." The reversal for First Investors amounted to $3,142,629; for Associated it was $781,425. (This "forgiveness" did not result in return of the cash to the contract companies, and was recorded as a debt owed by Principal Group to its subsidiaries. At the end of 1985, the debt would be "repaid" in a most extraordinary fashion.) This tactic effectively manufactured a profit for the contract companies.

The Code report analyzed the contract companies' statements and calculated the result of several conservative adjustments. First Investors' $1,040,128 profit became a $9,399,722 loss; Associated Investors' $117,888 profit became a loss of $2,904,576. (If even half the accrued/unpaid interest were written off, that would have increased First Investors' loss by $9.9 million, and Associated Investors' loss by $2.8 million.)

The statements of other Principal subsidiaries, including Principal Trust, were also signed off in February, and at the end of the month Hutchison completed the audit of the Principal Group consolidated statements for 1984. Those statements were also exceptionally rosy. Assets under administration totalled $895,685,000; total income was $80.6 million; net income (profit) was $4.4 million. The "improvements" made to the contract companies' statements were of course carried through to their parent's statements: there was no going-concern note, no mention of regulatory demands for capital, no disclosure of related party transactions, etc. The purchase of $12.5 million worth of Principal Group preferred shares by Athabasca Holdings, financed in the first instance by Principal Group, was not disclosed. Shareholders' equity was reported to be $10,455,000. The only reason for its existence was the fictitious injection of capital through Athabasca's share purchase, without which there would have been a deficit of $2,055,000.

McCutchen also audited the downstairs-cum-upstairs company, Principal Securities Management Ltd. (PSML), and was aware the company had been transferred from Principal Group to Collective Securities for $52,000. He testified that he considered its value to be about $20 million at that time. There was no disclosure in the Principal Group statement.

Code's analysis of Principal Group's bottom line, making the same conservative adjustments applied to the contract companies, turned Principal's $4.4-million profit into a $5-million loss. (If half the contract companies' accrued mortgage interest were written off, the loss would have deepened by another $12.7 million.)

Code concluded that the accounting policies used to paint these happy portraits of financial health were under Cormie's control. "The adoption by Donald Cormie of such aggressive policies is evidence tending to show an attempt to defer recognition of problems in FIC, AIC and PGL until the last possible moment. They presented what the evidence tends to show was a picture partly real and in the main fictional."

With Pennock's 1983 bad-news audit of Principal Group out of the way, McCutchen's 1984 audit was incorporated into the *Principal Group Ltd. 1984 Annual Report*. A message to the public, printed on the front of the full-colour glossy publication, advised: "Our 30th year was our best year ever. Earnings exceeded $4.4 million for the first time. The demand for our services and products remain strong as we look forward to our next 30 years."

PSML was prominently featured in the report. References to the mutual funds it managed ($253 million in managed assets, almost a third of $895 million in assets claimed to be under administration by Principal Group) implied that PSML continued to be a subsidiary. It was not disclosed that PSML had been transferred to Collective Securities, thus reducing the assets that Principal Group managed to $642 million.

A section on the contract companies advised that First Investors "had an excellent year in 1984, reflecting the corporate strategy of diversifying investments into superior quality corporate bonds and stocks, and de-emphasizing mortgage lending. The company holds over 52% of its assets in liquid, high yielding cash securities and fully secured collateral loans..." There was no mention of the fact that half the companies' assets consisted of largely non-producing mortgages and foreclosed real estate.

February 8, 1985

THE PRINCIPAL TRUST AUDIT WAS completed in early February and a news release followed immediately.

PROFITS DOUBLE IN 1984: Mr. John M. Cormie, President of Principal Savings & Trust Company of Edmonton, Alberta, announced today the release of the audited financial statement for the year ending December 31, 1984. Profit after tax for the year ending December 31, 1984, was $1,153,148 compared to $558,453 for the year ending December 31, 1983. Mr. Cormie, commenting on the 1984 results, stated that the strong financial position of the company is a result of an aggressive approach to the sale of mortgage and real estate assets and the continuation of investing in high quality financial assets...

Terry Pejnovik, Ken Marlin's executive assistant, quickly distributed the release to the sales force with a memo: "Please feel free to use this statement should any client or prospect question the financial health of our company." The memo advised that the news release was "the first of three marketing efforts to assure you and our clients of the stability of our company. The second is to advertise the three-year 11% RRSP (Principal Trust) beginning Wednesday, February 13. The third strategy is to forward to each of our offices a printed summary, financial statement of not only PS&T but also FIC and AIC."

Three documents were subsequently issued, each labelled SPECIAL BULLETIN, announcing the audited financial statements of Principal Trust, First Investors and Associated Investors. Christa Petracca took McCutchen's audits of these companies and worked the numbers into "summary statements," making them as attractive as possible. The contract companies' bulletins claimed that: "Due to continuing high interest rates, the Board of Directors continued to pass profits on to the certificate holders as additional credits."

What profits?

The statements were mailed to Principal salesmen. Marlin testified that the campaign—the first time in the history of the contract companies that information about their financial affairs was ever released—was in part a reaction to media rumours about problems with the trust company: "part of the effort to give comfort to our sales people, primarily."

February 23, 1985

THE COMFORT CAMPAIGN CONTINUED a couple of weeks later, when Ken Marlin gave an interview to *Financial Post* columnist Dunnery Best, insisting: "We deny being one of the 'group of four.'" In the article—circulated to "ABSOLUTELY EVERYONE" by Principal Group marketing manager Marie Ulrich—Marlin also claimed that Principal would soon be acquiring an Ontario trust company.

They weren't, in fact, close to a deal at all. By this time Ontario had already indicated its intention to block Principal's acquisition of Executive Trust, and the matter was under appeal.

Around this same time, Tewfik Saleh was asked by Ontario regulators for confirmation that the Principal contract companies were currently, and had been throughout 1984, in compliance with all aspects of the Alberta *Investment Contracts Act*. Saleh passed the letter to his assistant Bernard Rodrigues, with instructions for a reply that would dodge the question. Rodrigues wrote Don Reid, head of Ontario's trust and insurance investigation unit, on February 25, advising that the contract companies' 1984 regulatory statements, "as filed," showed that they had complied with the statutory requirements. "However, we cannot confirm to you the compliance of these two companies currently and throughout 1984 before completing our review of the statements which is in process. This process also involves inspection of the two companies by our staff auditors."

The next day, audit chief Burt Eldridge sent a memo to Saleh reporting that Associated Investors was deficient in all three of the Section 8 financial tests. This information was not relayed to Ontario.

Ontario was not alone in getting unsatisfactory answers from Saleh's office. In mid-February, investor Viola Pearson, a farm wife from Brooks, Alberta, had phoned Rodrigues seeking confirmation of assurances made to her and her husband Richard by Principal salesman Don Slater. Slater had given the Pearsons his usual pitch: their investment contracts were safer and better than federally insured RRSPs. According to Pearson, Slater always dismissed the guaranteed interest/additional credits breakdown as insignificant paperwork.

When Rodrigues explained that the contracts carried no insurance or guarantee, and that it was possible for the companies to fail, Pearson feared that she and her husband had been misled. "I was kind of panicky," she testified, "and Mr. Rodrigues said to me, he says, 'I am telling you not to panic, because at this moment, those companies appear to be in good standing.' " (Rodrigues testified that he did not recall making this statement.)

Pearson nonetheless wrote a letter of complaint, and Rodrigues ordered an investigation into Slater by the department's Lethbridge regional office. In mid-March, a letter was sent to Slater asking him to respond. He did so a week later:

> In my 26 years of service with the Principal Group I have at no time advised people that investment contracts provided 100% protection under the *Investment Contracts Act.* At no time in my 26 years of service did I mislead or misrepresent people to believe that the additional credits were guaranteed under the *Investment Contracts Act...* I am perfectly comfortable explaining the 4% base rate and the additional credit which in fact is not guaranteed. I explain it fully, completely and I explain it so it is well understood.

The investigator called the Pearsons to say that Slater had denied everything. That was the end of it. No one contacted other clients to determine what Slater was telling them.

The Pearsons had almost $100,000 in Principal Trust RRSPs and contract company certificates at this time. They immediately transferred a maturing term deposit to another institution, followed by other investments the next year. But $80,000 was still locked in when the contract companies went down.

March 4, 1985

DONALD CORMIE ANNOUNCED A major push on sales of Principal Group promissory notes. Sales staff were asked to sell the equivalent of $6 million worth of five-year notes by May 1985, and Jay Moulton, number two in sales administration under Ken Marlin, presented the sales committee with an action plan. Moulton's memo pointed out that Principal Group's failure to produce a 1983 audited financial report had hindered note sales during the previous year, and he advised that the 1984 report was being rushed into print. "It is not surprising that relatively sophisticated investors have reservations about the purchase of debentures from an institution that has not published a recent Annual Report," the memo said. "This publication will also play a pivotal role in the development of note sales outside the province, since the investor awareness of Principal outside of Alberta is consistently lower."

A few days later, Moulton met with a selected group of senior salesmen to discuss the note sale program and the security behind the notes. Jaimie Cormie, who happened to be walking past, was invited to join the discussion, and ended up demonstrating how to sell a note. As Jaimie talked, Moulton took notes, which show that Jaimie made numerous claims about Principal's stability. The note sale program had absolutely nothing to do with Principal's cash flow shortages, he said: "The program was designed to provide longer-term funding for the longer-term investment objectives of Principal Group." Principal had lots of cash and was very liquid; the trust company made all its profit in 1984 on bonds, and the contract companies were in "identical positions." We now know these statements to be false.

Moulton had his notes typed up, intending—given the absence of an annual report—to send them to the sales staff. He sent a three-page summary over to Jaimie's office for his approval. Jaimie made a few changes. "FIC/AIC are in identical positions" was altered to read: "FIC/AIC are in similar positions." As he worked, Donald Cormie appeared in the office. "Where's that from?" he asked, took the summary from Jaimie and made further changes in the wording, punctuation and structure. He titled the document "OBSERVATIONS PRINCIPAL GROUP," returned it to Jaimie and, according to Jaimie, instructed him to have Moulton get it checked out by the Principal legal department.

Moulton testified that he understood it would be illegal to distribute a copy of the document without regulatory approval. Instead, he marked "NOT TO BE COPIED OR DISTRIBUTED! VERBAL DISSEMINATION ONLY" on the front page, and sent it to Wally Noble, at that time general sales manager, with the expectation that the information would travel by word of mouth to sales staff.

The document formed the basis of a misleading publication, titled "Principal Group Corporate Notes Product Explanation," that was prepared in 1986 and widely distributed to salesmen and investors.

March 6, 1985

MEMO ON COLLECTIVE SECURITIES LETTERHEAD from Department 8 bookkeeper Diane Stefanski to Principal Group ("downstairs") comptroller Ginny Nicholson, copied to Donald Cormie:

> Further to our conversation of February 20, 1985, regarding PGL's payment to CSL [of] $16,000/month for management fees.
> Since the restructuring of PSML and as of August 31, 1984, when CSL began receiving 2% (less expenses) for management fees—is CSL still entitled to the $16,000 monthly mgt fee or should the diary card have been pulled? Or is this fee for other services not provided for under the PSML arrangement? Please advise.

Cormie's copy bounced back to Stefanski immediately, with an angry message scrawled across the bottom:

> No change authorized. D. Cormie.
> This is obviously a policy decision, and you should NOT take it up with Ginny. Also you disclosed information in a memo on CSL affairs without my authorization and this MUST NOT HAPPEN AGAIN.

The following Monday (March 11) Cormie wrote a calmer memo to Stefanski:

> You will recall that we set up a system whereby Collective Securities owns Principal Security Management Ltd., retaining one-half of all gross Mutual Funds proceeds from management. You are responsible to see that these Funds are received in cash every month, and that the necessary transactions are made to ensure that the Mutual Funds investments get made as arranged in [Cormie Ranch] as required. Please be sure that no months are skipped, and that I am notified immediately.
> Please also follow up to ensure that all funds are properly collected and accounted for, and that no month goes by without this being done. I would also ask that you advise me on a continuous basis throughout each month until this has been achieved. There is a tendency in PGL's accounting department to hold onto funds belonging to the other companies as long as possible without paying interest, and we have to ensure that this does not occur.
> Each quarter would you give me a photostat of the final Mutual Funds list indicating the respective deposits and the balances. Remember that this is highly confidential, and the information is not available to anyone except Rob Pearce, Jaimie and myself.
> —D.M.C.

March 28, 1985

AMONG THE WORST OF THE SPECULATIVE LOANS made by the contract companies during the 1982 lending frenzy were mortgages for land known as the Spectrum/Eckstrand properties. One property was 250 hectares of mountainside land at Three Sisters peaks, near Canmore, Alberta, at the eastern edge of Banff National Park; the other was an abandoned subdivision in Olds, north of Calgary. The mortgages had a book value of $4.5 million, but by 1984 they were in default. When the loans were made, Don Cormie testified, the properties were "red hot." Two years later they had been appraised at $152,000 and Cormie considered them valueless.

The contract companies had also made loans worth about $9 million to companies connected to deceased Vancouver builder/brewer Ben Ginter—famous for his smiling portrait on the label of his Uncle Ben's malt liquor. Those loans were also in default. Part of the money had gone to Rocky Mountain Breweries Ltd., in Red Deer, Alberta, which had been sold by Ginter to Calgarians Dick Slevin and Bob Lawson in 1981. Most of that loan had been rolled over to cover an earlier loan from another lender, leaving the final lenders, the Principal contract companies, in the lurch. Another loan had been made to Wexford Developments Ltd., a company related to the brewery. (The Wexford mortgage, for land in Bragg Creek west of Calgary, was actually shared 50/50 with Principal Trust, and was among the trash transferred from the trust company to the contract companies in early 1984.)

Cormie had different plans for these two sets of mortgages: he wanted to get the Spectrum/Eckstrand mortgages off the contract company books without having to take a write-down, but he wanted to foreclose on the brewery and take it over. There were, however, barriers to the contract companies taking over the brewery. As the owners of foreclosed (but licenced) hotels, they were prohibited by the Alberta *Liquor Control Act* from also owning a brewery. Also, second and third mortgages on some of the brewery property were held by another Ginter-related company, Pinch Penny Investments Ltd.

In April 1984, Cormie took steps designed to resolve these problems. First, First Investors and Associated Investors acquired the second and third mortgages held by Pinch Penny. Cormie flew to Vancouver to arrange this with Royal Trust, which was the executor of Ginter's estate. In exchange for the mortgages, which were extremely high-risk and of very limited value to the estate, Royal Trust agreed to take the Spectrum/Eckstrand mortgages off Cormie's hands. The trade was recorded on the contract companies' books at the mortgages' book value of $4.5 million.

So far so good. Then, at the last minute, one of Ginter's beneficiaries wanted immediate cash, as well as an undertaking that the Spectrum/Eckstrand properties would be worth a minimum of $600,000. "What happened at that stage," Cormie testified, "is that since the deal was closed and it looked highly favourable for First, I had Wyocan Resources [Ltd.] undertake to give them $600,000 on demand for those properties, if they decided that they would want the cash instead of the properties."

Wyocan—an inactive company owned by Cormie sons Jaimie, Neil and Bruce—was soon required to cough up $600,000 and take over the properties.

Wyocan, with no resources of its own, received help from Department 8. On April 30, 1984—the same day that Jim Darwish was attacked by Connie Osterman after criticizing Cormie's business activities—$600,000 was loaned from the Principal promissory note fund to Collective Securities, which loaned it to County Investments, which loaned it to Cormie, who loaned it to Estate Loan and Finance, which passed it to an Edmonton law firm, which handled Wyocan's purchase of the Spectrum/Eckstrand properties. The entry was subsequently revised to go through Cormie Ranch. The $600,000 was never repaid, and was still on the Cormie Ranch books at the time of the Principal collapse. (The property became attractive in 1992 after developers announced plans for a nearby golf course; it is now valued at around $500,000.)[6]

Meanwhile, the deal gave Cormie access to the brewery. After a court application, Peat Marwick Ltd. was appointed receiver/manager of the brewery's assets. Those assets were sold, pursuant to a court order, in January 1985 to a recently-created numbered company owned by the contract companies. The companies had also foreclosed on the property which secured the brewery-related Wexford loan, and that property was also sold, at book value, to the numbered company. Both of these purchases were financed by the contract companies, which recorded a total loan due from the numbered company in the amount of $14,534,400.

The day after the numbered company bought the brewery, the contract companies sold the numbered company's common shares (a hundred shares at $1 each) to Principal Group. Four days later, the numbered company was renamed Rocky Mountain Brewing Corporation. This transaction removed the forbidden brewery from the contract companies' portfolio, but left it with a $14.5-million loan to the brewery company now owned by Principal Group.

Cormie took care of that in his own way on March 28, when Athabasca Holdings directors Donald Cormie and Christa Petracca signed a resolution creating several series of Athabasca preferred shares which carried a dividend rate of 6%. The shares were purchased for $14 million from Athabasca's treasury by Principal Group, which paid for them with five promissory notes.

The shares were immediately transferred to the brewery company, along with $360,000 worth of Athabasca preferred shares acquired by Principal in the Carma transaction the year before. The brewery now owned $14.4 million worth of Athabasca shares, and owed Principal the $14.4 million.

That same day, the brewery company transferred the $14.4 million worth of Athabasca shares to the contract companies, thus paying off the debt it had incurred two months earlier when they financed its purchase of the brewery and Wexford properties.

At the end of the day, the contract companies—relieved of the Ginter and Spectrum/Eckstrand mortgages and spared a write-down—were left holding another $14.4 million in Athabasca preferred shares. Already saddled with $36.3 million worth of Athabasca shares during the Carma deal, this transaction pushed their total holdings up to $50.7 million.

Meanwhile, Cormie assigned a group of Principal Group and Collective Securities employees to run the brewery and turn it around. They were successful; the brewery showed a profit of $1 million in both 1985 and 1986.

Jaimie Cormie testified that they "parked" the brewery with Principal Group until they could figure out what to do with it. That decision would be made at the end of 1985.

April 22, 1985

DONALD CORMIE THOUGHT HE'D FOUND a way to use public money to solve the contract companies' capitalization problems. In late 1984, he decided to take First Investors public, assigning Christa Petracca to seek Alberta Securities Commission approval for a $50-million offering of new preferred shares. The idea was that the Principal sales force would push these new shares on investment contract holders as their certificates matured, effectively swapping their contracts not for cash, but for glossier corporate paper.

In December 1984, in preparation for the offering, Petracca filed an application with the Commission for an exemption order allowing Principal Consultants Ltd., which already had a licence to sell mutual funds, to also sell the new preferred shares of its affiliate First Investors—even though its salesmen weren't licenced as securities dealers. (Securities dealers are normally required to take a demanding course which, among other things, teaches them how to properly advise clients of the relative risks of various investments.)

In March 1985, Petracca filed a preliminary prospectus describing the offering. A prospectus is supposed to provide potential investors with comprehensive information about the company's affairs and must, by law, provide "full, true and plain disclosure" of all relevant facts—risks as well as potential benefits. The document filed by Petracca provided less than full disclosure, but it did place on record in the public domain, for the first time, some ugly truths about First Investors' mortgage situation. At the end of 1984, 63% of the company's $117-million mortgage portfolio was at least 90 days in arrears, but the reserves for losses totalled only 6.5% of the portfolio.

These revelations led to an hilarious exchange of correspondence between Petracca and Commission analyst Mark Brown, a chartered accountant. On April 22, Brown wrote Petracca a 12-page letter which trashed not only the prospectus, but the company, its management and its auditors. Brown dissected First Investors' circumstances, questioning the shabby intercorporate transactions of the previous year, the bizarre "appropriation of a deficit" in the financial statements and the failure to write down deteriorating assets. He pointed out that the wretched condition of the mortgage portfolio, combined with the continuing economic decline, cast doubt on the company's ability to meet its ongoing obligations. Brown continued: "The company will be required to use money from new investment contracts to repay old ones coming due. This is unacceptable." He identified almost a hundred deficiencies in the prospectus, and the bottom line was: Not in the public interest.

Brown's letter was copied to auditors Deloitte Haskins & Sells and to securities regulators in every province where First Investors' contracts were sold.

Petracca, undeterred, went back for another round. On May 2 she wrote again, claiming, among other things, that the $23-million "tender" of assets from the trust company to the contract companies had the "consent" of the Superintendent of Insurance, and that he had "agreed that the transaction was in the best interest of the certificate company." She made the same claim about Tewfik Saleh's approval of the Carma transaction and the acquisition of the Athabasca Holdings shares by the contract companies. Petracca behaved as if she were still dealing with the credulous Saleh: she was evasive, argumentative and patronizing, and actually suggested that the Alberta Securities Commission should butt out of administrating a company under the jurisdiction of the province's Superintendent of Insurance.

In her letter, Petracca claimed that the liquidity of First Investors "is certain, in particular, given the overall strength of the group." Not much of a claim, given that Principal Group had been insolvent for a year. And irrelevant: First Investors was making the offering, and had to stand or fall on its own. Challenged during the Code inquiry, Petracca testified: "You have to realize that I was trying to paint the most positive picture I could, given the environment, to achieve the corporate objective. It seemed reasonable to me at the time."

Brown replied in mid-May, trashing Petracca's arguments again. Copies of his letters went to Principal Group lawyers and the Deloitte accounting firm, each of whom had been sceptical of the offering in the first place. They recoiled in horror and urged a quick retreat. Petracca, however, felt they were "making progress," and Cormie gave her permission to continue. She proceeded to a commission hearing, where Principal Consultant's application for a securities licence exemption was rejected. Finally she wrote to the commission, withdrawing the share issue "pursuant to significantly favourable real estate transactions currently pending."

In early July, shocked at First Investors' financial disarray, the commission called in early July for the revocation of its registration under the *Trustee Act*, and the cancellation of its registration as a mutual funds dealer. We will recall that the company's application for the *Trustee Act* revocation went to the Cabinet office and disappeared; the mutual fund registration was cancelled, but in strictest confidence.

During the commission's investigation, Saleh and the department auditors were highly protective of First Investors. Audit chief Burt Eldridge met with Brown to discuss Petracca's prospectus, and advised that in his opinion the document—which claimed that First Investors had qualified assets which exceeded its obligations by $17.9 million—fairly reflected the company's affairs. There was a grotesque tug-of-war between the two offices, which reported to the same minister, for financial information about First Investors. Saleh and the auditors reluctantly allowed commission officials access to the files, but didn't want them to take away copies of any records.

Commission deputy director Marguerite Childs wanted copies of financial statements going back to 1976, but was resisted first by Saleh, and then her own superior. "Marc Lemay [the commission director] requested I not proceed with obtaining copies," she wrote in a memo on July 11—three days after First Investors had delivered its request to Cabinet for revocation under the *Trustee Act*. "The Lieutenant Governor in Council (Cabinet) will handle this matter from here."[8]

April 30, 1985

IN SEPTEMBER 1984 THE FEDERAL Progressive Conservatives swept the Liberals from power in a landslide victory, giving them the largest majority ever held in the House of Commons. The following spring, Prime Minister Brian Mulroney's government issued a green paper on regulation of the financial industry and Barbara McDougall, Minister of State (finance), went on tour to promote the proposed new policy. In Edmonton she appeared as guest speaker at a dinner hosted by the Alberta Society of Financial Analysts, joined at the head table by—among others—Donald Cormie and Member of Parliament Don Blenkarn, chairman of the House of Commons standing committee on finance.

Cormie, seated next to Blenkarn, seized the opportunity to complain about harassment of Principal Trust by the federal Department of Insurance. "I remember him," Blenkarn told me, "being pretty upset about the way the supervisors in Bob Hammond's office were demanding he put up more security for his trust company." When Blenkarn got back to Ottawa he looked up Hammond. "I have a very high regard for Bob Hammond and his ability to administer and follow up on trust companies and insurance companies and the like, and so I wanted to find out what the score was. Was he in fact beating up on poor old Cormie unfairly or what? Hammond told me that he thought Cormie's company was badly undercapitalized and so on and that he was paying close attention to Cormie's trust company—that was the only thing we were concerned with, was the trust company. So Ottawa had advised Alberta—and everybody else, I understand—that they were concerned about the Cormie company and I guess that's the reason that Cormie wasn't able to operate in Ontario and Quebec."

The CDIC's Section 25 notice had been dropped in September 1984, but hostilities resumed almost immediately. As early at mid-October there was a demand for $100,000 in additional capital. At the end of that month, Cormie won an Order-in-Council from the Alberta Legislature establishing Principal Trust's borrowing-to-capital ratio at 20:1. (We have no information about how this was accomplished.) The CDIC continued to enforce its more stringent ratio of 15:1.

Cormie remained furious about having to sell off some of the company's long-term Canada bonds. The bonds had dropped in value since their purchase, and Cormie told Blenkarn that the company was losing several million dollars by selling them at this time. (Cormie was right: the value of long bonds soared in 1985 and 1986, making them the top-performing security class in those years.) Cormie blamed the situation on "eastern prejudice," Blenkarn said. "My conclusion was that Bob Hammond was doing the kind of work we wanted him to do. I gotta tell you, in 1985, with trust companies falling apart right left and centre, it was exactly what I wanted Bob Hammond to be doing." Blenkarn laughed heartily. "We were in a disaster time. We had a collapse almost every month, you know. It was one trust company or bank after another. I mean," he laughed again, "tough supervision was the order of the day."

Unfortunately, tough supervision was the order only for federally-insured Principal Trust. Federal regulators well understood the disaster lurking inside the Principal tower, but felt neither empowered nor obliged to move on the larger, cross-corporate problem. They had authority over the trust company, but the rest of the Principal conglomerate was Alberta's turf. Within their own jurisdiction, federal officials acted admirably: they firmly regulated Principal Trust, forcing compliance with all the federal rules. Unfortunately, Principal responded to the feds' pressure by ruthlessly stripping the trust's sister companies of desperately needed assets. Federal officials witnessed the abuse of the investment contract companies, noted the likely insolvency of the parent company Principal Group and discussed the nature of the Principal "pyramid." They twiced offered to work collaboratively with Alberta, but were rebuffed. Then they politely closed their eyes and made damn sure the trust company's finances were in order.

Federal regulators emphasize now that they had no power to force the Principal contract companies into compliance with the *Investment Contracts Act.* True enough. There were, however, a couple of weapons at hand—if Ottawa had seen fit to wield them.

First, the CDIC had jurisdiction over events which occured within the premises of Principal Trust. That included the right to investigate sales pitches made in the Principal Financial Centres, where the trust branches were located. Federal regulators—indeed, much of the Canadian regulatory community—understood that Principal customers were often confused about the investments they purchased.[7] The fact that investment contract holders sometimes believed they were CDIC-insured should have been of grave concern to Ottawa. In April 1985—in the wake of the collapse of the Canadian Commercial Bank (See Chapter 15) and other institutions—CDIC chief executive officer Charles de Léry released a circular to insured institutions instructing them to stamp warnings on application forms where investments were not insured by the CDIC. John Cormie sent a letter agreeing to comply. That was it. The CDIC decals stayed on the doors, and the bait and switch continued.

Second, the Tory government in Ottawa could have applied moral pressure on the Tories in Edmonton to clean up the situation. Don Blenkarn wasn't the only federal politician to whom Donald Cormie complained about the CDIC. For three years Cormie bitterly protested Ottawa's treatment to anyone who would listen.

Several in that audience were members of the federal Conservative government; some were powerful members of Cabinet. Those who went to Hammond doubtless received the same briefing that Blenkarn did. If any of these people tried to talk sense to their Alberta counterparts, we certainly know nothing about it.

May 5, 1985

CONNIE OSTERMAN ROSE IN THE Alberta Legislature to offer a moving commendation of the Consumer Affairs regulatory staff:

> I think the effort of employees who operate in the six regions across the province has also been superb, Mr. Chairman... I have made the observation that regulation is a little bit like taking medicine. When the officer stops at your doorstep and starts to ask you questions and begins to conduct an investigation, it is like medicine. It's tough medicine, and a teaspoon of honey isn't going to make it go down any better. So as Minister I certainly give my full support to these people operating in the field, where they are constantly met with the frustrations from both sides, and say again that I think they have been doing a superb job.

Two months later, Tewfik Saleh again sought permission to rein in the contract companies. On July 18, spurred by audit staff reports—and, likely, recent criticism of First Investors by the Alberta Securities Commission—Saleh advised Deputy Minister Barry Martin that the situation with First Investors and Associated Investors "appears to be alarming and requires reporting to you and the Minister." Saleh, accompanied by Burt Eldridge, had met recently with Ken Marlin, he said. "I brought this serious situation to his attention and advised him that his two companies need substantial capital injections in order to be able to continue as a viable operation. I have not yet sent any formal demands to the companies pending direction from you and the Minister in this regard."

Saleh testified that he had a discussion with Martin and Osterman at this time, and again raised the issues of updated property appraisals and engagement of outside consultants. No steps were taken. Martin testified that he believed Saleh's memo was forwarded to the Cabinet financial institutions task force; Osterman says it was not. Interestingly, it was on July 29—only eleven days after Saleh wrote his memo— that George Kinsman, the Treasury bailout analyst, gathered information from Consumer Affairs about the affairs of Principal Trust and had his staff prepare their organizational chart detailing the relationship among the Principal Group companies.

Four days later, on August 2, Saleh sent a letter to Marlin expressing his discomfort with the contract companies' financial situation. The letter noted that the two companies had lost another $7 million during the first quarter of 1985. First Investors needed a capital injection of $9,476,068, and Associated Investors needed $1,668,536. These deficiencies, he said, were calculated without taking into consideration any write-down of the companies' real estate holdings. Saleh requested a reply outlining steps to rectify the problem. The letter flexed no muscle: there was no threat to deregister, cancel, or suspend the companies' licences.

Donald Cormie responded with a challenge to Consumer Affairs' long-established method of calculating the capital deficiencies. On August 8, during a meeting with Eldridge, finance vice-president Bill Johnson advised that Cormie, as a lawyer, had reviewed the *Investment Contracts Act* and disagreed with the way that government auditors calculated the three Section 8 financial tests. (The method proposed by Cormie would have turned deficits into surpluses.) A surprised Eldridge later reported to Saleh about the new strategy:

These tests have been consistently calculated since I joined the Department in 1976. Mr. Johnson stated that the original tests we were using were foisted upon the companies by former Superintendent Darwish… I recommend that we reject the companies' interpretation of the tests and insist that they continue to follow the ones in use.

Eldridge also told Saleh about a confidential chat he had with Johnson regarding the overall financial situation of the Principal Group of Companies:

He stated there are not any resources within Principal Group Ltd. to provide further funding for FIC and AIC. He stated that he had not seen financial statements on Collective Securities Ltd. (P.G.L.'s parent) but was aware of what was here and did not think there was a great deal of resources available. Mr Johnson was speaking for himself in this matter and not on behalf of the company…

Mr. Johnson was very candid in his discussion of the affairs of the contract companies.

Cormie's challenge of the Section 8 tests was not new. The tactic had been used at least once before, during the regulatory struggles with Jim Darwish and Deputy Minister Jack Lyndon in the mid-1970s. At that time, Darwish had cut the game short by simply calling in his Ontario counterpart. The official conducted a review, then reported that he agreed with Alberta's calculations and that the same calculations would be used in Ontario. Darwish called in the companies' external auditors to hear these unwelcome views. Checkmate.

This time, however, Cormie's strategy was astoundingly effective. Meetings were held, letters were written and various lawyers converged on the discussion, which dragged on for many months.

June 6, 1985

Donald CORMIE WROTE CHRISTA PETRACCA a letter raising her salary to $100,000 a year, plus an annual bonus equal to 1% of the consolidated net profits of Principal Group. The bonus—granted about a week after auditors Deloitte Haskins & Sells urged that Petracca be pulled off the First Investors share offering—would not be in cash, but would be applied against her interest-free house mortgage. (Based on the $4.4 million profit that accounting games had created for Principal in the 1984 financial statement, the bonus would amount to $44,000 for that year.)

Several company benefits were detailed in the letter, including an agreement to indemnify Petracca "in respect of any matter or claim which may be made against you as a result of the performance of your duties for any of the companies in the Group, including the provision of legal costs."

Petracca had received another promotion—of a sort—three months earlier, when Cormie appointed her the contract companies' third director. Among her first duties was the April 13 signing of a board resolution, also signed by Ken Marlin and Eric Espenberg, which named Cormie as one of four persons authorized to buy and sell land on behalf of the companies. Ten days later, another resolution gave Cormie and sons John and Jaimie full authority to buy and sell securities for the contract companies. Cormie testified at the Code inquiry that he was unaware of either resolution.

On June 7, the day after Petracca's raise, Cormie wrote a memo to Bill Johnson announcing his plan to have Petracca lead a small management team for the contract companies and the U.S. companies "so that these companies can get the kind of full-time management attention that we have found so successful on a number of other companies." Ten days later a memo to all Principal vice-presidents announced implementation of the plan. Petracca would head a "three-man management group" (her SWAT team) which would include Lance Frazier, hired by Cormie earlier that day. Frazier, a commercial real estate specialist, had jumped ship from North West Trust, which carried a devastated real estate portfolio twice the size of the one held by the Principal contract companies. Frazier's assignment was "to dispose of $20 Million worth of real estate in First Investors Corporation and Associated Investors of Canada with no book loss."

Cormie's memo also announced his plan to have Petracca gradually replace Ken Marlin as the contract companies' president. Petracca was fully aware of the mess the companies were in—she had, she testified, pulled her investments out of them in 1984—and it may seem odd that she'd want responsibility for them. This was, however, a way for her to become president of a high-dollar company so as to join the Young Presidents Organization. Petracca had to qualify for membership before she was 40, and time was running out.

As the companies deteriorated, Petracca's presidency disappeared. Cormie testified the companies were "having some serious problems with the regulatory people, and it was essential that Ken Marlin stay in these companies." Petracca turned 40 in December 1987, several months after the collapse of the Principal empire, her dream to join the YPO unfulfilled.

June 17, 1985

PRINCIPAL TRUST MANAGER GEORGE ABOUSSAFY found a couple of old

Vancouver contacts to help with Principal's problems. The trust company had bonds it didn't want to lose, and the contract companies had real estate they needed to get off their books—so Vancouver developers Fred Jaremchuk and Ron Downey agreed to have the assets parked with them for a while. (Downey is a prominent realtor with extensive roots in his community; he has served on the boards of the Real Estate Board of Greater Vancouver, the British Columbia Real Estate Association and the West Vancouver Police Board. In 1987, around the time his role in this transaction was revealed at the Code inquiry, he was elected president of the Downtown Vancouver Association.)

The bonds—$10 million worth of long-term Canada bonds the CDIC was demanding be dumped by the trust company—were "sold" to Shucksan Properties Inc., a company with Jaremchuk and Downey as its only directors. Shucksan paid for the bonds with a $10-million low-interest loan (7.5%, 3% below prime) from the trust company, and the bonds were pledged as security for the loan. A retroactive agreement signed a year later allowed the trust company to buy and sell the bonds and to take any gains on trading them as a "management fee."

At the same time, Jaremchuk and Downey, through General Equities Holdings Ltd. (Shucksan's parent company), borrowed money from First Investors to buy the Norscott Shopping Centre in Surrey, across the river from Vancouver. Its purchase price was $4,850,000, but they had in hand an appraisal from Royal LePage which estimated its market value at $8.1 million. First Investors agreed to loan General Equities 75% of the appraised value—$6,080,250—at the incredibly generous interest rate of 6.5%. The difference between the loan and the purchase price—$1,230,250—was to be used to bail Principal out of some of its bad real estate and mortgages.

Using that money—First Investors' own money—General Equities made a 10% downpayment on the purchase of six owned properties and two mortgages from First Investors, Associated Investors and Principal Trust. The sale was recorded at $12.2 million; the market value of the assets at that time at approximately $5 million. All three Principal companies took back mortgages on the remaining 90% of the purchase price. These loans also had generous interest rates: 7.5% for the trust company, and 6.5% for the contract companies.

The bonds held by Shucksan—earning approximately $1 million a year in interest—were pledged to guarantee the interest payments on the mortgages. Thus, tarnished real estate and mortgages, in serious danger of write-down on the three companies' books, were transformed into shiny new mortgages.

The loans to General Equity were non-recourse, which means there was no security beyond the properties themselves. Jaremchuk and Downey would share in any profits, but were at no risk; if things went badly, they could walk away.

At the Code inquiry, the rationale offered by Aboussafy, Donald Cormie and others for this transaction was that it would put the properties in the hands of better managers who would improve and hopefully sell some of them. But none were ever sold and General Equities was unable to generate enough revenue from them to cover the cost of the mortgages. Some of the bonds had to be sold to cover the difference.

So First Investors took the hit again. It loaned $6,080,250 in cash to General Equities; a loan secured by a shopping centre worth only $4.85 million. First Investors received $456,000 back in the form of a downpayment, and the balance of the loan—about $5.6 million—earned interest at 6.5% a year, less than what it had cost the company to borrow the funds from the public in the first place.

August 14, 1985

MEMO FROM DONALD CORMIE to comptroller Ginny Nicholson:

> I am attaching a form of Confidentiality Agreement which I would like each of those individuals on the distribution list for financial statements to sign. Any further individuals who become entitled to receive copies of financial statements will have to execute this agreement prior to our releasing statements.

Summer 1985

INVESTMENT BROKER TIM MASON went to the Sunshine Hutterite colony, 100 kilometres east of Calgary, to purchase a windmill. He wanted one for his family farm and his advertisement had been answered by George Walter, assistant minister at the colony, who invited the Masons to visit. They spent the day admiring the colony's technologically sophisticated operation, then settled themselves around the Walter family's kitchen table with other colony members to enjoy a glass of home-brewed wine.

Mason worked at the brokerage firm Midland Doherty Ltd. in Calgary. Like most members of the local investment community, he knew the Sunshine colony had money with Principal Group, and tried to warn Walter off. "You're completely and absolutely mad having your money there," Mason argued. "You know, you people have worked very hard for the money that you've got. You've got 90 people in this colony and you're jeopardizing their future. Is that fair?"

"Now, Tim, it's a very good investment," Walter replied. "We're getting a half-a-percent more than we could get anywhere else."

"Yeah, but is it fair to jeopardize the future of the colony for a half a point? It seems to me to be poor business, when you can accept a slightly lower return, but in a quality investment. This one's in trouble."

Walter shrugged. "Well, we'll think about it."

Mason claims no particular prescience in predicting doom for Principal Group. "I had no facts to base that on: just rumour, innuendo, the way they operated," he told me in 1990. "But I think you'll find that all around the investment community there were stories that Principal Group was in trouble, living high on the hog, paying more for money than anyone else, and there was risk to it. I knew from some people who had been at Principal, that some of their sales practices were questionable.

"I told [the Hutterites] in no uncertain terms—my wife was a little embarrassed, I think, because I was fairly forceful about my opinions of Principal Group. I probably called them at least once every three months after that, saying, 'For God's sake, you must get out of this thing.' It was a good two years before it went."

Walter understood that Mason was an investment broker, and suspected that he might be fishing for the colony's business. Nonetheless he made a call to salesman Walter Green—then in his 30th year of selling Principal investments to his extensive Hutterite clientele—to seek reassurance. "I says, 'Walter, how is things?' " Walter testified. "He says, 'Everything seems to be all right.' "

Walter made other calls to assure himself that the investments were solid. "Well, when we asked him, he always said, he said, 'George, I don't know how often I have to tell you that your investments are safe.' "

At the time of the Principal Group collapse, the Sunshine colony held promissory notes which, with accrued interest, totalled $3,634,019.

15

"How much bad news can the system stand?"

September 1, 1985

THE TWO ALBERTA-BASED BANKS—each badly mismanaged and ravaged by the real estate crash—had been insolvent for at least two years before federal officials pulled the plug. The collapse of the Canadian Commercial Bank (CCB) and the Northland Bank in the autumn of 1985 further mortified the Alberta government. Despite the province's best efforts, its financial industry continued to crumble in its hands. The Lougheed administration was unable to stop the take-down of the banks: they were federally chartered and the decisions were made in Ottawa.

The Edmonton-based CCB collapsed in March, then staggered on for another half-year after the federal government assisted in a $255-million government/bank industry bailout. Alberta's share of the support package was $60 million, plus the purchase of $18 million worth of debentures.[1] The package, based on inadequate information, proved to be ill-conceived and insufficient; on September 1, 1985, the CCB went into liquidation. At the same time, the Calgary-based Northland Bank, surviving only with the help of liquidity advances from the Bank of Canada—and a $5-million debenture purchased by Alberta with Heritage Trust Fund money—was put in the hands of a curator and told to seek a merger with another institution. No such knight appeared. The collapse of the two banks eventually cost the CDIC $417 million.

On September 4, provincial Treasurer Lou Hyndman faced the Heritage Trust Fund watchdog committee and defended the small fortune the province had lost. "It is and it was and it is today basic Alberta government policy that Western-based financial institutions are important to this province and their future and therefore the government should help achieve growth and stability," Hyndman told the committee.[2]

Coincidentally, the House of Commons Standing Committee on Finance was sitting that day in Calgary. The drama of the session, one of many public hearings into Barbara McDougall's green paper on financial institutions, was heightened by the failure of the two banks just three days previously.

Donald Cormie flew south to address the committee. The politicians heard his views on conflict of interest and other issues raised by the green paper—but Cormie also wanted to talk about the CDIC's incessant "interference" in his trust company. The committee, headed by Don Blenkarn, listened for an hour as Cormie complained about the CDIC's demands that Principal Trust dump $40 million worth of Canada bonds, and about his frustration with regulators—including the Ontario officials who had blocked his company's entry into their province.

After his presentation, Cormie was asked about the recent failure of several institutions. Murray Dorin, an Edmonton MP, commented that a financial company is sometimes acquired by people who use depositors' money to finance real estate developments. Cormie proceeded to expound on the "fiduciary duties" of those in the financial services business:

> You have probably put your finger on one of the critical areas. There are inexperienced people in the financial business who have no fiduciary concept. I think the fiduciary concept of the principles of a financial institution is important. They have to start with the idea that it is not their money, they are only trustees. One of the principles of a trustee is you cannot have a conflict between your own interests and the other interest. That is one area definitely in need of some review. I gather that is in the wind. A lot of these disasters are where people who are active in real estate get ahold of a financial institution and think, 'See, this is money for my purpose.' There is no fiduciary concept, you see, in that.

While Cormie was lecturing the committee on management ethics, his vice-president of finance was whispering to a provincial official about the impropriety of transactions on the Principal books. Bill Johnson invited audit director Burt Eldridge to the Principal tower for an urgent chat about the June transaction with General Equities/Shucksan Properties, the Vancouver-based shell companies where the bonds and problem real estate were parked.

Johnson, upset with this deal from the start, had gone to Cormie's office before it was completed to protest the inflated appraisal of the Norscott Shopping Centre on which the entire convoluted transaction depended. Johnson had actually used Cormie's phone to call and quiz the appraisers. He remained unsatisfied with the assumptions on which the appraisal was based and told Cormie so, but the deal proceeded.

Eldridge wrote a memo to file, copied to Tewfik Saleh and Reg Pointe, about his remarkable conversation with Johnson:

> Mr. Johnson pointed out situations he was encountering whereby real estate sales proposals were brought to him for approval involving [First Investors,

Associated investors and Principal Trust]. These proposed real estate sales would result in little benefit to the companies as a mortgage was taken back, so, in effect, a mortgage had been substituted for real estate. He felt deals like this were being proposed as pressure was felt by company officials to reduce real estate holdings. I told him pressures for such deals were not coming from this office and that the audit section would see through them.

He cited the recent Northland Bank sale of $100 million of problem loans whereby a mortgage for a similar amount was taken back by the bank as well as further funds advanced to buy a strip bond which would secure the principal of the loan upon maturity.

Mr. Johnson appears to be wanting our support to prevent transactions as he described. He stated he would use his authority subject to overrule by Mr. Don Cormie or Mr. Ken Marlin to prevent such transactions.

Transactions of this type described by Mr. Johnson have been noted and questioned by the Audit staff in Credit Unions and Trust Companies. This evidences the feeling in troubled financial institutions that, through deals such as this the officials think they can improve their financial situation when, in most cases, the reverse occurs.

A couple of days later, Johnson called Eldridge again. "Mr. Johnson wanted to know," Eldridge wrote, "if I had passed his comments on to Mr. Saleh concerning real estate transactions which merely turns real estate into mortgages and are of little benefit to AIC and FIC. I told him I had and that Mr. Saleh agreed with his and my opinion of this type of transaction"—that they were of no true benefit to the companies.

The week after these conversations, Johnson flew to Toronto and met with Ed Reid, senior examiner for the federal Department of Insurance. The meeting, a wrap-up session at the conclusion of the CDIC's annual review of Principal Trust, gave Johnson an opportunity to enlighten Reid about the General Equities transaction. Reid had written to Johnson in July, after examining the trust company's 1984 financial statements, to say that deterioration in the value of properties held by Principal Trust required reserves totalling $6 million to be removed from the company's borrowing base. That was $3.9 million more than the reserve of $2.1 million already on the books, and most of the additional reserve was caused by three properties which were "sold" in the General Equities/Shucksan Properties transaction in June. In his July letter, Reid advised that he was aware the properties had been sold and indicated that the $6-million reserve would be reduced once complete details were received.

Johnson's explanation of the transaction during the September 10 meeting threw a different light on the situation. On October 18, Reid's superior, Dick Page, wrote to John Cormie to say that, after looking over the General Equities transaction, they had concluded that the deal did not improve the trust company's position and that the full amount of the reserve for the three properties was required.

They did, however, subsequently give in on one important point. The $10 million worth of bonds held by Shucksan Properties—through a loan provided by Principal Trust—could be treated as a demand loan, rather than as a long-term asset, for purposes of the mismatch formula (a formula that established reserves on the trust company's capital when it failed to match assets and liabilities as to term). This effectively added $1.9 million to the company's borrowing base; at a borrowing-to-capital ratio of 15:1, it increased the company's ability to borrow from the public by $28.5 million.

On November 28, CDIC chief executive officer Charles de Léry wrote John Cormie to acknowledge that Principal Trust's mismatch problem had, finally, been largely corrected. However, the company was still exceeding its authorized borrowing-to-capital ratio of 15:1, and was at that time operating at a multiple of 20.9:1. The problem was the reserve required because of "a series of 'contentious' real estate transactions," de Léry said. An immediate injection of $2.2 million in capital was required.

September 12, 1985

MEMO FROM PRINCIPAL FINANCIAL ANALYST Rick Mathes to the Principal Group Sales Committee:

> Sales Committee has devoted much of its time in 1985 to the problem of cash flow in FIC/AIC. This is in spite of the fact that FIC/AIC's term certificate balances have increased by $33,000,000 since December 31.
>
> I would like to point out a problem which may be more serious: Mutual fund redemptions have been $51,448,000 in 1985 [to August 31] versus only $39,503,000 for the same period in 1984...
>
> I hope that this information is of some use to Sales Committee now that Sales Committee's attention will be primarily on mutual funds.

The next month, Principal salesmen were advised of an adjustment in their sales commission structure. Commission for selling Principal Group promissory notes was doubled from $3 to $6 for every $1,000 sold. At the same time, commission for selling investment contracts dropped from $3.00 to $2.25 for "qualified consultants," and from $3.68 to $2.52 for the more senior "account executives."

Commission for selling mutual funds had been increased in July—from $30 to $34 for qualified consultants, and from $36.80 to $40.10 for account executives. Commission for selling the trust company's CDIC-insured RRSPs remained at a nominal $1.50 for qualified consultants and $1.90 for account executives.

Plainly, it was now most lucrative to sell (in order) mutual funds, Principal Group promissory notes, investment contracts and, lastly, trust company RRSPs.

These changes also had the effect of channelling investors' cash further up the corporate chain, into the parent company Principal Group and even higher into Principal Securities Management Ltd. (PSML), the mutual fund management company which, since August 1984, had been owned by—and paid management fees to—grandparent company Collective Securities.

September 17, 1985

MEMO FROM PRINCIPAL TRUST general manager George Aboussafy to Principal VP Bill Johnson and members of Christa Petracca's SWAT team:

SUBJECT: SALE OF REAL ESTATE
We need one or two more General Equity type deals before the year-end.
I suggest we meet Friday, September 20, at 10:00 a.m. in the 29th floor
Boardroom to put together the packages and a list of potential buyers. Plus, if
there are any potential sales we are working on, let's find out how we can close
them ASAP.

October 14, 1985

THE MONEY RUSTLERS HIT BOOKSTORE SHELVES in the autumn of 1985. Authors Paul Grescoe and David Cruise, who wrote admiringly about several Canadian entrepreneurs, had swallowed whole the Cormie mythology. They reported that Cormie had predicted the end of the real-estate boom in 1981, "even while speculators were scooping up all the land they could. This kind of foresight bordering on clairvoyance, coupled with technology that would be at home on a space shuttle, has made Donald Cormie worth nearly $200 million at the age of sixty-two." The pair extolled Cormie's cycle theory:

He and his staff plot a vast array of statistics, including U.S. commodity prices
since 1820, the cost of labour in England since 900 A.D., the history of Dow
Jones trading since 1885, the U.S. monetary schedule—to name a few. All
these charts are overlaid, adjusted for inflation and then digested by Cormie,
who, when he travels, bounces the ideas off others, testing to determine if the
conditions shown by his charts are consistent with reality. Once Cormie is
satisfied, he announces, "I've done my homework," lays out his plans and
relentlessly executes them. As a result he has a remarkable record of accurate
predictions, much of which he attributes simply to smart analysis of historical
trends. "If you can see the cyclical patterns you are much more comfortable
about when to borrow and not to borrow… There are a lot of little signposts;
they give you a little advance notice. It's not 100% right—you're following a
trail." Cormie's ability to follow a trail has powered an incredible 60% growth
of Principal's total assets from $627 million in 1982 to $1 billion in 1985.
During the same period virtually every other financial institution operating in
the West was writing down their assets.
Cormie's foresight has saved the company from more than one disaster…

Grescoe and Cruise described Cormie as being so "firmly anchored in the basics of his legal training and the fundamental lesson of thrift he learned as a boy that he can conjure up the technical genie and bend it to his will without straying beyond the boundaries to sound business practice." There was more:

> The reason Cormie's public image is so powerful is because it is grounded in reality. A handsome man, just under six feet tall, once slim and whip-cord lean, the years have broadened his frame, leaving it stocky and powerful. He looks like actor Rod Taylor without a smirk. Cormie radiates sombre competence, underlined by the kind of confidence usually only enjoyed by those with inherited fortunes. His calmness inspires instinctive trust. He's the kind of man you'd want in charge during a crisis: the surgeon performing a triple bypass on your heart when the operating-room power fails; the pilot when your plane is hijacked by terrorists; the banker protecting your life savings during a recession. He is studiously the quintessential professional—controlled, highly motivated from within, even a little mean in his single-minded pursuit of achievement.

On October 14, the *Financial Times of Canada* published an excerpt from the book. It was immediately photocopied and distributed throughout the Principal sales force.

September 6, 1985

PROVINCIAL AUDITOR NICK ROMALO inherited the contract company file when Al Hutchison headed south to Arizona. He also took on Hutchison's biggest headache: how does an auditor measure the value of a company's mortgages and real estate when his supervisors refuse him the money or authority to acquire appraisals? Neither Romalo, nor his supervisor Burt Eldridge, even bothered to ask for appraisals during their annual examination of the contract companies' 1984 financial statements. This would have cost only $60,000, but the lid was screwed on tight.

The appraisals obtained a year and a half before indicated that real estate held by the two companies should be written down to about a third of book value. The market had not revived in intervening months, and the obvious thing to do was re-use the figures applied by Hutchison the year before. Eldridge, unfortunately, didn't feel "comfortable" doing so. "I think I would have been criticized for that," Eldridge testified. By whom? "I—don't know," he replied nervously, glancing around the hearing room. By Tewfik Saleh? No. "He wouldn't complain. I was concerned that they were passed on somewhere else."

Instead, Romalo conducted the 1984 examination using numbers provided by Principal, and ignored the massive write-downs included in Hutchison's reports. (Romalo testified that Eldridge told him to do this; Eldridge testified that the two men reach the decision by "consensus.") Using this method, Romalo calculated First Investors' capital deficiency at approximately $10 million as of December 1984.

That's far less than the $62.5 million that had been identified in December 1983, and the $80.1 million in April 1984. (Using the same method, Associated Investors's capital deficiency as of December 1984 was reported as $2.7 million—an apparent improvement from the $24.8 million reported at the end of 1983.)

Incredibly, Romalo also recalculated the 1983 figures which were to be included in the 1984 report for purposes of comparison. By throwing out the write-downs, the $62.5-million capital deficiency reported for First Investors at the end of 1983 was "recalculated" as only $1.4 million; a $59.8-million deficiency in reserves was reduced to $943,000. (The 1983 figures for Associated Investors were rewritten too: the $24.8-million deficiency in unimpaired capital became a modest $237,000; and a $21-million deficiency in reserves became a *surplus* of $263,000.)

Anyone reading Romalo's reports for 1984 would see relatively rosy numbers for both 1983 and 1984, and would not realize the size of the hole identified the year before—unless they had access to department files and pulled out the 1983 report. There was no note in Romalo's 1984 report advising readers that the 1983 numbers had been recalculated from the previous year. Eldridge and Romalo, both chartered accountants, conceded at the Code inquiry it would have been better to include a note advising that 1983 appraisals had indicated capital deficiencies in First Investors and Associated Investors of about $62 million and $24 million—and there was no reason to believe things had improved. "There is no intent, you know, to change anything or to cover up the situation," Eldridge testified. "I thought we covered it adequately in a later note."

That note, included in memos covering the reports, read: "The real estate has been accepted as presented by the company and its auditors. While we believe these figures to be highly optimistic we cannot, without having appraisals done, comment further on their valuation."

Romalo noted the change in auditors from Touche Ross to Deloitte Haskins & Sells, but did not, as procedure required, provide reasons for the change. And he did not include the fact that the going-concern note accompanying the 1983 audit had been dropped by the new auditors the following year.

The reports went to Tewfik Saleh on September 6. A month later, Saleh asked Eldridge for an update on the contract companies. That same day, October 2, Eldridge wrote a memo to Deputy Minister Barry Martin (copied to Saleh) expressing concern about the ability of the contract companies' parent, Principal Group, to pay back the money it had borrowed from the public through promissory notes. The debt at that time totalled $68.4 million and Eldridge sensed that Principal Group was extremely cash-poor.

> This lack of liquidity causes me concern should PGL be unable to roll over its notes payable at $68.5 million, the majority of which is due within one year. The flow of deposits from the Canadian Commercial Bank, Northland Bank and Heritage Trust illustrates how money flows out once there has been some adverse publicity. If there [should] be a run on the notes of PGL, the only opportunity for cash I am aware of for PGL would be through our regulated

companies and damage could be done to these companies before we are aware of it. Should the Principal Group of Companies experience financial problems, I believe it will come through PGL as it is the most vulnerable especially in the cash flow area.

Neither Martin nor Saleh replied to Eldridge's dire warning—a warning about a possible calamity that was, in fact, in progress. On October 22, Eldridge returned to Saleh with the requested update on the contract companies. Eldridge identified eight areas of concern: the companies' capital impairment; their continuing losses, totalling some $125.8 million as of October 1985; the overall lack of capital within Principal Group Ltd.; a recently recognized decline in deposits with Principal Trust and the contract companies; the companies' practice of speculating in real estate through granting loans at below current interest rates and participating in any profits on sale (as in the General Equities/Shucksan transaction); the real estate valuation problems; the eligibility of Athabasca Holdings preferred shares as a qualified asset; and the continuing dispute about proper calculation of the Section 8 financial tests.

The next week, Saleh asked Eldridge to help prepare a report for Connie Osterman on the Principal companies. The audit staff drafted a document dated November 5, 1985, summarizing—again—their major concerns. It included everything reported to Saleh the month before, and warned about Principal Group's liquidity problems and the debentures and promissory notes held by the public, about $20 million of that by certain Hutterite colonies.

The draft suggested that if the Hutterite colonies withdrew their money, Principal Group would collapse. This would have a "drastic effect" on the contract companies because of their substantial investment in Principal Group through their holdings of millions of dollars worth of Athabasca Holdings shares. "It is the Department's contention," the report advised, "that what kept FIC and AIC alive in the past few years was the vital cash flow from new customers..." It also said that Collective Securities, which controlled the Principal companies, as well as Athabasca, "does not come under the Department's jurisdiction and accordingly has always declined to make any of its financial statements available to the Department." It noted that both Principal and its external auditors had for many years accepted the department's method of calculating the Section 8 tests. "Now that the financial condition of these companies has gradually deteriorated to an alarming extent, Mr. Cormie and his senior people have suddenly changed their minds and no longer agree with the department's calculations."

The report was prepared for Saleh to forward to Osterman, but Saleh testified that he could not remember what he did with it. Eldridge didn't know either, but recalled that it was around this time—in the latter part of 1985—that he attended a meeting of Treasurer Lou Hyndman's financial institutions task force to discuss the contract companies. Hyndman, as we have seen, asked: "Do you see any light at the end of the tunnel?"

And Eldridge said: "No."

On November 11, Barry Martin and Connie Osterman sent the task force a briefing paper titled "Alberta Financial Institutions," which provided a snapshot of various provincial companies. A couple of days later, Martin asked Eldridge for a corporate chart to help him understand the inter-relationship of the Principal companies. "I was aware," Martin testified, "that there were intercorporate dealings between the companies involved in the Principal Group, and I understood that—it was my apprehension that a run or some adverse activity on any one of those companies had the potential to undermine the entire operation, the consequences of which I could only anticipate, but I felt that it would cause, as I called it—and that was my euphemistic term—cause a domino effect where the collapse of one company could, in turn, create the collapse of another and the ultimate outcome I felt would be calamitous."

All this activity unfolded against a backdrop of political pandemonium. Peter Lougheed had announced in late June his intention to retire, and provincial business had been disrupted for months by jockeying on the part of would-be successors. The frontrunner was Lougheed favourite Don Getty, who emerged triumphant from a convention on October 14. Getty was sworn into office on November 1, then spent six weeks distracted by his campaign to win a Legislature seat in a by-election in Edmonton-Whitemud. One of his first decisions as premier was to disband the existing task forces and committees of the Lougheed regime—including Hyndman's task force. Its last official act, in mid-November, was to deliver a report to Getty and the priorities committee which discussed the shaky state of Alberta's financial institutions. A two-page covering memo written by Hyndman laid out strategies to restore investor confidence "in Alberta and in Western financial institutions through a recovery strategy which will ensure the survival and safety of deposits."

Hyndman recommended an action plan "which would involve moving on three fronts simultaneously, with federal regulatory co-operation." He proposed that the province "continue the rebuilding" of the credit unions, and that it persuade the federal government to switch liquidators of the CCB and Northland Banks "to a new Alberta private sector/government rebuilding entity which would 1) reduce administrative costs/fees; 2) more efficiently handle sales of banks' assets; 3) be ready to accommodate less credit-worthy Alberta customers." He also recommended that the province "fold into a separate recovery/stability package all existing and future trust companies." (As we now know, the province followed this strategy with North West and Heritage trusts. The fate of Principal Trust was different.)

Under a section titled "Options to Build Depositor Confidence," Hyndman asked: "How much bad news can the system stand?" He listed three possible initiatives to rebuild deeply shaken public confidence: a four-province publicity campaign promoting the viability of Western institutions; independent audits to confirm their viability; and/or a selective, temporary guarantee of certain deposits, possibly for all Alberta-based institutions. The report demonstrates the depth of political distress about previous financial company failures and the determination to avoid another collapse.

Attached to Hyndman's memo was Martin and Osterman's report "Alberta Financial Institutions." It cautioned that Principal Trust "has perhaps the highest profile in Edmonton of all provincial trust companies," and warned: "Real estate and mortgage balance figures reviewed to June 30, 1985, were highly optimistic. Approximately 50% of the mortgage portfolio is in arrears six months or more."

The report also included a two-page briefing on the Principal contract companies which noted that First Investors, Associated Investors and Principal Trust were all members of the Principal Group. The memo advised that, according to the calculations of Consumer Affairs auditors, First Investors had a capital impairment of $10.1 million and Associated Investors was impaired by $2.7 million—as of the end of 1984. (These numbers, we'll recall, were arrived at by Romalo by throwing out the massive real estate write-downs of the year before.) It continued:

> However, the companies argue that they are in a surplus rather than a deficit position as suggested by the department. They base their argument on a legal interpretation by their counsel that the department's method of calculating the unimpaired capital is not in accordance with the provisions of The Act. In view of the legal issue the Department is obtaining a legal opinion to determine its course of action. In addition to the capital impairment issue, the department is concerned about the losses experienced from January 1985 to September 1985 which amounted to $10.4 million in FIC and $3.2 million in AIC as reported by the two companies.
>
> The valuation of company-owned real estate through foreclosure as well as real estate which forms the security behind mortgage loans in arrears has also been and continues to be a major concern. *The department had obtained appraisals on certain problem real estate in 1983 which indicate substantial write-downs in value. These write-downs have not been taken into account for the calculations referred to earlier as the Alberta real estate market is depressed and there is no real market for these properties.*
>
> As a result of the financial problems facing these companies, they have concluded transactions which resulted in the acquisition of certain assets, such as shares in related companies. This has caused some concern to the department in view of the fact that the eligibility of the investment in these assets and the market values placed by the companies appear to be questionable.
>
> Because the companies within the Group are so closely structured and related it is feared that the failure of any one company within the Group, regulated or unregulated, could seriously affect the other companies.
>
> These two companies have a total of $417 million in medium-term liabilities (averaging approximately 2 1/2 years) to their investment contract holders. Unless there is a significant improvement in the Alberta real estate market, the department is concerned that these two companies might not be able to meet their medium-term obligations to their contract holders.

Should the final determination of the outstanding legal and valuation issues
prove to be unfavourable to the two companies, the situation may call for the
suspension or cancellation of the registration of the companies unless the
principals have the financial resources and the willingness to cover the
deficiency. It is possible that the regulators might have to invoke the provisions
of The Act with respect to receivership and/or liquidation of the two companies
in the circumstances. [Italics added.]

Certain details were blurred—there was, for example, no information on the
precise size of the real estate write-downs recommended by department auditors—
but the crisis was unmistakable. The companies were in serious trouble, and there
was a good chance the province would have to take them down unless "the
principals"—the Cormie name was not invoked, but well understood—coughed up
some significant cash. It was also clear that taking down one Cormie company
meant taking down them all.

Nothing happened.

November 19, 1985

DURING THE AUTUMN THE CDIC AGAIN proposed that federal and
provincial auditors conduct a joint examination of Principal Group's three regulated
companies. On November 19—the day after the task force report was delivered to
Getty and his priorities committee—Barry Martin wrote a letter declining the
invitation. A joint examination was "premature," Martin said, just as he had a year
and a half before. This time his excuse was the dispute about the calculation of the
Section 8 tests.

November 18, 1985

AFTER WEEKS OF POLITICAL BATTERING, the federal government
announced a public inquiry into the failures of the CCB and the Northland Bank,
Canada's first such collapses since the Home Bank went down in 1923. The
commission would be headed by Mr. Justice Willard Estey of the Supreme Court of
Canada: Donald Cormie's old Harvard chum.

Estey chaired several days of hearings in Ottawa, then moved west. On
November 18—as Getty and his priorities committee were being briefed by Lou
Hyndman and Connie Osterman—the inquiry hit Edmonton with a splash.

The arrival of a Supreme Court justice was one of the season's social highlights,
despite the disgrace that had brought him. The world of lawyers is a small one;
Estey, known to friends as "Bud," was immediately embraced by his Alberta
colleagues and drawn into a lively whirl of social engagements.

"You see," Estey told me, "when you arrive in town running a banking inquiry,
you're an oddity, and people want you to go to dinner parties and there's always
someone you know who's sent his errand boy to drag you there. You can't be

anti-social, and besides I was curious, so if the hearings would stop early enough I would go." Among those who entertained Estey was, of course, his former class-mate. Estey remembers parties at Cormie's home on Grandview Drive, and possibly a lunch. "And don't forget he was a friend of the dean of the law school," he said. "The dean entertained me and a couple of old clients did too, and Cormie was probably at some of those parties too."[3]

One Cormie get-together was recalled with particular glee. "They kindly invited me to some party they were having and off I went and had a whale of a time." It was Grey Cup season and Estey spent the evening with one eye glued to the tube. "The great big house they had there had about six TV sets," he said, "and I went from room to room to meet all these people and shoot the breeze and there was always a television set. A typical western activity."

Estey remembers Cormie as a most amiable host. "He knew everybody in the place and he knew them all by name. And he was extremely good at introducing everybody and so was his wife." Estey met "a million lawyers" at Cormie's home. Wherever he went, Estey said, "you'd see an overlap of the same old gang." Despite their mutual interest in deteriorating financial institutions, Estey has no memory of discussing the issue with Cormie. But he did receive a lecture on the cycle theory across the dinner table. "I can remember him saying: 'I explained this to you once before.' He probably did, but it didn't mean anything to me."

Estey's inquiry was bound to hold a certain fascination for Cormie. During his first week in Edmonton, Estey heard from the CCB's auditors about the bank's "baseline value" strategy of evaluating real estate and mortgages. Told that properties were evaluated not by means of appraisals, but on the basis of some future value determined by management—and that bank management, not the auditors, determined the appropriateness of accounting strategies—Estey exclaimed: "That sounds to me like a formula for disaster!" It was, of course, the same formula being applied in the Principal tower.

The Estey hearings provided a forum for an unusual debate on accounting theory and the role of auditors, issues that had rarely been raised in public before. The CCB auditors had signed financial statements for 1984 showing no indication of impending insolvency, just four months before the bank went to the federal government for a bailout. The auditors had recommended modest provisions for losses in both 1983 and 1984, but were turned down by management. They did not protest, and did not qualify their audits.

In subsequent weeks Estey heard from bank management, who blamed the crash on the depressed Alberta economy, and from banking and accounting experts critical of the "baseline value" strategy and a string of outrageous transactions designed to avoid write-downs. In December, Estey returned to Ottawa to hear testimony from federal regulators, who said they relied on the auditors' reports to evaluate the banks' stability. The following March, he was back in Alberta, this time in Calgary, to hear testimony on the Northland collapse.

His progress was followed closely in the Principal tower, in auditor Don McCutchen's office at Deloitte Haskins & Sells and—with despair—in the office of Alberta's Superintendent of Insurance.

November 24, 1985

BURT ELDRIDGE, SCANNING THE BUSINESS PAGES of the *Sun*, came across a report that Principal Group was selling the Rocky Mountain Brewery to a company called Matrix Exploration Ltd. The name Matrix rang a faint bell.

Eldridge called auditor Nick Romalo to his desk and handed him the newspaper. "Wasn't Matrix included in the Principal transaction with Carma the year before? Why don't you have a look at what this is all about?" Romalo dug through the Alberta Securities Commission public files and reported a couple of days later. Eldridge passed the report on to Tewfik Saleh, with a memo noting that Matrix was a sub-subsidiary of Athabasca Holdings, which had sold the brewery to Principal a half a year before, "so ownership has not passed outside of the Collective group of companies controlled by Mr. Don Cormie Q.C."

Among the assets that came to Cormie during the 1984 Carma transaction was majority control of Matrix, a near-inactive company which traded on the Alberta Stock Exchange. Two-thirds of its common stock was owned by Allarco Energy, making Matrix a grand-daughter of Athabasca Holdings after the Carma deal. At the time of acquisition, Matrix (renamed Matrix Investments Ltd. in late 1985) had one undeveloped piece of acreage near Edson, west of Edmonton, with no real cash flow or earnings. Now, Cormie had activated the company, with the intention—as Eldridge speculated in his memo to Saleh—of developing it into an active public corporation that could raise capital in public markets.

Cormie's first step, effective September 1, 1985, was to have Allarco Energy sell its interest in certain oil and gas properties to Matrix, in exchange for 14,358,000 common Matrix shares and the assumption of bank loans. The Matrix shares, valued at 30 cents a share ($4,307,400), were issued from the company treasury. The developed gas acreage stayed with Allarco (including two gas plants and related producing fields), but the more speculative holdings—the undeveloped or partially developed oil and gas properties —went to Matrix.

Next, Rocky Mountain Brewing Corporation was moved into Matrix. As a result of the brewery/Athabasca transactions in March 1985 Rocky Mountain Breweries owed Principal Group $14.4 million, a debt subsequently turned into a debenture and preferred shares in the brewery. On November 21 (the same day that the Allarco Energy oil and gas properties were moved into Matrix) Principal sold its entire interest in the brewery—the preferred shares and debenture totalling $14.4 million—to Matrix. Matrix issued 44,500,000 common shares to Principal in payment, at a value of 30 cents a share, for a total of $13.35 million. Prior to this transaction Matrix was controlled by Allarco Energy; now Principal Group had controlling interest.

The book value of the brewery had skyrocketed during the year it was under

Cormie's control. In December 1984, the receiver had estimated its liquidation value at $3.2 million and its going-concern value at approximately $6 million. An independent appraisal at the same time concluded that its probable market value was about $5.8 million. A year later, a chartered business valuator with Deloitte Haskins & Sells—auditor Don McCutchen's firm—accepted that fair market value was $13.35 million, more than double what it had been the year before. A memo from the valuator indicated that his estimate was based on information from McCutchen that the Matrix board of directors was largely external to the Principal Group organization, "and therefore the price effectively reflects an arms-length transaction." In fact only three of the eight directors were outside directors, and one of them was also on the Allarco Energy board.[4]

From this point Matrix—loaded up with speculative oil and gas properties and an over-valued brewery—became a kind of currency within the Principal conglomerate. With little cash in hand, Cormie would conduct the convoluted business affairs among his companies with Matrix shares. Over the next year and a half the value of the shares, regularly traded among the companies, would climb and climb and climb.

The first of these deals occurred within weeks of swapping the brewery into Matrix. We'll recall that the contract companies paid administration fees and interest on subordinated notes each year to Principal Group. During preparation of the 1984 financial statements, several million dollars in fees and interest had been reversed to make the contract companies' books look better. The reversal had not been paid in cash, but was carried as a debt owed by Principal Group to its subsidiaries. Now, at the end of the year, this debt—and the debt for a similar reversal for 1985—totalled $10.79 million.

The debt was repaid on the last day of 1985—not in cash, but in inflated Matrix shares.

Principal Group could have simply transferred the stock to the contract companies. Instead, the game was played through Athabasca Holdings, which was handed both the debt and the means of paying it off. First, Athabasca entered an agreement with Principal Group to assume its debt with the contract companies, and received Matrix shares in "consideration" for doing so. Principal Group transferred to Athabasca 19,618,181 Matrix common shares at a value of 50 cents each— 20 cents more than their value when they been acquired by Principal four months earlier.

Then, the same day, Athabasca paid off its debt to the contract companies by transferring the block of Matrix shares at 55 cents a share—5 cents higher than their transfer value moments earlier. That 5-cent-a-share profit, totalling almost a million dollars, was termed a "handling fee." At the Code inquiry Cormie called this transaction a "gift" of $10.79 million to the contract companies.

The Code report accepted that the 30-cent-a-share transaction in September 1985 was done at market value; but it also accepted the opinion of chartered account Peter Schenkelberg, who testified as an expert on business valuations, that book value of Matrix shares—based on the value of the company's assets—was 19.725 cents a share through 1984 and 1985. Using Schenkelberg's evaluation, the total value returned to the contract companies was $3,869,686—not the $10.79 million claimed in their financial statements.

Meanwhile, Principal Group recorded a gain of $3,923,636 on the 20-cent-a-share profit; Athabasca recorded a gain of $980,909 on its 5-cents-a-share profit.

By moving the Matrix shares through Athabasca—owned by Collective Securities, and not consolidated in Principal's financial statement—Principal Group could record its paper profits in its statement. If the Matrix shares had not been moved temporarily outside the Principal Group of companies, the gain would have been eliminated in the consolidation.

December 12, 1985

PRINCIPAL NEO-TECH INC.—Ken Marlin's baby on the Toronto Stock Exchange—had been gobbling up subsidiaries for months. Now, suffering from indigestion, it needed something to settle the stomach. The cure, of course, was more cash, and Marlin was trying to raise new capital from the public. The plan was to sell $8 million worth of convertible debentures (with the option of later converting them to preferred shares). There had been nibbles, but no bites—until North West Trust in Edmonton indicated interest in half the offering.

Suddenly, the nibblers were jumping, and with North West's commitment for $4 million, the debentures were over-subscribed. It was decided to go about it a different way; the debentures would be left to other investors, and North West would buy Class A preferred shares from Principal Neo-Tech's treasury.

North West was interested, but only if certain favours were exchanged.

North West, in as much hot water as Principal, was suffering the same regulatory pressure to deal with its non-producing real estate. Within 14 months it would be taken over by the Alberta government—but for now it was alive, and struggling to keep on breathing.

North West agreed to buy the Class A shares, but it wanted to get rid of certain properties. If Principal Neo-Tech would buy them, with North West providing vendor take-back mortgages, North West would buy the treasury shares.

There was another condition. North West wanted a guaranteed return on its investment, which would have been the case had it continued with its purchase of the debentures. It wanted a "put" on the Principal Neo-Tech stock, granting it the option of selling the shares back at an agreed higher price, even if the market fell off. Principal Neo-Tech couldn't take a put on its own shares. So, Marlin testified, "I told them that First Investors would be the party to the put." Marlin, president of both First Investors and Principal Neo-Tech, signed the put agreement on behalf of the contract company. North West paid $3,531,500 for 350,000 Class A preferred shares at $10.09 a share, and paid First Investors $10 for the right to subsequently put the shares to First Investors at a guaranteed price of $4,185,000.

A year later North West exercised its put. The shares had declined in value and

First Investors was on the hook for approximately half a million dollars. Marlin justified First Investors' involvement in this transaction by arguing that it already had a substantial holding of Principal Neo-Tech shares. Also, the capital raised in the deal was vital to Principal Neo-Tech's success and would increase the value of its shares.

Actually, First Investors didn't receive its first block of Principal Neo-Tech shares until a couple of weeks after taking the put. On the last day of 1985, First Investors and Associated Investors bought $16.435 million worth of Class A preferred shares, at the wildly inflated price of $19 a share.[5] The stock, which was sold to the contract companies by Principal Group via Athabasca Holdings, was exchanged for a block of the controversial Athabasca preferred shares held by the companies since the Carma transaction in 1984.

This transaction, conceived by Principal finance vice-president Bill Johnson, was seen as a solution to the continuing protests of provincial regulators about the Athabasca shares held by the contract companies. Principal and the regulators had been arguing this point for half a year. The company had Parlee lawyer Keith Ferguson's opinion that the shares were qualified assets under the *Investment Contracts Act*, but Tewfik Saleh and the audit staff believed the shares were prohibited because of Donald Cormie's indirect controlling interest in the three companies. They were also sceptical of the book value assigned to the Athabasca shares, and considered them worth about half that figure.

Again, as with the earlier transfer of the Matrix shares, the Principal Neo-Tech share transfer was conducted through Athabasca because the company was outside the Principal Group consolidation. Principal Group booked a profit on the sale of the Neo-Tech shares to Athabasca of about $10.4 million.

The journeys of the Athabasca and Principal Neo-Tech shares would be reversed a year later.

December 18, 1985

THE CORMIE RANCH WAS LOSING MONEY hand over fist and had accumulated tax loss carry-forwards worth a couple of million dollars. Unfortunately, company losses can only benefit your tax picture if you have profits to apply against the losses, and the ranch didn't qualify.

Donald Cormie conferred with his accountants and decided to restructure the upstairs companies so as to let him use the ranch's carry-forwards to advantage. A new company was created and inserted between Principal Group and its parent Collective Securities Ltd. (CSL), turning the parent into a grand-parent. The new company—and the new parent of Principal Group—was named Collective Securities Inc. (CSI).

Before the reorganization, Cormie held 80.5% of CSL; Ken Marlin held 10.5%; and John and Jaimie Cormie each held 4.5%. CSL owned Principal Group and several other subsidiaries, most importantly Athabasca Holdings and PSML, the mutual fund management company. As a first step, the reorganization eliminated

CSL's other shareholders, so that Cormie owned the entire company; then CSL's subsidiaries were transferred down to CSI. Its shareholdings were in the same proportion as under the previous arrangement: 80.5% was held by CSL (now owned 100% by Donald Cormie); 10.5% by Marlin Management Inc., Marlin's newly-created holding company; and 4.5% each by John and Jaimie.

Thus the level above Principal appeared identical to what had been there before: CSI became CSL, and CSL became—Donald Cormie's.

Cormie, now sole owner of both CSL and Cormie Ranch, merged the two companies under the name CSL. All their assets, liabilities and tax losses were rolled in together, eliminating Cormie Ranch's $12.1-million debt to CSL. (See DIAGRAM 8: *Principal Group Corporate Structure After the December 31, 1985 Reorganization.*) Cormie (CSL) saved $1,087,000 in income taxes in 1985 by applying the ranch's losses against CSL's income; and there were further carry-forwards available for 1986 and 1987 of $1,048,027 and $1,148,410 respectively.

These numbers come from a memo written to Cormie by Rob Pearce, vice-president of CSL, a year after the reorganization. The memo continued:

The incomes we were able to shelter in 1985 were:
1) full years income from PSML net of admin fees to PGL
   —$2,250,000
2) Mutual Funds—capital gains realized
   —$200,000
3) Reverse deferred salaries set up in 1984
   —$930,000
4) Capital gain in [Athabasca] realized on sale of Bank to CSL
   —$1,900,000
   TOTAL: $5,180,000

Pearce, who acted as Cormie's financial advisor and helped manage the upstairs companies, wrote the memo during a discussion of the financial dealings between Cormie and Ken Marlin. Marlin had agreed to the reorganization as an accommodation to Cormie, Pearce pointed out. "This $5,180,000 is income sheltered from taxes by using [Cormie Ranch] write-offs that did not benefit Ken and therefore represents a savings to you of $2-2.3 million dollars."

In valuing CSL prior to the reorganization, provisions for taxes were made, and Marlin's share was calculated on the reduced post-tax amount. In fact, Pearce said, "after applying (Cormie Ranch's) losses and herd value to that income, no taxes were paid." As part of the reorganization, Marlin ended up with approximately $900,000 worth of preferred shares in the new CSL now owned by Cormie. Marlin also had an outstanding debt to Principal Group of about $1 million which continued to sit on Principal Group's books, accruing interest at the rate of 10% a year. At the time of the collapse, Marlin was stuck with a $1-million debt to a company under receivership and a handful of worthless shares in Cormie's personal company.

The fourth point on Pearce's memo referred to a transaction conducted at 1984 year-end. We'll recall that Athabasca Holdings had incurred a debt to Collective Securities (CSL) of $12.5 million during a circular deal that manufactured value for Principal Group by using Principal's money to finance Athabasca's purchase of new Principal preferred shares. That $12.5-million debt to CSL (owned at the time by the Cormies and Marlin) had somehow not been transferred down to CSI during the December 18 reorganization, and remained on the books of CSL—now wholly owned by Donald Cormie.

Cormie decided to cash in on the debt by taking over one of Athabasca's few valuable assets—the Cayman Islands bank. This transaction, conducted on the last day of 1985, gave Cormie complete control over one of the conglomerate's most prized assets: a blue-chip portfolio of highly liquid investments squirrelled away in a Caribbean tax haven.

Shares in Athabasca remained a significant portion of the contract companies' investment portfolios. After exchanging $15 million worth of the shares for stock in Principal Neo-Tech, as discussed earlier, they still held about $35 million worth of Athabasca stock. Now Athabasca (and indirectly its investors, the contract companies) had been relieved of a valuable asset and handed, instead, more debt.

In exchange for the Caribbean bank, CSL (Cormie) cancelled Athabasca's debts to CSL totalling $17 million (including the $12.5 million mentioned above). Athabasca also received $813,000 worth of stock and $1.5 million worth of mutual funds in companies owned by Cormie. And, alas, it received an unsecured promissory note from CSL (Cormie) for $3,696,896, bearing interest at 10% a year.

16

Burt & Bernie

February 6, 1986

BARRY, ARE YOU SITTING DOWN?" It was Consumer Affairs Minister Connie Osterman, phoning Deputy Minister Barry Martin in Toronto, where he was attending a regulators' meeting on the insurance industry.

"Connie, what is it? What's the problem?"

"I'm leaving the department. You've got a new minister, Barry."

"What are you talking about?"

"There's been a Cabinet shuffle. The premier's moved me out of the portfolio."

"Now?"

"God, yes, now. Do you believe it? He's sending me to Social Services."

Osterman was out, and Al Adair—"Boomer" to the world—was in. It was a bizarre time for Don Getty to be shuffling this portfolio. Short weeks before an election call, with Consumer Affairs knee-deep in bailout efforts, Osterman was being replaced by a man singularly disinterested in the regulatory system. "I damn near fell over," Martin testified. "I considered Mrs. Osterman knowledgeable, she had taken strong initiatives in other areas... I don't purport to question the premier and the right to put in who he will in his Cabinet, but this caused me a lot of personal anxiety."

Within minutes of Osterman's call, Martin heard from his new boss. "Al," he told Adair, "I think you have some situations we need to talk about."

Getty's choice of Adair was even odder than Peter Lougheed's appointment of Osterman three years earlier. Adair, MLA for Peace River, had been a sports broadcaster before his election in 1971. Like Osterman, he had little background for the job; unlike Osterman, he was unenthusiastic about taking it on.

Adair was sworn in on February 6. The next day, he returned to his constituency in northern Alberta to attend a nomination meeting. Then he flew east to honour previous commitments as Tourism Minister—appearances at winter carnivals in

Ottawa and Quebec City. Adair didn't meet with Consumer Affairs staff until February 17. During three days of initial briefings, he was told about the credit union bailout, then in progress, and about plans for rescuing the crippled Heritage and North West Trust companies. There was also discussion of Principal Trust and the contract companies, but Adair and Martin disagree on what was said. Martin testified that he told Adair that there were capital deficiencies in the contract companies, and that they were not in compliance with the *Investment Contracts Act*. Adair does not recall being given this information.

In any case, both agree that Adair's instructions were: business as usual. "I asked them to carry on as they had in the past and to keep me informed," Adair testified. He insisted there was no "policy." There was, however, a "direction"—to "try and work out a work-out plan." Martin says he took this to mean no action on the Principal front, and behaved accordingly.

At the February 17 briefing, "Mr. Adair indicated to us," Martin testified, "that if he was to be retained in Cabinet, he would probably be moved to another portfolio. I think his words were, 'I don't expect to be with you long.' He said, 'An election is coming, I expect over the next few months to be very much involved in the election process and in getting myself re-elected...' It wasn't difficult to assume that there were aspects of the portfolio that didn't exactly grab him."

Adair testified that he didn't remember saying he would be busy getting re-elected, or that he wouldn't be there long, but confirmed his other remarks. "I said... that I was not a regulator, I was a promoter, and if they were planning to get any regulations by me, they would have to show need. I was not going to put in new regulations just for the sake of new regulations."

On April 10, Getty announced the election, and Adair was rarely in the department after that. After the May 8 vote, he moved to another portfolio. Lawyer Elaine McCoy, Q.C., just-elected MLA for Calgary West, became Consumer Affairs minister. (She did not testify at the Code inquiry.)

Osterman testified that in the weeks preceding her transfer she considered the Principal contract companies to be in serious trouble, and felt the need for action. Osterman indicated that she protested the shuffle; she was not, most regrettably, asked at the Code inquiry what was said between her and Getty when he told her about the job change. Getty has never explained this decision. His declaration to the Code inquiry was silent on this matter, as it was silent on the fact that he met twice with Donald Cormie in 1986—the first time on January 20, less than three weeks before he pulled Osterman from the ministry.

What was said between these two men, who shared so many friends? Where did they meet? Who else was there? Did the premier know that Cormie had handed over $20,000 to Gary Campbell just a few months earlier to help finance his leadership campaign? And what was said about the Principal companies' problems? We have only a partial answer to the last question. "I would bring him up to date on what I thought was important in the financial services industry," Cormie testified, "and try and see if I could find out what the government's policy was, or any changes, if possible. It was nothing specific. It was just general discussion I did." The two men discussed Principal's real estate woes, but not specifically the contract companies, Cormie said.

Confronted with these revelations, Getty confirmed in May 1988 that he had met with Cormie, who told him that Alberta's regulatory environment was oppressive. "He was very concerned that we're tougher in this province on his operations than anywhere else he operates," Getty said.[1]

March 3, 1986

LETTER FROM DONALD CORMIE to Solicitor General Perrin Beatty:

Thank you for the most interesting dinner on January 28th and your letter of February 7th. You are certainly one of the most open-minded and concerned Federal Cabinet Ministers that I have met, and I would be pleased to meet with you again the next time you are in Edmonton.

I indicated to you that a major concern of the people within my acquaintance is the need for a drastic revision of the tax system.

There is a real need to eliminate the billions of dollars that flow out in tax rulings, purchases of assets for cash from public companies supported by taxes, fictitious research and development grants, as well as 90% of the cost of wells in the Arctic that end up in private hands. We certainly hope you are not going to further subsidize Arctic wells.

When all this is seen by the public in the West, as key civil servants and their former employers get what amounts to billions and billions of dollars out of the public treasury, it is difficult for anyone in the country to want to pay taxes voluntarily to cover these amounts.

While I know you have indicated that everything was done legally and everyone is entitled to the provisions of the tax laws, most people know that these benefits accrue to very few companies and people, and then are closed off as soon as the average businessman starts using them. The whole system develops a cynicism and distrust I find very unsettling. I am very disappointed to find a fresh Conservative government continuing these practices.

My main concern, that I expressed, is that we find a blatant "anti-Western" attitude among the civil servants in Ottawa when we are dealing directly with them. I suppose the solution is to get more Western businessmen to identify, document, name and publish the names of these various civil servants so that we can build up an accurate file on each person we can identify...

I have indicated specifically the situation with CDIC where an injudicious demand by them for us to sell $40 million in Canada Bonds within 60 days or have our insurance pulled, cost our Trust Company a direct loss of over $4 million, which was completely unnecessary. When these same people state that an Alberta trust company has no business spreading across the country, but should stay in its own province, we assume that that is the reason for their most arbitrary action.

At the moment, our Directors thoroughly resent the fact that CDIC is attempting to hold the capital ratio to 15 to 1 to prevent the company from growing, when many of the Ontario companies have been as high as 29.5 to 1, according to figures published one or two years ago, which is the latest industry information available. We thought, however, that we would wait and see what happens when this year's audited statements are filed before taking the next step to solve the problem.

Over the years, many regulatory people in Ottawa have developed an "advisory" role rather than a "supervisory" role, and now substitute their "opinion" for the rules and regulations, and the law.

However, we are anxious to look forward positively rather than back. Certainly your generosity in giving your time and attention to the dinner opens up lines of communication which certainly have not been available in the past.

January 14, 1986

LAWYER SYDNEY BERCOV'S OPINION ON THE on-going dispute concerning the calculation of the Section 8 financial tests was delivered to Tewfik Saleh in mid-January. He had found a way of supporting Principal's method of calculating the unimpaired capital and reserves tests—thus giving the companies more flexibility in valuing their assets.

The practice of the departmental auditors had always been to value company assets using the limitations set out in Section 29 of the *Investment Contracts Act*, which included the right to devalue stocks and bonds to market, and to reject some assets as not meeting the criteria under the Act. Now Bercov pointed out that the Act said the company "may" (not "must") value the assets according to Section 29's limitations—but could instead use GAAP or some other widely recognized method. However, he continued, the Superintendent retained the option of invoking another section of the Act, which gave him the right to require appraisals on properties that secured mortgages held by the company, and then have the mortgages written down to the appraised value. Even if the company were valuing assets according to GAAP, Bercov and the government officials agreed during the meeting, a "temporary" decline in value was one year or less.

Bercov also supported the department's view that contract company investments in affiliated companies were prohibited. Lastly, he advised that if the companies made investments not authorized by the *Investment Contracts Act*, Saleh could: (1) Refuse to renew registration pursuant to Section 7 of the Act; (2) Cancel registration pursuant to Section 10 of the Act; (3) Make a Special Report to the Minister; or (4) Cause a charge to be laid.

In February, Burt Eldridge was reading the weekly transaction summaries published by the Alberta Securities Commission when he discovered the year-end transactions between the contract companies and several affiliates. Eldridge and

Nick Romalo prepared a transactions analysis and corporate chart, and forwarded it to Saleh on February 17. Saleh testified that by mid-March, he well understood that all the intercorporate transactions were to the detriment of the contract companies. "What do I do about it?" he testified. "Short of what Mr. Bercov told me"—take one of the four steps allowed under the Act—"is that I reported the whole situation to the Deputy [Martin], because if I do what Mr. Bercov is telling me, then I'd bring the company down."

The outcome: the Section 8 tests were calculated according to the new company-preferred method; no appraisals were obtained; and the over-valued shares of affiliated companies remained on the company books.

March 1986

PRINCIPAL'S MUTUAL FUNDS, and the company which managed them, were Donald Cormie's ticket to the future. There was little overhead, little risk and a fortune to be made. Each year, Principal Securities Management Ltd. skimmed a 2% fee off the top of the funds it managed: no muss, no fuss, and scant opportunity for regulators to interfere. There was no question of minimum reserves, borrowing-to-capital ratios or capital injections; investors bought into a mutual fund and owned a portion of its assets. Their earnings were tied to the fortunes of the fund.

Bill Johnson, Principal Group finance vice-president, also saw the potential in PSML. In the spring of 1985, after the failure of the First Investors preferred share issue, Johnson looked into the possibility of taking the entire Principal Group conglomerate public. He contacted the brokerage firm Wood Gundy in Toronto to see if it would underwrite a public offering, and a number of draft prospectuses were prepared.[2] It quickly became obvious that taking the whole group public wouldn't work; the most likely means of attracting outside investment was to float a public issue of PSML alone. Johnson testified that he saw the offering as a way of generating rescue cash for the contract companies: if Collective Securities Ltd. transferred PSML shares to First Investors and Associated Investors, and the offering was made by those companies, it would provide them with capital and time to work out their problems. In the autumn he took the idea to Cormie. Cormie considered it a good idea, but "unnecessary" at that time, Johnson said—and it was shelved.

Then, in early 1986, Cormie pursued an ambitious plan to take PSML public through the back door, under the banner of Hollinger Inc., which trades on the Toronto, Montreal and Vancouver stock exchanges. Cormie began discussions with Toronto financier Conrad Black, majority shareholder of the billion-dollar holding company. The idea was to empty Hollinger of most of its assets (at that time energy, grocery, publishing and cable television companies); to roll PSML and other Principal assets in as new subsidiaries; and to have Collective Securities Inc. take controlling interest. Black confirmed that he met twice with Cormie in 1986, but did not take the idea as seriously as Cormie did. "Our discussions were perfectly cordial," Black told me by letter, "but they were very preliminary and were undertaken by us at the request of a mutual friend and with no optimism on our part that they would lead anywhere. It seemed to me at all times to be a somewhat far-fetched notion, but I met with [Cormie] twice to discuss it in general terms because I thought there was a possibility that we could leave to him the disagreeable aspects of the final disentanglement from the food business and expedite our positioning of our company in the newspaper business. The discussions quickly broke down when it became clear, as I thought it probably would, that he was interested in relieving us of a distinguished corporate name but not of the inconveniences that he was understandably reluctant to assume."

The mutual friend who bought Cormie and Black together was Maurice Colson, at that time vice-president and director of securities firm First Marathon Inc. Colson (brother of Hollinger Inc. director Dan Colson) had worked with Black in previous deals, and was aware that he wanted rid of certain Hollinger assets. In early 1986, when First Marathon arranged a private placement of 300,000 Principal Neo-Tech Class A shares, Colson ended up in Denver with Cormie and Ken Marlin, co-hosting a dinner for the offering's institutional purchasers. The clients toured Principal Neo-Tech's seismic operation, met with Principal management, and were taken to Aspen, the nearby skiing mecca, for a few days of fun.

After the dinner, Colson and a partner had a drink with Cormie and Marlin. "He said something about wanting to go public," Colson told me. "I didn't know anything about his operation, but just listening to him I suddenly realized: Maybe this is a way I could solve Black's problems and take this guy public." He went to work on the deal as soon as he reached Aspen—"I spent half my ski trip calling Black and Cormie every day"—and for several weeks dropped everything else to pursue the project. For Colson, it was "the deal of the century," and would have generated fees approaching a million dollars. "I'd go home at night and phone Black in Florida and Cormie at his place. It was very interesting and a real high trying to do it."

From the beginning, Black seemed sceptical of Cormie. "He must have asked me a hundred times: 'Is this guy for real?' " Colson said. As far as Colson could tell, Cormie was not only "for real," but top-drawer. "He had me out to Edmonton and showed me his offices, showed me where he had the cattle auction and all this stuff. He played a great game," Colson said. "He drove me around Edmonton and showed me all these properties he said he had owned and had sold—because he didn't believe real estate prices were going to stay up there and etcetera etcetera. It was all tied into his theory of cycles."

Lunch in the Principal tower with Cormie, Marlin, Jaimie Cormie and other company executives "was like having a meeting with the high priest," Colson said. "There was never any room for dissent. Whatever Cormie said they agreed on. He asked their opinions but they would formalize their opinions based on what he initially said... When I came back I remember saying, 'He runs that business like Jim and Tammy Baker. You have to have religion to work there.' "

Despite these discussions, neither Colson nor any of the Hollinger people got a close look at Cormie's assets. Jack Boultbee, Hollinger's chief financial officer, told me that when it came time for detailed information, the deal evaporated. "There was a proposal put to us at one point offering us a deal, and of course like any deal we said, 'We'll listen to you.' Then we spent some time waiting for some financial information that we never got."

In mid-June, during the Hollinger talks, Wood Gundy had estimated PSML's value at approximately $120 million, based on information provided by the Cormies. Donald Cormie decided to proceed with a public issue based on that figure, with Wood Gundy as the underwriters. Johnson's original idea, that a PSML offering be made through the contract companies, was long abandoned. Instead, it was decided that PSML would issue two million shares from its treasury, with an identical secondary offering by shareholder CSI. The company would apply for listings on the Toronto, Montreal and Alberta Stock Exchanges. The stock would be priced at about $10 a share; if all four million shares were sold, they would generate capital of $40 million. (The remaining 10 million outstanding common shares would remain in the hands of CSI, leaving the Cormies with majority control and the prospect of later selling those shares, presumably at a good price, through the stock market.)

A preliminary prospectus filed in August 1986 advised that the $20 million from PSML's offering, together with an equal amount to be borrowed by the company (the proceeds from parent company CSI's secondary issue), would be invested in mutual funds managed by PSML.

At the Code inquiry, Donald Cormie agreed that taking PSML public would have provided cash to allow CSI to free itself from its ever-escalating debt to Principal Group Ltd. But he insisted that the purpose of the offering was to help Principal Group pay off the promissory notes it owed to the public. When PSML began liquidating the mutual funds it had purchased six or eight months later, Cormie said, it would pay back CSI, which would pay back Principal Group, which would pay back its noteholders. That process wasn't outlined in the prospectus, Cormie admitted: "No, it is not written down. That was just the plan."

In preparation for the public offering, the Cormies arranged to change PSML from a "flow-through company" to a "stand-alone company." The management fees earned by PSML were no longer to be flowed through to CSI (and half on to Principal Group). Instead, they were retained in PSML to demonstrate the company's earning capacity. PSML's 1985 profit was $29,000; in 1986 it jumped to $2.156 million, the result of the mid-year change. There were other changes. Principal Group's entire investment department, a significant asset, was transferred to PSML. After July 1986, salaries for all investment staff and certain accounting personnel were paid by PSML, as well as two-thirds of Jaimie Cormie's salary and a fifth of the salaries of CSI vice-president Rob Pearce and in-house lawyer Lynn Patrick. PSML also signed an agreement with Principal Group for computer, clerical and marketing services. The administration fee, to be calculated as a percentage of the gross assets that PSML was managing—rather than half of PSML's income, as received previously—actually reduced the revenue Principal Group would receive from PSML.

Bill Johnson had an obvious interest in the offering, but he was pulled off the project and replaced by upstairs executive Rob Pearce when Wood Gundy officials appeared at Principal Plaza to conduct their evaluation of PSML. Johnson testified that Cormie removed him because he felt Johnson was negatively influencing Wood Gundy's opinion of value. Johnson thought PSML was worth between $75 and $90 million, far short of the $120 million finally included in the prospectus, and he feared that over-valuing it would endanger the offering.

Cormie was convinced the public could be persuaded that the offering was good value. He expected his own sales people—not then registered as securities dealers—to sell the PSML shares to the public. Christa Petracca had failed the previous summer to obtain the desired broker registration for Principal Consultants, but Cormie hadn't given up. He intended to transform the company into a national brokerage firm.

Cormie was angry that the Alberta Securities Commission wouldn't co-operate with the necessary exemptions. In late January, he wrote a memo to Lynn Patrick: "It appears to me that there is a political solution to the matter, since on speaking with a Cabinet Minister, he is absolutely amazed that we have been a broker in the United States for 23 years and can't get registered in the Province of Alberta because of policy decisions." He assigned Patrick to work with Cormie Kennedy lawyer Bill Connauton, who had provided an opinion in November 1985 supporting Cormie's method of calculating the Section 8 financial tests. The two lawyers consulted with commission officials and in mid-May, Patrick reported back, outlining the legal barriers to registration and suggesting that Cormie talk to "the politicians" about having the rules changed. The campaign continued, to little avail. That autumn, still without the coveted broker registration, the Cormies would embark on a cross-Canada tour to introduce PSML's offering to the country's investment community.

February 1986

CHRISTA PETRACCA WAS KEEN to get back to work. She'd had to slow down during the last weeks of her pregnancy, and was recovering in hospital—but that didn't mean she was out of the game. With her infant daughter beside her, Petracca called management consultant Peter Walsh for an update on his market study on the Rimrock Inn.

"I had a phone call from the hospital," Walsh told me. "'When are you going to have your report? I'm having a meeting here,' right from the hospital—right after the baby was born. 'I'll be back in my office next week,' she said. 'Could you come up and discuss the report?'"

Walsh, with Pannell Kerr Forster Management Consultants, was engaged by Petracca to advise her on the feasibility of a massive re-development of the Rimrock Inn. The 93-room hotel, located in Banff National Park, was perched on a cliff overlooking the Bow River valley, just down the road from Banff's Upper Hot Springs. It was one of two dozen foreclosed properties, and a top priority, on Petracca's SWAT team's "opportunities" list.

Principal became involved with the Rimrock in mid-1982 during the scurry to place high-interest investment contract money. The hotel, which went into receivership, was part of the collateral for a $14.3-million loan package to Banff developer John Pawluk Jr. Pawluk had run out of money during construction of a new wing on the then-36 room facility; the Principal contract companies[3] bailed him out with loans at 22.5% interest for three years. Pawluk had originally sought about $4.5 million for the hotel, but Principal's mortgage department strongly advised against this, arguing that Pawluk's finances were in a shambles.[4] The loan went ahead, greatly increased when Pawluk's father agreed to put up some of his own properties as security.

The progress of the loan was followed with great interest by Donald and Jaimie Cormie, then-mortgage manager Wayne Fuhr testified: "They were constantly phoning and asking how the loan was coming." The Cormies knew the Pawluk family, Fuhr said, and "at our investment level we were desperately looking for some investments to sop up the extra cash that we had not invested."

The majority of Principal's $14.3 million went to the Pawluks' earlier lenders to clear prior charges off the properties offered as security. Another $1 million went to clear liens, writs and related charges. Additional money was spent to cover outstanding taxes, insurance, legal, appraisal and other fees. In the end there was only half a million dollars left—about $129,000 of that for the Rimrock. The purpose of the loan was to refinance the hotel and complete Pawluk's renovations, but there was obviously no money left to do the job. Work on the new wing continued with other funding; meanwhile, the Principal companies' loans were almost immediately in default.

In late 1985, after a bitter court fight, First Investors and Associated Investors acquired title to the Rimrock Inn. Donald Cormie classified the hotel as a "hold," to be developed to the point where its increased value would cover the losses on the entire package of loans. The hotel was appraised at a market value of $4,475,000 in March 1984. Despite a deteriorating market, Cormie wrote a memo in mid-1985 advising that he assessed its value at $14 million—which would, not so coincidentally, cover the Pawluk loans. By keeping the property on the books at this value, he could avoid a write-down of the other Pawluk properties than had ended up in the contract companies' portfolios.

Upon acquisition, the Rimrock was transferred into Marquette Realty & Development Ltd., jointly owned by the contract companies, and was thus delivered into Christa Petracca's hands. She had big plans for the Rimrock. Encouraged by Cormie, Petracca envisioned a five-star luxury resort with spa and "stress centre," unique in western Canada. Cost: $25 million or more. The prototype was California's super-exclusive Golden Door, the most expensive such facility in America ($3,000 U.S. for a week's stay in 1986). Soon after leaving the hospital, Petracca sent Walsh to inspect the Golden Door and similar operations. "These aren't fat farms, but stress detoxification centres," Walsh told me. "They murder them—exercise, stress psychologists, baths, hot and cold showers."

Petracca was back at the office, her infant girl in a bassinet beside her desk, by mid-March. She immediately filed applications to government tourism offices for grants to help develop the Rimrock. Petracca wanted to expand it to 248 rooms and suites, three dozen of them with fireplaces. The stress rehabilitation program would include a medical diagnosis facility with direct access to an international stress evaluation computer network based in Arizona. There would be three restaurants, an entertainment lounge, ballrooms, indoor and outdoor pools, sauna, steam room exercise equipment and massage facilities.

Petracca was after a special clientele—business executives and "the exclusive international tourist who would not otherwise visit the Parks"—mainly rich Americans, as she said in a letter to the Alberta tourism department. The project tells us as much about Petracca and her interests as it does about this once-modest hotel—nothing but the best, and price no object. "Christa behaved as if she were used to having expensive things around her," Walsh told me. "She liked the project beyond the economic realities."

Petracca was involved in the development of other properties, too—among them the Prince Royal Hotel (formerly Charter Towers) on 5th Avenue and 6th Street S.W. in downtown Calgary. More than $2 million was spent on renovations before the 1987 collapse.

Another half a million dollars was poured into raw land in far-away Hawaii. The property, 26.6 ocean-view acres on the Kona coast of the largest of the Hawaiian islands, had been security for a $650,000 loan to Calgary-based Westmoreland Capital Ltd. (majority interest held by Calgary businessman Edward Fry) in November 1981. By February 1983, the account was in arrears, and by July 1983, foreclosure proceedings were underway. In March 1984, an Hawaiian court approved a foreclosure sale to First Investors for $480,000 U.S. (approximately $610,000 Can. at the then-current exchange rate).

The land had been appraised prior to the 1981 mortgage at $1.4 million U.S. "as is," but the appraisal had been based on assumptions that were no longer valid. A foreclosure appraisal prepared in March 1984 was for a mere $430,000 U.S. The land was adjacent to a posh resort complex with a golf course, and Petracca dreamed of creating a similar high-density development worth several million dollars. There were, however, significant drawbacks to the property: it was zoned agricultural; there were no water rights (and, because of an overtaxed and over-committed water system, it would be difficult to obtain any); the regional real estate market was depressed: the terrain was extremely steep; and there was an aboriginal land claim in dispute.

Petracca first attempted to sell the Kona property to an American who had shown interest at the foreclosure sale. She wrote him in August 1984 attempting to palm off the outdated 1981 appraisal, and offered to sell for $1.2 million U.S. He didn't bite. A year later, she engaged Honolulu-based appraisers to advise her of the land's market value. Their preliminary valuation of $665,000 U.S. was lower than she had hoped, so she dismissed them, and began spending money on rezoning and water rights. Despite the discouraging appraisal, Petracca and Cormie rejected an offer for more than $1 million U.S. (almost $1.4 million Can.) in September 1986. They kept spending; Petracca entered an agreement to have First Investors pay $150,000 for several acres adjacent to the Kona site. By 1987, First Investors' involvement in the Hawaiian property had climbed to about $1.6 million (Can.)

There were other less exotic—but equally inappropriate—development projects. The "Woodgreen" property, ten acres of raw land in Calgary which included the old Mannix House on the edge of Fish Creek Park, had secured a loan of more than $4 million. When it was foreclosed on, the land was appraised at approximately $1.2 million. Cormie and Petracca decided on a sub-division of single family lots; they put another $1.2 million into the street and engineering work necessary to qualify for rezoning. The zoning application, opposed by the local community centre, failed when it went before Calgary City Council in July 1987, shortly after the Principal collapse.

Throughout this cash-bleeding process, which continued for almost two years, little attention was paid to the legality of involving the contract companies in real estate development, or of having them acquire development subsidiaries. The *Investment Contracts Act* permitted a company to hold any property acquired by way of foreclosure, but required that it be sold within seven years. As Inspector Bill Code observed in his report:

> It is utterly inconceivable by any stretch of the imagination that FIC and AIC were real estate development companies. They were certainly not represented to the public to be such companies and they are not permitted under the [*Investment Contracts Act*] to become such companies. It is one thing to maintain property during the holding period by covering the payment of taxes and other charges necessary to maintain control of the property and by keeping the property in a reasonable condition. It is quite another to expend large sums of money on the redevelopment, expansion, additional construction, and completion of the property...

March 15, 1986

IN MID-MARCH A PRINCIPAL NEWS RELEASE appeared in the "Investment News" section of *The Globe and Mail:*

> Principal Savings and Trust Co. of Edmonton has reported an operating profit of $2,023,000 for the year ended Dec. 31, 1985, compared with $386,000 a year earlier. Principal Trust, a private company, expects to report higher profit for fiscal 1986, John Cormie, president, said. The company has $1 of shareholders' capital for every $8.40 of public deposits, compared with $1 of capital for $23 of deposits by the larger banks, Mr. Cormie said.

April 24, 1986

EDMONTON JOURNAL REPORTER JACK DANYLCHUK, new to the newspaper and the city, was handed Principal Trust's annual report and dispatched to Principal Plaza to interview president John Cormie. Danylchuk returned with a glowing account of the sumptuous corporate headquarters and the excellence of the company. His article, headlined "Principal 'is soundest' of financial institutions," appeared on the front of the business section with a photograph of John standing "in the impressive and luxurious marble and mahogany-styled foyer." The article began:

> "Status," whispers the elevator, as it whisks to the 29th floor of the Principal Savings and Trust head office at 10303 Jasper Avenue.
> "Money," proclaims the foyer of the executive suite—two storeys, as big as a suburban house, panelled in marble and mahogany.
> The ambience is even more luxurious than that so briefly enjoyed by executives of the Canadian Commercial Bank (CCB).
> But any similarity between the two institutions stops there, as abruptly as the ear-popping elevator ride to the top.
> CCB was a casualty of the last recession. Principal is a home-grown success story, "the soundest financial institution in Canada," boasts John Cormie, president. "I'll match books with any of the big banks," he adds.

Danylchuk repeated the old tale: Donald Cormie had predicted in 1978 that the real estate market was peaking and "ploughed" the proceeds of Principal's real estate portfolio into government bonds. Principal's joyous marketing department pounced on the article, sending copies to employees across the country with a covering memo:

> The following article appeared in the Thursday, April 24, 1986, edition of *The Edmonton Journal*, complete with a photograph of John M. Cormie, President, Principal Savings & Trust, pictured in the foyer of Head Office's 29th floor reception area. Both the picture and the following article will no doubt serve to impress existing clients and prospective clients by indicating both the stability and success of our company.

A year and a half later, Danylchuk, covering the Code hearings, heard his story—and the gloating memo—read into the inquiry record. He's embarrassed now about what he wrote, and upset about the media's failure to uncover one of the decade's most important business stories. "We're talking about the time that the Canadian Commercial and Northland banks had gone under, the credit unions were in difficulty, Dial Mortgage was in trouble," he told me. "You would think the press would have been watching every company and every regulatory agency. But we failed abysmally."

Two business writers who did know about problems in the Principal empire were afraid to say so. Patricia Best and Ann Shortell, co-authors of *A Matter of Trust*, a 1985 best-seller on the Canadian trust company crisis, wrote that Principal Trust had been "repeatedly barred from entering Ontario"—but left the impression this was because the province was uncomfortable with Principal's "financial supermarket" marketing concept. In fact, it was worried about much more than that. "Ontario definitely thought there was something really wrong there"—and they spelled it out to the two journalists in 1984, Best told me in 1993.

"I wish to God we'd said more," Shortell told colleagues during a national convention of the Canadian Association of Journalists in 1988. "I knew more and we couldn't say it at the time. Sometimes you have problems—libel is a real problem and libel laws in Canada preclude doing some things, particularly with financial institutions. There's the question of whether you're going to push a company over the cliff."

March 25, 1986

THE SPECTRE OF JUSTICE WILLARD ESTEY, still in Alberta hearing testimony on the accounting failures surrounding the collapse of the two provincial banks, hovered above the audit process this year. Auditor Don McCutchen was no longer willing to accept Donald Cormie's values for the contract companies' real estate. He and his colleagues were sniffing around the Principal mortgage department, trying to figure out what the stuff was really worth.

The wrangling continued for weeks. Cormie argued values property by property, dollar by dollar, while the auditors insisted on write-downs. The result: it took three months longer to complete the audits of the contract companies' 1985 financial statements than it had the year before. During this painful process, Cormie, backed by Petracca's SWAT team, called a meeting with mortgage department members to push the real estate values back up. Finance vice-president Bill Johnson, who attended, wrote a memo to file:

> Because of the fact that the Auditors revert to the Mortgage Department and their people for a final consensus of value, the write-downs requested by the Auditors are significant. Because of that, DMC felt the meeting was necessary whereby he would try to convince the Mortgage Department people (specifically Bill Green and Rick Charlton) to "alter" their values so that the reserves requested by the Auditors would be less. Bill Green and Rick Charlton impressed upon DMC that they felt they had gone as far as they could on the properties—that is, they had in fact tried to project a value three to four years down the road, rather than a current liquidation value. Much discussion ensued about general items and certain specific properties that DMC was familiar with and had viewed before and how he went about his own valuation. In other words, my opinion was that he was trying to pressure the Mortgage Department people into altering their long term values. He then suggested that the Mortgage Department...attempt to obtain third party letters of opinion or

appraisals that supported values higher than what the Mortgage Department gave. He insinuated that even though these may not be right values and the Mortgage Department may in fact be right, we needed third party information on the files so the Auditors could look at it and accept it.

McCutchen was arguing that under GAAP the properties had to be written off after three or four years of decline; Cormie wanted that time-line extended to seven years. (He got this number from the *Investment Contracts Act*, which required that any property acquired by foreclosure had to be sold within seven years.) The solution was simple: the statements were management's, and Cormie could say whatever he liked—but McCutchen's responsibility, as auditor, was to comment on their reasonableness. If they diverged from GAAP, then he would qualify them accordingly. In the end, he and Cormie agreed to disagree, and on May 9, McCutchen signed off on the contract companies' audits. The numbers were Cormie's, but McCutchen qualified his report as follows:

> The latest appraised value or estimated realizable value of certain owned properties and property securing certain mortgages which are carried at cost was [$9,833,069 for First Investors; $1,751,613 for Associated Investors] less than cost at December 31, 1985. The loss in value of the owned property and mortgages, in our opinion, is other than temporary and in such circumstances, generally accepted accounting principles require that the owned property and mortgages be written down to recognize the loss. The effect of this departure from generally accepted accounting principles is described in Note 2 to the financial statements.
>
> In our opinion, except that the loss in value of mortgage and owned property has not been recognized as described in the preceding paragraph, these financial statements present fairly the financial position of the company as at December 31, 1985...

Note 2 advised that it was "the opinion of management" that a decline in the value of property was temporary if the value could be expected to recover within a holding period of seven years, "allowed pursuant to the *Investment Contracts Act*." However, the note continued, such an assessment was not in accordance with GAAP.

Even with Cormie's inflated figures, First Investors showed a loss of $8,448,447. If the statement had been prepared with the GAAP-required write-downs identified by McCutchen, the loss would have climbed to $18,281,516. Associated Investors' loss, shown as $2,662,805, would have climbed to $4,414,418.

As in previous years, the companies claimed as income mortgage interest that was accrued but not actually received; in 1985, that amounted to $19.3 million for the two companies. Despite the extreme unlikelihood of ever seeing any of that money, only $6 million was booked as a provision for mortgage and owned property losses. (In 1983, 1984 and 1985, a total of $83.6 million in interest revenue was claimed by the two companies; of that, $57.9 million was accrued and unpaid. Provisions of only $12.3 million were booked during the three years.)

Richard Cormier, Inspector Bill Code's audit expert, found that the auditing standards employed for the 1985 statements had improved from the year before, but were still unacceptable. Essential disclosures about the year's intercorporate transactions were still lacking. By the end of 1985, the contract companies held shares in three affiliated companies—Matrix, Athabasca and Principal Neo-Tech— valued at a total of $62.3 million. That's an alarming one-seventh of all their assets; a quarter of the $62.3 million was the result of inter-company gains. These are figures that might have been flagged in the audit, but they were not.

Donald Cormie's primary concern was the impact of the subsidiaries' financial statements on the Principal Group consolidation. He tried in a late-April letter to talk McCutchen out of qualifying the Principal Group audit report, but was unsuccessful. McCutchen's report on Principal Group, completed at the end of May 1986, was deeply qualified—both on the failure to value property according to GAAP, and on the company's claim of profits on the intercorporate transactions discussed above. In the mundane language of accountants, McCutchen violently criticized Principal's accounting, management and real estate management strategies. The unusually long note concluded:

> In our opinion, except that the gain on sale of shares of the subsidiaries and the resultant increase in the excess of cost of investment in subsidiaries over acquired equity in net assets have not been eliminated, and that the loss in value of mortgages and owned property has not been recognised as described in the preceding paragraphs, these consolidated financial statements present fairly the financial position of the company as at December 31, 1985...

In an accountant's world, the message can't get much worse: "Everything's just fine on the ranch, ma'am—except that hail has destroyed the wheat crop, the cattle are dying in the barn and the hired hand has run off with your daughter." Everything normal here, except these guys have improperly claimed almost $26 million more in profit and assets on their books than the rules allow.

Using Cormie's inflated figures, the statement showed that Principal Group had a profit of $607,000. If the numbers had been recalculated in accordance with GAAP, there would have been a loss that year of $25.3 million.

It would obviously be disastrous, given the revelations in the auditor's report, to put the financial statement in the hands of the public; and yet it was essential that an annual report be released. Cormie, McCutchen and others put their minds to finding a solution.

March 26, 1986

THE CDIC THOUGHT IT HAD an agreement for a joint audit of Principal Trust and the contract companies. In a March 26 letter to Barry Martin, CDIC chief operating officer Jean Pierre Sabourin discussed the plan, saying it was agreed that federal and provincial auditors "exchange all pertinent information which might be useful in determining the true financial position of the Principal Group." At the last minute, Martin backed out. They could do a joint study of Principal Trust, he said, but the contract companies were off limits. In mid-April, four examiners—two from the CDIC and two from the Consumer Affairs audit staff—arrived at Principal Plaza to conduct their annual examinations of the trust company.

A month later, federal examiner Wayne Steele wrote a report, copied to provincial officials, which concluded: "Management have completed a number of transactions, which on the surface have improved the balance sheet although nothing important has changed." And further: "A marginal increase in [the borrowing-to-capital] multiple would not appear unwarranted if the company was not tied so closely to the contract companies and Principal Group Ltd. I have been led to believe that these companies are virtually insolvent..."

The CDIC's Charles de Léry followed up on July 10 with a letter to John Cormie. It observed that the trust company had begun to invest in Principal-managed mutual funds, and the investments totalled $11.9 million at April 1986.

> We are concerned, given the considerable attention that related party transactions have been receiving, that PST would now start making direct investments in the units of mutual funds managed by the Principal group of companies. We question the conflict of interest arising from PST's direct investment in mutual funds of the group and the necessity for a direct participant in the bond and stock markets such as PST to acquire units of an investment vehicle that usually caters to the smaller, unsophisticated investor.

(Of course, the purchase of these mutual funds benefitted the Cormie-controlled funds, while generating management fees for PSML and making it more attractive in its effort to go public. Every company in the conglomerate would soon be pumping loose cash into the funds.)

De Léry ordered the trust company to immediately sell the mutual funds, and again refused an increase in the borrowing-to-capital ratio. A month later, an urgent letter from Keith Bell, new head of the federal trust companies division, asked John Cormie to rectify an over-borrowed position of $17.8 million. Bell noted that in June 1986, while the company's borrowing was increasing—and an operating loss of approximately $300,000 was sustained—"the company saw fit to pay a dividend of $253,125 to its shareholders, thereby increasing the shrinkage of its borrowing base. We do not believe it to be a prudent business practice that a supervised financial institution will pay a dividend to its shareholders at a time when the position of the depositors has already been weakened due to the company being over-borrowed."

The July and August letters went unanswered until late September.

April 4, 1986

WHILE CORMIE BATTLED THE AUDITORS, another drama was being played out in the government offices. The contract companies' licences came up for renewal on March 31 each year; under the *Investment Contracts Act*, the companies were not supposed to be registered unless they complied with all the Section 8 financial tests. Earlier in his tenure, Tewfik Saleh had overlooked the fact the financial statements were late and issued the renewed licences anyway. This year he dug his heels in.

On April 1, while Boomer Adair was the department's absentee minister, Saleh was promoted from "director of financial institutions" to "assistant deputy minister, financial institutions." He retained the position of Superintendent, and, in that capacity, drafted a letter dated April 4 to Ken Marlin, noting the contract companies' failure to file their financial statements. Saleh advised that the licence applications would kept on hold until he had received the statements, then continued: "I should like to call your attention to the fact that in accordance with Section 3 of the Act, your companies shall not issue or offer for sale or sell any investment contracts until such time the renewal of your companies' registration is issued." This letter was not sent, and the companies continued to sell contracts.

In mid-April, Reg Pointe, director of trust companies, prepared a memo at the request of deputy minister Barry Martin summarizing the affairs of Principal Trust and the contract companies. Pointe said that the contract companies hadn't filed their 1985 financial statements, and had been given to the end of April, "failing which official notification will be given to the two companies prohibiting them from doing any further business in the province." This memo was written on April 16, six days after a provincial election call: a most inauspicious time to dump a crisis on the government. The deadline came and went and the companies, still doing business, failed to deliver their statements.

On May 1, a week before the election, Saleh finally sent his letter to Marlin; but it had been re-written. The request to stop selling contracts until the companies were re-registered was dropped, and the renewal deadline was extended to May 16.

Principal finance vice-president Bill Johnson met with Saleh during this time, and a mid-April memo to file indicates that Saleh expressed concern about resolving the dispute over the Section 8 financial tests. However, Johnson wrote:

> He did absolutely assure me that once he had the audited financial statements there is no problem and would be no problem in renewing the licences immediately. He then said that the unresolved differences between our calculations of excess capital and their calculations would be resolved in the normal course of events and the renewal of the licences would not be held up because of these differences.

The next day Johnson met with Donald Cormie, who was upset about the delay with the licences. As far as Cormie was concerned, Johnson wrote, "there were no unresolved differences as we had filed our calculations of the excess [in capital] four months ago and had filed with them two copies of legal opinions supporting our calculations. He then asked me to call Tewfik back and tell him that as far as we were concerned the differences had been resolved, we had heard nothing back from the superintendent's office refuting our calculations, and therefore the licences should be renewed regardless of whether the audit was done at this time."

Johnson called Saleh, who "back-tracked" from the position he'd held just a day before. He wasn't holding up the licence renewals because of unresolved differences, but because he was waiting for the financial statements.

> I suggested to him that in prior years this had been done and his comment to me was that he was made Superintendent of Insurance in November of 1983 and anything that had been done in prior years was not his responsibility. I then mentioned to him that the 1983 financial statements were not filed until May 7th, 1984, and the companies had received their renewals by March 31st, 1984. This was also when he was Superintendent of Insurance. He replied that because he had just started as Superintendent he did not know all the formalities and rules and policies involved, but now that he does he is not prepared to issue the license. He actually got quite belligerent with me on the telephone...
>
> He told me that he was going about it in a low key and quiet manner and that he was not going to send us any letter demanding that the audited financial statements be filed by a certain date (even though he would like to have them by April 25th, 1986) and that he did not want to do this and put us in a compromising position. He said if he did send a letter he would have to threaten non-registration and therefore we would have to stop selling certificates, etc. etc. until such time as he received the audit financial statements. Of course I told him that we obviously did not want to do this and that he would receive the audited financial statements as soon as possible and we were doing everything in our power to get them finalized.

On May 16, a week after Don Getty's Conservatives were returned to power, Johnson went to the Consumer Affairs offices to deliver the contract companies' financial statements. Saleh was out of town, so Johnson turned over the statements to Bernard Rodrigues, and was handed back the waiting licences for First Investors and Associated Investors, back-dated to April 1, 1986.

Johnson, in another memo, reported that he "sat down and discussed numerous issues with Burt & Bernie"—director of audits Burt Eldridge and Rodrigues— "specifically the presentation of the equity section of the balance sheet." That is the section where the capital deficiencies—$14 million for First Investors, and $4.9 million for Associated Investors, with the GAAP-required write-downs—were identified. The three discussed ways of rearranging the balance sheets and doing the capital calculations for the regulatory statements still to be prepared. If the calculations were done according to the method proposed by Principal a few months earlier, then the deficiencies would disappear. Johnson wrote:

> They informed me they had received a legal opinion and that they were prepared to live with my surplus calculations at this point in time. In other words, I got the feeling that they were prepared to live with our calculations and not rock the boat provided that they thought we were using our best efforts and had a good business plan to try and work our way out of the situation with respect to the contract companies.

Among the liabilities recorded on the companies' balance sheets were shareholder's subordinated notes totalling $22.2 million ($18 million for First Investors and $4.2 million for Associated Investors). The year before, Cormie had agreed that promissory notes totalling $8.4 million would be converted into share capital—in effect, replacing high-interest debt with a permanent injection of cash. The companies' financial statements for 1984 had been presented in accordance with this intention, thus moving the $8.4 million off the liability side of their balance sheets and onto the equity side. Now, the new 1985 financial statements advised that the contract companies' directors had rescinded their resolution to convert the notes to share capital.

During the regulators' discussion with Johnson, it was suggested that the notes should indeed be converted; Johnson agreed to take the suggestion back to the company. He went directly to Cormie and described in detail his conversation with the regulators. Later, in a memo to file, Johnson wrote:

> We came to the conclusion that rather than converting the subordinated notes to share capital that we should try and find a way that we can show the subordinated notes in the equity section as far as presentation goes and leave them as shareholders notes and to realize any unrealized security gains in the next month or two *so that the deficit is wiped out by the security gains.* Mr. Cormie would rather do this than have the notes converted to preferred shares. [Italics added.]

Two weeks later, Cormie took his "security gains" by selling a block of Associated Investors' Matrix stock—some of the same stock acquired from Athabasca Holdings in December—back to Athabasca. The contract company had paid 55 cents a share for the Matrix stock; it sold it back 4,100,000 shares at $1.20, thus creating a gain of $2,665,000, and erasing the deficit on the company books for that month.[5]

Associated Investors was paid for its Matrix shares with Athabasca stock—the same questionable stock that it had been relieved of in December.

First Investors would go through a similar transaction at the end of 1986—and would claim an even greater "gain" than its sister did here.

April 7, 1986

MEMO FROM PRINCIPAL OPERATIONS vice-president Grant Mitchell to all vice-presidents:

> Mr. Cormie has directed that, as was in the case of 1985, a bonus in the form of PNI [Principal Neo-Tech] and Matrix shares be given to salaried Principal employees. There are to be no salary increases...
>
> As you are all aware, the trading price of PNI stock has increased from $11.50 at the time of last year's bonus to $21.00 at present, while Matrix stock has gone from 22¢ to 85¢ over the same period. Principal's senior management expects further increases in value during 1986 with corresponding rewards to our employees.

June 2, 1986

ALBERTA'S ECONOMY HAD FINALLY SHOWN signs of improvement during the second half of 1985. The National Energy Program was scrapped by the Conservative federal government in May. Oilmen, celebrating the long prayed-for deregulation, watched the world price creep up past $30 U.S. a barrel. Farm bankruptcies decreased slightly, and the real estate market seemed to be stabilizing. Westerners dared a degree of optimism.

Then, in November 1985, a feud half-way around the world pushed Alberta back to square one. Saudi Arabian oil minister Sheik Ahmed Zaki Yamani, upset that other OPEC states were undercutting him on price, doubled his country's production and flooded the market. The price per barrel touched $28 in December, $22 in January, and in February crashed to under $15, a seven-year low. By late March, oil cost less than $10 a barrel, a dive of $20 in four dreadful months.

The industry, having learned from past mistakes, responded instantaneously. Budgets were slashed, rigs shut down and hundreds of people laid off.

Donald Cormie's cycle theory had failed to reckon with vendetta-bent Arabs, and his companies were battered by the price collapse. The impact on the Denver-based seismic company Neo-Tech Inc., part of the Toronto-traded Principal Neo-Tech conglomerate, was staggering. The seismic business was highly speculative, with millions of dollars poured yearly into data acquisition in areas that might (or might not) prove of future interest to oil exploration companies. When exploration stopped, so did the market for the data. (Think of Neo-Tech Inc. as a shop that stocked incredibly expensive video tapes, in a world where suddenly no one wanted to watch movies.)

Unfortunately, Neo-Tech Inc.'s development costs remained on the books. Normally, the costs, spread out over several years, were booked against income, and the company could show a profit. Now nothing loomed but an abyss.

Principal Group Ltd. was quick off the mark with damage control.

In 1983 and 1984, before Principal Neo-Tech had acquired its seismic subsidiary, Principal Group had financed several of Neo-Tech Inc.'s seismic shoots on a project-by-project, joint venture basis. The partnership continued after the acquisition, and by late 1985 Principal Group's investment in seismic data amounted to about $7.2 million. In December 1985, after oil prices began their collapse, Principal Group dumped its soured seismic investments into publicly-traded Principal Neo-Tech. The Toronto company paid about $6.5 million in the form of 418,790 Class A preferred shares valued at $4,397,295 ($10.50 a share, approximate market value at that time) and $2,084,361 cash—a generous payment for something that would soon be worthless.

Principal Neo-Tech was soon haemorrhaging horribly. It faced a massive write-down on the 1986 second quarter books of about $4.5 million, and by May 1986, there was talk of closing down Neo-Tech Inc. completely.

Principal Group held about 97% of Principal Neo-Tech's common shares. The anticipated loss on the second quarter books would have to be reflected in Principal Group's consolidated financial statement, unless Principal Neo-Tech could be shuffled into oblivion. But where? The answer was—upstairs, outside the Principal Group consolidation.

On June 2, Principal Group transferred its Principal Neo-Tech common shares to parent company Collective Securities Inc. (CSI—owned by the Cormies and Ken Marlin) at the extremely generous rate of $7.99 a share. (The common stock trailed the price of the publicly-traded Class A preferreds, which traded that month between $5.50 and $6.88, following a three-for-one split the month before). The sale brightened the look of Principal's books considerably. Predictably, CSI paid for the shares with a promissory note for $12.9 million dollars. That note was still outstanding at the time of the Principal collapse.

At the same time, the way was prepared for the contract companies to distance themselves from their Class A preferred shares. On June 2, 1986, the companies were granted an option giving them the right to sell the shares to Athabasca Holdings—again, outside the Principal Group consolidation—in exchange for Athabasca preferred shares. The option was exercised in December 1986 at exactly the same price paid to Principal Group for the Principal Neo-Tech shares 12 months before.

The contract companies, we'll recall, had traded Athabasca stock for the Principal Neo-Tech shares because of regulators' doubts about Athabasca's underlying value. Now, Athabasca was further weakened with shares of the crippled Principal Neo-Tech, while leaving the contract companies, owners again of the Athabasca stock, still indirectly exposed to the seismic operations write-offs.

Saturday, June 21, 1986

SEVERAL PRINCIPAL SALESMEN saw Ranch Day '86 from the Cormie Ranch parking lot. Only employees with several years of service were permitted to attend as guests; the junior staff had to work their way into the festivities. Some of the

Edmonton team were posted on the outskirts of the party site, and spent part of the day parking cars. Front gate workers handed out party souvenirs, including the Cormie Ranch leather coasters. Cut in the shape of a stylized legs-splayed steer, these were imprinted with the ranch brand: a backward "C" (for Cormie) above a T-shape with a rounded upper bar. The brand was called the "Anchor C," to recall (an information card explained) the "low water lake which forms the largest area of the ranch."

Ranch Day was like a country fair. Fifteen hundred people milled around, sipping Drummond Beer, courtesy of Principal's own Red Deer brewery. The balloon rides, unfortunately, were cancelled because of winds, but there were tours, by bus or haywagon, of the ranch facilities. Guests could watch herd dogs rounding up exotic Cormie cattle while, inside the barns, semen was extracted from blue-ribbon bulls. In the evening, guests dined on barbecued steaks an inch thick. *The Edmonton Journal* columnist Nicholas Lees[6] reported that guests consumed 700 pounds of aged beef, 300 bottles of wine, 20 cases of spirits and 100 cases of beer:

> RCMP were busy Saturday when most of the 1,200 guests making their way to the Cormie Ranch sped through the tiny community.
>
> "You're the 18th speeder I've stopped," said an officer guarding the approaches to the 15,000-acre spread near Lake Wabamun.
>
> "What's the hurry?"
>
> I wanted to tell him the Cormies had gone soft in the head and were giving away money.
>
> But a family running the largest beef seed-stock operation in Canada couldn't be called daft.
>
> And the $1,200 U.S. they were giving away was a shrewd move.
>
> It was a mutual-funds draw and publicized the family's $1.2-billion Principal Group, toast of North American investors...
>
> Amiable Don Cormie and wife Eivor welcomed all, while son James, president of Principal Securities Management Ltd., told folks the funds in the draw would quickly double in value.

After dinner, Cormie spoke about his economic theories. Jaimie drew names for door prizes, then everyone danced away to the music of a country band.

17

"This office requests that you discontinue selling voluntarily"

CHAIRMAN'S MESSAGE

...1985 was another outstanding year for Principal Group. In 1984, despite the overall weaknesses in the financial sector in Canada, we announced record profits of $4.4 million. In 1985 additional reserves in some of our subsidiaries reduced our profits to $607,000. For the first time, group assets under management exceeded $1 billion at year end, currently exceed $1.2 billion, and we anticipate will reach $4 billion by 1990 as our expansion continues.

This accomplishment is not merely luck. Principal Group manages our clients' investments and our corporate portfolios using in-depth analysis of long term cycles and trends within our economy. By understanding these trends, we have been able to act rather than react. Our success in moving out of real estate in advance of its subsequent collapse and moving into the stock and bond market at its low points are examples of how this strategic planning works for us and our clients. We continually monitor current cycles and trends within our economy and adapt our strategies accordingly...

Donald M. Cormie, Q.C.
Chairman and President, Principal Group Ltd.
Principal Group: 31st Annual Review 1985

WHEN IS AN ANNUAL REPORT not an annual report? When it's a "review," of course. Auditor Don McCutchen found a solution to Principal Group's dilemma concerning its qualified financial statement: instead of the usual annual report, which had always included details of the audit, why not publish a "review," featuring "highlights" of the year? McCutchen dug up a copy of such a review published by Winnipeg-based Investors Group—one of Principal's competitors— and sent it to Donald Cormie. Cormie thought it was a great idea, and gave the go-ahead.[1]

The review, put together during the summer of 1986, was a dazzling piece of work. Ambiguously titled *Principal Group: 31st Annual Review 1985*, it was printed on glossy paper and filled with graphs, charts and gorgeous full-colour photographs of company employees and the resplendent Principal Plaza. A photo of the marble foyer and mahogany stairway filled a page, as did one of a beaming Cormie in a pin-stripe suit. There were shots of Jaimie Cormie and his investment team studying a stock market monitor; photos of cameras and paints at Principal Neo-Tech's graphics facilities; white-coated production staff at the Red Deer brewery; Bill Johnson and comptroller Ginny Nicholson studying a balance sheet; and the Rimrock Inn ("propelled into the category of a true five star hotel that competes with and exceeds the standards of luxury resorts throughout the world"—even though the spa hadn't been started at that point).

Several pages highlighted PSML and its mutual funds. PSML's public offering was to be launched that autumn, and the publicity would help early sales. Graphs hyped the performance of the mutual funds and tracked Principal's phenomenal growth during the decade.

A "Condensed Summary of Operations" claimed, as did Cormie in his chairman's message, that Principal Group's consolidated income was a healthy $607,000. "Total assets under administration" were reported at $950,400,000; a pie graph imposed over an image of a maple leaf gold coin suggested that 46.1% of those assets were in government bonds and other marketable securities; 9.8% were in loans; 9.7% were in cash; 7.8% were in property and equipment; 10.1% in owned property; and only 16.5% were in mortgages.

It all looked, as investor Marjorie Givens would testify, "pretty good."

Nowhere in those seductive 46 pages were investors told what they really needed to know: that Principal Group's 1985 financial statements had been severely qualified by the outside auditor; that if they had been prepared according to generally accepted accounting procedures they would show not a profit of $607,000, but a loss of more than $25 million.

It wasn't even clear what corporate entity was being reviewed. The title said "Principal Group," and a back page identified as "directors" and "officers" the people who held those titles in the Principal Group Ltd. structure. But pages were devoted to PSML (owned by Principal's parent company CSI); Principal Neo-Tech (sold by Principal Group to CSI while the annual review was being planned); and the various mutual funds (owned by the mutual fund holders themselves and managed by PSML, no longer part of the group). Principal Group's relationship to these and other companies was not disclosed.

In his chairman's message, Cormie claimed that Principal Neo-Tech "had a banner year in 1985"—no mention of the fact that its seismic division had been demolished by the Arab oil price war one month after year-end.

The percentages shown in the captivating gold coin graph were based on the almost $1 billion claimed as "total assets under administration,"—even though more than a quarter of that was from mutual funds managed by PSML.[2] If the numbers were calculated based on the $677.4 million in assets reported on Principal Group's (unpublished) consolidated balance sheet, they would have shown that only 31% were in government bonds and other marketable securities—not the graph's impressive 46%. Owned property made up 14.2%—not 10.1%. Most startling, mortgages and secured loans made up 31.5%—twice the lean 16.5% that investor Givens had taken such comfort in.

The page devoted to First Investors and Associated Investors—graced by a photo of Christa Petracca and SWAT team member Lance Frazier—stated that the contract companies maintained with a Canadian chartered bank "qualified assets in excess of the cash surrender value of all certificates at all times." Not much of a boast, as we've seen. Then it continued with an astounding set of lies, authored by Petracca:

> Corporate investments are currently concentrated in bonds and securities offering excellent liquid returns. Because of the need for a balanced portfolio of secure investments, a large part of these companies' assets are in government and corporate bonds as well as blue chip stocks. Management's experience and financial expertise ensure the profitability of the Companies' investments and a safe, competitive yield to the certificate holders.

In reality, the contract companies were as liquid as chilled mud. At the end of 1985, two-thirds of their assets were invested in mortgages, owned property, notes receivable, debts due from affiliated companies, advance commissions receivable, Matrix and Principal Neo-Tech shares and the preferred shares of Athabasca Holdings. The investments produced little yield for certificate holders.

The review was published in September 1986; 12,000 copies were distributed to offices and customers across the country. Enthusiastic branch managers congratulated the public relations department on a job well done.

Meanwhile, during the weeks the Principal crew laboured on the review, the regulatory firmament had been shifting under Donald Cormie's feet. Officials from another province were once again showing an interest in the contract companies. Within a year, pressure from British Columbia would finally push Alberta into taking them down.

June 6, 1986

BILL SMITH HAD BEEN BRITISH COLUMBIA'S Acting Deputy Superintendent of Brokers only a few days when he discovered that the Principal contract companies had not filed their audited financial statements for 1985. The statutory deadline was March 31, 1986—the same as in Alberta—and Smith was shocked to realize that the companies had been operating unlicenced in his province for more than two months.

Smith, a chartered accountant, had worked for the B.C. government since 1969. In the 1970s, he was assistant chief accountant with the B.C. Securities Commission, and at the end of that decade became a policy analyst with Consumer and Corporate Affairs. During the early 1970s he was responsible for examining the Principal contract companies' financial statements, and for authorizing renewal of their registration; in 1974, he assisted in forcing the injection of capital into First Investors to shore up a deteriorating stock portfolio.

Smith well remembered contract companies president Ken Marlin from those difficult days, so he gave him a call. Marlin expressed "shock" that the companies weren't registered, and had their financial statements in Smith's hands three days later—70 days after the statutory deadline.

Smith was appalled at what he read. Auditor Don McCutchen's deeply qualified audit reports made it clear the companies were in serious trouble with their real estate holdings. When Smith looked at the valuation of securities held by the companies, "I noticed that there were a lot of investments in affiliated companies, which disturbed me." It appeared to Smith that the two companies were about $55 million short of the required qualified assets.

This sort of financial analysis wasn't really part of Smith's new job—his primary duties were related to processing prospectuses for the securities commission—but there was no one else available. The statements had actually come to him by accident, during a chat with an accountant in the filings department, but once Smith got started, he couldn't stop.

As B.C. Ombudsman Stephen Owen reported after the Principal collapse, the two contract companies had been operating in that province without proper supervision for many years. Owen found that there was "clear and long-standing negligence of public officials in B.C. in the performance of their statutory responsibilities," dating back to about 1978. During the entire period that B.C.'s *Investment Contracts Act*, enacted in 1962, had been in force, no written policy was ever developed to ensure that its requirements were met.

Lack of a policy wasn't a problem during the early years: the Superintendent's office was small, staff members interacted freely, and a single accountant kept an eye on both First Investors and Associated Investors. B.C. managed to keep a tight rein on the companies, and took the lead in collaborative efforts with Alberta regulators. As a result of that collaboration, Associated Investors lost its B.C. licence in April 1973, remaining unlicenced until January 1978. Owen found, however, that the practice of having one accountant responsible for the contract companies had ceased by 1978.

This, in combination with a move to Vancouver that same year, and the hiring of new staff who were not trained with respect to the requirements of the

Investment Contracts Act, led to a problem: no specific individual was left to regulate AIC and FIC. It was then that clear, written policy was most needed. Unfortunately, there was none, and AIC and FIC drifted into 1984 essentially unregulated.

After 1978, as a result of this disorganization, registration renewal certificates were issued automatically to the contract companies. The registration clerks didn't check whether financial statements had been received, let alone analyzed, because they were not aware it was necessary to do so.

In May 1984, the registration department demanded, and received, the Principal companies' statements for 1983. They went to then-Deputy Superintendent of Brokers Earl Jewitt (Bill Smith's predecessor), who found no statements on file for either of the companies for the past six years. Jewitt didn't order them to supply the missing statements, but he read the 1983 statements. Unfortunately Jewitt, a chartered accountant, found no particular significance in auditor Bruce Pennock's note that the statements had been presented on a going-concern basis. He did, however, understand that Alberta's depressed real estate market had seriously damaged the companies.

On May 29, 1984, Jewitt wrote to Tewfik Saleh to say he had identified a potential shortfall of approximately $20.8 million in the two companies. He asked to be advised of an upcoming meeting with the companies' officials, "and any other information you may have which you feel would be of interest to us."

Unknown to Jewitt, 18 days earlier Saleh had written his tough compliance letter identifying a $72-million shortfall in the two companies and demanding an immediate capital injection of $35 million. In mid-June, Saleh participated in the strained series of meetings between federal and provincial regulators and the company representatives. He never advised his B.C. counterpart—nor regulators in the other provinces where Principal did business—of either event, nor of the fact the companies did not comply with his capital demand.

Jewitt told Ombudsman Owen that he discussed with his superior, then-Superintendent of Brokers Rupert Bullock, the possibility of sending someone to Alberta to investigate the Principal companies, but "it seemed redundant for us to send someone there to do a job that was already being done." Bullock did not recall taking any action after learning about the companies' possible shortfall.

Jewitt also sent a copy of his letter to Saleh to Al Dilworth, Director of Investigations and Inspections in B.C.'s Department of Consumer and Corporate Affairs. Dilworth assigned senior inspector Bill Buxton to check out the companies' files. Buxton went to Jewitt for a briefing, then wrote a report to Dilworth at the end of May advising that Jewitt, who was monitoring the situation "along with his counterpart in Alberta," did not intend to use department inspectors to audit the companies, "and at this stage he prefers to keep the companies going in order to protect the investors' interests. He did not seem concerned about the 'new' investors."

Jewitt was copied with Buxton's report, and shot back an angry response to Dilworth. Buxton was wrong to suggest that he was not concerned about new investors, he said, but that didn't mean "that we should close down an operation on a suspicion that the financial condition of a company is suspect. The Alberta Superintendent of Insurance is well aware of the situation, and I have relayed my concerns to them. When they reply, a decision will have to be made as to our best course of action."

Dilworth marked the file to be brought forward again in two months. On several subsequent occasions he assigned it to a junior inspector, who gathered information during telephone conversations with Saleh and his assistant Bernard Rodrigues. There was no effort to obtain independent information.

Unfortunately—in a situation sadly reminiscent of the turf struggle then unfolding between Jim Darwish and Tewfik Saleh—Dilworth felt restrained from digging into the Principal problem. "I had been told on a number of occasions that certain functions were for the Superintendent and it was none of my business," Dilworth told Ombudsman Owen after the collapse. "That may be because I was upsetting [the] Superintendents by taking too active a role."

Several times over the next few years, B.C. officials were misled, or simply left in the dark, by Saleh and Rodrigues. Smith, testifying at the Code inquiry, described Saleh as a "brick wall." It was a very different situation, he said, from the atmosphere of co-operation and mutual support which had existed during the 1970s, when Darwish was the Superintendent.

On January 17, 1986, Bullock resigned as B.C. Superintendent of Brokers. He gave the usual three month's notice, but the government left the position vacant for almost half a year. His assistant Jewitt, ill and within a few months of retirement, temporarily filled the post as Acting Superintendent.

Notified in early April by the registration department that the Principal contract companies' financial statements were overdue, Jewitt called Rodrigues, who claimed that Alberta government lawyers had indicated that the companies were not in contravention of provincial legislation. (At that time, the companies were unregistered in both provinces and had been illegally selling contracts for two weeks.) At the end of April, Jewitt wrote to a lawyer in the legal services branch of the B.C Attorney General's department, stating that despite the financial problems of the companies, "it would appear that they still are not in contravention of the Act." What action could be taken under the circumstances?

At the end of May—exactly two years after first identifying the potential $20-million shortfall—Jewitt retired, without ever receiving the lawyer's opinion. It was completed in mid-June and forwarded to Jewitt's replacement.

Jewitt left before the new B.C. Superintendent was ready to take over. David Edgar, assistant deputy minister of Consumer and Corporate Affairs, stepped into the breach for 22 days. At the same time Bill Smith, also close to retirement, agreed to fill in as Acting Deputy Superintendent during June and July of 1986, until that position could be permanently filled as well.

Unlike his predecessors, Smith immediately grasped the significance of the companies' potential shortfall, identified the key capital requirements under the provincial legislation and took immediate and determined steps to find a solution. Smith briefed Edgar on the problem, and on June 13, a couple of weeks after taking up their new positions, they met with Director of Filings (chief accountant) Ted Affleck and the provincial legal services branch lawyer who had been queried by Jewitt a few weeks earlier. (The lawyer's opinion, produced on June 10, advised that the province had the right to inspect documents, procure property appraisals and force the companies to provide information.)

Smith wanted to bring in an outside firm of chartered accountants to look at the companies' books; Edgar ruled that out as premature. As Ombudsman Owen reported, Edgar felt that "it was important for Alberta, as the regulator of the primary jurisdiction, to take the lead and that it would not have been appropriate for B.C. to take regulatory action 'unless Alberta simply kept saying nothing.'" Edgar thought the companies should be asked to stop selling voluntarily. As far as Smith was concerned this idea was "always a non-starter," tantamount to "asking somebody to commit suicide," but he put the request in a letter and summoned Ken Marlin to Vancouver for a meeting the following Monday.

During the June 16 meeting, Smith handed the letter to Marlin. It noted the delay in delivery of the statements, the fact that the companies' registration was not renewed, and continued:

> When the financial statements were reviewed, they appeared far from satisfactory, and before registration can be issued, several concerns must be answered. In the circumstance, if you were selling certificates under the I.C.A., this Office requests that you discontinue selling voluntarily until the problems, perceived or real, are satisfactorily resolved.

The letter took a hard line with respect to valuation of the companies' assets, including the shares in three affiliated companies. Smith requested detailed information about the various assets, and gave the companies a week to provide it.

Marlin made it clear at the meeting that the companies would not "voluntarily" stop selling. His reply, Smith testified, was that "that would be just the same as putting them into bankruptcy... He may as well close the doors. And I take his point, that I think that this is precisely what would have happened." Marlin, shocked by Smith's forcefulness, went home and reported to Cormie. Smith's demands were given top priority, and the requested material was forwarded to him on June 20, a Friday, only four days after the meeting.

That same day, Cormie wrote a memo to comptroller Ginny Nicholson, taking himself off the list of signing officers for the contract companies.

The following Monday, Cormie wrote a confidential memo to Principal lawyer Lynn Patrick (copied to Marlin, Christa Petracca and finance VP Bill Johnson) instructing him to be prepared to appeal any direction that Smith might subsequently make to stop the selling operation. The memo continued:

It seems essential, however, that we have to locate people inside the government organization in British Columbia who are favourably disposed toward our Group and what we are doing and see if we can start working with some of these people so as to get them informed. I know several of the Cabinet Ministers and advisors to the Cabinet Ministers and once we have a clear picture of what is required, I will make a point of calling on them.

In the meantime, we should be sure to develop a straight-forward, friendly relationship with the people there on a continuing basis so they have enough information to be comfortable with everything we are doing.

Whether the lobbying campaign was actually pursued is not known. (Ombudsman Owen, who made no comment in his report about this memo, said he found no evidence of attempts by anyone to improperly influence B.C. politicians or public servants.)

After receiving Johnson's information package, Smith worked several evenings and through a weekend analyzing the material; it was B.C.'s first detailed review, since 1972, of the contract companies' circumstances. The package included the legal opinion obtained by the companies supporting their position that shares of Athabasca Holdings were a qualified asset under the *Investment Contracts Act*; Smith never knew that Saleh and other Alberta officials held the opposite view. Based on the opinion—and applying the grossly inadequate real estate write-downs used by Alberta regulators—Smith reduced the amount of the deficiency he had earlier estimated.

Nonetheless, by the end of June, Smith had determined that the two companies were insolvent, and estimated their shortfall in qualified assets at approximately $11.2 million. On July 2, he wrote a report to his new superior Michael Ross, who had become Superintendent of Brokers a week before.

Ross, 48, a chartered accountant with a commerce degree, was also certified as a management consultant. His mandate, he testified, was to "sort out the management problems of the department," and to prepare it for introduction of a new *Securities Act*. As Vancouver Stock Exchange experts David Cruise and Alison Griffiths wrote:[3]

Ross talked very tough at first: "If I find that our major purpose is being thwarted by people who are abusing the rules and procedures, I will take advantage of the discretion allowed in the legislation in order to make sure the market works. If I find that these people have been in trouble before, or even if we have suspicions about them, I will run them out of town." Any fear provoked by his words evaporated into sniggers when he announced to the media that he'd won a local songwriting contest.

Ross quickly proved unequal to the task of regulating the contract companies.

Smith's July 2 memo detailed the tangled affairs of the Cormie-controlled companies, advised that they were "cash poor and will remain so for some time," and concluded that various convoluted exchanges of one another's shares illustrated "the manoeuvring required to ensure that assets are qualified." He recommended that the Matrix stock (which had a book value of 55 cents and was then selling on the Alberta Stock Exchange in the range of $1.20 to $1.30 a share) be written down to 30 cents a share. The investment in Athabasca Holdings was unsuitable, Smith also said, and he was concerned that the best of Athabasca's assets, the Cayman Islands bank, had been "hived off" by parent Collective Securities.

Smith attached a letter to Marlin, demanding the insertion of qualified assets totalling $11,250,649, which Ross signed and mailed on July 4. The letter warned that the companies' licences would not be issued until the assets were inserted, and set a deadline of July 31.

On July 23, Smith received the contract companies' quarterly financial statements for the period ending March 1986 and discovered they had incurred additional operating losses of approximately $7.9 million during the first three months of the year. He dashed off a memo to Ross the same day, alerting him to this deterioration. Smith advised that he had telephoned Alberta auditor Burt Eldridge, who told him that Tewfik Saleh "was doing something but would give me no clear indication as to what that something was." He urged that Ross set up a meeting before the end of the month with Saleh, Marlin and Cormie to either work out a satisfactory solution or suspend registration—the deadline for the injection of the demanded assets was just a week away—and concluded: "Clearly, we cannot allow AIC and FIC to do business without registration with the full knowledge of this deterioration in their asset base."

Ross didn't follow Smith's advice. He decided, instead, that the demand for an additional $11.2 million was "sufficient at the time." Nor did a meeting seem necessary. Ross had recently learned that Saleh was no longer responsible for regulating the contract companies. Premier Don Getty had shifted jurisdiction for all financial institutions, including the contract companies, to the Alberta Treasury Department. Ross was well acquainted with Deputy Provincial Treasurer (Revenue) Allister McPherson, the official now responsible, and felt he could deal with him effectively over the telephone.

June 11, 1986

DON GETTY'S DECISION WAS MADE soon after the May election, and on June 11, an Order-in-Council transferred administration of the *Investment Contracts Act* from Consumer and Corporate Affairs to Alberta Treasury. In his declaration to the Code inquiry, Getty explained the shift as follows:

> Prior to becoming premier I had served on various boards of directors of public companies including the board of directors of the Royal Bank of Canada. In assessing the changes to Cabinet I concluded, based on my experience on these boards, that matters related to financial institutions should, if possible, be the responsibility of a single government department.
>
> I was also aware that when Alberta credit unions, North West Trust

Company and Heritage Trust Company, which were all within the responsibility of the department of consumer and corporate affairs, experienced financial difficulties, the department of the treasurer had become actively involved in the financial restructuring.

I therefore made the decision that, if possible, responsibility for financial institutions would be with one government department and I decided that that was the department of the treasurer.

I did not assess the performance of the department of consumer and corporate affairs or its personnel prior to making the decision. I did not discuss this with anyone and it was my own decision. The decision had nothing to do with First Investors Corporation Ltd. or Associated Investors of Canada Ltd. or any company within the Principal Group of companies.

It was a fast and sloppy transfer: the *Investment Contracts Act* was not amended to reflect the change, and the Superintendent of Insurance, still in Consumer Affairs, still held regulatory authority over the sale of investment contracts. Thus Tewfik Saleh remained nominally in charge of the Principal companies—but was, to his distress, immediately stripped of any real authority.

Alfred Kalke, Assistant Deputy Provincial Treasurer (revenue), became responsible for day-to-day regulation of First Investors and Associated Investors. He reported to Allister McPherson, who reported to Dick Johnston, appointed Treasurer after the May election. A couple of dozen Consumer Affairs employees also went over to Treasury, including Director of Trust Companies Reg Pointe and a staff of three auditors, among them Nick Romalo, who had conducted the last contract company examination. Inexplicably, Saleh did not move with them. He learned about the transfer by reading the newspaper, and was subsequently told to stay in Consumer Affairs, reporting to Minister Elaine McCoy, who would relay his information to Treasury.

After the transfer—and on the heels of news that the contract companies' licences were threatened in B.C.—Saleh demonstrated a sudden urgent desire to take action. Department auditors were pressed to complete their examination of the Principal contract companies' 1985 financial statements. In mid-July, audit chief Eldridge (who had remained with Consumer Affairs) delivered interim reports showing a combined capital impairment of approximately $15 million and failure to meet the other Section 8 tests.

Saleh included Eldridge's findings in a forceful report to his new minister—copied to Treasurer Johnston—stating that under the *Investment Contracts Act* he had a duty to act. The July 23 report advised: "I intend to make an official demand to the two companies for a substantial capital injection as determined by our auditors and ask management to provide me with a budget plan and business projection 'indicating what measure they intend to take in order to rectify their loss and deficit position." Saleh said B.C. had refused to renew the companies' registration unless they injected additional capital, and concluded: "It is apparent that FIC and AIC will continue to record losses unless there is massive injection of capital or replacement of low- or non-income producing assets for both companies." He requested "the opportunity for discussion and direction."

Johnston's office sent Saleh's report to McPherson with an "action request" for his comments and recommendations. The matter went down to Kalke with a request that he draft a memo from McPherson to Johnston, and Kalke sent the request to Pointe (the most senior Consumer Affairs official to go across to Treasury). Several versions of the draft bounced among the officials over the next few days. Pointe suggested, among other things, that an independent consulting firm should review the provincial examination reports.

Meanwhile, on July 23—the day Saleh sent his report to McCoy and Johnston—Bill Smith in B.C. reported to Michael Ross about continuing deterioration of the Principal companies' assets. Within a couple of days Ross was on the telephone to McPherson in Edmonton. The first time they spoke, Ross testified: "I said, 'Allister, do you know what's going on?' That's when the process started... He didn't know what was going on, no." Ross said he laid out his office's concerns; if McPherson wasn't worried before the conversation, "he would certainly have concerns after I talked to him." (McPherson, we'll recall, had been a member of the Cabinet financial institutions task force.)

Ross told Ombudsman Owen that he talked to McPherson about hiring a consultant to do an independent review of the two companies. According to Ross, McPherson suggested that B.C. hire the consultant, but Ross declined to do so because "if Allister is dealing with it, he is looking for a consultant who is on the spot." After these conversations, and in receipt of recently completed staff examination reports of the contract companies' 1985 financial statements, McPherson replied to Treasurer Johnston's earlier action request. His August 6 report included the staff reports, which warned:

> It is questionable whether FIC can earn a profit as long as a significant proportion of its assets are either non-performing or else produce an inadequate return. FIC relies heavily on making speculative gains on bonds and stocks for cash flow purposes as well as to reduce operating losses. It is questionable whether FIC can earn a profit on the new money taken in from customers... As long as FIC can attract enough new customers, it is likely it will be able to meet its cash obligations.

McPherson's report advised that "steps must be taken" to correct the companies' capital deficiencies, and continued:

> Contract holders are dependent on the financial ability of the company to repay their investments with accrued interest as investment contracts are not deposits covered by CDIC. It is unknown whether the companies will be able to correct the capital deficiencies. However, from past dealings with the companies, it is very likely that the companies will object to and disagree with the calculations used to demonstrate the deficiency. In view of the likely

disagreement by companies' officials and the seriousness of the situation we plan to use the authority of the Act to engage an independent consulting firm to review the internally prepared audit reports and to provide comments and alternatives for our consideration...

We will proceed accordingly unless you instruct us otherwise and we will provide you with further information and seek your direction after the independent review is completed.

McPherson also outlined three alternatives for dealing with the capital deficiencies: the companies could seek government assistance; new capital could be injected to restore them to economic health; or they could be permitted to fail, resulting in investors losing all or part of their money.

By the time that Johnston—a chartered accountant with an MBA—received this material, he knew a great deal about the Principal companies. He knew about the $23-million asset dump in 1984, the 1985 qualified audits, and the disputes between the companies and government auditors over calculation of the Section 8 tests. He knew about a combined capital impairment of $15 million and that there were conflicting opinions about the value of real estate holdings, and that the properties could be worth a great deal less than the companies claimed. He knew there were a number of non-arm's length transactions within the Principal conglomerate, and that both contract companies had a high proportion of their investments in related companies which in turn had assets of questionable value. Most importantly, he knew they were meeting past obligations with cash invested by new customers.

Johnston testified he wasn't alarmed by these early reports. The problems seemed typical of all Alberta's financial institutions at that time, and would have to be watched; but he assumed that somewhere within the Principal Group of companies were the resources necessary to make the required capital injection. He told McPherson to proceed with his recommendation for an independent audit.

June 25, 1986

THE TRANSFER OF RESPONSIBILITY from Consumer Affairs to Treasury wasn't discovered in the Principal tower until a couple of weeks later. In-house lawyer Lynn Patrick, who heard about it through contacts, reported it to a furious Donald Cormie. "I said that I had spoken to several people about what to do about this sort of thing," Patrick testified. One of those people was Gary Campbell, the Getty advisor who had collected Cormie's $20,000 contribution to the premier's leadership campaign the previous year. Campbell's advice, Patrick said, was to write to Johnston.

"We decided that Mr. Cormie would put down his thoughts in a letter and that I would take the responsibility of writing it," Patrick said. On June 25, Cormie dictated a three-page letter and sent it over to Patrick's office for his signature. Patrick signed, then had a careful look at it. The letter, typically aggressive in tone, included a veiled threat to move the Principal Group head office to another jurisdiction, "to a more responsive and supportive governmental environment." Patrick decided he didn't care to sign such a message, and pulled the letter back. A few weeks later he prepared a milder version. The letter, dated July 30, suggested that regulators would be dealing with both deposit-taking and non-deposit-taking institutions, and would confuse the investment contract companies with deposit-taking companies.

At the bottom of both versions was a notation: "cc: Mr. Gary Campbell." Patrick testified that the notation "wasn't necessarily" made so that Johnston would know Campbell was receiving the letter. He described Campbell this way: "Gary Campbell is a former law partner of mine [at Cormie Kennedy], and a business associate, and a neighbour and a good friend, and someone who I consider has got a pretty good view of what processes you might follow in dealing in a matter like this. I took an opportunity, either at a social occasion or some other time when I met with him, to talk about it."

The letter was not effective. In mid-August, Patrick received a polite reply from Treasurer Johnston—drafted by Al Kalke—assuring him that the decision to transfer all financial institutions to the Provincial Treasurer "was made with considerable thought." The letter advised that Johnston had asked Saleh and Kalke to meet with Patrick, and "Mr. Kalke will call you soon." The letter was sent August 15—the day after a new letter from Tewfik Saleh demanded a capital injection into the contract companies.

July 31, 1986

THE BRITISH COLUMBIA REGULATORS had set a July 31 deadline for injection of the demanded assets. That day, in mid-afternoon, Principal Group finance vice-president Bill Johnson showed up in Bill Smith's Vancouver office, not with confirmation of the injection, but with an argumentative letter to Michael Ross criticizing the assumptions and calculations used by Smith in identifying the $11.2-million asset deficiency.

The letter, signed by Ken Marlin, appealed for more time; the companies were negotiating with Alberta regulators regarding the First Investors deficiency, and wanted to complete an impending transaction which would replace Associated Investors' shares of Matrix Investments with cash. (The "sale" of Matrix shares for cash would not be completed for another half a year, and the deal—among the most outrageous of the transactions —would be achieved by Principal Group, not by First Investors.) As for the valuation of the Matrix shares: "Our external auditors satisfied themselves that 55 cents a share was a fair and reasonable carrying value," so Smith should also accept that figure.

The letter also said that because Principal Group was a private company, "the directors and shareholders of the company indicated they are not prepared to release the financial statements." Instead, Ross was offered Principal Group's annual report for 1984 and was promised the 1985 annual review when completed. That document, we'll recall, was hardly a frank reflection of Principal's circumstances.

As well, the letter said, "you are certainly welcome to review, or have Mr. Smith review, in Mr. Johnson's presence, the audited unconsolidated financial statements of Principal Group." Johnson appeared in Smith's office with the unconsolidated statements—much less revealing than the consolidated ones—and wanted Smith to look at them immediately. Smith declined to take the bait. "I refused to go over them on the grounds that I couldn't possibly make a review in the short time available," he testified. "And I wasn't prepared to have anybody say that I had been able to have a look at them." Smith was furious at the gambit: "I'm not going to be told by a registrant what I'm going to look at and how much time I'm going to spend on looking at it... I wanted to review the information. I didn't want to see it."

Johnson wrote a memo to file after returning home. During the impromptu meeting, he said, Smith "seemed annoyed" about the failure to inject the demanded assets, and he was "<u>very concerned</u>"—Johnson underlined this in his memo—about the two companies' continuing monthly losses.

> He repeatedly asked how the company was planning to overcome these losses. I told him that I didn't foresee a problem until the end of the year because we usually waited until year end to realize security gains and reverse levies. He said this wasn't concrete enough. (ie) too speculative. He needed something more definite. In fact, his comment was "We have to know if Cormie is willing to put some of his own blood into FIC and AIC."

The memo continued:

> 6. The rest of the conversation centered around the fact of the continuing <u>losses</u> in the companies.
> 7. It was clear Bill Smith wanted to protect his ass and go into a "soft" retirement.
> 8. In fact, he stated that he didn't want to get called to court three years from now and have to testify that he allowed renewal of the licences, when the continued losses hadn't been solved in his mind.
> 9. He was going to recommend to Michael Ross, the new Superintendent of Brokers, that they not renew the license until resolution of the continuing losses. He indicated that Ross should get together with Tewfik Saleh, the Alberta Superintendent to resolve the issue.

In other words, he was passing the buck to the new Superintendent as his term of Acting Deputy Superintendent was up on July 31st.

Smith considered the letter delivered by Johnson a tedious delaying tactic. "I was quite satisfied in my mind," he testified, "that I had enough information now that I would recommend that we stopped selling, and that if it came to a hearing before the B.C. Securities Commission, I would have enough information available to sustain it." The next day (August 1) Smith wrote a memo to Ross:

The continued non-arm's length transactions to generate book profits [do] not instil any confidence in me. I would not personally invest $1 in either company and I can see no reason why any other resident in this province would do so if he had possession of the financial information known to us.

I therefore continue to recommend that registration not be issued and that both companies be stopped from selling investment contracts or rolling over existing investment contracts. As you are aware, they are presently selling without registration, which is illegal, and registration should be granted or refused. Continued operation in the twilight zone cannot be encouraged.

This day marked the end of Smith's tour of duty as Acting Deputy Superintendent of Brokers. For the next few months, he commuted between Victoria and Vancouver, working as Ross' part-time assistant, then returned to his job as a policy analyst with the Ministry of Consumer and Corporate Affairs. However, until his retirement in July 1987, he continued to be involved informally with regulation of the contract companies.

Asked during the Code inquiry about Smith's memo, Ross laughed it off. "It made me smile," he testified. "We were both aware, to [some] extent, of what the situation with the companies was. Bill's personal judgment—or any regulator's personal judgment—is not something which should be conveyed specifically to the market. I viewed that as Bill making more of a personal judgment than a regulator's judgment at that time."

The company letter left Ross sympathetic to Principal's situation. "These guys really wanted to comply," he said. "They had to have their say and express their viewpoint, but they really were willing to comply and were making efforts to comply." Ross was "not particularly" concerned about the companies' failure to meet the July 31 deadline, and decided to give them time. "Because really we did not know whether the companies were long-term viable or not at that time. Until we actually knew and had done a complete examination to our satisfaction and to Alberta's, or Alberta had done an examination to our satisfaction, that action would have been, in my view at that time, precipitous." Ross' decision was made four months after the companies' registration had expired.

August 12, 1986

MEMO FROM DONALD CORMIE'S private secretary Jude Halvorson to Diane Cox, Principal director of public relations:[4]

CONFIDENTIAL

Unfortunately, Mr. Cormie's appointment with Don Getty on July 28th was cancelled. Mr. Cormie would like you to try to arrange for another time for them to meet. In this regard, Mr. Cormie will be away from the City from September 8 - October 15, 1986. Agenda items for this meeting will be a

general discussion on the development of the financial services industry in the
Province of Alberta, and further elaborations on DMC's meeting with the
Premier of January 20, 1986.

August 13, 1986

TWO WEEKS AFTER B.C.'S DEADLINE PASSED, Bill Smith called Ken
Marlin to ask again that the unregistered contract companies voluntarily cease
selling. The next morning he took a conference call from Marlin, Bill Johnson and
Lynn Patrick. He told them he was still waiting for the $11.3-million injection, and
set a new deadline eight days away. Afterward, Smith wrote a memo to Michael
Ross:

> I advised that my position had not changed from that outlined in my letter of
> July 4, 1986...
>   Late in the conversation, I was asked who our Minister was, and whether we
> had communicated the situation to him. I advised this was not currently a
> political matter, but that the Chairman of the Commission had been informed.
> Also said that you and I had spoken to Allister McPherson at Alberta Treasury.

After the conference call the Principal officials went up the street to
McPherson's office and were presented with a demand letter from Tewfik Saleh for
a combined injection of $15 million—$3.7 million more than B.C. was asking. The
letter[5] warned that unless the companies took immediate steps to rectify the
$15-million capital deficiency by August 31, "I would have no alternative but to take
appropriate action in accordance with the provisions of the Act."

Now there were two deadlines: B.C. wanted $11.3 million by August 22, and
Alberta wanted $15 million by August 31. The two provinces' calculations had been
based on different information, hence the different figures. Alberta wanted half as
much for Associated Investors as did B.C. ($800,000 as compared with $1,683,000),
but it wanted $4.6 million more for First Investors (approximately $14.2 million, as
compared with B.C.'s $9.6 million.)

Unfortunately, the Principal system was ill-equipped to plug the holes. Donald
Cormie's upstairs company Collective Securities Ltd. owned a Cayman Islands bank
with sufficient assets to do the job, but Cormie didn't care to go that route. Instead, a
scheme was worked out for the exchange of what has become known as the
"back-to-back notes." On August 26, Principal Group issued promissory notes to
First Investors and Associated Investors totalling approximately $11.2 million, as
demanded by B.C. In return, the contract companies issued identical promissory
notes back to Principal—making equal and opposite promises to pay the money
back—but subordinated to the claims of other creditors (including the investment
contract holders).

The next day, Marlin arrived in Vancouver with a letter to Smith reporting that
Principal had inserted the required "qualified assets" into the companies. The letter

claimed that the promissory notes were "collaterally secured by the equity in certain mutual fund holdings of [Principal Group]." Smith immediately wrote to Ross recommending that the contract companies' 1986/87 registration be issued; that was done the next day, with the licences backdated to April 1, 1986. (Company records indicate that during the five months the companies were unregistered in B.C., approximately 1,500 contracts totalling about $12 million were sold there.)

Smith testified that he took Marlin's letter at face value; he made no effort to ascertain that Principal Group's notes had the proper safeguards in place. The notes were only as secure as Principal Group itself, but Smith did not examine its financial statements or review its financial history. Nor did he investigate how cash could be realized, if necessary, from the collaterally secured mutual funds. He did not determine what mutual funds they were, what interest Principal Group had in them, or whether they were unencumbered by prior charges.

Smith's acquiescence seems odd, given his persistent pressure on the companies during the previous months and years. (In 1974, during a similar situation, Smith and then-Superintendent Bill Irwin had refused to allow First Investors to issue a subordinated promissory note payable to Principal Group unless the note included a subrogation clause, requiring the consent of the Superintendent prior to repayment. Registration was blocked until this was included.)

However, as Smith told Ombudsman Owen, he felt in 1986 that Principal contract holders were better off with the back-to-back notes—even without a subrogation clause—than they had been without them. He was relieved that the companies had come through to the extent they had, because "I really [didn't] know and still don't know whether anybody would have ever held a hearing or when they would have stopped selling."

In his report, Owen found Smith negligent in accepting the back-to-back notes, but praised his fast and efficient efforts to come to grips with a complex situation. Owen remarked:

> We have to ask why the effective and appropriate steps Mr. Smith took were not sufficient to resolve the problems. Whereas Mr. Jewitt's failure was at least to some extent individual, Mr. Smith's inability to resolve the situation was largely the result of inadequate and inappropriate responses from those to whom he reported.
>
> It is reasonable to conclude that these inadequate responses and lack of support for his recommendations discouraged Mr. Smith and affected his subsequent actions with respect to the companies, as it is otherwise difficult to explain why he was prepared to accept an injection of "assets" in late August without more than the most superficial review of what was actually tendered.

If Smith and his superior Michael Ross had investigated the new "assets," they would have discovered they amounted to a meaningless exchange of paper. Principal Group was insolvent and had been for two years. Some of the mutual funds claimed as collateral for the company's notes weren't owned by Principal Group at all, but by other Cormie-controlled companies; there was no paperwork authorizing Principal Group to pledge the other companies' assets. All the mutual funds were in accounts margined to the legal limit of 50%, and were subject to a prior charge in favour of the brokers. If the stock market fell, they had the right to sell out part or all of the accounts to cover their losses.

Having satisfied B.C., Cormie and Marlin turned their attention to the Alberta regulators. On August 29—the day after the delivery of the B.C. licences—Marlin sent a letter responding to Alberta's capital demand. He denied that First Investors and Associated Investors had the capital impairments identified in Tewfik Saleh's letter two weeks before, but advised that "pursuant to the request of another regulator" $1,683,000 of qualified assets had just been inserted into Associated Investors and $9,567,649 into First Investors. He enclosed a wildly optimistic nine-month profit plan already in the hands of the B.C. officials and concluded: "We consider the above steps to have rectified the situation."

The $11.3-million injection satisfied Alberta's concerns about Associated Investors, but left First Investors short by $4.6 million. There was no immediate protest. Alberta Treasury auditor Pat Visman was asked to look at the security behind the $11.3 million, and did some of the analysis that Bill Smith had failed to do. On September 9, she reported to Burt Eldridge, back at Consumer Affairs, that the mutual funds backing the promissory notes were already encumbered to 50% of their market value, and there was no guarantee that the contract companies would not at some time repay their subordinated notes to Principal Group without the province's consent.

Eldridge forwarded Visman's memo to Tewfik Saleh and suggested it was time for another talk with company officials. On September 10, Saleh wrote to Marlin, saying that the capital impairment identified for First Investors "still stands," leaving the company in the hole by $4.6 million. Then he bundled up the file and sent it to Al Kalke in Treasury, adding that neither he nor the staff auditors considered the "intercompany paper transaction" to be an acceptable capital injection. He recommended that a provincial lawyer be involved in the joint Consumer Affairs/Treasury review then underway.

18

"I don't think 'do nothing' is an option"

September 12, 1986

Psml's PUBLIC OFFERING BOMBED. Company brass crossed Canada to introduce the offering to major brokers and institutional investors, but half-way through the road show they knew they were in trouble. The Cormies blamed the lukewarm response on a precipitous drop in the stock market while they were making their pitch in Montreal. (On September 12, massive panic sell-offs pushed the Dow Jones industrial average in New York down 86.61 points, or 4.6%, its worst one-day crash since 1929.) "That tended to slow [the offering] down rather dramatically," Jaimie testified.

The markets, however, rallied within days. The PSML offering did not. Two other money management firms had floated more attractive offerings and brokers recommended those to their clients instead.

The real problem, of course, was that PSML was too expensive. Donald Cormie had insisted on valuing the company at $120 million, but there was little interest at that price. The offering was made on a "pro forma" basis, with a number of assumptions about value and earnings, because PSML had only become a stand-alone entity in mid-1986, it had no track record. Potential buyers weren't persuaded by Cormie's predictions of fabulous profits ahead.

Even the underwriter, Wood Gundy, seemed unconvinced. Ken Marlin testified: "I took it upon myself to phone the brokers who were part of the banking group or purported to be part of the banking group for the issue, and found that they had not accepted the pricing and had not really been contacted or consulted by Wood Gundy on the pricing, which convinced me that Wood Gundy themselves had not accepted the pricing. Even though they agreed to go ahead with the preliminary prospectus at $10 a share, I came to believe that they were the first ones to back off because they did nothing with their banking group to make the issue fly at all.

"I subsequently called on Wood Gundy in Toronto and had a frank discussion with them about what happened. True, the market had backed off and true, there had been other issues come out; but I felt strongly that seeing as we had gone that far with it, we should at least take the company public, and discussed with them their willingness to lower the size of the issue and lower the price. I felt that I had had a good meeting with them and that, in fact, they were prepared, at a reduced price and a reduced amount, to take the company public."

John Plaxton, at that time Wood Gundy executive vice-president, confirmed this version of events. "It just wasn't possible to do the issue on a basis that was acceptable to [Cormie]," he told me. "And I remember he discussed the matter with a couple of other investment bankers and they gave him the same view. I'll tell you something. If Wood Gundy had ever known that the conglomerate was in trouble they wouldn't have touched it with a ten-foot pole."

Marlin tried to persuade the Cormies that they should reduce the price by about 20%, but he was over-ruled. "I didn't get support on that idea from Jaimie, who felt strongly that the projections, as shown in the prospectus, were attainable and real and that the pricing at $10 was correct and that he wanted the opportunity to prove that that was correct. So the decision was made that we would pull the prospectus and go back to the marketplace in the spring."

There were renewed efforts to get the Principal Group sales force licenced as securities dealers so they could pitch the PSML shares directly to their RRSP and mutual fund clients. Jaimie testified that if they had been able to persuade the Alberta Securities Commission to grant the exemption, they might have gone ahead at $8 a share. The effort failed, and the offering was pulled in October.

Finance vice-president Bill Johnson, who had seen this as the conglomerate's last chance to raise capital, was bitterly disappointed. "The financial affairs of the contract companies were deteriorating," Johnson testified. "We were foreclosing on more property... The performance of those assets wasn't great by any means, and it was clear that capital was needed... In my own mind, I thought we would be probably approaching the government sooner rather than later for support."

The Cormies attempted to revive the PSML issue the following spring. Johnson, by then deeply alienated from his employer, watched the effort from the sidelines. In his view, when the offering failed in the autumn of 1986, it was "deader than a doornail." So, he believed, was Principal Group.

September 18, 1986

ABOUT A WEEK AFTER TEWFIK SALEH made his demand for capital for First Investors, half a dozen Consumer Affairs and Treasury officials met to discuss the situation. Representing Consumer Affairs were Tewfik Saleh, his assistant Bernard Rodrigues and director of audits Burt Eldridge. Attending from Treasury were director of trust companies Reg Pointe and Deputy Provincial Treasurer Allister McPherson's two lieutenants: Al Kalke, Assistant Deputy Provincial Treasurer (revenue) and Jim Drinkwater, Assistant Deputy Provincial Treasurer (finance).

Jim Rout, a lawyer with the Attorney General's department (civil law section), made an observation which should have been obvious to all: First Investors was insolvent and the company had to be stopped from taking deposits. Incredibly, the regulators paid little heed to Rout's advice, and did not discuss how it might be implemented. Instead, Pointe—responsible for supervising Principal Trust, whose branch offices sold the investment contracts—raised the regulators' years-old dilemma: if the contract companies failed, it would affect the entire Principal Group and could cause a run on the trust company.

Auditor Pat Visman's critique of the back-to-back notes was tabled during the meeting, as was a report prepared by George Kinsman, director of Treasury's loans and guarantees division. Kinsman, we'll recall, was in charge of the financial institutions rescue team, and had been keeping a file on the contract companies since 1984. After the transfer of jurisdiction in mid-June 1986, Kinsman monitored his Treasury colleagues' work. As we have seen, he had a detailed analysis of the companies' financial problems in Drinkwater's hands within a month of the transfer. Kinsman testified that he prepared this July 11, 1986, report, which he called a "high-spot review," on his own initiative. "I passed a copy to Mr. Drinkwater as general background," he said, "and I said something like, 'There is a problem here.' " The review was an alarming portrait of companies in very dire straits.

A month later, after Saleh's August 14 demand letter to Marlin had been drafted, Kalke asked Kinsman to look at it. A month after that, Kinsman handed Drinkwater a critical report on the back-to-back notes; it was this memo that Drinkwater distributed at the September 18 meeting. Kinsman analyzed the companies' nine-month profit plans, rejected most of their assumptions as unrealistic, and concluded that their long-term viability depended on whether Principal Group was able to refinance them as necessary.

At the end of the meeting, it was decided that Eldridge and Rodrigues should draft a letter to Marlin asking the companies to obtain two external supporting opinions: a legal opinion confirming the Principal Group promissory notes were qualified assets under the *Investment Contracts Act*, and an opinion from the external auditors confirming the security behind the notes. Those at the meeting came away with very different impressions about what was to happen next. Saleh said he believed that Kalke was going to review the matter with Deputy Minister McPherson, to follow up on a general feeling that the companies should be shut down. Kalke said he vaguely recalled a discussion about the possibility that the companies were insolvent and that steps should be taken to stop them from receiving new funds, but "I don't recall reaching a consensus, nor do I recall raising it with Mr. McPherson, and getting his specific advice either way." Pointe remembered Rout saying the companies must be stopped from taking new deposits, but said no one else discussed it. McPherson, who wasn't there, testified that he never heard about Rout's advice.

A week later (on September 25) Rodrigues, Kalke, Kinsman, Eldridge and Rout met again to look at the letter drafted to Marlin requesting supporting opinions.

During the meeting, Rout warned that the public relied on the fact that the Alberta government licenced the companies, thus exposing the province to "a degree of liability." Afterward, Kalke sent a hand-written memo to McPherson, marked "Quick Memo, Rush Urgent":

> Our group met on Thursday and I guess I really need your direction on two courses of action:
> (1) send letter as drafted
> (2) first seek an accountant's view on meaning of section 8(b) (copy attached)
>   The issue here is that the group is rather satisfied that these two companies do not meet requirements of section 8(b) [to have at least $500,000 in unimpaired capital]. Jim Rout feels very strongly that regulators have not done their job by insuring that section 8(b) was complied with, although the real serious financial problems of these companies occurred over past couple of years. Jim feels company should tell us with appropriate certification that companies meet requirements. We can then decide on next action. *Frankly, I don't think do nothing is an option.* Guess I feel that matter is very important & perhaps we should arrange another Martin/McPherson (& others) meeting. Kinsman's view is that if companies responded saying they agree they don't meet requirements of section 8(b) then where do we go from there. Again my view is we must do something (we already advised Minister of serious problems) but perhaps we should in advance decide in meeting of Deputies the move if companies say they agree they don't meet requirements. If you agree I will set up meeting. (Italics added.)

During the meeting, Kinsman opposed Rout's suggestion that the companies be asked for legal and audit opinions supporting their back-to-back note strategy; he feared the consequences of making a demand they might not be able to meet. A few days later, Kinsman wrote a memo recommending that Treasury should make up its own mind—without asking the companies for outside opinions—about the acceptability of the subordinated notes as a form of capital. He made this suggestion despite the fact that he had concluded a month earlier that they were not acceptable.

In the midst of this debate, the fact that First Investors was still $4.6 million short—even if the back-to-back notes were found satisfactory—was ignored. The draft letter, requesting outside supporting opinions, was abandoned.

In mid-October, senior Treasury and Consumer Affairs officials held the strategy meeting suggested by Kalke. Allister McPherson and Barry Martin, each backed by support staff, discussed their conundrum: What to do if the contract companies' capital wasn't sufficient and Principal refused to top it up? They again discussed engaging an outside consultant to review the companies' affairs, but made no decision.

October 24, 1986

FOURTEEN MONTHS AFTER THE FAILURES of the CCB and Northland Bank, Justice Willard Estey's report on the disasters was tabled in the House of Commons. His 641-page volume blasted bank managers, directors, federal regulators and the blue-ribbon external auditors who collaborated in hiding or ignoring the banks' financial problems for years. Ironically, Estey dismissed the rationale behind Alberta's promotion of a local financial industry during the Lougheed era. The two banks and other institutions had been supported by Alberta on the assumption that western institutions would be more attentive to otherwise neglected local interests. Estey rejected the rationale:

The evidence reveals that probably there was no neglected niche in this market by the time these banks commenced business [in 1975]. The evidence is more readily open to the interpretation that the improvident lending practices of these banks created a demand from those lacking in the capacity to repay their borrowings and to whom credit should not have been extended.

Estey described "survival tactics" that we now recognize as identical to the secret accounting and asset-juggling games being played in the Principal tower. The two banks' managements persuaded their auditors to value assets according to some projected future value after a prayed-for economic recovery some years later. This "future value" concept was used to justify some of the same flaky accounting strategies favoured by the Principal companies. The banks—like Principal—used their own money to freshen bad loans and avoid writing them down. New borrowers acquired old loans; their names were used in the transactions, but they faced no risk. Sometimes new companies were created to carry old loans; these shell companies held no other assets, and the banks took no guarantees from the people behind the shells. Often, the money "borrowed" in these ways covered not only the principal of the loan being refinanced, but all interest payments as well. Sometimes they simply began accruing the interest anew.

Estey found that Inspector General of Banks William Kennett relied on information provided by bank management and on audited statements signed without qualification by external auditors. Approached by auditors of the Northland Bank for help in resolving a dispute with management on the matter of accrued interest, Kennett would not intervene, and told the two parties to work it out themselves. Under pressure, the auditors bowed to the severely biased judgement of desperate management. Estey came down hard on the auditors who failed in their primary task, to determine whether the bank's financial statements fairly reflected its financial position. Anyone relying on these statements would have been misled.

Three of the Big Eight accounting firms, responsible for approving the two banks' financial statements, were criticized by Estey for their failure to apply proper accounting standards and principles in their audits. During a preliminary investigation by the Institute of Chartered Accountants of Alberta the eight auditors involved defended their judgements. In April 1989, however, they "volunteered to continue not to act as the partners responsible for expressing audit opinions with regard to the financial statements of deposit taking financial institutions" until January 1991. The offer, part of a settlement with the institute designed to avoid lengthy contested hearings, included payment of $210,000 in investigation costs and $425,000 towards the creation of an auditing and accounting research and education fund. The firms involved were Thorne Riddell, which audited the Northland Bank; Peat Marwick, which audited the CCB; and Clarkson Gordon, which audited both banks.

In November 1990, former officers and directors of the CCB, and the accounting firms Ernst & Young and Peat Marwick Thorne—successors to the firms named above—reached a $125-million court-approved settlement with the banks' liquidators in lawsuits launched against them in 1987. In doing so, none of the parties admitted any fault in the banks' collapse.[1]

October 30, 1986

Tewfik SALEH AND THE PROVINCIAL auditors understood instantly the implications of Willard Estey's findings for the Principal contract companies. During another high-level meeting at the end of October, four days after Estey's report was released, Saleh warned senior Treasury and Consumer Affairs officials that outside auditors would now be less willing to accept the notion of future value of real estate. If the companies' deficiencies weren't rectified before the end of 1986, the external audit report would include an unsurvivable going-concern qualification. Even worse, the auditors might decline to issue an opinion.

Minutes taken during the meeting, chaired by Deputy Treasurer Allister McPherson, show the group discussed a variety of factors forcing them to act. First was the sudden unwelcome attention being paid to the companies by regulators in B.C. If Alberta didn't make sure the companies were complying with the *Investment Contracts Act*, it faced the humiliation of seeing their licences pulled in another jurisdiction. There was also fear that the media—so far somnolent—might start asking difficult questions. The revealing First Investors prospectus, filed with the Alberta Securities Commission in 1985 when Christa Petracca tried to take the company public, was still on the commission files; anyone could have inspected it at any time.

The group discussed the painful ambiguity of the financial tests in the Act and decided they no longer wanted to follow a "legal approach" in dealing with the companies. Rather than wrangling with Principal over the interpretation of every point in the Act—and instead of taking the various steps available to them under the Act—the province would take a "business approach," involving the parent company in attempts to work out the problems, and bringing in a consultant to evaluate the companies' ability to continue.

Meanwhile, as feared, B.C. regulators began asking questions again. While the Alberta officials were huddled in Edmonton, Bill Smith was in his Victoria office poring over the companies' latest financial reports. Unaudited statements, covering the three-month period ending September 30, 1986, showed the companies plunging ever-deeper into the hole: their losses for the first nine months of 1986 totalled almost $7 million. On November 5, Smith faxed an alarm to Superintendent Michael Ross in Vancouver. Losses were up, and the companies had failed to provide requested information, Smith said:

> All in all these registrants are going to give continual problems and quite frankly a withdrawal of their registration must once again be considered. I recommend that you contact the Superintendent of Insurance, Alberta or Treasury Board with the view to jointly demand immediately, a further cash infusion in the amount of the combined unaudited losses for the 9 months ($6,973,000).

Ross responded by calling Allister McPherson to ask again that he appoint an independent consultant. Ross testified that he warned McPherson that if Alberta wouldn't hire someone, B.C. would. But neither province demanded more capital.

October 30, 1986

Aᴸ KALKE RECEIVED A LETTER from Margaret Ann Mailman, a contract holder in New Brunswick. Mailman said she understood that her "deposits" with First Investors were not covered by the CDIC, and she was concerned about a Principal consultant's assurances that the money was secure. Who, Mailman asked, actually administered the *Investment Contracts Act*? And who was responsible for assuring the company obeyed regulations?

Kalke replied that the Alberta Treasurer was responsible for administering the Act, with Treasury officials "carrying out the regulatory functions pursuant to the statute." He did not say that First Investors' affairs were a mess, nor that he had learned that very day that the company faced a going-concern note in its upcoming annual audit. Nor did he tell her that the regulators, abandoning their "legal approach," were no longer forcing compliance of the *Investment Contracts Act*. He continued:

> As you can appreciate we are not in a position to advise you whether or not your specific investment with First Investors Corporation is secure. You should regard it as an "investment" rather than a "deposit." We would, however, encourage you to obtain as much information as possible from the company or other investment advisors on the company's financial status.

How was Mailman, or any other investor, supposed to obtain information on the company's financial status when it was locked away at Principal Plaza and in government filing cabinets? Kalke testified that he wasn't aware that the company's financial information wasn't given to the public, and that he didn't recollect Jim Rout's advice, given two months earlier, that the company must be stopped from taking new deposits. His reply to Mailman, Kalke said, was standard practice for dealing with public inquiries at that time.

The following May, as the Mailman family prepared to move to Ottawa, they put more money into First Investors. In the intervening months their minds had eased: "They weathered the storm, so to speak," Mailman testified, "so we relaxed our scrutiny of the company for a while." They purchased another three-month First Investors certificate for $18,000 that matured on August 14, six weeks after the contract companies went down. At that time Mailman and her husband had a total of $101,105 in the company.

November 10, 1986

Ten DAYS AFTER THE DECISION to involve Principal Group shareholders in a "business approach" to straighten out the contract companies, Al Kalke phoned Ken Marlin and asked for a meeting. When Kalke, Tewfik Saleh and Burt Eldridge arrived at Principal Plaza, they were escorted to Donald Cormie's office for a chat. Cormie led, inevitably, with his cycle theory: Despite Alberta's depressed real estate market, they were still on the upside of the 55-year cycle, and good times were just around the corner. He talked about the mutual funds and PSML's public offering, then discussed a plan to syndicate the Rimrock Inn. Then he got to the matter at hand. Eldridge took notes:

> —with more trading in securities and shares on stock market he feels confident that any concerns with investment contract companies will be eliminated.
> —as Government is planning to bail NWT [North West Trust Company] out, and operate the trust company, perhaps the Alberta Government should do likewise with investment contract companies. He indicated that he will raise these matters with the Premier and Treasurer.
> —he indicated he also has some other ideas (not revealed to us) as to how investment contract companies and trust companies can and should operate in Alberta and nationally. He will discuss these ideas with the Premier and Treasurer.

The North West Trust bailout/takeover was at that time in the works through the Treasury department. The Cabinet priorities committee had been briefed a few weeks before, but it would not become public knowledge for another three months. The Eldridge memo continued:

> Cormie also expressed concern that he feels Alberta officials must be feeding bad information about Principal Savings and Trust Company to CDIC. He indicated that CDIC's behaviour has been strange recently and they asked all sorts of questions. He indicated that he has discussed their concerns with Hon.

D. Mazankowski Monday morning and Mazankowski stated he will look into the matter with his colleagues.

(That morning Cormie and Christa Petracca had driven to nearby Vegreville, the home of MP Don Mazankowski, then Deputy Prime Minister, Government House Leader and president of the Treasury Board. Petracca testified that she had arranged the meeting to discuss expansion of the Rimrock Inn, but Cormie went along to complain about a recent increase in pressure on Principal Trust by the CDIC. Cormie testified that he got no subsequent response from Mazankowski. Afterward, Cormie returned to Edmonton to be on hand for the afternoon meeting with the Alberta regulators.)

After an hour with Cormie, Marlin took the regulators on a tour of the facilities, then escorted them down to Bill Johnson's office on the 28th floor. Johnson detailed that meeting in a memo:

After a certain amount of general banter, Al Kalke started the meeting off by saying that the continuing losses in both the contract companies on a month-to-month basis were concerning them greatly. That is, Treasury was thinking of sending in an "independent consultant" to do an audit or valuation of both companies in order to see what the fair market value of the assets are. I made the point that sending in an independent consultant would not accomplish anything since if he wanted to know if the cash values or the net realizable values today of the assets—particularly the real estate—on the balance sheets of FIC and AIC were less than the audited amounts, then I said they didn't have to send in an independent consultant to determine this but I could tell him that factually, in fact, the cash values were less. Sending in an independent consultant would be a waste of time, effort and money on their part. In any event, I said, what would be the final purpose of such a valuation? We all know that an independent consultant would come up with valuations that are less than the "going-concern" value as shown by audited statements. Therefore, what would be the end result? Al Kalke did not answer this.

I also mentioned to him that I would be concerned about having an independent consultant in here at the time because it raises more questions than it answers. The most important thing was to keep the confidence of the public at this point in time and having independent consultants in doing an audit different from our external auditors would raise a number of questions even though the consultants would obviously keep their mandate confidential. As well, I mentioned to Al the fact that why on November 10th would they come in and ask for an independent consultant when our external auditors were already in here starting the year-end audit and by the end of February they would have year-end audited statements and could they not react with these statements? Al Kalke mentioned the fact that by the time the audit was completed and they had the financial statements it would be May and they felt that action was necessary now rather than in May. They also felt that because of the Estey Report, we may not get an audit completed this year. In other words, our auditors may be reluctant to issue an audit report...

We discussed the independent consultant and the continuing loss problem further. Al Kalke also mentioned the fact that he had received numerous letters indicating and asking questions about the high rates the contract companies pay and [the fact there was no CDIC insurance] on these companies.

The regulators identified two basic areas of concern: first, the continuing losses revealed in the monthly financial statements; and second, the true value of company assets (particularly real estate) used to calculate the Section 8 financial tests. Johnson continued:

Again, after much discussion on the recurring loss problem it seemed clear that if the monthly losses could be reduced or eliminated, they would "duck their head" as far as the valuation of the assets was concerned. These were Al Kalke's exact words. In other words, they would be willing to overlook the valuation question if the recurring losses didn't keep cropping up.

Kalke testified that, when he made this remark, he understood that appraisals would show that the companies' real estate, and thus their capital, was even more impaired than the statements indicated. "I simply meant," Kalke testified, "that recognizing that real estate values and the determination of those by appraisals is not exactly precise, and if you take that, you could be on one day and off the next day in terms of the requirements of the statute. I don't mean that to imply that we weren't concerned with the impaired capital position, but what I did try to convey was that if the companies were, indeed, making a very substantial profit month after month, our concern with respect to the impaired capital would not be as great."

After the meeting Johnson and Marlin went upstairs to report to Cormie. Johnson summarized the discussion:

[Cormie] came to the conclusion that there can be no more contract company statements filed showing a loss or, at least, an increase in the loss from the previous month. I explained to him that this would be extremely difficult to do since the non-performing real estate contributed a million dollars a month to the loss of FIC and about three hundred thousand dollars a month to the loss of AIC, and that increasing the yields in a short matter of time was next to impossible. Even after the properties are worked on for some time, the yield may increase only 1% or 2%. He then got into the interest expense problem and thought there was a way that interest expense [additional credits] could be reduced or recorded differently. Again, I told him that if this was the case why has interest expense been recorded in this way for years and years and years and all of a sudden he thinks it has been recorded incorrectly.

The dispute was one of many between Johnson and Cormie, and the coming months would be deeply frustrating for the accountant. The withdrawal of the PSML offering a few days earlier was a bitter blow, and it seemed to Johnson that Cormie wasn't facing up to the corporate crisis. "When you would talk about difficult problems or what I would call things that he didn't want to hear, we seemed to very quickly end up talking about something else," he testified.

A couple of days after the November 10 meeting Johnson wrote a memo to Cormie protesting his remarks:

> You indicated in the meeting with Ken and I that this was the first time you had looked at the financial statement projections for FIC and AIC since the year-end audit. This is not correct since in the spring of 1986 I gave you a position statement on both FIC and AIC with respect to the projected loss for the coming year. This projected loss is basically caused by the non-performing real estate that currently yields one and a half percent, the Matrix shares which yield nothing, the [Principal Neo-Tech] shares which yield us 2%, and the Athabasca shares which yield 4%. These position statements showed a significant loss and my question to you was "what is the corporate strategy with respect to eliminating or reducing this loss."
>
> You received the position statements and immediately went to Christa Petracca and asked for her comments. Apparently she told you that half the information in them was incorrect and presumably you believed this because at no time were you prepared to discuss these statements with me. Of course, the statements were entirely correct and hence the meeting with the regulatory people in November questioning us about the recurring loss problem.
>
> …I sent you the position statements on these contract companies…in the spring of 1986 indicating that because of this collapse in the real estate market (resulting from the collapse of oil prices in February 1986), we were going to be faced with a spread loss problem for a number of years to come…

November 10, 1986

CHRISTA PETRACCA AND DONALD CORMIE decided to go after Hong Kong investors to finance development of the Rimrock Inn. Wealthy islanders, eager to flee before China takes over Hong Kong in 1997, were looking for investments in Canada to take advantage of a lenient business immigration program. Investing in a hotel in the Rockies would facilitate their relocation, while giving Petracca the money she wanted to create her luxury spa. The plan was to fund the development (already improperly underway with contract company money) through the creation of a limited partnership. Marquette Realty and Development Ltd., owned by the contract companies, would transfer the hotel to the partnership at a value of $14.4 million. The partnership would consist of 612 units, priced at $50,000 each, and Marquette Realty would hold 32%; if the rest of the units were sold, it would raise $30.6 million to complete the expansion. This is, oddly, several million dollars more than the project's estimated cost.

An Offering Memorandum was issued by the Rimrock Resort Hotel Limited Partnership on November 10. The document was rushed to Hong Kong with realtor

Gordon Oxley, to be submitted to the Hong Kong Securities Commission for the purpose of obtaining approval to market the offering there. Prepared with the assistance of Cormie Kennedy lawyers (Petracca testified that Bill Connauton was the partner in charge), it was signed by Petracca as president of Marquette Realty and purported to carry the signature of lawyer Lynn Patrick, the secretary-treasurer. Patrick, however, had neither signed nor seen it. Petracca hadn't been able to secure his signature before it was time to send the memorandum to Hong Kong, so had taken the liberty of having Patrick's name typed in and placed within quotation marks.

On November 19 a copy of the document finally caught up with Patrick. When he realized what Petracca had done, he wrote her a furious memo, copied to Cormie:

> I have been advised that the Rimrock Offering Memorandum has been published and issued to the public purporting to have been signed by myself as to the Pro Forma, Balance Sheet and the Representation Certificates. I HAVE NOT SIGNED EITHER OF THOSE DOCUMENTS AND NO REQUEST WAS MADE OF ME PRIOR TO THE ISSUE AND DISTRIBUTION OF THAT DOCUMENT FOR MY APPROVAL OR MY SIGNATURE.
>
> To my mind, this is an extremely serious matter and I would remind you that you are not at liberty to do this under any circumstances whatsoever. As soon as you are back on the 24th of November, I want a meeting with you and Mr. D.M. Cormie about the implications of this action.

This meeting never occurred. "I called Mr. Cormie and asked if he would talk with me about it and he did, but Mrs. Petracca was not there," Patrick testified. He said that Cormie accused him of "exaggerated professionalism," and "that I was being negative about the project, and that I would be delaying it by taking this action."[2] When Patrick persisted, Cormie agreed to withdraw the memorandum and have it redrafted to Patrick's satisfaction. Patrick recommended substantial changes to the version reissued in January 1987, which went back to market the following month.

November 19, 1986

DURING HIS VISIT TO THE PRINCIPAL TOWER Burt Eldridge noticed Principal Group's glossy new 1985 "review" lying around the office. He asked for copies, and passed one on to Al Kalke. Kalke sent it to Reg Pointe, asking for a review, and Pointe passed it to auditor Pat Visman. On November 19, Visman wrote a scathing critique, calling the publication "materially misleading."

Two weeks later, Pointe, at Kalke's request, prepared a memo to go from Deputy Treasurer Allister McPherson to Treasurer Dick Johnston. This memo, almost identical to Visman's original, was delivered to Johnston on December 18. Johnston testified he probably didn't read it until early January, by which time outside consultants had been engaged. The memo raised serious concerns in his mind about the Principal companies, he said. "It certainly confirmed in my mind that the company was being less than honest with the consumers in this province, the investors in this province, by not fully disclosing the financial information." Despite this view, Johnston did not respond to the memo. Treasury took no further action, and the review, a major marketing tool, remained in circulation.

Meanwhile, Marlin and Johnson met with Kalke, Eldridge and Tewfik Saleh and on November 21 to again protest the plan for an independent consultant. Johnson handed over a letter, which he had signed, reading:

> To the best of my understanding, FIC and AIC are prepared to stay within the impaired capital limits placed on them by the *Investment Contracts Act* of Alberta. If any loss incurred in the course of this year and next year reduces or negates unimpaired capital calculations in accordance with the Act, the shareholders in FIC and AIC are prepared to inject capital such that the requirements under the Act are met.

Cormie testified that he authorized Johnson to make this statement to the regulators.

Four days later Kalke wrote Marlin advising that Treasury considered the contract companies' financial situation "serious enough to warrant an urgent examination," and that a consultant would be engaged. But, he said,

> In recognition of the concerns you expressed about having the consultant on your premises, we are prepared to allow the examination to be conducted away from your premises. All information and documentation needed for the examination would be obtained from you by our staff auditors who usually examine your companies' records.
>
> I am sure you will recognize the seriousness of the situation faced by your companies and will co-operate with this examination.

November 28, 1986

DURING THE SUMMER, THE CDIC had ordered that Principal Trust immediately sell off the millions of dollars worth of Principal-managed mutual funds in its portfolio. Its letters went unanswered, and in early September, CDIC president Charles de Léry again sought a response. John Cormie finally replied late that month to say he had obtained a legal opinion supporting the trust company's right to "invest in and lend on the security of unit trusts for which it is the trustee." On October 1, John and others appeared in Ottawa for a most unpleasant confrontation with federal officials. John testified: "We were told flatly that we were to consider ourselves under the federal Act and not under the Alberta *Trust Companies Act* any longer. We were now in a position where CDIC, which has no jurisdiction to regulate us, was regulating us. The Act that we were incorporated under is no longer the Act we were required to operate under."

The next day, Keith Bell, head of the federal trust companies division, wrote a follow-up letter, noting a capital deficiency of $2.5 million. Then, on October 7, de Léry replied to John's claims that the mutual funds were a legal investment. The CDIC's order to dispose of the funds had nothing to do with Principal Trust's trustee relationships, de Léry said, but was because of the related party nature of the transactions. "We are concerned that decisions by PST to acquire or dispose of units of mutual funds managed within the group may be influenced by considerations other than the best interests of PST." He then repeated his earlier demand.

Within two weeks, less than a million dollars worth of the mutual funds remained.

In early December, John, accompanied by Principal Trust general manager George Aboussafy, returned to Ottawa to again protest the CDIC's regulation. They brought with them a 22-page brief, and flogged it to as many bureaucrats and politicians as they could. The paper claimed that Principal Trust was more restrictively regulated than any other financial institution in the country. It also claimed: "Principal Trust has emerged as the only profitable Alberta-based financial institution left. This is due to the foresight Principal Trust had in redirecting its investments from the real estate market to the government bond market."

During a December 11 meeting, Aboussafy told the federal regulators that Principal was projecting a net profit for 1986 in the area of $1.2 million, "sufficient to cover the preferred dividends paid during the year." The regulators were naturally sceptical; the company had incurred a net ten-month loss of $131,000 to the end of October. Just how did Aboussafy intend to achieve such a profit?

There were a number of transactions in the works that would remove a great deal of the problem real estate from the books, Aboussafy confided. And so there were.

19

Creative transactions

PRIVATE AND CONFIDENTIAL

...In 1986 I think you should concentrate on competing directly with Neo-Tech and Matrix and aim for a $5 Million profit, net after tax. This may require some creative transactions, but I think we are in a position to help you with some of these if we keep concentrating on the specific objective...

Memo dated February 10, 1986 from Donald Cormie to John Cormie, with copies to George Aboussafy, Jaimie Cormie, Grant Mitchell and Christa Petracca

THE PRICE OF MATRIX STOCK had risen to about $1.20 by mid-October 1986, and would climb higher before the end of the year. Donald Cormie was looking forward to booking millions of dollars in gains in the Principal Group financial statements. There was a risk, however, that auditors or regulators might question the stock's true value, so a scheme was worked out to head off any such challenge.

During a meeting with Rob Pearce (president of Collective Securities and Donald Cormie's upstairs lieutenant), Cormie and Jaimie laid out the strategy. "Mr. Cormie had indicated that he felt that it would be beneficial to the companies to establish value to the Matrix shares, and he explained a method of doing that, which he termed as 'warehousing' of the Matrix stock," Pearce testified. "The explanation that was given to me, that it was undertaken to establish the fact that Matrix shares did have some value, and that if a third party would accept those shares under this type of an agreement, that that would give a reflection of the value to the marketplace."[1]

The plan was, basically, to park a large block of stock with an outside party, then buy it back a little later at a slightly higher price. The outsider would earn a fee for the service, take no risk, and would provide an invaluable service to Principal. Cormie suggested that Pearce pitch the project to Dr. Charles Allard, Edmonton's famous surgeon-turned-multimillionaire/entrepreneur, and Pearce contacted Allard in late October. In a follow-up letter on November 6, Pearce proposed that Allard's family investment company, Cathton Holdings Ltd., would purchase for cash approximately $8 million worth of Matrix stock (6,154,000 shares) from Principal Group at a price of $1.30 per share. (The stock was then trading at $1.22 a share, a plateau reached the day before because of purchases made by a Matrix vice-president.)

Principal Group, or one of its affiliated companies, would grant Cathton a "put" option giving Cathton the right to sell back the shares four or five weeks later at a penny and a half more a share than it had paid—creating a no-risk profit for Cathton of approximately $92,000. Allard would have the right to sell shares into the market, but only if he could find a buyer willing to pay at least $1.32 a share. At the same time, Cathton would grant Principal Group a "call" option giving Principal the right to buy back any Matrix shares that weren't sold by Cathton within five weeks of acquiring them.

Allard gave the proposal some thought but decided not to get involved at that time. He did, however, pass Pearce on to his broker Angus Watt at securities firm Levesque Beaubien. Watt, manager of its Edmonton office, had already been contacted by Allard's daughter Cathy Roozen (Cathton's vice-president of investments) for his views on the proposed deal. Levesque Beaubien had been willing to act as middleman in the transaction; now it took on the role of buyer.

Watt—another member of Don Getty's leadership campaign team—testified that he was already familiar with the Cormies and their companies. Watt did millions of dollars worth of business with Jaimie Cormie's investment department. His firm handled the purchase and sale of bonds and stocks, and had recently assisted in underwriting a related public offering. CSI held a margined mutual fund account with his firm. Watt also handled a Principal Group employees account which facilitated employees' sales of Matrix shares, and counted some of the Cormie family members among his personal clients.

The warehousing deal was consummated a few days later, much as discussed with Allard. On November 20, Principal Group sold the Matrix shares to Levesque Beaubien at $1.30 each. On December 22, Levesque sold them back at $1.3115. The buyer wasn't Principal Group, however, but Athabasca Holdings, outside of the Principal Group consolidation. Principal Group, relieved of the Matrix stock which it had acquired for 30 cents a year before, booked a gain of $6,149,500. The $8 million paid by Levesque to Principal Group was immediately loaned to parent company CSI, which deposited the money in a Levesque account which had been opened for Athabasca three days earlier. Athabasca put another $800,000 into the account (also borrowed from Principal Group), and the combined $8.8 million was used to buy Government of Canada bonds from CSI. The bonds were used to guarantee Athabasca's obligation to buy the Matrix stock back from Levesque.

A month later, Athabasca sold the bonds and used the money to buy the Matrix stock back from Levesque.

As a result of the transaction, Athabasca was in debt to CSI for $8 million; that was repaid with approximately $3.5 million worth of Matrix shares (at $1.36 each, creating a gain of $213,704 for Athabasca) and the assignment of a $4.5 million debt owed to Athabasca by Collective Securities Ltd. (Donald Cormie) since the sale of the Cayman Island bank in December 1985. Thus, a huge debt owed solely by Cormie slid down into the company he owned jointly with his sons and partner.

Both sides of the Matrix stock transaction (Principal's sale to Levesque and Levesque's subsequent sale to Athabasca) were reflected as open market trades on the Alberta Stock Exchange, located in Calgary. Under exchange rules, insider trading reports were required within 10 days. In this case they weren't filed until February 11, 1987—after a provincial investigator began questioning the transaction. The put/call agreements were not disclosed to the floor governor of the exchange, who authorized the trade.

Levesque Beaubien pocketed $128,157 in share gains and commissions; not a single share was sold on the market while the brokerage held the stock. Watt testified that he considered the stock "expensive" and had no intention of promoting it to his clientele.

Meanwhile, on November 25, Pearce wrote Allard again:

> Thank you for spending the time over the past few weeks to consider our proposal on the Matrix shares, and as well for putting us in touch with Levesque Beaubien. We were able to complete a sale to Levesque on substantially the same basis as discussed with you with the use of Levesque's capital. On a short-term basis, this was a much preferred method given the inconvenience Cathton would have to go through to adjust its investments to accommodate our proposal. Your suggestions on the structure of this transaction were most helpful in setting up the documents for the deal, and we are sure that Levesque will benefit from your suggestions over the period they hold the shares...

Allard and Donald Cormie had been acquainted for decades. Born in Edmonton, Allard was three years older than Cormie, and had also been a sessional instructor (in medicine) at the University of Alberta during the early 1950s, when he began to dabble in real estate development. He became chief of surgery at Edmonton General Hospital in 1955, but abandoned the post in 1969 to pursue his burgeoning business interests full-time.[2]

Allard was the financial wizard that Cormie only pretended to be. Always one canny step ahead of the market, he had unloaded his holding company Allarco Developments Ltd. on Carma Ltd. in 1980, at the height of the Alberta boom. He got prime prices for an incredible grab-bag of companies, which included everything from car dealerships to restaurants to a travel agency to a methanol production company to thousands of acres of land. It also included North West Trust and the affiliated North West International Bank and Trust Company, registered in the Cayman Islands in 1977. Before long, both the economy and Carma were in big trouble, resulting in Carma's asset swap with Principal Group in June 1984, and Cormie's acquisition of the Caribbean bank and an energy company.

Cormie had sent Pearce to Allard with his warehousing proposal because Allard, who had founded Matrix in 1969, was already involved with the stock. Allard's company Allarco Energy, had held approximately two-thirds of the Matrix shares when the company went to Carma in 1980. These passed into Cormie's hands during the 1984 swap with Carma. Allard kept a portion of the remaining Matrix shares, largely through Cathton Holdings. (Allard was Cathton's majority shareholder, with the balance held by five of his six children). Government records indicate that at the end of November 1985, Cathton held approximately 9% of outstanding Matrix shares.

Until that time, Allard's son-in-law Harold Roozen (president of Allarcom Ltd.) sat as a member of the Matrix board of directors. In late 1985, we'll recall, Matrix issued another 14 million shares from its treasury to Allarco Energy, in a swap for some of Allarco's oil and gas interests. The new shares severely diluted the Allards' interest in the company, and Roozen left the board. Cormie replaced him with Paul Lefaivre, recently retired as vice-president of the Royal Bank, who became Matrix chairman.[3] Soon afterward Cormie's 31-year-old son Neil was appointed president of the company.

After these changes, Cathton Holdings, Allard and family members slowly sold their shares into the ever-rising market: a hundred, a thousand, a couple of thousand, 5,000 at a time. The exception to this pattern occurred during February 1986, when Neil Cormie joined the Matrix board. On February 12 the Allard group sold a total of 10,500 shares into the market; the next day they sold 1,000; and on February 14 they sold 20,000 in a single transaction. The entire lot was picked up by Allarco Energy (then owned by Athabasca Holdings and controlled by Donald Cormie). This purchase of Allard's 31,500 shares was Allarco's first significant entry into the buy side of the public market. Over the next few months, it would buy a few hundred shares of Matrix here, a couple of thousand shares there, but it sold far more than it bought.

This changed in August 1986, shortly after B.C. regulators began questioning the value of Matrix stock held by the Principal contract companies. Suddenly Allarco was buying more than selling, as was Principal Group, the major shareholder. Pearce, an Allarco director, was in charge of Allarco's purchases. "Mr. Cormie had indicated that there should be somebody in the market willing to pick up the Matrix shares when there is a significant quantity put onto the market, either through employees getting them out of their bonus plans and wanting to sell them, or possibly another shareholder," Pearce testified. He routinely purchased stock in 2,000-share lots through the brokerage house Merrill Lynch. Pearce would put an order in for 2,000 shares, wait until it was filled, then bid again for more. "From time to time [Cormie] would come down to my office, you know, if for some reason there was no bid on the market to purchase shares, he would come down and want to know what's going on. Or somebody from James Cormie's department would come over and ask what's going on." The procedure could be a pain for the stockbrokers; if a block of, say, 10,000 shares became available, they would have to watch Pearce nibble it away in five separate bites.

Pearce made his purchases through Merrill Lynch broker Muriel Meier, based in Edmonton. Meier had been dealing with Cormie since the mid-1970s. She handled a handful of Canadian and U.S. dollar accounts for him, his wife Eivor, Cormie Ranch and Estate Loan and Finance. As well, the family's self-administered RRSP plans were held at her firm. Meier testified that a trading account had been opened there for Allarco in December 1985, shortly after it had acquired the additional 14 million Matrix shares.

During the Code inquiry, Pearce and the Cormies portrayed Allarco's interest in Matrix stock as a harmless effort to provide "liquidity" to the stock. Nonetheless, the inquiry heard damning evidence that Allarco's buy-backs were part of a larger scheme which effectively drove the price of Matrix stock upwards over many months. John Kolosky, who testified at the inquiry as an expert in market manipulation, analyzed the stock's activity and concluded that insider trades through Allarco and Principal Group created a false and misleading appearance of public trading and a public price. Prices climbed from 30 cents in late 1985 to a peak of $1.74 in mid-March 1987, an increase of almost 600% over 16 months. Every 10 cents of value in the price of Matrix shares produced a change of approximately $6 million in the market value of the 60-million-share block controlled by Cormie. (See DIAGRAM 9: *Trades of Matrix Investments Ltd. on the Alberta Stock Exchange between 1984 and 1987.*)

Kolosky has impeccable credentials. From 1979 to 1988, he was director of market operations at the Toronto Stock Exchange, responsible for market surveillance and for supervising and directing daily operation of the trading floor and its 150-person staff. For eight years before that, he was chief examiner on the Montreal exchange. Kolosky scrutinized hundreds of pages of evidence—stock trades recorded to the minute and second, insider reports, order tickets, a bid/ask summary and transcripts of several participants' testimony—and prepared a lengthy report on the Matrix scam.

During the period between August and November 1986, trading by Allarco and Principal Group in Matrix stock "was such that it was starting to get closer to a very clear indication of manipulation... The period from December 1986 to July 1987 there's no question in my mind that the market was manipulated," Kolosky testified. "In these situations here, it seems quite apparent that the orders were put in with the direct intent to maintain the market at a certain price, and in certain instances to move the market up, and they were put in by design to a certain extent rather than just being casual orders coming into the marketplace."

The standard of proper conduct for a free market is the interaction of many buyers and sellers operating at arm's length, with no single participant or associated group of participants being able to influence the price through their trading practice. But the public float of the Matrix stock was tiny, and by February 1986, all but 2.1% of the stock was held by Cormie-controlled companies (Allarco Energy, CSI, First Investors and Associated Investors, Athabasca Holdings and Principal Group). A year later, in February 1987, there was virtually no stock in public hands—only a minuscule four-fifths of one percentage point. Kolosky found no evidence of competition from outsiders "that would have caused them to bid [the price] up that high."

Kolosky found that insider trading through Principal Group's executive and employee stock bonus schemes further reduced the Matrix public float, facilitating the market manipulation. Cash-poor Principal Group gave salaried employees shares of Matrix and Principal Neo-Tech stock in lieu of salary increases; a handful of Matrix executives also received Matrix shares every time they put some of their own money into the stock. Even unionized employees at the Red Deer brewery agreed to accept Matrix stock in partial satisfaction of wage increases. The bonus schemes generated the trading of approximately 1.8 million shares—or about 41% of all the shares traded on the open market—during 1986 and the first half of 1987.

Stock bonus plans are usually used as vehicles to increase the public float in a stock; the company provides staff with stock already in hand and over time the employees sell it back into the open market. In this case, however, Principal Group went into the market to buy the necessary shares, at ever-climbing prices, to feed the bonus program. When employees sold their holdings into the market, they were snapped up by Allarco Energy, thus further reducing the public float. "This activity, coupled with the dominance in the market by Allarco and [Principal Group], assured market control and a steady increase in share prices," Kolosky said. "It is a common practice and almost a necessity for the public float to be reduced to a minimum in order to implement a scheme of market manipulation."

Principal Group's purchases of stock for the employee plan were handled by bookkeeper Diane Stefanski, through the Department 8 accounts. Stefanski testified that in September 1986, she was instructed by Jaimie Cormie to start buying the Matrix shares through a dealer at the brokerage firm Alfred Bunting. On September 11, the first day Stefanski did so—and the day after Tewfik Saleh wrote to Ken Marlin pressing his demand for a capital injection into the investment contract companies—$59,999 in Principal Group promissory note money was sent to Alfred Bunting to cover the purchase. Over the next couple of months, Stefanski testified, "there wasn't much of a market, so I was basically picking up everything that was on the market."

Kolosky focused on market domination during the period from December 1986 to July 1987, but he also found clear examples, going back as far as July 1986, of the Matrix price being pushed up. There were 93 "destabilizing trades"—share purchases made at a price above the preceding trade—during that period. Kolosky found that these trades laid the groundwork for several large block transactions, beginning with the $8-million deal with Levesque Beaubien on November 20 discussed earlier in this chapter. On November 18, Terry Myers,[4] a senior Matrix executive, bought 3,400 shares at $1.25, in blocks ranging from 100 to 1,000 shares. This took Myers 10 separate purchases, although five blocks were acquired from the same person at the same moment. The next day, Myers increased his bid to $1.26 and bought another four blocks totalling 9,000 shares.

During the morning of November 20, Myers kept the market at $1.25 bid and $1.29 offered. Then, at 1:19 p.m., 6,154,000 shares crossed the floor from Principal Group to Levesque Beaubien at $1.30, the price originally proposed to Dr. Allard two weeks earlier. Normally, such a trade, where buyer and seller are represented by the same broker, can only be executed on or in-between the market quotes; however, because the cross was treated as a "cash transaction," this restriction did not apply. Nonetheless, the outstanding $1.29 offering was satisfied 12 minutes after the Levesque block trade by Donald Cormie's son Bruce, who continued to buy Matrix shares for the rest of the day. His eight purchases totalled 14,000 shares, and upticked the price to $1.33.

Kolosky said this trading activity was "suspect," especially because of the close relationship between Myers, Bruce Cormie and Allarco.

> This trading appears to have prepared and maintained the market price of
> Matrix shares in order to justify the cross price of $1.30. The probability that
> the trading by Allarco, Terry Myers and Bruce Cormie is coincidental is highly
> unlikely. Since "cash transactions" do not set the high, low or last sale price, it
> was necessary to move the market to the cross price level so that the cross
> would appear to be within the market.

This trade in the public market, and other large block trades which followed, "unduly affected and created a false impression of public market activity in Matrix shares," Kolosky concluded. There was nothing wrong with Levesque holding stock for a client—large block trades are common enough—but "it is my opinion that none of these trades should have been transacted through the facilities of the market. I can further discern no reasonable business purpose for accomplishing these trades in the manner which they were completed."

Inspector Bill Code concluded that Cormie was behind the stock bonus plans and the large block trades.

> The purpose of the plan conceived by Donald Cormie, the evidence tends to
> show, was to create value, both by creating market activity through employee
> stock plans and initiating several large block trades through the market over a
> 6-month period. The creation of such value was necessary, for as noted else-
> where Matrix shares were used as currency within the Principal Group and had
> even been converted to loans... Having been transferred at prices of $1.30 or
> more with consequent large accounting gains, it was important that the shares
> stay at such prices at least until completion of the 1986 audit.

A year after delivery of Code's report, the Alberta Securities Commission issued a notice of hearing to Donald Cormie, Jaimie Cormie and Rob Pearce charging them with one of the most sweeping sets of stock manipulation and insider trading charges in Alberta history. The hearing, scheduled for March 1991, was aborted on its first day after the Cormies negotiated settlements with the commission agreeing not to trade on the Alberta Stock Exchange: Cormie for 10 years, and Jaimie for three years. Pearce,[5] who had settled with the commission two weeks earlier and agreed to testify against the Cormies, also agreed to cease trading for one year. The commission is a regulatory body responsible for protecting the investing public; the three settlements were not considered admissions of guilt, but a means of avoiding what promised to be a lengthy and costly hearing.

October 1986

PRINCIPAL TRUST GENERAL MANAGER George Aboussafy was a devoted Principal employee. He had carried Bruce Cormie's banner at the Conservative nomination meeting back in 1984; initiated the General Equities shopping centre deal with his Vancouver contacts in 1985; recruited Lance Frazier to Christa Petracca's SWAT team, then briefed him on problem real estate in both his own trust company and its sister contract companies. Then in late October—shortly after the CDIC began pushing again for a capital injection into Principal Trust—Aboussafy conceived another deal to relieve the trust company of trash real estate still on its books.

This plan, he testified, originated during a lunch meeting with Cormie Kennedy lawyer Bill Connauton.

Connauton had done plenty of work for the Cormie companies in the past year: He provided opinions interpreting the *Investment Contracts Act*, assisted Christa Petracca in the Rimrock Inn offering memorandum and was involved in the effort to take PSML public. But Cormie seems to have treated him as something of a errand boy. In a biting note, written at the end of October 1986, Cormie criticized a progress report from Connauton which requested Cormie's instructions on how best to have Principal Consultants registered as a broker dealer: "Bill: I assume C&K [the Cormie Kennedy law firm] have the best 'informal contacts' with the [Alberta Securities Commission] and would be able to 'advise' me how to proceed—not visa versa. I mentioned before we do not want you to keep asking for 'instructions' but to keep working on the matter until we succeed."

Aboussafy testified that during lunch with Connauton he happened to mention a warehouse/office building in the southeast end of Edmonton which he'd had his eye on. The property, the Derrick Plaza, was located in the Strathcona Industrial Park; it was 87% vacant, but Aboussafy said he thought it had "great potential." It had been built by a consortium of Edmonton businessmen in 1981—including, coincidentally, a 5% interest held by Don Getty's company D. Getty Investments Ltd. before he became premier—but was foreclosed on by the Toronto Dominion Bank in 1984. Aboussafy said he told Connauton he had made a offer on the building—the deal involved a swap of Principal Trust's second mortgage on another property—but the bank had turned him down. "And Bill said, 'Well, I know who bought the building!' I said, 'Fine, if you think they would take this deal...' " Aboussafy said he devised a scheme which involved the owner accepting $2.5 million in cash (the building's list price) and some real estate at a book value of $3 or $4 million. Connauton returned to his office and called his long-time client Jim Hunter, the Edmonton developer who was in the process of buying Derrick Plaza.

Connauton corroborates Aboussafy's version of events. He was not called to testify at the Code inquiry, but during a 1990 interview he took responsibility for bringing Hunter and Principal Trust together. "I said [to Hunter], 'Well, are you interested in selling your position?' He said, 'I'm always interested in selling.' That's Mr Hunter's game. He's a developer, he's a real estate man. So I said, 'Look, George Aboussafy is the guy who is interested, I'll call him, get him to call you.' Which I did... And so they called me, came up with a deal, and then the instructions were given to the lawyers."

This narrative assumes rather more significance in the light of subsequent events. Two months later, Principal Trust purchased Derrick Plaza from a numbered company controlled by Hunter in exchange for $2.58 million cash ($80,000 *more* than its list price), as well as several owned properties and mortgages at their book value of $3,871,413—an apparent total purchase price of $6,451,413. However, the properties and mortgages had been reserved down to about $800,000 on the trust company's books. Hunter testified he considered them close to worthless but was willing to take them off Principal's hands at book value, having been assured by Connauton the transaction was not illegal.

With the real estate discounted to zero, the real price Principal Trust paid Hunter for the building was the $2.58 million cash. Incredibly, Hunter had bought the building from the Toronto Dominion Bank for $1.75 million just minutes before transferring it to Principal Trust, and the flip generated an apparent instant profit of $830,000 (less transaction costs). Paperwork on the two sales was dated four days apart, but the transfers were registered on the same day, one right after the other.

If that's all there was to this transaction, we might conclude that Hunter was a wily businessman, that Principal Trust was a desperate sucker, and that Connauton, seemingly a lawyer with easily shifting loyalties, stood by while Principal, also his client, was ripped off. But there's more to the story.

First, Principal executives differ as to who knew what about how much Hunter paid for the building. Aboussafy and Donald Cormie testified that they weren't aware Hunter paid $1.75 million; Jaimie Cormie said the speculation was that he'd paid about $2.2 million; John Cormie swore an affidavit of transfer that the present value of the property was $6,451,413. Finance vice-president Bill Johnson, on the other hand, testified he knew exactly what Hunter was paying, and he complained to Jaimie about it prior to closing. The deal went ahead anyway.

In November, before the deal closed, Aboussafy says he called Hunter with another proposal. "We want you to buy some mutual funds," Aboussafy said. He assured Hunter of a generous profit. Aboussafy testified that the deal was Donald Cormie's idea, and Cormie put it to him well after the Derrick Plaza purchase had been settled. "He proceeded to explain a mutual fund purchase and a Matrix share purchase, that he was looking for individuals who had somewhere between $250,000 and a half a million dollars and asked if I knew any. At that point, you know, I reminded him that we were involved in the Derrick Plaza transaction and that I would ask the person we were dealing with, Mr. Jim Hunter, if he would be interested in such a transaction." The deal, a more complicated version of the stock warehousing scheme entered into a few days earlier with Levesque Beaubien, involved PSML-managed mutual funds as well as a large block of Matrix stock. In this case, the Matrix purchase did not cross the floor of the Alberta Stock Exchange.

Having secured Hunter's preliminary okay, "I went back to Don Cormie," Aboussafy testified, "and said that Mr. Hunter was interested as long as he was guaranteed no risk, and the return that he was looking for... Mr. Cormie said, 'Fine,' and asked me to turn that over to Lynn Patrick." Aboussafy testified that he went to company lawyer Patrick: "I explained my side of the transaction to him, what I was doing with the Derrick Plaza, and then I gave him the conceptual side of the other transaction and said that Mr. Cormie had asked him to go ahead with it." Aboussafy said he didn't know precisely how Cormie's deal would work, and assumed that Patrick went back to Cormie for instructions.

Patrick vehemently rejects this version of events. He testified that he knew nothing about the Derrick Plaza side of the transaction, and was involved only in putting together the paperwork for the Matrix/mutual fund purchase as instructed by Jaimie Cormie. Jaimie testified that Patrick handled the deal, and he wasn't involved until the closing.

Here's how the Matrix side of the transaction worked: On November 30 CSI (the Cormies and Ken Marlin) loaned $2.5 million to Hunter, who used the money to margin the purchase of $5 million worth of Matrix shares from First Investors. A total of 3,846,153 shares were purchased at $1.30 a share from First Investors, which loaned the other $2.5 million to Hunter to complete the sale.

Although the purchase appeared, from the perspective of First Investors, to be made on a 50% margin, Hunter had borrowed every dollar from Cormie-controlled companies. Hunter was at no risk; recourse on the First Investors loan was limited to the Matrix shares themselves, and put and call agreements were signed stating that CSI would buy the Matrix stock back from Hunter, at the same $1.30 he had paid for it, in a year and a half.

Then another Hunter-controlled company "bought" $5 million worth of PSML-managed mutual funds. The funds were purchased at the extraordinarily low margin of 10%; Hunter put up a mere $500,000 in cash and borrowed the other $4.5 million from First Investors. Again, he was at no risk. If the value of the stock went down, Cormie's companies would take the bite. The mutual fund units were also to be sold back to CSI in a year and a half, at the same price Hunter had paid for them—plus a "matured return" of $187,500, a 25% per annum profit on the $500,000 he put into the funds. Hunter's $500,000, documents show, was part of his profit from the Derrick Plaza flip.

In the end, Hunter's companies became the "owner" of $10 million worth of Matrix shares and mutual funds; the entire acquisition was funded with money from Cormie-controlled companies. Hunter, active in the Young Presidents Organization, was a prominent Edmonton millionaire and well acquainted with Donald Cormie; but both say they don't remember talking together about this bizarre set of deals. (See DIAGRAM 10: *The Hunter/Derrick Plaza Transaction.*)

Most of the parties in these transactions were represented by Cormie Kennedy lawyers. Senior partner Edwin Cook acted for the Toronto Dominion Bank during the Derrick Plaza sale to Hunter; Bill Connauton, assisted by partner Del Lewis, represented Hunter and his numbered companies during both his purchase and subsequent sale of Derrick Plaza, as well as during the Matrix/mutual fund deals. Principal lawyer Lynn Patrick represented Principal during the Matrix/mutual fund deals. A lawyer from a different law firm represented Principal Trust during the property purchase, but he was bypassed during the final phase of the acquisition. A $2-million-plus cheque, final payment for the building, was not sent, as would normally be the case, to the trust company's outside lawyer for dispersal. Instead, it went directly to Lewis with instructions that $500,000 be used toward the purchase of the mutual funds.

The three-part deal was a "creative transaction" deluxe, with the potential to help solve three of Principal's most crucial problems. It would remove millions of Matrix shares from First Investors, by that time under severe regulatory pressure, and allow the contract company to book a profit on the increased "value" of the stock; it would boost the amount of mutual funds under management by PSML by $5 million; and it would remove almost $3.9 million worth of bad real estate and mortgages from the trust company books. (Unfortunately, when it came time to do the financial statements, the auditors would not allow the trust company to eliminate existing reserves booked against the real estate transferred to Hunter, and the intended "gain" of $3 million disappeared.)

Curiously, the numbered company through which Hunter bought and sold Derrick Plaza (we'll call it Company #1)[6] was not the same numbered company which margined the mutual funds and was intended to receive the profit of $187,500 (which we'll call Company #2.) In effect, the owners of Company #2 received $500,000 belonging to the owners of Company #1, and used it to generate a massive profit for themselves. Hunter did not want to say who the beneficial owners of either company were, but confirmed during the Code inquiry that there were different people in each company. "That happens all the time," Hunter said, "and the answer is because we had accounting and tax advice that that would be a good way to do it."

During a bizarre interlude in the hearing, lawyers made lists of the categories of person who were *not* the beneficial owners of the companies: they were *not* owned by any Cormie family member, any employee of Principal Group or its associated companies, any government-elected representative, or any government employee—

but Hunter's lawyer refused to let him answer whether the owners included any person "in close association" with any of the above. The names were given in confidence to some of the lawyers attending the hearings, and investors' counsel Robert White appealed to Inspector Code to make them public, arguing: "There is still more to this than meets the eye." After discussion with other lawyers, White withdrew his appeal.

Corporate registry records indicate that Company #2 (356539 Alberta Ltd.) was incorporated on November 13, 1986—just days before the Matrix/mutual fund side of the transaction was completed—by John Cross, another Cormie Kennedy lawyer. Cross was replaced as director by his partner Connauton on December 30, the day of the Derrick Plaza flip. Connauton remained sole director of the company until July 16, 1987, a week before the Matrix/mutual funds deals were unwound as a result of the contract companies' collapse. At that time Jim Hunter became sole director and shareholder.

When the mutual fund deal was unwound, Company #2, which "owned" the mutual funds, received Company #1's $500,000 plus interest to date of $41,438; the total of $541,438 was distributed to "given individuals"—the beneficial owners of Company #2—who remain unknown.

During the Code inquiry, various Principal executives were at pains to argue that the Derrick Plaza transaction was not connected to the Matrix/mutual fund purchases. Bill Code found in his report that the evidence was inconclusive as to whether the deals were linked. He reached this conclusion despite Hunter's testimony that in his mind the deals were definitely linked. "I accepted all of that because I thought that if I didn't, the whole transaction might be jeopardized," Hunter said. "I really didn't spend a lot of time in thinking about the extra Matrix thing. All I was concerned about was that there was no liability on our part."

Bill Connauton agreed during an interview that the deals were connected; he portrayed the Matrix/mutual fund part of the transaction as a "deferral" of the payment of Derrick Plaza's purchase price. "It means that instead of getting all cash on the dash, Mr. Hunter received a portion of the purchase price later on in time," Connauton told me. "It's like me saying to you, 'I'll buy your property for $2 million, I'll pay you $500,000 cash now, and I'll pay you the other $1.5 million in two years. This is how I'll pay it to you.' The problem is people throw around this word 'profit' like it's a dirty word, and in fact there was an agreed purchase price, and it was to be paid in certain ways. One of the ways was cash, one was by transfer of other properties Principal Group had, and the third was by deferral payment which was secured by mutual funds." He, too, refused to identify the beneficial owners of the Hunter companies.

Letters show that Cormie Kennedy lawyers saw a connection between the deals, and they suggest that some of the Principal executives did as well. A letter from George Aboussafy to Del Lewis, accompanying a huge cheque to complete the purchase of Derrick Plaza, instructed that $500,000 was to "be used to conclude the mutual fund purchase in connection with the Matrix share sale." It continued:

"Should you have any questions with respect to the above, please do not hesitate to contact the writer or Mr. Lynn Patrick at the Principal Group of Companies."

Aboussafy testified that this letter was written on Patrick's instructions; Patrick denied it and once again insisted he knew nothing about the Derrick Plaza side of the deal. However, Lewis' letter of reply, addressed to Patrick, enclosed copies of documents dealing with the Matrix/mutual fund purchases and was captioned "Re: Derrick Plaza Building." Patrick testified that he never noticed the caption, and could not account for it being there.

Part of Aboussafy's enthusiasm for Derrick Plaza, he said, sprang from his conviction that the property could be quickly leased by someone with the right connections. Hunter appeared to have those connections, and during negotiations told Aboussafy he was close to signing leases totalling 60,000 to 75,000 square feet with two Alberta government-funded media outlets: Access Network and radio station CKUA. Leases of that magnitude would take up more than half the available space, boosting the building's value by millions of dollars. To encourage delivery of these tenants, the deal with Hunter included a generous leasing agreement with a third Hunter-managed numbered company (356538 Alberta Ltd.) There was potential for up to $750,000 in commissions if he could fill the almost-empty building. That same numbered company also received an agreement to manage the property on behalf of Principal Trust. Again, the beneficial owners of this third company are unknown, but corporate records show that it, like Company #2, was incorporated by Cormie Kennedy lawyer John Cross on November 13, 1986, and Connauton subsequently became its sole director.

During cross-examination, Hunter said that the two government-related leases were actually being negotiated by Edmonton entrepreneurs Les Mabbott and Graeme Young. Mabbott is another prominent Tory with close ties to Premier Don Getty, dating back to the early 1970s when he was deputy minister of intergovernmental affairs when Getty held that portfolio. In 1985, Mabbott was co-chairman of Getty's leadership campaign, and during the 1986 provincial election served as party campaign chairman.

Mabbott is also the man who, within days of the 1986 election, began assembling land for construction of Edmonton's downtown CityCentre luxury office tower, then sold the lots to Olympia & York Developments after persuading the Alberta government to become the main tenant. The province signed an expensive 37,500-square-metre lease in the still-to-be-completed complex without calling for tenders for office space. Around the same time, it also leased more than 11,000 square metres in Sterling Place, indirectly owned by Mabbott's company LPI Development Corp. Ltd. This, too, was done without a tendering process.[7]

When I contacted Mabbott to ask about his involvement with Derrick Plaza, he refused to answer several key questions. He did say, however, that he was a long-time business associate of Hunter's, that he became property manager of Derrick Plaza on a fee basis and that "there's no question I made some money on Derrick Plaza." During the negotiations leading up to Hunter's sale to Principal

Trust, Mabbott provided an appraiser with an opinion of value for Derrick Plaza of more than $8.7 million, based on replacement cost. Mabbott's opinion was provided after it was understood that Mabbott would manage the property once it passed to Principal Trust.

Mabbott said that Hunter "talked to me about our company managing the property and that was understood that we would, and he also then talked to me about—or he and an appraiser talked to me about—'How would you appraise the property?' And I said, 'On what basis are you looking for an evaluation?' And as developers they asked me to come up with a replacement evaluation. So I wrote a letter to somebody, and I forget who it was, whether it was to Jim, or to an appraiser; you know, at that time not knowing that Principal's involvement meant anything. Not that it would have made any difference, I just said, 'Well, I'm not telling you what value is, what I'm telling you is what it would cost to replace that building,' and then therefore I did a letter. So from that point, my name became associated with the project. But that was fair game because I was property manager or was either going to be or was, I don't know. But I did have that kind of involvement..."

By early 1987, Derrick Plaza lease negotiations with the Alberta government shifted from the media outlets to province-owned Alberta Government Telephones. In August 1987, AGT-funded Alberta Telecommunication Research Centre leased 11,853 square feet. AGT was considering taking another 60,000 square feet—according to Donald Cormie's son Neil, there was actually a letter of intent in hand—but the deal fell apart after the Principal collapse.[8] Another tenant was Lloyd McLaren, manager of Premier Getty's blind trust, who rented space soon after the Principal Trust purchase.

In March 1987—after it was understood that Principal Trust would not be able to book the expected gains on Derrick Plaza—George Aboussafy tried to flip the property again. A letter from Fred Jaremchuk, vice-president of General Equities of Canada—the Vancouver company that had taken over some of Principal's bonds and bad real estate during the shopping centre transaction a couple of years earlier—discussed its purchase for $4.2 million on behalf of a life insurance company. The purchase was subject to occupancy of about 90%.

This deal fell through, and the largely vacant building was still in Principal Trust's hands when the conglomerate collapsed.

December 24, 1986: 9:50 a.m.

PRINCIPAL GROUP AND LEVESQUE BEAUBIEN were so pleased with the outcome of their Matrix share swap that they agreed to do it again, for a longer period than the first time. The first deal was concluded on December 22; two days later Levesque purchased another $8 million worth of Matrix shares from Principal Group. This time the transaction took place on the basis of $1.50 a share, 20 cents higher than the value used at the conclusion of the first deal two days earlier. The trade, on December 24, was again recorded as an open market trade on the floor of the Alberta Stock Exchange.

This time CSI (the Cormies and Marlin) agreed to buy back the stock; however, the spread was much greater than before. Levesque had the right to sell the shares back to CSI at $1.57, seven cents more than it paid for them, in May 1987.

In the weeks between Levesque's first purchase in November, and the second transaction in late December, the stock's market price was held at $1.30, almost exclusively by Allarco purchases. Between December 22 and December 24, Allarco continually increased its bid from $1.30 to $1.45. The last purchase, at $1.45, was at 9:45 a.m. on December 24. Five minutes later, Principal Group sold 5,333,333 shares to Levesque at $1.50.

The sale of these shares, acquired at 30 cents, generated a gain of $1.20 a share—or a total of $6.4 million.

During the four months Levesque held the shares, it sold only 4,700. Then, on May 1, as agreed, Levesque put the rest of the shares to CSI, resulting in CSI paying $8,366,000 to Levesque. Levesque manager Angus Watt testified that when he asked why Principal was doing the transaction, he was told "for internal reasons." He did not inquire further. Kolosky sharply criticized Watt's involvement in the transaction: "Without the expectation that the shares would be distributed to the public, there was no benefit to the transaction than to create a false impression of its being an arms-length transaction handled by the public market."

Other parties were brought in on a couple of other Matrix/mutual fund warehousing deals similar to the ones worked out with developer Jim Hunter. These transactions were with East West Canadian Investments Inc., a syndicate of investors whose shares were registered in the name of a nominee, Edmonton lawyer David G. Finlay, who became a member of the Matrix board of directors in April 1987. The beneficial owners of East West are not known; Inspector Bill Code concluded there was no evidence that the company was in any way related to the Principal Group. Unlike the Hunter transaction, the Matrix shares warehoused in the two East West deals were traded across the floor of the Alberta Stock Exchange, and were thus reported in the financial press. The deals were consummated on December 30—the first at 9:57 in the morning, the second at 1:33 in the afternoon—at $1.47 a share. As with Hunter, the investors put up $500,000, First Investors loaned $7 million, and CSI loaned $2.5 million. For their half a million dollars, the East West investors became owners of $5 million worth of Matrix stock and $5 million worth of PSML-managed mutual funds.

In this case the investment period was to be two years, and the "matured return" was to be a stunning $1 million for each deal, without risk.

December 31, 1986

MINUTES OF A FIRST INVESTORS/Associated Investors control meeting on October 3, 1986 attended by Bill Johnson, Jaimie Cormie, Christa Petracca and comptroller Ginny Nicholson recorded the following plan:

[Matrix] shares held by First Investors are to be sold to a third party—[Athabasca Holdings]. SWJ [Bill Johnson] to check with DMC [Donald Cormie].

Action was taken at year's end, when First Investors traded back to Athabasca Holdings the Matrix stock it bought from the company at the close of 1984. On December 31, 1986, the contract company sold 4,869,308 Matrix shares, which it had bought at a cost of 55 cents, at a value of $1.48 a share. In exchange it received 7,206,570 Athabasca preferred shares, the same controversial stock it had unloaded a year before.

At the end of 1986, Principal Group and affiliates held a total of about 44 million shares of Matrix; the increases in the share price allowed the companies to claim paper profits in their 1986 books totalling about $51 million.

Christmas Eve, 1986

WHILE EVERYONE ELSE WAS PREOCCUPIED with last-minute gift-shopping and the office party circuit, Christa Petracca asked developer Jim Hunter to get involved in another flip. This proposal, made a few days before the Derrick Plaza deal was put to bed, was a little different: Hunter would buy not real estate, but a debenture secured by real estate in which Principal Trust and the contract companies had an interest—the Okanagan Park Resort in Kelowna, B.C. The plan was for Hunter to buy the debenture for $1.5 million, then sell it to the Principal companies for $5.1 million cash. Hunter would pocket $100,000 as his "commission," then apply the other $3.5-million "profit" toward the purchase of several foreclosed properties owned by the Principal companies. Their book value was $3,362,000, but Hunter would pay $6,862,000; the Principal companies would take the balance of the price back in mortgages. The debenture would appear on the books as an asset worth $5.1 million, and a gain of $3.5 million would be recorded on the "sale" of the properties.

Late on the afternoon of December 24, Hunter met briefly with Petracca and Bill Connauton at the Cormie Kennedy offices. They agreed to go ahead on the deal, Hunter said, subject to "lawyers being able to put it together over the holidays and, then, subject to Mrs. Petracca going through her auditors and, I presume, regulators and what-not, that we would do the transaction."

In this transaction lawyer Connauton appears to have acted for both parties. He prepared paperwork under Petracca's instructions, but also signed documents on behalf of Hunter's company (Company #1, the same one that had bought and sold Derrick Plaza).

The Lake Okanagan Resort, a 48-condominium complex with a common area and recreational facilities, was one of the properties assigned to Petracca's SWAT team. Principal Trust and the contract companies held first mortgages on the condominiums, but were in second place behind the Northland Bank on the common area. The debenture, held by the Northland (then in the hands of liquidators), was needed by the Principal companies to assume control of the entire development. Petracca had plans to further develop the money-losing resort, and was thinking of putting in a golf course to attract Japanese tourists.

With Connauton's assistance, Petracca had already arranged to directly purchase the debenture (and other related securities) for $1.5 million. After learning of Hunter's involvement with the Derrick Plaza purchase, however, she decided to approach him with a plan obviously patterned on that transaction. In both cases Hunter was to buy an asset in which Principal had an interest, then jack up the price. In one case, part of the purchase price was paid in trash real estate; in the second, the purchase was in cash and the "profit" was used to buy bad properties. Both transactions took problem real estate off Principal's hands, and in both cases most of Hunter's "profit" was used to purchase other Principal assets. Petracca testified that she conducted this transaction on her own authority, with Connauton's help. Cormie, however, was kept posted on its progress. "I encouraged her to go ahead," he testified, "and suggested that she get Bill Connauton to make sure that she was on solid legal ground as she went along because he was relatively familiar with these companies."

The deal had to be completed by December 31 if it was to affect the 1986 financial statements; Connauton laboured from Christmas through to New Year's Eve to get the documents in order and duly signed.

He was tying up loose ends in early March when the deal came unravelled. Auditor Peter Barnes, Don McCutchen's colleague at Deloitte Haskins & Sells, thought the deal smelled and refused to record it in the three companies' financial statements as Petracca intended. "The deal was reversed because we saw through it, the sham that it was," Barnes said in a note attached to the audit firm's working papers. "Hunte r paid $1.5 million for the debenture. Christa wanted to pay him $5.1 million for worthless properties improving the bottom line by $3.5 million. All along, Christa, John Cormie, D.M.C. were telling us that Hunter paid $5 million for the debenture which is not true."

Petracca testified at the Code inquiry that she hadn't actually said those things to Barnes about the value of the debenture, but had simply avoided discussing it with him. "My best recollection is that I did not say that," Petracca said. "I was trying to avoid discussing the whole transaction, and I believe I kept on repeating to him that 'I really don't wish to discuss it,' until we have determined whether this transaction can be done that fashion."

After the scheme was abandoned, Petracca arranged for First Investors, Associated Investors and Principal Trust to purchase the debenture from Hunter, who had already acquired it, for $1.5 million cash. Petracca called him and said that, because the deal wouldn't go through as conceived, she didn't want to pay the promised $100,000 commission. Because he was only middle-manning the debenture, and not taking all the trash real estate off Principal's hands, he deserved less compensation, she felt. "I believe that we had a perfectly legal and binding deal," Hunter testified. "When it didn't work, she came to me and said, 'Lookit, it is not fair that you should get $100,000. We think that maybe $10,000 for your time and trouble would be appropriate.' I said fine. The company got $10,000, and that was the end of it."

On March 9, Bill Connauton wrote to Petracca with a statement of account, including a bill for $19,165 for legal services. In the letter, he bragged about his foresight in withholding Hunter's $100,000 until the entire transaction was closed. "That is," Connauton said, "if he had received the monies and had spent them, it may not have been as easy to recover the same. (Christa, I'll give myself a pat on the back for this.)"

Part IV

Take-down

20

Look-see

January 7, 1987

IT TOOK THE ALBERTA REGULATORS a while to find an accounting firm willing to examine the contract companies' books. Several already worked for a Cormie company; another declined to become entangled in what it anticipated could be serious trouble.

Finally, in early January, Treasury officials hired Price Waterhouse Ltd., one of the Big Eight accounting firms. Insolvency specialist Tony Wooldridge agreed to conduct what he called a quick "look-see," and to report back in two weeks.

The engagement letter was signed January 7. That same day, Assistant Deputy Provincial Treasurer Al Kalke wrote to Marlin, saying that Treasury believed the companies' financial situation "warrants an urgent inspection." However, because of Marlin's earlier protests, Wooldridge wouldn't be allowed on the Principal premises. Instead, Treasury staff auditors would act as conduits between the companies and Price Waterhouse.

Kalke signed the letter as "Acting Superintendent of Insurance," having been appointed Tewfik Saleh's replacement earlier that day. Saleh was scheduled for retirement in April, but his departure date was moved up to February 1. He left with a handshake from Consumer Affairs deputy minister Barry Martin (who himself retired in mid-month) and thanks for a job well done; he testified that no one ever criticized his performance.

Shortly after receiving Kalke's letter, Marlin and Bill Johnson met with him in his office. They vigorously protested Wooldridge's appointment, but to no avail. Afterward, Johnson wrote a memo to file:

Ken Marlin and I left the meeting and decided that the best alternative was to get the audit of [First Investors] and [Associated Investors] completed as quickly as possible before the Price Waterhouse report was done. Therefore, our strategy involved sending the information over as quickly as possible but delaying certain information because in fact a lot of it hadn't been updated with recent computer runs, etc.

Marlin and Johnson also discussed the consequences of having Kalke's very disturbing letter in the company files while Deloitte Haskins & Sells conducted the annual audit. The fact that Treasury considered the situation "urgent" and had appointed a consultant was bound to adversely affect the auditors' treatment of the financial statements.

"Therefore," Johnson said in his memo, "Ken was of the opinion that we should have the letter taken back by Alberta Treasury so that the letter did not exist. Because of this, Ken and I met with Allister McPherson and Al Kalke on January 19th and McPherson at that time agreed to take the letter back, which was done." McPherson, Kalke and Treasurer Dick Johnston confirmed that this occurred. Not only did they take back Marlin's copy, they retrieved other copies that had gone to Tewfik Saleh and a government lawyer.

Wooldridge conducted his investigation entirely without direct access to Principal officials. Treasury auditor Nick Romalo was appointed the middleman and Wooldridge gave him lists of documents and information required. Romalo passed them on to Principal, then delivered the answers to Wooldridge. Getting information out of the Principal tower, Wooldridge found, was like pulling teeth. He wrote page after page of questions, but most answers came back scrawled on the margins of other pages. "Or, we would get 'yes' and 'no' answers to long, convoluted questions, that really provided no information," Wooldridge testified. "Unfortunately, I'm not so good an interrogator that I could ask all of the questions or ask the questions in such a way that I would get a complete answer the first time. So often answers would give rise to other questions, and this proved to be long and slow and tedious and frustrating."

Wooldridge's extensive background with troubled companies included his ongoing involvement in the liquidation of the Canadian Commercial Bank. He recognized disturbing similarities between the two situations, and wasn't satisfied with a cursory examination of the financial statements—he wanted detailed information on the value behind the assets claimed by the companies. He wanted real estate appraisals, he wanted explanations of various odd-looking transactions, and he wanted to know about the Principal-affiliated companies in which the contract companies had invested so heavily.

On February 2, past deadline for delivery of his report, Wooldridge wrote to Kalke to complain about the companies' stalling tactics. The next week, Marlin and Johnson met with Kalke to complain about Wooldridge. He seemed to be conducting a much more detailed review than they had been led to expect, they said. In fact, Johnson said in a memo:

the insinuation inherent in the questions was that there were a number of things going on in the companies that appeared to be not in [their] best interests.

Accordingly, Al Kalke agreed to talk to Price Waterhouse either himself or through Nick Romalo and explain to them that the nature and tone of their questions was not the best and from now on every question and information request that they sent to us had to be reviewed by Nick Romalo first.

January 20, 1987

In MID-JANUARY, BILL JOHNSON phoned B.C. Superintendent Michael Ross to suggest that he and Ken Marlin come by the next day to discuss the contract companies' year-to-date financial statements. "That's not necessary," Ross told him, "I've been keeping in touch with Allister McPherson and Al Kalke." As far as Ross was concerned, Alberta, the companies' home base, had the primary responsibility to regulate. He was aware that Alberta was undertaking a review, and once that was finished, Ross said, he and Bill Smith would visit Alberta, discuss the review, and take whatever steps were necessary at that time.

When Ross asked about the companies' finances, he was told they had not been capital deficient at year-end. Johnson later wrote a memo:

> [Ross] indicated that this was good and I told him that at any time the two companies were deficient under the *Investment Contracts Act*, that capital was put in. I also told him that if this were the case at any time in the future to the best of my knowledge the company was prepared to put capital in. He indicated to me that this was satisfactory to him.
>
> He also indicated to me that Bill Smith said to him that the statements…were "part numbers and part reality." In other words, the financial statements showed significant non-arm's length transactions which were part and parcel balance sheet accounting, but also that real capital had been put in when requested so by the regulatory people. He indicated that from here on in it was to be all "real" and not "numbers."
>
> Also he indicated to me that Bill Smith was the one who wanted to "shut us down." He said he still had Bill Smith on a "leash" and that Smith would be helping him with this review.

Smith was suffering that "leash." After all his hard work, Ross' regulatory action had amounted to half a dozen phone calls to Alberta in the half-year since the August injection of the back-to-back notes. Smith, fed up, had little interest when an early, unaudited draft of the contract companies' 1986 financial statements appeared on his desk in late January. He sent them back to Vancouver unread, and washed his hands of the matter.

Suddenly, on February 2, Ross unexpectedly resigned as Superintendent of Brokers. The previous year, he had accepted a free trip to the Super Bowl Game with Vancouver promoter Nelson Skalbania, as a guest of Denver Broncos owner Pat Bowlen. Both Skalbania and Bowlen were major players on the Vancouver Stock Exchange, and there was an ongoing investigation at the time into Skalbania's affairs. (No charges were ever laid.) Ross' indiscretion caused a stink, and he was forced to quit.[1] He left without briefing his successor on the Principal contract companies. No memos or files documented the steps and decisions he had taken during eight months on the job.

February 20, 1987

TONY WOOLDRIDGE NEVER DID get the answers to all his questions. Nonetheless, under pressure to produce something for the regulators, he delivered on February 20 a preliminary 53-page report advising that he had been stalled by the companies: "Our inability to obtain this information is of serious concern and is the cause of our inability to provide a final report on our review at this time." Wooldridge gained access to the files kept by provincial auditors; unfortunately, he didn't see the one kept in the office of the Superintendent of Insurance, and thus missed the damning reports of Jim Darwish and Al Hutchison prepared (and buried) in 1984. Nonetheless, Wooldridge's conclusions were remarkably similar to theirs.

"Although we have been unable to conclude on the value of the real estate related assets and intercompany investments, we are able to conclude that the companies are in serious financial difficulty," Wooldridge reported. "It is highly unlikely the provision of the additional information will cause us to view the companies' financial position more favourably."

Having analyzed the *Investment Contracts Act* and the *Canadian and British Insurance Companies Act*, Wooldridge concluded that they prohibited the companies' investments in Principal Neo-Tech, Athabasca Holdings, Matrix Investments, and the Principal Multiplier Fund (a Principal-managed mutual fund). He analyzed First Investors' 1986 year-end sales of the "highly speculative" Matrix Investments stock to Jim Hunter and the East West syndicate, and said he was unable to understand the business reason behind the way they were conducted. As for the movement of Athabasca Holdings shares during 1986, he concluded that the profit taken from their sale was not in accordance with GAAP and should be eliminated. He continued:

This series of transaction is an example of the shares of related companies being flipped within the group, the effect of which is to inflate the Companies' balance sheets and inflate profits. The measure of real benefit to the Companies of this series of transactions is dependent upon the value of the preferred shares of Athabasca Holdings Ltd. which were acquired. We have requested the financial statements of Athabasca Holdings Ltd. for the purpose of evaluating the investment but to date it has not been received.

At the end of 1986, according to company calculations, First Investors and Associated Investors had a combined excess of $32.3 million of qualified assets. Wooldridge did his own calculations, backed out a number of assets claimed by the companies, and identified a combined deficiency in qualified assets totalling $87 million. He also calculated a capital impairment in the two companies totalling $32.6 million. Company investments, he reported, were earning less than required to cover the interest and additional credits due to the contract holders. He criticized the companies' accounting strategies, including valuing mortgages and real estate according to some uncertain "future value."

Wooldridge offered a number of stern recommendations. The licences of First Investors and Associated Investors should be suspended or cancelled, on the grounds that they didn't meet any of the three financial tests in the *Investment Contracts Act*. The Superintendent of Insurance should recommend to the Minister that a receiver/manager or liquidator be appointed, and should enter the companies' premises to inspect their books and records. He should make a Special Report to the Minister that the companies were not complying with the Act, "and such failure may be prejudicial to the interests of the investment contract holders and creditors." If the province wanted to support the companies, Wooldridge continued, shareholders should be required to contribute additional capital to correct existing deficiencies. The companies should be required to dispose of their investments in related companies at no less than the recorded value on their balance sheets; their investment in non-performing real estate should be transferred to related companies at recorded values; and contract holders should not be paid more interest on their contracts than the companies were actually earning. "As we have not had the opportunity to review the financial position of other companies within the group we are unable to advise if they have sufficient financial strength to implement the above," Wooldridge reported.

This was, finally, the outside consultant's report that Tewfik Saleh had yearned for since 1984. Ironically, Saleh never received it; it was delivered three weeks after he made his exit from government service.

The Treasury officials who had replaced Saleh weren't surprised by Wooldridge's conclusion that the companies were in serious difficulty—Saleh and their own auditors had already told them that—but they were astonished to find that Wooldridge had suggested hard-hitting responses. "We had not asked for recommendations," Kalke testified. They were "premature," he said—Treasury wanted a measure of the size of the problem, but wasn't yet prepared to discuss how to deal with it. Fortunately—from the regulators' perspective—they had asked that the report be prepared in "draft" form, "for discussion purposes only," so it didn't really exist, and didn't warrant an official response.

On February 26, Treasurer Dick Johnston saw Wooldridge's draft report. Soon afterward, Premier Getty's priorities committee was alerted to the possibility of a serious problem with the contract companies.

When Treasury officials and Price Waterhouse representatives met again on March 3, they decided that Kalke should contact Ken Marlin, tell him about Wooldridge's report, and let him know the department wanted Wooldridge to continue to investigate. They also discussed the fact that Principal officials didn't want their auditors to know about Wooldridge's review. The auditors, ignorant of recent events, were preparing to sign off on the 1986 financial statements. At Wooldridge's urging, the Treasury officials conceded that they had a duty to apprise Deloitte Haskins & Sells of his findings.

February 9, 1987

MEANWHILE, THE FEDERAL REGULATORS were closing in on Principal Trust again. In early February, the Department of Insurance wrote John Cormie to say that as of November, the trust company was operating at a borrowing-to-capital ratio of 18.9:1. A capital injection of some $1.8 million was required to satisfy its authorized ratio of 15:1. No such injection was made. Instead, the trust company increased its borrowings from the public by 4.5% during the first two months of 1987. In mid-April, the feds wrote to say that the borrowing multiple was deteriorating badly. The ratio for February was 45.3:1, requiring a capital injection of some $6 million. Again, there was no injection.

February 24, 1987

"YOU'VE GOT TO BE fucking kidding!" Bill Johnson yelled into the long-distance telephone.

"Well, no, Bill, I thought you knew," Principal comptroller Ginny Nicholson said. "The trust company is selling another $9 million worth of real estate to First Investors. They started the paperwork just after you went on holiday."

"Oh, no, what's the CDIC going to say?"

Johnson, confident that work on the Principal Trust audit was completed, had taken his family to Mount Whistler for a ski vacation. While he was on the slopes, documents were drafted authorizing the sale of five mortgages and 32 properties, held by Principal Trust, to the contract company. John and Jaimie Cormie signed on behalf of the trust company, Ken Marlin signed for First Investors and Christa Petracca signed on both sides of the deal. The price was $9,220,322 in cash, retroactive to the last day of 1986. It was intended to have a wonderfully soothing effect on the trust company's 1986 statements.

Johnson hung up and dialled Donald Cormie. "We can't be doing this kind of thing," he argued. "It's no good for either of the companies." He was amazed that Cormie would try something like this, given the protests of the CDIC and Alberta regulators after the first asset dump in 1984. The transaction, Cormie replied, was proceeding.

There were several differences between this transfer and the one in 1984. This time, there was no talk of a "tender." The properties weren't to be transferred at book value, but at their "current market values" as previously estimated by the CDIC. A letter signed by Marlin portrayed the transaction as a solution to problems resulting from joint ownership of the mortgages. In fact, of the 37 properties transferred, only a quarter had been jointly owned before the deal. The rest were high-risk "development" properties wholly owned by Principal Trust: more trash.

March 3, 1987

THEY WENT TO DEVELOPER JIM HUNTER for help again. This time, the problem was Neo-Tech Inc., Principal Neo-Tech's seismic subsidiary in Denver, which had taken a loss of $9.5 million on the 1986 books. The publicly-traded Toronto parent company was desperate to sever its devastated subsidiary, and Hunter agreed to "buy" it. On March 3, he incorporated two new Denver companies, which quickly bought out the seismic operation. The deal was backdated to 1986 on Principal Neo-Tech's books. Little cash was exchanged. Instead, Hunter's new company Energy Holdings, Inc. gave Principal Neo-Tech a great deal of paper: preferred shares worth about $5 million and debentures worth about $12 million. It was a great comfort to the Toronto company's books. Unfortunately, the comfort proved temporary.

I spoke to Hunter twice about his involvement with the seismic operation. The first time, in 1990, he told me that he had gone to Denver to look it over, but declined to get involved. A year later, confronted with his name on the corporate registry records of his Denver companies, Hunter confirmed that he had bought Neo-Tech, but said it was a conditional purchase agreement, "and once we got into the books it just didn't make sense. So we had the right to toss it back to them or something." Having called his Denver lawyer, he called me back to say that the purchase was predicated on a business plan which wasn't implemented, so his interest in the company "was conveyed to Neo-Tech's attorney in Denver." That happened, he said, in December 1987, half a year after the Principal collapse. By that time, Principal Group trustee Collins Barrow Ltd. had taken over the control block of Principal Neo-Tech's common shares. When Hunter tossed the seismic business back, Collins Barrow caught it.

Soon after Collins Barrow assumed control, Principal Neo-Tech president Ken Marlin got the boot and a group of senior employees were asked to take over. The next spring, the trustee transferred much of its common stock to the new management group, who renamed the company The Laird Group Inc. They entered a partnership with the Principal Group estate to deal with the seismic enterprise, but have yet to realize any significant revenue. In 1988, The Laird Group determined that the Energy Holdings preferred shares and debentures were near-worthless and wrote them down to $4 million, a loss of about $13 million on that year's books. Since then, the seismic investment, worth $24 million in 1985, has been written down to almost zero.

At present, The Laird Group struggles heroically to survive. Crippled by the seismic crash, burdened with a mountain of debt inherited from the Cormie era and further wounded by a softening of the market for its graphic arts services, it posts huge losses every year: $13 million in 1986; $13 million in 1987; $3 million in 1988; $575,000 in 1989; $1.5 million in 1990; and $588,000 in 1991. The company has down-sized, refinanced, reorganized, unloaded unprofitable enterprises and now hangs on by the skin of its teeth. During 1991 and 1992 its Class A preferred shares traded on the Toronto Stock Exchange at between 1 and 5 cents each.

February 12, 1987

JAY MOULTON THOUGHT HE WAS making a courtesy call, but Paul Robinson wasn't in the mood. As soon as the young Principal executive walked in, Robinson started giving him hell about the Principal sales staff's lack of ethics. Robinson, chairman of the Saskatchewan Securities Commission in Regina, said he was considering a hearing to review Principal Consultants' registration to sell mutual funds in that province. Alarmed, Moulton tried to back out until he could get a company lawyer on the scene. Robinson, flanked by a government lawyer, told him to stay put.

Robinson told Moulton he was particularly concerned about an incident in Saskatoon the previous autumn. Four levels of the Principal organization were involved. The first-line manager, Thom Hanwell, had forged a document, then persuaded consultant Shelene Misselbrook to take responsibility. Doug Wilson, the area manager, attempted to cover up. When word got back to Edmonton, Wally Noble, the regional vice-president, recommended minuscule two-day and 14-day suspensions for Hanwell and Misselbrook. He also assured Misselbrook that her suspension would be removed from her personnel file in six months time.

Moulton, then a baby-faced 27-year-old, was a former lieutenant in the Canadian Armed Forces. Upon leaving the military, he attended the MBA program at Harvard University, where he was recruited by Donald Cormie in the spring of 1984. That June joined Principal as supervisor of field services, with responsibility for training the conglomerate's sales staff. In 1986, Moulton was "promoted" to vice-president of field services, Ken Marlin's second-in-command. (His duties remained the same, but he got a raise and a grander title). At the same time, Cormie appointed him director and secretary-treasurer of Principal Consultants, with an honorarium of $500 a year.

After Robinson's dressing-down Moulton wrote a six-page summary of the incident to Cormie and Marlin, advising that he had managed to "assuage" Robinson's concerns.

> I began, stating that when I became aware of Mr. Noble's recommendation, that I had instructed Mr. [Tom] Keogh [manager of field services] and Mr. Noble to have Hanwell and Misselbrook terminated. In fact, the correct action was taken.
>
> Furthermore, I advised Mr. Robinson that Mr. Cormie and Mr. Marlin insisted repeatedly upon maintaining the highest level of fiduciary duty. I have their whole-hearted support in matters of this nature.
>
> I stated that I have four years military experience and that the company

"policeman," Mr. Keogh, has 10 years military experience. This background enables Head Office Sales to enforce a high level of discipline.

Mr Robinson asked, specifically, what systems and procedures are in place for dealing with these matters. I advised that several policy memos had been issued, both prior and subsequent to the Hanwell/Misselbrook affair. He requested copies...

Moulton described to Robinson a high-quality training program and a personnel-selection test which "enables us to identify certain unethical behaviour and select only the best people." Then he lauded the company's internal audit department, which he said audited "the integrity of [Principal Consultants'] sales on a sample basis." By the end of the visit, Moulton reported, Robinson and the commission lawyer felt much more comfortable with Principal. Nonetheless, they wanted to interview and approve all staff being considered for management positions in Saskatchewan. They also asked for complete documentation of Principal's policies, training staff selection and internal audit procedures.

Moulton high-tailed it back to Edmonton and set up a crash program. Within three weeks he had stitched together a code of ethics, using bits and pieces of other codes in existence elsewhere. Then he wrote a memo announcing that all sales managers and trainees—everyone except the salesmen themselves—had to commit it to memory. The March 2, 1987, memo ordered that head office marketing personnel memorize the code by March 6; all area managers by April 1; and all branch managers by April 23. "All personnel will be required to sign a form acknowledging receipt of the code of ethics and understanding of the code of ethics," it said.

The code listed 17 standards that salesmen had to meet, or risk reprimand or termination, including: "Representatives shall not make misleading or exaggerated statements," and "Representatives shall offer clients full disclosure of pertinent product features including negative aspects as well as the positive." Moulton testified that he memorized the code to demonstrate his commitment, then recited it aloud at a meeting before Cormie, Marlin and Principal's most senior sales managers. No one else ever memorized it, but the code was welcomed with open arms as a peachy marketing gimmick. It was framed and prominently displayed in every sales office from coast to coast.

Saskatchewan officials did not follow up on Robinson's threat to hold a Commission hearing. Bill Wheatley, who replaced Robinson that year, later said that, according to official records, Robinson decided not to lift Principal's sales licence because "at least Moulton appears to take the matter seriously."[2]

This was one of only two known confrontations between Saskatchewan regulators and the Principal companies after their investment contract licences were reinstated in 1978 (Associated Investors) and 1981 (First Investors). The other incident took place in March 1984 when then-Acting Superintendent of Insurance Allan Higgs wrote to John Cormie, criticizing misleading claims made by two Principal salesmen. There is no record of any follow-up. (The Saskatchewan

Securities Commission was copied in April 1985 with the Alberta commission's letter to Christa Petracca trashing her prospectus for the First Investors preferred share issue. There is no record of any follow-up here either.)

Saskatchewan Ombudsman Gerald McLellan reported that the province's record was "virtually silent" during the period following the reinstatements, except to show that the companies' licences were renewed annually. Those licences, he said, "were issued solely [on the] assumption that the companies were suitable for licencing." The province's *Investment Contracts Act* required the delivery of annual and quarterly reports, but on a number of occasions they were not received. Those that were— including the 1983 audit report with the going-concern note, and the severely qualified 1985 report—were never read.

During his discussion with Robinson, Moulton cited Principal's internal audit department as an example of the company's efforts at quality control. There was in fact such a department, manned by a staff of four, which conducted routine audits of customer product knowledge. Robinson wasn't told, however, how the staff operated, what it found out, or what became of its reports.

In the early 1980s, the internal audit department had functioned as a limited branch inspection group, focusing on the trust company. Then-auditor Bruce Pennock reported to the "audit committee" in 1983 that the department lacked "leadership, commitment and a clear reporting vehicle through which it can cause change." Two years later, it began a series of client surveys to determine what customers understood about the investment products. These surveys were instigated by Tracy Barker, Principal's new internal audit manager, after salesmen made a product presentation to him which severely misrepresented the investment contract guarantee. (Barker, who joined Principal in late 1985, had worked for the Canadian Commercial Bank until its downfall earlier that year.)

A survey which sampled a mere 99 customers was conducted soon afterward, with alarming results. About a third of those questioned did not understand the *Investment Contracts Act*, the additional credits, or the fact that the contracts weren't CDIC insured. Another survey in April 1986 produced similar results. A final report submitted March 31, 1987—five weeks after Moulton was in the Saskatchewan hot seat—was even worse. Based on a sample of 150 contracts sold between July and September 1986, 41% of the respondents were not aware of the lack of CDIC insurance.

Moulton testified that he doubted these numbers were accurate. "I felt things were better than that," he said. He had an assistant contact the clients identified by the surveys, to make sure they were satisfied with their purchases. As well, he said, efforts were made to tighten up the training programs. It was a sad case of the blind leading the blind. Moulton himself did not understand how the contract companies' liabilities and reserves were calculated. He testified that he wrongly believed, like so many Principal clients, that assets equal to an investor's original deposit were held in a bank.

In most corporations, internal audit departments are independent bodies which serve as a check on company operations. The department communicates its findings to management but effectively acts as the eyes and ears of the board of directors, reporting to an audit committee whose membership is primarily made up of outside board members. It is the audit committee's job to review both the internal and external audit reports and to evaluate the action taken by management to rectify various problems. When internal audit staff are stymied by management, problems are referred to the audit committee for correction.

The situation at Principal Group was a travesty. The internal audit team reported to committee consisting of—Donald Cormie. Cormie testified that Barker reviewed the survey results with him, "but I didn't have to do anything because Marketing and the Sales Department picked it up on their own and put into effect a very aggressive ethics program, a better selection program, higher training standards and exam programs." It's like having a water quality analyst deliver his pollution readings to the guys who are dumping dioxin.

A week before the launch of Moulton's ethics program, there was another crisis. This one occurred in Calgary where, on February 4, salesman Arney Falconer traced the signatures of an elderly Drumheller couple—he maintains it was at their request—first on a withdrawal slip at Principal Trust for $4,840, then on an application form to transfer the money to a First Investors contract. Both documents were rejected by a trust company official because the signatures did not match those on file. Questioned by a member of Principal's internal audit team, Falconer said the clients, 79-year-old Jacob Leonhardt and his wife, had in fact signed. Then he called Leonhardt, a $100,000 client who was recovering from a second cancer operation, and persuaded him to back up the story. Confronted by a head office official, Falconer admitted what had happened. On February 26, at Moulton's direction, he was fired, fined $1,000, and lost his sales licence.

An internal investigation of Falconer's activities resulted in a report detailing other instances of tracing client signatures. "This is very evident on the original copies of applications," the report said, "as the signature appears to have been traced using carbon paper and then copied over in ink."

The situation was most unfortunate. Falconer was a valued member of the Principal team, having been named Rookie of the Year in 1985. In 1986, he joined the President's Club as Principal's top-selling qualified consultant, and was being groomed to take over the lucrative Hutterite accounts from retiring salesman Walter Green.

In April, Falconer met with Principal management and denied every accusation in the report. By early May, he was back on the team. On May 11, Tom Keogh—the "company policeman"—advised the Alberta Securities Commission that Principal Consultants would sponsor Falconer for his Investment Fund licence. "The event that resulted in Mr. Falconer's termination has been resolved internally, as it was limited to a contradiction in company policy/procedure," Keogh wrote. Moulton wrote a letter to Falconer on May 20 reinstating his benefits and President's Club membership, and promoting him to "account executive" status. He also received an advance of $4,000 a month for three months, $2,500 in back commissions, forgiveness of an $857 debt and repayment of the $1,000 fine. Most important, Falconer was assigned half the Hutterite business. And, Moulton wrote, the company would assist Falconer in obtaining a sales licence in Saskatchewan, because it wanted to develop Hutterite business there.

At the end of May, Keogh issued an "Internal Audit Bulletin" advising that "a consultant was terminated as a result of an apparent forgery," but that a subsequent internal audit review had determined that it was simply a matter of convenience. "Corporate counsel was consulted and felt the application was not a forgery since it was done with the client's knowledge."

March 2, 1987

THE FINAL VERSION OF THE RIMROCK INN offering memorandum to Hong Kong was printed at the end of January, and this time Principal lawyer Lynn Patrick actually signed it. Petracca forwarded the new memorandum on March 2 to the Agent General Asia/Pacific for Alberta—to none other than Donald Cormie's old law partner Jack Kennedy, who had been in the post for a year and a half. Petracca testified that she knew Kennedy "socially somewhat." In fact, he had recommended her to Principal Group nine years before, and she was hopeful that he would host a reception to promote the offering.

This same day, Treasury officials were questioned by colleagues in Alberta Tourism about the propriety of a huge federal/provincial grant to the contract companies toward completion of the Rimrock. By this point Acting Superintendent of Insurance Al Kalke had received the Price Waterhouse draft report, and was awaiting completion of the external audit of the contract companies. Nonetheless, he instructed department auditor Nick Romalo not to warn tourism officials about the companies or their financial difficulties, and the grant proceeded.

February 11, 1987

WITH MICHAEL ROSS OUT OF THE PICTURE, Bill Smith decided to try again. Nine days after Ross' sudden resignation as British Columbia Superintendent of Brokers, David Sinclair, a chartered accountant with the firm Coopers & Lybrand, was named Acting Superintendent. Smith immediately dashed off a note warning him about the Principal contract companies.

Alarmed, Sinclair called Al Dilworth, director of investigations, and asked him to check the companies' financial status. On February 26, Dilworth told Sinclair that he had called the Alberta regulators, who had assured him that "they had a good handle" on the matter. "Don't worry until we do something," Dilworth was told. The Alberta regulators said that the independent consultant's draft report had been received, and was to be discussed with company officials in early March. The next day Sinclair called Al Kalke in Edmonton and was promised a copy of the Price Waterhouse report. A week and a half later, Sinclair called again to ask why it hadn't arrived. Told that the document was not yet complete, Sinclair threatened to send Smith to examine it in draft form. Six days later the report arrived on Sinclair's desk.

The report, which arrived March 16, was dated February 20, and Sinclair concluded that Kalke had not levelled with him. The incident served as an early warning not to rely too heavily on Alberta, and Sinclair put this lesson to excellent use in coming weeks. B.C. Ombudsman Stephen Owen praised Sinclair's handling of the crisis:

> While in wanting more information Mr. Sinclair was not unlike the other [B.C.] regulators we have considered, the difference is that he took steps to pressure Alberta very hard to meet its responsibilities. He and Mr. Smith developed strategies to force Alberta both to provide the information [B.C.] needed and to keep up the pressure in order to ensure that they received maximum co-operation.

Sinclair was astonished at the harsh recommendations of the Price Waterhouse report. It was clear to him that a full-scale assessment was required, and that it should include the entire Principal Group, not just two contract companies.

March 6, 1987

TREASURY AUDITOR NICK ROMALO brought Ken Marlin and Bill Johnson together with Tony Wooldridge and his colleague Bob Sword at the Price Waterhouse offices. Copies of the draft report were handed to Marlin and Johnson, and everyone sat back while they read.

The two men testified that they were utterly shocked by its contents. "It became obvious after seeing the report on the 6th that what was going on was of major proportion," Marlin said. "That was the first time that we perceived the situation to be what it was." He and Johnson immediately went on the attack, arguing that the report was inaccurate, unreasonable and unfair. They went through it page by page, pointing out Wooldridge's "errors." Wooldridge didn't deny that he might have made mistakes—that "shouldn't have surprised anybody, considering the lack of information that we had," he testified. He saw the confrontation as an opportunity to collect replies to long-unanswered questions.

Wooldridge wanted to get inside the Principal offices and go through the mortgage and real estate files, but "Ken and I headed him off at the pass," Johnson reported in a memo. He and Marlin went to the Treasury offices and again persuaded Kalke that it was too risky to have Price Waterhouse on the Principal premises. According to Johnson, Kalke seemed relieved to be told that Wooldridge had made several errors, "because he gave us the impression that when he first reviewed the draft report he and Allister McPherson were both obviously shocked by its contents." Kalke "assured us that it definitely was not the government's intention to liquidate the companies regardless of what the Price Waterhouse report said," Johnson wrote.

He indicated that it was in their best interests and, they felt, in the best interests of the company, to agree on a workable solution whereby the companies could work their way out of the problems and that this solution should be reasonable and fair such that the government could approve it. He also recognized the fact that there were a lot of other businesses that could be affected, as well as people, and because of this concern he agreed that Price Waterhouse should in no way attend our premises at this point in time until the final draft was done and the Government had a chance to review it and a workable solution could be reached with the company.

But Marlin and Johnson lost an important skirmish. Kalke insisted that Wooldridge was to meet the contract companies' external auditor Don McCutchen, and that the audit reports weren't to be signed off until then.

March 1987

When DONALD CORMIE HEARD ABOUT the contents of the Price Waterhouse report, he decided it was time to seek the advice of a former premier. Cormie testified that: "I did at some time in here phone Peter Lougheed—he was a lawyer in Calgary at the time—and asked him for any suggestions he might have as to how I might handle it." Cormie did not volunteer, and was not asked, what suggestions he received.

March 12, 1987

Donald CORMIE DECIDED TO match the province's consultants with his own set of outside sharpshooters. He called Coopers & Lybrand Ltd., another of the Big Eight accounting firms, with which he was well acquainted. The firm had assisted in the 1985 reorganization which resulted in the insertion of Collective Securities Inc. between Principal Group and Collective Securities Ltd., had acted between 1983 and mid-February 1987 as receiver of the Rimrock Inn and was the auditor of both CSI and CSL.

Cormie originally dealt with Bob Brintnall, the partner responsible for the CSI and CSL audits. On March 12, Brintnall met with Cormie, Jaimie and Bill Johnson, to discuss strategy for dealing with the Price Waterhouse report. They were joined by Cormie Kennedy counsel Gary Campbell, who had just been appointed chairman of the reorganized North West Trust Company by the Alberta government. A couple of days later, Brintnall brought in Coopers & Lybrand president John Ryan, the firm's regional insolvency partner. Ryan, known as a specialist in "sick companies," was well known to federal and provincial regulators.

Meanwhile, Al Kalke, stung by questions from B.C., was pushing for a meeting with the contract companies' external auditors. This was set for March 16. The day before, a Sunday, Johnson and Marlin met with auditor Don McCutchen to prepare him for what was in store. This was McCutchen's first inkling of the regulators' January 7 letter or the Price Waterhouse investigation.

On the Monday, senior members of three accounting firms faced off over the contract companies' books. They met at the Coopers & Lybrand offices, but it was Wooldridge, of Price Waterhouse, and McCutchen, of Deloitte Haskins & Sells, who did most of the talking. Wooldridge went through his draft report, supporting his identification of massive capital and asset deficiencies. McCutchen and Johnson came back at him, defending the transactions and asset valuations. Johnson concluded later in a memo:

> In all, I thought McCutchen handled himself very well and, in fact, discredited Wooldridge to a certain extent as Wooldridge clearly did not understand the nature of the business, nor the GAAP techniques used in doing the audit. McCutchen also went into great detail in reviewing their excess statements that they file annually and also how the reserve system works.

Wooldridge remembered it differently. "This was my first opportunity to meet with Mr. McCutchen," he testified. "I did not know whether I would ever have the opportunity to meet with him again... I proceeded to go through much of the draft report with Mr. McCutchen and ask him questions and try to get as much information as I possibly could."

Afterward, as Johnson and Marlin headed back to the Principal tower, they burst into laughter. Johnson noted the moment in his memo: "We also laughed a bit about McCutchen's explanations of the reserve system and the contract liabilities as it was totally incorrect but it was convincing because Price Waterhouse and Coopers and Lybrand obviously thought they understood it but in fact they didn't."

Later that week, Marlin and Johnson, accompanied by Ryan, Brintnall and McCutchen, went to the Treasury offices for a meeting with Wooldridge, Kalke and Deputy Treasurer Allister McPherson. Marlin again attacked Wooldridge's report, Johnson wrote in a memo:

> Allister seemed to get very defensive at first and assured us there was no hidden agenda here and that he was looking for a workable solution regardless of what Price Waterhouse may or may not recommend in their report. He also pointed out that at this point in time they were on a hold position until the audit was completed but warned us that he would allow us a few weeks to get the audit completed, not a few months. In other words, he insinuated that we had stalled him before. John Ryan then took it upon himself to make a few comments and actually was quite rude in his comments with respect to the report and the fact that the report never should have been issued because conclusions were drawn in the report based on lack of information and not having all the facts. In fact, Tony Wooldridge conceded that he didn't have all the facts but yet he drew a conclusion based on that, and Ryan intimated that

this was irresponsible. Wooldridge didn't say anything but you could see that he was very upset over the comments.

March 19, 1987

ON THURSDAY AFTERNOON, a couple of days after the accounting firms got together, Al Kalke phoned B.C. Superintendent David Sinclair to discuss the contract companies. Sinclair made notes of their conversation: "Kalke indicated that unless the companies can put their house in order a liquidation may be necessary. Alberta is the prime jurisdiction of the matter. They appear to be taking a lead role and to be on top of the situation. Kalke will keep us informed."

The following Monday, Sinclair wrote a follow-up letter to Kalke: If no provision was made for a substantial injection of new equity into the contract companies, he considered suspension of their registration to be imperative. "As we have discussed, the British Columbia Securities Commission will look to Alberta as the lead jurisdiction to develop a course of action in this matter." But if Alberta was unwilling to act, B.C. was prepared to do so unilaterally, Sinclair said. In the meantime, "We have no choice but to renew the registrations, since to withhold approval would undoubtedly precipitate a collapse."

Next, Sinclair wrote to Mel Couvelier, B.C. Minister of Finance, advising him of the gravity of the companies' situation and alerting him to the likely magnitude of investor losses if the companies went down. That same day, Sinclair received suspension orders drafted by a lawyer in the Legal Services Branch. Sinclair testified that he requested the orders in case they were needed on short notice. From then on, he carried them around in his back pocket.

March 11, 1987

THE PRICE OF THE MATRIX stock floated in the $1.40 to $1.50 range during early 1987, then dropped to as low as $1.10 a share during early March after Principal Group and Allarco Energy withdrew temporarily from the market. On March 11, a Wednesday, Principal Trust president John Cormie's housemate/fiancee Pat Blakeney and his friend John McLay, a technical college teacher, went to the brokerage firm Alfred Bunting to open client accounts. Blakeney began buying Matrix stock at 7:40 that morning with a purchase of 600 shares at $1.25—up five cents from the previous day's closing. She made five purchases, and by lunch time the price was up to $1.40. That afternoon, McLay made two purchases totalling 1,500 shares, most of them also at $1.40.

Early the next morning Principal salesman Barry Hart made two purchases— 700 shares at $1.45, and 50 shares at $1.55. By 9:20 a.m., Allarco Energy was back on the market. During the morning, it made seven purchases totalling 3,900 shares at $1.45. At 11:41, the Principal Group employees account bought 100 shares at $1.50, then in the afternoon Allarco made another six purchases, totalling 5,000 shares, at

$1.50. On Friday morning, Allarco started buying again at $1.50, then at 9:05 a.m. upticked it to $1.55, and at 9:09 a.m. to $1.58.

This 38-cent increase in the value of a Matrix share during two days of trading would increase the value of the Cormie-controlled block by almost $23 million.

At 9:18 that Friday morning, two huge blocks of Matrix stock, totalling 3,125,000 shares, crossed the floor of the Alberta Stock Exchange at $1.60—a total of $5 million. This was the fourth and last of the "warehousing" transactions described in the last chapter. The deal was identical to the previous East West transactions, except that in this case the Matrix shares were "sold" to the investment syndicate by Principal Group instead of by First Investors.

The deal—conducted soon after Tony Wooldridge challenged the value and liquidity of Matrix stock—would have produced a profit on Principal Group's 1987 books of $4,062,500.

March 19, 1987

THE CDIC WAS NOT CHARMED by the Derrick Plaza transaction. By mid-March federal examiners had determined that the property had been flipped for a tremendous profit, and immediately passed the news to Alberta regulators. Then three CDIC auditors met with several Principal representatives—trust company president John Cormie was getting married, so Jaimie took his place—to request a capital injection of about $6.2 million.

March 26, 1987

DONALD CORMIE WAS FURIOUS with Principal mortgage manager Bill Green. While Cormie struggled to get the most favourable audit possible for the contract companies, Green was going behind his back and undercutting the valuation of properties on the companies' books. Deloitte Haskins & Sells auditor Peter Barnes had asked Green his opinion of the value of a number of the properties being handled by Christa Petracca's SWAT team. "Mr. Barnes presented himself in my office," Green testified, "and he was very concerned about the valuations that he had received on those properties from [SWAT team member Lance] Frazier and from Mr. Cormie, and he wanted another opinion. So I asked him to close the door, and I told him I would give them. And as he called them out I gave him values as best I could." Green's values were much lower than those on the books. A farm owned by First Investors, for example, had a book value of over $1 million, but Green said it was worth only $153,300.

The next day, during a weekly Friday morning real estate meeting, Green realized that Cormie had heard about his conversation with the auditor. "It was apparent at that meeting he was upset," Green testified. "I didn't have to guess why... I asked if I could speak to him in private, and I suggested to him I didn't appreciate his being upset with me, because I hadn't put the loans on the books [in the first place]. I'd come back to help the company"—Green had left in 1976, then returned in 1982—"and if I wasn't going to, I didn't want to be there. As well, I told him if he was upset he should be speaking with the people that approved the loans. He said that wasn't going to accomplish anything."

The next day, Cormie told Green that he had lost confidence in him. Green resigned the following Monday, and left at the end of the week.

Finance vice-president Bill Johnson, still grinding his teeth about the previous month's $9.2-million asset dump, tried to talk Green out of it, then tendered his own resignation the same week. Under the terms of Johnson's employment contract he owed Cormie six months notice, so he was stuck in the Principal tower until autumn.

April 6, 1987

DAVID SINCLAIR WAITED TWO WEEKS, then applied the pressure again. The B.C. Superintendent wrote another letter to Al Kalke, warning that the contract companies' situation could not be permitted to continue much longer "without firm action being taken." A meeting was arranged for the end of the month.

April 6, 1987

CHRISTA PETRACCA HAD LIVED in her luxury Wolf Willow condominium for five years; it was time to move up. In early April, she traded the $200,000 condo for a $345,000 house on one of Wolf Willow's most exclusive streets, bought with yet another interest-free loan from Principal Group.

April 15, 1987

AUDITOR DON MCCUTCHEN NEVER DID sign off on the contract companies' 1986 financial statements. Instead, at the request of both the companies and the Alberta regulators, he issued them in "draft" form—"For Discussion Purposes Only." According to John Ryan, the regulators feared the consequences if the statements were signed off with the going-concern note McCutchen insisted on including. "They indicated that they would be concerned if that was in there," Ryan testified, "not only from their viewpoint, but also their concern that while they are looking for a solution to whatever that problem was, that B.C. may lift the licences and there may not be a solution found."

The dispute with Donald Cormie over asset values continued right up until the afternoon the drafts were completed. In the end, the statements included extensive mortgage and real estate write-downs. Other inflated assets, however, were not written down. Profit on the "sale" of Matrix stock was recorded at the "market value" reflected on the Alberta Stock Exchange—Inspector Bill Code later called these "fantasy" values—at the time of the transactions. Nonetheless, the statements revealed a desperate situation. The companies admitted to a combined deficiency in qualified assets of almost $25 million ($15,320,557 for First Investors and $9,473,525 for Associated Investors) and a combined capital deficiency of more than

$46 million ($34,392,430 for First Investors and $11,664,437 for Associated Investors).

Worst of all, news of the Price Waterhouse investigation had forced McCutchen to include a going-concern note:

1. CONTINUING OPERATIONS
The continued operation of the company is dependent on the company and the regulatory body agreeing to a satisfactory resolution regarding the deficiency of assets to the certificate liabilities and reserves and other liabilities together with receipt of provincial licences that allow the company to continue to operate from year to year.

When the draft was prepared, McCutchen testified, he felt that the companies' cash flow situation raised doubt they could continue in business, irrespective of the regulatory crisis. But he neglected to include that observation in his going-concern note, and didn't mention it in later meetings with regulators. (McCutchen testified that the note wasn't more explicit because it was his "first cut," prepared under pressure of time. There was never a second cut.)

On April 15, McCutchen accompanied Ken Marlin, Bill Johnson and Coopers & Lybrand consultants John Ryan and Bob Brintnall to the Treasury Department offices to deliver the statements. Johnson again made notes:

Al Kalke was very concerned that [the continuing operations] note was there and Don [McCutchen] explained to him that the reason that the note was there was because he was unsure as to whether or not Alberta Treasury was going to pull the licences of FIC and AIC and because of this uncertainty he had to have a note with respect to continuing operations. John Ryan also read the note and became concerned that once the Province of B.C. saw this note they would be especially concerned. We agreed that we should meet with the Province of B.C. to bring them up to date with respect to the financial statements and Price Waterhouse's report.

The next day, Johnson and Marlin returned to the Treasury offices and tried to talk Allister McPherson into dumping Price Waterhouse. They suggested that Principal engage the Coopers & Lybrand accountants to prepare a "work-out solution." Johnson told McPherson that he felt uncomfortable with Tony Wooldridge, "in that I didn't think he had the foresight to come up with a solution that was acceptable to both Treasury and the company." McPherson, Johnson said in a memo, "reiterated the fact that he was most concerned that a solution be found that was acceptable to Treasury and the company and that in no way did he want the companies to be wound up if a proper solution could be found." McPherson agreed to think about it over the weekend and get back to them after meeting with Kalke and Wooldridge. "Ken and I agreed," Johnson recorded, "that we would withhold giving Tony Wooldridge any of the financial statements until such time as we heard from Allister or Al on Tuesday."

When Treasury officials met with Wooldridge on the morning of April 21, they authorized him to continue his investigation—but told him not to include any recommendations in the second report. Kalke passed the decision on to Johnson during a phone conversation that afternoon. Wooldridge was to review the Deloitte Haskins & Sells files and touch base with Treasury, Kalke said, but he wasn't to issue his next report until Treasury told him to. Kalke said that even though he wouldn't replace Wooldridge with Coopers & Lybrand, Principal should independently get them to prepare a "work-out business plan." If the plan was acceptable to Treasury, it wouldn't be necessary to actually receive the second report from Wooldridge.

The next day, a Wednesday, Johnson and Marlin met with Donald and Jaimie Cormie and a couple of finance department staffers to talk about ways of improving the contract companies' books. Donald Cormie's idea was to fail to declare full additional credits, creating yet another expense deferral on the financial statements. Johnson took notes: "Rick Mathes and I both stated that the regulatory people would not like this and would probably require us to notify our contract holders that the additional credits weren't declared in their full amount. However, DMC seemed to think we didn't have to do this."

Marlin had an even more extraordinary suggestion: they should raise another $100 million in investment contract money, then invest it in the stock market to earn a 25% return. He spoke as if this were a sure thing, and seemed not to grasp the impropriety of raising money from new investors to solve old problems. "My suggestion," Marlin testified, "was that rather than restrict the size of the company and wind it down, what we really needed to do was to increase the size of the company so the problem was smaller in relationship to the total assets. If we, in fact, could invest $100 million and, in fact, earn 25%, that would compensate for the non-producing assets... Bill Johnson was rather amazed that I would suggest that we should raise $100 million and invest it to earn 25%. He seemed more concerned that that would damage our credibility with the regulatory people and with Tony Wooldridge. I didn't share his concern about that. I was looking for a realistic approach that could, in fact, increase the income and make it workable."

The next day, Marlin and Johnson were back at Treasury to ask Kalke what he would need before he could give them a comfort letter for auditor McCutchen. Kalke said he would help them out by not pushing for delivery of the companies' financial statements as long as they were making progress on a work-out plan that would be acceptable to the province. But the solution had to be detailed and feasible, he emphasized, because he did not want to go through the same thing again the next year.

April 27, 1987

ALL KALKE MAY HAVE BEEN WILLING to give the Principal companies time, but his British Columbia counterpart was running out of patience. David Sinclair, accompanied by Bill Smith, arrived in Edmonton for an update on the Price

Waterhouse investigation. He again warned the Alberta regulators that if they didn't move soon, he was going to take action on his own.

During the meeting, Wooldridge briefed the B.C. officials on the circuitous method by which he was obliged to gather information from the contract companies. Then he explained that completion of his report was delayed pending receipt of their audited statements and described a number of suspect transactions, including the trust company's $9.2-million asset dump two months earlier. Smith learned for the first time about the lack of security behind the back-to-back subordinated notes he had accepted in lieu of a capital injection the previous August. Then there was the prickly reserve issue: should only the "guaranteed" 4% be reserved, or the entire amount of interest expected by investors?

"Frankly, as I think I said at the meeting," Sinclair testified, "I questioned the relevance of some of that discussion because I felt that there was a much deeper underlying issue, which was that of the financial position of these companies as a whole and what might be done to address that situation." Sinclair did not believe the problem was confined to the contract companies, and wanted a thorough assessment of the entire Principal conglomerate. It was the first time in a decade that anyone in authority had demanded that kind of analysis.

The group also discussed making another demand for capital. Participants' memories differ on this point, but Smith testified that he left with the impression that Kalke was going to write Marlin the following day, setting a two-week deadline for a capital injection of $50 million to $60 million. Sinclair, for his part, suspected that he might have to take unilateral action. Soon afterward, he engaged the services of a retired senior banking official to help him prepare for that eventuality.

Three days later, Ken Marlin and Christa Petracca arrived at Smith's Victoria office and asked how the meeting had gone. "I mentioned to him," Smith testified, "that he would have received a letter from Kalke, and he told me he hadn't... I said, 'Well, you would need about $50 million to make things right.' I said, 'You know, you could also make all of these things public and then we would see what happens.' " Nonplussed, Marlin and Petracca beat a hasty retreat.

Meanwhile, on April 27—as Alberta and B.C. were discussing the $50 million capital demand—Donald Cormie decided to bring out still bigger guns in his escalating battle with the regulators. Cormie met with Cormie Kennedy law partner Bob Duke, who contacted Jack Agrios, the high-powered city lawyer who served, with Gary Campbell, as co-counsel to the Cormie Kennedy firm (and was yet another member of Don Getty's 1985 leadership campaign team).

Agrios testified that Duke explained to him that Cormie's company had some problems, primarily to do with regulatory issues, and that he wanted to retain senior counsel. A couple of days later, at a briefing with Cormie, Marlin, Duke, auditor Don McCutchen and Coopers & Lybrand consultant John Ryan, Agrios was told that the problem centered on a debate concerning the values of certain real estate properties. At that time, Agrios said, he thought they were talking about a capital deficiency in the contract companies of a few million dollars.

Within a week, it was obvious to him that the problems were far greater.

Ryan and Agrios agreed to work together, with Agrios as "quarterback," to help the company work out a solution. Over the next few days, however, they handed Cormie a list of conditions: Bill Johnson, who had given notice, had to stay and assist them; they would have full access to the contract companies' books and personnel; they would be free to communicate with Treasury staff; and any capital expenditure over $25,000 had to be reviewed with them and cleared through the Treasury department.

April 29, 1987

PRINCIPAL'S SALE STAFF WERE NOTIFIED of a new push on promissory note sales. An April 29 interoffice memorandum issued by John Ritchie, Principal Group vice-president, marketing, introduced a call option on one-year notes, allowing clients to cash in their notes after 30 days. Salesmen would get the full one-year commission, even if these notes were cashed out just a month later.

April 30, 1987

WHILE KEN MARLIN AND CHRISTA PETRACCA were dropping in on Bill Smith in Victoria, Donald Cormie, Jack Agrios and John Ryan went to visit Allister McPherson and Al Kalke. This was Cormie's first meeting with the Alberta regulators since mid-November, and they were relieved to find that they had his full attention. Indeed, they were anticipating a request for government assistance. "The question is," McPherson told them, "what is required to fix, and who does it or assists in it?" For the first time, Cormie suggested that his mutual fund management company PSML could rescue the contract companies. PSML was going public in the near future, he said, and could easily generate sufficient cash for this purpose.

The Treasury officials asked for an explanation of several perplexing inter-company transactions which seemed to have no apparent business purpose. A meeting was set for the following week to hear the explanation.

May 4, 1987

THE CORMIES STARTED TALKING ABOUT resurrecting the PSML public issue in mid-March, around the time the Coopers & Lybrand consultants were hired. This time the plan was for a secondary issue only, with existing shares owned by CSI (the Cormies and Marlin) to be offered to the public. All the proceeds would go directly to CSI, presumably to pay down the Principal Group promissory notes.

Christa Petracca, meanwhile, seemed to have found a solution to the securities licence problem, clearing the way for Principal salesmen to sell PSML shares to the public. Efforts to persuade the Alberta Securities Commission to grant Principal Consultants a securities licence had been unsuccessful; the officials stuck by provincial rules prohibiting dual licences as both a mutual fund and securities dealer.

However, following an appeal to Consumer Affairs Minister Elaine McCoy (then responsible for the commission), they agreed to have a Principal subsidiary, newly created with a separate sales force, obtain the licence. In mid-March, an application was filed on behalf of Principal Securities Ltd., and an experienced broker was hired as president.

This plan came together quickly in the weeks after McCoy attended a January 20 luncheon with Petracca and Cormie.[3] Petracca testified: "We—Mr. Cormie finally decided that since Bill Connauton and Lynn Patrick were not achieving the objective via the normal process, that we should attempt to appeal to the political people involved." McCoy put Cormie in touch with a Calgary member of the commission, and later arranged for Cormie and Petracca to meet with then-commission chairman William Pidruchney. Petracca had several subsequent meetings with Pidruchney and other commission officials and eventually worked out a solution to the problem.

In a mid-April memo to McCoy, Pidruchney reported: "We have been working in a positive way to achieve the desired registration... if you intend to communicate with [Petracca] at the present time perhaps you might simply indicate that you are advised that the issues she raised earlier [about Commission policies] are being taken care of in this set of discussions and if that is not the case then perhaps she could let you know if she still requires any specific discussion with you." Then Pidruchney asked a question that would be the death of the long-coveted licence: Did McCoy, or the Provincial Treasurer, have any concerns about registering a Principal subsidiary as a securities dealer? "If you have any observations respecting any potential conflicts of interest between these subsidiaries, or any restrictions against self-dealing which you think should be put in place, this would be a good time to have these made known."

Pidruchney's memo sat on McCoy's desk for a couple of weeks. Then, on May 4, she passed it to Treasurer Dick Johnston, who passed it to Deputy Treasurer Allister McPherson with a request for a draft reply. It sat on McPherson's desk until early June, when discussions with Principal were reaching the crisis phase. On June 4, McPherson told Johnston he would be wise to suggest to McCoy that she "hold the application" until the situation was "clarified."

The next week, Johnston wrote a memo to McCoy, saying he was concerned about potential conflict of interest or self-dealing situations between the proposed securities dealer and Principal Trust, and that existing regulations didn't cover the potential problems. It was, therefore, "premature" to approve the registration; besides, "I do have some other concerns in this respect and would like to discuss this matter further with you." What was said between the ministers is not known.

McCoy had made no reply to Pidruchney's request by the end of June when the contract companies went down.

May 6, 1987

WHILE THE PRINCIPAL OFFICIALS huddled with their consultants in the Principal tower, and regulators assembled in the Treasury offices—each group preparing for the next day's (in Jack Agrios' words) "round table discussion, without prejudice"—Christa Petracca launched her campaign to have Donald Cormie pay her a huge bonus.

"She bugged me about her bonus and that she was entitled to it," Cormie testified. "And she did that from May 6th on." The money had been promised, he said, as an incentive to develop key real estate. (Cormie said he had first discussed a bonus with Petracca more than a year before. Ken Marlin and Cormie's sons John and Jaimie said the first they heard of it was in early 1987.) Petracca got the first installment within two days. On May 8, Cormie authorized a payment from Principal Group of $75,000. Cormie said the money was an advance against a total of $235,000—10% of an expected $2.35 million in government grant money negotiated by Petracca for the Rimrock Inn. The entire bonus was to be credited against Petracca's house mortgage with Principal Group.

The balance owing, Petracca calculated, was $160,000. She wanted it.

21

Two different planets

May 7, 1987

THERE WAS A GROWING SENSE of urgency now. British Columbia continued to press for a resolution of the contract companies' deficiencies, and seemed perfectly capable of unilateral action. There was a going-concern note in the financial statements, and a government consultant suggesting the companies be taken down. As Deputy Treasurer Allister McPherson said: "Time is of the essence. The press has picked up some rumours." (Not to worry, Jack Agrios replied. "We were able to stop the press.")

All the parties were finally in the same room, ready to thrash out the issues. Accompanying McPherson to the Thursday morning meeting were Superintendent of Insurance Al Kalke, Treasury auditor Nick Romalo, Treasury bailout analyst George Kinsman, provincial lawyer Jim Rout and government consultants Tony Wooldridge and Bob Sword, from Price Waterhouse. B.C. Superintendent of Brokers David Sinclair was there, accompanied by Bill Smith and Al Mulholland, the province's new Superintendent of Financial Institutions, responsible for trust companies.

Donald Cormie and Ken Marlin were flanked by advisors Jack Agrios and John Ryan and Deloitte Haskins & Sells auditor Don McCutchen.

McPherson led with a summary of Alberta's concerns, followed by Cormie, who blamed the problem on mounting real estate losses. Cormie plugged PSML as the group's future strength. Meanwhile, he suggested, a "bridge" was required to cover the real estate losses. This appears to be the first time that Cormie mentioned "bridge financing," which instantly became the negotiation buzzword. In testimony, Cormie described it as a sort of interim loan, repayable when the fortunes of the contract companies or Principal Group improved. The idea was that the government would provide money to help pay out maturing certificates and would somehow be paid back later as assets were liquidated.

At the regulators' request, McCutchen had spent the previous week diagramming half a dozen quirky deals: the 1984 Carma asset swap; the contract companies' acquisitions of Athabasca Holdings and Matrix Investments stock; the reversal of administrative charges; and the recent $9.2-million trust company asset dump into the contract companies. Now he walked the meeting through a 243-page binder which detailed the movement of money and assets among the various companies.

Then Agrios took over, proposing that he and Ryan develop "a proper business plan." The plan would take up to three weeks to complete, he said, and he suggested that Principal representatives report to Treasury officials every four days.

Sinclair thought Agrios' proposal meant definite progress. "I was impressed by Mr. Agrios," he said, "and I know Mr. Ryan to be an individual of competence and experience in these matters." (Sinclair and Ryan were both senior partners with Coopers & Lybrand.) Nonetheless, Sinclair wanted his own man on the scene, helping with Price Waterhouse's investigation. Sinclair repeated his demands for complete financial statements on all the Principal-affiliated companies, and for up-to-date valuations of the contract companies' loans and real estate.

The Principal group returned to Principal Plaza and formed a secret committee which was to meet every day with Agrios and Ryan in the penthouse boardroom. The group included Bill Johnson, finance vice-president of the downstairs companies, and Rob Pearce, familiar with Cormie's upstairs companies. Marlin and Cormie dropped in from time to time, as did Coopers & Lybrand partner Bob Brintnall and Cormie Kennedy lawyer Bob Duke. Cormie and Pearce told their secretaries the committee's work was highly confidential and not to discuss it with anyone.

Cormie instructed Ryan and Agrios to "seek any government help that we could get." Agrios testified that he conceived the objective to be an "orderly wind-down" of the contract companies that would allow the other Principal companies to continue. "Probably the best example of that was the manner in which the North West Trust bridging had been handled," Agrios said. North West Trust and Heritage Trust, we'll recall, had received extensive financial help from Alberta between 1984 and 1986; then, in February 1987, they were forced into a merger. The restructured trust company, also named North West Trust, was relieved of $293 million worth of bad assets, which were buried in a newly formed, unrelated shell company and quickly written down to 45% of their original value. Another $30 million worth of trash was sold at book value to the shell company over the next three years, helping North West Trust to proudly declare profits every year since the bailout.

North West Trust has an interesting history.[1] The company, one of the Allarco Developments assets sold to Carma in 1980, was dormant when purchased in 1958 by Dr. Charles Allard and built into a company with assets of $460 million. In November 1982, Carma sold it to Chateau Group, owned by Irving Kipnes and Larry Rollingher. When the company got into trouble, the province was quick to jump in, to the tune of $95 million in 1984 and 1985. After a vigorous search for a new investor failed—no one was interested without long-term government guarantees against future losses—Alberta took it over. The only other alternative, the liquidation of both it and Heritage Trust, was unacceptable, Treasurer Dick Johnston told reporters the day the merger was announced.

The federal and provincial Conservative governments worked together to backstop the restructuring, to prevent what Johnston described as political repercussions resulting from yet another collapse. The CDIC poured $275 million into the reorganization, contingent upon Alberta's support until the company returned to profitability. The merged North West Trust was owned 99% by the Alberta government, with Premier Don Getty's confidante Gary Campbell as chairman. The shell company which swallowed the real estate, 354713 Alberta Ltd., nicknamed "Softco," was jointly owned 99.9% by the province and its Treasury Branches. The remaining .1% was held by company director John Karvellas, a lawyer with Cruickshank Phillips, much of whose practice was on behalf of the Treasury Branches. Because the numbered company was not completely Crown-owned, the province's Auditor General was prohibited from making a public audit of the books. (Karvellas, coincidentally, had became Bill Connauton's new partner in early 1987 when Connauton left Cormie Kennedy to join Cruickshank Phillips. The firm was later renamed Cruickshank, Phillips, Karvellas and Connauton.)

Heritage's and North West's affairs, in both their pre- and post-merger forms, remain obscure. Unlike Principal Group and Alberta's two failed banks, they never endured the scrutiny of a public investigation, and we know very little about the events leading to their collapse and rejuvenation.[2] We do know that both were under intense scrutiny by the CDIC by 1984, forcing Alberta to address their problems. And we know that after the two trust companies were merged, North West's owners, Kipnes and Rollingher, and Heritage president Gordon (Bud) Conway lost their investments in their trust companies, but were allowed to remain involved. Conway, a former treasurer of the Alberta Conservatives, joined the management of the new North West Trust; Kipnes and Rollingher acted as consultants to help manage the assets in the shell.[3]

Cormie thought it reasonable to expect a similar solution.

Why then, finally, did the worst occur? There were two problems: first, the situation was worse than anyone imagined, and would be tough to keep hidden if provincial money were tossed in. More important, the egotistical Cormie was the mythic irresistible force. Unfortunately, when he tried to plough through Treasurer Dick Johnston, he encountered an immoveable object. Johnston, every inch as smart and strong-willed, would not be pushed around.

If Cormie had been a little more humble and a little less greedy, the story could have ended very differently.

May 7, 1987

THE FEDERAL REGULATORS HAD BEEN demanding a capital injection into Principal Trust for months. Finally Robert Hammond, the federal Superintendent of

Insurance, sent his Alberta counterparts a summary of his concerns. Besides being seriously over-borrowed, he said in a May 4 letter, Principal Trust's operations "are not being conducted in accordance with sound business and financial practices in that: it sells, through its branch system, the products of related companies when such companies are in serious financial condition."

On May 7—the same day the Alberta and B.C. officials were meeting with Donald Cormie—federal Department of Insurance investigator Denis Sicotte couriered a letter to John Cormie. The trust company's borrowing-to-capital ratio in March was 26.3:1 and its capital deficiency was now $3.8 million. John wrote back four days later, disputing the feds' method of calculating the ratio and complaining about its "alarmist and restrictive attitude." He proposed a different method of calculation which would have reduced the ratio to 8.41:1.

Sicotte wrote back a week later, agreeing to adjust the ratio for March to 22.6:1, requiring an injection of almost $3 million.

The federal officials made plans for a trip to Edmonton.

May 8, 1987

WITHIN A DAY OF THE MAY 7 MEETING, information was flowing from Principal Plaza to the Treasury offices and to David Sinclair in Vancouver. Jack Agrios sent Allister McPherson an organizational chart of all the Principal Group companies, showing their relationship to grandparent company Collective Securities Ltd. and the mutual fund companies.

At McPherson's request, Nick Romalo prepared a number of analyses, including a summary of the asset transfers from Principal Trust to the contract companies, and a schedule of administration, interest and distribution fees and the subsequent "forgiveness" of some of the charges. Romalo was also instructed to ask Jim Rout whether the sale of trust company properties to the contract companies was lawful. His supervisor Reg Pointe, Director of Trust Companies in 1984 when the first transfer occurred, knew perfectly well that the *Trust Companies Act* forbade such a transaction, but Romalo was told to ask again.

Romalo was also told to ask Rout whether the contract companies' investment in Athabasca Holdings was permitted under the *Canadian and British Insurance Companies Act*. This question had been answered by lawyer Sydney Bercov more than a year before, and Rout replied on May 13 with the same answer Bercov had given: the affiliated company was not a qualified investment.

Meanwhile, the first of the every-four-day meetings took place on May 11, a Monday. Agrios and John Ryan had prepared by studying balance sheets and cash flow reports. They sat down with McPherson and Al Kalke and admitted, for the first time, that the contract companies were not viable without outside support. They also pointed out that Principal Group—traditionally the contract companies' source of support—carried its own burden, in the form of $92 million worth of promissory notes to the public. Both McPherson and Kalke testified that they were astonished at the magnitude of the note sales.

On Thursday, the four men met again. Given that the contract companies were insolvent, the regulators acknowledged a responsibility to protect new investors. McPherson suggested that, rather than cancelling the licences or stopping all sales, new funds should be isolated in a trust fund, retroactive to May 1. Someone suggested creating a "soft company," similar to those created for the credit unions and trust companies, where the contract companies' "soft assets" could be dumped.

By this time everyone was aware of Christa Petracca's massive expenditures on a handful of development properties. Agrios testified that he was very sceptical about their propriety, particularly the fortune being poured into the Rimrock Inn. The four men agreed there were to be no expenditures in the companies of more than $25,000 without their mutual agreement.

Agrios and Ryan headed back to Principal Plaza for a long meeting with Cormie, Marlin and Petracca. The consultants quizzed Petracca about her development projects, and Agrios warned her against further major spending without his authorization. (Two days before Petracca had authorized the expenditure of $1.5 million for excavation and construction of a new foundation adjacent to the existing hotel—Phase I of her luxury spa. Excavation proceeded, resulting in a gigantic hole in the mountainside.)

After the meeting, Agrios wrote letters to Cormie confirming the points covered during the discussion. He emphasized that the $25,000-spending cap was essential to maintain the credibility he had established with the province. A second letter dealt with the plan to segregate new investors' money in a trust fund so "they can be separately identifiable and traceable." Provincial lawyer Jim Rout and Cormie Kennedy lawyer Bob Duke were asked to work out the details.

May 11, 1987

THE SAME DAY JACK AGRIOS AND John Ryan enlightened the astonished Alberta regulators as to the magnitude of the promissory note sales, Donald Cormie wrote a memo clamping down on information on the flow of the note money. The memo was addressed to Ken Marlin's son Byron, an employee in the Principal Group computer department, who prepared the weekly promissory note cash flow summary. He was ordered to restrict distribution of the summary to Cormie and his son Jaimie.

May 19, 1987

THE SECRET COMMITTEE SCRAMBLED to pull together all the requested data and produce an analysis of the situation. At the next of the every-four-day meetings, Jack Agrios gave Allister McPherson a mountain of documents, including a maturity analysis of Principal Group notes, the financial statements of the group companies, and a list of five future "scenarios." All but one involved a government bailout.

Scenario #1 showed what would happen if the Principal Group companies continued to operate without any intervention. The numbers were appalling: the contract companies would lose between $22 million and $42 million every year for the next five years, totalling losses of $201.6 million by 1991. Principal Group's losses would total $49.6 million by that same year. The scenario advised: "As can be seen from the attached five year profit plans, the earnings of FIC, AIC, and PGL show significant losses; and, therefore, the companies in their present state are not viable." And it concluded:

> It is clear, therefore, that to operate the investment contract companies and PGL under this scenario is not feasible. The losses in each of the companies are extremely significant and do not warrant continued operation. Also, financing of deficits in the subsidiaries would have to be done through the raising of additional PGL note money which is not an acceptable practice on a long-term basis.

Next came four bailout strategies, each based on different assumptions. Scenario #4, recommended by the consultants, would be the most expensive for the province. It called for immediate repayment of all investment contracts, including all accrued interest. The plan would require an initial government outlay of $386 million, which would be reduced to $177 million after the companies' assets were liquidated.

This document was prepared with the full knowledge of Donald Cormie and Ken Marlin. It seems odd, after fighting for so long to bury the companies' problems, that they would permit the consultants to so frankly admit a catastrophe. By now, however, they were anticipating some form of bailout—bridge-financing, or a "soft landing," as Cormie called it. According to Marlin, they got greedy. By maximizing the problem, they hoped to maximize government support.

Marlin and Cormie testified that they never believed the companies were insolvent, and felt the scenarios grossly exaggerated the problem. In the end, they blamed the consultants' presentation for the companies' collapse. "The worst case scenario presentation got out of hand," Marlin said, "and ended up creating a problem so big they couldn't help us." (Ryan, Agrios and Bill Johnson testified that they considered Scenario #1 an honest reflection of the crisis.)

Marlin said he complained to Cormie about the scenarios, but "I think you have to get it in context and realize that we, at this point, still believed that there was help on the way." Marlin made no strenuous objection because he had been led to believe "that the conservative approach, the worst case scenario would be a great confidence builder, and that was what was vital as far as getting government support. We had to show that we, in fact, needed support, so you make the hole as big as possible, and you understate your assumptions so that they have confidence that you're being realistic."

Cormie's testimony in this area was confusing. He said the companies weren't viable unless they received fresh capital, but he thought $20 million to $25 million would have done the job. He also said the companies could have continued indefinitely to meet their obligations as they fell due "if they had just continued in business"—continued, that is, to suck in public money. At the same time, he agreed, there "was kind of an indigestible block" of certificate maturities coming due during 1987. "So it was felt that there would have to be a bridge to be able to pay those people out in '87, those high maturities, and to recover it later on from a disposal of the assets in a more orderly fashion."

Cormie said he let his consultants take the lead. "I was told by Jack [Agrios] that he was confident that we were going to get something in the way of a bridge or help and—he didn't promise it, he said that, you know, it hasn't been decided, but he was confident something was going to come. So we just proceeded on that basis. We didn't see any point in interjecting something different." Cormie said he had always had a fall-back plan: "It was always our intention as directors, that if the government wasn't going to do anything and help in no way, then we would have put the capital in because we had it, and that's assuming we would have got the licences. If we got the licence, we would have got an unqualified audit."

Having delivered the scenarios, Agrios began to sell the Treasury officials on the benefits of a bailout. Basically, the government would provide money to help the contract companies wind down. Then money raised by a public offering of PSML would be used by CSI to pay down the approximately $66 million it owed to Principal Group, and Principal Group would pay off the promissory noteholders. Then the Cormies and Marlin, their trust company and the profitable mutual fund operation in hand, would continue on their merry way.

A letter written by Agrios to McPherson a day after the May 19 meeting listed 10 "benefits" of government assistance:

- avoidance of liquidation values on asset realization;
- avoidance of excessive costs on receivership proceedings;
- use of experienced personnel in asset realization;
- maintenance of Alberta financial institutions including all of the developed advanced technologies;
- protection to depositors being consistent with similar procedures in Alberta with substantially improved realizations;
- maintenance of the substantial commission income and cash flow from PSML;
- effectively creating a procedure to sell loss carry forwards and create increased cash flow;
- ensuring the protection of employment for approximately 500 in Alberta;
- establishing a procedure to effect a public issue of PSML which is available to reduce the Collective Securities Inc. loan; and
- moving any possible shortfall to Principal Group Ltd. noteholders and establishing a procedure to service the noteholders.

During the May 19 meeting, the participants discussed the public relations impact if the contract companies were wound down. The Principal representatives wrongly assumed that help could be provided secretly, with no one the wiser. "There's no way to keep the assistance quiet," McPherson advised them, acknowledging this could be a "major problem."

There was also some discussion of stopping promissory note sales. Agrios' follow-up letter advised that he was talking with Cormie about a program "whereby no new Notes to new investors will be effected." However, roll-overs (reinvesting maturing notes) would continue. "We will be confirming this with you within the next day." Despite this, note sales continued for weeks.

Two days later, on May 21, two more meetings took place. First, the Principal consultants met with Treasury staff, then Treasury officials met separately. At the top of both agendas was the fact that new investors' money continued to flow into promissory notes and investment contracts while lawyers attempted to work out new trust arrangements. (The idea was soon dropped as unworkable.) Regulators were also concerned about the impact on Principal Group's noteholders if the contract companies were liquidated, and asked the consultants for more information about the resources available to pay off the notes.

Later, the Treasury officials began work on a nine-point plan, preparatory to drafting recommendations to the Treasurer, and conversation turned to previous bailouts. George Kinsman's notes observed that: "Given precedents it is going to be very difficult to support the Cormies."

May 22, 1987

Tony Wooldridge COMPLETED THE SECOND VERSION of his Price Waterhouse report and delivered it to Superintendent of Insurance Al Kalke. At Treasury's request, it was again submitted in "draft" form. Wooldridge noted that he remained hampered by insufficient information. This time there were no recommendations, but the report concluded as before that the contract companies did not meet the Section 8 tests. The first draft had identified a combined capital deficiency of $32.6 million; this second draft reported deficiency of between $23 million and $61 million.

Just as serious was the fact that every month the companies dug themselves deeper into the hole. Wooldridge calculated that they were earning roughly 6% to 8% on their assets, while owing 10% to 12% on the investment contracts. "As a result the companies are incurring 4% to 6% negative margin on their operations before expenses." Vindicated by the doomsday scenarios presented earlier that week, Wooldridge pressed his point:

> On a very preliminary global basis it appears that the Companies require an
> injection of capital and/or earning assets in the order of magnitude of $150 to
> $200 million in order to have an opportunity to continue their operations on a
> potentially viable basis.

The Companies have prepared five year projections of their financial statements and cash flows under various sets of assumptions. We have had an opportunity to perform only a cursory review of these forecasts and have had no opportunity to discuss these with officials of the Companies. It appears, however, that these forecasts acknowledge that the Companies cannot continue on a viable basis without a substantial capital injection and that such capital is not available within the group.

By this time, Wooldridge had more information on the intercompany transactions. He reported that the contract companies' balance sheets and net income had been "inflated by transferring shares of a listed company," and suggested the shares of both Matrix Investments and Athabasca Holdings were seriously over-valued. As for the $12.5 million worth of Principal Group preferred shares held by Athabasca, Wooldridge was unable to satisfy himself of the quality of the investment: He had never received the requested financial statements.

A couple of days later, Wooldridge briefed Treasurer Dick Johnston on the report, after which his involvement in the Principal companies ground to a halt. Wooldridge received copies of the companies' "scenarios" as they were prepared, but wasn't asked to comment on them. He was never asked to finalize his report; events, he testified, "just overtook the need for issuing a final report."

Wooldridge said he felt at the time that the Treasury officials wanted to help the Principal companies stay in business. "I believe and feel that if the companies had come up with a halfway reasonable plan for working out of their difficulties, every effort by the regulators and others would have been put forward to make that plan successful... If they had spent less time shooting the messenger and more time working on a solution, we wouldn't be here today."

Johnston testified that he was open to a bailout, although it wasn't a foregone conclusion. "At that point," he testified, "I had not taken a decision as to what the government would or would not do. I was working up possible recommendations for discussions, and among those recommendations was a government-backed restructuring plan... In this case, we were applying certain rules which we had seen in other work-outs with other companies." There was no general policy approach, Johnston said—there's that slippery word "policy" again—"but it did follow an approach which we had followed in other financial institutions."

May 22, 1987

ANOTHER OF THE EVERY-FOUR-DAY MEETINGS. George Kinsman took notes: "The next meeting to discuss investment contract companies going down. [Agrios will] bring Ken Marlin along."

That meeting took place on Tuesday, May 26. This time, with Ken Marlin and three Cormies in attendance, they discussed the kind of assistance necessary to permit the rest of the Principal conglomerate to survive. Marlin suggested that a government guarantee of 8.5% interest on all the contracts (the 4% guaranteed interest and a portion of the promised "additional credits") would keep certificate holders happy. If all they got was their capital and the 4% guaranteed interest, with no additional credits, Marlin predicted it would destroy the Principal Group business, including the mutual funds. There was more discussion of the millions owed to Principal Group's noteholders. By this time, the regulators knew the company's largest receivable was a $67-million loan to grandparent company CSI (the Cormies and Marlin), half of which had been loaned further upstairs to Donald Cormie's company CSL. They had also figured out that PSML, the mutual fund management company owned by CSI—and designed to provide the cash to pay off CSI's debt to Principal Group—had been sold by Principal Group in 1985 for $52,000.

They kept asking questions.

May 25, 1987

A FEW DAYS AFTER COMPLETION of the Price Waterhouse report, the Alberta regulators sent a copy to Barry Kumpf, the retired banking official hired by B.C. Superintendent David Sinclair. Kumpf was assured that the companies had agreed not to issue any new investment contracts, although they would roll over existing ones until their capitalization could be improved or alternative corrective action taken.

Kumpf, until recently a senior officer with the Toronto Dominion Bank, recast the contract companies' balance sheets based on the liquidation value of their assets: He determined there would only be enough money to give First Investors customers 70 cents on the dollar, and Associated Investors customers 72 cents. Kumpf estimated the size of the hole at $130.2 million, based on the assumption of an orderly market which could absorb the real estate. But, he noted in a late May memo to Sinclair, the Alberta government already held a huge real estate portfolio because of previous bailouts. The economy was stagnant, and unloading the real estate could take a very long time.

Kumpf didn't like what he'd seen in Edmonton. He told Sinclair that company officers had said they had "no other means, corporate or private, to fund the deficit." It appeared to Kumpf that the Alberta Treasury Department was prepared to "let this matter drag on hoping that improvement of equity will come from sale of assets or raising of new capital." He suggested that setting a target date of July 1 for improvement of the companies' equity by at least $130 million would "force the hand of Alberta Treasury to support or otherwise."

May 27, 1987

THE FEDERAL REGULATORS ARRIVED in Edmonton for another chat with their Alberta counterparts. As always, they were primarily concerned about Principal Trust, but they pushed for information on the rest of the conglomerate.

Allister McPherson and Al Kalke, speaking for Alberta, admitted there was no longer any question about it—the contract companies were not viable. They were considering several alternatives, they said, ranging from shut-down and liquidation to some sort of government protection for contract holders and assistance to the rest of the group.

One of the Alberta officials said that the province had asked that the companies cease taking new money from the public. Alberta didn't want to see its "exposure" increased, he said. However, contract roll-overs (renewal and reinvestment of maturing contracts) were allowed, because this business was already on the books and would not increase the exposure. "Had we acted last month," he said, "these people would have been caught anyway."

Permitting the roll-overs was, of course, a form of essential support. As Ken Marlin testified: "There was a cash flow problem if we stopped taking money." Without roll-overs, ever-larger amounts of cash would have been needed to pay upcoming maturities, pushing the companies deeper into the hole.

The next day, McPherson and Kalke met again with Ryan and Agrios and actually set a deadline to stop the contract companies from taking in new money; the goal was the following Tuesday, five days away.

Over the next few days, Treasury officials prepared a discussion paper for Treasurer Dick Johnston. That paper, completed the following Monday (June 1), detailed the dilemma: First Investors and Associated Investors were bankrupt, and if intercompany debts could not be honoured, "which is quite likely," total capital deficiencies could exceed $200 million. If the contract companies failed, Principal Group would go down as well, imperilling the trust and mutual fund operations. If government protection was provided to the contract holders, the paper said, "serious consideration needs to be given to the PGL noteholders' situation. There is significant overlap between the two groups, and the same agents typically sold both forms of investments."

A simplified version of the paper, prepared at this same time, warned that B.C. regulators might very soon suspend the contract companies' licences. Johnston studied the paper, then scrawled a couple of notes: "STOP NEW CONTRACTS" and "LIFT LIC[ENCE] IN B.C. LIKELY." He did not question the propriety of permitting contract roll-overs; he did, however, seek further enlightenment on the subject of "complex intercompany transactions".

The next day, Johnston took this paper with him to a meeting of the Cabinet priorities committee, and used it as the basis of an oral report to his colleagues. "I would first of all describe for them," he testified, "the size of the hole in these two companies, provide to them my best view as to what it would require to restructure the companies, give some view as to the backdrop of assets in the other corporations, including a comment with respect to the [Principal Group] notes. And then we would have obviously a political discussion at the same time."

June 3, 1987: a.m.

LISTEN, I JUST DON'T THINK we can wait any longer." David Sinclair was determined to force a resolution to the Principal situation. He arrived in Edmonton, planted himself across from Al Kalke and George Kinsman, and pressed his point: the B.C. government faced charges of regulatory failure if it let the situation drag on. His superiors were asking why something hadn't already been done. If Alberta wouldn't clean up the mess, he wanted the contract companies put into receivership. Sinclair was also blunt about Principal's style of business: "These intercompany dealings just scare the hell out of me."

The regulators then met with Principal representatives, who were geared up to make another pitch for a government bailout. Jack Agrios laid out eight "salvage scenarios"—including the five already presented—for liquidating the contract companies so as to leave the rest of the conglomerate intact. Agrios recommended either Scenario #4 or Scenario #6; otherwise, he said, "there's going to be a major financial disaster." Scenario #4, as we have seen, involved the government immediately paying out all investment contracts, and injecting $385 million. Scenario #6 saw the government guaranteeing all contracts at 8.5%, at a cost of $210 million.

The next day, back in B.C., Sinclair wrote a briefing paper for Finance Minister Mel Couvelier. Sinclair reported that the Alberta officials had indicated their province might consider indemnifying Alberta investors in the event of a collapse, then urged that B.C. refuse to participate in financing a support package. While co-operation between the provinces was desirable, he said, B.C. might have to suspend the companies' registrations if Alberta let the situation drift on more than a couple of weeks. The paper was one of Sinclair's last official acts; he would return the next week to his chartered accounting practice.

Donald Cormie missed the meeting with the provincial officials—he was with securities dealers in Toronto preparing to take PSML public—but was back in Edmonton in time for an appointment with the Provincial Treasurer.

June 3, 1987: 4 p.m.

IT WAS AS IF THEY CAME from two different planets. Dick Johnston couldn't understand Donald Cormie at all.

Here the guy was, handing over a document requesting $385 million in provincial aid for his contract companies, but claiming that the hole was only $16 million. Fifty million in "bridge financing" would somehow set everything right. Cormie didn't seem the least embarrassed—none of this was his fault, after all.

Johnston wanted to help, but was deeply disturbed by what appeared to be very slippery dealings. Johnston well understood that some of the contract companies' money had been used in high risk investments and to shore up related companies owned by Cormie and his family, but Cormie was utterly unabashed, demanding that Alberta take the companies off his hands.

The two men faced off in Johnston's Legislature office and Cormie, oblivious, began a slow slice of his corporate throat. Johnston testified that he had met Cormie only twice before, both times at Conservative Party gatherings. He vaguely remembered Cormie saying something about a problem obtaining a securities licence, but this was the first time they had ever really discussed his business.

"I had indicated to him that our best information was that the losses were well over $100 million," Johnston testified. "For him to come back and say, 'Well, they're only $16 million,' I felt that either my credibility was being tested or I had missed something entirely, but I could not convince him that this was an urgent and pressing problem." Cormie talked about low oil prices and real estate failures, Johnston said, and "he shouldn't be blamed for the problems found in these two corporations. If any blame should be attached, it should be attached to the government because it's an Alberta-based institution operating here in this province and it was our responsibility, not his."

The man's audacity was stunning. Cormie seemed to feel, Johnston said, that "it would be appropriate for those people who had invested in First Investors and Associated Investors to simply move their money into the mutual fund business and live happily ever after, and in some fashion the government should accommodate that transaction... The impression I had, and the clear message was left with me was, you know: 'Don't bother me with these contract companies at this point, you solve the problem, I'll get on with dealing with mutual funds.' "

Johnston wanted some indication that Cormie was willing to share responsibility for the contract companies' losses, "and it just wasn't there." The Treasurer says he asked Cormie bluntly: "Are you willing to put up any money?"

"No," Cormie replied. "It's not my responsibility."

Like Cormie, Johnston visualized a Principal bailout along the lines of the Heritage Trust/North West Trust rescue. But he was hamstrung by the fact that the owners had lost control of their companies, as well as their capital. Since Willard Estey's report the previous autumn on the CCB and Northland Bank failures, it was no longer possible to leave management in place after a bailout, Johnston explained to Cormie. If provincial money went in, he said, the Cormies and Marlin were out. They would not be permitted to either manage the companies or assist in winding them down.

Cormie flatly rejected the idea. There was no way he would even consider a solution that did not leave his family in control.

Johnston replied that the province could simply lift the companies' licences and leave Cormie out in the cold, but Cormie didn't seem to get the message.

During the meeting Cormie talked at length, as always, about the golden future of PSML. The Cormies had tried to take the mutual fund management company public the previous autumn at a value of $120 million; now he handed over material projecting the value at up to $450 million before the end of the decade. Johnston suspected that PSML was worth significantly less. Curious, he agreed to have his people look into the matter.

June 2, 1987

THE PRINCIPAL CONSULTANTS HAD PROMISED Treasury that the contract companies would stop taking in new money by June 2, a Tuesday. That day, Ken Marlin prepared a brief memo instructing Principal sales staff to route new investors' money into trust company term deposits, mutual funds or Principal Group promissory notes. The only cash to go into First Investors or Associated Investors would be money rolled-over from maturing certificates. The memo was sent to Superintendent Al Kalke that day for approval. Before it was actually distributed to staff, however, the memo was intercepted by horrified Principal sales executive Jay Moulton, who went running to Marlin and Donald Cormie.

This was Moulton's first hint that something was seriously wrong in the Principal tower. Few company employees had any idea that there was a financial crisis in the contract companies, or that their licences were in jeopardy. Moulton knew more than most. He was aware of the secret committee which met in the Principal boardroom, he knew there had been discussions with the province and he had heard Donald Cormie make passing references to "bridge financing." But this memo put a whole new spin on the situation.

Moulton met with Cormie and Marlin on late Wednesday afternoon, soon after Cormie's confrontation with Johnston, and argued against the memo. "This was a shock to me," Moulton testified. "I had no idea that this was the magnitude of the strategy that was going to be implemented." The sudden severance of the investment contracts from the Principal product line, with no explanation whatsoever, would be a public relations disaster, Moulton warned: both with the clients and with the sales staff. "It appeared to me at that point that there were certain options that I suggested or questions that I asked that hadn't been fully considered," Moulton said. "And from that, I interpreted to some extent that the decision did not entirely lay with them. It was beyond their control." Moulton suggested alternate ways of handling the contracts but, he testified, no decision had been made when he left.

The next day, a Thursday, suffering what he later described as a nervous breakdown, Marlin entered hospital for a week.

On Friday, a memo was distributed to sales staff. The version that appeared, however, was significantly different from the one approved by Kalke three days earlier. After some misleading hype ("As an initial step toward further emphasizing mutual fund products, we will begin to offer FIC/AIC term certificate products to maturing term certificate customers only") it advised that customers rolling over their certificates would be allowed to add new money to the roll-overs—in direct contradiction of the agreement with the province. No one has ever admitted responsibility for this despicable change. Cormie, Marlin and Kalke testified that they had no knowledge of how the memo came to be altered; each insisted he was unaware of the change until it was drawn to his attention at the Code inquiry.

The following Wednesday (June 10) Jack Agrios wrote a letter to Cormie, copied to Marlin, complaining that new investment money was continuing to go into the contract companies. "It is imperative that this be terminated at once as there can be no misunderstanding in regard to the undertakings that have been given," Agrios wrote. "Any reoccurrences will seriously jeopardize our discussions with the B.C. and Alberta Governments." To no avail: More than $10 million in sales and roll-overs occurred during the month of June.

Agrios also inquired about a trust being established for all new investor money going into Principal Group promissory notes.

Of concern though is the fact that we have been apprised that major charitable institutions have been aggressively approached to invest in PGL notes. This is highly objectionable and cannot be condoned at this time. It is our understanding that new investors will not be aggressively sought for PGL notes and that the current program is merely being maintained to facilitate these investors expressing a desire to participate in the program.

The memo was ignored. Approximately $6 million worth of notes were sold in the subsequent month and a half.

June 5, 1987

THE ALTERED ROLL-OVER MEMO was distributed that same Friday evening to senior sales officials at a Principal area managers' meeting in an Edmonton hotel. Jay Moulton apprised the eager staff of a major shift in corporate focus. Principal was moving away from investment contracts and would increasingly emphasise mutual fund products; a task force was at work developing new products as they spoke. Principal was also moving into the brokerage business, Moulton reported. A new company, Principal Securities Ltd., would soon obtain its securities licence, and then it would be full speed ahead.

Then Donald Cormie took the podium. Unaware that Dick Johnston had, just the day before, thrown the new securities licence into limbo (See Chapter 20), Cormie painted his vision of a glorious tomorrow.[4] They were moving out of the "risk business," away from such things as investment contracts, and into the "fee business" of selling and administering mutual funds. Cormie wanted every Principal salesman to hold a broker's licence. "We'll sell our own stock, that way we can make our own market," he told the crowd. "The advantage to being a broker, we don't have to guarantee anything." Cormie outlined a plan to phase out the contract companies in three or four years, "the sooner the better." They were old-fashioned and obsolete, he explained. By getting rid of them, "we are getting rid of debt. We don't want this liability." There were new provincial restrictions on the contract business "that we can't live with," Cormie said. Then he confidently told the group: "The government will assist with bridging."

June 9, 1987

THE FURTHER THAT TREASURY OFFICIALS unravelled the Principal web, the greater their distress. The following Tuesday, George Kinsman and his colleagues completed a lengthy summary of the Principal situation which commented: "...the legitimacy of management is in serious question." The summary, received by Treasurer Dick Johnston that day, described the likely domino effect of bringing down the contract companies. Because Principal Group had an investment in them, and an additional $67-million loan to its parent company CSI, it too would be insolvent. If the contract companies went down, contract holders would receive at most 60 to 70 cents on the dollar. If Principal Group went down, its noteholders might recover as little as 8 cents on the dollar.

There had been "extensive self-dealing"—a filthy expression in the financial industry—among the Principal companies, and "the financial problems are exacerbated by the intercompany transactions and investments." Charts were attached, demonstrating the flow of cash inside the complicated corporate structure. They showed that almost half the $67 million owed by CSI to Principal Group had been loaned up the line to CSL, Cormie's personal holding company.

The summary analyzed the pros and cons of bailing Cormie out, and offered three reasons in favour of "providing protection to contract holders":

- FIC and AIC are regulated financial institutions selling contracts to public without requirement to comply with *Securities Act* and without requirement to disclose;
- FIC and AIC's contracts have evolved to a point where they are sold as alternatives to GIC's and deposit certificates; and
- Contracts have been sold out of the same premises as trust company deposits which are covered by deposit insurance...perhaps a third of contract holders may be assuming that CDIC insurance applies.

Then it listed five reasons for not getting involved. At the bottom of the list, but large in everyone's mind, was the horrendous "cost to the taxpayer." The list noted that the absence of CDIC insurance was disclosed on contract forms, and that investors had received higher interest than they would have on insured deposits. Thus, it was implied, the investors could be blamed as the authors of their own misfortune. The summary also remarked that government protection had previously been refused to investors in the half dozen mortgage broker companies which had failed in recent years. It ignored the logical error of comparing provincially-regulated contract companies, which had no disclosure requirements, with mortgage brokers, which had been required to file a prospectus before they could sell notes to the public. Finally, it noted: "Use of [same] sales agents may make distinction between certificate holders and PGL note holders very difficult." That is, if government helped contract holders it could, unhappily, be on the hook with noteholders as well.

The summary continued with a list of alternatives for dealing with the situation. The first option was to do nothing; but, "B.C. will take action to remove licence in B.C. precipitating need for action in Alberta." Second, the contract companies could be pushed into receivership without government support—devastating for contract holders and noteholders, as well as the rest of the conglomerate. The credibility of the sales force would be damaged, the mutual fund business would probably be severely disrupted, and there could be a run on deposits at Principal Trust. Receivership could also mean lower values when company assets were liquidated.

The third alternative was to protect the contract holders, either by redeeming all contracts immediately, or as they matured. Either option could be implemented without formal receivership "providing the owners co-operated." The summary referred to Cormie's idea that promissory noteholders could be supported by PSML, the mutual fund management company, either through earnings or the sale of part or all of the company. The fourth alternative, to support the entire Principal conglomerate, was based on Cormie's plan to save his mutual fund and trust companies by expanding into Ontario and Quebec. (There was no indication of how he intended to break down the Ontario regulators' resistance.) Cormie projected that trust company profits and mutual fund management fees would double over the next four years, and that the sale of PSML would bring in between $100 million and $175 million. "We are highly sceptical," the Treasury report remarked, "that the company plans are realistic and achievable."

Treasurer Johnston was also highly sceptical. Nothing in the report came as a surprise to him, and he considered the situation fraught with peril for the government. "My own judgment at this time was that the additional assets in the Principal entity itself were not at all of the order of magnitude described by Mr. Cormie," Johnston testified. "Moreover, I could see that if the government got involved here, the commitment of taxpayers dollars would probably be extensive and considerable and continuing, and that once the government obviously got involved, then of course, any other unforeseen problems or any other liabilities which may come due within the entity would also become our responsibility. That once you started the process on behalf of the government, it would never end until the company was either wound down or sold in some fashion. So I evaluated the risk to the government as extensive. I did not believe that the asset backing in the entity itself was there. And there was extreme reluctance on behalf of management itself, particularly the Cormie family, to move out of this process, to move out of the companies. And so while I can't say exactly when I concluded, I was coming close to the conclusion at this point... I'm not saying at this particular point I made a conclusion myself in my own mind, but I was moving in the directions I've indicated."

The question, for Johnston, came down to three points: Was Donald Cormie willing to plug the hole? Was he willing to do it quickly and quietly and then walk away? And did he actually have the assets to do the job?

Meanwhile, Treasury officials continued to dig into the self-dealing. That Thursday (June 11) Principal finance vice-president Bill Johnson replied to George Kinsman's questions about the $67 million owed by CSI (the Cormies and Marlin) to Principal Group, and the $31 million owed by CSL (Donald Cormie) to CSI. "To the best of my knowledge, and pursuant to discussions with management," Johnson wrote, "there are no notes covering these amounts, nor is there any security, repayment terms or call feature."

The whole thing smelled.

June 15, 1987

JAY MOULTON WAS INCREASINGLY PANICKY about the mounting crisis. In mid-June (he thinks it was June 15, a Monday) Moulton went to Bill Johnson for more information. Johnson showed Moulton the eight scenarios he'd helped prepare for the province, and talked numbers with him. Moulton knew that he was looking at a time bomb. Later that day, he received a phone call from Donald Cormie, who had heard about the meeting with Johnson. Cormie was furious; the matter was highly confidential and none of Moulton's business.

Stock market trading records show that during the Monday lunch-hour, Moulton called his broker and arranged to sell some of his Matrix stock. The best price he could get was $1.20, but he sold 1,000 shares at that price. (Allarco Energy, which normally picked up all offerings, had stopped buying on June 5. The price dropped from $1.45 to $1.25 over the weekend and within days reached the new low.) Two days later, on Wednesday morning, Moulton sold another 10,500 shares, also at $1.20.

Soon afterward, Principal Group returned to the market and the shares made a dramatic recovery. Over the next four weeks, Principal bought virtually all Matrix stock on behalf of its employee pension plan. Diane Stefanski, who handled the buying, testified that Cormie walked into her office, picked up the phone, and connected her with the stockbroker who would be handling the purchases. Within minutes of Moulton's early morning sale, the price was up to $1.25, then $1.35. Within an hour it was at $1.40. After lunch it reached $1.50, the highest it had been in weeks. By the end of the day, Matrix was still at $1.50 and Principal held it there until June 25, when it pushed the price to $1.55.

June 19, 1987

A COUPLE OF WEEKS AFTER their first confrontation, Donald Cormie and Dick Johnston met again. Cormie's position had shifted somewhat; now, he said, he was willing to consider helping out the contract companies.[5] But he didn't offer cash or his Cayman Islands bank. Instead, he wanted to assign half of PSML to the benefit of the contract holders. Cormie suggested he sell half the company to the Alberta government for $75 million, then turn the proceeds over to the contract companies. He would continue to own the other half; then, as Alberta's business partner, would run PSML, somehow using his half of the revenue to "backstop" the Principal Group promissory noteholders.

But there was a condition, Cormie said. "If I put my money into the contract companies, then I should be able to stay with them and work it out." He wanted a restricted licence from the government, allowing him to wind down the companies under a manager's supervision—the long-anticipated "soft landing."

Johnston was appalled. "Look, it's political," he said. "I can't use government money to help your companies and then let you stay in control... If we're going to do anything for these companies, you're going to have to be right out of them."

"Well, how far out?"

"Right up to the top."

Impossible, Cormie said. No management role, no deal. Then he argued that the hole in his companies was much smaller than Johnston believed. Auditor Don McCutchen's 1986 audit of the contract companies (still in draft form) had identified a deficiency in qualified assets of only $25 million, not the almost $300 million Johnston kept talking about.

PSML was a growing enterprise and could easily finance any shortages, Cormie continued. The Treasurer well remembers this presentation: "There was no doubt in his mind the value of the company was growing," Johnston sighed at the Code inquiry. "Every time I talked to him it grew again."

Despite his bravura, Cormie began to understand the scrape he was in. "On the 19th," he testified, "I got my first inkling that this wasn't going to be an easy or a favourable arrangement... that maybe we wouldn't be the kingpins in the wind-down... Then we tried to persuade them the following few days about PSML, how valuable it was." Cormie's first inkling was a trifle late. As far as Johnston was concerned, the game was almost over.

"Mr. Cormie had not moved very much," Johnston testified. "He had offered to put up an asset, Principal Securities Management Ltd., which in my view probably would suffer considerably once it was known that the Principal Group of Companies was in difficulty; and secondly, which was assigned a value far greater than anything I could believe in or in fact anything the department could recommend to me. And that value, even at the 50% level or at the 100% level was not, indeed, adequate to deal with the size of the losses, in my judgment now, in the contract companies."

There was still no indication Cormie was willing to throw in any of his personal assets.

Johnston and Cormie met on a Friday. The Cabinet priorities committee would meet Monday afternoon, and Principal would be on the agenda. Johnston had a pretty good idea what he was going to say.

Having said goodbye to Cormie, Johnston asked Jack Agrios to meet him on Sunday. Agrios agreed, then immediately called Cormie and asked that he and Ken Marlin come to his home for a meeting on Saturday.

That Friday evening, Johnston's officials laboured deep into the night on preliminary paperwork for a take-down of the contract companies. Superintendent Al Kalke completed a Special Report as required under the *Investment Contracts Act.* It advised that a state of affairs existed of a serious nature prejudicial to the contract holders or creditors, then recommended that a receiver/manager be appointed. Treasury officials discussed the timing of this appointment, the necessary public announcement, the possibility of a depositor run on Principal Trust and the province's response to that eventuality.

June 19, 1987

THE FEDERAL REGULATORS' LATE-MAY MEETING with their Alberta counterparts hadn't reassured them about Principal Trust's future prospects. Three weeks later, they again demanded a capital injection—this time for $2.9 million— and criticized a number of "unsound business and financial practices." This letter, written by CDIC president Charles de Léry, laid out a "plan of action" and asked for a response within three weeks.

June 21, 1987

JACK AGRIOS HAD A BETTER FIX than his client on the urgency of the situation. During the Saturday meeting, he pressed Donald Cormie to sweeten his offer to Johnston. Cormie reluctantly agreed to throw all of PSML into the pot and told Agrios he could say so when he met with Johnston the next day.

On Sunday afternoon, before seeing Agrios, Johnston met with his officials and went through the situation one more time. The high-level group, which included Deputy Treasurer Allister McPherson, bailout analyst George Kinsman and his supervisor Jim Drinkwater, discussed the province's potential liability to contract holders if no assistance was provided. Kinsman's notes of the meeting recorded Johnston saying: "Did such a bad job on regulatory side that we have compassion for them." Then this: "government is exposed to some extent." And finally: "[Consumer Affairs] expressing concern." But, Drinkwater said, there was "no basis for saving this business, since when they get their money back—there will be a lot of bad press."

After this meeting, Johnston summoned Agrios and John Ryan to his Legislature office. Agrios announced what he hoped was wonderful news: Cormie was willing to turn over all of PSML to assist the contract companies. "You're too late," Johnston told them. He had made up his mind to recommend that the companies' licences be pulled and the companies be put into receivership; when he met with his Cabinet colleagues the next day, he would oppose a government bailout. "I made it clear," Johnston testified, "what I would be recommending to my colleagues and ultimately to Cabinet, and that it would be a Cabinet decision, not a Treasurer's decision. But I made it clear what I would recommend."

Johnston said he also made it clear that there were two conditions to be met—Cormie had to contribute his personal assets to the bailout, then walk away—before he would consider helping the companies. Agrios confided that he was having a hard time convincing Cormie of the seriousness of the situation.

The next morning, before the priorities committee met, Agrios brought Cormie and Marlin back to the Legislature building for another round with Johnston. What if he turned over all of PSML? Cormie asked Johnston. What if he put up the assets of the grandparent company CSI?

Not that he was actually offering to do so; he just wanted to discuss the idea. What if he turned CSI over to the province and there was money left over after taking care of the contract holders and noteholders? What if CSI operated for a while and generated profits? Cormie thought he should have half the "upside."

"There were discussions of that order," Johnston testified, "and that's when, I think, I advised Mr. Cormie that the government would not use its dollars or take the risk. That the losses intrinsic in all these companies was greater than anything we ever imagined or calculated. And at no time would we allow him to take the upside if the government took all the risk." Anyway, Cormie was still not willing to cede control of the companies. "Although, you know," Johnston said, "he would vacillate. At one moment, he might say, 'Well, maybe I'll step down,' or 'Maybe we'll find someone else,' but then he would come right back and say, 'You know, the only way this thing can be saved is if I'm involved.' It was not clear what his position was at all."

Cormie was suggesting that his conglomerate be severed at the CSI level and everything below the line would be turned over to the province. CSI, owned by the Cormies and Marlin, held the undercapitalized trust company, the bankrupt Principal Group, and shares in Principal Neo-Tech, Athabasca Holdings and Matrix Investments: all troubled companies of highly questionable value. There was no mention of assets further up the line, of Cormie's holding company CSL, where the real prizes —the Cayman Islands bank, Cormie Ranch, and Principal Securities Ltd., the embryo brokerage firm—were held. Nor was there any mention of the Cormie houses or yacht, of Estate Loan and Finance, County Investments or the mutual fund accounts at various brokerage firms.

Finally, Johnston asked: "Is that it? Have you put everything on the table?"

Yes, Cormie said, that was everything.

Johnston said he would discuss the matter with the priorities committee that afternoon and get back to him.

When Johnston met with his fellow politicians that afternoon, he persuaded them that there was only one way to deal with Cormie. They had to put his contract companies into receivership and cut the man loose. The situation was impossible: There would be political fallout, no doubt about it, but they had to walk away. The losses in the contract companies were staggering, and the parent company was in even worse shape.

Our only information on the discussion among that powerful group, which included Premier Don Getty, comes from testimony given by Johnston during the Code inquiry. One deciding factor, he said, was the cost of a bailout. Where would they find the money necessary to do the job, and how could they explain it to the voters? "Given the fact that we have been hard hit by the economy," Johnston said, "given the fact that this was a very significant loss amount, given the fact that there was not much co-operation on behalf of Mr. Cormie and his family to find a reasonable alternative in terms of putting their own assets up, this was the balanced position to take and this was the decision that was made by priorities committee."

No bailout. Agrios heard the news several hours later, and got on the phone to his client.

June 22, 1987

"NO DAMN WAY," GINNY NICHOLSON muttered as she read Donald Cormie's memo. Here was her boss, up to his ears in bailout negotiations, facing the collapse of his companies, arranging another bonus for the Cupcake.

The memo—written the same day the Cabinet priorities committee met—instructed comptroller Nicholson to pay Christa Petracca 10% of any government grant received for development of the Rimrock Inn. The bonus was to be paid by First Investors, not as cash, but to Principal Group to be applied against her recent $300,000 house loan. In May, Petracca had received a $70,000 advance against her total expected bonus. Now Alberta Tourism had sent a cheque for $321,000, and Cormie wanted Petracca to have her cut of that immediately.

Part of Nicholson's job was to query inappropriate expenditures, and this bonus sure as hell looked the part to her. Intimidated by her forceful employer, however, she decided to deal indirectly with the problem. She stared at the memo in disgust and buried it in her deepest drawer.

June 22, 1987

ALBERTA AUDITOR NICK ROMALO was reading the weekend papers when he saw an article in *The Edmonton Journal* about 2,000 depositors, including 350 Albertans, who were suing the B.C. government for regulatory negligence in the failure of an investment and housing co-operative that was declared insolvent in late 1985. Romalo clipped the article and on Monday morning sent a copy to government lawyer Jim Rout with a note: "Have you seen this in the *Journal?* We better be prepared for the same kind of actions—depending on the solution chosen for FIC/AIC."

June 23, 1987

DR. CHARLES ALLARD'S HOLDING COMPANY Cathton Holdings hadn't traded its Matrix shares for weeks. Suddenly, the day after the priorities committee decision, Cathton began a furious dump of its stock. The action began just after the lunch hour with the sale of 10,000 shares. Over the next two days, another 19,500 shares were sold; Principal Group picked up most of them at $1.50 each, but in mid-morning on the 25th kicked the price up to $1.55.

Cathton then went on hold until the afternoon of June 30, when it sold another 2,000 shares.

June 23, 1987

ON TUESDAY AFTERNOON, the day after the priorities committee meeting, Dick Johnston summoned Donald Cormie to his office to inform him of the committee's decision. Cormie appealed for time to work something out. "Mr. Cormie wanted us to defer the decision," Johnston testified. "He did not want us to come to the conclusion, obviously, as we were reporting to him. He said, 'I need more time, we should do something else, we should defer this, we should not deal with it today'—in other words move it sideways.

"I said, 'We can't, we have got to make a decision on this process.' "

Cormie still didn't offer his personal assets, Johnston said.

At 9:30 that evening, the men met again. Cormie tossed around more ideas, but nothing was resolved.

Meanwhile, late that afternoon, Jack Agrios and John Ryan convened a meeting of Cormie Kennedy lawyers and government officials, including Allister McPherson and Jim Drinkwater, to discuss the best way to wind down the contract companies. Rather than appoint a receiver/manager under the *Investment Contracts Act* (as already recommended by the priorities committee), and rather than follow normal procedure under the *Bankruptcy Act*, Agrios and Ryan suggested an unusual strategy they thought would least affect the other Cormie companies.

The *Companies Creditors Arrangement Act* (CCAA) was a little-known, rarely-used piece of federal legislation which allowed a company in trouble to apply to the court for time to come up with a restructuring plan which had ultimately to be approved by creditors. Under the CCAA, a company, controlled by a court-approved manager with the assistance of former management, could continue to carry on business, protected from any lawsuits by its creditors (in this case, the contract holders) until the court order expired. There were other advantages to the CCAA, which in subsequent years has become a popular device for coping with insolvency. In a normal bankruptcy process, liquidation takes place under the eye of the court, and the receiver/manager has a duty to conduct a detailed examination of the company's affairs on behalf of the creditors, with the power to set aside improper transactions. These things wouldn't happen under the CCAA.

There was a catch, however: the CCAA applies only to companies which have issued bonds, debentures or stock issued under a trust deed. The Principal contract companies didn't qualify; but, the lawyers agreed, it would be simple enough to correct that oversight. "The best course of action," Cormie Kennedy lawyer John Cross said in a memo the next day, "appears to be to create new indebtedness for a nominal amount..."

Agrios, Johnston and others testified that they favoured the CCAA because it would prevent a fire sale of company assets and result (they hoped) in the maximum yield for contract holders. Then Johnston continued: "Oh, and finally, I guess, the arguments of the company were that if you moved under this piece of legislation, they may well be able to send a different message to investors generally interested in putting money into Principal Group Ltd., in that they would have an opportunity to soften the terms of the wind-down of the two contract companies, and that might give the company an opportunity to dispose of their interests in PSML, and to maintain, a confidence in mutual funds as well."

The CCAA, a relic of the 1930s, had been conceived as a way of allowing a troubled company to continue as a going concern while working out its problems. No one questioned how the insolvent contract companies were supposed to continue in business when their licences were about to be pulled.

It was quickly agreed that Coopers & Lybrand should become manager of the contract companies under the CCAA. This, of course, was Principal consultant John Ryan's accounting firm, which had a number of earlier connections with Cormie and the Principal empire. Treasury raised the question of a possible conflict of interest with Ryan, who was to be in charge of the file, but Ryan wrote to McPherson, assuring him that neither his recent advocacy work for Principal, nor the firm's previous audit work for CSI and CSL, created any conflict. On the contrary, its knowledge of the companies and their inter-relationships would "substantially enhance" its ability to get on with the task.

June 24, 1987

THE CABINET MEETING WAS ON Wednesday, two days after the priorities committee meeting. Dick Johnston explained the committee recommendation to pull the contract companies' licences. Then, he testified, there was an extensive discussion which took a couple of hours. "I think everybody looked at the alternatives, and we discussed fully the broad range of recommendations, looked at the political side of it, but agreed that the decision of priorities was the only decision which could be made." This is the only information we have on what went on behind those closed doors.

Toward the end of the day, Johnston stepped out of the meeting and gave his officials the go-ahead on the take-down.

That afternoon, while Cabinet met, Cormie and Marlin sat down with Deputy Treasurer McPherson to pitch PSML's ability to rescue the entire conglomerate. Cormie again argued that PSML could be worth up to $450 million by the end of

1989. "I felt that they weren't grasping the significance of that company and its earning power to solve the problems," Cormie testified. "They thought that some of our figures were exaggerated and I wanted to show them that they were real. So that meeting was specifically to deal in detail with PSML and why it was in a stronger position than other management companies, because it did have control of its customers through the consultants; whereas most mutual fund managers deal through brokers and any time the broker says, 'Gee, I like another fund better,' zip, out goes the fund. So this was a much more stable operation than the usual mutual fund management."

McPherson didn't buy it. Treasury's investment specialists had done their own calculations of PSML's value, which they thought might even be dropping. They placed it in the range of $30 to $100 million.

The next day, in a panic, Cormie contacted Bill Comrie and Allan Olson, two of the best-connected people he knew. Comrie, we'll recall, had helped collect Principal Group's $20,000 for Don Getty's leadership campaign in 1985; Olson was co-chairman of the campaign. "These two men had wide business experience and were well-regarded in the government circles," Cormie testified. He passed them a handful of paper, including material on PSML, and argued there was no need for the province to bring the contract companies down. Then, he testified, they went off to make "discreet inquiries."

On Saturday, Cormie met with the two men in Comrie's office. The news was bad: "They just told me that Dick Johnston was adamant he wasn't going to do anything."

We have very little information about the efforts made by Comrie and Olson on Cormie's behalf, except for Cormie's impression that they had seen Getty. Johnston was very reluctant to discuss the matter. Pressed by investors' counsel Robert White, he admitted to a brief phone conversation with Olson, "indicating that he had heard that Principal was in trouble and was I aware that it was a fairly significant financial institution that, in fact, it had political elements and I said yes, and yes...

"It was the normal kind of phone call that you would receive from people who are listening to things. Now, my memory is that they did not advise me they were doing this on behalf of the company. They simply said they had heard about it and wanted to be sure that I understood they were generally concerned about the political implications and was I on top of the issue. That was essentially the tone of the conversation that lasted maybe two or three minutes."

With the elimination of his last hope, Cormie said, he "collapsed." Then he got on the phone to Ken Marlin and his sons.

June 28, 1987

KEN MARLIN HELPED CONVENE a Sunday meeting of staff and advisors to discuss damage control. The group planned a conference call with area sales managers; news releases and employee memos were drafted. For the first time, Marlin heard about the *Companies Creditors Arrangement Act*. A small detail needed to be taken care of to make the companies eligible under the CCAA: arrangements were made to sell a couple of $50 bonds, one for each contract company, to one of Marlin's friends.

Marlin testified that he wasn't too worried at that point. He liked the sound of the CCAA, comparing it to a Chapter 11 bankruptcy in the United States, which allows a company's officers to prolong its affairs for months or even years. "At that point, I was optimistic that a plan could be presented that would see everyone receive their money," he said. "I believed that we could maintain public confidence as long as it was not billed as a financial failure or that the companies were going down."

Marlin, like Cormie, still expected to somehow move the contract holders into mutual funds. Both understood that the province intended to pull the companies' licences on Tuesday afternoon, but neither was concerned about the consequences. At that point, Marlin said, "I was still convinced that it would get very little press coverage, it was not a big item, and that between the new manager and ourselves, with the benefit of the value of [PSML] and what we were in a position to put behind it, we would be able to maintain public confidence."

Jaimie Cormie wasn't so sure. He spent Sunday evening sorting through the corporate securities portfolio and on Monday morning started "selling madly"— pumping up cash levels in the mutual funds, and to a lesser extent the trust company, in preparation for a run. "I knew the ramifications of going under the CCAA would not be very positive to the public," Jaimie said. Other Cormies were also evaluating their portfolios. First thing Monday morning, Matrix president Neil Cormie sold 5,000 shares of his company's stock. He got $1.50 a share, compliments of Principal Group.

Donald Cormie spent Monday and Tuesday trying to hold his mutual fund business together, "because, remember, somewhere between 70% and 85% of our business was mutual fund business and it was still a flourishing business. I was very concerned if there was any way at all that we could avoid the fallout, that we had to do what we could. So I was really more concerned about that and the sales force and the executive group."

June 29, 1987

On MONDAY, THE DAY BEFORE the contract companies were to go down, Superintendent Al Kalke reversed Principal Trust's February sale of $9.2-million worth of mortgages and real estate to First Investors. After months of navel-gazing Treasury had finally concluded, with the help of provincial lawyers, that the transaction was prohibited under the *Trust Companies Act* and the properties were "probably not authorized investments" for the contract company. The reversal increased First Investors' asset base by several million dollars in badly needed cash, and placed Principal Trust in very hot water with the already impatient CDIC.

That same day the trust company issued a news release:

PRINCIPAL RECORDS PROFIT—5 MONTHS, 1987

EDMONTON—Mr. John Cormie, President of Principal Savings and Trust Company of Edmonton, Alberta, announced the unaudited financial results for the five months ending May 31, 1987 showing gross profits of $1,039,000.

Mr. Cormie stated that the company has always believed in a diversified investment strategy which continues to prove itself in the current economic environment. Based on the healthy financial position of the company, Mr. Cormie is looking for a further increase in earnings during the balance of 1987.

June 29, 1987

GINNY, THIS IS Christa Petracca."

"Oh, hello, Christa," Ginny Nicholson replied, glancing at her bottom drawer.

"Don sent you a memo last week about a bonus for me. Can you tell me where my money is?"

"Gee, I don't know. Didn't it arrive?" Too bad: Petracca would have to get Cormie to send down another memo, authorizing Nicholson to write another cheque.

Later that day, Cormie told bookkeeper Diane Stefanski how to record Petracca's bonus. The next day, a $50,000 cheque was cut on the Principal Group account and sent to Bill Johnson for signature. Mid-afternoon, a couple of hours before the contract companies were to go down, an outraged Johnson took the cheque to consultant John Ryan; together they phoned Jack Agrios.

Agrios, up to his eyebrows in the CCAA court order, quickly ordered the cheque cancelled.

June 29, 1987

IN ONE OF THE MOST BIZARRE INCIDENTS of the entire Principal saga, Connie Osterman's records of her tenure as Consumer Affairs minister—including whole boxes of documents and notes dealing with her 1984-1986 treatment of the Principal contract companies—were destroyed the day before the companies went down.

Alberta Ombudsman Aleck Trawick, who investigated the matter a year and a half later, concluded that their destruction was inadvertent. "I was unable to establish any evidence to indicate any conscious effort by anyone to destroy files in order to hide the content, nor is there any evidence to link the destruction of the files to any events surrounding the regulation of any company within the Principal Group."

Trawick found that after the 1986 election a project was established to have ministers' files, stored in over-crowded vaults in the basement of the Legislature, reviewed and then either archived or destroyed. The project was undertaken by Joyce Ingram, deputy secretary of Cabinet, and carried out by Wanda Kolba.

A year later, on April 1, 1987, various ministers' assistants began cleaning out their vaults. The material in Vault Number 5, assigned to the Consumer and Corporate Affairs Department, was reviewed by several previous ministers—with the exception of Osterman. Kolba contacted Osterman's executive assistant Doug Cameron, who said he was too busy to deal with the matter. Then Kolba went to Tom Burns, Osterman's executive director in the Department of Social Services, where she was then minister.

There are two conflicting versions of what happened next.

Kolba says Burns left her with the impression that she was to co-ordinate the destruction of Osterman's files with the minister's secretary Theresa Boyes. Kolba claims that she dealt with Boyes, who indicated that Osterman only wanted her constituency files. The rest were referred to then-Consumer Affairs Minister Elaine McCoy, who had the department's director of records review the files and make a decision.

Osterman's staff say they never instructed Kolba to destroy the files.

With remarkable speed, the records were taken to the Fort Saskatchewan Correctional Centre, a few kilometres north of Edmonton, and burned. Trawick discovered that the centre's incinerator had been destroyed in 1984; the method used to eliminate Osterman's files was "to dig a hole on the bank of the river at the rear of the old jail, place the documents into the hole, obtain permission from the Fire Chief at Fort Saskatchewan, and then light the documents in order to destroy them."

June 30, 1987

A FEW HOURS BEFORE FIRST INVESTORS and Associated Investors ceased doing business, Jaimie Cormie instructed Ginny Nicholson to advance $361,000 in contract company money to Principal Group, as prepayment of a monthly levy for administrative services. The levy was for July, a month when the companies would no longer be in business, and no administrative services could conceivably be provided.

Nicholson did what she was told, then asked Jaimie to sign a memo authorizing the transfer. He refused, and suggested she ask his father to sign. Cormie also refused, but sent an instruction via his secretary to leave the prepayment on the books.

"I was aware that there were negotiations under way with the government, and I was aware that First and Associated were, you know, in financial duress, and I wasn't sure that this was the proper thing to do," Nicholson testified. She wrote a memo to Bill Johnson, summarizing the incident "for the record."

June 30, 1987: 5:00 p.m.

ON TUESDAY AFTERNOON, Donald Cormie went down to the 29th floor foyer and made a speech to head office staff. His secretary Jude Halvorson was there: "Mr. Cormie indicated to the group that was there that they had made application to the court under the CCAA and the licences for First and Associated were not being renewed. There was discussion about the fact that the Alberta real estate economy was poor. There was also mention that the companies could have prevailed and gone on if they had received the financial assistance that they hoped to receive from the provincial government."

In the crowd was Eric Espenberg, a director of First Investors and Associated Investors. "I was shocked!" he testified. It was the first he had heard that the companies were in trouble.

Jay Moulton had scheduled a telephone conference call with area sales managers for five o'clock. Neither Cormie, speaking to head office staff, nor Marlin were immediately available—Marlin had been at the court house with Cormie Kennedy lawyers most of the day, and was still there awaiting the judge's decision—"so we kept delaying the call." Finally, Moulton began the announcement on his own and Cormie took over when he arrived.

Louis Gratton, manager of the Northlands area, took the call in his office on the 9th floor of Scotia Place, a few blocks up Jasper Street. He remembers Cormie saying that the disappearance of the contract companies wouldn't hurt the rest of the Principal companies, "that we were still strong. It was mentioned that this is probably favourable, because now, without these [contract] companies being a problem, the company wouldn't have to be putting cash into them... We would still be moving ahead and moving on, and that everything would be okay... My thoughts were that he was trying to be upbeat, but his voice didn't have quite that crispness that he usually had when he spoke."

There was no need to worry about their investment contract clients, Cormie assured the sales managers. The investors should get 100% of their principal and the 4% guaranteed interest, and there was a good possibility some of their additional credits would be returned as well.

After he hung up the phone, Gratton went to Principal Plaza to see Ken Marlin, finally back from the court house. In the corridor he ran into Christa Petracca. "What happened? What happened?" he asked her. Petracca blamed it on the government regulators. They had badly undervalued the companies' real estate, she said: the Rimrock Inn, the Prince Royal and other properties. "You know, these guys," she told Gratton, "I don't think they know what they are doing, because those assets are good." Then Petracca, a director of the contract companies, said something so chilling that Gratton would never forget it: "I've been telling Mr. Cormie for years not to put so much money into these companies."

June 30, 1987: 5:30 p.m.

TELEVISION CAMERA LIGHTS WENT ON, pens were poised over notepads and Dick Johnston approached the microphone. While Donald Cormie was giving his version of events to the sales managers, Johnston read a statement to the reporters. At the same time a news release was distributed:

> Provincial Treasurer Dick Johnston today confirmed that First Investors
> Corporation and Associated Investors of Canada, subsidiaries of Principal
> Group Ltd., applied to the Court of Queen's Bench for an Order appointing

Coopers & Lybrand as a manager under the *Companies Creditors Arrangement Act* and have been granted the Order. The application followed provincial cancellation of the registration of the two companies to raise money from investors pursuant to the Alberta *Investment Contracts Act.*

Mr. Johnston indicated discussions have been ongoing with the companies as a result of provincial concerns about their ability to make full payment of their obligations under outstanding investment contracts. The Treasurer stated that the utilization of a plan of arrangement under the *Companies Creditors Arrangement Act* was chosen based on providing the Investment Contract holders with the greatest chance for maximum recovery of amounts owed to them. Investments by contract holders are not insured deposits.

Mr. Johnston indicated he regretted the necessity for these two contract investment companies to take these steps but that protection of the investment contract holders required it be done.

Cormie saw Johnston's speech on the six o'clock television news. "Oh my God, what's he saying?" he gasped. "What's he talking about the licences for?" He sat stunned for many minutes while the implications sank in.

22

"How could Mr. Cormie let this happen?"

THE WORST MOMENT FOR salesman Scott Schroder was the afternoon an elderly client attacked him with her purse. Shrieking "Liar!" and "Bastard!" and "Thief!" she struck repeatedly at his arms and shoulders. Weeping, she begged for her life savings back.

"I had to stand there and take it," Schroder told me. "There was nothing I could do." That night, and for each of the 41 nights between the contract companies' collapse and the day the rest of the Principal house of cards began to tumble, Schroder joined his colleagues at the Schnitzel House restaurant below Principal Plaza and drank himself blind.

He wasn't the only Principal salesman to be attacked; almost every one of them, sooner or later, was called a crook. "How could Mr. Cormie let this happen?" they asked themselves. Every day the abuse got worse, and every night they gathered at a corner table to recount the latest nightmares: the widow forced onto welfare, the truck driver who said he'd be waiting in a dark alley. Sodden and exhausted, they didn't bother to look away whenever one of their group began to sob.

July 1, 1987

HE WALKED INTO A NEWS conference on Canada Day and cut the contract holders loose. No, of course Principal Group wouldn't guarantee the investment contracts, nor would it make up any losses in the two subsidiaries. First Investors and Associated Investors were separate entities, and neither he nor Principal Group was liable for their losses. "The parent company has no responsibility to these companies whatsoever," Donald Cormie told the assembled reporters. "They are stand-alone, limited-liability companies." He had to raise his voice to be heard above the heckling of investors waving their certificates in protest.[1]

Cormie pared down somewhat the predictions he had made to sales executives the day before, but the new numbers were almost as ludicrous. This time he said the 67,000 investors would get their original investments back, but their interest and additional credits were at risk. They might see half their principal with six weeks, and the rest over three years, he said.

Cormie emphasized what to him was the most important point: the contract companies' problems would not affect Principal Trust or Principal's eight mutual funds, all of which remained the best buys in town. For the rest of the conglomerate, it was business as usual.

Among those in the media crush was Rod Ziegler, business columnist for *The Edmonton Journal*. "This is a disaster," he whispered to Cormie's son Neil. Ziegler, the paper's leading business analyst—and formerly its business editor—is, we'll recall, an old family friend of the Cormies. After the news conference, Ziegler joined them at a council of war. "I went over to the Eagle's Nest and we sat around in the big stuffed chairs and Don said, 'I understand you don't think the interview went well,' " Ziegler told me. He talked with the Cormies often over the next couple of years, discussing media coverage of the collapse and of the subsequent Code inquiry. "Neil calls me, and he asks, 'How's the scuttlebuck?' " Ziegler said. "That always makes me laugh, that he thinks it's scuttlebuck, not scuttlebutt."

The Cormies were bitterly frustrated by their inability to control the media spin on their story, and were thrilled to find at least one journalist open to their version of events. They occasionally slipped Ziegler a detail or two, which would appear as a scoop the next day in his column. "I did well with my columns by playing friendly broker," Ziegler told me cheerfully in 1990.

After the collapse, Ziegler wrote dozens of columns about the Principal affair. They were, with rare exception, strongly sympathetic to the Cormie viewpoint and critical of the Alberta government, which both Cormie and Ziegler blame for not quietly bailing Principal out of its troubles.

On the Thursday and Saturday after the Eagle's Nest meeting, Ziegler wrote columns based on what he'd been told by Cormie. The first quoted Cormie as saying that people would get all their money back, that the contract company collapse wouldn't affect other companies in the conglomerate, that the government spurned a request for help from the contract companies that could have avoided the crisis and that the contract companies were victims of the real estate crash. Two days later, Ziegler attacked Treasurer Dick Johnston's decision to shut down the contract companies. "For the record," Ziegler wrote, "it's clear to me that, with the best of motives, Don Cormie and his people moved heaven and earth to keep First Investors and Associated afloat... They are the only failures in the phenomenal string of successes that is Principal Group."

This ringing testimonial so pleased the Principal forces that they immediately distributed copies across Canada to the demoralized sales staff.

Few others were buying Cormie's line. On Thursday—the first business day after the national holiday—there was a rush on deposits at Principal Trust offices.

Mutual fund clients started pulling their investments out; assets under PSML's management had dropped from a record $522 million on June 30 to $373 million when Principal Group went down six weeks later. By the second day, contract holders were phoning reporters and consumer advocacy organizations. They wrote letters to the newspapers, telephoned regulators and provincial politicians, contacted lawyers and repeated their stories again and again: salesmen had assured them that the entire Principal Group was standing behind their investments, that the Alberta government stood behind them. Where were Principal and the government now? Where was Donald Cormie?

Where was their money?

By the end of the first week they were organizing. *Journal* columnist Linda Goyette wrote: "On Friday they frantically tried to find one another. They bought the morning papers, circled the names of other victims in the complicated stories, dialled unknown numbers to share fury and frustration. They begged for collective action on open-line radio shows."

When Edmonton investor Don Logan's name appeared in the *Journal,* his phone never stopped ringing. "There were hundreds and hundreds of calls," he told me, "one sob story after another. One elderly lady was crying. She said: 'I've never been on welfare.' She had $110,000 in what she called 'the bank' and now she was broke. That's how little she knew, she thought First Investors was a bank." Logan and his wife were about to build a house. Their First Investor money—$24,000 tied up for three months in what they thought was a CDIC-insured term deposit—was earmarked for the downpayment, due a week after the collapse. "It was terrible. My wife was eight and a half months pregnant, and I ended up returning calls between her contractions. Everyone I talked to, I said, 'Will you come to a meeting? If we get a group together, will you help?' And then it snowballed.

"I was driven by anger," Logan said. "I was consumed by this. I couldn't go to a party or a social function or meet anybody, without people saying, 'Oh, you're that guy with Principal. Well, why the hell did you bank there anyway? Jeez, I could have told you they were in trouble.' I got sick of this. All these people with perfect hind vision. That raged on for a long, long time."

By that first weekend, Logan was calling for a public meeting; the next day, he and a fledgling Edmonton investors group held a news conference. By Tuesday, groups in Calgary, Lethbridge and Medicine Hat were also planning meetings. Groups in other provinces formed over the next few weeks. They all wanted the same things: government help and a public inquiry into the collapse.

The media attention was persistent and aggressive. The story made the front page of Alberta's newspapers the first day and was rarely off for the next couple of years. Reporters ran with the stories fed to them by investors, and quickly dug up information of their own. By the third day of the collapse, the *Journal*—which for 30 years had written nothing but flattering fluff—reported that the Alberta Securities Commission knew in 1985 that the contract companies had serious problems with their mortgage portfolios; that Johnston admitted knowing six months earlier that the companies were in trouble; that the already-burdened contract companies had recently bought millions of dollars worth of property from their sister trust company. On Saturday, the paper wrote about the misleading *1985 Annual Review*. Over the next few days it reported that the province had allowed the companies to continue sales while regulators took months to evaluate the problem; that Ontario had blocked Principal's entry into that province because of the condition of its contract companies; that Principal salesmen hadn't had a clue about the companies' finances.

And then there was the first public meeting. On July 9, *The Edmonton Journal* published a front page article titled "Investors unleash anger: 'I want my money back,' tearful senior demands":

> More than 1,000 furious investors crammed a convention centre hall
> Wednesday night, demanding the return of cash frozen in two troubled
> Principal Group companies.
>
> "I want my money back," said one man of retirement age, as he entered the
> convention centre. "I lost everything," he sobbed as he covered his face and
> turned away...
>
> Organizers of the "Last Investors Defense Fund" meeting circulated a
> petition calling on the premier to order an immediate public inquiry into the
> collapse...
>
> [Don] Logan said he invited Johnston, Principal Group officials and
> provincial regulatory officials to the meeting. They didn't attend.

For Donald Cormie, local darling for three decades, the uproar was horrifying. He blamed it all on Dick Johnston's news conference. Cormie hadn't imagined in his darkest dreams that Johnston would actually tell the truth about the companies' situation, or breathe a word about cancelled licences. "I was really stunned when I heard the press conference," he testified. "Instead of being a soft, co-operative wind-down to do the least damage to the certificate holders, it seemed to me it was like a publicity event that was going to indicate that there were great problems and wrong-doing, and I just found it stunning... The fallout was unbelievable."

There were feeble attempts to overcome the awful publicity. During the first week John Cormie, as Principal Group vice-president and treasurer, told the *Calgary Herald* the parent company had spent as much as $50 million trying to keep the contract companies afloat. The next week, as chairman and president of Principal Trust, John told *The Globe and Mail* that after an initial rush on deposits, customers were starting to return. He denied suggestions that company salesmen had misled their customers, and said "little would be accomplished by a public inquiry."

The day after that—following coverage of the weeping seniors—Donald Cormie bought two full pages in the *Journal* to publish "An Open Letter to Customers of Principal Group Ltd. and its Related Companies". The July 10 letter blamed the contract companies' problems on the decline of the Alberta real estate market, and promised:

I am determined to see that all our customers are treated honourably and fairly.

I am deeply concerned by this turn of events. Since I helped form the Principal Group in Edmonton 33 years ago, thousands of people have invested their money in various investments distributed by us and **they have been repaid with financial success.**

This is the first lapse from a string of unbroken successes. It's an exception and I am determined it will be the only exception...

The Principal Group management is supporting Coopers & Lybrand with the best people in our organization, because we are determined to see the return of the maximum amount of the funds invested in the shortest possible period of time. We want this cleared up with minimal loss to any FIC or AIC customer as soon as possible...

We want your continued confidence and trust. We're working like the dickens to prove it to you.

And he repeated his key theme: the basic financial strength of Principal Group and its member companies was undiminished. To those with Principal mutual funds or Principal Trust deposits he promised that the contract companies' problems "are not your problems. Your funds are secure."

After his press conference Cormie dropped from sight. To some Principal executives, struggling to keep the ship afloat, it appeared their captain had gone into hiding; others feared for his health. In fact, he was engaged in a campaign— "working like the dickens," you might say—to sell off the rest of the conglomerate before its value deteriorated to nothing.

While Cormie and his son Jaimie worked the phones, Ken Marlin hit the road. The sales chief spent his time propping up the battered sales force, and in mid-July issued a memo to all salesmen confirming that they had not known that the contract companies were going down at the end of June. Incredibly, the still-mesmerized sales force held firm. Only three dozen members of the 418-person team bolted over the next six weeks. Marlin, intent on bolstering promissory note sales and roll-overs, also laboured to maintain the good will of Principal Group's noteholders. He focused on the 22 Hutterite colonies which held a third of the approximately $90 million in outstanding notes. The week after the contract companies went down, Marlin travelled the province meeting with the Hutterites. Many of the colonies' leaders believed they had the option of cashing out their notes early, but Marlin corrected them. Then he explained that despite the failure of the contract companies there was no need to panic.

Jacob Kleinsasser of Big Bend colony near Cardston—with about $3.15 million in notes—attended the Lethbridge meeting and testified that Marlin "gave us real comfort... I can't remember what all was said, but the way he sounded, if my memory serves me right, he says, with those two subsidiaries now being no longer with Principal Group, we are still more secure than what we had been, because, to the example, if you have something that doesn't do well for [you] and you can dispose of it, naturally that is strength, that gives added strength to what you have left over."

Hutterite specialist Arney Falconer followed up with a new sales pitch to Kleinsasser. Principal was working on an even more secure investment plan for the colonies, Falconer told him. "He says, 'It had been good up until now, but it will be still more, that much better now,'" Kleinsasser said. "And, he says, 'We are working much closer with the government, too, and your investments will be more secure than what they ever had been.' But he says, 'I can't give you a firm answer of what it will be, but it should be coming out in the near future, maybe as early as the coming week.'"

Fortunately for the Big Bend colony—and many other potential buyers—the new "more secure investment plan" was not to be. In mid-July, after a secret hearing, the Alberta Securities Commission finally revoked Principal Group's right to sell promissory notes.

In the days after the contract companies' collapse, commission staff had asked for up-to-date financial information on Principal. After a week's discussion, and after learning the information was not available, the staff brought the matter before the commission during a two-day hearing on July 16 and 17. At its conclusion, with the concurrence of the company, the commission issued an order withdrawing from Principal Group the *Securities Act* exemptions which had enabled the company to sell its notes. The order was made retroactive to July 1, and Principal was ordered to return all note money received after that date (more than a million dollars in three weeks).

The commission originally made its order confidential. Five days later it reconsidered, amended the order and made it public.

DONALD CORMIE WASN'T THE ONLY one to cut the contract holders loose. Dick Johnston took the line that the investors were to blame for their own predicament; they knew their investments weren't insured at time of purchase. Principal Group might be held liable for some of the losses, Johnston said, but Alberta certainly wouldn't. Premier Don Getty—who spent part of Canada Day at the race track, and much of the following weeks on the golf course—followed Johnston's lead: it was a shame some "unsophisticated investors" had lost money, but taxpayers would not stand for the province bailing them out.

The usually efficient Johnston suddenly demonstrated a curious amnesia. He originally claimed that the companies' licences were pulled after a "routine audit" indicated there was a possibility they wouldn't be able to make full payment on their contracts; only when pressed by a reporter did he admit he'd known about the problem for months. On July 2, asked by the *Herald* about risk to the parent company, Johnston responded: "I'm concerned. But I'm fairly sure they're in a very liquid position." Liquid, hell. Principal Group was the walking dead, and he knew it. In his rush to blame investors, he also seemed to have forgotten recent briefings on such matters as the misleading *1985 Annual Review* and the fact that an estimated third of the contract holders somehow believed their contracts were CDIC-insured.

Johnston coyly suggested the contract holders' losses might be more than Cormie had indicated, but wouldn't admit what he knew: that they were likely to lose about half their money.

As protests grew, Johnston's department prepared a communique laying out the official government line. The memo, drafted July 9—the day after the Edmonton investors' rally—told provincial MLAs: "It is important for you to realize that while some concern was raised about the financial position of the companies earlier, it was not confirmed until June that the companies would not be able to meet their commitments to contract holders."

That night, a thousand Calgarians met at a community centre to call for government action. During the meeting, investors learned for the first time about the CCAA. The quick sale of a couple of $50 bonds had spared the contract companies the embarrassment and scrutiny of bankruptcy proceedings.

The next day, investors Don Logan and Suzanne Mah went to court to challenge the court order which froze the contract companies' assets under the CCAA. Mah, a lawyer, and Logan, an economic development advisor for Indian groups, made a strong team,[2] and they found a formidable advocate. The next week lawyer Robert White—soon to be appointed investors' counsel at the Code inquiry—argued in Court of Queen's Bench that the two companies were insolvent and should therefore be dealt with under the *Bankruptcy Act* or the *Winding-Up Act*, where their financial situation could be properly examined.

The day after Logan and Mah announced their lawsuit, Conservative backbenchers began breaking party ranks to join in demands for a public inquiry. Johnston and Getty struggled, unsuccessfully, to resist the mounting pressure. A public investigation wouldn't help investors get their money back any faster, Getty told the *Herald* on July 15. "By far the easiest thing to do is call an inquiry like they did into the banks thing...and forget about it for two years," he told the paper. "But that ties up the money for two years. What I'm trying to do is help the investors and not get this off my shoulders onto the shoulders of a judge." He did not indicate how he was helping investors.

That same day, Johnston announced he had expanded receiver/manager John Ryan's powers; he had told Ryan to hold "a complete public hearing and investigation" into the operations of First Investors, Associated Investors and affiliated companies. The order—which had to be approved in court—would allow Ryan to subpoena witnesses, compel them to testify and "look for fraud, dishonesty and claims of misrepresentation." (Most of the investigation could be held in public, but certain information would have to be kept confidential, Johnston said.)

This decision followed the Edmonton investors' appearance at the city court house. Justice Allan Wachowich, who had signed the original court order, authorized a limited investigation of the contract companies, giving Ryan authority to determine if Principal Group did anything "prejudicial" to the investors.

That was the day the *Journal* reported that Ryan's firm Coopers & Lybrand was also the auditor of upstairs company CSI. Ryan denied a conflict of interest, and Johnston said he was unaware the firm had done the work for the grandparent company. "I didn't know that," he said flatly; he had received a letter from Ryan assuring him there was no conflict, and had relied on that. (In fact, minutes of a June 21 Treasury meeting attended by Johnston show that the firm's work for CSL was discussed at that time.)

On July 17, Johnston suddenly discovered wrong-doing in the Principal organization. A front page story quoted him as saying "he now believes there is strong evidence to suggest 'misleading representation was made to investors.' " He wanted Coopers & Lybrand to find out exactly what had occurred. Donald Cormie, the article continued, welcomed this move as an opportunity to "show that we have worked long and hard, and at great cost to other Principal Group companies, to help these two companies... I hope the public hearing will take place as soon as possible, because these companies were managed competently and honourably, and the evidence will support that."

Several days passed between Johnston's announcement expanding Cooper & Lybrand's power, and a court appearance by provincial lawyers seeking amendment of the original order. By that time, the accounting firm's credibility had been further undermined by a *Journal* story on July 21 revealing that Coopers & Lybrand had worked for the contract companies as receiver/manager of the Rimrock Inn as recently as February 1987.[3]

That day, a Wednesday, provincial government lawyers finally made their way to the court house. Their efforts to seek expansion of Cooper & Lybrand's mandate under the CCAA was opposed by both the Edmonton investors' group and by its Calgary counterpart, which wanted to overturn the entire CCAA order. Calgary investors—represented by insolvency lawyer John McNiven, who would later join White as investors' counsel at the Code inquiry—announced plans to seek court permission to file a bankruptcy petition against the contract companies. On Thursday, Saskatchewan investors joined the campaign.

That was the day the *Journal* discovered the Derrick Plaza flip of December 1986. The July 24 article noted the connection of several prominent Conservatives with the building and reported the government was considering leasing space there. It also detailed the extraordinary increase in price during the one-day flip. John Cormie, in a careless moment, told the paper the reported price was deceptive, because the deal included a swap of "soft assets," properties which Principal Trust had foreclosed on and were no longer worth their recorded mortgage values. It was the first hint of the conglomerate's accounting games, and would come back to haunt him at the Code inquiry.

July 8, 1987

THE FEDERAL REGULATORS WERE back in town. The CDIC's letter of June 19, demanding a capital injection of $2.9 million into Principal Trust, had gone unanswered. On July 8, with no advance warning, the CDIC's Jean Pierre Sabourin came to John Cormie's office, handed over a letter from CDIC chairman R.A. McKinlay and announced an inspection to determine the solvency and continued viability of the trust company. Sabourin, accompanied by Edmonton chartered accountant Bruce Robertson of B.I. Robertson Associates, immediately went to work. The next day, a Thursday, Sabourin raised with John Cormie the matter of the capital injection and advised that a response would be required before the CDIC board of directors met in a week's time. The following Monday, the two met again. "I was informed," Sabourin said in a subsequent court affidavit, "that the shareholders had determined that, because of the volatile situation, the best course of action would be to await CDIC's examination results prior to the injection of capital."

On July 16, the CDIC board learned of the current status of Principal Trust. On Sabourin's recommendation, the board agreed to postpone the capital injection until he completed his inspection. However, the delay was conditional on receiving confirmation and security from trust company shareholders that financial resources were available to inject capital as required.

On July 22, after a lengthy meeting between CDIC executives and Principal Group shareholders, the Cormies made a number of promises, including assurances that adequate capital was on hand. None of the promises were kept.

July 23, 1987

THE DAY AFTER THE meeting with the CDIC—and the day after the Alberta Securities Commission made public the fact it had revoked Principal Group's right to sell promissory notes—Donald Cormie wrote letters to Christa Petracca and to Jaimie, John and Neil, forgiving their interest-free mortgage loans. The sons' mortgages amounted to $32,000, $158,500 and $66,000 respectively. Cormie's letter to Petracca said:

> Dear Christa: As you realize, the Group is under tremendous demands at the present time, and we are starting to lose some of our key executives. As an inducement to have you stay and work out the existing problems, at least to year end, we are prepared to pay you a bonus by discharging the [$300,000] loan against your house, with no further payment, effective immediately. You will, however, remit $200,000.00 on the sale of your condo whereupon that mortgage will be discharged. The other will be discharged immediately...

The condominium was not sold until autumn, which means that at this time Petracca owed a cool half-a-million to Principal Group.

There was also the matter of Petracca's quarter-of-a-million-dollar bonus. On June 22, we'll recall, Cormie wrote Petracca a memo tying the bonus to 10% of any government grants received for the Rimrock Inn. She had received a $75,000 advance, and had been clamouring ever since for the rest of the money.[4]

On July 9—the day after the CDIC began its inspection of the trust company—Cormie wrote another memo confirming the bonus but stating Petracca was immediately entitled to it. The money was to be paid to her by the contract companies "at a rate equal to 10% of the cash coming in on the grants to a maximum of $250,000. I must acknowledge that you have in fact done the work which fully entitles you to the bonus, and that our original agreement did not require that you wait for the grant money."

Toward the end of August, after Principal Group went down, Cormie returned the memo to his secretary Jude Halvorson, with a couple of handwritten corrections. The revised version said: "We agreed that your bonus would be paid to you by the Group"—no longer by the contract companies—and continued: "The cash came in on the grants"—in fact, the government grants had disappeared, and only the first $333,000 was ever received—"and although you have been entitled to the bonus for some time, you should now receive it immediately in cash." Cash: no longer was the bonus to be applied against her mortgage, which had been written off a few weeks before.

The memo was backdated to June 22, prior to the corporate collapse.

Under cross-examination Cormie testified: "Mrs. Petracca was complaining about having been ill-used on her bonus arrangement, I was harassed to death at this particular time, July and August, we were working 15, 18 hours a day with buyers, and I said that I would simply dictate a memo to set out the arrangement to clarify it." He said he had unilaterally tied the bonus to the grants, and denied that the memo had been backdated in an effort to make it appear it had been written before the collapse. Petracca, who testified several weeks before Cormie, insisted that she had received the final version of the memo in June "at the time that he wrote it," definitely not in July.

Inspector Bill Code found there was evidence tending to show that Cormie acted dishonestly and fraudulently in backdating the memo, and that it was done "with a view to having [Principal Group] make a valid payment of funds to Petracca so as to avoid the possibility that Petracca may not be paid from [First Investors and Associated Investors] which were by then [July 9, 1987] under the control of the manager, Coopers & Lybrand Ltd."

This matter was one of very few where Cormie admitted to a mistake. He should, he said, have simply given Petracca the bonus in May. "I should have paid it and applied it on the house and let it go at that, but I didn't."

There were other interesting cash flows after the Alberta Securities Commission stopped note sales. On July 22, there was a sudden rush of cash through Department 8 down into the Principal Group promissory note fund. On that day, CSI (the Cormies and Marlin) cashed in several mutual funds and made a repayment of about $1.54 million toward its debt to Principal Group, which at that point had reached about $69 million. Over the next two weeks, five more payments were made—doubtless delivered in a desperate attempt to fund note maturities in the absence of new noteholders' cash —reducing the debt by another $4.3 million. About two-thirds of the $69 million had been borrowed interest free; the remaining portion carried interest rates ranging from 7.875% to 9.5%. The repayments were applied against the highest interest loans.

Meanwhile, on July 28 the "PEP plan" was paid out. This was an remarkably generous investment program offered by Principal Group to company employees and selected others; members of the plan earned a premium of about 4% over the market interest rate on trust company deposits. The payout totalled about $1.8 million, and included almost half a million dollars to Cormie family members and close family friends—several of whom had never worked for the company. The largest payments were $141,577.85 to Cormie's sister Helen Esau, and $157,833.24 to Cormie's brother Gordon and his wife Phyllis (all of whom lived in Sidney, B.C., not far from the Cormie mansions). There was also $40,558.11 to Cormie's father-in-law, who had died the year before.

July 27, 1987

THE SEARCH FOR A BUYER wasn't going well. Several parties were briefly interested, but not at Cormie's prices, and not under the companies' present circumstances. In late July, a potential buyer, alerted by telephone to the Alberta Securities Commission order revoking Principal Group's right to sell promissory notes, stood up and walked out of the Principal board room.

A month earlier, Cormie had been bragging that PSML alone was worth at least $140 million; now he was praying for a fraction of that amount. On July 27, he wrote the Vancouver Belzberg family's First City Financial Corporation offering PSML (including $10 million cash on hand), the Principal Group computer and software and Principal Consultants Ltd. (conglomerate's sales arm)—all prized assets before the crisis—in exchange for First City assuming responsibility for payment of $50 million worth of promissory notes, plus interest.

The deal fell through; the price kept plummeting.

July 29, 1987

DICK JOHNSTON WENT BEHIND closed doors with Principal officials and investors' representatives. When they emerged, there were the makings of a deal; the investors had wrung from the province a promise to finance an independent investigation into the failure of the contract companies. Coopers & Lybrand would be reduced to its original manager's role, under the control of a five-person committee dominated by investors, and the inquiry would be conducted by an independent inspector.

Johnston continued, however, to block a public investigation of the government's role in the collapse. "I think the Ombudsman will do that," he told the *Herald*. (An Ombudsman usually conducts investigations out of the public eye and delivers his report to the government, which may or may not make it public.) The province agreed to pay the costs of the Investment Contract Holders Committee and the investors' special counsel. But Johnston retained the right to nominate the inspector, the investors' lawyer and the committee's chairman. (The investors would meet to nominate their four representatives on that committee.) The next day, however, Justice Ronald Berger made it clear that the Court of Queen's Bench, not the Getty government, would run the Principal investigation. Berger refused to sign the agreement until it was rewritten. Several hours later, he signed an order saying that the court would make the appointments, and any party to the action could suggest names.

Meanwhile, investors went to the Legislature to meet with Johnston, Getty and Consumer Affairs Minister Elaine McCoy. During the meeting, Getty made an end-run around his Treasurer, promising that the still-to-be-appointed inspector would be empowered to investigate the government's role in the Principal collapse.

Two weeks later, Justice Berger expanded his court order, allowing the inquiry to "summon and compel attendance of witnesses, including Ministers of the Crown...and their deputies and employees." Afterward, Getty announced he would order all government ministers to fully co-operate with the investigation.

During that August 13 hearing Berger also approved the appointment of prominent Calgary lawyer Bill Code, Q.C., as inquiry Inspector. Code, 54, appointed under the Alberta's *Business Corporations Act*, was known as a hard-hitting corporate lawyer with a penchant for bow-ties and race horses. His strong ties to the Liberal party—he ran as a Liberal candidate in Calgary West in 1984—were touted as evidence of his objectivity.

July 29, 1987

WE'VE GOT A PROBLEM HERE," the Merrill Lynch broker told Diane Stefanski. "For some reason the EL&F accounts are frozen. Coopers & Lybrand has gotten a court order. What's going on?"

"I don't know," Stefanski said. "Send me a copy of the order and I'll find out." Then she went looking for Donald Cormie. "He was always in the secret meetings those days," Stefanski told me, "so when I heard him stomping in the corridor I came out and called him, and showed him the court order."

"They can't do that," she remembers Cormie saying furiously. "They have no right to do that."

Here's what had happened: In August 1986, we'll recall, Principal Group had issued $11.2 million in promissory notes to the contract companies to satisfy B.C.'s demand for injection of assets. Principal's note to First Investors, for $9.6 million, had been secured with a pledge of mutual funds in a Merrill Lynch margin account held in the name of Estate Loan and Finance. Now Coopers & Lybrand was unwinding the contract companies' affairs, and made a demand to collect on the note, plus interest.

(While the Cormies were making public statements about "working closely" with Coopers & Lybrand to produce the best results for contract holders, the accounting firm made it clear from the outset that the less it had to do with former management the better. Still "selling madly"—July 1 was a Canadian holiday, but stock markets were open south of the border—Jaimie Cormie was in the Principal penthouse the day that Coopers & Lybrand took over the contract companies. "I was talking quite a bit to the Coopers people when they were in on July 1st, and I must admit, I was very surprised by what I was hearing," Jaimie testified. "What I literally heard from Coopers initially was, 'Goodbye, we are in control now, and by the way, give me all of your information.' ")

A court order intended to freeze the pledged mutual funds had ended up briefly freezing all seven cross-collateralized accounts held by Estate Loan with Merrill Lynch. (There was a total of about $23 million in the brokerage accounts; after dissolving them and paying back the brokerage's margin advances, a balance of about $12 million remained. When Coopers & Lybrand claimed its $9.7 million, Cormie was left with only about $2.3 million.)

"He was so upset over the fact that a court order without his knowledge could freeze something so easily," Stefanski testified. So Cormie decided to take what was left in the Merrill Lynch account, to dissolve the mutual fund accounts he controlled at other brokerages and to send the money across the border. "He indicated that it would be more difficult in the States to get a court order to automatically freeze his account without his knowledge."[5]

On July 29 and 30, Cormie, using the services of the Toronto Dominion bank, wire transferred a total of $4.2 million to Bear Stearns and Co., a major brokerage firm in New York City, long involved in handling U.S. securities portfolios for the Principal companies. Ten new accounts were opened with Bear Sterns, identified as "Estate Loan & Finance Account Number 1," then Number 2, Number 3, and so on all the way to 10.

During that two-day period, a portion of the cash from the liquidated mutual funds was sent by cheque to the University of Alberta. The year before, Principal Group had pledged $500,000 to the university's Faculty of Business during a province-sponsored fund-raising drive. Cormie had put $250,000 into five Principal mutual funds, promising to make up the difference if the investments didn't double within three years. By the end of July, 1987 the account had grown to $305,878, and Cormie decided, Stefanski testified, "that under the circumstances" it would be better if the university managed the money itself. (To understand Cormie's philanthropy it helps to know the family connection: Cormie's youngest son Robert was engaged to marry Jennifer Meekison, daughter of Peter Meekison, the university's academic vice-president.[6])

August 5, 1987

DONALD CORMIE HAD WRITTEN a letter promising to forgive Christa Petracca's $300,000 mortgage, but hadn't gotten around to doing the paperwork. Then on August 5, Ken Marlin testified, he was at a meeting in Cormie's office, "and Christa came in the door. I'm not sure what was said, but Don Cormie immediately said to me, 'Look, we've got an emergency, we've got to take care of this.' He asked me to step outside and said that he was concerned that Christa was leaving, that she had been interviewed by, I believe it was a gentleman from Trizec, and that she had received an offer. [He said] that Christa was upset about the fact that she had not received her bonus, that he wanted to discharge the mortgage because the money had been advanced by way of a mortgage, and he wanted to discharge the mortgage to make sure that she was happy."

Marlin thought they were talking about $30,000 or so, 10% of the $333,000 that had been received in Rimrock [Inn] grant money, "so we proceeded to Christa's office and I signed the discharge." Marlin says he didn't know how much the mortgage was, and didn't ask. "It doesn't show on the face of it. I made an assumption."[7] Later he felt there was "a bit of a charade going on in that immediately following it, there was conversation to the effect that 'Now are you satisfied? You're going to be satisfied now that this is done?' Christa agreed she was, and we left the office."

Marlin followed Petracca back to her office and learned that she had lunched with the Trizec official, but received no job offer.

August 7, 1987

Dick JOHNSTON FINALLY DECIDED to call in the Mounties. On Friday morning *The Edmonton Journal*[8] reported:

> Evidence has come to light which may require a criminal investigation of Principal Group, Treasurer Dick Johnston said Thursday.
> "We've received information that would suggest that an RCMP investigation is warranted," Johnston told reporters.
> The department approached the police on the advice of the Attorney General's department after receiving several complaints from people who have investments in [First Investors and Associated Investors]...
> RCMP in Saskatchewan have been looking into Principal Group for two weeks after complaints from investors in that province.
> Johnston said that pertinent information suggesting an investigation might be needed only came to his attention a few days ago...

The Cormies were on the verge of a deal when the police investigation was announced. Great Lakes Group Inc. of Toronto, a member of the Edgar and Peter Bronfman conglomerate, was willing to buy the sales arm, the trust company and PSML. The Principal assets would be rolled up with Great Lakes' own mutual fund into a newly formed company and later taken public. Great Lakes was offering less than $20 million in cash—to be used toward paying off the Principal Group promissory notes—but another $40 million in preferred shares in the new company.

Unfortunately there was, as Great Lakes vice-president Don Hilton later told the *Journal,* a "liability impasse" that proved insurmountable. What with the danger of lawsuits against the crumbling Cormie empire, and now the added complication of an RCMP investigation, the deal was just too risky to consummate—unless somebody was willing to provide an indemnity. The Cormies needed a government guarantee, and they went looking for one on Thursday afternoon, the same day Johnston announced the police investigation. Alberta was offered $40 million in preferred shares in a new Great Lakes company in exchange for protection against any subsequent legal action. A wretched Donald Cormie told Johnston it was the province's last chance to halt the collapse of the entire Principal conglomerate. If the Great Lakes proposal didn't go through, he said, Principal Group would have to declare bankruptcy on Monday.

Johnston didn't immediately reply. "They said they were going to be holding meetings the next day with Great Lakes and, obviously, Great Lakes would let us know what their final decision was," Jaimie Cormie testified. The next day, very late on Friday, Great Lakes called to say the deal was off.

As their negotiators climbed on a plane, Donald Cormie picked up the phone and called a Calgary bankruptcy specialist.

August 10, 1987

ON MONDAY MORNING, Donald Cormie, sons John and Jaimie and Ken Marlin held their last meeting as directors of Principal Group Ltd. They met in Cormie's penthouse office, signed a resolution putting the company into bankruptcy, and Marlin went down to the courthouse to file the necessary papers. The preliminary statement of affairs reported liabilities of $94.7 million and assets of $85.3 million, resulting in a deficiency of $9.4 million. Chartered accountant J. Stephens (Steve) Allan, chairman of the Calgary-based firm Collins Barrow Ltd., was appointed the company's trustee in bankruptcy. (In 1991, Allan joined Ernst & Young Inc.)

Treasurer Dick Johnston followed up with a drastic action of his own. To the Cormies' dismay he issued a ministerial order freezing an estimated $135 million in deposits at Principal Trust. The order, signed by Director of Trust Companies Reg Pointe, said that, pursuant to the *Trust Companies Act*, he was taking possession of the company, its property and the conduct of its business. He appointed Bruce Robertson (the same accountant assisting the CDIC in its inspection of the trust company) to handle the company's business.

During the day, it was business as usual at Principal Trust branches across Canada. Then on Monday afternoon at 5:00 p.m. Alberta-time, tellers were ordered to disconnect the automatic banking machines. The next morning, customers found the doors locked.

During a Monday evening news conference, Johnston told reporters the trust company would be closed until a buyer was found or the company was wound down. He lashed back at a news release issued by Marlin which blamed the province for failing to back the deal with Great Lakes. Principal's collapse was the result of company management and the recent recession, Johnston said. As for the Great Lakes deal, it could have cost the province "hundreds of millions" of dollars.

The *Calgary Herald* reported: "He also implied Principal shareholders would be able to walk away with some still valuable companies without fear of or the expense of fighting potential lawsuits, some of which could arise from management decisions."

The next day, Johnston took even more aggressive action in the public relations war with a call on *The Edmonton Journal's* editorial board. (He met with the *Herald* board a few days later.) "Johnston said letting Principal file for bankruptcy was preferable to the government spending $200 million to keep the troubled firm afloat," the *Journal* reported. "'It would be unfair to ask the taxpayers of Alberta to pick up these losses—full stop,' Johnston said. 'The losses were very, very high.' " For the first time, he admitted the extent of the contract company losses: Investors might end up getting only 60 cents on the dollar.

Meanwhile, on Monday afternoon, the Cormies told CDIC chief operating officer Jean Pierre Sabourin, still in town on his Principal Trust inspection, about the bankruptcy of the parent company. They told him they had not prepared a business plan for the continuing operations of the trust company; that there were no remaining potential purchasers interested in Principal Group; and that the bankruptcy of Principal Group would probably result in millions of dollars of withdrawals in deposits and mutual funds. Then Sabourin talked with Steve Allan, Principal Group's new trustee, who said he was not in a position to consider injecting capital into the trust company.

An emergency meeting of the CDIC board of directors was called that same day. Board members were advised that Robertson, who by that time had substantially completed his examination of the company, believed that Principal Trust was insolvent. A resolution was passed authorizing Sabourin to apply to the court for the winding-up of Principal Trust and the appointment of a liquidator. Then Sabourin, with the resolution in his pocket, gave trustee Allan a couple of days to sort out the company's affairs.

On Wednesday, August 12, Allan put out the word he was conducting a fire-sale of the Principal Group assets. Seven companies were interested, he told reporters, but a deal had to happen by the weekend. On Monday, the CDIC would go court to apply to wind up the affairs of Principal Trust, among the most attractive of the assets. He announced a Friday afternoon deadline for bids.

Allan had spent the weekend with the Principal Group shareholders, taking a crash course in the complexities of the byzantine Principal conglomerate. The Cormies suggested a compromise deal for settling their upstairs debts to Principal Group. Principal's largest asset was the debt owed by CSI (the Cormies and Marlin), at the time of bankruptcy about $64.4 million. CSI's primary assets were its shares in PSML, Principal Neo-Tech and Matrix Investments (which owned the Red Deer brewery), and the $33.4 million owed by CSL (Donald Cormie). They proposed that Cormie's Cayman Islands bank, valued at $23 million, be transferred to Principal Group in full satisfaction of the $34.4 million owed by CSL; and that the balance of CSI's debt be settled in exchange for transfer of all the company's assets.

With this basic understanding, Allan let it be known that the assets on the auction block included PSML, Cormie's coveted mutual fund management company. Despite a stampede of investor withdrawals, PSML still managed about $350 million worth of mutual funds, and it attracted a lot of attention.

By Friday afternoon, there were offers from Great Lakes Group, First City Trustco Inc., Oxford Company Ltd., Counsel Corp., and Ottawa-based Metropolitan Life Holdings Ltd., the Canadian division of New York-based Metropolitan Life Insurance Co. Each offer contained a sliding purchase price dependent on the level of the mutual funds under management at future dates; in each case, the purchase price was offered in negotiable securities.

After a day's evaluation, Allan notified Metropolitan Life of its winning bid. Metropolitan had offered approximately $27.5 million for PSML and some of the assets of Principal Group, Principal Trust and Principal Consultants. Like the other bidders, Metropolitan wanted Principal Trust and the sales operation, but it wasn't willing to buy them as existing entities because of potential lawsuits down the road. Instead, it offered to take over pieces of the companies (salesmen, investment company staff, computers, office space and trust company facilities), thus giving it the resources to run the businesses; the liabilities stayed with the emptied shells. Metropolitan planned to create a new subsidiary, roll PSML and the other Principal assets in, then create subordinated debentures that would be used to pay for the purchase. A portion of the debentures would be redeemed for cash within a month of the deal closing.[9]

Sabourin went to court the following Monday with an application for Robertson's appointment as "provisional liquidator" for Principal Trust. This was granted with the proviso that he was not to begin liquidation until September 1, 1987, giving Allan time to finalize the Metropolitan deal. The offer was, of course, conditional on Allan gaining legal control of PSML. While newspapers portrayed the sale to Metropolitan as a *fait accompli*, Allan went behind the scenes to see if he could hammer out a solid deal with the shareholders. It was a difficult process. Cormie, Allan told me in 1990, was "really stressed out" during this period. "He would absolutely explode, then later be quite calm."

Cormie held a great deal of leverage during these discussions. First of all, the clock was running, and assets were deteriorating day by day. For Allan to get his hands on PSML without the Cormies' consent would require petitioning CSI into bankruptcy, which would take a lot of time and trouble. Just as important was the fact that the only asset Cormie had personally offered, the Cayman Islands bank, could not be accessed without his assistance.

"We've been questioned many times about our deal with Cormie," Allan told me in 1990. "We arrived in August 1987 and Cormie had this bank, it's in a foreign jurisdiction, and we were very concerned. The [Alberta] government was going to appoint an inquiry, and we knew he was going to be dragged through the mud... The bank was very liquid and beyond our grasp. They were mobile; they could take off and leave us with nothing."

Allan took what he thought he could get. He accepted the bank as full compensation for Cormie's CSL debt to CSI, swallowing a loss of $11 million.

The Cormies held on to everything else they personally owned and controlled—the ranch, yacht, houses, art and foreign investments (the $4 million sent to New York City, for example)—and would, as well, receive $1.5 million from the Principal Group trustee to cover potential income tax liability. Cormie also got copies of computer software used by Cormie Ranch (for genetic selection, cattle management and accounting purposes) and by his U.S.-based investment companies.

Marlin got $50,000 and a chance to earn $5,000 a week over 26 months as a consultant to the trustee (a total of $180,000). His $1-million debt to CSI would not be pursued unless he became bankrupt during the next three years.

John and Jaimie Cormie agreed to repay the balance of the housing loans which their father had written off a month before. Meanwhile, the Cormies and Marlin would transfer all their shares of CSI to Principal Group, making the CSI assets available for application against the Principal Group debts; then CSI would assign itself into bankruptcy, appointing Allan as the trustee. Cormie would keep CSL. The Cormies and Marlin also got to keep their U.S. investment companies Principal Management, Inc. (the investment advisor to all the U.S.-based funds) and Principal Investors Corp. (the registered broker-dealer). Allan agreed not to pursue about $1.8 million owed by the two Arizona-based companies to Principal Group. Then Cormie had Principal Investors forgive $262,573 U.S. owed by his CSL.

The agreement stipulated that the Cormies, Marlin and their U.S. companies were "fully and finally" released from all claims, debts and actions that Principal Group might encounter in the future, with the exception that the release should not apply to any claims by reason of fraud.

On August 17, as Allan entered into these negotiations, he told the *Herald* that he found nothing deceptive about the way the Cormies had shuffled assets around the conglomerate. "They moved things around like crazy, but it was for tax or regulatory purposes," Allan said. "Everybody's suspicious but there's nothing there." As we have seen, by the time he testified at the Code inquiry he had reached quite a different conclusion. After a detailed examination of Principal Group affairs—and after hearing the testimony of bookkeeper Diane Stefanski[10]—he had concluded there was possible fraud involved.

The compromise deal was announced on August 25. Three days later, Allan went to court to seek approval of the arrangement. Justice Berger approved the sale to Metropolitan, after considering and rejecting a last-minute bid of $30 million by First City Trustco from the courtroom floor. But he withheld judicial approval of Allan's deal, saying he lacked information about the Cormie family assets. Cormie lawyers provided some information—the assets were said to be worth only $5 million—in a sealed envelope, but these values had been determined by Cormie without independent confirmation. "There are just too many unanswered questions to warrant judicial concurrence," Berger said.

Nonetheless, he ruled that it was clearly within Allan's authority to make the deal with Cormie under the emergency powers provided in the *Bankruptcy Act.*

A month later, after the deal had closed, Allan assured company creditors: "We negotiated the best deal possible in the circumstances and consider it a sound commercial transaction."

August 17, 1987

J UDE HALVORSON WAS INCREASINGLY ANXIOUS about the goings-on in the Principal tower. As Donald Cormie's secretary, she continued to answer his phone, type his letters, deposit cheques and serve as a shareholder/director of his upstairs companies Cormie Ranch, County Investments andEstate Loan and Finance. On August 17—as Cormie' s negotiations with Steve Allan continued— Halvorson decided it was time to withdraw as shareholder of County Investments, where the Cormie family investment accounts were held. She approached her boss, asked to be relieved of the position, and requested her share capital from the company. "Mr. Cormie asked me if I would retain one share in the corporation so that they would be able to have one shareholder," Halvorson testified. (County president Heather Lindsay had resigned in mid-July and quickly redeemed her 35 shares.) Halvorson was paid $6,400 of her $6,500 share capital, leaving her with one share valued at $100.

At the end of the month, Cormie returned to Halvorson his July 9 memo to Christa Petracca and instructed the secretary to retype it and backdate it to June 22. "After I had typed the June 22nd backdated memo," Halvorson testified, "I became very concerned... Because it was long past the time that Mr. Cormie had control of the Principal companies. It was at a time when the trustee in bankruptcy had been appointed... After I had left the retyped memo on Mr. Cormie's desk, I went to my memory-writer and I made an extra copy."

Then she went looking for Rob Pearce, Cormie's upstairs lieutenant, "to see how I should handle this.... That evening, [he] phoned me at home and indicated to me that I should be taking all the documents I had with respect to the memo to Steve Allan... The next morning when I arrived at the office, I accessed my memory-writer and I ran a copy of the July 9th, 1987 memo and took a copy of the June 22nd memo, which had not been signed at that point in time, to Mr. Allan."

Several days earlier, Halvorson had asked Pearce about her position as County director and shareholder. "I had some concern with respect to [being a director/shareholder] because I was not aware of what the company had done," she said. "I was aware that there were other depositors at County Investments Ltd., and I became concerned that if they weren't paid the money they had on deposit, I would be liable for payment to them of their deposits." Pearce suggested that she speak to Cormie about obtaining an indemnity, as he had done in May, "and if I had more concern that I obtain some legal counsel."

Halvorson went into the County minute books and, copying the indemnity provided to Pearce that spring, drafted a document she hoped would protect her if any legal action were taken against Cormie's upstairs companies. Later, she consulted legal texts and prepared a more detailed version. Then, on August 31, a Monday, she testified: "I asked Mr. Cormie if he would give me an indemnity on behalf of Collective Securities Ltd. and a personal indemnity with respect to my having acted as a director for County Investments Ltd.... Mr. Cormie said that he would be prepared to give me an indemnity on behalf of Collective Securities Ltd., but he would not give me a personal indemnity. I took the documents back to my memory-writer and I deleted the line where Mr. Cormie was to sign in his personal capacity. Mr. Cormie had indicated to me that I should affix the seal for Collective Securities Ltd. on the document and to leave the documents on his desk." She did so, then waited to hear back from him.

The next day, the Cormies began clearing out their offices, which took them the rest of the week. "When the move occurred," Halvorson recalled, "Mr. Cormie's family members, his daughter, two daughters-in-law and his sons helped Mr. Cormie pack storage boxes." Records relating to Cormie Ranch, County Investments and the other upstairs companies were packed away, as were many works of art, including the Group of Seven paintings that had been on display in the executive offices.

Both Halvorson and Diane Stefanski, Cormie's bookkeeper, remember steady traffic to the shredding machine during Cormie's last few weeks in the Principal tower. Stefanski testified that the normal production of the machine, located near her desk, was about a bag of trash or so a month. During June, July and August of 1987, she said, the output leapt to a bag or two a day. At 2,000 pages per bag, that's 100,000 to 200,000 pieces of paper chewed to tiny ribbons.

At the Code inquiry, Cormie bristled at the suggestion that he may have ordered the removal or destruction of incriminating documents; but could not explain why the shredder was working overtime.

On Wednesday of that last week, still waiting for her indemnity, Halvorson had another run-in with Cormie. Stefanski had left, and Halvorson was attempting to cover for the bookkeeper. "I was having problems with the computation that was required," Halvorson testified, "and I indicated to Mr. Cormie I was having problems with this. He said that it is just an arithmetic matter, you should be able to do this on your own, and I didn't understand what I was doing. I ended up in tears and after I had regained my composure, I went into Mr. Cormie's office and Mr. Cormie indicated to me that he wanted to pay me a bonus. He didn't indicate to me the denomination of the bonus, but he said that I had been a loyal secretary and that he would like me to have a bonus. I indicated to Mr. Cormie that it was not necessary, that I had been well paid, and that I had done my job just like everyone else at Principal Group had done."

The next day, a Thursday (September 3), Cormie again offered a bonus, "and I again indicated I didn't need a bonus."

That afternoon, Halvorson received a phone call from lawyer Bill Connauton who, with his new partner Rick Cruickshank, was helping Cormie deal with the legal consequences of the Principal Group/CSI bankruptcies. Connauton wanted

Halvorson to drop in to the Cruickshank Phillips office to sign some documents for Cormie Ranch Inc. and County Investments. "I arrived at Cruickshank's offices about five to five and I was met at their side entrance door by Mr. Cruickshank's secretary, and shown into their boardroom," Halvorson said. "Mr. Connauton and Mr. Cruickshank were there, and Mr. Cruickshank presented me with a document to sign or to acknowledge, acknowledging a debt that County Investments Ltd. had owing to Collective Securities Ltd."

The debt, Halvorson saw with horror, was for about $6.9 million. An "X" marked the spot where she was to be the sole signing authority on behalf of County Investments. "Well, sir, I was very upset," Halvorson testified. "I was not aware of the fact that County Investments had a large debt like that, and I indicated to Mr. Cruickshank that I couldn't sign the document." At no point during this meeting, she said, was she told she might require independent legal advice.

"After I had indicated that I would not sign the document, Mr. Cruickshank and Mr. Connauton discussed between themselves as to whether or not the assignment document would be enforceable without the acknowledgment of County Investments Ltd. [Then] Mr. Cruickshank asked me if I was going to have problems in signing any other documents with respect to Cormie Ranch Inc., and I had indicated that at this time I wasn't prepared to sign anything and that I should be resigning."

A few minutes after Halvorson's arrival, Cormie showed up, followed soon afterward by Jaimie and John Cormie, and then by Ken Marlin. "While I was waiting, Mr. Cruickshank made arrangements to have my Cormie Ranch Inc. resignation typed, and while I was waiting for the resignation to be typed, there was a general discussion going on with respect to the use by the U.S. companies, the use that they would be allowed to have on the [corporate computer] once the sale of assets was completed to Metropolitan. Mr. Cormie"—unaware she had refused to sign the acknowledgement—"asked me my opinion as to how long it would take to transfer some of the information from the [computer] with respect to names, addresses, number of shares, to an Apple computer that they were going to be using in their new offices."[11]

CSL was the Cormie holding company that had just escaped a $34.4 million debt to Principal Group by handing over a $23-million Cayman Islands bank to trustee Steve Allan. County Investments, which had borrowed $6.9 million from CSL, had loaned the money upwards to Cormie family members, who then loaned it upstairs to Estate Loan and Finance where the family houses and other property was held. Now, CSL—no longer obligated to pay the complete debt back to Principal Group—was assigning County's debt to a new numbered company (368198 Alberta Ltd.) which had been incorporated just weeks before. Donald and Jaimie Cormie were the shareholders and directors of this new company, which now had the right to collect on the $6.9 million receivable. (A balance sheet prepared for County Investments as of October 31, 1987, showed total assets of $11.1 million, almost all of it in the form of money owed by Cormie family members.)

The day after the meeting at the Cruickshank Phillips office, Cormie told Halvorson that he had been advised by his lawyers not to provide her with the CSL indemnity he had promised her. "He said to me that although I had turned the bonus down on two different occasions, he insisted that I write a cheque for $5,000 payable to me and to draw my payroll cheque up covering the period from the first of September to the fourth of September. Mr. Cormie also apologized to me at that time for leaving me in a mess with respect to County Investments."[12] (As Inspector Code observed during his inquiry: Cormie left Halvorson "hanging out to dry," while he was protected by director's insurance elsewhere.)

What Halvorson really wanted was an explanation of County's $6.9-million debt to CSL. "I was concerned to ask Mr. Cormie about the debt because I had refused to sign the acknowledgement on behalf of County Investments Limited," she testified. The question went unasked. "Mr. Cormie, at that point in time, was quite volatile in terms of his personality. I was nervous to ask Mr. Cormie because I had refused to sign the acknowledgement." Then she phoned her husband. "I indicated to him that Mr. Cormie was not going to sign the Collective Securities' indemnities for me, and that he apologized to me with respect to County, and he had indicated to me that he wanted me to take a $5,000 bonus. My husband said that I should take it, I didn't know what kind of a situation I was going to find myself in with respect to any potential liabilities that I had for County." Halvorson cut two cheques on the CSL account and took them to Cormie, who signed them and said goodbye.

The next week, after hiring a lawyer, Halvorson dumped her remaining share in County Investments and resigned as company officer. The week after that, on September 14, Metropolitan opened the doors of 12 former Principal Trust outlets. Halvorson, like many former Principal employees, went to work for the new company.

Her first day on the job, Halvorson went to the Silk Hat, a Jasper Avenue diner, for a late lunch. Cormie, eating there with Marlin, confronted her in her booth. "Mr. Cormie indicated because I had returned to work that I had a moral obligation to pay the $5,000 back to him," Halvorson testified. She kept the money.

September 20, 1987

IN THE EARLY AUTUMN, PETER LOUGHEED emerged briefly from political retirement to blame the Principal collapse on Ontario and the National Energy Program. (See Chapter 7.) Don Getty's government, scrambling desperately for a scapegoat, seized on the preposterous explanation, and began espousing it as the party line. Lougheed faded back into his legal practice and a bouquet of corporate directorships, never to comment again on the subject of Cormie or the Principal collapse.

In mid-August, while on an Edmonton radio talk-show, Getty made his own unsuccessful stab at damage control with a promise that if the province were proven negligent "and the court orders us to pay," Alberta would compensate Principal investors. And, he said, the regulations governing financial institutions might need revision. "I have a feeling that there is something wrong with the damn regulatory process. But I want to find out." His disingenuous guarantee—the Code inquiry, a quasi-judicial investigation under the *Business Corporations Act*, had no mandate to recommend compensation, let alone order it—cut little ice with critics.[13] A month later, under attack in the Legislature, Getty was driven to a more credible pledge: "I would say that the government will—if there is negligence, any proof that the government has in some way damaged the investors, then the government would make up that damage, no question about it."

That November, as the Code inquiry got underway, bargain-hunters picked over the remains of the Cormie empire at a public auction. Among the items were two well-used shredding machines, a champagne cooler, four deluxe refrigerators and audio-visual equipment once used to prepare motivational tapes for the sales staff. Cormie's prized leather-inlaid mahogany desk went for $650.

23

Evidence tending to prove

STUART ELGIE WATCHED THROUGH his kitchen window as the car wound its way up the driveway to his old farmhouse. "Look at that," he called to his wife Betty. "It's that Cormie fellow, the one in the papers all the time."

It was Thanksgiving Day weekend, 1989, a few months after the release of Inspector Bill Code's sensational report—two years after the collapse of Donald Cormie's empire. Cormie and two of his sons had chosen the old Fergus homestead as a holiday rendezvous point. Ex-trust-company president John, now living nearby, drove south. Law student Robert drove west from Toronto, and they all gathered at the town's old inn.

Elgie, owner of the Cormie farm for many years, could see Donald and Eivor, with John and his wife Patricia, in the car. He invited them inside and strolled with his unexpected guests through the rooms, while Cormie told handed-down tales of the house and his ancestors. Then they settled in for tea. "This is quite a coincidence," Betty told Cormie. "We were just talking about you." His face darkened momentarily, but Betty hurried on. "Stuart was working in the barn, there was a beam above the window that had to be replaced, and we..." Stuart Elgie rushed out of the room and returned with a small green bottle in his hands.

"We found this lodged in the middle of the wall," Stuart said. "Look what's inside." He pulled out a faded slip of paper, crumbling at the edges, with the message "Borrow Your Requirements from the Traders Bank" embossed at the top. A hand-written note was scrawled across the page:

George M. Cormie
Fergus, Ontario
1909

"Why, that's my Dad!" Cormie exclaimed.
"We thought so. It's been plastered up inside that wall a mighty long time."

"Think of that—1909! He would have been 17—this must have been just before he went off to college." Cormie beamed, turning the bottle over and over in his hands.

They sat for a while longer, nibbling on cookies and talking about recent renovations to the house. The Cormies seemed very happy there, Elgie told me a couple of years later. "When they were here you wouldn't have thought they had a worry in the world. There wasn't a word about all of his trouble. He didn't bring it up and I didn't bring it up."

BILL CODE'S INQUIRY TURNED INTO a minor industry for Alberta's depressed economy. The hearings continued on and off for 14 months and generated work for six dozen lawyers, more than a dozen accountants, numerous court reporters and bevies of journalists. The provincial tab came to $25 million, including a $1.1-million contribution toward Donald Cormie's $2 million legal bill.

Despite his early endorsement of the process, Cormie was dragged protesting through the public hearings. His lawyers argued repeatedly that the inquiry violated the *Charter of Rights and Freedoms*. They took their protest to Alberta's Court of Queen's Bench, and ultimately to the Supreme Court of Canada, which twice refused to hear their appeals.

Unlike a trial in criminal court, where evidence has been accumulated and charges laid in advance of testimony being heard, new information was uncovered daily as witnesses were summoned to tell their versions of events. The paper chase continued unabated, with each person's testimony leading to the discovery of new evidence, and new perspectives, on what transpired behind the Principal and regulatory curtains. It wasn't until a few months into the hearings, for example, that any hint emerged of the mysterious Department 8. Suspicions abounded about the ultimate use of money loaned by Principal Group to parent company Collective Securities Inc., but it wasn't until book-keeper Diane Stefanski testified that the upstairs games became comprehensible.[1]

Albertans gorged on the scandal. They read about it in their daily newspapers, talked about it nightly at their dinner tables. The inquiry was broadcast live on local cable television, a day later in Calgary and Victoria. Thousands tuned in to hear the blow-by-blow testimony of 154 nerve-racked witnesses.

"It's our version of *Dallas* [the television soap-opera]," Edmonton-Strathcona MP David Kilgour said to me. "And we've all vomited so much we had to stop reading the stories."

Unfortunately, investors stuck to the Principal flypaper find it's not so easy to forget. Every time they pay rent or put gas in the car, every time they open a chequebook, their stomachs lurch. Money they worked so hard for, saved so carefully, is gone, some of it never to be returned. Some investors are as upset today as they were the day Principal went down.

Throughout the inquiry Cormie expressed his regret at the investors' losses, but insisted he was not responsible. He claimed he was a hands-off shareholder with little knowledge of the affairs or activities of the companies he owned. He pointed the finger at various vice-presidents, claiming they were the ones who had committed any improprieties. Only John and Jaimie supported his claim. The others, including Christa Petracca, fought back vigorously.

Code's report described Cormie as unco-operative, evasive and self-serving. "As the central figure in the Group, I expected Donald Cormie to provide the key evidence as to the operations of these companies, but this proved not to be the case," Code said. "For the most part, Donald Cormie was more interested in acting as his own counsel and in arguing than he was in giving evidence. He continually evaded answering questions and, when answering, gave argument rather than facts. Numerous occasions will be pointed out in this Report where Donald Cormie changed his evidence depending upon his view of how it would best serve his interests." Code grew increasingly impatient with Cormie as time went on. "This is back to bafflegab," he complained while listening to Cormie's incomprehensible explanation of why the impoverished contract companies were drained of all "surplus funds." A few days later, he flatly rejected Cormie's efforts to deny control of the Principal conglomerate. "Mr. Cormie, there is no doubt who had the final decision in every one of these companies and that was you; isn't that true?"

Cormie termed Code's interpretation "absolute nonsense." He insisted that the directors and officials he appointed to the various companies controlled those companies, and he did not. "I would not make day-by-day decisions," he testified. "Final corporate responsibility sits with me as chief executive officer, yes. I could over-rule if I knew something was there. Most of the time I wouldn't know about it, but I supported the officers."

Code criticized Cormie's lawyers for failing to question corporate executives about the wide-ranging powers that Cormie would later attribute to them during testimony. During the inquiry, lawyer after lawyer—representing various other interests—hammered away at Cormie, confronting him with document after document, incident after incident, that demonstrated his vital grip on every aspect of the corporate operation.

In the end, no reasonable person could buy Cormie's claim that he was a hands-off shareholder. His fingerprints were everywhere, even though he stayed behind the scenes. Others signed the documents, made the phone calls and attended meetings, but little happened without his knowledge, and he was always in control. When the existence of his companies was threatened in 1987, he emerged to deal directly with the government. Nonetheless, to this day Cormie maintains that he was the victim of a biased investigation, hostile officials and a sensationalist media.

Cormie admitted that in the final weeks he had "never even considered" paying back any of the money he and his family owed to County Investments (which owed money to CSL/to CSI/to Principal Group, which owed money to the public). The $4.2 million he sent to New York was family money, Cormie said, and County Investments hadn't demanded its return.

Cormie also testified that he felt no obligation to be "fair, open and honest" with customers, or to disclose the companies' financial circumstances "when half or part of the load will do." He complained of lawyers' "trick questions," and said he could not remember the thousands of answers he had given in testimony. The remark was a perfect opening, and Ed Molstad, representing secretary Jude Halvorson, made the most of it: "I emphasize, sir, you don't have to remember your answers if you stated the truth."

Code's report was made public on July 18, 1989. It found—no surprise—that Cormie controlled the Principal Group of Companies through his controlling shareholding of Principal Group Ltd. and the offices he held. It also found "evidence tending to prove" that Cormie and others were frauds, thieves, liars, stock manipulators and tax-evaders; then it condemned the Alberta government for failing to ensure that the Principal contract companies met the safeguards built into the *Investment Contracts Act* for the protection of contract holders.

When the report was released, Premier Don Getty ducked out of question period in the Legislature, opting instead to attend a Red Deer cattle show. Then he claimed that because everything had been answered during the investigation, he didn't have to respond in the Legislature.

Regrettably, everything was *not* answered. Code left untouched the larger, most essential political questions. He noted the failure of two Alberta governments to clean up the vastly inadequate *Investment Contracts Act*, but never addressed the reasons behind such a crucial oversight.

Code did note that Connie Osterman made occasional reports to Cabinet's financial institutions task force regarding the Principal contract companies, and that the task force was advised of continuing legal and accounting disputes between the companies and the regulators. He reported that George Kinsman, Treasury's bailout analyst, knew about the contract companies' problems as far back as 1984; and he reported Eldridge's testimony that Lou Hyndman had asked about a "light at the end of the tunnel" in late 1985. Code also noted Hyndman's alarming report to Getty around that time, and Getty's subsequent declaration that he had no knowledge of any financial trouble in the Principal companies until February 1987. But Code made no comment on any of this evidence.

Several potentially important witnesses were not called. Former Attorneys General Merv Leitch and Neil Crawford, now both dead, did not testify. Nor did Assistant Deputy Treasurer (finance) Jim Drinkwater[2], who supervised bailout analyst George Kinsman, knew about the contents of Kinsman's Principal contract companies file and was his link with the Treasurer and Deputy Treasurer during 1984 and 1985. Others were not called: Jack Lyndon, Consumer Affairs deputy minister during the 1970s; Alberta Securities Commission director Marc Lemay and deputy director Marguerite Childs; Julian Koziak, Osterman's predecessor as Consumer Affairs minister and a member of the financial institutions task force; Gary Campbell, who attended a strategy meeting with Cormie in early 1987; George de Rappard, priorities committee member and deputy minister to the Cabinet, from whose keeping disappeared the 1985 request to remove First Investors from a list of approved trustee investments. Former Deputy Provincial Treasurer Chip Collins, Peter Lougheed's key financial advisor and a member of the Cabinet priorities committee, might have had something to share. Collins, who followed Lougheed from the Mannix Co. into government service, was involved in all provincial financial issues, from creation of the Heritage Trust Fund in 1975 to the credit union rescue in the 1980s. He should have been asked what he heard at the priorities committee meetings, and what he knew about the Principal companies during his decade-and-a-half in a crucial post.

Efforts to take cross-examination into the political arena produced some of the hearings' most hostile confrontations. Government lawyers leapt to their feet whenever questions were raised about Conservative party members.[3] This resistance—most passionate when the names of Lougheed or Getty were invoked—was not limited to government counsel. Inspector Code made it clear he had little patience with this line of questioning, and occasionally lost his temper. A remarkable clash occurred when Gary Greenan, one of the investors' lawyers, quizzed Cormie about a possible meeting with Lougheed in 1975. Greenan asked Cormie whether he had discussed with Lougheed the possible suspension of the contract companies' licences. Challenged by defence counsel, Greenan said he was working on information received from an unidentified source and confirmed by Ken Marlin. Marlin's lawyer clarified that Marlin believed there was a meeting around that time, but he didn't know what was discussed.

Then, rather than simply rule Greenan out of order—if he considered that the right call—Code launched into a tirade: "Well, here we go. That's the danger of it, Mr. Greenan. Now you have brought Premier Lougheed in as something and we know what the papers will pick up from that, and I find that extremely unfortunate when what appears to be baseless cross-examination is used. And particularly—you see, we don't know if—Mr. Marlin has told his counsel that he didn't say that to you, what you just put to him. And you say you have other sources, which you are not disclosing, and I just find that unfair and improper."

After a recess Greenan asked his question again, and Cormie replied that he didn't recollect meeting with Lougheed on the licence matter in 1975. Then Code went back at Greenan: "Okay. I gather you are not going to carry on and I find that a bit unfortunate that already you have asked the questions which embarrass the former premier..." Despite the Inspector's resistance, Greenan and his colleague Claus Thietke continued to scratch away at the political questions. Some of their hard-won answers proved invaluable in the writing of this book.

However, Greenan and Thietke were junior counsel, subordinate to John McNiven, who made the key decisions. (McNiven, one of the two lawyers appointed to represent contract holders, volunteered to handle regulatory issues, while his Edmonton counterpart, Robert White, dealt with business-related matters.) It was McNiven who decided to pull the punches in his submission to Code on the regulatory issues. He made reference to the fact that Cormie was a "substantial financial supporter" of the Conservative party, and that he "had ready access to Alberta Cabinet Ministers, met them on social occasions and periodically entertained Ministers and members of the Legislature." McNiven noted Cormie's discussions with Merv Leitch and Bob Dowling in the early 1970s, and Cormie's persuasive argument that hurting his contract companies would hurt Alberta's developing financial industry. But he did not place these events within their larger political context.

The premiers' names were mentioned only in passing. McNiven noted that Consumer Affairs Minister Bob Dowling's letter to Cormie in 1973 was copied to Lougheed, and that Cormie wrote to Lougheed in 1975 protesting proposed amendments to the *Investment Contracts Act*—but McNiven drew no significance from these facts. Getty was only mentioned once: to quote his promise in the Legislature of compensation for investors if the government were proven negligent.

This soft-pedalling, McNiven told me in 1991, was the result of a decision mid-way during the hearings not to pursue senior politicians' responsibility for Alberta's regulatory failure. It was quite simple, McNiven said: "Certainly I didn't want to have Getty any more embarrassed than he was by the inquiry—because any cheque that was going to be cut would be cut by his say-so. I didn't want to go out and point fingers deliberately at the very people that I'd have to be negotiating with to get an offer of settlement. You don't call somebody an SOB and then sit down and have a beer with him the next day. I was concerned about holding Getty to his promise that if the evidence exposed wrong-doing he'd make it good, and my whole argument was addressed to that point. It wasn't concerned with the broader dimensions of public morality and all the rest of it. My job was to get money for the investors."

There were gaps in the picture, McNiven acknowledged, and more witnesses could have been called to help fill in the blanks. But after Barry Martin had detailed the strategy he followed to protect the Principal companies, little more seemed necessary. "We reached a point in the evidence... when I was satisfied we had enough to hang our hats on to get the money out of the government. I wasn't trying to make political hay out of the testimony of these people. After we got Martin's testimony I wasn't really too concerned about hanging anybody else out to dry, or getting into all of the ramifications of the minute details about what went on. The broad picture to me was pretty simple. The government knew they had screwed up, Martin admitted they screwed up: end of case. We're holding Getty to his commitment. Essentially that's the thrust of my argument. There were any number of questions that could have been asked, but in terms of what I was trying to do, I wasn't going to waste any more time."

McNiven is another good example of just how small-town Alberta really is. In the 1950s, he was a class-mate and Delta Upsilon fraternity brother of Peter Lougheed and Merv Leitch, and a student of Donald Cormie's, while studying law at the University of Alberta. After graduating, he practised in Calgary, and a few years later replaced Lougheed as corporate counsel at the Mannix Co. McNiven is a long-time Progressive Conservative, is acquainted with many Cabinet ministers and claims Lougheed as a friend. Despite these long-standing ties, McNiven gave no thought as to whether he might be in a conflict of interest in the role of investors' counsel investigating government negligence. "I never felt there was any conflict there at all, just because I knew these folks," he told me. If it had been necessary to put Lougheed on the witness stand, McNiven said, he would certainly have done so. But he didn't have to, "because at that point I had the evidence I needed. That's one thing any good trial lawyer will tell you, don't ask the unnecessary question. When you've got what you want, sit down and shut up. I didn't care what involvement Peter had... It didn't matter a whit to me. I got the evidence I wanted. After that I didn't care much what happened."

Later, we talked about Connie Osterman, left holding the bag for an entire government's failure. Osterman, we agreed, had done little more (or less) than several ministers before and after her: she gave Donald Cormie time to solve his companies' problems. "Frankly, I think she was set up," McNiven told me cheerfully. "Let's face it, somebody had to take it. Can you think of a better fall-guy, sorry, fall-person?"

No, I can't.

Loyal soldier to the end, Osterman made no effort during the inquiry to tell the entire story. She rambled on, in sentences so long they were sometimes incomprehensible. She answered the questions that were put to her, but offered no elaboration unless directly asked to do so. Several important questions were not asked.

Ten days after the release of the Code report, Getty booted Osterman, then Minister of Career Development and Employment, out of Cabinet. First she was asked to resign. When she refused, Getty announced in the Legislature he had fired her. "The Minister was in breach of her public duty to carry out the purpose and objects of the legislation for which she was responsible," Getty said. "As personally painful as I find it to be, I believe that public finding [in the Code report] requires that the Minister step down from Cabinet."

Osterman maintained her equanimity until she was axed, then rushed home to give interviews to constituency newspapers. She lashed out at Getty, saying she had warned him in November 1985 about the Principal companies' problems. But Getty had cancelled the financial institutions task force, and paid no heed to her warning memo. "I wasn't sure why because I was used to a certain style of action with the former [Lougheed] administration, and then I got moved from the portfolio," she told the Three Hills *Capital.*

On her return to Edmonton, she was cornered by party faithful, reminded of her oath of confidentiality, and urged to keep silent. Since then, she has held her tongue, except to remark that she looks forward to seeing Cormie's lawsuit against the province, filed in 1989, come to trial. Perhaps then the whole story will be told, she says.

Osterman bitterly regrets her performance at the Code inquiry, and wishes she had shared everything she knew about the involvement of some of her Cabinet colleagues in the Principal matter. She now feels that her interests were possibly quite different from those of the Alberta government's, whose lawyers represented her. "At the time of the inquiry I should have gotten my own lawyer and I should have made sure I was asked all the questions I should have been asked," she told me. "I thought for sure I would be told if there were *any* meetings to do with financial institutions, and then I find out Mr. Getty met with Mr Cormie." She was referring to evidence that the two men met in 1986, shortly before she was removed from the Consumer Affairs portfolio. "Anyway, it was a wonderful number on me." Osterman languished for three years on the backbenches, then in May 1992, she resigned from politics.

Concurrent with Osterman's firing, Getty announced a partial bailout of the contract holders. Alberta's offer, to cover up to $85 million in losses, amounted to 18 cents on the dollar for First Investors customers and 15 cents for Associated Investors customers. The offer was "fair and final," Getty said. Because Code had assigned only partial blame to his government, it wasn't responsible for all losses. Investors could take it or leave it—but if they took it, they had to sign a document waiving their right to sue the Alberta government, past or present Ministers or any government employee. In exchange, the province would finance investors' lawsuits against third parties (such as the Cormies); but it would also t ake the first $25 million arising from these suits to compensate itself for financing the Code investigation.

The offer enraged investors—too little to satisfy, too much to refuse—but in the end most gritted their teeth and signed.

Earl Rose, co-chairman of Calgary's Seniors Principal Investors Group, tried to persuade the group to reject the offer and launch a class-action suit against Getty and the province. It was hopeless: of its hundreds of members, only six were willing to go to court. Many were desperate for money. Others doubted they would survive the years of litigation looming before them. Rose held out for months, then finally signed the agreement in early 1990. "There's no point in me, with my limited resources, trying to sue the government by myself," he told me a few days later. "It was the hardest thing I ever signed." Rose's fury still claws at his gut. He feels betrayed not only by the company, but by the province, which gambled with his life savings when it decided to not enforce the law. Rose and his wife Pat had $49,000 in Associated Investors when it went down.

Alberta's offer was extended to contract holders across Canada, more than half of whom lived outside Alberta, but held good only if any compensation from their own provincial governments was pooled and shared with all investors. Since then, contributions from B.C., Saskatchewan and Nova Scotia have totalled 7.8 cents on the dollar. Liquidation of company assets has—as of late 1992—amounted to 54 cents on the dollar. Another 4 cents is expected to be realized by First Investors, and 7 cents by Associated Investors. Thus, investors in the four pooling provinces are expected to eventually recover 83.8% of their "valuated claims" (principal plus interest and additional credits to June, 1987, with no compensation for lost income during the years the money was out of their hands). Alberta has sweetened the pot for its own residents—to the indignation of those elsewhere—by throwing in another 3.7 cents to compensate for the cost of liquidating the contract companies' assets. This pushes the total anticipated recovery for Alberta investors up to 87.5%.

If New Brunswick makes a contribution, as expected, investors there will make the same recovery as those in the other pooling provinces. Investors in Newfoundland, whose government is not expected to make an offer, will recover only 76% of their investments.

The promissory noteholders, second-class victims of the Principal fiasco, are far less fortunate. Getty, calling them "sophisticated" investors who knew they were risking their money in unregulated securities, has refused any compensation.[4] He acknowledges no responsibility on Alberta's part, despite the fact that it allowed Principal Group Ltd. to borrow money from the public for three years after it was known to be in trouble. There were about $87 million worth of promissory notes outstanding at the time of the collapse (496 notes affecting more than 11,000 people, about a third of the money owed to 22 Hutterite colonies). Their relief will be limited to the proceeds of the liquidation of Principal Group assets—about 45.8 cents on the dollar—and any funds resulting from successful lawsuits. (Alberta noteholders received another 8.8 cents from the province to cover administration costs of the estate.)

Soon after the contract company bailout was announced, Principal Group trustee Steve Allan launched a campaign to protest Alberta's indifference to his noteholder clients. These people were hardly fast-buck speculators and they were far from sophisticated, Allan argued; he presented a survey showing most of them had a high school education or less. Almost all the respondents were over 60. Their money often came from insurance proceeds on the death of a spouse or from the sale of a house, farm or business at the time of their retirement. Allan argued that they were seduced by the same sleazy sales techniques that lured many of the contract holders—techniques understood and ignored by the regulators. They ended up with promissory notes instead of investment contracts simply because they had a larger amount of money to invest.

If Alberta had pulled the licences of First Investors and Associated Investors in 1984, as it should have done, Principal Group would have fallen and note sales would have halted. If Barry Martin had not blocked an investigation into sales practices in mid-1984, perhaps the misrepresentations would have ceased. Instead, aggressive sales campaigns pushed note sales from $54 million at the end of 1983 to $87 million at the time of the bankruptcy in 1987. Of the notes outstanding at that time, nearly 90% had been sold since January 1985. During this period, the province knew that the contract companies were insolvent, and it knew that if they went down the whole conglomerate would go with them.

The noteholders' last hope was Alberta's Ombudsman, whose report was due a few weeks after the Code report. If Getty did not understand his government's moral obligation, surely Aleck Trawick would point it out.

Trawick let the noteholders down.

In his report, Trawick called their situation "tragic," and confirmed that most of them "could not be said to be sophisticated investors in any sense of the word." They had, indeed, been confused by salespeople who represented the promissory notes as "another form of deposit within the guaranteed or insured aura maintained by the Group because of the regulation of some of its subsidiaries..." It was also clear, Trawick said, that salespeople "took advantage of the fact that these investments were exempt from any regulation in marketing them, and revealed little financial information. When financial information was required to close the sale of a note, there was no hesitation and even encouragement to use erroneous and misleading information..."

Nonetheless, Trawick rejected Allan's claim that the province should have protected investors from Principal Group's tactics. The notes had been sold in Alberta's exempt securities market, freeing them from any prospectus or registration requirements, and therefore the government had no duty to regulate them, Trawick said. He observed there had been no complaint from any noteholder about Principal Group's sales practices (until after the collapse), and concluded: "While hindsight may show that improper practices were taking place in the Principal Group's 'financial centres,' the actions of the department must be considered in accordance with the knowledge that they had, or should have obtained, and in these circumstance I do not find administrative error having regard to the knowledge [Consumer Affairs] had, nor do I find any administrative error in their practices and procedures in obtaining such knowledge."

Trawick made this finding despite extensive evidence of Consumer Affairs' longstanding knowledge of misleading and manipulative sales practices. He did not note that Treasury officials, including Treasurer Dick Johnston, were aware that Principal Group's 1985 Annual Review was misleading, but made no effort to remove it from circulation. Nor did Trawick comment on evidence that Consumer Affairs officials made a concerted effort to withhold information on the contract companies from their colleagues at the Alberta Securities Commission.

In Trawick's view, Alberta was off the hook because officials in two independent but related branches of government—Consumer Affairs and the securities commission (both of which reported to the Consumer Affairs minister)—did not, and were not obliged to share information that might have enabled them to put together the big picture. Trawick did not address the systemic regulatory failure in Alberta which allowed this lack of communication to occur, except to say that, "in hindsight," the policies and procedures in place were designed to deal with the traditional "four pillars" of the financial industry (banks, trust companies, securities dealers and the insurance industry). "The financial supermarket concept utilized by the Principal Group was difficult to regulate in accordance with that system," he concluded.

But that's no excuse. Having permitted a financial supermarket inside its jurisdiction, the province should have established mechanisms to deal with it, instead of erecting roadblocks to proper regulation. A recommendation for exactly this kind of body, with the power to examine the entire conglomerate, had been made as early as 1971 by consultant Gordon Burton.

In a responsible system, information would have been shared not only between Consumer Affairs and the securities commission, but among officials within each department as well. In 1985, one section of the commission was trashing Christa Petracca's efforts to take First Investors public, while another was investigating Principal Group promissory notes and making comparisons to a "Ponzi scheme." If these two groups had communicated with one another, and talked with their colleagues in Consumer Affairs, a major disaster could have been averted. If Consumer Affairs officials had shared their doubts about the value of Matrix Investments stock with the securities commission, perhaps the commission would have caught the bizarre "warehousing" transactions and price elevations—instead of being embarrassed into action several years later during a public inquiry.

Trawick also criticized the investment contract holders for not checking out First Investors and Associated Investors before putting money into them, and he endorsed Alberta's offer of only partial compensation to them.

Since the 1987 collapse, investors have watched the ugly spectacle of the contract companies and their parent squabbling over the pitiful remains of the corporate corpse. Pieces of an enormous jigsaw puzzle in life, the companies in death are separate and hostile, each at the other's throat for control of the few remaining assets. Pathetically, most of those assets are pieces of one another. Whatever the Principal salesmen suggested, whatever the investors believed—and however the companies actually functioned—in law they were independent stand-alone entities with separate assets, liabilities and obligations. The companies behave now, not as the collective victims they mostly definitely were, but as the scavenging creatures the law requires.

This struggle is played out through the battles of Principal Group trustee Steve Allan with contract companies receiver/manager John Ryan. Allan, doing his best for the noteholders, argues that Principal Group was the bigger fish, that First Investors and Associated Investors took advantage of their parent in the form of capital injections. Ryan, represented by investors' counsel Robert White, argues that the contract companies were drained of "surplus funds" for years and were by far the more abused. In 1988, the contract companies' receivers, demanding the proceeds of the Cayman Islands bank, threatened to sue Principal Group for misrepresentation and mismanagement. The Principal Group trustee complained about money advanced to the contract companies in 1984 and 1986 in the form of subordinated notes. They even fought over the tax losses.

Principal Group has since filed a lawsuit asking the court to order that the assets of all three companies be pooled for the benefit of all their creditors. The contract companies have fought this action and want each party to forego its claims, leaving the others with the assets they held at the time of the collapse. Faced with costly and lengthy litigation, the parties are now attempting to negotiate a solution. Talks got serious last autumn and a settlement is expected soon.

There are other lawsuits. Principal Group has sued the Alberta government; a motion by the province to strike the claim was rejected by Chief Justice Kenneth Moore of Court of Queen's Bench in March 1991. The contract companies have sued their auditors. Principal Group has sued Principal Trust, now under the control of liquidator Bruce Robertson, for $20 million, including return of the $11.3 million injected by way of promissory notes in late 1984. Both Principal Group and the contract companies have sued Donald Cormie and other family members. So has the Alberta government, which in 1990 accused Principal Group's directors of conducting the affairs of the contract companies "in an improper, unreasonable, unfair, deceitful, wrongful and fraudulent manner." The suit named Cormie, his sons John and Jaimie, his wife Eivor, Christa Petracca, Ken Marlin and five upstairs companies: Collective Securities Ltd., Cormie Ranch Ltd., Cormie Ranch Inc., Estate Loan and Finance Ltd. and County Investments Ltd.

Cormie, in return, has gone after the Alberta government with a suit against three (former) Alberta Cabinet ministers—Dick Johnston, Connie Osterman and Elaine McCoy.

Some investors are also suing the CDIC, arguing that since their contracts and promissory notes were sold on Principal Trust premises, the trust company's insurer should be held responsible.

Meanwhile, the Code inquiry was monitored with interest by RCMP officers, Revenue Canada officials and investigators with the federal Consumer and Corporate Affairs Department. The day after Code's report was released, federal officials laid four charges of false advertising against Cormie, his son John, Marlin and Petracca under the *Competition Act*. In January 1992, days before he was to go to trial on the first of these charges, Cormie entered a surprise guilty plea to the charge that he had misled investors in his chairman's message in the 1985 Annual Review. He was fined $500,000, the largest fine ever levied against an individual under that act, and the other three charges were stayed. Cormie paid the fine that same afternoon.

Revenue Canada has served Cormie with $15 million worth of tax notices; he has disputed the reassessment.

Six years after the collapse, the RCMP continues to investigate whether there is sufficient evidence to lay criminal charges. Alberta's Attorney General will decide whether to prosecute, but such decisions are usually based on an RCMP court brief that recommends charges and details the case. RCMP investigators and lawyers in the Attorney General's department continued to discuss the legalities of the affair, but as of early 1993, no brief had yet been delivered. It is increasingly unlikely that Cormie would be convicted if charges are ever laid; the courts take a dim view of marathon delays, and the memories of potential witnesses fade month by month.

Meanwhile, after weathering the Principal scandal and several conflict-of-interest crises, Alberta government members voted themselves a retroactive 30% pay raise in the summer of 1989. The wage hike was only the most recent in a series of increases which jumped their salaries by 310% in 10 years. The raise was announced on August 28, 1989, the same day that Ombudsman Aleck Trawick released his report.

Alberta's adventures in the financial services industry have cost the province almost half a billion dollars. The federal government lost more than double that. Two-thirds of the $1.7 billion lost by the CDIC in the 1980s came from bailing out depositors in eight Alberta companies. The CDIC's vigilance in the case of Principal, however, has paid off. It expects to recover all monies paid out to Principal Trust's federally-insured RRSP holders.

In 1987, the federal regulatory system, desperately inadequate in its response to these failures, was re-organized. The Department of Insurance and the Office of the Inspector General of Banks were merged into the new Office of the Superintendent of Financial Institutions, whose powers were broadened. An overview body, the Financial Institutions Supervisory Committee, was established, consisting of the Superintendent of Financial Institutions, the Governor of the Bank of Canada, the Chairman of the Board of the CDIC and the Deputy Minister of Finance. The committee meets to discuss the general health of Canada's financial institutions and anticipate possible problems.

Would such a body have been able to avert the Principal Group disaster? Probably not: These new federal bodies are—still—concerned only with *federally-regulated* and *federally-insured* institutions. They remain terribly understaffed, and they still have no authority to seek information from the unregulated components of a conglomerate, including a parent company.

The Conservative federal government came to power in 1984 promising to thoroughly revamp Canada's antiquated financial institutions legislation. Seven years later, a four-bill package demolishing the four pillars of the financial services industry received royal assent, becoming law in the spring of 1992. The new legislation loosens the barriers between the various kinds of financial institutions, in effect clearing the way for the spread of Donald Cormie's "financial supermarket" concept across Canada. It paves the way for the creation of a handful of massive conglomerates, composed of banks, trust and insurance companies, securities dealers, investment counsellors, mutual fund distributors and real estate brokers and developers. Existing institutions will be able to move into one another's markets, both by offering one another's services and by purchasing companies in other sectors. (For example, banks can buy trust and insurance companies, trust companies can buy real estate companies, and so on.) Most services, with the exception of insurance, could be peddled across the counter at a single location.

It is not difficult, after wading through the Principal grime, to see the potential for abuse in such conglomerates. The new legislation, attempting to deal with some of these dangers, sets out an number of restrictions against self-dealing and conflicts of interest. Will these rules prove adequate to the challenge? We wait with dread. Trust companies have already threatened to exchange their federal charter for a provincial one if they don't like the new rules. Massive bank-owned real estate development companies are already in the works. In any case, the federal initiative affects only federally-regulated companies. Cormie's companies were, as we know to our sorrow, under provincial jurisdiction. There is very little—except, perhaps, Alberta's shame—to prevent the same sort of operation in that (or any other) province again.

In the days before the Code report was delivered, Alberta introduced tough consumer protection legislation forcing financial services companies to provide their customers with detailed information about their products. The legislation, while welcome, does not address the essential question: Who will watch the watchdogs?

SNOWBIRD COUNTRY: PALM TREES and cactus, Mercedes Benz and Cadillacs. This is Phoenix, Arizona, winter home of tens of thousands of Canada's retired wealthy. The Cormies bought a villa near here in 1982 and it was here that Donald Cormie turned his attention, after the Edmonton operation went down, with a plan to build up the U.S. investment companies. Relieved of PSML and the Canadian mutual funds he had nurtured so carefully, Cormie wanted to develop the same sort of operation in the American market. Company headquarters were in nearby Scottsdale, on the second storey of an upscale office complex.[5]

In halcyon pre-bankruptcy days the U.S. companies were linked to the entirely unrelated Principal Group companies. A sign in the window of the Scottsdale office proclaimed: "The Principal Group of Companies, Assets under administration $1 billion." (No mention was made of devalued Canadian dollars.) After the collapse, the Scottsdale companies went solo; the sign disappeared, and worried investors were assured the Canadian debacle posed no problem for the U.S. companies.

At the end of 1987, the connection was severed when the names of the U.S. companies were altered: "Principal" was changed to "Sea." (DMC's ranch brand was called the "Anchor C" and the yacht was called the *Anchor Sea*. Principal Management Inc., investment advisor to all the U.S.-based funds, became Sea Investment Management Inc. Principal Investors Corporation, the registered broker-dealer, became Sea Investors Corporation. See?) Around the same time, Cormie and his son Jaimie applied to emigrate to the U.S. under a family sponsorship plan made possible by Eivor Cormie's former American citizenship. The outcome of their applications is unknown.

The next year, the Principal name and management of a couple of Cormie's mutual fund companies were sold for a reported $400,000 to an unrelated company in Des Moines, Iowa (which, confusingly, took the name Principal Management Inc.) After that, Sea Investors laid off its sales staff and vacated its Scottsdale office, in favour of more modest digs in Phoenix proper.

In 1987, soon after settling with Principal Group trustee Steve Allan, Sea Investors' officers and shareholders received payments totalling $489,000 U.S. In 1988, they received another $111,000 U.S. The company had barely broken even in 1986 (there was a modest profit of $9,000 U.S.), and in 1987, it declared a loss of $412,000 U.S., a direct result of the hand-outs. The next year's payments pushed the 1988 loss to $364,000. By 1990, the company reported a net operating loss carry-forward (for tax purposes) of about $852,000. (Ironically, this loss, which can remain on the books for more than a decade, makes Sea Investors valuable. If acquired by a profitable company, its losses can be applied against the purchaser's income and used to reduce its taxes.)

In 1988, the U.S. Securities and Exchange Commission (the SEC) launched an investigation into Sea Investment Management Inc. and Sea Investors Corp. Fourteen months later, in May 1989, the SEC censured the companies and their chief operating officer, Christa Petracca. In an eight-page judgement the SEC ruled the companies had wilfully violated 18 sections and sub-sections of American investment law, including: incorrect calculations of net asset values; improper custodial arrangements for company assets; failure to maintain proper records; sale and redemptions of shares based on incorrect net asset values; and failure to file and distribute timely financial reports. No fines were levied, but the companies were ordered to recruit outside directors and to hire an independent consultant, acceptable to the SEC, who would closely supervise their activities for three years. Cormie told the *Calgary Herald* he considered the SEC's actions to be little more than a slap on the wrist.

In the spring of 1989, after learning that Sea Investors had been selling mutual funds in Arizona for 13 months without a licence, the Arizona Corporations Commission began investigating the Cormie companies. Their dealer registration was not renewed in 1991 and they are now inactive.

In late 1990, Cormie's son Neil told the *Herald* the U.S. operation was essentially dormant and would stay that way until the legal battles were resolved. His father couldn't concentrate on any new business ventures, Neil said, until he extricated himself from lingering problems in Alberta. "Until everything is resolved up here, there won't be any other plans."

Meanwhile, in 1989, Cormie said he was retired; at the same time he talked about taking his business to Europe. "I'm fascinated by the common market and getting a foothold in there," Cormie told the *Financial Post*, "because with the computer business today, you can run your business from almost any place. We think there are going to be some real opportunities coming up there."

In early 1989, Cormie Ranch went up for sale and the next spring a deal was struck with a group of Japanese investors who planned to develop a billion-dollar tourist mecca. The province and lawyers for the contract companies moved in with the lawsuits mentioned earlier, to block the Cormies from collecting the $5.5 million offered for the ranch. A subsequent court order allowed Cormie to receive a third of the bank interest on the proceeds of the sale to pay his legal fees. (At 12.25% a year, that was about $225,000 annually. Plummeting interest rates have proportionately reduced this sum.) Cormie's wife Eivor was allowed to keep $125,000 of the $400,000 paid for her small share of the ranch, and half the interest on the remaining $275,000. The rest of the money, including two-thirds of the interest, is in a trust fund pending outcome of various lawsuits.

In early 1991, Cormie pleaded poverty in court during a bid for an immediate hearing of his appeal to have the Alberta and investors' suits against him quashed. Cormie had been using interest from the sale of the ranch to pay his legal bills, but that was insufficient, his lawyer told the Court of Queen's Bench. The court denied the request for an immediate hearing.

The Cormies are hardly impoverished. The yacht *Anchor Sea*, owned by Estate Loan and Finance, continues to moor near Victoria, B.C., a quick jog from the family mansions—properties with an estimated joint value of $2.6 million. The Edmonton home has been sold, but the family held on to the elegant lakeside retreat, worth an estimated $650,000, near Stony Plain. The "cottage," owned by sons Bruce, Neil and Robert, is leased to their parents. The 250 hectares of mountainside land at Three Sisters peaks, acquired by Wyocan Resources (Jaimie, Bruce and Neil) during the 1984 takeover of Rocky Mountain Breweries, has an estimated value of $500,000. The Phoenix house, owned by Jaimie, was sold in mid-1991 for $640,000.[6] There's also the $4.2 million sent to New York in the days leading up to the collapse and an unknown amount of money in overseas investments.

Cormie's involvement with the Cormie Kennedy law firm was severed in 1987. The firm, renamed Cook, Duke, Cox, Tod & Kenny, has billed Cormie millions of dollars to represent him since the collapse. Cormie, 71 this summer, was still a dues-paying member of the Law Society of Alberta in 1992, although he has been classified as non-practising since October 1987.

Collective Securities Ltd. rents space on the top floor of a downtown Edmonton office tower. Another tenant told *The Edmonton Journal* in 1992 that Cormie or Christa Petracca came by occasionally to clear away the mail that accumulated outside the door.[7]

Petracca has been involved in condominium development in Phoenix. She owns a Scottsdale home that she bought in 1989 for $252,000 U.S. For a while, she also spent time in Calgary, managing the Prince Royal Inn, purchased from the contract companies' receiver by a consortium in which she is believed to have held a 50% silent interest. The hotel was sold again in early 1990 at a healthy profit.[8] After the collapse, the Principal Group trustee sued Petracca for repayment of her discharged $300,000 mortgage and other money advanced to her during the company's last weeks. In November 1991, she gave up the house, valued at $440,000, and handed over another $70,000 in cash to settle the matter out of court.

John Cormie sold his Edmonton home and moved to Collingwood, Ontario, to work for a real estate company. His entry in the *Canadian Who's Who*, describing him as president of the defunct Principal Trust, was deleted in 1992.

For a while, Neil Cormie lived near Victoria, B.C. and was listed in the telephone directory as resident on the yacht *Anchor Sea*. His brother Donnie sometimes answered the phone at the nearby Victoria mansions.

Principal Group in-house lawyer Lynn Patrick went to work for The Churchill Corporation in 1989 as president of a new subsidiary. A couple of years later, he became Churchill's corporate counsel.

Former Cormie Kennedy lawyer Bill Connauton continues to practice law in Edmonton. He was appointed Queen's Counsel in early 1992.

Tewfik Saleh moved to Bermuda to become senior counsel in the chambers of the Attorney General. His former assistant Bernard Rodrigues became Superintendent of Insurance soon after the Principal collapse.

Barry Martin is in retirement in Victoria. He remembers with pleasure the huge retirement party thrown for him in 1987— attended, he told me, by many Cabinet ministers.

Principal finance vice-president Bill Johnson joined Coopers & Lybrand during the Principal collapse as administrator of the contract companies' files. He's now a principal with the firm, and hopes to wind up the contract companies' affairs in 1993.

Ken Marlin worked for a few months for Principal Group trustee Steve Allan, answering questions about the operation of the company. He spent three weeks testifying at the Code inquiry, attended many of the hearings, and was invariably co-operative and charming with the media.

Unlike Cormie, Marlin had no nest-egg to help him weather the storms. Everything he had was built on the Rock of Cormie. Two months after the Principal collapse, the National Trust Company was chasing Marlin for overdue mortgage payments on his house (two months, a total of $1,792); a few months later, he gave up the property. Four houseboats were seized by two banks. Then Marlin transferred his few shares in Cormie's Arizona companies to one of his sons. In September 1988, Marlin—once worth $15 million—declared personal bankruptcy, reporting $7.6 million in liabilities and total assets of $22,000.

After the Code inquiry, Marlin moved to Richmond, B.C., near the home of his son Rod. For a couple of years, he worked in real estate sales, commuting periodically to Edmonton to meet with his defence lawyers, make court appearances and answer the questions of RCMP commercial crime investigators. In October 1992, the last time we talked, he was doing some work for Rod at Marlin Travel. His bankruptcy remained undischarged as officials continued to search for hidden assets.

Marlin rarely speaks with Cormie any more, but he ran into him during an Edmonton court appearance in 1990 and stopped to answer a question about a sales job he had taken. "Well, it puts the bread on the table," Marlin told his former partner, then he drifted away.

Meanwhile, THINGS ARE QUIET at Principal Plaza. The lights went out at the top of the tower in the months after the collapse, and eventually *PRINCIPAL* was replaced by *METROPOLITAN*. The penthouse corporate headquarters were briefly occupied by trustee Steve Allan and staff, then stood vacant for several years.

In 1989, the building's owners sent demolition experts to jackhammer the marble and chain-saw the mahogany staircase. The space was considered too expensive for prospective tenants—probably jinxed, some thought—and it was decided to gut the 29th and 30th floors. Doors were taken down, plumbing was removed, tiles and carpets were lifted. Walls were reduced to rubble, and the rubble was carted away. While wrecking Donald Cormie's office, workmen discovered a small safe cleverly concealed in one of the walls. There was, of course, nothing to be found inside.

The doors and railings went to the offices of a construction firm. Some of the marble went to friends of the demolition team to be transformed into kitchen cutting boards. They tried to give away Cormie's bathroom tiles, with the St. George logo on them, as souvenirs, but no one wanted them.[9] The mahogany staircase also ended up in the dump.

When I visited the 30th floor in the spring of 1990, nothing remained but concrete, dust and insulation hanging in clusters from the ceiling ducts. The once-majestic staircase was gone, leaving only a gaping hole in the concrete, through which I peered down to the 29th floor. It was a glassed-in cavern, and echoed when I spoke.

The layout of the walls was still visible in the concrete, and I spent a few minutes tracing offices and pathways. Here was Donald Cormie's walk-in vault; here was his shower; here was the secret passageway. There was Diane Stefanski's desk, Rob Pearce's office, Jaimie Cormie's investment department, Christa Petracca's suite. That was the corridor Petracca would have travelled to get to Cormie's door. Here's where the security cameras were mounted. This would have been the dining room—the Legislature Building visible from its window—and there's where St. George, etched in glass, endlessly battled the Dragon of fear, doubt and want.

"A Well - Watered Stock Transaction"
The Transfer of Athabasca Holdings Ltd. in 1959

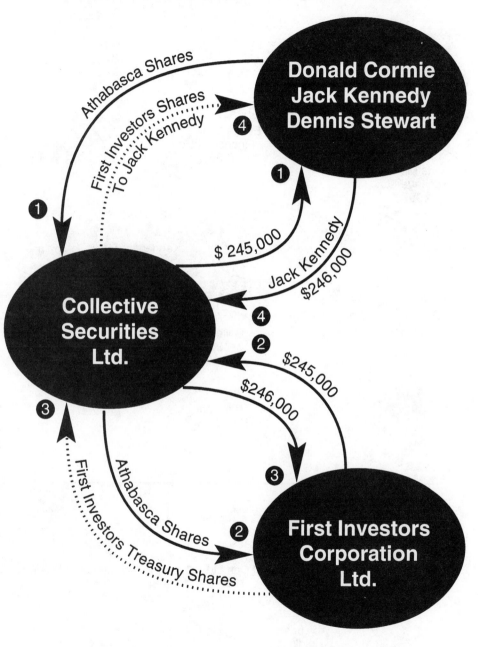

Diagram 1

Principal Group Corporate Structure
1967

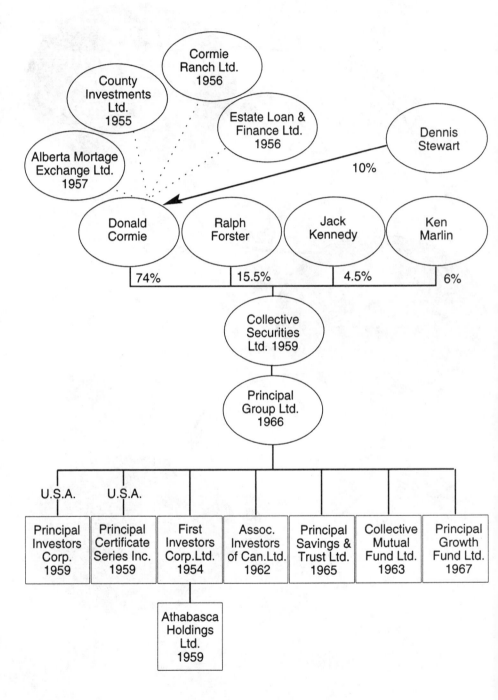

Diagram 2

The Carma/Allarco Transactions
June 29, 1984
(in thousands)

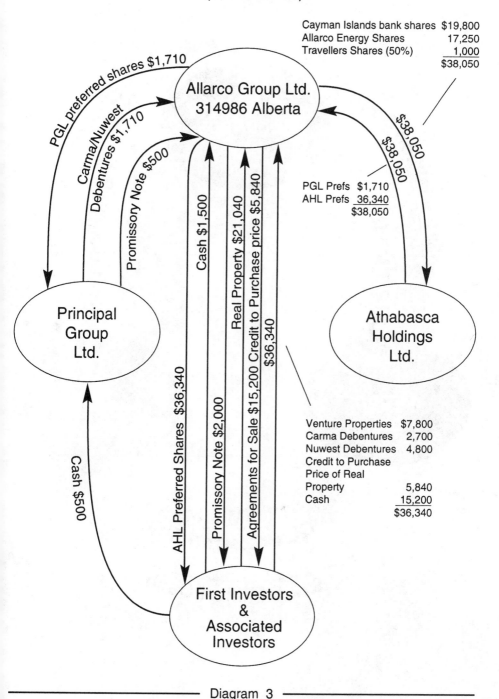

Cayman Islands bank shares $19,800
Allarco Energy Shares 17,250
Travellers Shares (50%) 1,000
$38,050

PGL preferred shares $1,710

Carma/Nuwest Debentures $1,710

Allarco Group Ltd.
314986 Alberta

$38,050
$38,050

PGL Prefs $1,710
AHL Prefs 36,340
$38,050

Promissory Note $500

Cash $1,500

Real Property $21,040

Credit to Purchase price $5,840

$36,340

Principal
Group
Ltd.

Athabasca
Holdings
Ltd.

Venture Properties $7,800
Carma Debentures 2,700
Nuwest Debentures 4,800
Credit to Purchase
Price of Real
Property 5,840
Cash 15,200
$36,340

AHL Preferred Shares $36,340

Promissory Note $2,000

Agreements for Sale $15,200

Cash $500

First Investors
&
Associated
Investors

Diagram 3

Athabasca Holdings Ltd. Purchase of
Principal Group Ltd. Preferred Shares
in December 1984

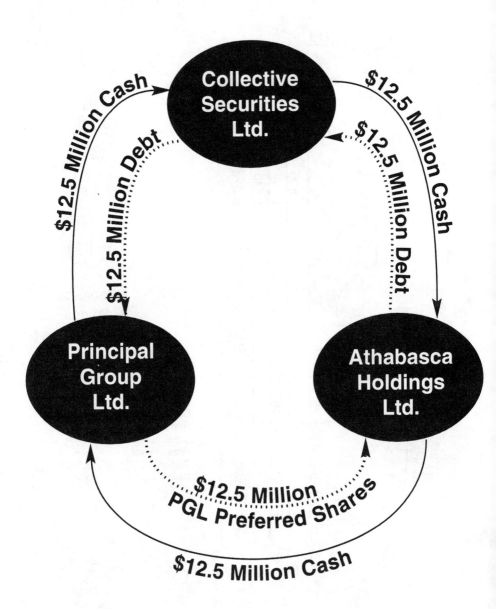

Diagram 4

Department 8:
Flow of Cash to the Upstairs Fund

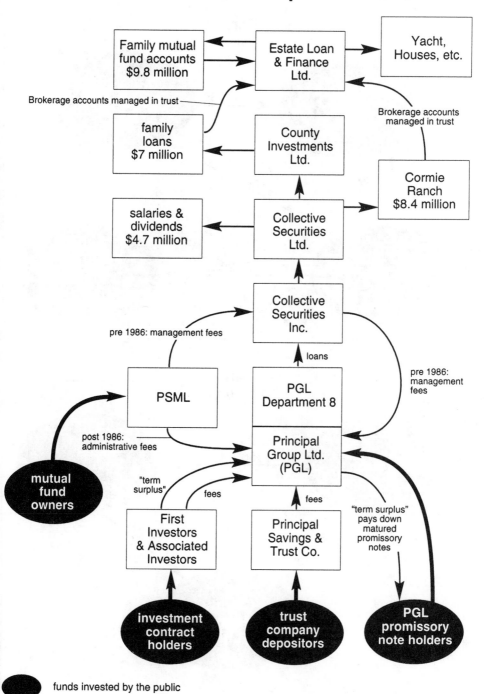

Diagram 5

The Year-End Interest Adjustment,1981

(in thousands)

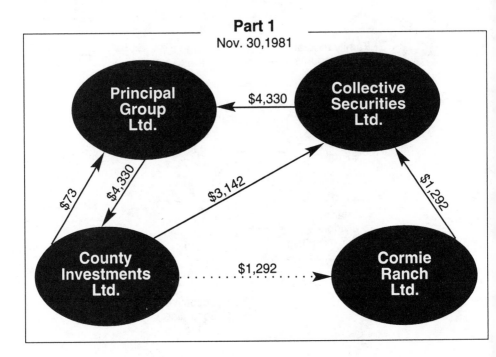

Part 1

Nov. 30,1981

Principal Group Ltd. ← $4,330 Collective Securities Ltd.

$73 · $4,330 · $3,142 · $1,292

County Investments Ltd. ····· $1,292 ·····▸ Cormie Ranch Ltd.

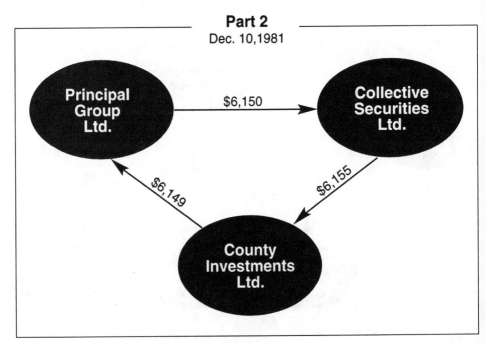

Part 2

Dec. 10,1981

Principal Group Ltd. → $6,150 → Collective Securities Ltd.

$6,149 · $6,155

County Investments Ltd.

Diagram 6

Interest Rate Roll Down
October 14, 1982

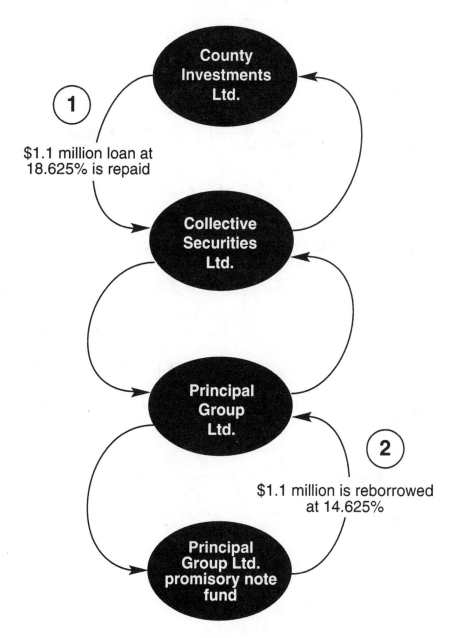

County
Investments
Ltd.

1

$1.1 million loan at
18.625% is repaid

Collective
Securities
Ltd.

Principal
Group
Ltd.

2

$1.1 million is reborrowed
at 14.625%

Principal
Group Ltd.
promisory note
fund

Diagram 7

Principal Group Corporate Structure
after the reorganization (Dec. 31,1985)

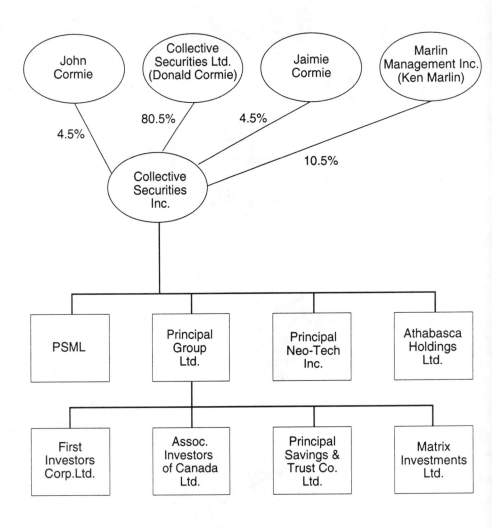

Diagram 8

Trades of Matrix Investments Ltd.
on the Alberta Stock Exchange Between 1984 and 1987

1) Nov. 20, '86 - Levesque Beaubien buys from Principal Group at $1.30
2) Dec. 22, '86 - Athabasca buys back from Levesque at $1.3115
3) Nov. 30, '86 - Jim Hunter buys at $1.30
4) Dec. 24, '86 - Levesque Beaubien buys again at $1.50
5) Dec. 30, '86 - East/West buys at $1.47
6) Mar. 11, '87 - East/West buys more at $1.60

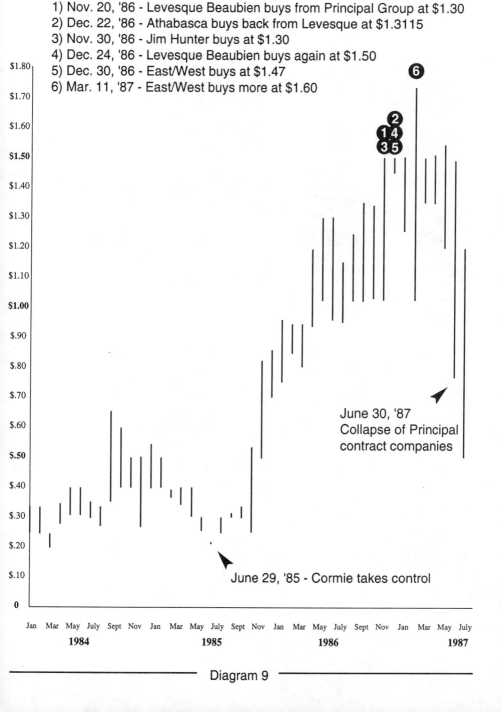

June 30, '87
Collapse of Principal
contract companies

June 29, '85 - Cormie takes control

Diagram 9

Hunter/Derrick Plaza Transaction
November 1986

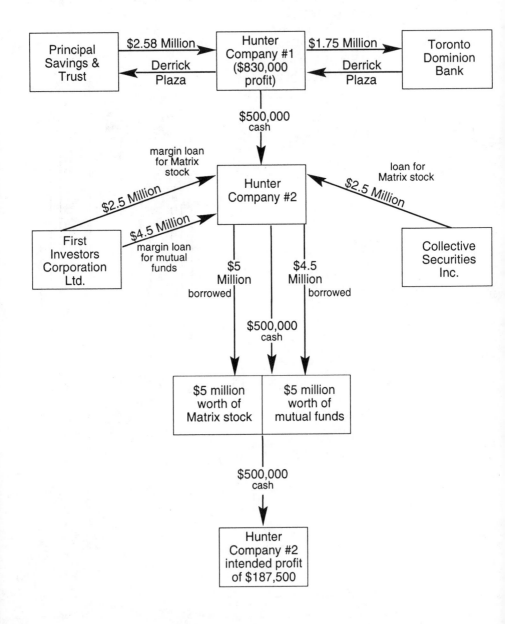

Diagram 10

Chapter notes

2: Green Plymouth

[1]Little is known of John Cormie's brother Alexander, who disappeared from view. John's eldest son John Alexander Cormie (Donald Cormie's uncle) earned his Bachelor of Arts degree at the University of Toronto in 1901. After graduation he became a minister in the Presbyterian (later the United) Church, moved to Manitoba, married there, and in subsequent decades was posted to a series of small-town churches in the southwest part of the province. In 1920 the church brought the Rev. Cormie to Winnipeg to take an administrative post. He was recorded in the 1936-37 *Canadian Who's Who* as the Superintendent of Missions, United Church of Canada: the first Cormie to enjoy the distinction of an entry until Donald Cormie's name appeared in 1973.

[2]Hecht(1).

[3]Mathew Ingram(1).

[4]MacGregor. EDMONTON: A HISTORY, p.249.

[5]Hecht(1).

[6]In his last year at the university Cormie offered two courses. The first, on sales law, was described in the calendar as: "A comprehensive examination of the law relating to the sale of goods, Formation of the Contract, Effects of the Contract, Who can give good Title. Representations, Conditions and Warranties. Actions for breach of the contract. Unpaid seller's remedies. *Bills of Sale Act. Conditional Sales Act. Bulk Sales Act.*" The second

was described as: "The Law of principal and surety. The Statute of Frauds in its application to the contract. The Construction and Effect of Guarantees. The rights of a surety. Release of the surety. Co-sureties. Illegality. Infancy."

3: The richest man in Babylon

[1]See Chapter 15: "A Master of Mass-Suggestion," in Fyfe. NORTHCLIFFE.

[2]Maurice. THE TANK CORPS BOOK OF HONOUR.

[3]Ab Coyne went on to acquire the Yamaha Piano franchise for northern Alberta and the North West Territories. Now retired, he says he became wealthy practising the lessons he learned from the rich man of Babylon: "Hold back 10% of what you earn and blow the rest."

[4]Some of First Investors' minority shareholders held on to their First Investors stock and were bought out over the next few years.

Stan Melton continued to pursue his real estate interests and that same year took his company public with a listing on the Toronto Stock Exchange. He died suddenly in 1973, and the Melton board of directors appointed Cliff Willetts (another First Investors founder) as chairman of the board. In 1975 Melton's son Timothy was elected president of the company, subsequently renamed Melcor Developments Ltd.

[5]Obtained from Forster's nephew Ralph W. Forster, who is writing his uncle's

memoirs.
[6]Cormie's block included 4,500 shares he was voting for his law partner Jack Kennedy, and another 1,840 he was voting for First Investors' then-accountant Gerald Bright.
[7]The exchange of paper as a strategy for increasing a company's asset base became popular in the summer of 1984, when a handful of Canadian banks and trust companies bought and sold hundreds of millions of dollars worth of one another's preferred shares. See Critchley(1).
[8]Preferred shareholders have no vote but are entitled to dividends at predetermined rates of interest, which must be paid before any dividends are paid to common shareholders. Common shares entitle the holder to a vote in the selection of management and give him a claim on a proportionate share of any profits, which are declared as dividends. Thus, if you own 10% of a company, you are entitled to 10% of all profits—and 10% of the votes at a shareholders' meeting.
[9]According to the testimony of Cormie's secretary Jude Halvorson and others. See Chapter 13.
[10]Obtained from Ralph W. Forster.
[11]CODE REPORT, p.27.
[12]Schreiner(1).

4: A suite deal for heifers

[1]Chalmers(3).
[2]Part of the mill property was sold to Qualico Construction Co., which built high-rises on the site. The original Edmonton Milling Co. Ltd. remains on the property and has been designated an historic site.
[3]Ketchum(2), 3Carlisle(1) and Twigg(1).

6: "My favourite nit-picking accountant"

[1]Solomon(6).
[2]Gordon Miniely wrote me in 1990: "I have a faint recall that they were required to transfer certain assets into one of the companies in order to meet reserve requirements."
[3]Foster, THE BLUE-EYED SHEIKS, p.321; Wood, THE LOUGHEED LEGACY, p.42.
[4]Cormie was referring to Harry Rose and Jim Darwish, who he blamed for the fiasco resulting from the purchase of Associated

Investors in 1962. He had been threatening the Alberta Securities Commission with legal action.
[5]The directions included the following: elimination of Associated Investors' capital impairment within six months; any introduction of capital in the future was to be by way of permanent share capital, and any capital introduced by other than cash had to be acceptable to the Superintendent; delivery of monthly financial reports to the Superintendent; and investment only in qualified assets as identified in the Investment Contracts Act. The companies were not to enter any intercorporate transactions with shareholders, directors, officers or affiliated companies, or any other directly or indirectly related party without the written consent of the Superintendent.
[6]Solomon(2).
[7]Pratt, "The Lougheed Party," in Nikiforuk, Pratt and Wanagas, RUNNING ON EMPTY, pp.93-94: "...commanding fear as much as respect from grown men who worried incessantly whether they were in or out of the boss's favour... By persuasion, manipulation, and sheer force of personality, Lougheed imposed his will on a deferential caucus fearful of the consequences of resistance." See also THE LOUGHEED LEGACY by David Wood, a Tory insider with liberal access to Lougheed and his personal papers, who wrote with admiration of Lougheed's considerable manipulative skills: "One of his favourite devices is to get someone else to ask the question, or make the controversial statement." (Pp.192-193).
[9]Solomon(4).
[9]For excellent accounts of the American collapses, see: Adams, THE BIG FIX; Singer, FUNNY MONEY; Sprague, BAILOUT; Zweig, BELLY UP; and Davis(1).
[10]War Barry Enterprises Ltd., "Report Regarding the Effectiveness and Suitability of the Restructured Departmental Organization: Alberta Consumer and Corporate Affairs." This document was not entered into evidence at the Code inquiry.
[11]In September 1980, before the department shuffle, Ken Marlin had attempted to sidestep Superintendent Jim Darwish on the U.S. depository issue with a phone call and letter direct to Minister Julian Koziak. Koziak sent an "action request" to Darwish asking for input on the matter, and received back a four-page memo summarizing the department's turbulent history with the Principal contract com-

panies, including their constant lack of capital. Darwish referred to the Ernst & Ernst report and the Shortreed/Gardiner reports and mentioned the huge management fees and dividends which drained the companies. He explained the rationale behind the prohibition against holding assets in the United States—if Principal companies in the U.S. got into trouble down there, American authorities could seize or freeze the assets held in their jurisdiction, and Canadian regulators would have no way of bringing them back—and advised he had received a legal opinion from the Attorney General's Department supporting his position. Koziak, convinced, asked Darwish to draft a letter for him to be sent to Marlin. The letter, requesting the securities be returned to Canada, was sent to Marlin the same day. It was a gratifying moment for Darwish—the last he would have on the matter for two years.

Several months later more letters had gone back and forth and the assets were still in New York. When Ron Kaiser took over Darwish's responsibilities, one of his first actions was to overturn the decision to force the return of the assets to Canada. He and Barry Martin met with Principal Group vice-president Christa Petracca and decided against pressing the issue. Petracca had obtained her own legal opinion from lawyer Peter Owen, who indicated there was no legal problem with keeping the assets down south. Darwish fretted, but there was nothing he could do. That was it for two years.

[12]In the weeks after the Osterman/Darwish confrontation, appraisals were acquired for Paramount's real estate holdings. Eventually the accounting firm of Clarkson Gordon was brought in to investigate the situation. After that, things happened fast. "Once they got in and got their report, they went down to the minister and told her all about it," recalled Darwish. "But until that happened, we were having a series of meetings with company officials, and the company officials were complaining about who they wanted to attend meetings from the department and different things like that, and it drifted along for quite a while." In January 1984, after demands for capital were not met, Tewfik Saleh put Paramount under a limited licence, blocking any further sales. In June an administrator was appointed and the company went down.

[13]This is Darwish's version of events.

Barry Martin denies that Darwish either talked to him about this document or handed it to him—and claims he received it through departmental mail. However, documents support Darwish's version. A handwritten note from Darwish to Martin on the cover of the April 24 memo says "Extra copy for Minister as per our discussions." A subsequent memo delivered by Darwish to Osterman on May 23, 1984, said he had discussed the memo with Martin and the method of sending it to her, prior to sending it.

[14]The fact that Darwish's side of the conversation was broadcast over the speaker did not come out at the Code inquiry, and Darwish was not aware of it until I discussed it with him in 1990. I learned of this during an interview with Mark Gregory earlier that year. In subsequent interviews both Barry Martin and Connie Osterman said they could not recall whether the speaker was on—Martin added that "it would not be a proper thing to do"—but neither denied it had happened.

7: Hopes and prayers

[1]Catherwood(1).
[2]Wood, THE LOUGHEED LEGACY, p.92.

[3]These statistics come from economist Robert Mansell, who testified at the Code inquiry. Mansell a specialist in macroeconomic analysis of the Alberta economy, is a professor of economics at the University of Calgary. He conducted a computer simulation of the provincial economy (leaving such factors as high interest rates as a constant) to determine the impact of the NEP. Without the program, Mansell concluded, Alberta would have escaped the 1981-82 recession that hit other parts of Canada. The recession was relatively mild in the East, over in 15 months, but Alberta was devastated. It took until 1987 for the province's employment level to recover to that of pre-recession 1981.

[4]The Battleford default was part of a larger scandal involving Liknaitzky's misuse of a large sum of trust monies held by his partners in the law firm Brower, Johnson, Liknaitzky and Robertson. Some of that money was used to pay monthly interest payments to investors, maintaining the illusion of the company's financial health.

[5]See Hutchinson(1), Pratt(2), Pratt(3), Pedersen(9) and Sheppard(1).

[6]In mid-1991 the Alberta Securities Com-

mission handed down cease-trading orders against the Rogers brothers because they violated commission regulations through their involvement with two Abacus-related blind pools, Glacier Resources Ltd. and Zigold Resources Ltd. (The Alberta Stock Exchange permits new companies without assets to sell stock to the public before developing any business plan; these "blind pools" are prohibited in other provinces.) Ken Rogers was suspending from securities trading for 25 years; two 15-year orders were handed down on William Rogers. Nine other associates were also banned for varying periods of time. [Shilliday(1), CP(3), Pedersen(1)].

[7]Peter Pocklington would eventually collect $67 million in financial assistance from the Alberta government to bolster his ailing businesses. The province took over Gainers in 1989 after Pocklington defaulted on a government-backed loan, then filed a $70 million lawsuit against him in mid-1991, alleging a series of Pocklington-controlled companies derived "unjust, inequitable and unconscionable benefits" through a complex series of inter-company transactions between 1985 and 1987. [Barrett(1).]

[8]Kerr(2), Trigueiro(1), Trigueiro(2), Dunn(1) and Pratt(1).

[9]Morton(1), Morton(2), Morton and Kerr(1), Best(1) Mackey(1) and Slobodian and Bunner(1).

[10]The Canadian Commercial Bank and the Northland Bank went down in September 1985. See Chapter 15.

[11]The Alberta Treasury Branches, created in 1938, was one of the few financial institutions in Alberta not in trouble during the early 1980s—largely because it was owned, financed and guaranteed by the province. See: Barstow, "Treasury Branches score big in free-enterprise Alberta," which notes the irony of Albertans' ardour for this government-owned institution in a province devoted to free enterprise. In 1987 the Alberta Treasury Branches ranked as the 20th largest financial institution in Canada. Between 1982 and 1991 its province-guaranteed deposits climbed from $2.6 billion to $7.1 billion. During this period the Treasury Branches lost money every year; its capital deficit finally bottomed in 1989 at $149.4 million, then began a slow improvement.

[12]For a discussion of jurisprudence regarding the duties of public authorities,

see CODE REPORT, pp.493-506.

[13] Source: a government memo on Associated Investors dated April 15, 1973.

Neil Crawford remained with Cormie Kennedy until 1968, while serving a term as Edmonton alderman. Family members say Cormie asked him to leave because his political activities were taking up too much of his time. Crawford was elected to the Legislature in 1971, and immediately joined Lougheed's Cabinet. In 1979 he was appointed to the dual posts of Attorney General and Government House Leader, where he stayed until 1986.

[14]Under the *Trustee Act*, the company was approved as an appropriate recipient of funds invested by trustees on behalf of others; one of the requirements of the Act was that the company have $1 million in unimpaired capital.

[15]Danylchuk(3).

[16]Bergman and Walker(1).

[17]Solomon(2), Powell(2) and Slobodian(1).

[18]Records filed with the chief electoral office show that in the crisis year of 1986 the Principal Group companies donated a total of $19,100 to the Alberta Tories— most of that to the re-election campaigns of the party and individual candidates. Neil Crawford and Neil Webber received donations, as did long-time Cabinet minister Horst Schmidt and MLAs Nancy Betkowski and Rick Orman, who joined the Cabinet after the 1986 election. Liberal Grant Mitchell also received a $10,000 contribution before the 1986 election. Mitchell now sits as MLA for Meadowlark—and was Liberal finance critic in 1987 when Principal Group went down—but from 1983 to 1986 he was Principal vice-president of operations and a member of the board of directors of Principal Trust.

At least one federal politician received a contribution as well. Yellowhead MP Joe Clark received $15,000 from Principal Group, as well as $1,000 from Cormie's son Bruce, during the 1984 federal campaign. The Cormies were very active in Clark's riding, where the family ranch was located. After Bruce's unsuccessful bid in the spring of 1984 for the Tory nomination in Edmonton South, he became vice-president of, and fund-raiser for, Clark's riding association. Bruce later upped his political profile with membership in the federal Conservative 500 Club, whose members have contributed at least $1,000 to the party.

[19]In 1986, hard hit by the real estate collapse, The Churchill Corporation received millions of dollars from Vencap Alberta Equities Ltd., a publicly traded venture-capital company set up by the Conservative government in 1982 with a $200-million loan from the Alberta Heritage Trust Fund. Vencap invested $3 million in Churchill common shares and $6 million in Churchill preferred shares; another $5 million went into Allan Olson's construction company (which, through its various branches, also won more than $53 million worth of government contracts during the 1980s). As well, publicly-traded Churchill SBEC (Small Business Equity Corporation) Ltd., owned 17% by Churchill, was established to take advantage of the province's 1985 Small Business Equity Company program which effectively offered investors a $3 grant for every $10 they invested. Later, the pension fund of the then-Alberta owned AGT (Alberta Government Telephones) Ltd. bought a $3.15-million debenture from Churchill. See Pedersen(4), Pedersen(11), Donville(1) and Cernetig and Moon(1).

Despite this support, Churchill has fared poorly. Once valued at more than $100 million, it is now worth only a fraction of that. It announced losses of several million dollars in 1990 and 1991, and some of its subsidiaries have gone into receivership. The company went public in 1987 at $2.60 a share; the same shares traded in September 1991 at three cents each.

[20]The Young Presidents Organization was founded around 1950 in New York with three stated aims: to share fellowship, to make members better presidents and to foster free enterprise. But as early as 1956, when the first Canadian chapter was established in Toronto, members acknowledged its economic/political benefits. "You can't be a member and not make thousands of dollars worth of contacts," a Canadian member told the *Financial Post* that year. [Perry(1).]

These days the YPO emphasizes self-development and family values. Members and their wives get together in exotic locations for seminars on topics such as wine-tasting, stress management, art, jewellery and world affairs: a kind of college of culture and poise for folks too important to attend a night-school class. There are four conventions a year and countless local gatherings at 120 chapters worldwide. The protective Texas head office refuses to release the membership list.

Cormie testified that he often came away from YPO conventions with valuable ideas—for example, the concept of structuring his conglomerate according to a functional approach, with each component providing a different service to the whole.

[21]Neil Webber, MLA for Calgary Bow from 1975 to 1989, is an old friend of Principal vice-president Christa Petracca. She studied mathematics with him circa 1970 when he was an instructor at Calgary's Mount Royal College. Webber told me that during his years in Cabinet he sometimes met Petracca socially, usually for lunch, and had wide-ranging chats about politics, business, news of the day and their respective jobs. "We both worked for—had interesting jobs, and we talked about them in an interesting way," he told me. Webber said that his friendship with Petracca resumed in Edmonton some time after she joined Principal Group in 1978. "I either ran into her or heard from her one day, I can't remember now."

One Principal insider says that Petracca used her meetings with Webber to sniff the political wind. "It proved to be a useful contact," the person told me. When questions arose about the government's intentions regarding financial institutions, "Christa would say, 'I'm having lunch with Neil Webber on Tuesday and I'll see what I can find out.'"

Webber denied saying anything to Petracca that would have breached Cabinet confidentiality, but agreed their "general discussions" might have touched on the topic of the financial services industry. Webber said he abruptly ceased his association with Petracca in early 1987, when Treasurer Dick Johnston brought his concerns about Principal to the priorities committee. "I felt that given the situation between government and Principal Group that I would be not in a comfortable position by talking to her. Even about other things, because of the problem between government and Principal Group. I never called nor did she call me after that." Webber said he had no memory of even a passing mention of the Principal companies prior to 1987.

8: Going-concern

[1]The unaudited regulatory statements, copied on Touche Ross letterhead, in-

cluded only the first seven notes which appeared in the GAAP statements. (The final notes, which were excluded, were the ones Bruce Pennock had insisted on, regarding contingencies, the subsequent event of the $23-million transaction and the exposure faced by First Investors as a result of that deal.)

[2]This despite the fact that Bernard Rodrigues specifically drew Tewfik Saleh's attention to Burt Eldridge's memo in a note regarding preparations for the June 15 meeting.

[3]"CDIC has refused to increase PST's [ratio] because of the manner in which management have been conducting PST's affairs." Affidavit sworn by Jean Pierre Sabourin, CDIC chief operating officer, on August 13, 1987, In The Matter of the Winding-Up of Principal Savings and Trust Company.

[4]Memo written by Allan Hutchison on June 28, 1984.

9: Under the Principal umbrella

[1]This letter was written in the heat of a commission battle with another top-selling salesman, Arney Falconer. We'll return to Falconer, and related sales ethics issues, in Chapter 20.

10: Caribbean hideaway

[1]The Venture Properties Securities were mortgages on downtown Calgary property granted by, and to secure a loan to, Venture Properties Ltd.; two guarantees of its shareholder, Paul D. Kuffler; foreclosure actions on both mortgages; and legal actions on both guarantees. Principal auditor Touche Ross & Co. had pressed the contract companies to write a $4.4-million contingency for loss against the Kuffler loan for the year ended 1983. According to Marlin, Kuffler owned 25% of a building in Denver in which Carma held a 50% interest.

[2]Naylor, MONEY AND THE POLITICS OF DEBT.

[3]By the autumn of 1984, wrangling between the United States and Cayman Islands governments over bank secrecy resulted in an agreement to provide the U.S. with limited access to bank records in drug money cases. The decision resulted in a minor exodus of laundered narcotics money, but the colony still remains among the most favoured of the world's money

hideouts.

[4]It is known that the Cayman bank's "expenses" almost doubled in the year after Cormie took over. The bank's audited financial statement shows that expenses for the second half of 1984, after the takeover, amounted to $181,000 (or about $362,000 for the entire year.) The next year this figure had jumped to $688,000. What these expenses involved—besides office space, three employees and accounting services—remains unknown.

[5]Hemingway(2).

[6]Tewfik Saleh testified that he had no memory of this conversation, but he did not deny it. Whatever happened to spark the incident is not known.

11: Donald and the Cupcake

[1]Adams(3).
[2]Koch(1).

12: Virtually insolvent

[1]The test for qualified assets on deposit equal to the "cash surrender value" was calculated on the basis of the face value of the certificates.

[2]Grant Mitchell, like many Principal zealots, seems to have functioned with his eyes glazed. He became director of Principal Consultants Ltd. in 1983 and director of Principal Trust in 1985. He testified that he had access to weekly spread reports prepared for Cormie and the financial reports of several Principal companies. Despite his directorships and signing authorities for the two companies, however, he had little interest in their financial workings. Mitchell testified that he was aware after becoming trust company director that in 1984 $23-million worth of non-producing mortgages were transferred from the trust company to the contract companies. He was also aware that the trust company announced and widely publicized a record profit in 1985, but made no connection between that profit and the $23 million contribution from its sister companies. Mitchell said he was aware that Principal had many mortgages in arrears and that some of them had to be foreclosed, but "wasn't in a position of perspective" to understand how serious that might be for the company.

[3]Bankruptcy trustee Steve Allan testified that Principal Group was arguably insol-

vent by the end of 1983, but after this transaction the company was definitely bankrupt.

13: Department 8

[1]Grescoe and Cruise, THE MONEY RUSTLERS, p.275: "The 10 percent rule has been passed on to his eight children like a dominant chromosome. 'My father might pay a dollar for shovelling the sidewalks and at the time that job might be worth 25 cents,' says Bruce Cormie, 'then he would sit down and say, 'Now, Bruce, do you want to spend that money on candy and get bad teeth? Or do you want to put it in the bank so it's working for you when you're in school, when you're in bed, when you're sick?'' "

[2]Ironically, the firm was Lucas, Bishop and Fraser, whose partner Robert White would tackle Cormie as investors' counsel at the Code inquiry.

[3]As of November 30, 1981, Cormie Ranch owed Collective Securities a total of $8,663,085.21 (interest-bearing loans totalling $6,362,683.16 and interest-free loans of $2,300,402.05). Source: letter from Collective Securities to Cormie Ranch dated December 2, 1981.

[4]"Metro Edmonton Hospital District #106" continued to roll its money back into Principal Group as its investments matured. At the time of the collapse it held $2,471,734.23 in promissory notes.

[5]These figures include $20,900,402 paid by the contract companies between 1983 and 1986 which was subsequently "waived" by Principal Group Ltd. Unfortunately the repayment was made with the grossly overvalued shares of an affiliated company, a promissory note and a reciprocal waiver, and was thus partly illusory. These transactions will be discussed in later chapters.

[6]This application was for recognition as an exempt purchaser under the *Securities Act*, enabling Estate Loan and Finance to buy securities which had been issued without filing a prospectus to the Alberta Securities Commission.

14: A teaspoon of honey

[1]Stockland(1).

[2]Allan Hutchison would have been investigated by the Alberta Institute of Chartered Accountants if he had remained in the province. However, when he moved to Arizona he resigned his membership in the institution, removing himself from its jurisdiction.

[3]The notice of suspension issued August 30, 1991, by the Institute of Chartered Accountants of Alberta said that: (1) McCutchen failed to comply in all material respects with the generally accepted auditing standards of the profession including those set out in the CICA (Canadian Institute of Chartered Accountants) Handbook as amended from time to time; (2) the financial statements failed to comply with the generally accepted accounting principles including the Recommendations set out in the CICA Handbook as amended from time to time; and (3) McCutchen failed to fully document or retain documentation or working papers that reasonably evidenced the nature and extent of the work performed.

[4]Properties were classified as (1) land held for development, (2) income producing property or (3) land held for resale. Ninety percent of the real estate held by the contract companies were included in the last two categories, which only required a writedown if management was of the opinion there was a permanent decline in value. Valuations of some of these properties were based on development scenarios and contemplated rezoning or subdivision. This was a highly innovative treatment, and highly inappropriate, given that the companies were prohibited under the *Investment Contracts Act* from developing real estate, or from holding properties over the long term for investment purposes.

The new strategy had the effect of allowing the contract companies to avoid recognizing an additional $5.4 million in losses on owned properties. Instead of booking the losses as a contingency, as would have happened the year before, they were instead shown as an "appropriation of the deficit"—a curious accounting strategy which equates roughly to the contingency booked the year before.

Clarkson Gordon: Final Report, pp.11-13: "An appropriation sets aside a portion of retained earnings for specific purposes so that the retained earnings are not available for dividends or other distributions... We have not previously seen an appropriation of a deficit... [It] would seem to serve no useful purpose other than to reflect the effect that a contingent loss

might have if it were recognized... As the appropriation is not shown on the balance sheet its existence is not prominently disclosed. The appropriation has no effect on the income or mortgage values reported and is not a substitute for an appropriate loan loss provision."
[5]Best(2).
[6]Ketchum(2).
[7]As we saw in Chapter 9, complaints about Principal's sales practices went back many years. As recently as January 1984 a letter from J. Henry Thomas, Superintendent of credit unions, co-operatives and trust companies in British Columbia to John Cormie complained that "many depositors enter your doors on the assumption that they are dealing with a trust company, the investments in which are all guaranteed by CDIC." This letter, which complained of a tendency to "bait and switch", was copied to Dick Page in the federal Department of Insurance.
[8]Marc Lemay, the Alberta Securities Commission's most senior official, had been familiar with the Cormie companies for more than a decade. In the spring of 1973, as the Commission's senior financial analyst, Lemay was involved in capitalization meetings with Associated Investors. The next year, as deputy director, Lemay agreed not to make a report to Cabinet about First Investors' finances in exchange for an agreement not to accept trust funds under the *Trustee Act*. (See Chapter 7.)

15: "How much bad news can the system stand?"

[1]The province was trying to protect not only the bank but the already bailed-out North West Trust, which held an 8% interest in the CCB.
   Francis, CONTROLLING INTEREST, pp.205-206: "Alberta and Ottawa encouraged pensions and co-ops to contribute tens of millions of dollars to give [the two banks] their start. Among initial shareholders and depositors were the Alberta teachers' superannuation funds, Alberta and federal civil service pension funds, a number of Western co-ops, as well as the funds of employees working for federal Crown Corporations such as Canadian National Railways, Air Canada, and others."
   The banks were in trouble years before their bankruptcy. As Francis reported, directors Bill Siebens and Jack Pierce

resigned in disgust from the Northland and CCB boards respectively. Pierce said that in 1979 he took his concerns about the CCB and its absentee chairman Howard Eaton directly to Deputy Treasurer Chip Collins, Premier Peter Lougheed's right-hand man. "Pierce says he told Collins he was concerned that fees due to the bank were possibly being skimmed in Europe. Pierce does not believe his allegations were ever checked. Collins, under questioning in the legislature, was reported to have said he could not remember the conversation."
[2]Kerr(1).
[3]Frank Jones, dean of the University of Alberta law school from 1976 to 1986, refused an interview for this book, but did not deny his friendship with Cormie.
[4]Don McCutchen testified that he told the valuator that it was the audit committee of the Matrix board, not the board itself, which was largely external to Principal Group.
[5]For several months the Principal Neo-Tech Class A stock traded lightly in the range of $10 to $14. Suddenly in December 1985 trading jumped ten-fold and ranged as high as $19.50. Half the shares that Principal Group sold to the contract companies for $19 had just been received from Principal Neo-Tech at a value of $10.50 as partial consideration for the purchase of seismic data owned by Principal. (See Chapter 16.) At $19 the stock was trading at six times its book value (equity per share), which most financial analysts would consider an excessive premium. The Toronto Stock Exchange has never investigated this company's curious trading history.

16: Burt & Bernie

[1]EJ(3).
[2]An underwriter negotiates with an issuing company on the price, quantity and timing of a new stock issue, assists in preparing the prospectus, then distributes blocks of the shares to investors.
[3]Principal Trust was also involved, and loaned approximately 10% of the $14.3 million. These mortgages were among those transferred by the trust company to the contract companies in 1984.
[4]A February 1982 report prepared by consultant Bill Green (a former Principal employee who would soon return as mortgage manager), advised that John Pawluk's company, Banff Investments

Ltd., had a capital deficiency of about $1.7 million and owed hundreds of thousands of dollars in trade and supplies accounts. Despite this crisis, Pawluk took over $1 million out of the company in its 1981 fiscal year. Green commented in his report: "To bail this project out and to complete the hotel as planned will require at least $10,000,000... this investment proposal has an unusually high degree of risk... The company is technically bankrupt, and in view of the way the principal shareholder has conducted the affairs of the company it is doubtful at this time if he will find a prudent lender willing to advance him the required funds."

[5]This transaction was conducted privately (not through the stock exchange), but it is interesting to look at the public trading of Matrix shares in the days leading up to the sale. The stock, buoyed by enthusiastic promotion and a bull market, had traded on the Alberta Stock Exchange during most of May between 93 cents and $1.09. Then on May 29, SWAT team member Lance Frazier and his wife Elaine suddenly started buying. Their buying began during the lunch hour at a price of $1.08, concluding at the end of the day at $1.10. The next morning Frazier bought at $1.12, ending that afternoon at $1.15. During the 26-hour period the Fraziers acquired 26,500 shares of Matrix stock at a total cost of $28,750. Several thousand of those shares were bought at $1.12 from Allarco Energy (owned by Athabasca Holdings), which turned around and bought more shares at $1.15.

Meanwhile, two unknown investors jumped in to buy a total of 800 shares at $1.20. It was at this unprecedented price that Associated Investors, on May 30, transferred its Matrix stock to Athabasca.
[6]Lees(1).

17: "This office requests that you discontinue selling voluntarily"

[1]Principal Group's appropriation of the annual review format does not reflect in any way on Investors Group, which produced an annual report as well as a review.

Don McCutchen testified that although he brought the idea of a "review" to Principal Group, he was not consulted in the review's preparation and did not read it until after its publication. He also testified that he protested to Donald Cormie that it contained financial information with which

he disagreed and which was not in accordance with his qualified audit opinion. He could not recall Cormie's response.
[2]A similar brochure published around the same time to promote PSML claimed that the company's "assets under management" totalled $630 million. Grilled on the conflicting claims, Jaimie Cormie agreed the "assets under management" were the same in the two companies—but insisted that they were being "administered" by Principal Group and "advised" by PSML.
[3]Cruise and Griffiths, FLEECING THE LAMB, p.250. Also see Francis, CONTREPRENEURS, p.147.
[4]Diane Cox was not called to testify at the Code inquiry and refused to be interviewed for this book.
[5]The August 14 letter, the collaborative effort of Treasury and Consumer Affairs officials, was sent after being approved at a meeting attended by Deputy Treasurer Allister McPherson and Consumer Affairs Deputy Minister Barry Martin.

18: "I don't think 'do nothing' is an option"

[1]Peat Marwick managing partner G. Douglas Carr, who provided Christa Petracca with an appraisal of the Cayman Islands bank in 1984, was one of the auditors caught in the CCB squeeze.
[2]Donald Cormie testified that this statement had been made at a vice-presidents' meeting and was not directed at Patrick on this matter. Inspector Bill Code concluded: "I prefer the evidence of Patrick over that of Donald Cormie."

19: Creative transactions

[1]"Warehousing" is a stock market term normally used to describe the deceptive practice of accumulating control of a large block of stock by distributing it among apparently unconnected parties. The strategy creates the impression that the stock is widely held, when in fact it is controlled by one person or a small group. Sometimes, while the stock is warehoused, its "owners" sell the shares among themselves at ever-increasing prices, create an impression of value, then "blow it off" on an unwitting public. This process is sometimes called "wash trading" and is illegal. In the case of Matrix, almost all of the stock remained under Donald Cormie's control until Principal

Group collapsed in 1987.
[2]After selling Allarco, Allard went on to found the Bank of Alberta in 1983 and to develop his broadcasting and communications empire, including Superchannel, the Western Canadian pay-TV network. He died in August 1991 at the age of 71, after a lengthy battle with cancer.
[3]Paul W. Lefaivre was budget director of the Alberta Progressive Conservative leadership convention in 1985. He sat on a number of prestigious boards: vice-chairman of Alberta Blue Cross, chairman of the board of provincial crown agency Alberta Opportunity Company, and was a member of the review committee of the Alberta Heritage Fund Small Business and Farm Interest Shielding Program.
[4]Terry Myers became Matrix Investments vice-president of acquisitions in 1986. He was with Nu-West Development Corporation from 1976 to 1982, then worked as a consultant to business and government for four years. During that period he served on the review board of the Alberta Heritage Fund Mortgage Interest Reduction Program.
[5]In accepting this shorter period for Robert Pearce the Alberta Securities Commission took note of the conclusion of Inspector Bill code in his report: "The evidence tends to show that Pearce's activity degenerated over time as he caused Allarco [Energy]to become more and more the only buyer of Matrix stock. His conduct was, however, legitimate, from the perspective of my mandate, because the evidence before me tends to show that he had no dishonest intent when he carried out the day to day trades. I am not satisfied that Pearce intended to create a fictitious premium on the stock although such a premium was created."
[6]Company #1 is known as 321635 Alberta Ltd. Corporate registry reports show its sole shareholder at that time as K.K. Jay Holdings Ltd; that company's shareholder is Jim Hunter's associate Donald Brewster. According to a transaction summary prepared for the inquiry by the accounting firm Clarkson Gordon, Brewster held the shares of Company #1 as sole trustee of the Hunter Childrens Trust.
[7]EJ(8), Thorne(3).
[8]Macdonald(1), Thorne(1) and Thorne(2).

20: Look-see

[1]Francis, CONTREPRENEURS, p.147; Cruise and Griffiths, FLEECING THE

LAMB, p.250.
[2]Danylchuk(7).
[3]Elaine McCoy was sufficiently impressed with Petracca during the lunch to request a copy of her resume. Petracca testified that she thought that McCoy wanted it for a file she kept on potential candidates for appointment to government-selected boards.

21: Two different planets

[1]Best and Shortell, A MATTER OF TRUST, pp.311-317; Mackey(1), Gallagher(1), Morton and Kerr(1), Morton(1), Morton(2), Best(1), Slobodian and Bunner(1), MacDonald(3) and Ziegler(1).
[2]During the Code inquiry, Donald Cormie's lawyers tried repeatedly to enter evidence regarding Alberta's dealings with other failed financial institutions. Code refused to allow this, ruling it was outside his mandate. The lawyers appealed to Justice Ronald Berger, who rejected the application, ruling the focus of the investigation must be the Principal companies.
[3]In September 1988 the numbered company, or "Softco," wrote off 83% of Bud Conway's $98,000 debt. John Karvellas told The Edmonton Journal the agreement was worked out between Conway and Softco on a priority basis at the request of Assistant Deputy Treasurer Jim Drinkwater. MacDonald(3).
[4]The following summary is based on the notes of executive Doug Haydock.
[5]Participants in the Johnston/Cormie meetings of June 1987 have slightly different recollections of what was offered, and when, by Cormie. The following account is pieced together from participants' testimony; it relies most heavily on the versions given by Dick Johnston and Allister McPherson, and is backed by McPherson's notes.

22: "How could Mr. Cormie let this happen?"

[1]Because the Code inquiry focused on the failure of the Principal contract companies, few witnesses were asked questions about events after Dick Johnston's June 30 news conference. However, the intense media interest during this period generated dozens of newspaper articles on which I partly relied to piece together events between July and September of 1987. Particularly helpful were: Adams(1),

Adams(6), Adams and Pratt(1), Beaty(1), Beaty(3), Bertin(1), Cox and Waddell(1), CH(1), CH(2), Chalmers(2), Chalmers(4), Chalmers(5), Chalmers and Laghi(1), Chalmers and Laghi(2), Danylchuk and Pedersen(1), EJ(1), EJ(2), EJ(6), EJ(7), Goyette(1), Hryciuk(1), Kondro(1), Kondro(3), Kondro(4), Kondro(5), Laghi(1), Laghi(2), Laghi(3), Laghi(4), Laghi and McClure(1), Laghi and Wood(1), Mayer(1), Mayer(2), Mayer(3), Mayer and Laghi(1), Mayer and Pedersen(1), McClure(1), Morchuk(1), Pedersen(2), Pedersen(3), Pedersen(5), Pedersen(6), Pedersen(7), Pedersen(8), Pedersen (10), Pedersen(12), Pedersen and Laghi(1), Pedersen and Laghi(2), Pratt and Beaty(1), Sadava(2), Solomon(1), Thorne(4), Thorne(6) and Ziegler(5).

[2]Don Logan went on to become national chairman of the Principal Investors Protection Association, which now has more than 400 chapters across Canada. Tragically, Suzanne Mah became one of more than 2,000 investors to die without seeing the return of her money; she died in August, 1989 at the age of 36 after a year-long battle with cancer.

[3]Investors Mah and Logan made a formal complaint of conflict of interest before the Institute of Chartered Accountants of Alberta, which conducted an investigation into the conduct of Coopers & Lybrand and concluded a year later there was no conflict. The professional conduct committee of the Canadian Insolvency Association, which subsequently investigated the matter, reached the same conclusion. Both organizations' rules prohibit a firm from liquidating a firm it previously audited; work done for subsidiaries, a parent or affiliates doesn't count.

[4]This version of events came from Donald Cormie during testimony at the Code inquiry. Petracca denied making any complaints or demands.

[5]At the Code inquiry, Cormie explained his decision this way: "The Canadian brokers and the Canadian banks were becoming very difficult. They were concerned about the consequences of First and Associated, and the logical thing to do was to manage it in an environment where we had the ability to manage it freely."

[6]Peter Meekison, academic vice-president of the University of Alberta between mid-1984 and 1991, was deputy minister of Federal and Inter-Governmental Affairs in Peter Lougheed's government; for many years he was considered one of the premier's most valuable advisors. His daughter Jennifer, a university student in 1985, had a summer job at Principal that year preparing a preliminary version of Principal Group's 1985 annual report. Cormie testified: "Her family would often help her on a lot of things in the way of grammar and structure and organizational expression, so I thought she would be a good person to come up with the preliminary draft."

[7]Cormie testified that he did tell Marlin the discharge was for a $300,000 mortgage.

[8]Laghi and Chalmers(2).

[9]The balance of the mutual funds managed by PSML continued their drastic slide over the next few weeks, resulting in a reduction of the purchase price. The Metropolitan deal ultimately generated about $5 million in cash and debentures worth $15 to $20 million.

[10]Stefanski went to work for trustee Collins Barrow after the Principal Group bankruptcy, but was quickly terminated.

[11]Donald Cormie's testimony on these dealings with Halvorson was confusing and did not match Halvorson's recollection of events. Originally Cormie said he had no memory of being asked for a personal indemnity, nor of saying that he would give her a company indemnity. He did remember her presenting him with an indemnity, that "sat on my desk for a few days," but he refused to sign it. Later he said he had said to lawyer Bill Connauton by telephone that he would give Halvorson a company indemnity—normally privileged conversation—without realizing that she was in Connauton's office during the conversation. Cormie denied seeing Halvorson at the Cruickshank Phillips office, and denied even knowing that she went there. He also said he didn't know anything about his lawyers asking Halvorson to sign the acknowledgement, and didn't know Halvorson refused to do so.

[12]Cormie has denied making this remark.

[13]The following week Court of Queen's Bench Justice John Agrios released a judgement on a years-old lawsuit in the Battleford Mortgage collapse which made it doubtful that Principal investors would ever win a lawsuit against the province (except in the unlikely event that malice could be proven). In the suit, 18 Battleford creditors who collectively lost over $1 million sued the Alberta Securities Commission, the province and the Law Society of Alberta for negligence. Justice Agrios

ruled that the investors were not entitled to compensation because the Commission had a duty to supervise deposit-taking companies in the general public interest, with no special responsibility towards individual members of the public. Judege Agrios ruled that investors should not have assumed such a far-reaching and stringent system of supervision guaranteeing that all registered deposit-taking companies were sound and fully trustworthy.

23: Evidence tending to prove

[1]According to Diane Stefanski, she almost wasn't called to testify. She says that Inspector Code's accountants Clarkson Gordon couldn't make sense of what she was saying about Department 8, and inquiry staff had ruled her out as a witness. After the collapse Stefanski worked briefly with Ken Marlin, whose lawyer alerted them to her significance. Stefanski told me: "It got to the point where the Code people were asking me, 'What questions should we be asking you?'"

[2]Jim Drinkwater left Treasury in 1989 and went to Edmonton-based Canadian Western Bank as its vice-president, treasury and corporate finance. Among his duties was providing corporate and government clients with specialized financial and economic advice. Two years later he joined AGT (Alberta Government Telephones) Ltd., the largest subsidiary of Telus Corp., a former Alberta Crown corporation.

[3]Lawyer Jack Major, Q.C., led Alberta's defense of its handling of the Principal affair and the battle to keep Peter Lougheed's name out of the inquiry; he acted for all government witnesses, including Connie Osterman. At that time Major was a senior partner in the Calgary firm Bennett Jones Verchere, where Lougheed has been a partner since leaving politics. In August 1991 Major was appointed a Justice of the Alberta Court of Appeal. Sixteen months later Prime Minister Brian Mulroney appointed him to the Supreme Court of Canada.

[4]Don Getty commented that the province would not provide compensation to noteholders because the inquiry had not provided any new information on the matter. This is very coy, as Code did not—and was not intended to—focus on reasons for the Principal Group failure. Trustee Steve Allan appealed in November 1987 to Court of Queen's Bench to have the Code inquiry expanded beyond the contract companies into the failure of the parent and affiliated companies, but was unsuccessful. As a result, information about the Principal Group collapse was, and is, spotty in many areas.

[5]Adams(2), Adams(4), Danylchuk(1), Fisher(2), Fisher(3), Fisher(4) and Fisher(5).

[6]Ketchum(2).

[7]Danylchuk(6).

[8]MacDonald(2).

[9]Chalmers(6).

Bibliography

BOOKS

James Ring Adams. THE BIG FIX: INSIDE THE S&L SCANDAL (HOW AN UNHOLY ALLIANCE OF POLITICS AND MONEY DESTROYED AMERICA'S BANKING SYSTEM). New York: John Wiley & Sons, Inc., 1990.

W. Steve Albrecht et al. HOW TO DETECT AND PREVENT BUSINESS FRAUD. New Jersey: Prentice-Hall, Inc., 1988.

Patricia Best and Ann Shortell. A MATTER OF TRUST: GREED, GOVERNMENT AND CANADA'S $60 BILLION TRUST INDUSTRY. Markham, Ontario: Penguin Books Canada Ltd., 1985.

The Canadian Institute of Chartered Accountants. REPORT OF THE COMMISSION TO STUDY THE PUBLIC'S EXPECTATIONS OF AUDITS. Toronto: June, 1988.

CANADIAN WHO'S WHO. Toronto: University of Toronto Press, 1936-37, 1973, 1989, 1990, 1991, 1992.

Terrance Corcoran and Laura Reid of the *Financial Times of Canada*. PUBLIC MONEY PRIVATE GREED: THE GREYMAC, SEAWAY AND CROWN TRUSTS AFFAIR. Toronto: Collins Publishers, 1984.

John Craig. THE NORONIC IS BURNING! Don Mills, Ontario: General Publishing Co. Ltd., 1976.

David Cruise and Alison Griffiths. FLEECING THE LAMB: THE INSIDE STORY OF THE VANCOUVER STOCK EXCHANGE. Vancouver: Douglas & McIntyre, 1987.

Peter Foster. THE BLUE-EYED SHEIKS: THE CANADIAN OIL ESTABLISHMENT. Toronto: Totem Books, 1980.

Diane Francis. CONTREPRENEURS: STOCK-MARKET FRAUD AND MONEY LAUNDERING IN CANADA. Toronto: Macmillan of Canada, 1988.

Diane Francis. CONTROLLING INTEREST: WHO OWNS CANADA? Toronto: Macmillan of Canada, 1986.

Hamilton Fyfe. NORTHCLIFFE. London: George Allen & Unwin Ltd., 1930.

John F. Gilpin. EDMONTON: GATEWAY TO THE NORTH. Canada: Windsor Publications (Canada) Ltd., 1984.

Paul Grescoe and David Cruise. THE MONEY RUSTLERS. Markham, Ontario: Viking Books Canada Ltd., 1985.

Allan Hustak. PETER LOUGHEED. Toronto: McClelland and Stewart Ltd., 1979.

J.G. MacGregor. EDMONTON: A HISTORY. Edmonton: M.G. Hurtig Publishers, 1967.

Major R.F.G. Maurice. THE TANK CORPS BOOK OF HONOUR. London: Spottiswoode, Ballantyne & Co. Ltd., 1919.

R.T. Naylor. HOT MONEY AND THE POLITICS OF DEBT. Toronto: McClelland and Stewart Ltd., 1987.

Peter C. Newman. THE ACQUISITORS. Toronto: McClelland and Stewart Ltd., 1981.

Andrew Nikiforuk, Sheila Pratt and Don Wanagas. RUNNING ON EMPTY: ALBERTA AFTER THE BOOM. Edmonton: NeWest Press, 1987.

Peggy M. Pasternak, ed. WHO'S WHO OF CANADIAN WOMEN. Toronto: Trans-Canada Press, 1986, 1987, 1988.

Mark Singer. FUNNY MONEY. New York: Alfred A. Knopf, Inc., 1985.

Irvine H. Sprague. BAILOUT: AN INSIDER'S ACCOUNT OF BANK FAILURES AND RESCUES. New York: Basic Books, Inc., 1986.

G.R. Stevens, O.B.E. A CITY GOES TO WAR. Brampton, Ontario: Charters Publishing Company Ltd., 1964.

David G. Wood. THE LOUGHEED LEGACY. Toronto: Key Porter Books Ltd., 1985.

Phillip L. Zweig. BELLY UP: THE COLLAPSE OF THE PENN SQUARE BANK. New York: Crown Publishers Inc., 1985.

GOVERNMENT AND COURT REPORTS

CENSUS OF CANADA. 1851, 1871, 1881, 1891.

Clarkson Gordon (Richard Cormier). ANALYSIS OF FIRST INVESTORS CORPORATION LTD. AND ASSOCIATED INVESTORS OF CANADA LTD. ACCOUNTING POLICIES, PRACTICES AND FINANCIAL STATEMENT DISCLOSURES. (Code Inquiry Exhibit 600.) Oct. 15, 1988. (Cited as Clarkson Gordon: Final Report.)

William E. Code. FINAL REPORT OF THE INSPECTOR WILLIAM E. CODE, Q.C. Calgary, Alberta: In the Court of Queen's Bench of Alberta, July 18, 1989. (Cited as the Code Report.)

House of Commons Standing Committee on Finance, Trade and Economic Affairs. CANADIAN FINANCIAL INSTITUTIONS. The 11th Report to the House. Ottawa: Nov., 1985.

The Honourable Willard Z. Estey. REPORT OF THE INQUIRY INTO THE COLLAPSE OF THE CCB AND NORTHLAND BANK. Ottawa: Minister of Supply and Services Canada, 1986. (Cited as the Estey Report.)

Guy MacLean, Ombudsman of Nova Scotia. IN THE MATTER OF THE REGULATION OF FIRST INVESTORS CORPORATION LTD., Feb., 1990.

Gerald McLellan, Ombudsman of Saskatchewan. SPECIAL REPORT ON THE REGULATION OF FIC LTD. AND AIC LTD. BY THE SASKATCHEWAN SUPERINTENDENT OF INSURANCE (THE PRINCIPAL INVESTIGATION), 1989.

Stephen Owen, Ombudsman of British Columbia. THE REGULATION OF AIC LTD. AND FIC LTD. BY THE B.C. SUPERINTENDENT OF BROKERS (THE PRINCIPAL GROUP INVESTIGATION). Public Report No. 19, Sept., 1989.

Stephen Owen, Ombudsman of British Columbia. THE SALE OF PROMISSORY NOTES IN BRITISH COLUMBIA BY PRINCIPAL GROUP LTD. Public Report No. 28, Oct., 1991.

Lyman R. Robinson, Q.C. REPORT TO THE MINISTER: In the matter of the *Trade Practice Act* and In the Matter of First Investors Corporation Ltd., Associated Investors of Canada Ltd., Principal Consultants Ltd., Principal Savings and Trust Company, and Principal Group Ltd. Province of British Columbia, Oct. 14, 1987.

Aleck Trawick, Ombudsman of Alberta. SPECIAL REPORT: THE ROLE OF THE PROVINCIAL GOVERNMENT IN THE REGULATION OF THE PRINCIPAL GROUP OF COMPANIES. Office of the Ombudsman, Province of Alberta, 1989. (Cited as the Trawick Report.)

War Barry Enterprises Ltd. "Report Regarding the Effectiveness and Suitability of the Restructured Departmental Organization: Alberta Consumer and Corporate Affairs." Feb. 12, 1982.

Robert B. White, Q.C. SUBMISSIONS OF SPECIAL COUNSEL TO THE CODE INVESTIGATION, WILLIAM E. CODE, Q.C.—INSPECTOR. Volumes 1,2 and 3. Edmonton: April 20, 1989.

ARTICLES

Abbreviations
AR *Alberta Report*
CH *Calgary Herald*
CP *Canadian Press*
EJ *The Edmonton Journal*
FP *Financial Post*
GM *The Globe and Mail*
ES *Edmonton Sun*

Jeff Adams(1). "Attempts to save companies failed." **CH**. July 4, 1987, p.A3.
Jeff Adams(2). "Cormies trying to rise again." **CH**. May 20, 1989, p.D1.

Jeff Adams(3). "Disagreements threaten to undermine the unity of Cormie clan members." **CH**. May 20, 1989, p.D1.

Jeff Adams(4). "Inquiry looms over Phoenix hopes." **CH**. May 20, 1989, p.D1.

Jeff Adams(5). "Legal fight puts crimp on Cormie's U.S. comeback." **CH**. Dec. 5, 1990, p.D2.

Jeff Adams(6). "$50 bonds saved 2 firms from red faces at wind-up." **CH**. July 10, 1987, p.A1.

Jeff Adams and Sheila Pratt(1). "Investors scramble for funds." **CH**. July 3, 1987, p.A1.

J. Stephens Allan, Letter to the Editor. "Principal noteholders not skilled investors." **CH**. Aug. 13, 1989, p.C5.

Angela Barnes. "Trust firms forced to raise capital to cover loans." **GM**. Jan. 5, 1985, p.B7.

Tom Barrett(1) (**EJ**). "Province, Gainers launch suit against Pocklington." **CH**. July 30, 1991, p.A1.

Robin Barstow. (Financial Times News Service.) "Treasury Branches score big in free-enterprise Alberta." **EJ**. Aug. 26, 1987, p.G3.

Bob Beaty(1). "Government actions leave Cormie family bitter." **CH**. Aug. 12, 1987, p.A5.

Bob Beaty(2). "Lawyer claims no evidence of links." **CH**. July 24, 1987, p.B2.

Bob Beaty(3). "Principal sale, firings possible." **CH**. Aug. 7, 1987, p.A1.

Jonathan Beaty and Richard Hornik. "A Torrent of Dirty Dollars." TIME. Dec. 18, 1989, pp.44-50.

Eric Bergman and Roberta Walker(1). "The Man of Principal." ALBERTA BUSINESS. Oct., 1985, pp.8, 17-18.

Oliver Bertin(1). "Alberta cancels licence of 2 investor firms." **GM**. July 2, 1987, p.B1.

Dunnery Best(1). "$50 million to keep the rain off NW Trust." **FP**. Jan. 12, 1985, p.13.

Dunnery Best(2). "Good Sport in the West." **FP**. Feb. 23, 1985, p.12.

Ruth Bowen. "Seven Travelling Cormies." **EJ**. Sept. 16, 1965, p.17.

Don Braid(1). "Alberta's secret scandals." TORONTO STAR. July 21, 1987, p.A11.

Don Braid(2). "Apathy finally laid to rest." **EJ**. April 10, 1984, p.A7.

Don Braid(3). "Osterman close to getting boot." **CH**. Aug. 15, 1989, p.A3.

CH(1). "Failed firms anger investors." July 2, 1987, p.A1.

CH(2). "Principal deal hinges on Cormie OK." Aug. 30, 1987, p.A1.

CP(1). "A 'formula for disaster'." **CH**. Nov. 21, 1985, p.C2.

CP(2). "Auction sells off bits of financial empire." **CH**. Nov. 23, 1987, p.A3.

CP(3). "Alberta places ban on Rogers: Ex-Abacus chief out for 25 years." **GM**. Sept. 7, 1991, p.B8.

CP(4). "Cormie wants proceeds of sale to pay legal bills." **GM**. Feb. 22, 1991, p.B4.

CP(5). "Estey questions practice of two bank auditors." **CH**. Nov. 23, 1985, p.E2.

Tamsin Carlisle(1). "Cormie property worth millions." **FP**. July 21, 1989, p.3.

Robert Catherwood(1). "Bugles, purple Cougars pass but policyholders linger on." **FP.** June 10, 1972, p.A1.

Miro Cernetig and Peter Moon(1). "Getty's job 'tough' on living standard: Alberta Premier has taken out mortgages, sold off assets since being sworn in." **GM.** Nov. 26, 1990, pp.A1, A3.

Ron Chalmers(1). "2,000 join in move to sue B.C. gov't." **EJ.** June 19, 1987, p.C1.

Ron Chalmers(2). "Alberta inquiry into Principal stalled." **EJ.** Aug. 8, 1987, p.A1.

Ron Chalmers(3). "Former swamp a showplace of technology on the hoof." **EJ.** March 12, 1985, p.B3.

Ron Chalmers(4). "Investment firm's woes known in 85." **EJ.** July 3, 1987, p.A1.

Ron Chalmers(5). "Investors not told of mortgages." **EJ.** July 4, 1987, p.C2.

Ron Chalmers(6). "Principal offices scrapped." **EJ.** Aug. 16, 1989, p.A7.

Ron Chalmers(7). "University uncertain about pledge." **EJ.** Aug. 26, 1987, p.F1.

Ron Chalmers and Brian Laghi(1). "Investors face $60-million loss." **EJ.** July 2, 1987, p.A1.

Ron Chalmers and Brian Laghi(2). "RCMP reviews Principal complaints." **EJ.** Aug. 7, 1987, p.A1.

Roy Chandler, secretary to the International Auditing Practices Committee of the International Federation of Accountants. "Cementing the ties that bind auditors and bank regulators." THE BOTTOM LINE, Aug., 1989, p.18.

Anna Cormie. "The Cormie Family." Included in Pat Mestern. LOOKING BACK: THE STORY OF FERGUS THROUGH THE YEARS, 1833-1983, VOL. II. 1983. Fergus: R&R Printing, 1983, pp.377-380.

John Cormie. "The Cormie Family." Included in TWEEDSMUIR HISTORY: ENNOTSVILLE WOMEN'S INSTITUTE. Marguerite Skeoch Metcalf and Isobel Cunningham Burr, Curators. 1972. Privately printed.

Kevin Cox and Christopher Waddell(1). "Weekend will determine fate of Principal firms." **GM.** Aug. 15, 1987, p.B4.

Barry Critchley(1). "Preferred shares: Cozy trusts and banks are under scrutiny." **FP.** Oct. 6, 1984, p.7.

Jack Danylchuk(1). "Cormie just 'another snowbird' among Arizona's wealthy." **EJ.** Aug. 14, 1988, p.A1.

Jack Danylchuk(2). "Deal paves way for Cormie ranch sale." **EJ.** May 19, 1990, p.C1.

Jack Danylchuk(3). "Fate of FIC request remains mystery." **EJ.** Sept. 3, 1989, p.A10.

Jack Danylchuk(4). "Principal 'is soundest' of financial institutions." **EJ.** April 24, 1986, p.E1.

Jack Danylchuk(5). "Principal's founder keeping profile low." **EJ.** July 18, 1987, p.D1.

Jack Danylchuk(6). "Remnants of a once-mighty empire." **EJ.** Jan. 23, 1992, p.B3.

Jack Danylchuk(7). "Sask. threat prompted ethics plan." **EJ.** Dec. 2, 1987, p.A1.

Jack Danylchuk(8). "Vacuum salesmen launched myth-driven firm." **EJ.** July 7, 1989, p.A4.

Jack Danylchuk and Rick Pedersen(1). "Principal official admits losses could exceed $60 million." **EJ.** July 10, 1987, p.H1.

L.J. Davis(1). "Chronicle of a Debacle Foretold: How deregulation begat the S&L scandal." HARPER'S. Sept., 1990, pp.50-66.

Bernd Debusmann (Reuters News Agency). "Caymans' siren call of secrecy." **GM.** Sept. 16, 1991, p.B7.

Caroline Doggart. "The World's Best Tax Havens." REPORT ON BUSINESS MAGAZINE. Aug., 1990, pp.58-65.

Ric Dolphin. "The Tainted Fortunes of Donald Cormie." CANADIAN BUSINESS. Oct., 1988, pp.32-37, 122-138.

Christopher Donville(1). "Churchill wins a reprieve." **GM.** April 2, 1991, p.B7.

Madelaine Drohan(1). (**CP**). "Banks didn't know what they were in for." **CH.** Dec. 28, 1985, p.D1.

Madelaine Drohan(2). (**CP**). "More than one gallows needed after bank failure." **CH.** Dec. 27, 1985, p.C6.

Kate Dunn(1). "More credit union help planned by province." **CH.** Feb. 28, 1985, p.C1.

EJ(1). "Angry investors demand answers." Aug. 12, 1987, p.A1.

EJ(2). "Alberta needs a public inquiry." Editorial. July 31, 1987, p.A4.

EJ(3). "Getty says he has no record of meeting Cormie in 1987." May 7, 1988, p.B1.

EJ(4). "Hold Last Rites for Mrs. Cormie." March 16, 1933, p.11.

EJ(5). "Mrs. G.M. Cormie Called By Death." March 15, 1933, p.11.

EJ(6). "No conflict over Principal, firm says." July 16, 1987, p.A1.

EJ(7). "Province to aid investors if found at fault—Getty." Aug. 21, 1987, p.G8.

EJ(8). "Secret deals." Editorial. March 30, 1987.

EJ(9). "Secret trials must be justified." Editorial. July 21, 1987, p.A6.

EJ(10). "Well-known city businessman, traveller of the world, dies." March 22, 1972, p.64.

Jim Farrell. "Cormie neighbors happy with resort plan: Local authorities say Japanese proposal would be a boon for the area." **EJ.** May 3, 1990, p.B3.

Matthew Fisher(1). "Papers reveal past criticism of Principal." **GM.** June 1, 1988, p.B1.

Matthew Fisher(2). "Principal's Cormie courts investors in United States." **GM.** Feb. 15, 1989, p.B1.

Matthew Fisher(3). "SEC investigated operations in U.S. after collapse of Principal." **GM.** Feb. 15, 1989, p.B13.

Matthew Fisher(4). "Two Cormie firms wilfully broke law, U.S. regulator rules." **GM.** May 19, 1989, p.B19.

Matthew Fisher(5). "'Wild West' setting for Cormie family's revival bid." **GM.** Feb. 15, 1989, p.B13.

Tim Gallagher(1). "Shaky trust." **AR.** Sept. 16, 1985, p.41.

Virginia Galt. "OSC may be asked to probe Bomac sale." **GM.** Sept. 23, 1983, p.B1.

GM(1). "TSE stages comeback after miserable week." Sept. 16, 1986, p.B9.

GM(2). "U.S. market has worst day since 1929." Sept. 12, 1986, p.A1.

Linda Goyette(1). "Rueful investors unite to share financial fiasco." **EJ**. July 4, 1987, p.A5.

Lorne Gunter. "When the trough runneth over: Premier Getty's unabashed cronyism anger voters and alarms Conservatives." **AR**. Aug. 5, 1991, pp.9-12.

Armin Hecht(1). "He Lost His Job At 47, Now He's Glad It Happened: Broken Leg Changed His Plans." **EJ**, May 22, 1963, p.58.

Maureen Hemingway(1). "Hi, society!" **EJ**. July 11, 1982, p.H3.

Maureen Hemingway(2). "Hi society! (Hoedown winds up day on ranch.)" **EJ**. July 1, 1984, p.B3.

Dennis Hryciuk(1). "No need to shut savings firm—Cormie." **EJ**. Aug. 13, 1987, p.A1.

Brian Hutchinson(1). "Rapping de Rappard." WESTERN REPORT. Dec. 4, 1989, p.11.

Darcy Ingram. "Connie Osterman speaks out." THE CAPITAL, Three Hills, Alberta. Aug. 2, 1989, pp.1,3.

Mathew Ingram(1). "Cormie breaks the silence." **AR**. March 12, 1990, pp.29-30.

Gordon Jaremko. "Reform urged in Alberta investment set-up." **CH**. July 17, 1974.

D'Arcy Jenish. "Rebellion on the home front: Angry Calgarians stop payments and sue their lenders." **AR**. Nov. 28, 1983, p.36-37.

Jerry Kammer. "Canada has own scandal similar to S&L debacle." THE ARIZONA REPUBLIC. April 22, 1991, p.A1.

Parker Kent. **CH**. "Agency Rule." Aug. 26, 1965.

Kathy Kerr(1). "Hyndman defends loss of millions." **CH**. Sept. 5, 1985, p.A1.

Kathy Kerr(2). "Rescue bid could cost $40 million." **CH**. March 21, 1985, p.A1.

Brock Ketchum(1). "Firm claims it was in dark over town purchase." **CH**. July 24, 1987, p.B2.

Brock Ketchum(2). "How the rich keep their riches: Family's personal wealth intact after financial empire caves in." **CH**. April 12, 1992, ppB1-B2.

Halyna Koba. "Donald Cormie's Ten Percent Solution." *The Insiders* column of YOUR MONEY, Oct., 1986, pp.87-88.

George Koch(1). "Code's new conundrum." **AR**. Feb. 29, 1988, p.5.

George Koch(2). "Cracking the code." **AR**. June 31, 1989, p.9.

George Koch(3). "Scrutinizing the auditors." **AR**. Jan. 25, 1988, pp.8-9.

George Koch(4). "So much for special friendship: Christa Petracca's lawyer lashes out at Donald Cormie." **AR**. May 30, 1988, p.9.

George Koch(5). "When the water's high, buy." **AR**. May 23, 1988, p.10.

Wayne Kondro(1). "Met picks up pieces of Principal." **CH**. Aug. 18, 1987, p.A1.

Wayne Kondro(2). "NEP blamed for Principal failure." **CH**. Sept. 20, 1987, p.A1.

Wayne Kondro(3). "Other subsidiaries healthy, Principal Group says." **CH**. Aug. 8, 1987, p.A3.

Wayne Kondro(4). "Principal's spoils up for grabs." **CH**. Aug. 13, 1987, p.A1.

Wayne Kondro(5). "Terms reached to dissolve Principal empire's assets." **CH**. Sept. 3, 1987, p.A3.

Lafferty, Harwood and Partners Ltd. A CONFIDENTIAL CLASSIFICATION LIST OF CANADIAN SECURITIES, prepared and published by Lafferty, Harwood and Partners Ltd., Montreal, Jan., 1985.

Brian Laghi(1). "Collapse a problem for Tories." **EJ**. Aug. 12, 1987, p.C1.

Brian Laghi(2). "Getty open to Principal inquiry." **EJ**. July 15, 1987, p.A1.

Brian Laghi(3). "Insurance head knew 2 firms short of cash." **EJ**. July 17, 1987, p.D1.

Brian Laghi(4). "Principal investigation not full inquiry—critics." **EJ**. July 17, 1987, p.A1.

Brian Laghi and Matthew McClure(1). "Principal files for bankruptcy." **EJ**. Aug. 11, 1987, p.A1.

Brian Laghi and Duncan Thorne. "Pay hike draws flood of protest." **EJ**. Aug. 30, 1989, p.A1.

Brian Laghi and Roy Wood(1). "Government to pay if negligent, investors say." **EJ**. July 31, 1987, p.D1.

Nicholas Lees(1). "Western beef and mutual funds great barbecue draw". **EJ**. June 24, 1986, p.E3.

Patricia Lush. "Three real estate firms finding escape from bankruptcy painful." **GM**. Jan. 9, 1984, p.B1.

Jac MacDonald(1). "Business property 'flip' investigated." **EJ**. Sept. 23, 1987, p.G8.

Jac MacDonald(2). "Receiver chasing profits in sale of Principal subsidiary." **EJ**. April 20, 1991, p.D1.

Jac MacDonald(3). "Secretive gov't firm writes off big debts." **EJ**. Jan. 13, 1989, p.A1.

Jac MacDonald(4). "Taxpayers should have been told: Auditor general on North West Trust disclosure." **EJ**, Jan. 26, 1989, p.A1.

Allan Mayer(1). "Cormie to receive $1.5 million in 'compromise'." **EJ**. Aug. 28, 1987, p.A1.

Allan Mayer(2). "Insurance giant bids for Principal." **EJ**. Aug. 19, 1987, p.A1.

Allan Mayer(3). "Public inquiry rejected in Principal collapse: Calgary lawyer named to investigation." **EJ**. Aug. 14, 1987, p.A1.

Allan Mayer and Brian Laghi(1). "Buyer must act quickly to get Principal Group." **EJ**. Aug. 13, 1987, p.G1.

Allan Mayer and Rick Pedersen(1). "Investors strike back with lawsuit." **EJ**. July 11, 1987, p.A1.

Lloyd Mackey(1). "Taking over the trusts." **AR**. Feb. 23, 1987, p.4.

Matthew McClure(1). "Liability blocked bail-out scheme." **EJ**. Aug. 12, 1987, p.C1.

Gord McIntosh **(CP.)** "Check of trust firms uncovers $1.5 billion in doubtful loans." **GM**. Jan. 4, 1985, p.A1.

Brian Milner. "Banks' auditors settle." **GM**. Nov. 3, 1990, p.B10.

Judy Morchuk(1). "Gov't killed Principal investors' confidence—analyst." **EJ**. Aug. 12, 1987, p.C1.

Lasha Morningstar. "A suite deal for heifers." **EJ**. July 18, 1983, p.A1.

Gordon F. Osbaldeston, P.C., O.C. "Keeping Deputy Ministers Accountable." National Centre for Management Research and Development, University of Western Ontario, 1989.

Peter Morton(1). "Alberta, Ottawa tackling NW Trust." **CH**. Nov. 21, 1986, p.E1.

Peter Morton(2). "North West Trust part of complex network." **CH**. Nov. 12, 1986, p.G1.

Peter Morton and Kathy Kerr(1). "Province rescues dying trust firms." **CH**. Feb. 10, 1987, p.A1.

Rick Pedersen(1). "Abacus affair's key figures named in blind pool probe." **EJ**. May 3, 1990, p.D1.

Rick Pedersen(2). "Allegations of conflict investigated." **EJ**. July 22, 1987, p.A1.

Rick Pedersen(3). "Angry investors band together to push probe." **EJ**. July 24, 1987, p.D1.

Rick Pedersen(4). "Churchill list a business who's who." **EJ**. Nov. 3, 1990, p.D3.

Rick Pedersen(5). "Court orders limited probe of failed pair." **EJ**. July 16, 1987, p.D1.

Rick Pedersen(6). "Investors unleash anger: 'I want my money back,' tearful senior demands." **EJ**. July 9, 1987, p.A1.

Rick Pedersen(7). "Ontario stymied Principal plans." **EJ**. July 11, 1987, p.D2.

Rick Pedersen(8). "Principal hearing mired in legal row." **EJ**. July 23, 1987, p.C1.

Rick Pedersen(9). "Regulators labored in a communications gap during Dial affair." **EJ**. Oct. 7, 1989, p.G1.

Rick Pedersen(10). "Sales allowed during audits—Johnston." **EJ**. July 7, 1987, p.D1.

Rick Pedersen(11). "Source of Churchill's woes buried in maze." **EJ**. Nov. 3, 1990, p.D1.

Rick Pedersen(12). "Up to court who runs inquiry—Berger." **EJ**. July 31, 1987, p.D1.

Rick Pedersen and Brian Laghi(1). "Investors win inquiry control." **EJ**. July 30, 1987, p.A1.

Rick Pedersen and Brian Laghi(2). "Principal says losses less than expected." **EJ**. July 8, 1987, p.F1.

Tom Philip. "Off the hook: A quiet end to the CCB-Northland lawsuit." **AR**. Nov. 19, 1990, pp.25-26.

Tom Philip and D'Arcy Jenish. "Signature's collapse: A $4.5-million mortgage firm failure." **AR**. Nov. 28, 1983, pp.37-38.

Gretchen Piere. "Cormie's kingdom: Scottish thrift and Lady Luck built tiny firm into an empire." **EJ**. July 18, 1982, p.D5.

Robert L. Perry(1). "Here's Exclusive Club For Men Under 40: But You Have to be Head of Firm Doing $1 Million a Year in Business." **FP**. Feb. 25, 1956, p.21.

Johanna Powell(1). "Bowlen launches countersuit." **FP**, Sept. 11, 1989, p.7.

Johanna Powell(2). "Defiant Cormie vows to keep up fight." **FP**, Dec. 14, 1989, p.19.

Johanna Powell(3). "Principal Group's investors suing Cormie firm for land." **FP**. Jan. 4, 1991, p.3.

Sheila Pratt(1). "Credit unions to get transfusion." **CH**. June 20, 1985, p.C1.

Sheila Pratt(2). "De Rappard investigator fired." **CH**. Jan. 22, 1984, p.A1.

Sheila Pratt(3). "No politics in firing, says Koziak." **CH**. Jan. 26, 1984, p.A1.

Sheila Pratt and Bob Beaty(1). "Getty rejects probe into collapse." **CH**. July 15, 1987, p.A1.

Joanne Ramondt. "Ruth Hogue: Like Death". **CH**. May 23, 1989, p.C2.

Mike Sadava(1). "Clark aide plays down Cormie gift." **EJ**. Aug. 27, 1988, p.A10.

Mike Sadava(2). "Investors upset to discover funds not with Principal." **EJ**. July 5, 1987, p.A1.

John Schreiner(1). "Principal Group is After New Markets." **FP**. Dec. 17, 1983, p.A1.

Robert Sheppard(1). "Alberta to drop curbs for probes of public figures." **GM**. Sept. 14, 1984, p.9.

Karen Sherlock(1). "Subtle barriers block climb into management." **EJ**. Oct. 19, 1986, p.H10.

Karen Sherlock(2). "Management climbing tips." **EJ**. Oct. 19, 1986, p.H10.

Gregg Shilliday(1). "Son of Abacus Cities: Unscathed after the infamous crash, Ken Rogers gets caught." **AR**. Sept., 23, 1991, p.35.

Linda Slobodian(1). "Don Cormie: Principal founder vows to carry on." **ES**. Feb. 25, 1990, p.4.

Linda Slobodian and Paul Bunner(1). "A profitable bail-out: North West & Heritage Trust merge and make money." WESTERN REPORT. June 8, 1987, pp.24-25.

Howard Solomon(1). "Clients win first round of probe." **CH**. July 30, 1987, p.A1.

Howard Solomon(2). "Cormie won't try to block Code report." **CH**. May 3, 1989, p.A1.

Howard Solomon(3). "Ex-minister keeps mum on role." **CH**. May 23, 1989, p.A9.

Howard Solomon(4). "Former minister doesn't regret 1973 decision." **CH**. July 19, 1989, p.A6.

Howard Solomon(5). "'Investors were shafted': Subsidiaries' profit margins always thin, executives say." **CH**. July 19, 1989, p.A9.

Howard Solomon(6). "Lougheed has stayed silent." **CH**. July 29, 1989, p.A9.

Peter Stockland(1). "Trusts sound: Media slammed." **ES**. Jan. 6, 1985, p.8.

Marina Strauss. "More companies buy time by invoking little-used law." **GM**. March 11, 1991, p.B1.

Elsie Tanner. "History of Class '44." EVERGREEN & GOLD, University of Alberta, 1944, p.73.

Duncan Thorne(1). "AGT leased space from Principal 9 days before collapse." **EJ**. Feb. 7, 1988, p.D7.

Duncan Thorne(2). "Code urged to look at property flip." **EJ**. Feb. 11, 1988, p.B5.

Duncan Thorne(3). "Ex-MLA linked to firm awarded controversial lease." **EJ**. March 28, 1987, p.B1.

Duncan Thorne(4). "Government lease for Principal considered." **EJ**. July 23, 1987, p.B1.

Duncan Thorne(5). "Landlord group dreads impact of new tower." **EJ**. May 8, 1989, p.D1.

Duncan Thorne(6). "Probers worked for Principal." **EJ**. July 21, 1987, p.A1.

David Trigueiro(1). "Struggling credit unions taken over." **CH**. May 5, 1984, p.D6.

David Trigueiro(2). "Alberta stands behind credit unions." **CH**. Sept. 14, 1984, p.E3.

David Trigueiro and Don Martin. "Banking watchdog groups taking a lot of heat." **CH**. Sept. 5, 1985, p.C1.

John Twigg(1). "Cormie's role on Vancouver Island: rich, withdrawn, mysterious stranger." **EJ**. July 18, 1987, p.D1.

Geoff White. "CCB kept silent on bad loans: Fancy deals made." **CH**. Oct. 10, 1985, p.A1.

Rod Ziegler(1). "A $290M-shell that's proving hard to crack." **EJ**. June 25, 1987, p.G1.

Rod Ziegler(2). "Alberta's regulatory system a failure for investors." **EJ**. July 4, 1987, p.C2.

Rod Ziegler(3). "Big question of trust for Principal Group." **EJ**, July 2, 1987, p.C2.

Rod Ziegler(4). "Canada stuck a long way from debt-reduction track." **EJ**. May 2, 1989, p.E1.

Rod Ziegler(5). "Government rejection forced Principal's move—Cormie." **EJ**. Aug. 11, 1987, p.F1.

Acknowledgements

Many people talked with me during research for this book. I particularly thank Ken Marlin and Connie Osterman, who each spent many hours answering difficult questions without any assurance as to the outcome. I also thank The Hon. Willard Estey, who was frank and forthright regarding his friendship with Donald Cormie where many others were not.

Thanks also to Ken Pennifold, Don Logan, Ab Coyne, Diane Stefanski, Bill Johnson, George Blochert, Barry Martin, Joe Ostermann, Neil Webber, Helene Wekherlien, Colin Henderson, John Pullishy, Mark Gregory, Darlene Tuttle, Rod Ziegler, Frank Hutton, Robert White, John McNiven, Claus Thietke, Gary Greenan, J. Stephens Allan, Grey Clarke, Peter Mason, Jim Devonshire, Peter Walsh, Tim Mason, Bill Connauton, Jim Hunter, Les Mabbott, Angus Watt, Jack Lyndon, Julian Koziak, Alex McEachern, Don Blenkarn, Jim Edwards, David Kilgour, Robert Hammond, Hal Veale, Conrad Black, Maurice Colson, Jack Boultbee, John Plaxton, Steven Glover, Bill and Marilyn Macleod, George Field, Eleanor Tufford, Ian Young, Bob Purvis, Graham Fletcher, Ken Pawliuk, Frederick Widmann, Lorna Jean Romanko, Bill and Barbara Hall, Albert Milton, Earl and Pat Rose, Margaret Ann Mailman, Dorothy Forster, Ralph W. Forster, Ivan Cormie Cunningham, Rev. Keith Wettlaufer, David Beattie and Betsy and Stuart Elgie. Thanks also to Code inquiry counsel Neil Wittmann, Jim Eamon and Linda Taylor. Many others spoke with me on the understanding their names would not be revealed. I thank them for their help and for their trust.

Last but by no means least I thank Jim Darwish—the only hero in this sordid tale—with whom I had a very interesting visit. What goes around does, sometimes, come around.

Thanks are due many friends and colleagues who assisted me during the preparation of this book. Most particularly I thank Susan Ruttan, the *Calgary Herald's* former news editor, and former managing editor Gillian Stewart, who assigned me to cover the Code inquiry in 1987; and former *Calgary Herald* reporter Howard Solomon, who replaced me at the hearings when I moved east and kept me posted on subsequent developments. Thanks also to former Principal salesman Scott Schroder of Edmonton, who urged me to write this book. Thanks also to Dennis Stacy, John Sawatsky, Wayne Kondro, Sandy Hunter and Mathew Ingram for help along the way.

Thanks as well to *The Edmonton Journal* reporter Jack Danylchuk, my competition at the Code inquiry. His enthusiasm for the story fed mine. And thanks to Colonel Alec Manson, who first taught me the quiet but extraordinary drama of accounting scams.

Thanks to *The Edmonton Journal*, Ray Giguere, Larry Arbour and Principal Group trustee J. Stephens Allan for their generous permission to use the photographs which appear in the book. I am also indebted to *The Edmonton Journal* librarians Pat Garneau and Pat Beuerlein. Thanks to the library staff of the *Calgary Herald* , and to the research staffs of the National Archives of Canada; the National Library of Canada; Ottawa Public Library; Carleton University Library; Transport Canada; and the Department of National Defense—all in Ottawa. Thanks also to Mary Bartram, assistant archivist at the Archives of Ontario in Toronto; Jeff Gilbert, land registrar in the Ontario Land Registry Office in Guelph; and to archivist Ena Schneider of the Edmonton Public School Archives. Thanks to Matt Neubert, assistant director of securities, Arizona Corporations Commission. And an especially heartfelt thanks to the very patient Joan Capp, formerly of Exhibit Central in the Law Courts Building in Edmonton.

Posthumous thanks to Gordon Montador, publisher of *Summerhill Press* until his death in May 1991. Gordon's belief in the project kept me returning to my computer day after day after day. His warmth and wit are deeply missed.

Posthumous thanks also to my life-long friend Bruce Cummer, whose support for this book continued after his death and resulted in the creation of *Bruce Press*.

Thanks to my lawyers Bruce MacDougall and Vivian Bercovici for their patience and support.

Others cannot be named. To the anonymous friends of *Bruce Press*: I couldn't have done it without you.

Finally, thanks to friends (not named above) who supported and encouraged me during four very difficult years, among them Debbie O'Rourke, Melanie Dickstein, Jack Hanna, Joy McKinnon, Maureen Adamac and MorningStarre.

Unavoidably, my interpretation of events in this book will not coincide with the views of all participants. In the end the conclusions drawn are mine, and responsibility for its contents lies with me.

Index